THE
REFERENCE
SHELF

FREE TRADE
VERSUS PROTECTIONISM

edited by DONALD ALTSCHILLER

THE REFERENCE SHELF

Volume 60 Number 3

THE H. W. WILSON COMPANY

New York   1988

THE REFERENCE SHELF

The books in this series contain reprints of articles, excerpts from books, and addresses on current issues and social trends in the United States and other countries. There are six separately bound numbers in each volume, all of which are generally published in the same calendar year. One number is a collection of recent speeches; each of the others is devoted to a single subject and gives background information and discussion from various points of view, concluding with a comprehensive bibliography. Books in the series may be purchased individually or on subscription.

Library of Congress Cataloging-in-Publication Data

Main entry under title:

Free trade versus protectionism / edited by Donald Altschiller.

    p. cm. — (The Reference shelf ; v. 60, no. 3)
    Bibliography: p.
    ISBN 0-8242-0767-X
    1. Free trade and protection. 2. United States—Commercial policy. 3. United States—Commerce—Japan. 4. Japan—Commerce--United States. I. Altschiller, Donald. II. Series.
HF1713.F765   1988
382.7'0973—dc19   88-24067
                                               CIP

Printed in the United States of America

CONTENTS

PREFACE 5

I. FREE TRADE AND PROTECTIONISM:
   INTELLECTUAL AND HISTORICAL BACKGROUND

Editor's Introduction 7
W. M. Corden. Tariffs and Protectionism ....
.......International Encyclopedia of the Social Sciences   7
Adam Smith. Tariffs and Free Trade ....
...........................The Wealth of Nations   22
John Maynard Keynes. Proposals for a Revenue Tariff ..
.... Essays in Persuasion   30

II. THE CASE FOR PROTECTIONISM

Editor's Introduction   34
Gus Tyler. The Myth of Free Trade .... Dissent   34
Susan Strange. Protectionism, Why Not? . . World Today   46
John M. Culbertson. The Folly of Free Trade ....
.... Harvard Business Review   55

III. THE CASE AGAINST PROTECTIONISM

Editor's Introduction   70
W. Allen Wallis. Protectionism: A Threat to Our Pros-
      perity .... Department of State Bulletin   70
Beyond Protectionism .... World Policy Journal   79
Bernard K. Gordon. Truth in Trading .. Foreign Policy   95

IV. TRADE POLICY WITH JAPAN AND CANADA

Editor's Introduction   108

Karel G. van Wolferen. The Japan Problem ....
.... Foreign Affairs   109
Clyde V. Prestowitz, Jr. U.S.-Japan Trade Friction: Cre-
ating a New Relationship ....
..................California Management Review   120
Paul D. Wolfowitz. Protectionism and U.S.-Japan Trade
.....................Department of State Bulletin   133
Adam Bromke and Kim Richard Nossal. A Turning
Point in U.S.-Canadian Relations ... Foreign Affairs   138
Denis Stairs. Free Trade—Another View ....
.... International Perspectives   148
David Peterson. Neo-Protectionism: Déja Vu All Over
Again .... Vital Speeches of the Day   163

Bibliography   170

PREFACE

No nation was ever ruined by trade.

—BENJAMIN FRANKLIN (1779)

After more than three decades of relatively few trade restrictions, many Americans are rethinking their opposition to protectionism. Tariff proponents cite the growing malaise of the American economy—mounting trade deficits, a weakening dollar, and the loss of thousands of industrial jobs—and then blame the problem on the unfair advantage enjoyed by America's trading partners, especially Japan. In the past few years, several protectionist bills have been introduced in Congress. Although most of this legislation was never enacted, some American industries have benefited from special governmental regulations to raise the price of imported goods. In addition, a recent study found that the share of foreign imports subject to tariffs rose from 8 percent in 1975 to 21 percent in 1984.

The growing debate over free trade vs. protectionism has raised many questions for the American public, especially during this Presidential election year. Will protectionist legislation help revitalize the American economy? Should the government help resuscitate American industries by imposing import quotas, even though many of these companies are not as efficiently run as their foreign competitors? Are workers losing their jobs because foreign industries are permitted to sell their lower-priced products in America? Should the U.S. threaten to limit imports as a way of persuading other nations to drop restrictive trade policies aimed at American exports?

This anthology discusses these and other topics and provides some answers offered by both the proponents of free trade and of protectionism. Although the debate may seem to be dominated by economics, trade policy also touches upon a wide range of fields, including philosophy, science and technology, and, even, political nationalism. Some articles in this anthology were selected because they offer these varying perspectives.

The first section traces the intellectual and historical background of the free trade debate. The next two sections present detailed arguments for and against protectionism. In the concluding section are discussions of trade issues involving America's two largest trading partners, Japan and Canada.

The editor wishes to thank the authors and publishers who have granted permission to reprint their material in this compilation.

DONALD ALTSCHILLER

August 1988

I. FREE TRADE AND PROTECTIONISM: INTELLECTUAL AND HISTORICAL BACKGROUND

EDITOR'S INTRODUCTION

The question of free trade versus protectionism has been debated for more than two centuries. Although this economic dispute first arose in pre-industrial Europe, it now confronts a largely post-industrial world economy. This section traces the intellectual and historical origins of the free trade debate. The first essay, an entry from the *International Encyclopedia of the Social Sciences*, surveys the history and theory of protectionism. The next article contains a long excerpt in support of free trade from Adam Smith's classic work, *The Wealth of Nations*. In a widely quoted passage, this Scottish economist declared, "It is the maxim of every prudent master of a family never to attempt to make at home what it will cost him more to make than to buy . . . what is prudence in the conduct of every private family, can scarce be folly in that of a great kingdom." On the other hand, the British economist John Maynard Keynes argued in the early 1930s that the imposition of tariffs would help solve his country's economic difficulties. The article "Proposals for a Revenue Tariff" from his collection, *Essays in Persuasion*, concludes this section.

TARIFFS AND PROTECTIONISM[1]

In international economic usage, *protection* usually refers to acts of government policy which protect an industry from foreign competition, thus enabling the industry to earn higher incomes than it otherwise would. It can also be interpreted more broadly

[1]Excerpted from an encyclopedia article by W. M. Corden. *International Encyclopedia of the Social Sciences*. David A. Sills, Editor, v. 8: 113–121. Reprinted with permission of MacMillan/The Free Press, Division of MacMillan, Inc. © 1968 Crowell Collier and MacMillan, Inc.

to include all government policies which assist industries that are either competing with imports or are actual or potential exporters. The four main protective devices are subsidies to domestic producers, taxes on imports, quantitative restrictions on imports, and state trading. Taxes on imports are historically the principal device. These taxes are usually called tariffs or customs duties, though sometimes other terms, such as import surcharges or equalizing duties, are used. Tariffs may be classified by motive and by form. Since a tariff will normally produce customs revenue, protect domestic output, reduce consumption of the protected product, and reduce imports, in motive it may be a revenue tariff, a protective tariff, a tariff designed to reduce consumption of a product, or a tariff to improve the balance of payments. The principal distinction is between the first two motives—revenue and protection. In practice, motives and actual effects are usually mixed. Individual tariffs may be classifed by form according to whether they are ad valorem (a percentage of the value of the unit), specific (a fixed sum for each unit), or a combination of the two, whether ad valorem percentages are fixed or variable with the price of the import, and whether the tariffs allow for exemptions—for example, of imports destined for re-export.

A tariff schedule is a complicated document consisting often of several thousand different items. Not only may there be a separate tariff rate for each item, but in addition a tariff schedule may have several columns, so that there is more than one duty for each item. Historically, most countries have had at least two columns in their tariff schedules, the distinction being usually between a conventional and a general column, the conventional tariff applying to some or all imports from countries with which a tariff agreement has been concluded and the general tariff to the remaining imports. Most trade agreements include the so-called most-favored-nation clause, which provides that (when countries A and B sign an agreement) country A will not discriminate in any tariff item against imports from country B. When countries are linked by a network of trade agreements, all containing such a clause of general application, a system of nondiscriminatory tariffs results. If a country is part of a preferential area a third column will state the preferential tariff applying to some or all of the imports from fellow members of the area, this tariff being normally less than the conventional tariff. If all trade between members of the preference area is free of duty, though each member still has its own tariff on imports from other sources, there is an extreme form of preference area, a free trade area. One step beyond the free trade area is the customs union. As in the free trade area, all trade between the members is free of duty and other trade restrictions, but in addition the members of a customs union have a common external tariff applying to all imports from outside the area. They are in fact a single unit for tariff purposes.

History of Protectionism

The history of commercial policies—that is, government policies affecting international trade—is difficult to sum up. Tariff schedules and other instruments of protectionism are complex, and there is no easy way of aggregating the individual elements. Moreover, movements toward or away from protectionism in different parts of the world have not been synchronized and have had many different causes, some special to particular countries. From the tariff histories of the principal industrial countries there does not emerge a consistent causal relationship to explain why tariffs or quotas were imposed, raised, or reduced at certain times. Much prominence is usually given to the arguments of the advocates and the critics of protectionism, and to the interplay of tariff policy with class or regional divisions. It is not always clear to what extent the arguments provide actual explanations or mere rationalizations of the course of events.

One may also wonder how important specific books and economic theories have been in influencing the course of tariff history. Adam Smith's *Wealth of Nations* (1776), Hamilton's *Report on the Subject of Manufactures* (1791) and List's *National System of Political Economy* (1841) were influential works, the first providing the intellectual support for the British and Continental free-trade movement, and the latter two for protection of infant manufacturing industry in the United States and Germany, respectively. But the British free-trade movement did not get under way until 50 years after the publication of Smith's book, United States protectionism lagged 25 years behind Hamilton's *Report*, while the Zollverein (the German customs union which preceded the establishment in 1871 of the German Empire) had a very moderate tariff, and when Germany did become protectionist after 1880 it was agriculture much more than manufacturing industry that was protected. The influence of "scribblers" was perhaps less than many tariff historians suggest. The legitimization by J. S. Mill in his *Principles of Political Economy* (1848) of the infant industry argument for protection, while convincing to most English economists, did not have any noticeable effect on tariff history. More recently, the terms of trade argument for protection, in the form in which theoretical economists have given it so much prominence, has made no apparent impact on actual commercial policies.

Some generalizations which may serve as guidelines through the tariff histories of the major Western industrial nations are, however, possible. The first is that war often leads to increases in protection. War usually gives rise to additional revenue needs. The revenue duties which are imposed have an incidental protective effect; after the war, when the extra revenue need disappears, the tariff is maintained so as to safeguard the infant industries established under the shelter of the tariff. War leads to a boom in demand for a wide range of industrial goods; after the war, tariffs may be imposed to compensate for the fall in demand. War may cut a country off from imports and thus provide a form of natural infant protection; after the war, this protection is replaced by tariff protection to ensure survival of the infants. Finally, special measures may be taken in wartime to develop industries producing goods essential to the military effort or to the living standards of a nation cut off from outside supplies. After the war these industries are maintained, both to preserve employment and capital values and in awareness of the strategic argument for protection. The protectionist histories of Britain, France, the United States, and Australia all provide support for this generalization. The beginnings of American protectionism can be traced to the effects of the War of 1812 in protecting infant American industries from British competition. High protectionism in the United States originated in the Civil War. Industry in the North boomed in response to the war-generated demand and naturally created pressures for its survival after the war. More important, the federal government's revenue needs soared during the war, and the customs were its principal source of revenue (Taussig 1888). Yet when the revenue needs fell after the war, the tariff was not reduced.

Another generalization which sheds some light on tariff history is that depressions, whether of the general cyclical type or long-term depressions in prices of particular products, generally lead to increases in protection. Falling prices automatically increase the protective incidence of specific duties. More important, the principal motive for protection is defensive—to protect sectional income levels from decline—and it is natural that when demand for the products of a country's industries falls, commercial policy should try to reduce or exclude foreign competition. The revival of protectionism in France and Germany in the late nineteenth century can be explained principally by the depression of 1873-1879 and by the more prolonged fall in agricultural prices produced by the new supplies from Russia and the New World. A great increase in protection all over the world resulted from the depression of the early 1930s. In particular, Britain, which had been completely free trade from 1860 to World War I and remained predominantly free trade during the 1920s, finally became protectionist in 1931.

The converse of these two generalizations is that peace and prosperity usually encourage movements toward free trade. Prosperity and economic growth reduce protectionist pressure. In prolonged prosperity, industries become less dependent on protection and are less likely to insist that a trade barrier be maintained as an insurance against intensified foreign competition in the future. Moreover, prosperity is usually associated with rising prices and thus with automatic decline of the protective incidence of specific duties. Nevertheless, these generalizations do not, of course, explain all changes in tariff policy; for example, they do not explain the very high Hawley-Smoot tariff of the United States, which, though enacted in 1930, was conceived and lobbied for in the prosperous 1920s.

At the risk of some oversimplification, the state of world commercial policies in the 1960s may be summarized as follows. The nonindustrial countries use tariffs primarily for revenue, not protection, purposes. Taxes on trade, whether import taxes, export taxes, or the profits from a multiple exchange rate system, are usually the largest source of government revenue. In the semi-industrial or recently industrialized countries—notably, Canada, Australia, India, Brazil, and Argentina—tariffs or other restrictions on imports are primarily protective in intention and are essential to the preservation of substantial manufacturing industries. The protective tariff rates are usually high, and quantitative controls sometimes prohibitive; yet over-all tariff levels appear moderate because imports which are noncompetitive with domestic production, in particular raw material imports, are usually admitted free of duty. It is in these countries that industrial protection is a major element of economic policy and a topic of debate. In the advanced countries it is agricultural protection which is most important; the rates of protection are often high, varying between countries and products. Many European countries operate complex schemes, involving quantitative restrictions and variable import levies. Industrial protection in the advanced countries is much less significant, and recent years have seen important moves toward the freeing of world trade that affect mainly the trade in manufactured goods between the advanced countries. On the whole, the industrial protection of the advanced countries bears most heavily on "cheap-labor" products, such as textiles from Japan and Hong Kong, in which the advanced countries have lost their comparative advantage. The tariff structures of the advanced countries, as of the semi-industrialized ones, display in general the characteristic of "tariff escalation": tariff rates rise with the degree of processing contained in a product, basic materials often paying no tariff at all. Finally, in the communist countries the concept of protection as generally understood cannot be said to have any real significance.

Theories of Protection

An elaborate structure of economic theory concerned with the gains and losses from protection has grown up alongside the actual ebb and flow of world protectionism—sometimes influencing actual policies, as in the free trade movement of nineteenth-century Britain, and sometimes being influenced by them. The construction of a rigorous case for free trade was one of the earliest contributions of modern economic theory, and the free trade versus protection issue has preoccupied economists of most countries since Adam Smith. Much of this theory has developed out of attempts to refute crude protectionist beliefs or the advocacy of interest groups. To a lesser extent it has given precision and set boundaries to popular arguments. Sometimes it has even produced essentially new propositions.

The method of approach of most economic theorists to the problem is simple. The foundation is the classical case for free trade, first developed by Adam Smith and David Ricardo. The latter originated, in *On the Principles of Political Economy and*

Taxation (1817), the formal law of comparative costs upon which the free trade case is now based. This classical case has been modified by a whole series of "arguments for protection." While the extent of the modification must depend on the circumstances of each situation, so that, strictly, nothing can be said without specifying situations and relevant magnitudes, it is probably a fair summary to say that most economists regard the free trade case as only modified and not refuted by the various protectionist arguments.

EMPLOYMENT

A perennially popular argument is that protection preserves or increases employment in the protected industries. The free trader's usual answer is that while employment will certainly be diverted into the protected industries, employment will be less elsewhere; the effect is thus a reshuffling rather than an increase in aggregate employment, a reshuffling into less productive activities which causes a real income loss. Full employment can always be maintained by fiscal and monetary policy along Keynesian lines, together with exchange rate adjustment to maintain external balance. The modern amendment to this free trade logic is that exchange rate adjustment may not be possible for one reason or another, and the internal cost level may be inflexible downward. One can imagine a situation of unemployment and external deficit which ideally calls for exchange devaluation to divert expenditure from foreign to domestic goods. In the absence of exchange rate adjustment, or of substitute protectionist devices, fiscal and monetary policy would have to be used to reduce expenditure so as to restore external balance, thus increasing unemployment instead of reducing it. This result can be avoided by tariffs, which would take the place of devaluation as a device to shift spending from foreign to domestic goods. In this sense tariffs can maintain full employment. But the issue of an *optimum* pattern of tariffs remains; while various sets of tariffs will raise employment, some will achieve a given employment increase at less cost or a greater welfare gain than others.

A slight variant of the basic employment argument is the "population-sustaining" argument popular in countries such as Canada and Australia, where population growth by immigration is an object of policy and where the inflow of migrants is responsive to employment opportunities. The assumption is made that export demand is expanding only very slowly. To maintain growing employment and external equilibrium it may then be necessary, if free trade is to be maintained, to associate the requisite monetary expansion with frequent exchange devaluations—the latter to prevent the growth of imports exceeding the slow growth of exports. But frequent devaluations may not be possible. One way out is to sacrifice the monetary expansion for the sake of external balance; but this would discourage immigration. The other way out is to sacrifice free trade—to steadily widen the scope of tariffs, or to raise tariffs, as a second-best alternative to frequent devaluation. An essentially similar argument applies in underdeveloped countries where the employment-seeking work force is growing rapidly through natural increase while export demand is growing more slowly.

INCOME REDISTRIBUTION

A second argument for protection is that it alters the distribution of internal real incomes in a desirable direction. Clearly protection will make the income earners in the protected industry better off, particularly if the service they supply or the capital equipment they own is quite specific to the industry. It is obvious that protection, while usually benefiting some, harms others, notably consumers of the protected products and competing users of labor and materials. These conflicts of interest are at the core of the political activities surrounding tariff making. Opposition to protection in Britain and the United States in the early nineteenth century was founded at least as much on the sectional interests of manufacturers (in Britain) and cotton growers (in the United States) as on any abstract case for free trade. But for a long time the common economic teaching was that while a small section could gain from protection, a large section—such as the aggregate of wage earners—could not, since its gains as protected producers would be more than offset by its losses as consumers. But an interesting theoretical development (Stolper & Samuelson 1941) has shown that, given certain assumptions, a gain to a large group *can* result. Whether such a redistribution of real income represents a gain or loss in national welfare is a question within the province of welfare economics.

The "pauper-labor" argument, which was the protectionist's stand-by in the United States in the period of the high McKinley and Dingley tariffs of the 1890s and which crops up whenever protection for labor-intensive industries is sought, is a variant of the income distribution argument. Imports of labor-intensive goods do tend to reduce the demand for some types of labor and so lower the real wages of this labor. But it is also true that the gains to other sections of the community from free trade may be so great that the gainers could compensate the losers. Aggregate welfare would then perhaps be maximized by free trade combined with compensation. But if the institutions of the society do not in fact ensure that compensation takes place, who is to say whether there is a net social gain or loss from protection— whether one man's gain is greater than another man's loss? Popular statements of the "pauper-labor" argument, however, usually contain fallacious elements. Cheap labor does not necessarily mean low prices for given qualities of product, and low prices for some products do not mean low prices for all. If a country's labor is really so cheap or efficient that it can sell everything cheaper, then clearly appreciation of its currency is required, though, indeed, tariffs imposed on its products by other countries may be a second-best alternative.

INFANT INDUSTRY

The infant industry argument for protection is the oldest and most respectable of the protection arguments. It has undergone considerable refinement. The main distinction is between the argument based on falling costs, which represent economies internal to firms and the benefits of which are reaped by firms themselves, and the so-called external economies. Support for protection on the grounds of internal economies—that a firm's costs will fall with increased scale of output or over time—can only be given with reservations or for special cases. For, if a firm will eventually recover its initial losses, why should it require a subsidy, either direct or indirect? Can it not cover these losses from borrowed funds—to be repaid when costs later fall? One can readily think of situations where this is not possible or just would not happen; and in these situations the argument based on internal economies may be valid. Economists have given more attention to the case for protection based on external economies and have refined and classified the possible types of external economies. Most interesting are the external economies that are generated with the over-all growth of a manufacturing sector— economies external to the individual firms making up the sector, although internal to the sector as a whole. These economies provide the main justification for a general policy of industrial protection in countries which are semi-industrialized or show potentialities for industrialization. The discussion about the virtues, or otherwise, of a policy of *balanced growth* is closely related. This concept hinges on the interdependence of industries, especially of the different industries making up a manufacturing economy, an interdependence through both demand and supply. Any individual firm or industry may not find it profitable to expand, but if all expand together, maintaining some appropriate relation, they will all turn out to be socially and perhaps even privately profitable (Nurkse 1953). Against this must be set the advantages of unbalanced growth, among them the economies of specialization and the benefits to be derived from trade. A lively controversy is here unresolved.

Terms of Trade

A country which restricts its trade, either by import tariffs or by export taxes, is likely to improve its terms of trade as a result. Restriction of demand may lower the prices at which foreign suppliers provide imports, and restriction of supply may raise export prices. On balance the gains from the terms of trade improvement may outweigh the losses from the country's reduced use of the international division of labor. A country, in fact, can act as a monopsonist or a monopolist. This is the terms of trade argument for protection. The element of gain which a country derives is at the expense of its trading partners, whose terms of trade will decline. Much elaborate theory has been spun around this general proposition, and it has yielded the concept of the "optimum tariff"—optimum to one country and not the world. Account has been taken of the possibility that other countries will retaliate against an "optimum tariff." If so, the terms of trade improvement may disappear and all countries may finally be worse off; although it is at least possible that when both countries restrict trade optimally, each responding to the other's restriction, on balance one of them may still finally be better off than before the whole exercise began. The terms of trade argument in the form in which it appears in the theoretical literature has not been of much practical significance. But in the process of growth countries have sometimes chosen to develop import-competing rather than export industries for fear that their terms of trade would otherwise deteriorate, and industrial protectionism in primary-product exporting countries is rooted to some extent in a belief in the price-inelasticity of demand for their exports.

SECOND-BEST POLICIES

In underdeveloped countries the average income in the industrial or the "Westernized" sector of the economy is usually higher than that in the agricultural sector. There are various possible reasons for this; and to some extent the discrepancy may be only in money income and not real income. But it has been argued recently that insofar as there is a discrepancy not only in average real incomes but also in *marginal* returns—that is, insofar as a transfer of labor from the agricultural to the industrial sector would raise aggregate real income—protection of the advanced sector to encourage this labor transfer may be justified. This argument for protection needs to be carefully qualified and is not accepted without reservations. But it is interesting as an argument which is more or less special to underdeveloped countries. It is really a particular case of what has lately been recognized as a much larger category, the *second-best* argument for protection (Meade 1955). This argument applies whenever there is some distortion or disequilibrium in the internal economy, so that prices do not correctly reflect marginal costs. One remedy would be to eliminate the distortion directly; another would be to compensate with internal subsidies and taxes. But the politically and administratively most convenient remedy is often to compensate the distortion through carefully chosen commercial policies, such as tariffs. This is a second-best remedy because in compensating indirectly for internal distortions it creates new distortions—for example, in consumption patterns.

In a sense all the arguments for tariffs so far discussed are second-best arguments, justified by the impracticability of the "first-best" policies. It can be held that the best policy to maintain full employment is to combine fiscal and monetary adjustment with exchange rate variations. Internal incomes are best redistributed by nontrade taxes (such as income taxes), which finance direct subsidies. Infant industry protection is best provided by direct subsidies which benefit infants irrespective of whether they are import-competing or potential exporters. And the income of one country can be raised at the expense of another by direct international aid, so avoiding the trade-restricting effect of the optimum tariff. Yet to subsume all these arguments into a single second-best argument is to ignore the distorting by-products and administrative costs of what appear on the surface to be first-best policies.

Economic Growth

Is there a special argument for protection on the grounds that it facilitates or stimulates economic growth? While the growth of the protected industries will no doubt be stimulated, the question is whether the over-all growth of the economy would have been less under free trade. Part of the answer is in the infant industry argument for protection: infant protection can be summed up as the incurring of a current loss for the sake of a future gain; if the expected future gain is indeed realized, then growth will have been fostered, although the issue still remains whether the current costs of this growth justify the future benefits. Another part of the answer is in the employment, or demand-generating, argument for protection; the incentive to invest will be lower in an underemployed than a fully employed economy. If protection is really needed to maintain full employment it also stimulates growth. There remain two ways in which protection can raise or lower growth rates. First, it may redistribute internal incomes toward or away from sections with a relatively high propensity to save; for example, savings out of industrial profits are generally higher than out of peasant incomes or out of rents, so that industrial protection tends to foster savings. Second, protection may raise the inducement to invest by increasing some or all profits or by reducing the risk element in investment. Thus investment is usually more responsive to profit increases in some than in other industries, so that protection of particular industries at the expense of other industries may affect the over-all growth rate. Furthermore, protection may bring about an over-all redistribution of real income away from wages or rents and toward profits, and so stimulate investment. A particular case of these relationships is the role of high and secure profits in protected industries in attracting foreign capital inflow. In all these cases the returns from growth may or may not outweigh the costs of protection.

All these arguments for protection do not distinguish between the methods of protection. There exists a fairly simple body of subsidiary analysis to assist the choice between the main methods—subsidies, tariffs, and quantitative import restrictions. Economists have tended to prefer the methods in that order—to prefer subsidies to tariffs because they distort only the production pattern and not the consumption pattern, and because their "cost" is more clearly apparent; and to prefer both subsidies and tariffs to quantitative import restrictions because of a predisposition in favor of the price mechanism and because of the monopoly profits that may be reaped under a scheme of quantitative restriction by holders of licenses to import. But beyond general arguments for protection and the broad choice of method, economic theory has provided little help in the construction of protective systems. We have seen that tariff schedules are usually complicated documents and that tariffs may assume many forms. The complexities in the tariff systems of most countries result from the piecemeal way, usually in response to numerous sectional pressures, in which tariff systems are constructed and amended and from the mixture of motives at work. One aim is often to tailor a tariff precisely to the object in view—for example, to achieve the desired protective effect with the minimum rise in prices to consumers and thus with the minimum incidental revenue effect. It is the pursuit of this aim which leads tariff makers in some countries (for example, Australia) to make detailed comparisons of production costs between countries and to construct complex tariffs which are finely adjusted to the estimated cost differences for those products which they have resolved to protect. But economists have not subjected the details of tariff making and the logic behind tariff structures to the same thorough analysis as they have the welfare effects of protection as a whole.

Measurement of Protection

Increasing attention is being paid to the need to measure the magnitudes and effects about which economists generalize. The various exercises in measurement connected with tariffs may be classified as follows. First of all, specific tariff rates and nontariff protection must be converted into ad valorem equivalents if one tariff or protective device is to be comparable with another. A problem is to discover the typical or "average" price to which each specific tariff rate applies. In the case of nontariff devices, the object is to discover the net result—the excess of the price received by the producer over the price of potential imports, expressed as a percentage of the latter. The main difficulty here is similar—to establish the prices of potential imports in those cases where actual imports have either been completely excluded or are unrepresentative of free-trade imports. A second step is to relate tariff rates to value added domestically rather than to the gross value of domestic output (which includes imported materials) and to allow for tariffs on imported materials. Such calculations yield *effective* protective rates (Barber 1955). For example, an apparent tariff rate of 10 per cent on cotton yarn will represent effective protection of 20 per cent when half of the yarn value (before duty) is raw cotton content, which would pay no duty if imported in that state. If the tariff on raw cotton were also 10 per cent, then the apparent and effective protection for yarn would both be 10 per cent. Calculations of effective protective rates are needed to determine the true impact of a protective system on an economy but have only recently been made systematically. They require detailed knowledge of the materials content in protected industries.

A further step is to calculate averages of tariff levels. Since one must sometimes sum up complex tariff schedules if one is to generalize at all, averages of tariff levels have frequently been calculated, though not always with awareness of the methodological traps. These averages usually refer to apparent, not effective, rates. The simplest and commonest method is to relate customs revenue to the value of total imports. The result is an average weighted by the value of imports after tariffs have been imposed. The higher a tariff, the more imports will be excluded, so that this method underweights the high tariff items. Indeed, a particular tariff which is so high as to be prohibitive will not enter the index at all. To avoid this bias, "unweighted" averages—that is, arithmetic averages of tariff rates—are sometimes calculated. The result then depends on the method of tariff classification and really has no coherent meaning. Yet another method is to weight by the value of the domestic production of items to which tariff rates apply. A practical difficulty here is that tariff classifications usually do not coincide with classifications of production statistics. This method in a sense yields the average, not of all tariffs, but only of the protective tariffs. It might be regarded as yielding an overstatement since it does not allow for items where there is no tariff but where a protective tariff could have been imposed. Other methods are to weight by consumption (imports plus domestic production) after tariffs have been imposed, to weight by the value of world trade, or to weight by the value of exports from some leading supplying countries. These latter methods are all approximations to what is often regarded as the preferable weighting system, namely, weighting by what imports would have been in the absence of tariffs. In fact, no method is ideal, since an average tariff, however calculated, cannot be a measure of the welfare or other effects of the tariff structure. Indeed, since the dispersion of tariffs has welfare implications, the use of a single figure to represent a complex tariff system may tend to obscure important implications.

Yet a further step is to estimate the effects of tariffs on output and employment (Salant & Vaccara 1961). The primary and the secondary effects of tariff imposition must here be distinguished. The primary effect consists of the direct rise in output or employment, when cost and exchange rate levels are given and when possible multiplier repercussions of the rise in incomes due to the initial rise in output are disregarded. It includes not only the effect on output and employment in the protected industry itself but also in industries which supply materials and components to it. The secondary effect allows for further repercussions. One possibility is that over-all employment and external equilibrium are maintained by exchange appreciation or by a rise in internal cost levels associated with the tariff increase. These adjustments would somewhat reduce employment in the newly protected industries. The other possibility is that the primary employment effect is not offset by deliberate policies—whether of exchange adjustment, cost adjustment, or demand reduction by fiscal or monetary policies—and is instead allowed to set off a multiplier process. A secondary rise in employment or in prices must then be added to the primary increase in employment.

Recently economists have become interested in the measurement of the welfare effects of protection (Corden 1957). The methodological problems involved are considerable. What is welfare? What is the precise configuration of the alternative situation with which the protection situation is being compared? The "cost" of protection, presumably, is the excess of free-trade welfare over protection welfare. How are changes in the distribution of income due to protection to be incorporated in the welfare measure? The simplest approach is to assume full employment in both situations, hold the terms of trade constant, ignore income distribution effects, and assume that free trade represents an optimum in the neoclassical sense. The cost of protection then results from a distortion of production and a distortion of consumption, both of which can be approximately measured, provided the effects of protection on the quantities produced and consumed are known or can be estimated.

An interesting approach is to measure what has been called the *cash cost* of protection, namely, the value of the production subsidy which would be needed to achieve a protective result equivalent to that of tariffs or other trade restrictions (Young 1957). This cash cost is the excess of the value of protected output over the value of duty-free equivalent imports (at the current exchange rate). It has been estimated for Canada and Australia. It states the cost of protection in the same form as the costs of other subsidizing activities of the government are stated. It is thus not a net social cost; rather it is a gross cost against which the various benefits of protection must be offset.

TARIFFS AND FREE TRADE[2]

Adam Smith (1723-90) is considered the founder of modern economics. He made his name first as a moral philosopher, holding the chairs of logic and of moral philosophy at Glasgow, and publishing his *Theory of the Moral Sentiments* in 1759. He then became tutor to the Duke of Buccleuch, which enabled him to travel abroad with his pupil, and from the mid-1760s to live on a comfortable pension. His travels were in part responsible for his interest in economics, which culminated in 1776 in *The Wealth of Nations*, a book that influenced not only future generations of economic theorists, but also important political figures of his own day.

---

[2]Excerpted from *The Wealth of Nations* by Adam Smith (1776).

*Of Restraints upon the Importation
from Foreign Countries of Such Goods
as Can Be Produced at Home*

By restraining, either by high duties, or by absolute prohibitions, the importation of such goods from foreign countries as can be produced at home, the monopoly of the home market is more or less secured to the domestic industry employed in producing them. Thus the prohibition of importing either live cattle or salt provisions from foreign countries secures to the graziers of Great Britain the monopoly of the home market for butcher's meat. The high duties upon the importation of corn, which in times of moderate plenty amount to a prohibition, give a like advantage to the growers of that commodity. The prohibition of the importation of foreign woollens is equally favourable to the woollen manufacturers. The silk manufacture, though altogether employed upon foreign materials, has lately obtained the same advantage. The linen manufacture has not yet obtained it, but is making great strides towards it. Many other sorts of manufacturers have, in the same manner, obtained in Great Britain, either altogether, or very nearly a monopoly against their countrymen. The variety of goods of which the importation into Great Britain is prohibited, either absolutely, or under certain circumstances, greatly exceeds what can easily be suspected by those who are not well acquainted with the laws of the customs.

That this monopoly of the home-market frequently gives great encouragement to that particular species of industry which enjoys it, and frequently turns towards that employment a greater share of both the labour and stock of the society than would otherwise have gone to it, cannot be doubted. But whether it tends either to increase the general industry of the society, or to give it the most advantageous direction, is not, perhaps, altogether so evident.

The general industry of the society never can exceed what the capital of the society can employ. As the number of workmen that can be kept in employment by any particular person must bear a certain proportion to his capital, so the number of those that can be continually employed by all the members of a great society, must bear a certain proportion to the whole capital of that society, and never can exceed that proportion. No regulation of commerce can increase the quantity of industry in any society beyond what its capital can maintain. It can only divert a part of it into a direction into which it might not otherwise have gone; and it is by no means certain that this artificial direction is likely to be more advantageous to the society than that into which it would have gone of its own accord.

Every individual is continually exerting himself to find out the most advantageous employment for whatever capital he can command. It is his own advantage, indeed, and not that of the society which he has in view. But the study of his own advantage naturally, or rather necessarily leads him to prefer that employment which is most advantageous to the society. . . . To give the monopoly of the home-market to the produce of domestic industry, in any particular art or manufacture, is in some measure to direct private people in what manner they ought to employ their capitals, and must, in almost all cases, be either a useless or a hurtful regulation. If the produce of domestic industry can be brought there as cheap as that of foreign industry, the regulation is evidently useless. If it cannot, it must generally be hurtful. It is the maxim of every prudent master of a family, never to attempt to make at home what it will cost him more to make than to buy. The taylor does not attempt to make his own shoes, but buys them of the shoemaker. The shoemaker does not attempt to make his own clothes, but employs a taylor. The farmer attempts to make neither the one nor the other, but employs those different artificers. All of them find it for their interest to employ their whole industry in a way in which they have some advantage over their neighbours, and to purchase with a part of its produce, or what is the same thing, with the price of a part of it, whatever else they have occasion for.

What is prudence in the conduct of every private family, can scarce be folly in that of a great kingdom. If a foreign country can supply us with a commodity cheaper than we ourselves can make it, better buy it of them with some part of the produce of our own industry, employed in a way in which we have some advantage. The general industry of the country, being always in proportion to the capital which employs it, will not thereby be diminished, no more than that of the above-mentioned artificers; but only left to find out the way in which it can be employed with the greatest advantage. It is certainly not employed to the greatest advantage, when it is thus directed towards an object which it can buy cheaper than it can make. The value of its annual produce is certainly more or less diminished, when it is thus turned away from producing commodities evidently of more value than the commodity which it is directed to produce. According to the supposition, that commodity could be purchased from foreign countries cheaper than it can be made at home. It could, therefore, have been purchased with a part only of the commodities, or, what is the same thing, with a part only of the price of the commodities, which the industry employed by an equal capital would have produced at home, had it been left to follow its natural course. The industry of the country, therefore, is thus turned away from a more, to a less advantageous employment, and the exchangeable value of its annual produce, instead of being increased, according to the intention of the lawgiver, must necessarily be diminished by every such regulation.

By means of such regulations, indeed, a particular manufacture may sometimes be acquired sooner than it could have been otherwise, and after a certain time may be made at home as cheap or cheaper than in the foreign country. But though the industry of the society may be thus carried with advantage into a particular channel sooner than it could have been otherwise, it will by no means follow that the sum total, either of its industry, or of its revenue, can ever be augmented by any such regulation. The industry of the society can augment only in proportion as its capital augments, and its capital can augment only in proportion to what can be gradually saved out of its revenue. But the immediate effect of every such regulation is to diminish its revenue, and what diminishes its revenue is certainly not very likely to augment its capital faster than it would have augmented of its own accord, had both capital and industry been left to find out their natural employments.

Though for want of such regulations the society should never acquire the proposed manufacture, it would not, upon that account, necessarily be the poorer in any one period of its duration. In every period of its duration its whole capital and industry might still have been employed, though upon different objects, in the manner that was most advantageous at the time. In every period its revenue might have been the greatest which its capital could afford, and both capital and revenue might have been augmented with the greatest possible rapidity.

The natural advantages which one country has over another in producing particular commodities are sometimes so great, that it is acknowledged by all the world to be in vain to struggle with them. By means of glasses, hotbeds, and hotwalls, very good grapes can be raised in Scotland, and very good wine too can be made of them at about thirty times the expense for which at least equally good can be brought from foreign countries. Would it be a reasonable law to prohibit the importation of all foreign wines, merely to encourage the making of claret and burgundy in Scotland? But if there would be a manifest absurdity in turning towards any employment, thirty times more of the capital and industry of the country, than would be necessary to purchase from foreign countries an equal quantity of the commodities wanted, there must be an absurdity, though not altogether so glaring, yet exactly of the same kind, in turning towards any such employment a thirtieth, or even a three hundredth part more of either. Whether the advantages which one country has over another, be natural or acquired, is in this respect of no consequence. As long as the one country has those advantages, and the other wants them, it will always be more advantageous for the latter, rather to buy of the former than to make. It is an acquired advantage only, which one artificer has over his neighbour, who exercises another trade; and yet they both find it more advantageous to buy of one another, than to make what does not belong to their particular trades.

Merchants and manufacturers are the people who derive the greatest advantage from this monopoly of the home-market. The prohibition of the importation of foreign cattle, and of salt provisions, together with the high duties upon foreign corn, which in times of moderate plenty amount to a prohibition, are not near so advantageous to the graziers and farmers of Great Britain, as other regulations of the same kind are to its merchants and manufacturers. Manufactures, those of the finer kind especially, are more easily transported from one country to another than corn or cattle. It is in the fetching and carrying manufactures, accordingly, that foreign trade is chiefly employed. In manufactures, a very small advantage will enable foreigners to undersell our own workmen, even in the home market. It will require a very great one to enable them to do so in the rude produce of the soil. If the free importation of foreign manufactures were permitted, several of the home manufactures would probably suffer, and some of them, perhaps, go to ruin altogether, and a considerable part of the stock and industry at present employed in them, would be forced to find out some other employment. But the freest importation of the rude produce of the soil could have no such effect upon the agriculture of the country.

If the importation of foreign cattle, for example, were made ever so free, so few could be imported, that the grazing trade of Great Britain could be little affected by it. Live cattle are, perhaps, the only commodity of which the transportation is more expensive by sea than by land. By land they carry themselves to market. By sea, not only the cattle, but their food and their water too, must be carried at no small expence and inconveniency. The short sea between Ireland and Great Britain, indeed, renders the importation of Irish cattle more easy. But though the free importation of them, which was lately permitted only for a limited time, were rendered perpetual, it could have no considerable effect upon the interest of the graziers of Great Britain. Those parts of Great Britain which border upon the Irish sea are all grazing countries. Irish cattle could never be imported for their use, but must be drove through those very extensive countries, at no small expence and inconveniency, before they could arrive at their proper market. Fat cattle could not be drove so far. Lean cattle, therefore, only could be imported, and such importation could interfere, not with the interest of the feeding or fattening countries, to which, by reducing the price of lean cattle, it would rather be advantageous, but with that of the breeding countries only. The small number of Irish cattle imported since their importation was permitted, together with the good price at which lean cattle still continue to sell, seem to demonstrate that even the breeding countries of Great Britain are never likely to be much affected by the free importation of Irish cattle. The common people of Ireland, indeed, are said to have sometimes opposed with violence the exportation of their cattle. But if the exporters had found any great advantage in continuing the trade, they could easily, when the law was on their side, have conquered this mobbish opposition. . . .

There seem, however, to be two cases in which it will generally be advantageous to lay some burden upon foreign, for the encouragement of domestic industry.

The first is, when some particular sort of industry is necessary for the defence of the country. The defence of Great Britain, for example, depends very much upon the number of its sailors and shipping. The act of navigation, therefore, very properly endeavours to give the sailors and shipping of Great Britain the monopoly of the trade of their own country, in some cases, by absolute prohibitions, and in others by heavy burdens upon the shipping of foreign countries. The following are the principal dispositions of this act.

First, all ships, of which the owners, masters, and three-fourths of the mariners are not British subjects, are prohibited, upon pain of forfeiting ship and cargo, from trading to the British settlements and plantations, or from being employed in the coasting trade of Great Britain.

Secondly, a great variety of the most bulky articles of importation can be brought into Great Britain only, either in such ships as are above described, or in ships of the country where those goods are produced, and of which the owners, masters, and three-fourths of the mariners, are of that particular country; and when imported even in ships of this latter kind, they are subject to double aliens duty. If imported in ships of any other country, the penalty is forfeiture of ship and goods. When this act was made, the Dutch were, what they still are, the great carriers of Europe, and by this regulation they were entirely excluded from being the carriers to Great Britain, or from importing to us the goods of any other European country.

Thirdly, a great variety of the most bulky articles of importation are prohibited from being imported, even in British ships, from any country but that in which they are produced; under pain of forfeiting ship and cargo. This regulation too was probably intended against the Dutch. Holland was then, as now, the great emporium for all European goods, and by this regulation, British ships were hindered from loading in Holland the goods of any other European country.

Fourthly, salt fish of all kinds, whale-fins, whale-bone, oil, and blubber, not caught by and cured on board British vessels, when imported into Great Britain, are subjected to double aliens duty. The Dutch, as they are still the principal, were then the only fishers in Europe that attempted to supply foreign nations with fish. By this regulation, a very heavy burden was laid upon their supplying Great Britain.

When the act of navigation was made, though England and Holland were not actually at war, the most violent animosity subsisted between the two nations. It had begun during the government of the long parliament, which first framed this act, and it broke out soon after in the Dutch wars during that of the Protector and of Charles the Second. It is not impossible, therefore, that some of the regulations of this famous act may have proceeded from national animosity. They are as wise, however, as if they had all been dictated by the most deliberate wisdom. National animosity at that particular time aimed at the very same object which the most deliberate wisdom would have recommended, the diminution of the naval power of Holland, the only naval power which could endanger the security of England.

The act of navigation is not favourable to foreign commerce, or to the growth of that opulence which can arise from it. The interest of a nation in its commercial relations to foreign nations is, like that of a merchant with regard to the different people with whom he deals, to buy as cheap and to sell as dear as possible. . . .

To expect, indeed, that the freedom of trade should ever be entirely restored in Great Britain, is as absurd as to expect that an Oceana or Utopia should ever be established in it. Not only the prejudices of the public, but what is much more unconquerable, the private interests of many individuals, irresistibly oppose it. Were the officers of the army to oppose with the same zeal and unanimity any reduction in the number of forces, with which master manufacturers set themselves against every law that is likely to increase the number of their rivals in the home market; were the former to animate their soldiers, in the same manner as the latter enflame their workmen, to attack with violence and outrage the proposers of any such regulation; to attempt to reduce the army would be as dangerous as it has now become to attempt to diminish in any respect the monopoly which our manufacturers have obtained against us. This monopoly has so much increased the number of some particular tribes of them, that, like an overgrown standing army, they have become formidable to the government, and upon many occasions intimidate the legislature. The member of parliament who supports every proposal for strengthening this monopoly, is sure to acquire not only the reputation of understanding trade, but great popularity and influence with an order of men whose numbers and wealth render them of great importance. If he opposes them, on the contrary, and still more if he has authority enough to be able to thwart them, neither the most acknowledged probity, nor the highest rank, nor the greatest public services, can protect him from the most infamous abuse and detraction, from personal insults, nor sometimes from real danger, arising from the insolent outrage of furious and disappointed monopolists.

The undertaker of a great manufacture, who, by the home markets being suddenly laid open to the competition of foreigners, should be obliged to abandon his trade, would no doubt suffer very considerably. That part of his capital which had usually been employed in purchasing materials and in paying his workmen, might, without much difficulty, perhaps, find another employment. But that part of it which was fixed in workhouses, and in the instruments of trade, could scarce be disposed of without considerable loss. The equitable regard, therefore, to his interest requires that changes of this kind should never be introduced suddenly, but slowly, gradually, and after a very long warning. The legislature, were it possible that its deliberations could be always directed, not by the clamorous importunity of partial interests, but by an extensive view of the general good, ought upon this very account, perhaps, to be particularly careful neither to establish any new monopolies of this kind, nor to extend further those which are already established. Every such regulation introduces some degree of real disorder into the constitution of the state, which it will be difficult afterwards to cure without occasioning another disorder.

How far it may be proper to impose taxes upon the importation of foreign goods, in order, not to prevent their importation, but to raise a revenue for government, I shall consider hereafter when I come to treat of taxes. Taxes imposed with a view to prevent, or even diminish importation, are evidently as destructive of the revenue of the customs as of the freedom of trade.

PROPOSALS FOR A REVENUE TARIFF[3]

John Maynard Keynes (Baron Keynes), 1883–1946, the most influential economic thinker of the 20th century, departed from the classical pre-

[3]Excerpted from *Essays in Persuasion* by John Maynard Keynes, pp. 271–280. MacMillan and Co., Limited, 1931.

cepts of the free economy when, in 1929, he endorsed a political plan to promote employment by government spending. During the Depression of the 1930s, his views influenced a number of Western governments to implement large-scale economic plans, such as the New Deal in the USA. His main precepts are laid down in *The General Theory of Employment, Interest, and Money* (1936).

Do you think it a paradox that we can continue to increase our capital wealth by adding both to our foreign investments and to our equipment at home, that we can continue to live (most of us) much as usual or better, and support at the same time a vast body of persons in idleness with a dole greater than the income of a man in full employment in most parts of the world—and yet do all this with one quarter of our industrial plant closed down and one quarter of our industrial workers unemployed? . . .

I am of the opinion that a policy of expansion, though desirable, is not safe or practicable today, unless it is accompanied by other measures which would neutralise its dangers. Let me remind the reader what these dangers are. There is the burden on the trade balance, the burden on the Budget, and the effect on confidence. If the policy of expansion were to justify itself eventually by increasing materially the level of profits and the volume of employment, the net effect on the Budget and on confidence would in the end be favourable and perhaps very favourable. But this might not be the initial effect.

What measures are available to neutralise these dangers? A decision to reform the grave abuses of the dole, and a decision to postpone for the present all new charges on the Budget for social services in order to conserve its resources to meet schemes for the expansion of employment, are advisable and should be taken. But the main decision which seems to me to-day to be absolutely forced on any wise Chancellor of the Exchequer, whatever his beliefs about Protection, is the introduction of a substantial revenue tariff. It is certain that there is no other measure all the immediate consequences of which will be favourable and appropriate. The tariff which I have in mind would include no discriminating protectives taxes, but would cover as wide a field as possible at a flat rate or perhaps two flat rates, each applicable to wide categories of goods. Rebates would be allowed in respect of imported material entering into exports, but raw materials, which make up an important proportion of the value of exports, such as wool and cotton, would be exempt. The amount of revenue to be aimed at should be substantial, not less than £50,000,000 and, if possible,

£75,000,000. Thus, for example, there might be import duties of 15 per cent on all manufactured and semi-manufactured goods without exception, and of 5 per cent on all food stuffs and certain raw materials, whilst other raw materials would be exempt. [In a subsequent article I agreed that this precise scale of duties could not be relied on to produce so large a revenue as that suggested above, and that £40,000,000 was a safer estimate.] I am prepared to maintain that the effect of such duties on the cost of living would be insignificant—no greater than the existing fluctuation between one month and another. Moreover, any conceivable remedy for unemployment will have the effect, and, indeed, will be intended, to raise prices. Equally, the effect on the cost of our exports, after allowing for the rebates which should be calculated on broad and simple lines, would be very small. It should be the declared intention of the Free Trade parties acquiescing in this decision to remove the duties in the event of world prices recovering to the level of 1929.

Compared with any alternative which is open to us, this measure is unique in that it would at the same time relieve the pressing problems of the Budget and restore business confidence. I do not believe that a wise and prudent Budget can be framed to-day without recourse to a revenue tariff. But this is not its only advantage. In so far as it leads to the substitution of home-produced goods for goods previously imported, it will increase employment in this country. At the same time, by relieving the pressure on the balance of trade it will provide a much-needed margin to pay for the additional imports which a policy of expansion will require and to finance loans by London to necessitous debtor countries. In these ways, the buying power which we take away from the rest of the world by restricting certain imports we shall restore to it with the other hand. Some fanatical Free Traders might allege that the adverse effect of import duties on our exports would neutralise all this; but it would not be true.

Free Traders may, consistently with their faith, regard a revenue tariff as our iron ration, which can be used once only in emergency. The emergency has arrived. Under cover of the breathing space and the margin of financial strength thus afforded us, we could frame a policy and a plan, both domestic and international, for marching to the assault against the spirit of contractionism and fear.

If, on the other hand, Free Traders reject these counsels of expediency, the certain result will be to break the present Government and to substitute for it, in the confusion of a Crisis of Confidence, a Cabinet pledged to a full protectionist programme.

II. THE CASE FOR PROTECTIONISM

EDITOR'S INTRODUCTION

The world has never known genuine free trade as envisioned by Adam Smith. Indeed, the Western creed of free trade is an alien concept to our contemporary Asian trading partners. The economies of Japan, South Korea, and Taiwan are successful, in part, because of the protectionist policies of their governments. This Asian prosperity has, in turn, led many Americans to re-examine the rationale for free trade. This section discusses the case for protectionism. In the first article, Gus Tyler, writing in *Dissent,* presents historical and economic arguments to dispel the "myth of free trade." The second article, appearing in the British journal *World Today,* offers economic arguments in support of European protectionism. The section concludes with an article from the *Harvard Business Review* entitled "The Folly of Free Trade." The author, University of Wisconsin economist John M. Culbertson, declares that "our blind allegiance to free trade threatens our national standard of living and our economic future."

THE MYTH OF FREE TRADE[1]

Free trade is a myth. It does not exist; it never did exist, with the possible and limited exception of a brief period when Britain practiced it as well as preached it to expand its near-monopoly over world manufacture.

It is a myth that has bred a progeny of myths: the Peace Myth, that the "century of peace" between the Treaty of Vienna (1815) and the outbreak of World War I (1914) was due to free trade;

[1]Reprint of a magazine article by Gus Tyler, assistant president of the ILGWU. *Dissent.* 35:212-218, Spring '88. Reprinted by permission.

the Depression Myth, that the Smoot-Hawley Tariff Act of 1930 caused or prolonged the Great Depression; and the Current Myth, that the great nations of the world in the post–World War II era have been working toward free trade.

The myth is so powerful that it dominates virtually all thinking of America's academics, who continue to reiterate classic clichés that never did and certainly do not today square with reality. The myth nourishes the high-flown rhetoric of statesmen who prate of free trade while practicing all sorts of protectionism. The myth is embraced by conservative businessmen who use it to promote their special economic interests, and it is dear to liberals, who see it as a way to curb monopolies, to help Third World countries, and to promote internationalism.

That free trade is a myth does not necessarily mean that it is bad. History is full of myths that have served mankind well. But this is a mischievous myth: It conceals the real problem of the world economy, maldistribution of income; it speeds the collapse of the American economy; it turns to globalized *laissez-faire* at a moment when the countries of the world need massive and collective intervention by governments in their highly interdependent economies.

Disraeli saw free trade for what it was when, in the 1843 debate over repeal of the British Corn Laws, he said: "Free trade is not a principle, it is an expedient." In the following century, however, free trade did indeed become a "principle" of prevailing economic dogma. "I was brought up, like most Englishmen," wrote John Maynard Keynes, "to respect free trade not only as an economic doctrine which a rational and instructed person could not doubt, but almost as part of the moral law. I regarded ordinary departures from it as being at the same time an imbecility and an outrage."

As an "expedient," free trade served the interests of the rising British textile manufacturers in the years following the Napoleonic Wars. England was the workshop of the world, far ahead of any possible competitors in its manufacturing potential. To open all markets everywhere meant to allow British manufactured goods to be sold everywhere and to deny other countries the opportunity to develop their own "infant industry." In addition, repeal of the Corn Laws meant that British bread would be cheaper and employers, heeding the "iron law of wages," could pay less to their employees.

John Stuart Mill understood the political dynamic behind Corn Law repeal. "A cause seldom triumphs unless somebody's personal interest is bound up with it. It would have been long before the Corn Laws would have been abolished in Great Britain [if] those laws had not been contrary to the private interests of nearly the whole of the manufacturing and mercantile classes."

The "expedient" became a principle in the hands of Adam Smith, who saw economics as a subhead of theology—as a modern way to prove the existence of God "by design." Smith, a professor of moral philosophy, envisioned a world governed by a "divine being whose benevolence and wisdom have, from all eternity, contrived and conducted the immense machinery of the Universe so as at all times to produce the greatest possible quantity of happiness." God did not do this by personal appearances but by applying "the invisible hand." To prove that the Great Designer of the universe could work his benevolent will despite man's selfishness, Smith wrote *The Wealth of Nations* to reveal a grand design wherein even man's greed served the common good. To interfere with the working of the "immense machinery," the "invisible hand," was an immoral act, a sin against the "divine being." The true believer would not get in God's way but would let things be (*laissez-faire*) in both domestic and international trade. To do otherwise was to imply that man was wiser than God—a blasphemous thought.

The working of the "invisible hand" was, of course, visible for those who would see through the eyes of Adam Smith. Providence had seen to it that each country should be more adept at producing a given product than some other country. (Richardo later called these superior talents "natural attributes" that gave each country a "comparative advantage.") Each land would do what it could do best and exchange its wares with those of another country, thereby blessing the earth with "the greatest possible quantity of happiness." In this mysterious way, egoism became altruism. (No wonder that Keynes was taught to think of free trade as "part of the moral law.")

So profoundly and devoutly did Britain believe in the credo of free trade that it was ready to use armed force to impose this divinely ordained freedom on others—as in the Opium Wars. In 1839, China confiscated shipments of opium that the British, contrary to agreement, were smuggling into China. Britain, on behalf of the smugglers, declared war on China. In Parliament the action was defended as a necessary step to preserve "free trade."

When other countries began to develop manufacturing capacity, English free traders demanded that an embargo be placed on British-made machinery and on British coal so that other nations might not catch up with Britain. When, despite British efforts to keep other nations dependent on its manufactures, competitors did appear on the scene, Britain turned to the idea of empire as the answer. Trade barriers would be removed within the "commonwealth" while duties were imposed on those outside the commonwealth. Although such a move was clearly massive "protectionism," Joseph Chamberlain found suitable language to present the proposition as an improved form of free trade. "I say that such a proposal might commend itself even to an orthodox free trader," said Chamberlain in 1896. "It would be the greatest advance that free trade has ever made, to extend its doctrines permanently to more than 30 million of the human race."

Thus was the myth of free trade perpetuated as Britain set forth to organize the biggest protected market in the world—a model repeated in the next century by the European Common Market, a device to minimize trade barriers within a circumscribed zone while raising barriers against all those outside the zone. The interplay between "free trade" and empire is brilliantly documented by Bernard Semmell in a book with the oxymoronic title of *The Rise of Free Trade Imperialism*.

Although the myth of free trade was to provide the rhetorical rationale for imperialism, the real reason for Britain's expansionism was its need to deal with the perennial problem of "glut," the simultaneous "glut" of commodities, capital, and people—the Achilles' heel of any capitalist society cursed by a lopsided maldistribution of income. An empire provided a place to invest surplus capital, a place to ship surplus wares in exchange for cheap raw material, and a place to export surplus population—the jobless, the poor, the criminal riffraff.

This British "solution" became the European solution, turning the century after the Treaty of Vienna into the Age of Imperialism, with its bloody and brutal conquest of tens of millions of "lesser" peoples in Africa, Australia, Asia, and Latin America. In the lexicon of the free trade mythologists, however, this war-drenched era was defined as the "century of peace." Thus, Milton and Rose Friedman:

The century from Waterloo to the First World War offers a striking example of the beneficial effects of free trade among nations . . . one of the most peaceful [periods] in human history among western nations, marred only by some minor wars—the Crimean War and the Franco-Prussian War are the most memorable—and, of course, a major Civil War within the United States.

The peace myth is based on the fact that among the "western nations" there was no *major* conflict for a whole century—a fact that has little to do with free trade but much to do with the great powers' fear of another French Revolution and its bastard child Napoleon. As Viscount Castlereagh put it: "The existing Concert [of Powers] is their only perfect security against the revolutionary embers more or less existing in every state of Europe; true wisdom is to keep down the petty contentions of ordinary times, and to stand together in support of the established principles of social order."

In line with that policy, the great powers combined their forces to put down revolutions both in Europe and the Americas; they agreed to hold down wars among themselves for fear of revolution; instead they turned their militaries loose upon the defenseless peoples of continents still unblessed by Christianity. The result was a century of unending war. As Queen Victoria—the epitome of the Imperialist Age—put it: "If we are to maintain our position as a first-rate power, we must, with our Indian Empire and large Colonies, be prepared for attacks and wars, somewhere or other, CONTINUALLY." (The capitals are Victoria's—G.T.) The century of "peace" was a century of war—CONTINUALLY.

Sooner or later, these continual wars, directed against weaker peoples, had to become wars between the great powers. The earth did not expand with the expanding needs and appetites of the imperialist nations. They began to collide in China, Africa, India, Persia, Latin America, the Middle East, and the crumbling remnants of the Ottoman Empire. The Great War (World War I) was the inevitable consequence of the Age of Imperialism, the bloodiest conflict in human history up to that time. Yet, the myth hath it, this was a century of peace—cradled by "free trade."

In this case, the myth rests on another myth, since there was virtually no free trade as well as no peace. Britain had given up the practice, although mumbling away at the preachments, well before the turn of the century. Both Germany and the United

States—soon to challenge British dominance in manufacture—rejected "free trade" because they saw in it "perfidious Albion's" trick to enslave other nations eager to develop their own industries.

American manufacture was reared behind a protectionist fence almost from the day of the nation's birth. In 1789, on July Fourth—Independence Day—the infant United States decided to protect its "infant industries" by passing a tariff bill, among whose stated purposes was "the encouragement and protection of manufacturers." In his *Report on Manufactures* (1791) Secretary of the Treasury Alexander Hamilton outlined a comprehensive plan for the development of manufacture that called for outright bans on certain competing imports and subsidies for exports. The War of 1812 spurred American manufacture; but when the war ended, Britain set out to destroy this competition. As Henry Brougham put it to Parliament in 1816: "It was well worth while to incur a loss upon the first exportation, in order, by glut, to stifle in the cradle, those rising manufacturers in the United States, which the war had forced into existence, contrary to the natural course of things." The United States struck back. In 1816, Congress passed a tariff act whose stated intent was purely protectionist, lifting rates by 42 percent over the prewar level. In 1828, Congress enacted a law that free-traders, mainly southern agricultural interests, called the Tariff of Abominations.

After southern influence was weakened by the Civil War, protectionism ran rampant, like a wild pig. Although there was only one nickel mine in the United States, owned by Joseph Wharton, an act of 1870 protected the company against all foreign competition. Then there were the McKinley Tariff of 1890, setting duties on manufactured goods higher than ever before; the Wilson-Gorman Tariff, which, despite Democratic President Cleveland's efforts, did virtually nothing to lower the existing high tariffs; the Dingley Act, passed in McKinley's administration, which restored the 1890 schedule; and the Payne-Aldrich Tariff of 1909, which continued the tradition. Even under Democratic President Woodrow Wilson, the Underwood-Simmons Act lowered tariffs by a mere 10 percent.

Whatever the merits or demerits of these acts—protectionism plus piggishness—they make a mockery of the myth that the century prior to World War I was an era of "free trade" so far as the U.S. went.

As for the European powers, they were involved in amassing their empires with their systems of preferences and exclusions.

Increases in tariff levels did not end with World War I. The Emergency Act of 1921 and the Fordney-McCumber Act of 1922 lifted the tariff to the highest level ever—with no apparent negative effects on the American economy as a whole. Indeed, in 1929 America's output in goods and services hit the highest point in the nation's history.

Then in the fall of 1929 came the Great Depression. Glut had returned! The capacity to consume could not keep up with the capacity to produce—the ancient inevitable of a gross maldistribution of income.

The following year, the Smoot-Hawley Tariff was enacted. It was not a response to the depression. It started as an effort on the part of American agriculture to get the same kind of protection afforded American manufacture. All its major features were clearly in place *before* the depression and it did not become effective until *after* the depression. Nevertheless, free trade mythology charges that Smoot-Hawley caused the Great Depression of the 1930s.

Thus, Edward E. Yardeni, economist for Prudential-Bache, writes:

The single most catastrophic cause of the Great Depression was the Smoot-Hawley Tariff of June 1930. Not the stock market crash of October 1929. Not the collapse of the Austrian Kreditanstalt bank during May 1931. Not the sharp increase in the Federal Reserve's discount rate during October 1931. Not the tax increase of 1932. Not the bank failures and not the collapse of the money stock. All these events contributed to the explosion, but the detonator was the tariff.

Yardeni's is a 1985 version of a myth that is so widespread that it is accepted as a "given." Yet all the facts run to the contrary.

The Great Depression began *before*, not *after*, Smoot-Hawley. The slump in the economy started in June 1929 (a few months before the stock market crash) and continued on to June 1930 (when Smoot-Hawley was enacted) and beyond. The decline in the eleven months *before* Smoot-Hawley was far more precipitate than in the eleven months after.

Smoot-Hawley had virtually no impact on the downward trend at all: the decline just continued downward on an almost straight line graph. The tariff had insignificant influence, because the tariff itself was statistically insignificant.

In 1930, American imports came to about $3 billion, which was 3.3 percent of the Gross National Product. Of the $3 billion in imports, two-thirds came in *free*. The actual duties calculated for 1930 came to $482 million—a sum equal to one-half of 1 percent of the Gross National Product. Of the duties collected, moreover, Smoot-Hawley was only responsible for about 32 percent of the sum. So the final impact of Smoot-Hawley was about one sixth of 1 percent of the GNP.

To allege that such a trivial sum could have triggered or prolonged the Depression is a myth. It is also a mischievous myth because it attributes the Depression to Smoot-Hawley instead of to the gross maldistribution of income in the years leading up to 1929. Yet the myth had (has) its appeal to conservatives who prefer to point to Smoot-Hawley rather than income imbalance as the cause of the depression and to progressives waging their traditional war against monopolies.

Free trade enjoyed a brief revival in the immediate post–World War II period, almost exactly a century after the repeal of the Corn Laws. This time the prime mover was not Britain but a United States that in the post-Hitler era found itself in almost exactly the same position as Britain in the post-Napoleonic period. The U.S. was now the "Workshop of the World," the source of manufactured commodities, machinery, and of capital. The strong American dollar could buy raw materials, such as petroleum, cheaply. "Free trade" for the U.S. meant a world market for its goods made with inexpensive raw materials, as it did for the British a century before.

Once more history repeated itself. Just as Britain was soon challenged by the United States and the European continent by producers who had risen from infancy behind protected walls, so too did the United States find itself challenged by the European Common Market and by Japan and, later, other countries—including recently "backward" nations. The challenge came quickly this time because American producers, unable to export their products to closed markets, simply exported their production, locating their facilities in lands where wages and taxes were low and where "protective" walls were high. For American producers who did their work in such favored lands, the idea of free trade *in the United States* was a delight, allowing them to produce and sell in "protected" markets overseas while exporting to the United States with its "unprotected" market.

Although the United States also began to devise its own protective measures, by relative standards, America—mired in a muddy myth—became an island of free trade in a protectionist ocean whose waves were washing away American manufacture. The myth, however, was not the only reason that America began to suffer the deindustrialization that Britain had experienced at the end of the last century. For American manufacturers who could produce and sell in protected markets overseas or who could produce cheaply in Third World countries and sell expensively in America, "free trade" in the United States was their updated version of "protectionism." For American importers and retailers, ditto. For American bankers who had made bad loans to Third World countries, their chief "protection" was a "free trade" policy in the United States that would allow debtor countries to export to the United States far more than they would import from the United States.

To these economic reasons for favoring "free trade" in the United States must be added a major *political* reason: the purchase of allies in exchange for pieces of the American market—so many bases in exchange for allowing so many cars, panties, or television sets to be sold in the United States.

Despite these many pressures of special interests and of the State and Defense Departments in favor of "free trade," the United States was compelled—as was Britain toward the end of the last century—to turn toward "protectionism." But so powerful was the hold of the free trade myth on the thinking of the world, especially the Western world, that protectionist practices had to be garbed in free trade dress. Thus, the great nations met in "round" after "round" to announce reductions of *tariff* barriers and then rushed home to erect nontariff barriers, thousands of little pieces of red tape to break the legs of anyone trying to penetrate their boundaries with foreign goods that they did not want. To encourage exports, they all—including the United States—concocted super-sophisticated forms of subsidies, a no-no of classic free trade policy. They "negotiated" VERs (voluntary export restraints), which were quotas. Then they indulged in the ultimate and most deceptive form of protectionism, devaluation of currency, under the universal explanation that it was a way to ensure a "level playing field."

To the United States, the world's greatest creditor nation now turning into the world's greatest debtor nation thanks to annual trade deficits of more than $100 billion a year, devaluation of the dollar appeared to be a natural solution. By cheapening the dollar vis-à-vis other currencies, American-made products could be bought inexpensively by people with yen, francs, lire, or marks, and foreign-made products would be more expensive for Americans making purchases with weak dollars. The resultant rise in exports and decline in imports would reduce America's trade deficit.

What made this "solution" appealing is that it did not involve tariffs, quotas, nontariff barriers, or subsidies. Hence, it was touted as "nonprotectionist," even as "antiprotectionist," because it was a way to relieve pressure for quotas, tariffs and subsidies in the United States.

Once more the power of the free trade myth displayed itself, because the deliberate devaluation of the American dollar was pure-and-simple *protectionism*. When the dollar declined by 50 percent against the Deutschmark and the Japanese yen, as it did through most of 1987, the cost of any import from these countries was automatically doubled: what cost one dollar now cost two dollars. In effect, this was exactly the same as imposing an additional tariff of 100 percent on imports from these countries.

This "protectionist" measure worked—at least in part. By 1987, the *volume* of imports to the United States fell and the *volume* of exports rose—as expected. But, in terms of dollars and cents, the trade deficit was rising instead of falling, because whatever was imported required many more dollars. The consequence was that trade deficits—measured moneywise—rose to unprecedented heights.

There were other negative features of dollar devaluation. Because world oil is priced in dollars, some of America's competitors were able to buy petroleum at bargain rates, while America could not. To pay for imports, the United States had to borrow money from abroad, requirng it to allocate an ever larger percent of its products to pay interest on overseas loans. Dollar devaluation was also witlessly discriminatory, giving "protection" to some industries that did not need it and got it anyhow because they were competing against German and Japanese producers, but denying protection to other industries, primarily labor intensive, that were competing against Hong Kong, Singapore, Taiwan, and

44

The Reference Shelf

South Korea (whose currencies were pegged to the American dollar) or against Latin American countries whose currencies were falling even more rapidly than the dollar.

In sum, dollar devaluation is PROTECTIONISM in a form that is clumsy, irrationally discriminatory, a longtime drain on the nation's funds, and a fatal threat to the future of America once overseas investors conclude that to invest in dollars is to invest in a vanishing value. Yet—alas the myth—dollar devaluation is presented as "free trade's" answer to "protectionism."

The sad story is that the world today is probably more heavily "protectionist" than at any time in world history. Trade wars are being waged without halt. If they are less visible than in the past, it is due to the near abandonment of crass old weapons like tariffs and prohibitions in favor of sly supersophisticated stratagems such as government financing of production at home or consumption overseas with interest-free (low-interest) loans, suppression of worker rights to reduce production costs, and the government's purchasing obsolete machinery, designating inaccessible ports of entry for imports, revaluating currencies, specifying purchasing restrictions, *etcetera, ad infinitum, ad nauseam.*

The world war in trade is heating up because in the present world market no nation can make it without waging war against others, for the very simple reason that the world market cannot consume what the world can produce. There is a global imbalance between the planetary power to produce and the people's power to consume—that is, to buy. The ancient plague is back. The world is glutted with commodities, capital, and people without work.

This inherent and natural ailment of a capitalist society was somewhat countered in the near half century from 1930 to 1980 by policies of growth and redistribution (Keynesianism?) to contain the suicidal instincts of a capitalism left to the capitalists. In the years following World War II, however, governments have found it increasingly difficult, almost impossible, to continue such policies—even when they want to—because they are increasingly losing control of their national economies. The great corporations that governments tried to control are now getting out of control as the multinational replaces the national company. These global corporations—globally owned and operated, gathering capital from many lands, and locating their operations in many lands—are able to thumb their noses at governmental regulations. If the "business climate," as interpreted by a corporation, is not attractive in one part of the globe, the company moves its activities to another part. The old "natural attributes" that once provided "comparative advantages" to a company in a given land are now replaced by unnatural attributes—such as tariffs, quotas, subsidies, nontariff barriers, and currency devaluation—that bestow the "comparative advantage" on given geographic sites for corporate location. The natural propensity of such corporations, as Adam Smith noted, is to maximize gain, which—in a modern world where virtually all the factors of production are portable—means to locate where wages and taxes are low and protective walls are high. In the long run, this means relocation of the centers of production from high-wage to low-wage countries, from lands with progressive social policies to those with oppressive social policies. Such relocation means a redistribution of world income, a polarization with more income to a tiny top and less for everyone else.

The decoupling of corporation from country is nowhere better exemplified than in the American experience over the last two decades. In 1966, American multinational corporations had 17.7 percent of the world market; in 1983, American multinationals had exactly the same share of the world market. But the United States that enjoyed 17.5 percent of the world market in 1966 had only 13.9 percent in 1983. The reason for this odd development? American-headquartered multinationals do much of their production in other lands. Indeed, American multinationals in Japan do such a thriving business there that, if their sales in Japan were to be reckoned as American "exports" to Japan (which, of course, they are not), the balance of trade between Japan and the United States would be in America's favor.

Among the nations first to be adversely affected by the flight of the multinational operations to low-wage, low-tax, protectionist lands is the United States. Its relatively high wages and social programs make it a place to be avoided by the corporations. The consequence has been a steady deindustrialization of the United States, a deindustrialization inflicted on America by many of its most prominent multinational corporations.

One of the immediate effects has been the polarization of income in the United States as many of the blue-collar jobs—the upward escalator in America—have been wiped out. An equally devastating effect has been the increasing inability of the government to stimulate the economy by borrowing and spending. The stimulants that the government seeks to pour into the economy by deficit spending are wasted, as the "stimulant" goes to purchase wares made in other countries. In effect, America's "free trade" commitment has meant that government expenditures have stimulated economies in other countries.

The end result is to weaken the American economy and, simultaneously, to make it more difficult for the government to come to the rescue by traditional Keynesian strategies. Although this is at the root of America's present troubles, the United States is not alone. The global corporation is a threat to every advanced economy.

At present there is no supranational political institution to play a balancing role vis-à-vis global corporations in the way that past national sovereignties did vis-à-vis their national corporations. While the world economy has been (or is being) transformed into a global "factory" in a global "village," no corresponding political institutions have, as yet, emerged. Nor can they, so long as our thinking is bemused by an eighteenth-century myth, yclept "free trade."

PROTECTIONISM, WHY NOT?[2]

We seem to be surrounded these days by important people who tell us that protectionism is a terrible thing, and that the creeping tide of trade restrictions must be turned back if we are ever to escape from world recession. At the April Summit of Heads of State, all seven were agreed (so we were told) that one of the most important challenges facing the industrial countries is to find ways to stop the growth of protectionism. Here in London, the Commonwealth Secretariat produced a report in 1982 called "Protectionism—threat to international order—impact on developing countries." In April this year, the organisation's Sec-

[2]Reprint of a magazine article by Susan Strange, professor of international relations at the London School of Economics. *World Today* 41:148-50. August/September 1985. Reprinted with permission.

retary-General followed up with a memorandum on development prospects which declared that "the central problem is the increase in protectionist pressures and measures—especially in major economies—over the last decade." (*Development Prospects, Policy Options and Negotiations*, p. 26. London: Commonwealth Secretariat, April 1985)

President Reagan was most anxious that the Summit meeting should set a date for new multilateral trade talks. It did not because President Mitterrand said he thought monetary reform was more important and he would not agree to setting a date for trade talks. The Americans are backed by the secretariat of GATT (General Agreement on Trade and Tariffs).

Their last report concluded its introductory chapter by declaring that

When discrimination in international trade becomes acceptable, the general level of protection *cannot but rise*. Indeed [it went on] there is *no way* of maintaining an international trade *system* in the full sense of the word, referring to regularity, orderliness and predictability, without the most-favoured-nation commitment. If the system was to be maintained [it ended], parties to the GATT would have to indicate in some binding manner their willingness to return to the nondiscriminatory trading system embodied in the General Agreement. ("International Trade," 1983/4, pages 20 and 22)

The same message has come not only from the GATT secretariat in Geneva but also from UNCTAD (United Nations Conference on Trade and Development).

The Indian delegate, speaking for the Group of 77 in March this year said he thought the most immediate concern of the Trade and Development Board should be the trading system. Here, "the supreme task was to restore confidence in the system by implementing commitments already undertaken on stand-still and roll-back of protectionism and on increasing the access of developing countries to the markets of the developed countries." (UNCTAD Bulletin, April 1985, p. 7)

On all sides we are told that, if the creeping tide of protectionist measures is not turned, things will get progressively worse; that trade disputes will become trade wars, possibly breaking up the western alliance even if they do not lead (as it is said of the 1930s) to something much worse still. Already, some people are pointing to the American Congress voting $2 bn to help American grain exporters undercut the French in the Algerian market. The downward slide to economic perdition, they say, is already beginning.

In short, there are at present many distinguished people—economists and academics as well as officials—all saying more or less the same thing: "If we don't do something about the 'new protectionism', the world economy will never recover, developing countries will never develop, things will go from bad to worse."

I believe this to be a great myth; it is a piece of conventional wisdom that asks to be challenged. I shall argue that world trade is not seriously jeopardised by protectionism and that behind the conventional unwisdom there is a coalition of vested interests with particular reasons for going on at such tedious length about the dangers of protectionism.

What I do believe is that the real weakness of the world economy lies elsewhere, and results from 10–15 years of monetary mismanagement and financial uncertainty. It is the instability of the banking system; the unpredictability of perverse exchange rates; interest rates far too high for productive investment as distinct from speculative investment; a volatile and uncertain market for oil; and the shrinkage of the less developed countries' (LDCs) purchasing power in the aftermath of debt repayment problems that is the real trouble.

The wringing of hands over protectionism only serves to distract our attention from these real problems.

I also believe that there is little danger of protectionism spreading like some kind of infectious disease and that the general outlook for world trade is not too bad.

The Facts

The GATT report for 1983–84 noted that the volume of world trade in that year was at an all-time high. In the first half of 1984, it actually increased by 9 per cent. This was nearly double the rise in world production in 1984. Despite the drop in the volume of trade in oil (8 per cent) and other minerals, trade in manufactures rose 4 per cent. The overall rise in trade in the period covered by the report was 2 per cent, more than making good the relatively small fall in trade experienced in 1982–83. In short, we were back to 1980–81, despite the weak oil market, and despite the continued problems of debtor countries. World trade in manufactures, indeed, which suffered a rather milder hiccup in 1981–82 than it suffered in 1974–75 was back again on the upward trend which, if continued, will be double its 1973 level well before the end of the 1980s.

From the way the Commonwealth Secretariat and some champions of the Group of 77 talk, one would think that the LDCs were the chief victims of trade policies. So it is rather surprising to see from the GATT figures that LDC exports of manufactures rose by 9 per cent, more than twice the overall figure. That was in terms of volume; by value, and largely because of the rising dollar, they rose by 15 per cent. Some victims!

Particular attention is given in such circles, as I have quoted, to the infamous Multi-Fibre Agreement and the restrictions it has put on LDC exports of textiles and clothes. The record suggests, however, that it has not been very effective. "Of the two main areas of supply," says GATT, "exports from industrial countries declined, while those from developing countries increased." The latter now take 25 per cent of the world market for textiles and 42 per cent of that in clothing. In 1983, textile "imports from developing countries increased faster than total imports" into the United States and were up $14\frac{1}{2}$ per cent in 1982. As an exporter, Hong Kong increased the volume of its textile exports by 30 per cent, of its exports of clothes by $6\frac{1}{2}$ per cent. The colony's overall clothing trade surplus went up from $1.27 bn in 1973 to $3.51 bn in 1983. South Korea's record is similar. Its exports of textiles and clothes to the United States in the thick of the world recession rose steadily from $162m in 1981 to $260m in 1983. Its exports to Japan were nearly three times as great in 1983 as they had been in 1980.

In automotive and electronic manufactures the story for the exports from LDCs is the same. It also shows that Voluntary Export Restriction (VER) agreements are not entirely effective. Japan—the object of both American and European protectionism—increased its exports of cars and automotive parts by $9\frac{1}{2}$ per cent. "Despite the various import restrictions," says the same GATT report, "the rapidly expanding North American market took one half of these exports, or 19 per cent more than in the preceding year." Its share of world exports of automobile parts is worth nearly $6bn: it rose in 1983 by 27 per cent. And Mexico and Brazil (not to mention other newly industrialised countries like Spain and South Korea) are rapidly increasing their market shares. Mexican and Brazilian exports of parts to North America rose by 45 per cent in 1983 to $1\frac{1}{2}$ bn.

In electronic products, trade is booming: up 13 per cent despite the large number of bilateral "voluntary" export restraint agreements. Most of the growth is in Japanese exports to the United States, but seven Asian countries are also busy expanding their exports of electronic components and semi-manufactures.

We can conclude from these facts that protectionism is no great threat to the prosperity of the international system. It may well be that, without the protectionism we have, the shift of manufacturing industry from North to South would have been even greater and even faster. No-one knows. What is clear is that it has not been bad enough either to stop the growth of world trade or to stop the growth of LDCs' exports of manufactures. In dollar value, LDCs' exports of manufactures are now five times what they were in 1973 while trade in manufactures is three times what it was in 1973 and LDC exports of primary products are only three times what they were in 1973 (in dollar value, that is).

It should be added that we do not know for sure that there has been a net increase in protectionism. It is true that there has been an increase in trade restrictions—but there has also been an increase in opportunities, opportunities opened up by bilateral agreements, by tariff liberalisation in the past and by joint production arrangements and so forth. We do not really know what the net figure is or how to measure it.

Secondly, there is the question of efficiency. Predictably, the International Monetary Fund (IMF) joins the general cacophony of voices about 'the new protectionism'—indeed it was one of their staff who first coined the phrase. The IMF says that counter-trade, which is a kind of bilateral trade, adds 12–15 per cent to transaction costs in international trade. Yet if you spread that 15 per cent over all the transaction costs for an export industry or for an importing company, the difference in average transaction costs may be much less, while the marginal benefit both to the company and to the exporting country may be rather more than 15 per cent. The fact is that some trade in certain circumstances may be better than no trade, even at some increased cost.

How, then, are we to explain all the weeping and wailing and gnashing of teeth that has been going on about the new protectionism?

The Explanations

The first point is that people do not look at the facts. They do not actually read the GATT report. They rely on tribal memories, and tribal memories are often more based on tribal myths than on historical facts. The facts are that the 1980s are very different from the 1930s and that most of the tribal memories of the 1930s are wrong. It is true that from 1929 to 1933 there was a drop in world trade of the order of 26 per cent. The drop this time was only 2 per cent. What was the same was that the cause of the slump, of the slow growth and the unemployment was the lack of purchasing power due to sudden shrinkage of credit. After the Wall Street crash in 1929, the world economy suffered from a sudden sharp shrinkage of American credit and of British credit. That then brought about shrinkage of trade from people who no longer had the purchasing power to buy imports. All over the world, governments responded with protectionism. But protectionism was only the response to the financial disorder. And when economic historians got around to writing at the end of the 1930s about the world depression, most of them said that the increase in tariffs had made very little difference, and that some parts of world trade had gone on increasing and others had not. But by the time they were writing that sort of stuff, everyone was engaged in the Second World War and their conclusions were ignored.

So why, in contrast to the 1930s, has trade held up so well this time? There must be an explanation for the difference between that 26 per cent figure and the 2 per cent figure. And why is it that protectionism has been so ineffective?

There are two answers. One is the internationalisation of production. Big companies have to produce for a world market. It was Professor Fred Meyer, of Exeter University, who got the answer when he said that one had really to look at changing technology, because in most sectors of the world economy the new plant that a company put in was going to be more expensive and was going to be obsolete faster than the plant it was replacing. This had happened so often since the Second World War that it was increasingly impossible for any company to make a profit out of a purely national market. It needed an international market in order to get the returns back fast enough to be ahead with the next new process or plant. The way to get market access to other na-

tional markets in order to sell on the world market is very often
to negotiate a joint production arrangement.

The second reason why trade has held up so well is, simply,
bilateralism. Now 'bilateralism' is a dirty word with most international organisations. Yet the fact is that there was a lot of bilateralism in the 1930s and one of the reasons for the admittedly slow
recovery of trade in the late 1930s lay with the bilateral agreements that the Latin Americans made, the Germans made, the
Americans made. Everybody was up to it. It only got such a bad
name because Dr. Hjalmar Schacht used it exploitatively, in
southern-eastern Europe in conjunction with the political intimi-
dation of his boss, Adolf Hitler. Yet, bilateralism was trade-
creating then and so it is now. Some bilateralism is state-to-state,
as with the recent French-Soviet agreement. Some of it is between state enterprises and foreign companies, and some of it is
between companies. One of the commonest and fastest-growing
forms of bilateralism is known as counter-trade. The GATT estimates that counter-trade only accounts for 8 per cent of world
trade. But the United States Department of Commerce says it is
already something like 20–30 per cent; it reckons that it will rise
to 50 per cent of world trade by the end of the 1990s. Certainly,
88 countries are engaged in counter-trade today instead of only
13 in 1972.

The third reason why we hear so much weeping and wailing
about protectionism is that there is a lot of vested interest in per-
petuating the conventional myths about it. One of these vested
interests is certainly the GATT secretariat, which has come to a
dead-end. It had a ministerial meeting in November 1982, which
was a fiasco; the French predicted correctly that it would be so
and nothing much has changed since then. I am not sure that it
will. Indeed, if GATT were to close down, all its people given a
golden handshake to go away, nothing much would happen to
world trade. Secondly, the United States government has a vested
interest in insisting loudly but in a very hypocritical way, on the
importance of liberalising trade. It is interested in only two
things.

It is interested in the liberalisation of trade in agriculture because it does not like the EEC's Common Agricultural Policy
(CAP) and it is interested most of all in liberalisation of trade in
services. The figure for American exports in services continues
to rise at a meteoric rate and the United States government is

keen to see that it should continue to rise, in order to make up for the increasing failure of American industry to sell its manufactures. But manufactures are not nearly as profitable as trade in services. And so the Americans pretended that there was once a multilateral system for the regulation of world trade. As GATT says, such a system implies regularity, order and defined rules. In those terms, there never was a system. The United States kept on changing the rules to suit itself. There was no golden age of the GATT to get back to. It is a great illusion to believe there was—an illusion shared by many liberal economists. Some are much tempted to get very emotional, not to say evangelical about problems of trade. Politicians, they say, are a rotten, spineless lot who give in to political pressures and if it were not for them everything would be fine. Academic economists find it much easier to tell students that this explains any tendency by governments to protectionism and to explain the world economic recession in these simple, moralistic terms. It would be much more difficult to explain the complications of the world financial system, to which none of them (and no politician either) has a simple or an easy answer. That is why I think they are "clerical traitors."

But does protectionism matter? It is clear that it does not matter to the world economy. However, it may matter—and it probably does—to individual states in some economic stores. That it does is a further, third reason why we need not stay awake at night worrying about protectionism as a major problem of international economic relations. Like corporations, enough states are realising that they will not be able to survive unless they can compete in world markets. They cannot afford too many inefficient, uncompetitive manufacturing industries or service sectors, especially where trade is growing and where, therefore, they must liberalise in order to survive.

The South Koreans are saying that they are not going to make the same mistake as the Japanese. They are going to open up the domestic market to make sure the Korean corporations and enterprises stay competitive at home in order to stay competitive on the world market. The Brazilians are now designing their arms industry for a world market from the very beginning. Regardless of what the Brazilian army or air force wants, they are selling tanks and aircraft designed specially for war in the Middle East and making sure that there is competition in the industry. Even the Australians who have been habitually protectionist have adapted policy to this imperative. Despite the unions, the Prime Minister, Robert Hawke, has said that Australia must liberalise its restrictions on automobile imports in order to make its own domestic producers more competitive.

The Conclusions

The policy implication of this analysis is that we in Europe should follow the example of the United States. Just as the United States has been, we should be pragmatic about protectionism. We should not be the prisoners of somebody else's ideology. In certain sectors, the United States has always been highly protectionist. Look at meat, at wool, at shipping and shipbuilding, steel and textiles. There are lots of other sectors where the United States has not been consistently protectionist, but where it is a mixed picture. The United States has also used government procurement very effectively in some newer industries, particularly in computers and integrated circuits. American companies would not be nearly so far ahead of everybody else if they had not started with the security of very large, no-risk government contracts. In short, the United States has felt free to be inconsistent about trade policy and to change its mind. Europe, too, should be pragmatic about protectionism. There are two good grounds for protectionism.

One is on social grounds where the state may be acting quite rationally if, in seeking that to maintain social cohesion, it finds it better to give some protection to a threatened domestic sector, whether it is agriculture or textiles, rather than to have an expensive, disruptive riot to cope with or to nurture a disaffected minority that may disrupt, if not destroy, the state. For all the faults of the European Community's Common Agricultural Policy (CAP), it appears rather more rational when compared with the policies of the United States as they have affected American farmers in recent years. They have been sold up in large numbers because the banks foreclosed on them. By comparison with the uncertainties of American agricultural policy, the CAP seems less wasteful in social as well as financial terms.

Second, there is sometimes a strong case for protection in the form of preferential government procurement. To many liberal economists, preferential procurement is a kind of protectionism. But the American experience suggests that it may be a rather more efficient and more easily controlled kind of policy. The advantages of preferential procurement for one's own corporations are plain enough. Only last April, the head of Phillips, Mr. Wisse Dekker, warned European governments of the need to get their act together and to provide a truly common market, a common procurement and a common research and development policy. If they failed to do so, he said, some of the big companies like Siemens and Phillips would increasingly invest their money elsewhere and move their operations elsewhere.

To sum up, from the point of view of national policy pragmatism is the watch-word. Protectionism is rational if there are very good social reasons for it and/or if there is plenty of competition in the domestic market. If there is concentration in an industry or it is ridden by cartel agreements over prices, it may be dangerous in the long-term national interest to go in for too much protectionism. But preferential procurement is probably highly necessary in certain high-technology sectors such as biotechnology, lasers, communications systems, electronics, informatics. In all these, Europe has to compete with the United States which has the advantage of a tremendously large defence budget. It also has to compete with Japan, with its immense concentration of corporate and state purchasing power and a large, highly impervious national economy. Since in Europe we cannot imitate Japan, we surely need to take a leaf out of America's book. Narrow nationalism here is probably the great danger to the European economies, not protectionism.

THE FOLLY OF FREE TRADE[3]

Any manager who tries to create a strategy out of worn-out clichés and unexamined nostrums is dismissed. Yet in the United States and other Western countries we have grown comfortable with the government following outworn nostrums about free trade. We have elevated the economic theory of free trade to the

[3]Reprint of a magazine article by John M. Culbertson, professor of economics at the University of Wisconsin in Madison. *Harvard Business Review.* 64: 122–128. S. /O. '86. Reprinted by permission of the Harvard Business Review. © 1986 by the President and Fellows of Harvard College; all rights reserved.

status of a national theology, and we follow its simple dictums as if they were immutable laws. We appear prepared to follow the precepts of free trade wherever they lead us, even if that means plunging lemminglike to our economic ruin.

Today the evidence should be clear to anyone who wants to look at it: our blind allegiance to free trade threatens our national standard of living and our economic future. By sacrificing our home market on the altar of free trade, we are condemning ourselves and our children to a future of fewer competitive businesses, fewer good jobs, less opportunity, and a lower standard of living. These unacceptable outcomes threaten us in ways that are all related to our practice of free trade.

American business's stake in these matters is clear. If we do not wish to live with these outcomes, then we must construct a new and effective way to think about trade that will serve the interests of both business and the nation.

Threats of Free Trade

As we practice it, free trade has profoundly destructive results for the United States and other Western nations. First, nations that do not play by our rules practice unequal competition. Second, free trade puts us in direct competition with low-wage nations, countries that have a lower standard of living than the United States. Third, by allowing these nations to take over big sectors of our market, we permit the permanent interruption of an important relationship between demand and supply that has been the main engine of economic growth in American history.

UNEQUAL NATIONAL COMPETITION

Classical economics teaches us that free exchange works to produce the best results for all, whether the exchange takes place within one nation or across national boundaries. But this concept works only when the exchange is an equal one that occurs within a common framework of laws, customs, rules, and regulations. Economic competition conducted under the law of the jungle leads to chaos and failure. The price system becomes a guide to nothing that is sensible or tolerable.

The laissez-faire approach to economics fashionable in the United States permits distorted outcomes precisely because it neglects the essential role of rules and regulations in preventing destructive competition. When each nation creates self-serving rules, free trade across national boundaries becomes destructive—an unequal competition under inconsistent and inharmonious rules.

Most American companies facing international competition have encountered the problem. Most governments are playing a simple game: they use their myriad powers—subsidies, favorable banking practices, local content requirements, exchange control, and the like—to win jobs and gain higher incomes for their people or to achieve a favorable national balance of payments.

American companies, therefore, end up competing not with foreign companies but with sovereign foreign states—states intent on winning jobs and sometimes whole industries for themselves. Foreign competitors are able to beat out a U.S. company not because of superior economic efficiency but because of subsidies. Japan grants favorable credit terms to certain industries, and many countries give cheap export-finance loans. European nations have special treatment for the value-added tax on exported goods. Most of the Pacific rim nations have weak or nonexistent environmental regulations, and Taiwan often fails to enforce its patent and copyright laws. Laborers in places like China lack the rights of U.S. workers.

WAGE COMPETITION AMONG NATIONS

Among nations, competition over wages causes desirable industries and jobs to move from countries with higher standards of living and higher wages to countries with lower standards of living and lower wages. It is an unequal form of competition that explains much of the recent movement of industries and jobs out of the United States, undercutting our production.

Low-wage nations can raise their standards of living at the expense of ours in two ways: export their people to the United States or import U.S. jobs to their people. The result of either approach would be the same—our wages and standard of living would fall to match the level of the lower-wage nation while, at least temporarily, those of the lower-wage nation would rise.

If there were free immigration and truly open borders, workers from the lower-wage countries would stream into the higher-wage countries. These new arrivals would compete for jobs, accept work for lower pay, and force the existing jobholders to accept either lower wages or unemployment. Precisely for this reason, of course, no one accepts or supports the notion of free immigration.

We do, however, accept and support the notion of free trade, which has the same effect. Instead of exporting workers to the United States, lower-wage countries simply import our jobs and industries to their workers. As the higher-wage nation suffers cutbacks in production, failures of companies, and losses of jobs, the market dictates that workers accept lower wages and a reduced standard of living to match the lower-wage foreign competition.

For example, Japan, Taiwan, and, most recently, South Korea have had rapid increases in desirable jobs in major industries and in their standards of living. Through unbalanced exports to us, they have taken over U.S. markets and jobs. They have gained industries and jobs that we have lost. These countries could not have risen so rapidly if they had based their advance on their home markets or on balanced and mutually beneficial trade with other nations.

Under either free immigration or free trade, however, the lower-wage nation enjoys only a short-term benefit. Rapid economic advance based on taking over the markets, the industries, and the jobs of high-income nations is likely to be a blind alley. Gradually, the higher-wage nation, deprived of its economic base, becomes poorer and its market shrinks—or it belatedly begins protecting itself from one-sided imports. The low-wage nation then may wish it had followed a pattern of economic growth that was sustainable and not parasitic.

Either free migration or free trade would work to turn the world into a "population commune," drifting into global poverty, pulled down by the negative-sum game of international wage competition.

DEMAND AND MARKETS

Our present-day economics fails to recognize the importance of demand and markets—and thus exaggerates what production alone can accomplish. Yet a nation's productive capabilities are decisively limited by the levels and kinds of its domestic demand and its access to foreign markets. But in the United States, we persistently fail to see the importance of our vast, prosperous, and accessible domestic market. We don't appreciate the key role that the demand side of our domestic market has played in generating economic growth for our country. As a result, we are now about to give away our great advantage to our foreign competitors.

America's rise to economic preeminence was based on the interaction between the market's demand and the pace-setting industries that developed to meet that demand. The process was self-feeding. Favorable circumstances—the size of the U.S. market, extraordinary resources, freedom from overpopulation, a favorable position in the two world wars—gave the U.S. market a unique richness and diversity. This market was the magnet that drew forth the new industries that, in turn, created even more wealth. In the interaction of demand and supply, the U.S. economy became the pathbreaker for the world.

But recently this self-feeding interaction has been interrupted, as Japan and other countries of the Pacific rim have taken over large shares of the U.S. market. These nations have recognized the role of demand in fostering industrial growth and, by using government subsidies and lower-wage workers, have simply substituted their industries for American industries in the demand-supply relationship. With the U.S. market switched over to fueling the meteoric advance of foreign industries, U.S. industry has begun to decline.

Unlike the historical demand-and-supply relationship between market and industry, the new relationship that substitutes foreign industry for American industry represents an economic blind alley. The domestic markets of these foreign producers have neither the size nor the wealth to support their own industries. As they undercut U.S. production, however, they will gradually weaken the American economic base that they have come to depend on. Rather than a self-sustaining, self-reinforcing process, this new relationship becomes self-liquidating.

Underlying Myths of Free Trade

Much of the debate over trade today is conducted within a narrow range of thinking, a set of ideas dictated by classical economics. If the United States is to develop a realistic trade policy, we first need to examine these underlying notions, recognize them for the myths that they are, and then substitute more practi-

cal attitudes toward the role of trade in our economy. Seven
myths in particular dominate conventional thinking about trade.

Comparative advantage governs international trade. To justify free trade, laissez-faire economists from Adam Smith to the
present have claimed that international trade and competition
work totally differently from trade within one nation's borders.
They argue that international trade and competition are not
based on price comparisons—that is, that trade is not subject to
the rule that low-priced goods undercut high-priced goods and
that low-priced labor undercuts high-priced labor. Rather, they
say, international trade is governed by comparative advantage. It
depends on differences in the internal structures of prices in the
trading countries and is not affected by differences in their absolute levels of costs and prices.

To support this contention, economists offer an example in
which two nations with different wage and cost levels nevertheless have a pattern of trade that is balanced and mutually beneficial. They then say that the example shows how free trade will
result in balanced and mutually beneficial international trade and
competition. What it actually illustrates is that if the two nations
require their trade to be in balance, then the trade will be governed by comparative advantage and absolute price levels will not
matter. When trading nations require their trade to be in balance, the low-wage, low-price nation cannot pull away the industries and jobs of the other nation. Under this condition,
differences in the nations' absolute costs will not matter.

Most of international trade is not governed by comparative
advantage. Rather, it reflects wage and price competition on the
part of countries seeking jobs and economic growth.

**Exchange rate adjustments automatically keep foreign
trade in balance.** According to our classical economics, the huge
U.S. trade deficit and the export of American industries and jobs
indicate only the need for an adjustment in the exchange rate: a
decline in the international value of the dollar would make everything all right again. The implicit argument is that a decline in
the dollar would balance U.S. trade and improve the competitiveness of U.S. industries without forcing a domestic decline in real
wages and the standard of living.

Again, this argument is fallacious. A decline in the dollar is
simply a way for the United States to become poorer. It is a way
for the American economy to accede to the inevitable results of

competition from lower-wage and lower-standard-of-living nations by becoming itself a lower-wage, lower-standard-of-living nation. A devalued dollar is, quite simply, worth less. By reducing the value of the dollar we cut real wages, diminish U.S. buying power, and bring the U.S. economy more in line with the lower-standard-of-living countries against which free trade has pitted us.

U.S. companies can become competitive through cost cutting. Others argue that the way to bring U.S. trade into balance is for American companies to compete by cutting costs. But in global competition, there is no way U.S. production at wages of $10 an hour can become competitive with efficient foreign production at wages of $1 an hour. Efforts to compete by cutting costs are suicidal.

Frantic cost cutting to accomplish what is impossible destroys the future capabilities of companies as well as the nation. Abandoning research and development, chopping investment, decimating staff is a formula for self-destruction. The U.S. oil industry is warning the nation that it is being forced to cripple its future capabilities by lowering costs to survive the flood of cheap foreign oil. Many other industries are also going through massive cuts in future-oriented expenditures.

First, they can find ways to economize within their companies—always a useful measure at the start. But the company that chooses to go this route will eventually find itself faced with deeper and deeper cuts. Almost inevitably, the process changes from cutting fat to cutting meat to cutting close to the bone. Some American companies have already reached the last steps—firing skilled people, abandoning research and development, scaling back investment. These actions, taken in the name of achieving competitiveness, will only destroy the company's capabilities.

The second path is more direct but leads to the same outcome: to lower costs, American companies can turn to offshore sources and buy components or finished products from lower-cost foreign companies. If begun on a small enough scale, this approach can delude an American business into thinking it has restored its competitiveness. In fact, it is an admission of defeat—one that the foreign source will understand and gradually exploit by capturing more and more of the product's value-added and eventually discarding the empty shell of the American business. Companies that shift production abroad through outsourcing, closing U.S. factories, building new ones abroad, establishing joint ventures with foreign companies, and giving up products become essentially importers of foreign goods. Such a shift has been prevalent in automobiles, apparel, footwear, computers, telephone equipment—perhaps in most manufacturing industries. It does not take much imagination to see what lies at the end of this road.

Low-cost goods are efficiently produced goods. Economists often assert that the production of something more cheaply in one country than in another is evidence that it is produced there more efficiently and therefore should be produced in the cheaper country. In the United States, this argument is used to support the conclusion that goods that can be made abroad more cheaply—and presumably more efficiently—should be made abroad.

This argument is based on a false assumption. Lower cost is linked with efficiency only when the goods under examination are of equal quality and the producers are all operating under the same rules, including government and labor policies that reflect accepted social and environmental values. To shift production from the United States to low-wage foreign labor may cut costs but does not necessarily raise efficiency. This is because low-cost labor, by definition, means a lower standard of living. If the standard of living in a low-labor-cost economy is low, how can anyone sensibly call that economy efficient?

In shifting production to countries with low wage rates, with large government production subsidies, or with lax production regulations, free trade actually *reduces* economic efficiency—as does producing goods for the American market on the opposite side of the world in order to take advantage of cheap labor. In international trade, the price system works perversely. Low cost does not imply efficiency.

All it takes to make free trade work is a level playing field. A popular argument designed to deal with the rising flood of foreign imports is the notion of the level playing field: since most of our foreign competitors do not play by the same trade rules as the United States, these countries must admit our goods to make things fair. Then we will be playing by the same rules—our rules.

Two things are wrong with this argument. First, since many other nations do not suffer from our delusions about free trade, they will not be threatened, cajoled, or pressured into adopting our rules against their self-interest. Second, since they generally have cheaper labor and yet increasingly use more of the advanced technologies of advanced nations, our foreign competitors will actually exploit the U.S. market even more under universal free trade. Our trade would not be brought into balance—certainly not at any acceptable standard of living—by other countries adopting free trade. We would only suffer more broadly the destructive consequences of free trade.

The United States should give LDCs unlimited market access. The argument that the United States has a responsibility to help less developed countries by granting them free access to its market has a humanitarian ring. For two reasons, however, such a position is good neither for us nor the LDCs.

First, granting unlimited access to our market is like signing a blank check—which nobody should ever do. Moreover, while less developed countries could cumulatively cause serious erosion in the U.S. standard of living, for each of them the benefits could be so small as to produce no marked improvement in their standard of living. Also, their basic economic underpinnings would remain unchanged.

Second, in encouraging LDCs to base their economic advancement on exploitation of the U.S. market, we are guiding these nations into a blind alley. The experiment can only fail, either because the United States belatedly wakes up to the ruinous effects of this approach and limits imports or because the wage competition causes the U.S. economy to decline and the U.S. market to shrink. A far more humanitarian approach would be for the United States to advise these nations to tie their economic programs into a pattern that would prove workable and sustainable over the long run.

The change to a global economy is inevitable and desirable. These days it is increasingly fashionable for Americans to say that the separate national economies must inexorably evolve into a global economy. This is simply the latest version of the kind of wave-of-the-future rhetoric that economists and others have applied to many movements now dead and forgotten.

The proposition is that the spread of free trade and international economic integration will proceed because all nations approve and desire it and because it will be successful. Put this way, the argument falls of its own weight. It is not true that all nations desire thoroughgoing international economic integration, with its implied override of national economic objectives, interests, and policies. For example, Japan—a model of realism and success in so many recent competitive undertakings—is hardly rushing to submerge itself in a one-world economic commune. And the destructive effects of free trade are now so obvious that at some point the United States and other high-income nations will wake up before worldwide economic integration drags them down into worldwide poverty. Rather than blithely assuming that a world economy is inevitable, we should expect worldwide economic integration to stop before it spreads much further. No nation is willing to preside over its own economic ruin.

Despite its fashionable ring, this one-world doctrine is dangerous. It simply reinforces the folly of free trade. The correct course is for nations to get their own economic affairs and their own international trade under control and to use the only functional structure that works—a world of effective national economies, engaged with one another in mutually beneficial trade and constructive competition.

A Realistic Trade Policy

With imports pushing them against the wall, American companies in many industries have seen only a narrow choice: leave the industry or move production overseas. The decision of AT&T to give in to foreign competition and shift production of telephones from Shreveport, Louisiana to a new factory in Singapore typifies one reaction to these inexorable pressures. Given this choice, which leaves out the prospect of a constructive U.S. trade policy opening a third option—remaining competitive at home—most companies, preferring foreign production to corporate failure, are moving their production abroad or buying foreign production for resale. But while it may be hopeless for these companies to try to compete from their U.S. production base under existing trade policy, managers choosing to move overseas should realize that there is no guarantee of success abroad. In fact, the American exodus to foreign production bases may bring about the very circumstances that will undermine that move.

From pressure in Congress to a new pragmatism about trade in the Reagan administration, the signs are clear: America's willingness to play victim to the free-trade doctrine is unlikely to continue much longer. At some point in the not-too-distant future, the United States will put limitations on foreign imports to balance America's trade. When that happens, companies that have moved abroad will find themselves on the wrong side of the fence. As a more reasonable U.S. trade policy begins to reconnect the powerful domestic market with U.S. companies—restoring the self-reinforcing process of economic growth in this country—American companies that have gone abroad will be on the outside looking in.

Moreover, in a world in which nations generally will be hard-pressed to meet domestic demands, the operations of American companies in other countries are unlikely to receive favorable treatment or political support. American companies will be the natural target of frustration and disappointment. The prospect of operating in such an environment—with but limited access to a rehabilitated U.S. economy and a flourishing U.S. market—should give American executives pause before they leap over the fence. Under U.S. trade policy, they are being asked to choose between two losing strategies: they can cease production now in the face of unfettered importation or they can move abroad and find themselves on the wrong side of the fence when the change in U.S. trade policy finally comes. The solution, of course, is for American business leaders to support a change in trade policy now, before it is too late.

A realistic trade policy would end the general underselling of American production by foreign production. It would set limits on the proportions of U.S. markets that could be taken by imports and ensure for U.S. industry a market on which it could rebuild and resume its advance. The new policy would put U.S. exports on a strong foundation by tying them to U.S. imports as in the principle of comparative advantage rather than by allowing low-wage foreign producers to generally undercut U.S. exporters through their absolute cost advantage.

These accomplishments will be possible only if we move beyond the slogans that dominate the trade debate: "Free trade is good." "Protectionism is bad." A revolution in ideas that replaces sloganeering with pragmatic analysis must underlie the revolution in accomplishments. American business must play the decisive leadership role.

A number of principles should guide this effort at understanding and shaping a new and pragmatic U.S. trade policy:

1. In a world of diverse nations, free trade works perversely, causing destructive competition among nations, including wage

competition that tends to reduce all nations to a lowest-common-denominator standard of living.

2. Making trade among diverse nations constructive means balancing it and preventing destructive shifts of industries between nations. Just as they need a fiscal budget to keep expenditures in line with incomes, nations need a trade budget to keep imports in line with exports.

3. To balance its trade and continue its economic growth, a nation with a high standard of living and an attractive market will find permanent limitations on imports necessary, just as limitations on immigration are.

4. In balancing its trade, the high-income, high-cost nation will tie its exports to its imports through trade packages or through exports subsidized from the proceeds of import licenses. These arrangements could bring about balanced international trade that would correspond to comparative advantage.

5. Import limitations supposed to be nondiscriminatory—such as tariffs—are actually very discriminatory. For example, uniform U.S. tariff rates high enough to balance U.S. trade with low-wage nations would virtually exclude imports from other high-income nations and would thus discriminate against those with high incomes.

6. Countries must manage their trade in ways that meet their particular needs and capabilities. National differences in circumstances, ideologies, administrative capabilities, and other factors are too important to permit any uniform and general system for arranging international trade.

7. National governments have a legitimate and necessary role in arranging constructive international trade. Government is the only agency that can assume the responsibility for managing a nation's trade budget in a way beneficial to the interests of the nation. The interest of the nation in balanced trade is in concert with the interest of American business in guaranteed access to the American market.

Balancing U.S. Trade

The U.S. economy urgently needs immediate action to stop unfairly advantaged imports from undercutting U.S. production. Month by month, American companies are sinking, failing, or giving up on U.S. production and moving their operations offshore. The once mighty U.S. automobile industry, located in the nation with the world's greatest market for automobiles, is being liquidated through joint ventures with Japanese companies, shifting the design and production of its cars abroad, producing American cars largely with foreign-made components, abandoning the small-car market to imports, and shifting its capital to secondary industries. The longer we allow this process to go on unchallenged, the dimmer our economic future will be.

Two kinds of trade policies, therefore, need to be put into place: some first steps to hold the line, halt the erosion of the American economy, and begin to move in the direction of balanced trade and some permanent measures that will ensure balanced and mutually advantageous trade among nations.

To hold the line, we should immediately impose quotas on certain goods, at least halting their increase in market share and, in some cases, reversing recent rapid growth. The inadequate quotas on autos, steel, textiles, apparel, footwear, and machinery can serve as a point of departure. The goal is a comprehensive trade policy that protects and defends the interests and future of the United States—that protects the nation rather than any special interest. The imposition of quotas would be a step in the direction of import limitations to balance our trade; quotas would begin the process of designing a system of mutually beneficial trade between us and our trading partners.

The United States should quickly establish provisional targets for the maximum share of its market available to various foreign-made products. Over time these targets would be tied to a balanced pattern of trade. In establishing the targets, we would send foreign producers a clear signal of what to expect in the way of access to our market. Even more important, the targets would tell American producers how much of the domestic market would be reserved for them so that they could begin gearing up for U.S. production and at the same time spell out the clear dangers of moving more production overseas.

Some quotas should be based on existing legislation and on the findings of the U.S. International Trade Organization regarding the economic injury that foreign competition has inflicted on such U.S. industries as footwear, textiles, and apparel. But we should reject the notion—on which ITO is based—that quotas are only a temporary remedy designed to give domestic industries time to shrink or become competitive.

Our new trade policy should make it clear that we want permanent limitations on imports to the American market. The basis of a realistic U.S. trade policy is a permanent system of limitations on imports to the American market, coupled with the promotion of desired exports within the framework of balanced and mutually advantageous trade with other nations. A trade policy that tries to force free trade on the world is doomed to failure—and would ruin us if adopted.

A permanent system limiting imports to the U.S. market and maintaining balanced trade should eventually replace these temporary measures. Such a system must serve a number of goals. It must:

• Preserve the United States as a high-income nation with a great market for advanced goods.

• Produce balanced and mutually advantageous trade plus debt dealings with each nation, nation-group, and the world.

• Produce an industrial composition of trade that serves U.S. interests and reserves a defined share of the home market for U.S. producers by taking into account factors like the defense implications, the development of breakthrough technology, the kinds of jobs produced, and the kinds of jobs required.

Creating and administering a trade policy that meets these goals is a demanding task—but so is running a corporation in today's world. In either case, simple slogans that promise easy success are unrealistic. A successful trade policy requires foresight, realism, judgment, honesty, knowledge, administrative effectiveness, and toughness in enforcing rules and regulations, just as the operations of large companies do. At both organizational levels, that of the company and that of the nation, adapting successfully to a complex, uncertain, and changing economic environment is a hard-won achievement. The hope of the United States lies in recognizing and tackling this difficult task rather than in waiting for Providence or free trade to bring us success on a platter.

The permanent system of balanced trade should be based on the inherent value of the U.S. market. Its size and wealth give it great value to foreign producers and other nations. We should capture this value for the benefit of all Americans through two mechanisms: quid pro quo trade packages arranged with other nations and the sale at market price of a limited number of import licenses. We should use part or all of the revenue generated by these sales to support particular U.S. industries whose products we want to export to further national interests.

The United States should enforce these import-limiting arrangements rigorously and promptly—not in the way that the government now handles these matters. We should strive to detect trade violations quickly and take immediate action. Moreover, punishment must provide real remedies rather than the long-delayed hand slaps delivered now. We must treat the import limitation program as a set of serious business contracts between nations—not as a theater for acts of political symbolism.

A Time to Rethink

In touting free trade to other nations, the United States has not only invited its own economic destruction but also misled other countries in their expectations from international trade. It is time for America to reject this false god and accept the blame for preaching an unrealistic doctrine. We must repudiate the notion that the rest of the world can achieve economic growth by unbalanced sales to the U.S. market.

Mutually beneficial and balanced international trade is the only trade policy that makes sense. Apart from transition problems, it would do no violence to any nation's valid claims. By moving to such a policy we would be helping low-income nations develop sustainable economic programs and safeguarding the living standards of high-income nations. We owe it to all countries of the world to put to an end the unrealistic idea that more countries can emulate Japan and achieve economic advance through a parasitic relationship with the American market.

The delusion that free trade is the road to worldwide affluence has influenced many countries; the delusion will hurt many of them. We need to escape from this belief and build a new system of international trade—one that rests on realism and mutual benefit for all nations.

III. THE CASE AGAINST PROTECTIONISM

EDITOR'S INTRODUCTION

Most of the leading business executives in the U.S. are opposed to greater protection from imports, according to a *Fortune* magazine poll. A recent Harris poll found that more than 80% of Americans felt the U.S. must produce better products rather than depend on artificial trade barriers. Despite these polls, protectionist sentiment is still strong among many politicians and their constituents. This section examines the case against protectionism. In the first article, W. Allen Wallis, Under Secretary for Economic Affairs in the Reagan administration, explains why protectionism poses a threat to the American economy. The next article features excerpts from a Georgia forum entitled "Beyond Protectionism." The authors, including former Senator Gary Hart and M.I.T. Professor Lester Thurow, discuss various proposals to make the American economy more competitive without resorting to protectionist legislation. In the final article in this section, University of New Hampshire Professor Bernard K. Gordon aims to debunk the myth that importation of foreign goods weakens American industry.

PROTECTIONISM: A THREAT TO OUR PROSPERITY[1]

The subject I have been asked to address is international economic policy. At the outset, I want to point out that the term can be misleading. International economics is governed by the same fundamental laws as domestic economics. The modifier "international" does not mean we are dealing with something ex-

[1]Excerpted from testimony by W. Allen Wallis, Under Secretary for Economic Affairs, before the National Association of Business Economists, Washington, D.C., February 26, 1985.

otic or arcane that must be handled with a different set of rules—
not at all. Economic cause and effect on the international scene
are no different than on the domestic scene. What is different is
the politics, and even the politics are more domestic than foreign.

Trade policy, for example, seems to be a quintessential example of international economic policy. But the essence of trade policy was illuminated by the 19th-century humorist, Ambrose
Bierce. Bierce defined tariffs as devices "to protect the domestic
producer against the greed of his consumers." Trade policy involves diverting the income of some groups in a country (for example, consumers of automobiles) for the benefit of other groups
in the same country (for example, producers of automobiles).
The policy may be carried out at the border by limiting access to
the U.S. market, but both its beneficiaries and its victims are primarily domestic and only secondarily foreign. My comments on
protectionism today may, therefore, be taken as equally applicable to the domestic and international economies.

The Dangers of Protectionism

The most serious threat to the world economy—and to our
domestic economy—is the swelling tide of protectionism. People
who would never condone protectionism at home somehow accept that it should be practiced internationally. To illustrate this
point with a hypothetical example, suppose that the State of Virginia decided that North Carolina tobacco was making excessive
inroads in the Virginia market, and suppose that Virginia (defying the constitutional prohibition against internal tariffs) managed to impose a special levy on all tobacco entering the state. Of
course, North Carolina would retaliate against products from
Virginia. Clearly, total economic activity—and our prosperity—
would be reduced. No one in this room would consider that trade
barriers among the 50 states would be anything but a disaster; but
many people (economists included) appear to assume that a different set of economic rules operates on the international scene.
By this same logic—or lack of logic—they assume that with impu-
nity we can introduce protectionist measures at our international
borders without hurting all parties concerned—ourselves more
than others.

Protectionist measures invite a spiral of retaliation, and, even
in the absence of retaliation, they foster inefficient uses of scarce

resources and raise the cost of living in the country introducing the protection. A favored group or industry may initially benefit from a quota, for example, but even greater additional costs are borne by the majority of the population.

It may seem strange that in the United States, historically the champion of the free market, I should feel the need to make a plea for a free and open trading system. But, while most persons would readily agree that such a system is demonstrably superior in principle, I often find them advocating policies that would produce the opposite result. When individuals, industries, or even whole sectors perceive their economic interests to be threatened, they often rationalize a course of action that has, over and over again, proven to be a failure: protectionism. "We believe in free trade," they say, "but it must be fair trade." "Fair trade" is not defined, but implicitly it means trade in which we win.

Protectionist measures, and trade-distorting measures in general, are not really actions taken by one country against another country. Instead, they are actions that benefit one domestic group at the expense of other groups in the same country. Producers oppose consumers, and industries that compete with imports oppose industries that export. It is disheartening but not surprising that protectionism's advocates are found in all nations, and always have been, but that does not validate their cause. Their arguments, in whatever language they may be phrased, are founded on the same fallacies, and neither eloquence nor vehemence will alter the fundamental fact that protectionism is inevitably self-defeating. Protectionism is like a disease—not only pernicious but contagious. When it appears, it spreads and leaves a trail of economic disability.

By "protectionism," I mean any measure that gives a domestic producer an artificial advantage over foreign producers. I include tariffs, quotas, voluntary export restraints, subsidies, unnecessary licensing, health and safety standards, and all other measures that distort trade.

On the surface and in specific cases, protectionism may, at first glance, seem advantageous—at least to the naive. It is often claimed, for example, that import restrictions save jobs. It may be true that employment in one industry is higher with protection than without, but jobs lost in other sectors are often greater.

Why are jobs lost in other sectors? In many cases, one industry's output is another industry's input. As a case in point, you will recall that last summer President Reagan refused to yield to demands for restrictions on copper imports. He recognized that the domestic copper industry suffered serious problems, but he also recognized that any benefit that might accrue to the copper producers would be more than offset by increased costs to those industries using copper as a raw material. To maintain international competitiveness, U.S. firms need to have access to the highest quality and lowest cost products available in the world market.

More generally, to the extent that protectionism restrains imports, it will cause the dollar to appreciate. This, in turn, will encourage imports and discourage exports, with an adverse effect on employment. Economists have long understood that, when all the interrelationships within our economy are taken into account, an across-the-board import duty has the same effect as an across-the-board tax on exports. Unfortunately, this is not understood by those who argue for an import surcharge or other protectionist policies. Protection alters the distribution of employment among industries, but it does not affect the total level of employment.

It is sometimes argued that protection is "fairer" to low- and middle-income families. The opposite is more likely to be true, since protection raises prices in the protected industry—and who pays for that? Higher prices always impose a higher proportionate burden on low-income consumers than on high-income consumers.

Finally, we cannot ignore the risk of retaliation. If we limit a country's exports of a given product to us, that country's ability to buy from us is reduced, and it may also retaliate directly against some of our exports. The result will be that a different U.S. industry will lose an export market and, thus, employment. In such a situation, our overall employment level could possibly remain the same, but, through government intervention in the marketplace, employment will have been redistributed. Furthermore, the redistribution will be from more efficient to less efficient industries, for which all of us will pay, both as consumers and as producers. It is far better to allow the market to work and to transfer employment from an uncompetitive industry to one that is more efficient.

This leads me to the often-heard argument that we must protect our "basic" industries. This argument ignores the fact that, in a dynamic economy such as ours, what may be a basic industry in one period of time may not be at all "basic" in another. This argument mistakes the prospects for continued vitality in our economy as a whole with the prospects of particular industries. New industries develop, and old ones decline. For example, would any of you hesitate to call computers a basic industry? But was it a basic industry in, say, 1950? Obviously, the mix is constantly changing and will continue to do so. Then why should government intervene to decide what industry is "basic" and merits special protection? I submit that the marketplace will demonstrate what is "basic" and what isn't and that if a particular industry is declining, the marketplace is telling us something.

Protection is often invoked to provide an industry an "adjustment period" to modernize and become more competitive. The theory is that it will become healthy and that the protection can then be eliminated. Unfortunately, the opposite is usually the case. Not only does protection obviate the need for the protected industry to become more efficient, but the protection entices more resources into a sector that probably already has excess capacity. For example, for several decades textiles has been one of our most protected industries, yet a study in 1982 showed that fully one-third of all the clothing and textile establishments in the country had not been in the industry 6 years earlier. In France, one-fifth of all new manufacturing firms in recent years have been in the clothing and textile industry.

Let us remember that in the 1960s the protection sought by industrial countries for their textile industries was described as "temporary." Would we not all be better off if scarce resources, instead of being attracted to textiles, had been invested in new industries where we enjoy a comparative advantage? Furthermore, we would now have a serious problem on our hands if we were to remove protection for textiles except over a prolonged period; and the industry has accumulated huge vested interests that lead to increasing rather than decreasing its protection.

We should also note that some forms of protection not only reduce our welfare but actually help foreign producers by enabling them to charge higher prices for the restricted exports. This is generally true of quotas or so-called voluntary export restraints. U.S. protection of steel in the 1970s, for example, is estimated to have increased the annual profits of Japanese steel producers by about $200 million, or about half of the Japanese expenditures on research and development in steel. The current restraints on Japanese automobile exports to the United States are adding considerably to the profits of those Japanese automobile manufacturers who are allowed to export to the United States, thereby generating an influential voice in Japan for continuing the restraints.

Protectionist measures can cause distortions without achieving their original intent. In 1977 we signed an orderly marketing agreement with Japan covering color television receivers. At that time, Japan accounted for 90% of our imports. Two years later, Japan accounted for only 50% of our imports—but the share of other Asian countries increased from 15% to 50%. Thus, we merely succeeded in changing the source of imports.

Protection at international frontiers is often the outgrowth of government intervention in the market. A good example is provided by agriculture, which is subsidized in most industrial countries, including our own. Subsidies are designed to improve the income of a privileged group at the expense of other citizens—in this case, consumers. Subsidies artificially stimulate the production of goods that are neither wanted nor needed. More of the subsidized goods are produced than would have been without subsidization—witness farm surpluses in the European Community. As is true of all subsidies, they shift resources away from other sectors of the economy to the subsidized sector. The result is that resources are used less efficiently, total output is reduced, and investment in other sectors lags. Part of the blame for the European Economic Community's poor economic performance in the past decade or two can be attributed to the rising burden of agricultural subsidies, which attract capital and labor into farming at the expense of the rest of the economy.

Having pushed commodity prices above market-clearing levels and having enticed new producers into the market, subsidizing nations then resort to protectionism. They impose import barriers to keep out the cheaper products that would undercut the artificial price structure that has been built up. Then, with excessive production and saturated markets, producing nations move to the next stage: subsidizing exports to move their stockpiles.

That protectionism is economically harmful, particularly to the nation that imposes the restrictions, is not just an abstract theory. It is an observable fact for which I have given a few examples here and for which many more examples could be readily produced. It follows logically that our policies should be directed toward the reduction of protectionism. We need greater public awareness that protection that, in the short run, appears to be a benefit is, in the long run, detrimental. Spreading this awareness is a task for which I count on your support.

Opening Foreign Markets

Other countries, of course, have an even bigger stake than we do in preserving and extending the open trading system, for they lack our huge internal free market. Japan, for example, has benefited greatly from the access it has enjoyed to our market, as have we. But barriers that Japan maintains to its domestic market limit the ability of U.S. firms to sell there on terms comparable to those enjoyed by Japanese firms in the United States. Both countries would be better off if Japan were to remove as many of these obstacles as possible.

It is for this reason that President Reagan and Prime Minister Nakasone agreed earlier this year to launch an intensive series of sectoral trade negotiations. Late in January, I led a mission to Tokyo to initiate the discussions, which will initially include telecommunications, electronics, forest products, and medical equipment and pharmaceuticals. High officials from the Office of the U.S. Trade Representative, the Department of Commerce, the Department of Agriculture, and the Treasury are very active in the negotiations, which are unique in that the negotiators on both sides have been given the same instructions—to identify barriers to Japan's markets that are susceptible to corrective action by government. Secretary Shultz and Foreign Minister Abe have been instructed to provide a progress report to President Reagan and Prime Minister Nakasone at the time of the Bonn economic summit in May.

We have no illusions that success will be instantaneous. The political forces of protectionism are stronger in Japan than in most countries. Nevertheless, we seek early progress in the telecommunications sector and will persevere with our efforts.

If we are to be successful in breaking down foreign protectionist barriers and in opening foreign markets, we must ourselves avoid resorting to protection. Just as we object to protectionism in others, we should not expect them to welcome it in us. Nor should we be surprised if they retaliate or use our actions as excuses to justify their own protectionism. The question of retaliation reminds me of one of President Reagan's favorite analogies. He said, if two people are in a boat and one of them shoots a hole in the bottom, it will not help the other person to shoot another hole in the bottom. Some call that getting tough, the President said, but he calls it getting wet. Our markets are more open than most, but we have our share of highly protected, inefficient sectors. But to halt and reverse the tide of protectionism, it is obviously not sufficient to practice self-discipline just at home. We need the cooperation of the international trading community.

Forming a Coalition for Free Trade

I have spoken a great deal of the danger of protectionism in terms of reaction and retaliation, but I do not want to leave you with the wrong impression. The main reason we should work toward free trade is not fear of retaliation, but that we gain by it, whatever other countries do. I am advocating a hard-headed policy to maximize our own welfare. Of course, open markets here help our trading partners, and it helps them and us still further if their markets are open, too. The debt-ridden less developed countries, for example, can hardly even service that debt unless they, we, and the other developed countries keep our markets open to them.

In considering policies for opening trade, it is necessary to consider the political process on which such policies must be based. Phrases like "political will" are empty rhetoric. The important consideration is political capacity.

If those interested in an industry have an influence over the government, they have a chance of gaining protection. This is strikingly true in the case of nationalized industries—for example, international airlines in most countries. Modern democracies increasingly have become fragmented. Some of this is due to methods of electing legislatures—for example, by proportional representation or by electing several representatives from a single constituency—and other devices which effectively prevent any one party from gaining a majority, so that coalitions have to be formed. Even in countries where the two-party system prevails, such as the United Kingdom and the United States, party discipline is weakening, and it is necessary to form coalitions among many special interest groups in order to achieve any legislation.

Comprehensive negotiations, such as would be involved in a new round of comprehensive trade arrangements, offer the best chance for putting together a coalition for free trade. Each party to the coalition may lose some special benefit. But if it can be assured that the special benefits lost by all of the other members will gain it enough to offset its loss, it is possible to get a working coalition for free trade. This is a case in which it may be easier to clean the whole Augean stable at once than to clean it one stall at a time.

We must, therefore, push aggressively forward on a comprehensive multilateral trade negotiation under the auspices of the General Agreement on Tariffs and Trade (GATT). The object of such negotiations is twofold:

First, to hold the line and eventually reverse the global trend toward protectionism that has already cost us dearly and, if permitted to spread, would eventually cause a contraction in world trade and a reduction in our standard of living;

Second, to create new market opportunities for our own (and others') most efficient and dynamic industries so that they may realize their full potential as engines of future growth.

We have much to gain from a new round of trade negotiations, and so do our partners.

But the problems are immense. The less developed countries have shown little interest in a new round of negotiations, and, in many of the industrialized countries, high unemployment has encouraged governments to shield industries from competition. Highly protected industries in this country, for that matter, do not want import competition. Many people, both at home and abroad, have to be shown where their best interests lie. We have to persuade governments that the best reason for them to reduce trade barriers is that it is in their best interest to do so. Despite the difficulties, this Administration is determined to continue its efforts to produce a freer and more productive trading system.

In closing, I ask all of you, as professional economists, to contribute your skills and your prestige to this common effort to increase our prosperity—not only the prosperity of the United States, but that of the whole world.

BEYOND PROTECTIONISM[2]

The following forum is based on a discussion sponsored by the Center for a New Democracy, the Georgia World Congress Institute, and the World Trade Club of Atlanta on November 23, 1985. Martha Keys, executive director of the Center for a New Democracy, served as moderator.

GARY HART is a former U.S. Senator from Colorado.

LESTER C. THUROW is Gordon Y. Billard Professor of Economics at the Massachusetts Institute of Technology and author of *The Zero-Sum Solution: Building a World Class American Economy* (1985).

STEPHEN MARRIS is a senior fellow at the Institute for International Economics and the author of *Dollars and Deficits* (1985).

SALLY SHELTON-COLBY is a vice-president of Bankers Trust Company. She has previously served as the U.S. ambassador to the Eastern Caribbean and deputy assistant secretary of state for Latin America.

RICHARD N. GARDNER is Henry L. Moses Professor of Law and International Organization at Columbia University. He served as deputy assistant secretary of state for International Organization Affairs from 1961 to 1965 and as the U.S. ambassador to Italy from 1977 to 1981.

JACK SHEEHAN is the legislative director and assistant to the president of the United Steel Workers in Washington, D.C. He is a member of the United States Special Trade Representative's Trade Advisory Committee.

SIDNEY TOPOL is chairman of the board and chief executive officer of Scientific Atlanta.

RYAN C. AMACHER is dean of the College of Commerce and Industry at Clemson University, South Carolina. He has served as a senior international economist for the U.S. Treasury.

DENNIS LOCKHART is vice-president and area manager of Citicorp and is based in Atlanta, Georgia.

RICHARD REAGAN is vice-president and managing partner of Booz Allen & Hamilton and is based in Atlanta.

[2]Excerpted from magazine forum *World Policy Journal*. 3:157-81. Winter 1985-86. Reprinted by permission.

Hart: Just 10 years ago, our nation enjoyed a trade surplus. The transformation of that surplus into a record deficit has implications that go far beyond the jobs, profits, and market share of America's workers, farmers, and businesses. Fundamentally, what's at stake is America's self-esteem.

I think all would agree that until very recently trade was a relatively low priority on this administration's agenda. Partly as a result, Congress moved to fill the vacuum, and in recent months has debated the trade crisis at length. Hundreds of legislative proposals have been introduced. Many of them propose tariffs, quotas, and other trade barriers in an effort to protect American workers and industries.

We are not here to debate the merits of such protectionist policies. Some on this panel, including myself, oppose that approach. Others of us endorse it. But we all agree that protectionist measures are at best a partial, short-term answer, and that there are many other steps our nation must take if we are to recapture our mantle of leadership in world trade. As the title for this seminar suggests, our goal is to look "Beyond Protectionism"—to discuss the long-term policies that will make our products and industries more competitive. On that subject, I suspect we will discover many points of agreement.

For myself, I believe there are five keys to regaining our trade competitiveness. First, we must remedy the overvaluation of the dollar—the single greatest cause of our trade deficit. To do this, we must reduce our budget deficits, but we can also take other steps—such as calling a new international conference to reform the world's exchange-rate system.

Second, we need to help our workers and industries adjust to a dynamic and often turbulent world economy. We need stronger education and retraining programs, and greater trade adjustment assistance, so that our workers will not be held hostage to economic forces beyond their control.

Third, we need to do more to defend our nation's trading rights and to eliminate unfair practices by our trading partners. We should also be pushing to expand world trade rules to cover trade in services, agriculture, high technology, and intellectual property.

Fourth, we need to modernize America's industries. We need new partnerships between labor, management, and government to ensure reinvestment in our older, keystone industries. Ultimately, we can only be more competitive in trade if our key industries as well as our newer sectors are more competitive.

Finally, we can dramatically increase American exports by revitalizing the economies of the world's developing nations. Recessions and debt burdens have forced many of those nations to reduce their consumption of American products, and we must reverse that trend.

Our trade policy is a projection of our values. We need a trade policy that reflects both a concern for our people and a confidence in their ability to compete and win in the international marketplace. Our trade policy should project a determination to shape—not hide from—our economic destiny.

To project those values, we need a clear vision that will join America's technological prowess, skilled work force, and international influence to ensure we are the world's most competitive economy. We need to strengthen our older industries as we encourage the new information industries that hold so much promise for our future. And we must address the true causes of a trade crisis that today is robbing too many hard-working Americans of the self-esteem they deserve.

Thurow: I think that such issues as international trade and protection are best considered not in some abstract international context, but rather in the context of our own country's general economic future. For I would argue that, in a real sense, the American economy has died and been replaced by a world economy. The very phrase "American economy" today means something quite different from what it meant even 15 years ago.

In 1929, for instance, the United States exported or imported about 5 percent of its gross national product. In 1969, we still exported or imported just slightly more than 5 percent of GNP. So for these 40 years, international trade was a very small tail on a very big economic dog—there was no significant change. But between 1969 and 1980, a revolution occurred in the world economy. By 1981, we were exporting 13 percent of GNP, by 1984, largely because of the overvalued dollar, we were importing 13 percent of GNP. Thirteen percent may not sound like much compared to small countries like Switzerland, whose trade with other nations is on the order of the commerce between different states in America—between New York and New Jersey. But how does America's 13 percent compare with that portion of GNP that Japan exports? For Japan, the figure is 17 percent. And if you exclude intra-European trade and consider only exports and imports in and out of Europe, you see that the European countries don't export or import much more than the United States does. For all practical purposes, Europe, Japan, and the United States are equally dependent on world trade.

This is an enormous change for America, which has never had that kind of involvement in the world economy. Today, about 70 percent of all the goods and services produced in the United States are subject to actual and potential foreign competition. And most of the remaining 30 percent is affected in some way. For example, a nation cannot devote 11 percent of its revenue to health care expenditures if its competitor devotes only 6 to 8 percent. Thus even though American doctors do not, technically speaking, compete with German doctors, the whole U.S. health industry is eventually going to be turned upside down because of international trade. America's integration into the international economy will have more far-reaching effects than one might expect. In some ways, we are just one country like any other in this larger economic system.

Another major shift America faces has to do with the relative quality of its technology. After World War II, the United States practiced economic isolationism—and was *able* to do so because it possessed superior technology. The country could live comfortably behind that technological superiority without competing in the world economy. During the 1950s, we had a per capita GNP double that of the next best economies in the world (excluding Canada) and eight times that of the Japanese. No matter how you looked at it, we had tremendous technological advantages. The American Boeing 707 flew; the British Comet crashed.

But by the 1980s, the entire situation had changed. In a recent survey, the *Nihon Kezai Shinbun*—the Japanese equivalent of the *Wall Street Journal*—asked the 2,000 largest firms in Japan if they thought their technology was equal to that of their American competition, ahead of the American competition, or behind the American competition. Eleven percents said behind; 64 percent said equal; and 25 percent said ahead. Whether or not they are correct, the fact that 25 percent of these Japanese firms think they have technology superior to their American competitors' tells you that the world is different. For if that survey had been done in 1955, I would guarantee that no firm in Japan would have claimed that its technology surpassed America's.

What makes the situation all the more critical is the convergence of these two trends. The United States lost its technological edge at the same time that it was being absorbed into the world economy. Most goods must now compete not just in an American market but in a world market. Thus America has had to face increased economic competition just when relative U.S. economic strength is weaker than at any point since World War II.

What this means, I would argue, is that our world economic institutions, originally built between 1945 and 1955, now need to be rebuilt. It is as though the world is moving from the horse-and-buggy era to the automobile era. The driving regulations and rules of the road are still more suited to horse-drawn vehicles than to automobiles; and if you try to drive automobiles at automobile speeds on horse-and-buggy roads, you're going to run into trouble. The United States is having difficulty adjusting to the fact that the whole world economic situation has changed. Americans are used to a world where all U.S. economic problems can be solved at home, inside the United States. But that is no longer the case—many economic problems involve the rest of the world, and the rest of the world has to be involved in their solution.

I'd like to mention five problems that I think must be addressed if the American and world economies are to work. First, we must increase the extent to which different countries coordinate their monetary and fiscal policies. Second, we must find a way to stop the wild fluctuations in value that the major currencies are subject to under the current system. And then each of the three major economic actors in the world—Europe, Japan, and the United States—has a local problem that it must solve at home if the world economy is to run smoothly.

Europe's problem is employment—or rather, unemployment. The European countries have not produced any new net jobs for the past 15 years. This creates a sense of failure; and to stay in the world economy you have to feel like a winner. As in a ball game where the players who lose take their baseballs and bats and gloves, go home, and refuse to play, so European nations have gradually begun withdrawing from the world economy. For example, consider automobile quotas. U.S. quotas allow Japan to export 2.3 million cars to the United States, whereas Italian quotas allow only 300. Japan is being kicked out of the Italian car market because otherwise the Italian automobile industry would lose jobs. In effect, Italy is taking steps toward pulling out of the world economic system.

Japan has problems of its own. Bluntly put, the Japanese are drug addicts—and their drug of choice happens to be exports. The structure of the economy they have built requires exports to grow faster than imports. That's possible for a very small country in the global economy, but not for the second largest industrial power in the world. The international economy cannot function with Japan running a trade surplus of $60 to $80 billion. The Japanese are going to have to take action on this matter.

The serious problem America faces is low productivity. Even if we had a reasonably valued U.S. dollar, U.S. firms would still be in trouble. For with productivity growing in the United States at only one percent a year but growing at 3 percent a year in Europe and 4 percent in Japan, the United States can compete in world markets only if the dollar falls every year, forever, and if the American relative standard of living falls every year, forever. I don't think Americans will or should tolerate that. To avoid that scenario, however, we're going to have to address the productivity problem. If the rest of the world can maintain productivity growth at 3 or 4 percent a year, the United States has to do so as well, for if we are a failure we will gradually pull out of the world economy.

No one can produce a high-quality product out of low-quality components; no one can produce a high-quality economy out of low-quality inputs. And if we compare the quantity and quality of the inputs going into the American economy with those going into the European and Japanese economies, we always find that the U.S. inputs are not as good or not as large. For example, in plants and equipment we invest two-thirds of what the Europeans do, and only half of what the Japanese do. Do we think we can keep investing half as much as Japan and still compete with their industries? The Japanese will have two robots for every one of ours—and so on down the line.

This is not a problem that can be solved by government alone. Certainly some kind of government action will be necessary, but there will also need to be a lot of changes in the private sector. A further question is whether it is in the American character to take the kinds of steps required to bring the U.S. economy up to world-class levels.

One major problem is this: no economy can compete if it has an inferior labor force. And the educational credentials of the U.S. work force do not measure up. In large U.S. cities, 8 percent of workers test out as functionally illiterate: they cannot read at a fifth-grade level. In Japan, on the other hand, one-half of one percent of the labor force tests as functionally illiterate. How can you compete with someone when you have 16 times as many illiterates on the payroll as they do? Furthermore, if you give math exams to 17-year-olds leaving high school, the average American 17-year-old knows precisely half as much mathematics as the average Japanese 17-year-old. Eighth-grade graduates in Japan score better on math exams than MBAs in America do. Seven percent of U.S. college students graduate as engineers and scientists as opposed to 40 percent of German and Japanese college students. Is it any surprise that German and Japanese products are a little better engineered than American products?

To raise the quality of American education, there are many things we could do. For example, our children go to school 180 days a year, Japanese children go to school 240 days a year, Swedish children 220 days. It's a form of American chutzpah to think we can learn in 180 days what it takes the rest of the world 220 or 240 days to learn—especially considering that in those days these other students go to school an hour and a half longer than ours do. If I were to walk into American schools and announce, "Well, boys and girls, we adopted a 180-day school year in 1863 when America was an agricultural society, but in a modern world we're out of date. So you've got to up your school year to 230 days"—I don't think the students would exactly roll out the palm branches. But these are the kinds of steps we must take: part of being competitive is doing things you don't necessarily want to.

There are important considerations in the private economy as well. When you mention low productivity, most people immediately think of lazy, low-quality, blue-collar, assembly-line workers in Detroit who aren't doing their jobs particularly well. But that's not the heart of the problem. Consider these statistics. Between 1977 and 1983, U.S. manufacturing companies laid off 2 million blue-collar workers—7 percent of their work force. Over the same period of time, their output rose 14 percent. To produce 14 percent more with 7 percent fewer workers—that's basically a 21 percent gain in productivity, which over six years averages out to roughly 3 percent productivity growth per year.

This means that the U.S. blue-collar work force had a world-class level of productivity.

Unfortunately, though, this is not the whole story. In the same period that those companies were laying off 2 million blue-collar workers, they hired 10 million white-collar workers—a 41-percent increase in white-collar employment that produced only 14 percent more. So white-collar productivity fell 7 percent, wiping out much of the gain in U.S. blue-collar productivity. If there is negative productivity in America, then every high-rise office building in Atlanta is a monument to it. The famous studies of productivity on the Escort, which sought to explain why the Japanese produce the Escort for $2,500 less than the Americans, attributed 40 percent of this difference to Japan's lower white-collar overhead. And that's not just white-collar overhead in Japan—Japanese companies operate in the United States with lower white-collar overhead than U.S. companies operating here.

American companies need to revolutionize their management practices. For example, if you go to the Toyota assembly line at the end of the day, you will find the inventory control being done by blue-collar workers instead of by a white-collar star up in some office. This means you don't need management information systems to get the inventory statistics to the white-collar workers. Similarly, quality control circles in the shop reduce the work force needed in the office. Thus you save by using participatory management techniques. As far as I know, U.S. companies could implement these kinds of systems on a much broader basis than they do.

But in fact, there are real obstacles. If blue-collar workers are to do quality control, they have to be able to learn a little bit of simple operations research—which means that they already need to know a little bit of mathematics. It's a lot easier to teach Japanese workers that operations research than it is to teach American workers, because those Japanese workers know that little bit of mathematics they need. So here we are back at the education problem again. The whole problem of productivity ties together. An inferior education system keeps U.S. industry from being able to use certain techniques that would help boost productivity. To deal with our productivity problem, we have to address some very basic issues.

Marris: It is dangerous to propose solutions to a problem before defining the problem. Therefore, I would like to begin by asking: what is the main cause of the U.S. trade deficit? The answer is overwhelmingly clear. It is the strong dollar. According to my calculations, approximately 75 percent of the deterioration in the U.S. trade balance since 1980 can be attributed directly to the strong dollar. That isn't really surprising. If you're in business, and your prices increase 40 percent, and your competitors' prices decline 30 percent—which is, roughly speaking, what has happened since 1980—you're in deep trouble.

What is the cause of the strong dollar? By now, half of this story is only too familiar. The combination of excessive U.S. budget deficits and inadequate private savings at a time of strong economic recovery was bound to generate abnormally high interest rates, and these high interest rates have in turn attracted money to America from all over the world. In 1985, 50 percent of all net investment in the United States has been financed by foreigners.

The other half of the story, however, is much less well known because it relates to what's been going on in the rest of the world. The fact is that America's major allies—Japan, West Germany, and the United Kingdom—have been doing exactly the opposite of the United States. While the United States has been running excessively large budget deficits—a structural budget deficit of around 5 percent of GNP—these other countries have been cutting their structural budget deficits. In fact, Japan, West Germany, and the United Kingdom together have cut their deficits by an even larger amount in relation to their GNP than the United States has increased its budget deficit. Why did they do this? They did this because they thought they would be freeing up domestic savings for investment in their own countries. But what they failed to realize is that they live in an open world economy, and if they freed up their domestic savings when the United States was desperately short of its own, their savings would flow across the Atlantic and Pacific, which is what has happened. As a result, Europe and Japan have had very weak recoveries, the weakest since the war, and unemployment in Europe has risen steadily throughout what was supposed to be a world economic recovery.

What happens if we go on like this? In other words, what happens if we continue with these diametrically opposed policies? The short answer is that the world economy will have a hard landing. The dollar will in time go down too far and there will be a very unpleasant recession, not only in the United States, but in the rest of the world. This recession will, moreover, create a very serious risk of a major financial crisis both in the debtor developing countries, and also in the indebted sections of the U.S. economy, such as in the farm belt.

It is true that the dollar has come down quite a lot since last February, but it hasn't fallen nearly enough. My calculations suggest that if from now on the U.S. economy grew somewhat more slowly than the rest of the world—up to this point it has been growing much faster—and if the dollar stayed where it was yesterday, November 22, then the U.S. trade and current account deficit would rise to $250 billion by 1990. What is worse, by that time the United States would have become the largest debtor country in the world, to the tune of over $1 trillion. But that is something that cannot happen and will not happen. It is not possible for the United States, the world's most powerful country, to become the world's largest debtor. As investors gradually realize that they are making the same mistake as the banks did when they lent to Mexico and Brazil, the dollar will decline a lot more. At that point, people will no longer be willing to increase their exposure in dollars.

Now what about possible solutions? The economics of the situation, quite frankly, are not all that difficult. The right solution to the present problem is to correct its basic cause. In short, America must reduce its excessive reliance on foreign savings and that means a very substantial cut in the U.S. budget deficit. At the same time, America's allies must begin making more use of their own savings at home to finance an investment-led expansion and get unemployment down. The crucial point—and Lester Thurow has already made it—is that the United States at this point cannot solve its economic problems, particularly the problem of its trade deficit, on its own. It has, in fact, become a hostage to the whims of foreign investors and the policies of other countries.

Let me illustrate that briefly. In order for the United States to solve the problem of its trade deficit, two things must happen. The budget deficit must be cut *and* the dollar must come down. Either one without the other would severely depress the economy. If the budget deficit is cut but the dollar remains strong, the economy will be crowded out by the strong dollar, as it has been recently, and there will be a recession. On the other hand, if the dollar declines because foreign savings dry up, but the budget deficit has not been cut, the economy will be crowded out by a sharp rise in U.S. interest rates, and this will force the economy into recession. Either way, you lose. Thus, both the budget deficit must be cut and the dollar must be brought down.

But in order to get the dollar down in a manageable way and not provoke a crisis, we need both a cut in the U.S. budget deficit *and* a shift by other countries to more expansionary policies. If the United States cuts its budget deficit but the other countries continue on their present course, we shall have an increasingly soggy world economy. Investment demand in the rest of the world will weaken, the dollar will remain too high, and protectionist pressures will continue to increase. Thus, we need a cooperative effort.

In addition to these opposite shifts in fiscal policies, we will need close cooperation among the central banks of the major economies, both with regard to monetary policy and to intervention in the foreign exchange markets. To start the dollar on its way down, the Federal Reserve should be pursuing a relatively easy monetary policy, which at the moment it is. But in order for this to be effective, Japan and Germany should also temporarily tighten their monetary policies. The Japanese recently seem to have learned this lesson: they made a small move toward tighter money in early November and it had the dramatic effect of pushing the yen up. Regrettably, our German friends have not cooperated. Not only has Germany not taken monetary action to help push up the mark, but the president of the Bundesbank has categorically denied either that he was ever asked to do so, or that if he had been asked he would have ever agreed—a rather sorry comment on the present state of international monetary cooperation.

Nevertheless, there are a few signs of movement in the right direction. The meeting of the Group of Five—Britain, France, Germany, Japan, and the United States—in New York on September 22 was an encouraging sign. But its significance should not be overstated. What really happened in New York was simply that the U.S. Treasury rejoined Planet Earth. For the past five years, the Treasury has taken the untenable position that the market would solve all problems—that if each country looked after its own affairs the world economy would look after itself. This laissez-faire approach led to the divergent and inconsistent fiscal and monetary policies, which are heading us toward a crisis. It is therefore major progress that the U.S. Treasury now recognizes that the strong dollar is not something to be proud of, but is in fact a huge problem. And it's equally important that the administration has publicly recognized that the solution to that problem requires action not only by the United States, but also by other countries.

Yet we still have a long way to go. For if you read carefully the annex of the New York communiqué you will find that what each of the five countries committed themselves to are essentially the same policies they have been pursuing for the last few years: in short, the same policies that got us into this mess. Beyond the economics of the matter, the crucial element in a solution to these problems is a renewal of American leadership in the world economy. It is true, of course, that America must itself adopt sensible economic policies. But that alone is not enough. It is also essential that U.S. policies be compatible with those of the other major countries in the world, and vice versa.

We have reached a very tricky stage in the evolution of the world economy—one of the most fascinating stages intellectually, but also perhaps the most difficult to manage successfully. The United States is still by far the largest economy in the world, but it is no longer predominant. What happens elsewhere now matters a great deal. For most of the early postwar period, that wasn't true. If the U.S. economy was doing well and America was exercising leadership, most other things in the world economy looked after themselves. But the world today is so interdependent that if the policies of the major countries are incompatible, there are massive capital flows through the foreign exchange markets. This is what has happened over the past five years. We have had major fluctuations in exchange rates; serious distortions in world trade; and increasingly large movements of migrant labor from the less dynamic to the more dynamic parts of the world economy.

We need American leadership at several different levels. First, we need American leadership in the battle of economic ideas. Let's be honest. The economics profession has not performed very brilliantly in the last 10 years as far as macroeconomics is concerned; the old adage that if you have five economists you have six solutions is not so far from being true. At this point President Reagan, on the one hand, and Chancellor Kohl, Prime Ministers Nakasone and Thatcher, on the other, are equally convinced of the rightness of their fiscal and monetary policies, policies that are quite different but equally wrong. It is not enough for them to simply meet and agree to differ, which is basically what's happened at the last four or five summits. To be sure, they have set up working groups to study this and that. But the relatively low-level officials on these working groups have known that their governments were not really interested in intervention in the exchange markets or reform of the IMF, or in SDRs (special drawing rights). Thus, it is hardly surprising that their reports have generally consisted of a timid and tepid defense of the present system.

The truth is that it is just as important for our future that our heads of state understand how monetary and fiscal policies work, and how they interact in an increasingly interdependent world economy, as it is for them to understand the technical issues involved in defense policies. After all, if we make a mess of the world economy, we may not be able to defend ourselves.

A second area where American leadership is required is to breathe new life into the international economic institutions. They were, after all, set up precisely to provide a global view of the way national economic policies fit together, and to provide objective criticism when—as often happens—these policies do not. It is very symptomatic of the present state of affairs that the managing director of the International Monetary Fund was not even present at the meeting of the Group of Five in New York when important decisions were taken concerning the world's key currency. In fact, it is worse than this, as I know from my own personal experience. The major international organizations have become so frightened of losing what influence they have left that they spend much of their time simply saying what they think their major shareholders want to hear. So let me make just a few institutional suggestions.

First, summits. These have become media events with hopelessly overloaded agendas. There should be at least one if not two additional "working" summits each year devoted exclusively to the management of the world economy. At least one or two key developing countries should attend, while one or two of the present participants should be dropped. The heads of the major international organizations should participate directly in the meetings and be instructed to follow up on the decisions taken. Ways should be found to bring Congress and the private sector more closely into the preparation and follow-up of these "new style" summits.

Second, monetary cooperation. We need some kind of "open market committee" to manage the key exchange-rate relationships. Basically, this means setting up a triumvirate in which the key role would be played by the Federal Reserve, the Bank of Japan, and the Bundesbank. This open market committee should consult on planned changes in monetary policy and should have $100 billion or more of mutually agreed credits at its disposal to use when intervening in the exchange markets. It should report directly to the heads of state and be required to indicate what changes in fiscal and other policies may be needed to maintain sensible exchange-rate relationships.

Third, the Bretton Woods institutions. It is ridiculous that many of the most important types of trade restrictions lie outside the legal mandate of the General Agreement on Tariffs and Trade. It is ridiculous that the GATT secretariat is still far too small to police properly those restrictions that do fall within its legal mandate. It is even more ridiculous that international trade is dealt with by the GATT in Geneva, while international finance is dealt with by the International Monetary Fund and the World Bank in Washington—and never the twain do meet. There is no time to say more. But the fact is that if we were to sit down today to draw up sensible arrangements for effective economic cooperation for today's world, they would look quite different—given all that has happened since 1945, and all that we have learned since then.

Finally, we need better political leadership, especially political leadership on the part of the United States. I am struck by the political and diplomatic skills and energies the Reagan administration has marshalled on behalf of something like Star Wars. I only wish that it would exercise that same skill, leadership, and political pressure on behalf of something as critical as the better management of the world economy. For in the long run that is far more important.

Comments by Panelists

Sheehan: We need to rethink the use of the term "protectionism." The fact is that other countries engage in unfair trade practices against us, both in competing for our markets and in blocking our exports overseas. Taking action against these practices should not be called protectionism but instead should be seen as a necessary and appropriate response: as a way of pressuring other countries to comply with the rules of the game.

If an industry does receive safeguard relief, however, such relief should be tied to that industry's efforts to modernize. In other words, relief should be made conditional upon that industry meeting certain guidelines for reinvesting and restructuring.

With regard to Professor Thurow's remarks on education and retraining, we have an immediate obligation to those in our steel mills and other factories to ensure that they are not thrown out in the street. We need a much greater emphasis on educating and reeducating our workers. We also need to encourage greater worker participation in the production decisions of their companies.

While this conference is dealing with trade issues, we have to realize that trade policy must be part of a national economic policy, and we must ensure that our economic policies produce economic growth. Otherwise, we will continue to experience a sharp decline in our industrial section where the median-income workers are to be found.

Topol: I would like to make two comments. First, we should do more to encourage nations like China to export to us because they represent an enormous market for U.S. industry, especially for our high-technology goods. I am therefore very much opposed to our restricting textile imports from the Chinese as the congressional bill would do. Such a move, in my opinion, would be highly self-defeating. The Chinese are approaching the whole issue of trade in a responsible fashion, agreeing to purchase goods from us in proportion to what we import from them. To restrict their goods would only hurt ourselves.

Second, I am very disappointed that the Reagan administration has chosen to ignore the report of its Commission on Industrial Competitiveness. It is a well-thought-out report by conservative businessmen and academics, by people in both industry and government. Even though Professor Thurow does not believe it goes far enough, at least it is a step in the right direction. It recognizes what we have to do to become competitive in the world: devise a better tax structure, manage our economy as other countries manage theirs, and raise the level of concern for competitiveness to the highest level of our companies.

Amacher: I agree wholeheartedly with Mr. Sheehan on one point; namely, that we should use the term "protectionism" cautiously. The textile bill before Congress does not do anything that was not agreed to five years ago in bilateral negotiations with each of the countries that would be affected by the bill. We should view our markets as a public good and say to our competitors that they will have to pay for access to them either in the form of tariffs or by giving us access to their markets.

We should also be careful about expanding trade with the People's Republic of China, because it is a planned economy. I think that China's experiment with capitalism will be as short-lived as those in Hungary, Czechoslovakia, and Poland. And then, will we have given away the U.S. textile industry for the sake of a short-lived Chinese experiment with capitalism?

Reagan: Peter Drucker once commented that most people and most organizations spend most of their time trying to keep yesterday alive. I think that is especially true today. The fact is that we are in a new economy and the economy that we once knew is gone, probably forever. That means that we have to face up to international competition. While I oppose protectionism, I think it is one thing for our country or an industry to be disadvantaged because of a lack of productivity, and another because a foreign government is subsidizing or in another way favoring one of its corporations. In that situation, I would like to see our government become more involved. For example, if a foreign corporation bids $20 million because it has government support, and an American company is forced to bid $40 million because of the lack of U.S. government support, we should find a way to help our company. We should say to foreign companies that whatever price you set, we will match it. In this way, competition would be based on technical merits and not on government-supported price cuts.

Lockhart: Our salvation lies in restoring our competitiveness, and that will require business leadership more than political leadership. I therefore wholeheartedly endorse the focus of Professor Thurow's remarks on productivity, not on macroeconomics. In the coming years, we will find the dollar weak at times and strong at other times. We will need to compete under both conditions. A focus on macroeconomics will do little to address the underlying competitiveness of our economy, company by company, person by person. For example, we need to improve our product design quality, reduce excessive white-collar overhead, and adopt a "just-in-time" approach that would reduce costs and improve discipline in the handling of inventory. And we have to cultivate what I would call a trading culture in the United States, a culture that understands that we trade or perish. We need to give the same kind of attention to marketing as do the Japanese, who now outman our sales personnel by twenty or thirty to one in China and who educate their executives in foreign languages far more than we do.

Although they are not the key, policymakers can help create the environment that is necessary for improving competitiveness. They can relax restrictions on antitrust ventures, improve SEC and other government regulations so as to alter business's current short-term focus on quarterly earnings, provide tax incentives to encourage exports, and make export financing more competitive with that of other countries. Finally, I question whether we are going to be able to compete globally without a stronger sense of teamwork between the government and the private sector.

TRUTH IN TRADING[3]

Congressional demands for trade protectionism have reached dangerous—and largely needless—proportions. The first alarms sounded last spring, when the Senate voted, 92-0, to allow the president to retaliate against Japan's allegedly unfair trade practices. In the House of Representatives, nearly 300 protectionist bills were introduced between January and the summer recess. When Congress reconvened in September, protectionism dominated the agenda.

Behind this protectionist revival is the widespread belief that the United States faces a "trade crisis" that, in the words of Speaker of the House Thomas P. O'Neill (D.-Massachusetts), is rapidly

[3]Reprint of a magazine article by Bernard K. Gordon, professor of political science at the University of New Hampshire. *Foreign Policy* 61:94–108. Winter 1985–86. Reprinted by permission.

bringing about the "de-industrialization" of America. He and his colleagues warn that American jobs are being lost "every hour" to foreign imports and that export-hungry countries such as Japan and some of its Asian neighbors are profiting hugely from open U.S. markets while shutting American goods out of their own.

Those resisting the protectionist tide, such as President Ronald Reagan, are dismissed as "philosophical free traders" unwilling to face the "facts." But the facts—as found in such official sources as the International Monetary Fund's *Direction of Trade Statistics Yearbooks* and the U.S. Department of Commerce's *Highlights of U.S. Export and Import Trade* and *U.S. Trade Performance in 1984 and Outlook*—are that the United States remains the world's leading exporter. The U.S. share of world exports has stayed remarkably steady at about 12 per cent since the late 1970s, and the trend is not down, but up. The United States also still ranks as the world's leading exporter of manufactured goods. In 1984, U.S. manufactured exports rose in value by 8.3 per cent (to $151.2 billion), and in the market outside the United States this share has become the world's largest over the past 6 years—rising from 17 per cent in 1978 to about 20 per cent in 1985. In contrast, West Germany has fallen into second place, currently accounting for 18 per cent of the global total, and Japan ranks third, with 16 per cent.

Studies of American trade, moreover, debunk the myth that foreign goods are hastening the decline of American industry. A recent report by Norman Fieleke of the Federal Reserve Bank of Boston examined the impact of imports in 73 U.S. industries between 1980 and 1984 and concluded that "the 'deindustrialization of America' by foreign competition is more nearly a matter of myth than of substance." In addition, the report found no correlation during the same period between rising unemployment and rising net imports.

What then feeds the view that international trade victimizes the United States and that something drastic must be done? The answer lies in the enormous attention given to U.S. imports and the almost complete neglect of America's robust export performance, which results in a misguided emphasis on the so-called trade deficit. As a September 13, 1985, editorial in the *Wall Street Journal* entitled "Trade Deficit Bogeyman" correctly argued regarding the U.S. trade situation:

The words "surplus" and "deficit" should be avoided insofar as possible. . . . These words are frequently taken to mean that the developments are "good" or "bad." . . . Since that interpretation is often incorrect, the terms may be widely misunderstood and used in lieu of analysis.

Just as the *Wall Street Journal* warned, the terms have badly twisted the current trade debate. The trade "deficit" does not necessarily mean trouble for the United States—much less that the country is going bankrupt. As the president's Council of Economic Advisers (CEA) observed in its 1985 annual report, "Large external deficits and associated capital inflows are in large part the consequences of successful recovery in the United States, rather than problems requiring separate, new policy actions." The CEA correctly warned that an "emphasis on the bilateral trading balance [with any partner] in a multilateral trading system is misplaced"—recognizing the potential danger in congressional demands for trade restrictions on Japan and other Asian countries.

Despite the steady growth in its exports, the United States has of course been buying more merchandise from abroad than it has been selling—causing a trade deficit of $60 billion in 1983 and $123 billion in 1984. But policymakers must understand what even those figures mean.

U.S. merchandise trade statistics leave out, for example, the export of American services. Contrary to popular wisdom, services are not the preserve solely of poorly paid short-order cooks and janitors, but include overseas banking, insurance, shipping, advertising, and other sectors. When the Bechtel Group, Inc., of San Francisco wins a $200 million construction contract in the Persian Gulf, for example, the jobs involved are hardly low-paying, and this services transaction never shows up in the merchandise trade statistics.

Moreover, the United States leads the world in these service industries and regularly runs a surplus in its services account. In 1983, this surplus topped $28 billion, and it exceeded $20 billion in 1984. Further, these figures represent conservative estimates, because it is more difficult to measure trade in services than in merchandise. Yet trade statistics ignore this services surplus. Thus $20–$30 billion in U.S. exports is generally ignored when measuring the country's trade balance.

Figures on U.S. imports also mislead by including roughly $55–$60 billion in annual U.S. oil imports. Oil imports do not threaten American jobs or signal any decline in American industry. Yet by pumping up the size of the deficit, the large oil figure adds to the false sense of crisis surrounding U.S. trade and strengthens protectionist voices. Indeed, a New York Stock Exchange study concluded in mid-1984: "The U.S. non-petroleum trade balance has been positive since 1973." Even in 1984, when the "$123 billion deficit" gave protectionism its big push, oil represented almost one-half that total. That year, moreover, the rest of the world was slumping economically while America was booming. If economists know one thing, it is that an expanding economy sucks in imports.

Inefficient and uncompetitive American industries can manipulate fallacious trade data. The American shoe industry, for example, much of which has failed to modernize and thus offer competitive products, has based its call for footwear-import restrictions on the crisis allegedly facing U.S. industry. But more innovative American shoe producers, such as the Timberland Company of Newmarket, New Hampshire, have racked up big sales both at home and abroad. Not even the allegedly damaging effects of the high dollar have seriously hurt these firms. And they did not petition Congress for quotas against shoe imports.

U.S. policymakers must resist the current protectionist sophistry. For as the world's leading exporter, and with billions of its exports unaccounted for in trade figures, the United States is hardly a loser in international trade.

Japan Will Buy

Because the erroneous belief in a trade crisis is so widespread, the pressures for a "new trade policy" and for shorter-term fixes may be irresistible. Something useful can be done, but the United States needs first to put its trade difficulties in proper perspective and then to recognize not only changes that have taken place in U.S. trade, but also the opportunities they hold out.

In 1984, America's $37 billion trade deficit with Japan brought Japan-bashing back into vogue on Capitol Hill. Yet in the same year, America imported more from Canada ($67 billion) than from Japan ($60.4 billion). About 70 per cent of U.S. imports from Canada were manufactured goods; automotive imports alone totaled $22 billion. The United States also ended 1984 with a $20 billion merchandise trade deficit with Canada—a figure considerably lower than the $37 billion deficit with Japan in 1984 but hardly different from the $21.6 billion deficit with Japan in 1983. Yet U.S. trade imbalances with Canada evoked hardly a whimper.

Similar patterns—and inattention—are evident concerning U.S. trade with Western Europe. Bonn is rarely mentioned as a source of U.S. trade problems, but West Germany, which buys fewer manufactured goods from the United States than does Japan, rolled up a 1984 trade surplus with the United States of $8.7 billion—nearly twice the 1983 figure. In fact, America's 1984 merchandise trade with Western Europe as a whole ran $16.9 billion in the red—an increase of 3,600 per cent over 1983. But U.S. trade legislation rarely targets West European imports.

The trade figures for Canada and Western Europe do not imply that the U.S. trade deficit with Japan is unimportant; this gap can and should be reduced. But its 70 per cent rise in 1984 was topped by the 94 per cent rise in the U.S. deficit with West Germany, and it was positively dwarfed by the 730 per cent jump in the U.S. deficit with European Community (EC) members (from $1.6 billion to $13.3 billion) and by the 3,600 per cent leap in its deficit with Western Europe as a whole.

But more important than these deficit figures, and almost completely overlooked, is the scale of U.S. exports to Japan. This figure is already enormous and is growing steadily. As early as 1983, as Under Secretary of State W. Allen Wallis remarked, American sales to Japan equaled U.S. exports to "France, West Germany, and Italy combined." By 1984 they reached almost $24 billion—and the 7.7 per cent increase that this figure represents was recorded during a year in which the Japanese economy grew by only 4 per cent. In contrast, U.S. exports to the EC countries declined by $4 billion in 1982–1983 and grew by a mere 3.6 per cent the following year.

The large-scale and steady growth of U.S. exports to Japan refutes the myth that the Japanese won't buy American goods. Another myth holds that America sells mostly raw materials and food to Japan—constituting a "colonial" economic relationship.

Yet agricultural goods accounted for no more than one-fourth of American exports to Japan in 1984, and their share is declining. American manufactured goods, including aircraft, electronics, and computers and other automatic data processing equipment, made up more than one-half of the $24 billion in U.S. exports to Japan in 1984, and, according to Commerce Department figures, this portion has been increasing steadily since 1977, when it stood at 30 per cent.

The U.S. share of these manufactured imports has been much bigger in Japan than in Western Europe. In 1983, American products represented 38 per cent of Japan's purchases of manufactured goods, and the U.S. share has risen over time. In contrast, America's smaller share of Western Europe's manufactured imports has remained flat over the past decade, at about 8 per cent. Only in Great Britain and Ireland has this share normally exceeded 10 per cent.

The export of high-technology manufactured goods indicates a similar pattern. U.S. high-technology exports to Japan have increased by more than 51 per cent since 1980—to $6.1 billion in 1984. To the much larger, 10-member EC, these U.S. exports rose only 14.3 per cent, and the increase in dollar terms from $17 billion to $19.5 billion was not much larger than that for high-technology exports to Japan.

American exports to Japan carry a high "value-added" component, and Japan's per capita imports from the United States are correspondingly high; Japanese economist Kiyohiko Fukushima pegged the figure at $182 in 1983, compared with $157 for Western Europe. ("Japan's Real Trade Policy," *Foreign Policy* 59 [Summer 1985]: 38.) Moreover, the West European figure is declining; in West Germany it fell from $151 in 1982 to $147 in 1984. The reverse is true in Japan. Indeed, its per capita imports from the United States now exceed $200—not much lower than the $250 worth of America's per capita imports from Japan in 1984.

Since 1979 the American trade picture has been dominated by the shift to the Asia-Pacific region. By 1981, U.S. trade with East Asia—at $139 billion—was almost $15 billion larger than with Western Europe. In 1983 the difference alone had doubled, to $30 billion; U.S. trade with Western Europe stood at $117 billion, and trade with East Asia, at $147 billion.

The common argument, that most of these Asian totals represent U.S. imports, ignores the two main economic reasons that the Pacific region is significant to U.S. trade: the vitality and sheer size of the Pacific economies (despite their frequently small population bases) and the receptivity to U.S. products that has made them America's best customers. Both points emerge clearly after comparing East Asia with Latin America. Reflecting geography and history, Latin America traditionally has been seen as an especially promising market for U.S. goods, and for decades it was much more important than Asia in American trade. But East Asia's higher economic growth rate, along with its massive purchases from the United States, has now reversed that pattern.

In 1968, for example, even the then five-country Association of Southeast Asian Nations (ASEAN)—Indonesia, Malaysia, the Philippines, Singapore, and Thailand (Brunei joined in 1984)—paled against South America as a market for the United States. ASEAN's imports from the United States added up to only $942 million, while South America's were $2.78 billion, a ratio of 1:3. By 1983, ASEAN's purchases from the United States had soared to about $12 billion, compared with a South American figure of $10.6 billion. And imports from the United States have consistently made up 15 per cent of total ASEAN imports.

Further, these patterns were evident well before the Latin American debt crisis depressed Latin imports. Throughout the 1970s, South America's imports generally were growing at a slower rate than ASEAN's, and with few exceptions, the U.S. share was declining steadily.

Typical of that pattern is Brazil, which alone regularly accounts for almost 40 per cent of all South American imports. Imports from the United States have dropped steadily as a proportion of the Brazilian market, from 32 per cent in 1968 to 16 per cent in 1981. For Latin America as a whole the decline for that period was from 38 per cent to 27 per cent.

The consequences of this ASEAN–South America divergence have been dramatic for U.S. exporters, and they have been repeated in the larger markets of the Pacific and Latin America. In 1968, putting Japan and Mexico aside, imports in each market were roughly the same, at somewhat more than $3 billion. By the 1980s, however, U.S. sales to the Pacific region had reached $33–$34 billion because of strong overall import growth and the U.S. ability to maintain a market share of roughly 17–18 per cent. But in Latin America, where both overall imports and the U.S. market share declined during this time, American imports never exceeded $21 billion.

Yet these contrasts—particularly the strong U.S. export performance in Asia—have been masked by America's near-obsession with imports, by the misplaced attention given to the "trade deficit," and by the country's tradition of close economic ties with Western Europe and Latin America. Americans accordingly have come to regard Japan, Singapore, South Korea, Taiwan, and other Asian countries as their principal competitors. In fact, far from being trade enemies, they have turned out to be America's best markets—and vice versa.

The profitability of American trade with the newly industrializing countries (NICs) is especially impressive. Singapore, for example, despite its tiny 2.5 million population, imports more American goods (4.2 billion in 1983 and 1984) than either the People's Republic of China (PRC) or Brazil, and about the same quantity as either Italy or Australia.

South Korea is one of America's 10 largest customers, purchasing $6 billion from the United States in 1984. Heavy industrial goods represented nearly one-half this total. South Korea's U.S. imports rank with France's—even though France has more people and a per capita income five times higher. Moreover, South Korea's 1985 U.S. imports, according to a projection by the U.S. embassy in Seoul, will rise at about twice the rate of its better-known exports to the United States.

Similar considerations apply to Taiwan, now much criticized for its large trade surplus with the United States. Yet Taiwan's imports from the United States in 1984 exceeded $5 billion—more than triple the value of U.S. exports to India and more than $2 billion larger than American sales to the PRC. And like South Korea, Taiwan's American imports, projected to reach $6 billion in 1985, are rising much faster than its exports to the United States.

Further, the Asian NICs, ASEAN, and Japan will continue to provide the greatest spur to America's export growth. From 1980 to 1984, U.S. manufactured exports to the NICs and exports in the separate high-technology category rose by 20 and 41 per cent, respectively. In the same period, U.S. general and manufactured exports to Western Europe fell by 14 and 7 per cent, respectively. U.S. high-technology exports to Western Europe rose, but by a mere 14 per cent.

America's strong export performance in East Asia is all the more impressive considering Japan's heavy presence in that region—which makes its markets the world's most competitive. Yet the import-obsessed United States, with a zero-sum approach to trade, has increasingly adopted a begrudging and niggling posture toward these customers.

The NICs are repeatedly accused of unfair labor and trade practices. Congress continues to move toward restricting their goods because, among other things, these countries participate in the GSP program. GSP refers to the Generalized System of Preferences, under which the United States and other advanced industrialized countries allow limited duty-free access to manufactured goods from the newly industrializing states. The American program took effect in 1976, and Taiwan and South Korea—strong U.S. customers—have also been the biggest beneficiaries. Congress recently renewed the GSP program, but in response to complaints from competing domestic industries, greatly lessened GSP allowances for East Asian countries. Congressional support is still strong, moreover, for special new duties on textiles that would most seriously affect the East Asian NICs. Such protectionism is neither healthy nor necessary, because high mutual export growth is clearly the chief characteristic of trade between the United States and these countries.

U.S. policymakers must also recognize that, contrary to much conventional wisdom, the strong dollar does not greatly skew America's trade with Japan. That currency values are not among the leading determinants of bilateral trade balances does not deny the general proposition that a cheap currency, if it lowers final prices, should promote exports, and that an expensive currency, if it raises prices, should hurt them. Yet strong evidence indicates that, in practice, this proposition does not always hold. An important 1983 study by the International Trade Commission (ITC), for example, found that there is "often little direct correlation between the percentage change in the value of the U.S. dollar . . . and trade balances."

U.S.-Japanese trade patterns demonstrate this clearly. Since 1980, the dollar has risen much more in relation to Western Europe's currencies than it has against the yen, but America's trade imbalance with Japan has been greater. Research conducted by the economic consultants H. C. Wainright & Company of Boston, Massachusetts, indicates similarly that "where the dollar appreciated most, the trade balance deteriorated least, and vice versa."

Indeed, U.S.-Japanese trade has evolved largely independent of the yen-dollar rate. Between 1976 and 1980, for example, each country doubled its exports to the other, even though the yen grew 30 per cent stronger in that period. Former Under Secretary of Commerce Lionel Olmer, who dealt with U.S.-Japanese trade when the dollar's value was rising most sharply, fully recognized the limited importance of exchange rates. In congressional testimony in 1984 he remarked that "our deficit with Japan is chronic" and "long preceded the strong dollar. . . . the trend toward large and increasing deficits with Japan is an independent problem [that has existed] across changing business cycles and fluctuating yen-dollar rates."

One main reason for the relative unimportance of currency changes is what economists call the "pass through" effect—specifically, the fact that fluctuating currency values generally are not passed through fully, or at all, to consumers. Americans who recently have contemplated buying a Mercedes, BMW, or Peugeot automobile have run into this phenomenon. Despite the great strength of the dollar against the deutsche mark and the franc, U.S. importers of those cars certainly have not lowered their dollar prices.

Moreover, as several studies have found, when the dollar has fallen, U.S. exporters simply have realized larger profits rather than lowering their prices to reflect the change. Japanese producers, however, with very different capital sources than U.S. firms, and determined to maintain market shares when the yen has risen, have accepted lower prices and profits.

Price itself, as the ITC study also concluded, is only one of the criteria that determine purchasing patterns. In some cases, as automobiles again illustrate, it is low on the list: Despite increases of $5,000 or more in the price of a Mercedes or a BMW, demand has not fallen off, and there is some reason to think that high price actually promotes demand in the luxury-car market. More generally, elements of quality, design, reputation, and service are often more important than low price in selling goods with a "technological component"—and that is mainly what industrialized countries like the United States and Japan sell to one another.

Consequently, the anticipated decline in the dollar's value will probably not greatly reduce the U.S.-Japanese trade imbalance. And a falling dollar will certainly have only a small effect on U.S.

exports unless American firms do a more effective job in the Japanese market than they have so far. Some years ago, for example, when Japan's nontariff barriers (and before that, its tariffs) were blamed for the trade imbalance, the House Ways and Means Committee undertook what has come to be known as the Jones Report. Its conclusions remain valid today: "Any long-term improvement . . . will depend more on improved [U.S.] performance . . . in promoting exports than on the removal of remaining non-tariff barriers."

How to Do Better

Indeed, perhaps the most striking aspect of U.S. trade and exports to Japan, especially in comparison with Western Europe, is how well America has done with so little effort. A good measure of that effort is found in Commerce Department figures for 1977 and 1982 that show that American businesses other than banks stationed many more employees in Western Europe than in Japan.

In 1977, when the United States exported $27 billion worth of goods to EC members, there were 11,703 American citizens working for U.S. firms in these 10 countries. In Japan that year, U.S. sales totaled $10.5 billion, but the comparable number of American employees was only 338. The EC market for U.S. exports was 2.5 times larger than Japan, but the U.S. employee contingent in the EC countries was 32 times greater.

The comparable figures for 1982 show only a slight change. By 1982, U.S. sales to Japan had doubled—to $21 billion. But the number of American employees based there approached only 800. In the EC countries the U.S. employee figure had dropped to 6,500—still eight times that of Japan—while imports from the United States, reflecting a significantly lower growth rate than sales to Japan, stood at just under $48 billion.

The ridiculously small number of U.S. business employees based in Japan reflects America's long-standing diffidence toward Japan and, except for the PRC, toward Asia in general. But the mere 800 or so Americans working in Japan puts in a different light frequent complaints about the closed Japanese market. Moreover, there are now about 96,000 Japanese nationals living in the New York City area alone. Obviously not all are working in sushi bars. At least 25,000–30,000 Japanese citizens are now estimated to be working for Japanese firms in the United States. Language and custom, obviously, make the Japanese market difficult. But as the Commerce Department, which is hardly unsympathetic to exporters, itself has said, "On balance . . . entry into the Japanese market is not significantly more difficult than entry into other industrially advanced national markets."

The Commerce Department also counsels patience and a willingness to absorb higher-than-average initial costs to set up in Japan, and American firms that have succeeded agree. A 1983 report by the consulting firm of McKinsey & Company warned that American exporters have been "needlessly discouraged by misleading assumptions about Japan's . . . domestic market entry problems." The report specifically chastised both the U.S. government and the media for placing "too much emphasis on the merchandise trade deficit . . . while largely ignoring other measures of business penetration in which the U.S. performs better." As measures to punish Japan for its trade practices come closer to enactment, the U.S. government and especially American businesses must listen to that advice. Corporate executives must re-examine why they send about the same number of representatives to Australia, comfortable and English-speaking, as to Japan—while they export as much to Japan in 2 months as to Australia and its surrounding market in an entire year.

Today's panaceas will not cure the supposed trade deficit problem. Bringing the dollar down may help over the very long haul, but it will have little meaning for the largest single component of the deficit—oil—because imported oil is largely denominated in dollars. In fact, a strong dollar helps restrain the price of imported oil.

Moreover, if Congress were serious about reducing the trade deficit with Japan, it would remove the restrictions on U.S. oil sales there. Annual Alaskan oil production stands at $20-$30 billion, and perhaps $10 billion of that could be sold to Japan. This step alone would immediately reduce the deficit to a figure no larger than America's deficit with Canada, but there is little evidence of major steps in this direction.

To avoid the protectionist cycle now in the making, the United States should seize the opportunity presented by its genuinely symbiotic trade relationship with East Asia and try to open these markets even wider. Charting an important new direction in U.S. trade policy, the CEA recommended in early 1985 that if Washington could not achieve the grander goal of "comprehensive trade liberalization," it should move instead to establish free trade areas (FTAs)—in which the United States and a number of other countries, independent of the worldwide General Agreement on Tariffs and Trade (GATT), would greatly lower or eliminate trade barriers against each other.

The president already has the authority to do so, and last year, then Special Trade Representative William Brock proposed talks on a US-ASEAN FTA. Progress along these lines already has begun. In September, a U.S-Israeli FTA was established, and discussions toward a U.S.-Canadian FTA are now under way—with strong support in both capitals.

Canada's incentive is to avoid U.S. protectionism, and America's closest trade partners in the Pacific are no doubt thinking the same way. For the United States, the FTA approach promises to open markets and also represents, in the CEA's words, a "free trade . . . lever against protectionist countries that are recalcitrant in fully multilateral negotiations."

Washington should pick up on Brock's ASEAN idea and eventually apply it to South Korea, Taiwan, and ultimately Japan. The United States and these East Asian countries already greatly depend on each other, and as the CEA recognized, once one FTA is established, other countries that need the American market will not want to be left out. The United States can obtain the market access it wants and other goals by using its most powerful bargaining lever: the enormous American market.

The FTA agreement with Israel also demonstrates that countries are willing to give up the trade tactics America resents. The Israelis have agreed to phase out their export subsidies and to protect American copyrights and patents in exchange for greater access to U.S. markets. This concern about intellectual property has also been one of the sore points in America's dealings with Taiwan and Singapore. It is also precisely the kind of issue that is souring current US-ASEAN trade talks and that Brock presumably sought to transcend when he made his FTA proposal.

Trade negotiation is not easy and will not bring overnight results. Nevertheless, opening trade remains a far better policy than erecting trade barriers and waging the sort of export-subsidy wars currently proposed. As the report by the CEA observed, FTAs are a "second-best" strategy. But in politics and economics that is often the best a country can obtain—and probably all it really needs.

IV. TRADE POLICY WITH JAPAN AND CANADA

EDITOR'S INTRODUCTION

Trade policy involves more than economic considerations: it touches upon the history, culture, and identity of a nation. These factors are especially influential in the policies of our two largest trading partners, Japan and Canada. This section examines the complexities of the trade relationship between the U.S. and these major industrial nations. In the first article, Dutch journalist Karel G. van Wolferen analyzes American misperceptions of the Japanese economy which contribute, in no small part, to U.S.-Japan trade problems. In the second article, former Reagan trade official Clyde V. Prestowitz, Jr., writing in *California Management Review,* discusses the history of trade friction between the U.S. and Japan and offers some solutions to lessen the tension. Finally, in his testimony before the House Foreign Affairs Committee, Assistant Secretary of State Paul Wolfowitz asserts that Japan must assume its responsibilities as the number two economic power by resisting protectionist measures.

U.S. trade policy with Canada is the focus of the second part of this section. Writing in *Foreign Affairs,* Canadian professors Adam Bromke and Kim Richard Nossal describe the political and historical factors which led to the signing of the comprehensive trade accord between the two countries on January 2, 1988. In a related article which appeared in the Canadian journal *International Perspectives,* Dalhousie University Professor Denis Stairs analyzes the arguments for and against the bilateral trade agreement and its implications for Canada. Finally, in a speech to the Americas Society in New York, Ontario Premier David Peterson advocates a policy of modified free trade that distinguishes between "protectionism to shelter inefficient industries, and legitimate economic development efforts to bolster efficient ones."

THE JAPAN PROBLEM[1]

The relationship between the world's two greatest economic powers is in serious trouble. With a frightening momentum economic disputes between Japan and the United States are growing into a political conflict. Still, attempts by both sides to create a situation they can live with are unpromising. The Reagan Administration gives the impression of preferring to avoid thinking about it. Although the "Japan problem," as the fundamental conflict has become known, is already many years old, what must pass for a Japan policy in Washington is so unrealistic that it may make the situation considerably worse.

There is much more at stake than America's growing trade deficit with Japan. If present trends are allowed to continue they will eventually lead to a gradual loss of industrial capacity in the United States. At some point an irate Congress is likely to apply the brakes to these trends by passing undifferentiated trade legislation that is even tougher than what is being contemplated today. Uncontrollable consequences in Japan, including political instability and a xenophobic reaction, could follow.

What makes conflict between Japan and the United States so menacing is that the two countries do not know how to cope with each other. The United States does not understand the nature of the Japanese political economy and thus cannot accept the way it behaves. Americans can hardly be blamed for this, as the Japanese themselves present their country as simply another member of the community of democratic nations committed to the free market. Japan is largely unaware of the threat posed by America's unwillingness to accept it for what it is. Never having experienced its wrath, Japan does not believe in the powers of the American legislature. The Japanese make things worse with ritualistic arguments and empty promises that only convince congressmen, businessmen and other Americans that they are being deceived.

I believe that two fictions are central to the outsiders' inability to come to grips with Japan. . . .

[1]Excerpted from an article by Karel G. van Wolferen, correspondent for the Dutch newspaper NRC Handelsblad. *Foreign Affairs* 65:288–303. Winter '86/'87. © 1986 by the Council on Foreign Relations. Reprinted by permission.

First there is the fiction that Japan is a sovereign state like any other, a state with central organs of government which can both recognize what is good for the country and bear ultimate responsibility for national decision-making. This illusion is very difficult to dispel, since diplomacy must take it for granted.

In fact, statecraft in Japan is quite different from that in the rest of Asia, Europe and the Americas. For centuries it has entailed the preservation of a careful balance between semiautonomous groups that share power. Today, the most powerful components of what I will call the Japanese System are certain groups of bureaucrats, some political cliques and clusters of industrialists. There are lesser ones, such as the agricultural cooperatives, the police, the press and the gangsters. These semiautonomous components, each endowed with great discretionary powers, are not represented in one central ruling body.

It is crucial to distinguish Japan from other nations with governments that are besieged by special interest groups or that cannot make up their minds because of interdepartmental disputes. We are not dealing with lobbies but with a structural phenomenon not encompassed by the categories of accepted political theory. A hierarchy, or rather a complex of overlapping hierarchies, is maintained, but it has no top. There is no supreme institution with ultimate jurisdiction over the others. Thus there is no place where, as Harry Truman would say, the buck stops. The buck keeps circulating.

The second fiction that hampers the formulation of an effective policy toward Japan is the premise maintained by the United States and Europe that Japan belongs with them in that loose category known as capitalist free-market economies. Although the Japanese economy is very extensively commented upon in the West, it still causes tremendous conceptual difficulties for foreigners and Japanese alike. Japanese officials usually bristle with indignation at the suggestion that their country is something other than advertised. Yet Japanese economists I talk with often remind me that Westerners writing on Japan commonly exaggerate the function of the market mechanism. On the other hand Western academic economists, including current presidential advisers, appear horrified at the suggestion that Japan does not in fact belong in the club of capitalist free-market nations. For many of them, the idea that there can be a successful economy which is not based on the free play of market forces is tantamount to heresy.

As Japan also clearly does not belong in the category of the centrally controlled Soviet-type economies, does it then belong to a category of its own, as quite a few commentators have implied? The rapid rise of South Korea and Taiwan as industrial states suggests that this is not the case: even when shorn of its cultural and psychological specifics, the Japanese "economic miracle" constitutes a model that can be pursued by at least some others. South Korea and, to a lesser extent, Taiwan—both states having a strong central government—have economies that appear to be driven by a phenomenal force similar to that of Japan, even in the absence of Japanese-style "harmony," lifelong employment, management techniques—all of which are often cited as reasons for the Japanese success. Analysis shows that a third category of political economies can exist, besides the Western type and that of the communist world. Chalmers Johnson of the University of California, Berkeley, has isolated this category of industrial nations and has labeled the type Capitalist Developmental State. (See, for example, his *MITI and the Japanese Miracle: The Growth of Industrial Policy, 1925–1975*, Stanford [Ca.]: Stanford University Press, 1982.)

The strength of the CDS is a partnership between central bureaucrats and entrepreneurs. The bureaucrats never attempt to gain absolute power over the nongovernmental corporations. They guide the economy while using the entrepreneurs as antennae. The central planners of the CDS know what is happening at the periphery through constant monitoring of the experiences of capitalists trying to find new ways of making money. The mistakes the planners undoubtedly make are more than compensated for by the unified forces they bring to bear on industrial development. The economy prospers because promising areas of industry are stimulated by central policies favoring investment. Those that appear to have reached a dead end are more easily abandoned through policies forcing reorganization. In other words, it is a partnership that has an industrial policy and a trade strategy. Freedom of the market is not considered a desirable goal in itself, but only one of several instruments for achieving predetermined effects that are totally subordinated to the ultimate goal of industrial expansion.

The CDS is structurally protectionist in the sense that all kinds of informal, if not official, barriers to imports must ensure that foreign competition will not undermine its aims. It has to remain so if it wants to continue enjoying the proven benefits of this model. But, as is becoming abundantly clear, in the long run this causes political problems in its relations with other states. The question is whether the bureaucratic-entrepreneurial partnership will continue to flourish after its industries face market saturation at home and inhospitable markets overseas. Related to this is the even more important question of whether the international free trade system, made up of countries without a trade strategy, can survive as it struggles to accommodate the CDS.

It is not likely that the partnership between the state and private enterprise in Japan will break up. The official line is that the various forms of governmental guidance (if acknowledged at all) now carry much less weight with the private sector than in the past. This contention is habitually accompanied by a demonstration that current tariff regulations make Japan about the freest market in the world. In Japan, quite often—and always more frequently than in the West—what is true on paper is not true in practice. Japanese spokesmen widely advertise the fact that a number of foreign firms that have tried hard enough have been successful in their market. These firms are well known because they belong to the same small sample always mentioned in this context. A select few foreign firms receive assistance to serve as fresh examples of Japanese openness. What we should look at, however, are distribution systems in a few controlling hands, regulations dictated by Japanese competitors, new product standards, and other barriers that a potentially powerful foreign competitor faces in the Japanese market. The bureaucrats in Tokyo are extremely inventive when it comes to subtle controls and euphemisms for rendering them more palatable to foreigners.

Moreover, what has given the Japanese CDS system durability is the obliteration of the line dividing private and public sectors. Japanese power relationships have evolved into something far more intricate than a "bureaucrats-businessmen partnership." In South Korea one can distinguish the government from the entrepreneurs; in Japan, however, it is not only impossible to locate a center, it is also not possible to separate the realms of public and private business. In the higher reaches of Japanese economic activity, bureaucrats, former bureaucrats in top business positions, and bureaucratically inclined leaders at the top of the business hierarchies are as one as they mingle with each other busily monitoring the economy. Antagonisms exist in the higher reaches of the system—quite a lot in fact—but they rarely, if ever, pit the formal organs of state against the industrial organizations. The great rivalries and territorial wars between the different ministries are significant and publicized, whereas genuine confrontations between the bureaucrats and recalcitrant corporations are almost never heard of. Only much lower down, among the newer firms and especially the vitally important sectors of small subcontracting firms, can one find more traditional entrepreneurs without strong ties to the bureaucracy.

Because it is impossible in Japan to extricate the state from the socioeconomic system, monumental communication problems arise when foreign businessmen or government representatives at the higher levels attempt to negotiate with what they think are their Japanese counterparts. The confusion is made even worse by the peculiarly Japanese institution of the "buffer," the person who is entrusted with the task of making contacts with foreigners as smooth as possible. Resident foreign diplomats and businessmen usually deal with the Japanese through an intermediary community of English-speaking, "internationalized" Japanese who absorb the shocks that an unpredictable outside world might deliver to their institutions. These buffers can be amazingly frank, can convey genuine understanding of the foreigner's difficulties and create the impression of willingness to cater to his wishes.

Japan has a handful of super buffers who spend much time traveling the globe, troubleshooting and explaining the Japanese case at international conferences. Two of them, Saburo Okita and the late Nobuhiko Ushiba, were even made ministers for external economic affairs. This increased the confusion further because they had no actual mandate to decide or negotiate anything. Ministers more influential than these two, or leaders of economic federations, and even the prime minister himself, often play the buffer role when speaking with foreign trade envoys. The foreign negotiator who arrives home yet again with the news that this time he has *really* talked with the proper authorities, who have impressed him with their readiness to take effective action, is deceiving himself. Such persons with the necessary broad authority simply do not exist in Japan.

Thus the communication gap appears as unbridgeable as ever, and the Japan problem grows worse all the time. It is generally summed up by record-breaking trade surpluses: $45 billion in 1984 and $61 billion in 1985. For 1986, the Organization for Economic Cooperation and Development has projected a Japanese surplus of up to $85 billion; more than $50 billion of that will show up as a bilateral trade deficit with the United States. Japanese competitiveness and the inhospitality of its own market to foreign products are helping to bring about further deindustrialization in the United States and Europe. After the virtual loss of the motorcycle and consumer electronics sectors in the United States, the Japanese are gaining leverage over such crucial industries as semiconductors, machinery and telecommunications equipment.

The number of trade bills introduced in Congress demonstrates that Americans think this is intolerable and that patience is wearing thin. But protestations from Washington, accompanied by demands that the Japanese market be opened wider, are met by little more than Japanese rhetorical assurances of their commitment to free trade. Efforts by the bureaucracy to ameliorate the situation are designed to keep the Americans quiet. They do not get to the root of the problem, for as things stand nothing can. As far as the politicians are concerned, many, if not most, have a stake in what is euphemistically known as *boeki masatsu,* or trade friction. They want to keep it from doing too much damage, and they instruct bureaucrats accordingly, but if *boeki masatsu* disappeared so would a lucrative source of income. This is because the sectors of the business community that most fear foreign competition at home through liberalization measures urged by the United States are also the most generous with political donations. As the various ministries involved in "liberalizing" blame each other for being the bigger obstacle to effective measures, they come up with minute compromises, presented together as "market-opening packages." The effect of the half dozen of these presented thus far has been practically nil. In mid-1985 much propaganda accompanied a so-called Action Program, but the nature of that effort was succinctly characterized by Foreign Affairs Minister Shintaro Abe, who called it a table of contents without contents.

To be sure, Nakasone has made quite a difference when compared to his four predecessors. He has continued a campaign, begun by former Prime Minister Kakuei Tanaka, to increase the leverage of the LDP politicians over the bureaucrats. For this, he has utilized the talents of the experts whom Tanaka had collected in his group, the largest and unquestionably the most powerful of the *habatsu*, or political cliques, of which the ruling party is a coalition. He has been helped by the circumstance that bureaucratic territorial wars over newly developing industrial sectors, like telecommunications, have given the politicians a relatively new function as arbiters. Nakasone has also found a new use of the *shingikai*—advisory committees expected to present high-minded schemes, long on abstract ideals and short on concrete proposals, which previous prime ministers could pass off as policy. He has handpicked *shingikai* chairmen and key members and does not leave it to their imagination as to how he expects to be "advised." But all this falls very much short of what Japan needs in the way of centralized power to cope with the problem of its economic relations with Europe and the United States.

Increased congressional pressure on the Reagan Administration has brought to the fore a double formula to help reduce the trade imbalance: push up the value of the yen and make Japan stimulate its economy.

Nakasone has shown his willingness to cooperate by directing an advisory committee under the chairmanship of former Bank of Japan Governor Haruo Maekawa to present guidelines for making domestic demand, rather than exports, the main engine for economic growth. However, the final version of the Maekawa report has been picked clean of the originally suggested concrete proposals by éminences grises from the important ministries, notwithstanding the fact that an angry Nakasone had ordered it rewritten in order to reflect an awareness of the hostile international situation that the Japanese economy was faced with.

While Nakasone was presenting this most recent token of Japanese goodwill in Washington last April, his countrymen were pulling the rug out from under him. LDP politicians said that they could not accept the Maekawa report. Top bureaucrats leaked their worries that Nakasone was misleading Reagan. The *Nihon Keizai Shimbun* (Japan's version of *The Wall Street Journal*) tore the report to pieces. And the *Asahi Shimbun* commented in an editorial, "Every time a political leader says one thing abroad and something else at home, distrust of Japan in the world community grows. It is ironic that Nakasone, who is proud of his diplomatic prowess, now repeats the same mistake." (April 21, 1986)

Finally, the Ministry of Foreign Affairs weighed in with a statement that the report did not represent Japanese policy.

All this did not deter President Reagan, Secretary of State George P. Shultz, *The New York Times* and others from praising it. But suppose the Maekawa report were a truly serious blueprint for a campaign to stimulate the domestic economy of Japan, what good would it do America? The idea that Japan can help tow the world's less powerful economies has become untenable after all the years in which its domestic growth has not had any significant influence on the level of imports from the United States or Europe. When things are booming, raw materials find their way to Japan, of course, but not the finished products that America wants to sell there.

Perhaps in no other area is the inapplicability of conventional economic theory as blatantly obvious as in the case of the yen-dollar exchange rate. The current Administration in Washington is probably like no other recent government in its firm conviction of the healing powers of the free market. It is therefore no wonder that its favorite theory as to why Japan is competitive in America but America is not competitive in Japan revolves around prices. If only those Japanese goods in American shops could be made expensive enough, and American goods in Japanese shops cheap enough, everything would fall back into place again. Or at least the incredibly lopsided trade balance could be brought to proportions that one could live with.

Japanese officials and economic commentators had for years been pleased enough with the conclusion that the yen was undervalued, as this meant that the dollar was worth too much, which put the ball in America's court. Thus it was difficult for the Japanese monetary authorities to object when, in September 1985, the finance ministers and central bank governors of the five largest economies of the Western community agreed in New York to manage a decline in the value of the dollar. Nine months later the Japanese currency had appreciated by roughly 40 percent against the dollar, much more than either side had anticipated. This currency realignment is said to be a better reflection of fundamental economic realities.

Is achievement of American aims in sight with more expensive Japanese goods in American shops? Only in the cases where the higher prices will not endanger the market share that Japanese firms have in the United States. In some areas there is no longer any competition. In others, it is possible for Japanese exporters to subsidize vulnerable items with surplus funds from highly profitable company divisions.

Or, if need be, domestic prices will go up in order to offset losses in the overseas market. Cheaper American goods in Japanese shops? Japan's newspapers and magazines have been searching for months for instances where the benefit of the strong yen has been passed on to the consumer. Their findings all show that the effect is marginal at best and that in some cases prices of imported goods have actually gone up. Nakasone has repeatedly told his ministers to instruct those below them to see to it that not only the importers but the whole nation profits from the lower import prices. But the bureaucracy itself sets a bad example: officials who administer the government import programs of beef and wheat use their exchange gains to help subsidize the highly inefficient domestic agricultural sector.

In some industries the high yen is causing an acceleration of the shrinking that has been going on for years. In others, plans to move simpler production lines to the much cheaper labor markets in other parts of Asia have been accelerated.

But from the viewpoint of Japan's Western trade partners the most important thing that is happening is that the subcontracting firms are being forced to streamline. These are the hardworking, often tiny, outfits that occupy a key position in Japan's dual economy. They form a shock-absorbing cushion underneath the large conglomerates. They are currently being asked to absorb much of the exchange rate losses, and are therefore trimming their costs as never before. While more automation is introduced in these small- and medium-sized subcontracting firms, the larger Japanese manufacturers are buying parts in South Korea and Taiwan. Both measures enable them to continue exporting to the United States at roughly the old dollar prices.

In short, the Japanese System continues to shield the home market against imports, and Japanese firms are going to extremes in order to hang on to overseas market shares. There is a good chance that when the American effort to "talk the yen upwards" runs out of steam, the value of the yen will drop to the lower, fluctuating levels desired by the system. At that point the workers who were dismissed from the subcontracting firms, who have spent some time in the parasitic distribution system (which is a large reservoir of the would-be unemployed) or who have cultivated a few square yards of heavily subsidized rice paddy, will return to help make new cheap export products. With more efficient subcontractors, Japan will be commercially more battle-ready than ever. An intensification of the conflict appears inevitable as many billions of dollars are added to the bilateral trade deficit, as expectations in connection with new unrealized Japanese plans are frustrated, as Japanese attitudes begin to grate on members of Congress, and as new moral shortcomings are discovered of the kind conveyed by Nakasone's recent remark that America's minorities have lowered the nation's average intelligence level. . . .

What does make sense, however, is for the United States to decide quickly on measures constituting a Japan policy, to stave off an otherwise seemingly inevitable confrontation that would harm the non-communist world and destroy what remains of the international free trade system.

A Japan policy must necessarily contain ingredients that diverge widely from accepted diplomatic practices between countries at peace. To see that clearly, it is useful to recognize how the Japanese System itself handles conflict. In Japanese society conflict is avoided, ignored, denied, exorcised by ritual, but rarely solved. There is no tradition of appealing to universal principles or of using legal procedures to keep order in society. Individuals and groups accept their positions and their lot because a stronger power holds them in place, although subtle acts of sabotage are expected and condoned. The ins and outs of the general balancing act among the semiautonomous components of the system are not finally determined by reason, but by power. Conflicts between parties that have no hierarchical relationship with each other and refuse to accept subordinate positions fester and cannot be resolved. Conflicts with the outside world are comparable, as Japanese groups will not subordinate themselves voluntarily to foreigners, while the reasoning that outsiders bring to bear can never be convincing enough. The situation is insoluble unless, of course, the other country adopts the means of the system and forces recognition of proper positions.

If he listens carefully, the foreigner will quite often hear his contacts in Japan say that there will be no essential shift in policy until relentless and consistent outside pressure forces the change. The Japanese political-economic system fosters inward-looking attitudes. It is incapable of selfless gestures, but it can react with alacrity once it is imbued with a pervasive sense of crisis. In the growing conflict with America no significant Japanese adjustments can be expected until the entire establishment has been thoroughly imbued with the idea that there is a new reality to which it must adjust, like the reality created by OPEC. No verbal threats serve this purpose, because they have for many years proved quite empty.

International trade legislation of the most general kind is unlikely to have enough effect on Japan. Only action that specifically singles out Japan, in a carefully measured dose, will imbue the Japanese System with the sense that the situation has become intolerable for the United States. The Reagan Administration could usefully give up its efforts to remind Japan of the teachings of Adam Smith and jettison the fiction that Japan has a free-market economy similar to those of the West. It is one thing to fight the growth of government control over one's own economy but quite another to blind oneself to the Japanese reality of a highly controlled economy. To make the point perfectly clear it is necessary for the United States to stop agreeing diplomatically with the Japanese argument that American companies also must try harder to penetrate the Japanese market.

When the Japanese System has become fully alerted to the new reality, a modus vivendi must be arranged with it. One part of the new set of conditions could be direct fixed commitments between Western and Japanese economic institutions for an international division of labor. The "voluntary" quotas on car exports demonstrate the feasibility of such agreements. The cartelization that they necessitate is nothing new to the Japanese System, and would even be preferred by some of its components. Yoshihiro Inayama, the former chairman of Keidanren (the most influential club of Japanese industrialists), has actually stated that it would be better if the United States decided unilaterally to restrict the import of Japanese products until the trade imbalance is rectified.

It must be remembered that the essence of the problem is not that Japan exports much more than it imports, but that its exports systematically undermine Western industries. Peter Drucker calls this adversarial trade, as distinct from competitive trade whereby a country also imports manufactures of the same kind as it exports. Germany's trade surpluses are very large too but

Germany practices such competitive trade, as does the United States.

The important thing for the American government to realize is that in order for the relatively free international trade system to survive, the world needs a different kind of discipline. The increasing impact of Japan's imitators and the possibility that China will in the future develop a CDS apparatus make it all the more urgent. The hue and cry in Japan that almost inevitably will follow such American measures may give the impression that the Japanese are being punished. But that will not be the case at all. Quite the contrary, by preventing waves of uncontrollable retaliatory protectionism, these measures will most probably preserve the health of the Japanese economy, considering how dependent it is on exports, and thereby promote continued political stability.

U.S.-JAPAN TRADE FRICTION: CREATING A NEW RELATIONSHIP[2]

Forty years after the end of World War II, Japan and the U.S. are again engaged in conflict. Trade frictions, which began as minor irritants in an otherwise smooth relationship in the 1960s, have gradually escalated over the years. Today, they threaten to explode into a full-scale trade war which could seriously damage, if not destroy, what has been termed the "most important bilateral relationship in the world bar none" by Ambassador to Japan, Mike Mansfield.

The conflict is more dangerous than it appears because its real nature is partially hidden. It masquerades as a banal and sometimes grubby dispute over widgets with the stakes being whether American or Japanese big business makes more money. In truth the issue is strategic and geopolitical in nature. Japan is once again challenging the U.S., only this time the issue is not China or the Pacific, but world industrial and technological leadership and the military and economic powers which have always been its corollaries.

[2]Reprint of a magazine article by Clyde V. Prestowitz, Jr. *California Management Review* 29: 9–19, Winter 1987. © by the Regents of the University of California. By permission of the Regents.

If things continue on this present course, Japan will come to dominate many of the world's industries, in particular, high technology. This will have two major economic consequences. First, the U.S. will become increasingly poorer compared to Japan. The terms of trade will continue to go against the U.S. and its *relative* standard of living will decline. Indeed, average family income in the U.S. has already dipped compared to ten years ago. Second, the U.S. will become militarily dependent on Japan for the technology of its weaponry. The U.S. continues to make economic concessions and accepts unequal circumstances in the name of larger political objectives. For example, the U.S. hesitates to act against Japanese policies that effectively close its market to superior American-made satellites and supercomputers because it hopes to achieve Japanese participation in the space station. The U.S. also long hesitated to act against Japanese dumping of semiconductors because it hoped to obtain Japanese participation in Star Wars. At the same time, because of its relative economic decline, the U.S. will be less and less able to afford the military establishment it must have to bear the burdens of leading the West. The end of this road is not hard to see. It is the British postwar experience, only without a U.S. to whom to pass the ball. It is clearly a problem which intensely concerns the entire free world, not just the U.S. and Japan.

The Origins of U.S.-Japan Trade Friction

The origins of the situation are rooted in postwar history, in very different concepts of the purpose and theory of market capitalism, in a fundamental American misunderstanding of the character of Japanese society, and in flaws in the American policy-making machinery.

In the postwar period, the U.S. focused on containment of the Soviet threat. Japan became the foundation of the U.S. position in the Pacific. To shore up this foundation, the U.S. adopted a policy of aiding Japan's industrial recovery. This was similar, of course, to U.S. policies in Europe and was based on similar reasoning. In the case of Japan, however, two extremely important exceptions were made, or at least allowed to develop. One was the anti-military clause written into the Japanese constitution by the occupation authorities. The other was the view of Japan as an underdeveloped rather than as an industrial economy, which meant that Japan was permitted to engage in "infant industry policies" to a much greater extent than the Europeans.

However noble the anti-military clause, its economic consequences were destined to and have become enormously significant. While Japan spends less than 1% of its GNP on defending itself, the U.S. is spending close to 7% of its GNP in defense of itself and other free world countries—including, especially, Japan. Thirty years ago, when Japan's GNP was one-tenth that of the U.S., this kind of disparity was unimportant. But today, with Japan's absolute level of investment equalling that of the U.S., it is simply going to be impossible for the U.S. to compete while putting such a comparatively large percentage of its GNP into products that are put in holes in the ground. A different way of looking at it is to note that if the U.S. spent only 1% of GNP on defense, there would be no budget deficit and an extra $200 billion available for productive investment.

UNILATERAL CONCESSIONS

The view of Japan as an underdeveloped rather than as a developed country led the U.S. into a big brother posture toward Japan that was not adopted toward Europe. The result was a lopsided economic and trading relationship. The U.S. made unilateral concessions. It permitted Japanese exports into the U.S. market and Japanese investment in the U.S. while the same was denied to the U.S. in Japan. This was justified on the basis of Japan's need to develop "infant industries." Whatever one might have thought of such policies 30 years ago, they are clearly inappropriate today. Nevertheless, the situation of unilateral concessions persists, and the longer it does so the more difficult it will be for the U.S. to compete.

DIFFERING THEORIES OF ECONOMICS

A second major cause of conflict is a very different view of what economics is all about. The U.S. is conditioned by a history of wealth and ready opportunity presented by an abundance of resources. We have not had to work too hard to get rich—we simply turn potential wealth into real wealth. Consequently, we have tended to take wealth for granted. We have tended to focus on individual opportunity and have concluded that the purpose of economics is to maximize consumer welfare. We believe a system of perfect competition ensures maximum opportunity and maximum consumer welfare. Thus, we see the legitimate role of government as that of establishing rules that ensure a competitive system and then acting as referee to assure compliance with the rules.

In Japan, economics is a matter of national security. Japan is not naturally wealthy. From the time of Perry, it has been struggling to catch up to the technological and industrial level of the West, not primarily to increase consumption, but to provide the leverage to maintain its national independence and autonomy. The legitimate and necessary role of government is seen to be that of leading this effort.

Thus, whereas in the U.S. we believe comparative advantage in trade arises from factor endowment more or less automatically, the Japanese believe that comparative advantage is something to be conquered through the concerted efforts of all elements of society—and, once achieved, defended. This gives rise to extensive industrial policies aimed at fostering infant industries and restructuring aging ones. To operate effectively, these policies must protect the domestic market to some degree. Such protection, however, is not necessarily of the classic tariff or quota type. It may be nothing more than informal consensus among participants in the market not to buy foreign goods.

This, of course, leads to conflict with the U.S. which accuses Japan of closing its markets. From the U.S. point of view, Japan is engaging in sneaky trade practices. The Japanese, on the other hand, feel that the U.S. is attacking the very essence of their ability to survive as a first class nation. The difference is simply alternate views of what economics is all about.

MISCONCEPTIONS AND FALSE ASSUMPTIONS

A third major problem is U.S. misunderstanding of the nature of its adversary. Japan presents itself to the world as a democracy and market economy. The U.S. infers that it is therefore more or less like the U.S. and that its economy will react to stimuli in a manner similar to the U.S. economy. This could not be further from the truth. Japan's keiretsu, lack of effective antitrust, lack of effective systems of adjudication and appeal, tradition of administrative guidance, strong trade associations, lack of consumer advocates, etc., all mean that the Japanese economy is an entirely different thing from the U.S. economy. Japan is one of the world's most hierarchical, most highly structured, most homogeneous, most traditional, and most conservative societies. The U.S. is among the least hierarchical, least structured, least homogeneous, least traditional, and least conservative societies. Japan may be a democracy and have a market economy, but it is not at all a democracy and market economy like that of the U.S.

Not recognizing this, however, the U.S. develops negotiating demands based on the assumption that Japan works like the U.S. Since the negotiating goals are based on false assumptions, they are usually not achieved or, if achieved, do not fulfill expectations. The result is growing dissatisfaction and even bitterness on both sides.

An example of the stickiness of the Japanese market is the famous soda ash case. Japan manufactures soda ash through a process which is energy intensive. Since energy is very expensive in Japan, Japanese soda ash is also expensive. Conversely, soda ash occurs naturally in the U.S. and is mined at Green River, Wyoming. Soda ash is very inexpensive in the U.S., and even though the transport costs to Japan are substantial, U.S. ash can be delivered in Japan for about $75 per ton less than Japanese ash. Despite this cost advantage, up until two years ago, American suppliers sold only 60,000 tons per year in a market of 1.4 million tons. Investigation revealed that while unloading charges at world ports such as Antwerp, Cape Town, and Genoa were on the order of $20 per ton, in Japan they were $50–75 per ton, just nullifying the American cost advantage. Moreover, it was discovered that there was only one unloading facility for soda ash in Japan. It was called Toko Terminal and it was owned by a consortium of Japan's soda ash manufacturers and large trading companies such as Mitsui and Mitsubishi. Members of this consortium were also linked to Japan's major soda ash users, and they threatened the users with possible restriction of supply in the future if they did too much business with foreign suppliers.

When it was suggested to the Japanese government that this looked like a cartel in restraint of trade, the government issued heated denials and counterattacked with the old, familiar charge that the Americans had not tried hard enough, that their service was unreliable, and their quality poor. Finally, the U.S. government brought this case to the attention of Japan's FTC. Embarrassed, the FTC investigated, found that there was indeed a cartel, and issued a cease and desist order. U.S. sales almost immediately climbed to the 200,000 ton per year level. Interestingly, however, they then leveled off and have remained stuck at the same amount despite a 40% depreciation of the dollar against the yen.

This is not to say there is a lack of competition in Japan or that the Japanese government controls the fall of every sparrow. That is patently not the case. But it is clear that the Japanese market does not respond in the same way to the incentives and stimuli that drive activity in the U.S. There is not necessarily anything wrong with this; after all, there is no law that says all economies have to work the same way or be based on the same assumptions.

However, it makes it very difficult to achieve significant results if one negotiates with Japan while assuming that the Japanese economy is very similar to those of the other industrial countries. But this is precisely what the U.S. has insisted on doing. The focus of American negotiation is always on process. The belief persists that if we can just get some tariff lowered, or some standard revised, that our businessmen will then be able to operate in Japan just as they do in other markets or in the American market. When this does not occur, the businessmen are either blamed for being lazy or the Japanese for cheating through some nefarious means. That the fault may be the assumptions of the negotiators never seems to occur to anyone. But that is the problem, and all the negotiations, agreements, and attempts at coordination are all doomed before they begin because their premises are false.

This, in turn, dooms American industry to continuing to compete at a disadvantage. Since the American negotiators will not achieve anything that will result in real market share increases for U.S. industry, the industry will continually be faced with a situation in which its opportunity to obtain volume will be limited to the U.S. market and Europe, while Japanese industry will have volume opportunities in those two markets plus Japan. We know that in many industries, and particularly in high-tech industries, decreases in cost are directly related to volume. Thus, if the Japanese always have more opportunity to obtain volume in fast-growing industries, they will always become the low-cost producers even if the technology originates elsewhere. U.S. industry knows this and increasingly doesn't even bother to produce in the U.S., but makes what accommodations it can with Asian suppliers. In effect, American industry is preempted by a situation that arises at least in part from the determined myopia of its own government's trade negotiators.

The U.S. must understand that the driving forces of the Japanese economy are very different from those in the American economy. Since the U.S. cannot remake Japan in its own image, it must deal with the reality. This means managed trade based on the general principle of reciprocity. Such a formula sounds simple, but to execute it will require a complete rethink of U.S. trade policy and the creation of a new relationship with Japan.

Towards a New Relationship

For the past five years, from Prime Minister and President down, all of our key ministers, subcabinet officers, legislators, and businessmen have been involved in literally hundreds of discussions aimed at creating deeper mutual understanding and resolving trade problems. We have created a large number of groups, including the Subcabinet Group, the Trade Committee, the High Tech Working Group, the Energy Group, and the Investment Group. These groups have been supported by private business advisory groups on both sides. In addition, there have been two sets of wise men and several ad hoc businessmen's groups. Of particular importance has been the relationship between President Reagan and Prime Minister Nakasone. We have discussed every facet of our relationship from agriculture to high technology to defense to finance. Thus, no one can accuse either side of insufficient time or effort.

What has been the result of all this effort? Clearly, there has been some real progress and we have deepened understanding on both sides. In the broadest sense, our relations are closer than ever before.

We have cooperated closely in resolving the problem of debt in the less-developed countries. In the trade area, which has been our main problem, there have been a number of forward steps. We were finally able to reach agreement on beef and citrus. Minister Takeshita and other officials at the Ministry of Finance were able to agree to take important steps to liberalize Japan's financial markets. We were able to agree with MITI on a mutual reduction of tariffs on semiconductors. Through the efforts of Chairman Ezaki and others, Japan took steps to revise some of its laws on standards and certification, to establish the Office of the Trade

Ombudsman, and to speed up some tariff cuts. Dr. Shinto also made major efforts to open NTT to foreign bidding and took positive steps to encourage foreign companies to establish relationships with NTT.

On the U.S. side, great progress has been made in alleviating the problem of the unitary tax. Also, as a result of Chairman Morita's efforts, the Semiconductor Protection Law was amended to give Japan a grace period for better protection. In Japan, we were able, through the efforts of former Minister Hayashi, to testify before the Diet on the problems of VAN and software protection. Diet Members Fujio, Kanemaru, Kuranari, Hashimoto, and others also participated in these discussions.

Continuing Doubts about Real Progress

In spite of all this, we must ask ourselves: Have we made progress proportional to our efforts? Do we have concrete results to show for our trouble? Have we really dealt with the problems or have we just spent an inordinate amount of time dealing with symptoms?

Five years ago, our bilateral trade deficit was $10 billion. Despite all our efforts, this trade deficit will be about $60–70 billion this year. These numbers indicate that we have little in the way of concrete results to show for our efforts.

It has been argued that the increase in the deficit is due to fundamental macro-economic factors. Some point to the U.S. budget deficit, low savings rates, and large defense expenditures. Others contend that success in Japan depends on the efforts of private companies. They argue that U.S. companies are satisfied with the big U.S. market, or their quality or service is poor, or that they don't adapt their products to consumer needs in Japan.

There is some truth to this point, but it is not the whole truth. Although the dollar was strong, U.S. satellites were still less expensive than those made in Japan, but the Japanese didn't buy them. Yes, sometimes U.S. quality has not been as good as it should have been, but while the U.S. leads the world in VAN technology, a restriction on foreign-owned VANs in Japan was almost written into Japanese law last year. Yes, some U.S. companies haven't tried very hard, but others, like Corning Glass, tried for years to sell in Japan and were turned away because of Japanese self-development policies.

Let's assume for the sake of argument that all criticisms of the U.S. are correct. Let's assume that U.S. quality is poor, service abysmal, and so forth. What about other countries. Germany is a great trading nation; half of its GNP is based on trade. Switzerland is a small mountain country with no natural resources and must export to survive. The Koreans are aggressive exporters, and no one ever accused the Hong Kong Chinese or the Taiwanese of being poor traders. How do these nations fare in the Japanese market? In a word, poorly. They have just as much difficulty penetrating the Japanese market as those poor, bumbling, hopeless Americans.

We are forced to the conclusion that, despite all our efforts, there is something about Japan which makes it a relatively closed market. One of the problems is that we have a different definition of "open."

Informal Barriers

There is a tendency in Japan to focus on formal barriers and to argue that if tariffs are low and quotas non-existent, the market is open. We in the U.S. tend to look at things more in terms of the total conditions for doing business.

This last summer, my son persuaded me to take him to a baseball game in New York. I hadn't been to a game for a long time and was really enjoying myself—especially since my team was winning. Then, in the seventh inning, the pitcher began to tire. So, the manager called to the bullpen for a new pitcher. When I glanced at the bullpen, I was surprised because the pitcher was climbing into a car to be driven to the mound. (I must be getting old, because in my day the pitcher walked to the mound.) Then I blinked again because the car was a Toyota.

This tells us a lot about trade. It tell us that Japanese cars are good, and inexpensive, and that Japanese salesmen work hard and persevere. But it also says something about the U.S. market. It says that even though there are voluntary restraints, Japanese cars still have 20% of the U.S. market. It says that when Japanese cars come into the U.S., they are not inspected. The U.S. allows self-certification and, most importantly, distribution in the U.S. is easy. It takes years and a lot of money to build a nationwide dealer network in a country the size of the U.S. But Japanese auto manufacturers didn't have to do that. GM, Chrysler, and Ford had already built networks. Japanese manufacturers went to their dealers and asked them to sell Japanese cars too. One might expect that GM or Ford would have put pressure on their dealers not to carry the Japanese cars. But in the U.S., such pressure is illegal and the executives of GM and Ford could be put in jail for such behavior.

What is the picture in Japan? Japan's tariffs on autos are low and it has no quotas. Japanese officials argue that it is an open market. However, Japan does not grant self-certification. Every car must be inspected. Moreover, no Japanese auto manufacturer would allow his dealers to carry a foreign competitor's car. Thus, while Japan may have no formal restraints, the reality is that the market is not as open as the U.S. market and foreign penetration is less than 2%.

At this point, someone always says, "Yes, but the Americans don't adapt to Japanese needs. They don't put the steering wheel on the right side." But manufacturers in Britain, Australia, and Germany *do* put the steering wheel on the right side, and they haven't gained a significant market share either. In sum, the absence of formal, easily identifiable barriers doesn't necessarily mean a market is actually open to foreign penetration.

Take, for example, another aspect of this situation. The Commerce Department has authority to administer fishing in U.S. waters. It determines how many fish can be taken, over what period of time, and with what kind of equipment. These rulings have a great impact on the fortunes of Japanese and other fishermen. When rules are changed or new policies considered, the Commerce Department posts notices and then holds public hearings. Everyone is free to come, learn, and comment upon the plans. And everyone comes—Japanese, Portuguese, French, British, etc.—and they voice their opinions. These remarks are taken into consideration and the rulings are drawn up based on them.

Over two years ago, I suggested to several officials in Japan that Japan could remove a lot of suspicion and perhaps even improve its planning if it provided a similar opportunity for public hearings in which representatives of foreign companies in Japan could participate in discussions of Japanese government planning. I suggested it because of our experience with the proposed software legislation. We in the U.S. were only made aware of the legislation at a very late stage. In order to register our feelings, we had to make it into a major political issue. Had we had a chance to be informed and to be able to discuss it at a much earlier stage, I believe we could have settled the problem quietly and easily.

The Japanese ministries reacted somewhat negatively to my suggestion. In fact, a story was leaked in Japan that I had demanded that foreign nationals be made members of the industrial council, although I had never demanded such a thing. I had simply requested that we be given a chance to be informed regularly and allowed to comment on proposed plans. Eventually, this was agreed to, but only after difficult discussions and only in a few instances. And because there is still little transparency in the regulatory and law-making process in Japan, we have little choice but to consider this another major element of trade friction.

Despite the frustration, this situation is not surprising. The U.S. is a nation of immigrants. It is an artificial nation in the sense that at its foundation, people sat down and consciously thought of how a nation should be built. It was created out of people from all over the globe, from all races, religions, and cultures. To make this kind of society work, it was very important that the rules be clear and fair and known to everyone; it was important to have it written down; and it was important that the process be transparent, so that no one would feel suspicious or cheated.

Japan, however, is a traditional society. It is very homogeneous. It has never had to wrestle with the problem of integrating others into its society. The rules in Japan are less formal and based more on personal relations where everyone knows more or less what to expect. While there is nothing inherently wrong with this, it makes Japan a relatively difficult country for an outsider to become part of. This in itself would be no particular problem except for the fact that Japan has taken advantage of the openness of the U.S. system to become, in fact, a very large part of it. And that in itself is fine. No serious observer in the U.S. wants to expel Japan or protect the U.S. market. But when Japan takes big shares of foreign markets, while Japanese markets and processes remain difficult to penetrate, a feeling of unfairness inevitably arises.

The real problem is a growing attitude in the U.S. and elsewhere that Japan does not play by the same rules. The U.S.-Japan Advisory Commission described the problem as "an unacceptable level of friction" that is eroding goodwill and mutual trust on both sides. Put strictly in terms of trade, patience is running out because our access to Japan's market is seen as no where near equal to Japan's access to other markets. This perception is expressed with greatest vehemence in Europe and runs the risk of derailing any progress toward global trade liberalization.

It is a mistake to think that this is strictly a bilateral problem. In the end, failure to open the Japanese market could be the single most important barrier to realizing the growth potential of the Pacific region. Indeed, it may well poison the whole free trade system.

Active and Mutual Concessions

What then is it that we seek? I believe the ideal we both agree on is two economies, interrelated and interdependent, in which opportunities for foreigners to do business are essentially the same as for nationals. I believe we both want maximum transparency in policy-making and rule-making processes, and relations which are as close as the best of friends can be. I suggest that if this is our goal, it is not enough simply to remove barriers. We must determine if we are reaching the goal, and if not, we must take positive steps to assure its achievement.

This situation is not unprecedented. Forty years ago, the U.S. had an enormous trade surplus with all other nations. We realized that while such a surplus might benefit us in the short term, it would be destabilizing for the rest of the world—and, therefore, for ourselves—in the long term. We took active steps to reduce our surplus. Indeed, Ambassador Sherman of the U.S. State Department once told me his first job as a diplomat in Japan was to encourage Japanese companies to export to the U.S. (I often remind him that he did too good a job.) The U.S. Department of Commerce in those days sent representatives to U.S. companies to encourage them to buy foreign products. We didn't just relax barriers, we took active steps to make sure foreign products were *actually* imported and *sold* in the U.S.

Another example of this is the work of Dr. Shinto regarding NTT procurement. He didn't just drop barriers to foreign bidding, he actively encouraged it. He printed his bids in English and sent people to the U.S. to find products to buy.

If we agree on our objective, and if we agree that we are not reaching it, then we should mutually take these kinds of positive steps on a grander scale to reach the objective. I would like, therefore, to offer the following prescription to help assure the health of the U.S.-Japan relationship. Simply stated, I recommend positive action by each party.

In the U.S.:

• We must continue to tackle our own economic problems, including the fiscal deficit.

• Our companies must make the long-term commitment to develop difficult markets like Japan.

• We must restore our commitment to quality products and to a genuine pride in a job well done.

• We must make sure that our educational institutions turn out students who are qualified not only to live in the twenty-first century, but to govern and direct it.

For its part, Japan must step forward and publicly claim its rightful place in the community of trading nations:

• Japan must abandon the security of the rich outsider without responsibilities. As the second largest economy in the free world, Japan has enormous responsibilities, in the Pacific region and in the larger world trading system, which cannot be met by protecting its domestic industries.

• Japan should *establish imports of foreign goods and services as a national priority at least equivalent to its long-standing goal of exporting*. It should establish a goal of perhaps doubling its imports of manufactured goods and of substantially reducing its trade surplus. It should establish plans and procedures for concretely realizing these goals.

• Japan must abandon outgrown reliance on the markets of others to stimulate its economic growth. Japan must stimulate its own internal demand and encourage imports from the new industries in the developing nations of the Pacific region and the rest of the developing world.

I am confident that with goodwill on both sides we can reach the objective of truly intertwined and interdependent markets and economies—a new relationship without friction. And then I may see the day when the Yomiuri Giants carry their pitchers to the mound in Chevrolets.

PROTECTIONISM AND U.S.-JAPAN TRADE[3]

This is a good time to think and talk about U.S. economic relations with Japan. Actions since the beginning of the year—the result of the President's January 2 meeting with Prime Minister Nakasone—have produced a period of relative progress in addressing a number of the trade problems between us. Despite this, the striking increase in our bilateral trade deficit with Japan last year has provoked strong concern in the Congress, our business community, and the popular press. Pressures for protectionist action, which could have a major detrimental impact on this relationship as well as on the global trading system, have mounted to a dangerous level.

Our relations with Japan are too vital strategically, politically, and economically for us not to resolve current and underlying difficulties on an urgent basis. There is a need for urgent action, not to close U.S. markets but to open Japan's. We are determined to do this and are engaged in a comprehensive effort to realize these goals. Japan must also meet this challenge, as Prime Minister Nakasone and Foreign Minister Abe have vowed to do.

My theme today is simple: the most serious threat to our domestic economy, the world economy, and our bilateral relationship is the swelling tide of protectionism. As the Secretary indicated last Saturday, protectionism is not a cure—it is a disease, and one that can spread like the plague. To counter this threat, the United States and Japan are working together urgently in a cooperative effort to remove barriers to imports in Japan. We are also cooperating to launch a new multilateral trade round to strengthen the world trading system.

It is important to ask a number of questions. What is our "trade problem" with Japan, and what are its causes? What is our strategy to deal with it? Why is this strategy different from previous efforts? What progress have we made to date? What are our prospects for future success? What conclusions follow?

---

[3]Excerpted from a statement by Paul D. Wolfowitz, Assistant Secretary for East Asian and Pacific Affairs, before the subcommittees on Asian and Pacific Affairs and on International Economic Policy and Trade of the House Foreign Affairs Committee, April 17, 1985.

Attitudinal Perspective

Let me briefly give some perspective on the attitude toward imports in Japan.

After Japan was opened to the West, Japan imported foreign products primarily to sell to foreigners living in Japan, not to Japanese. Businesses which catered to the dometic market did not carry foreign goods. If something was considered to have merit for the larger Japanese market, it was manufactured locally. The attitude that foreign goods are imported to be sold to foreigners and, conversely, that imports are not really meant for Japanese or are not part of the mainstream of Japanese life, still lingers in sectors of Japan's economy. To the Japanese, imported products historically have always been expensive and exotic. They were not considered an alternative to a Japanese product; they were something apart.

After the war, when Japan began its march toward economic recovery, the Japanese Government implemented an "import-saving structure" to ensure that its precious foreign exchange would be used to import only those items most essential to industrial recovery. Japan's trade deficits in this period were high, and the bilateral trade balance with the United States ran overwhelmingly in our favor by 3 or 4 to 1. Duty rates on most imported products were high, either to limit the imports of "luxury" items or to protect recovering industries. Stores literally sold foreign goods "under the flag," placing little American, French, and British flags around the products to emphasize their foreign origins and to justify the high price charged. If you go into a Japanese department store today, you still will find little American flags or stickers around these products—again, to emphasize that they are somehow "different."

For more than 100 years, therefore, the attitude has developed that Japan will import only what it does not have—raw materials which it needs or products that it does not make. For other items, the preference—then, as now—was for local manufacture. In addition, many Japanese are convinced that direct imports are not suitable for the average Japanese: fit and finish will not be there; instructions will not be in Japanese; and they may not be able to get repairs made. This inability of the Japanese, including many government officials, to think of foreign products as equal and an alternative to Japanese goods, to be sold on the same basis rather than as something apart, lies behind much of the difficulty we have in opening the market.

In order to promote local manufacture—the preferred alternative to direct imports in both the Meiji and the postwar periods—Japan erected a wall of protectionist barriers. These included visible barriers such as high tariffs, quotas, or outright import and investment restrictions, and invisible barriers such as various regulatory regimes, standards, legal cartels, and tax breaks. Local companies could grow in strength in a protected market sanctuary that allowed them to develop a base to eventually move out into foreign markets. These barriers stayed up long after the initial recovery of the Japanese economy. Following Japan's entry into the OECD [Organization for Economic Cooperation and Development] in 1964, foreign governments began putting pressure on Japan to remove those barriers. The government—then, as now—was caught between powerful competing forces: foreign criticism from its trading partners, and domestic forces which had an interest in the continuation of their protected status. Lowering these protectionist barriers has been an extremely emotional issue in Japan.

After continued pressure from the United States and other countries and multilateral trade rounds to reduce barriers, the great bulk of formal barriers (tariffs, quotas, and investment restrictions) to trade in Japan have been dismantled. Today, Japan maintains quotas on 27 product categories, compared to 490 quotas at the end of the 1960s. Japanese tariff rates, on average, are the lowest in the industrialized world; it also accelerated the tariff reductions negotiated in the MTN [multilateral trade negotiations]. Many Japanese state that their market is among the most open in the world.

Why, then, do we still have trade friction? There are many answers. One answer is the attitudinal aspect I have just described. Problems with market access, of course, are the most well-known cause. Another has to do with the structural aspects of the problem.

Structural Aspects

While the $37 billion U.S. trade deficit with Japan has been the focus of attention in our bilateral relationship and the cause of much of the growing demand for protectionist measures, the more meaningful measure of Japan's external imbalance is Japan's overall trade surplus, estimated at $44 billion in 1984. In short, these imbalances reflect an overreliance on export-led growth.

Even if we achieve everything we want on market access, that still will not eliminate our bilateral trade deficit with Japan because it is responsive to other major considerations such as exchange and growth rates. Another important factor, as Secretary Shultz stated in a speech on April 11 in Princeton, is the imbalance between Japanese savings and investment. The Japanese could reduce their trade surplus with the world by pursuing policies to offset the impact of their high savings rate.

Gross private saving in Japan is over 30% of GNP [gross national product]—about 50% higher than the average of the other OECD countries. (Net savings, after depreciation, is 16% in Japan, compared to only 2% in the United States.) This high rate of savings means low consumption. It also means that Japanese companies, and especially mature industries, must look overseas for growth. The excess of savings over investment, and the excess of production over domestic consumption, finds its way abroad. Or, to put it another way, under current conditions, Japan relies on an excess of exports over imports to maintain full employment. Export at that level cannot but impact on the world trading system and on the United States, in particular—traditionally Japan's best overseas market.

As Secretary Shultz suggested in his Princeton speech, opening up investment opportunities within Japan would be one way to use savings resources and reduce the pressure to export. The needed decisions are more difficult for Japan politically than economically. The structural rigidities in the Japanese economy constrain access by even Japanese firms and investors. If the Japanese Government would improve incentives and reduce constraints that currently inhibit domestic and foreign firms from investing in Japan, all nations, especially Japan, would benefit. As the Okita report stated, "active measures (to encourage direct investment) will be needed in view of the fact that direct investment into Japan is currently much less than Japanese direct investment overseas."

Steps are already underway to liberalize the Japanese capital market so as to channel Japanese savings more efficiently to both foreign and domestic uses and to widen the financial opportunities facing Japanese firms. This agreement was reached last May and resulted from the understanding reached between the President and the Prime Minister during the President's visit to Japan in November 1983. This agreement was a landmark one, and the sector-intensive approach used to look at every aspect of these financial issues has been adopted as the model for the approach that we now are using in other sectors. As the capital market liberalization proceeds and as the international role of the yen expands, we would expect the value of the yen more fully to reflect the strength of the Japanese economy. But Japan will have to deal with its savings-investment imbalance if its chronic imbalance in trade is to be corrected.

Are we singling out Japan for special attention? Prime Minister Nakasone answered this in his statement of April 9 when he said that: "It is Japan that most benefited from free trade," and "Therefore, it is Japan's fundamental national policy to cooperate with the world in fighting protectionism." The answer, then, is that Japan is not being singled out. It recognizes that it has benefited most from the global trading system, that it is now the number two economic power in the world, and that it must share the burdens and responsibilities of its position and do what is necessary for its own people and for the world. In addition, the size and potential of Japan's market for our exports is another reason for us to pay particular attention to Japan.

Policy Response

Market access is another reason for our trade deficit with Japan. The United States and Japan are working together to deal with this problem.

The President and the Prime Minister agreed to a new approach in Los Angeles on January 2—the market-oriented sector-selective approach (MOSS). This new approach addresses the full array of barriers in a particular sector to eliminate any problems in the market system which inhibit import of any product or service in the sector. Through these negotiations, microeconomic concerns about products and services in particular sectors are being addressed in an intensive and comprehensive fashion. As Secretary Shultz and Foreign Minister Abe agreed on last Saturday, both sides will accelerate their efforts in the four sectors in recognition of the need to quickly resolve problems.

Initially, we are focusing on telecommunications, electronics, forest products (including paper), and medical equipment and pharmaceuticals. These were all launched during January and February. Telecommunications received the most attention because of the April 1 date for implementing the new laws in Japan which "privatized" [Nippon Telegraph and Telephone] and liberalized the telecommunications market in Japan. Though much more needs to be done, there has already been significant progress, particularly if commitments for the future are fully implemented. These talks are being undertaken on an urgent basis.

A TURNING POINT
IN U.S.-CANADIAN RELATIONS[4]

U.S.-Canadian relations are at a turning point. Negotiations aimed at reaching a comprehensive trade accord between the two countries have entered a final phase. To be considered by Congress, a draft treaty must be ready by October. A successfully concluded pact will be an important step forward in consolidating cooperation between the two North American neighbors; moreover, in a world rampant with protectionist tendencies it will provide an effective example of liberalizing international trade. Conversely, failure to reach a mutually satisfactory agreement will not only be a distinct setback in bilateral relations beween Ottawa and Washington, but will also encourage nationalist and protectionist trends. Whatever the outcome of the trade talks with the United States, it will have profound consequences for Canada, reaching to the very heart of the country's politics.

For the United States, close economic ties with its largest trading partner are important; for Canada, with three-quarters of its trade going to the United States, they are essential. But the present negotiations also have a symbolic significance. The success or failure of the talks will affect the overall climate of relations between the two countries on such issues as acid rain, Arctic

[4]Excerpted from an article by Adam Bromke, political science professor at McMaster University, Hamilton, Ontario and Kim Richard Nossal, associate professor of political science at McMaster University. *Foreign Affairs* 66:150–169, Fall 1987.

sovereignty and cooperation in North American air defense. Indeed, the outcome of the trade negotiations may influence the countries' readiness to cooperate on various global issues, both within NATO and in the broader realm of East-West relations. Last but not least, since the trade issue is likely to play a major role in the Canadian elections that are expected in 1988 or early 1989, the outcome of the negotiations may determine the pattern of Canadian-American relations for a number of years to come.

II

The massive electoral victory of the Progressive Conservative Party under Brian Mulroney on September 4, 1984, promised to bring an end to the increasingly unpleasant friction between Canada and the United States. Since 1980 a number of differences over both bilateral and global issues had marred relations between the two North American neighbors. (For an assessment of Canadian-American differences in the early 1980s, see Adam Bromke and Kim Richard Nossal, "Tensions in Canada's Foreign Policy," *Foreign Affairs,* Winter 1983/84, pp. 335–53.) Canadians were embittered by the continued disputes over both Atlantic and Pacific fisheries, and the lack of attention paid by the Administration of Ronald Reagan to controlling acid rain pollution of lakes and forests north of the border. Americans were irritated by what they viewed as the nationalist measures of the Liberal government of Pierre Elliott Trudeau: the establishment of the National Energy Program, designed to "Canadianize" the oil and gas industry through a retroactive nationalization of 25 percent of any oil discovery; and moves to strengthen the Foreign Investment Review Agency, which monitored and regulated foreign investment. As a result of American pressure both these initiatives were considerably diluted, but criticism from Washington continued, highlighting the basic differences in approach to the proper role of the state in the economy.

The United States was also disappointed by what it considered Canada's unsatisfactory contributions to the defense of both North America and Western Europe. Even after the Liberal government substantially increased its defense outlays in the late 1970s, the image of Canada as an ally not pulling its weight persisted in Washington. There were, moreover, marked differences over various global issues, notably over the deterioration in East-

West relations. Prime Minister Trudeau looked back with nostalgia to the era of détente, a view that set him apart not only from President Reagan, but, after changes of government in Britain, West Germany and France, from other major NATO leaders as well.

Finally, the two men did not get along well. Trudeau was openly critical of Reagan's sharp anti-Soviet rhetoric, and Reagan had little use for Trudeau's fall 1983 "peace initiative." This effort by the prime minister to use personal diplomacy to bring the nuclear powers to the negotiating table was virtually doomed when he received only lukewarm support from Washington. (For differing evaluations of Trudeau's peace initiative, see Adam Bromke and Kim Richard Nossal, "Trudeau Rides the 'Third Rail,'" and Michael Tucker, "Trudeau and the Politics of Peace," *International Perspectives* (Ottawa), May/June 1984, pp. 3–10; and Michael Pearson, Gregor Mackinnon and Christopher Sapardanis, "'The World Is Entitled to Ask Questions': The Trudeau Peace Initiative Reconsidered," *International Journal* (Toronto), Winter 1985–86, pp. 129–58.)

It is thus not surprising that the Reagan Administration could barely conceal its satisfaction with the outcome of the 1984 general elections in Canada. The Progressive Conservative government appeared to be more attuned to Washington on both domestic and foreign policy. During the preceding campaign Mulroney was highly critical of how the Liberals had handled Canadian-American relations. He pledged not only to introduce a "new era of civility" in North American affairs, but also to provide the United States with greater support in global policy. He promised to enhance Canada's military capability and to increase Ottawa's contribution to NATO.

The two men, moreover, appeared to get along well at their two White House meetings in 1984. The first was in June, while Mulroney was still leader of the opposition; the second was held just a week after he became prime minister. The timing of the visits underlined the importance the new Progressive Conservative government attached to relations with the United States. On the latter occasion, the two leaders agreed to hold annual reunions to review and improve relations between the two countries.

III

Early in its tenure the Mulroney government showed its eagerness to live up to its campaign pledges. The offending sections of the national energy program left untouched by the Liberal retreat in the early 1980s were eliminated; the Foreign Investment Review Agency was symbolically renamed Investment Canada, and its operations were sharply curtailed. In a speech to the corporate community in New York in December 1984, Mulroney grandly declared that Canada was "open for business again."

The new government also wanted to expand free trade with the United States. This proposal was not entirely novel: in 1983 the Liberal government began exploratory negotiations with Washington on a series of trade pacts in limited sectors of the economy—using as a model the 1965 Auto Pact, which had created a continental free market in automobiles. During his short tenure as prime minister in 1984, Trudeau's successor, John Turner, seemed prepared to continue this policy. But the Progressive Conservatives embraced a more sweeping approach. Taking their cue from President Reagan's own campaign promise of 1980 to conclude a "North American accord" between the United States and its two neighbors, the Conservatives proposed to negotiate a comprehensive and formal bilateral trade pact.

Mulroney also appeared ready to make good his election promise to enhance Canadian defense. To boost the morale of the Canadian armed forces he ordered that the distinctive uniforms of the three services—eliminated when they were integrated by the Liberals in 1966—be restored. The Canadian contingent in Europe was increased by 1,500. And Defense Minister Robert Coates was dispatched to Washington and London to explain the new direction in defense to Canada's most important allies.

The culmination of this initial spurt of activity came at the summit meeting between Mulroney and Reagan in the city of Quebec in March 1985. It appeared to confirm all the predictions of a closer relationship between the two neighbors after years of estrangement. "We are more than neighbors or friends or allies," declared President Reagan, setting the tone for the meeting. "We are kin who together have built the most productive relationship between any two countries in the world today. . . . For the United States there is no more important relationship." The atmosphere in Quebec was warm, even jovial. It had been dubbed the "Shamrock Summit," not only because it fell on St. Patrick's Day, but also because both leaders liked to stress their common Irish ancestry.

There was a substantive side to the summit, however. Two major agreements were signed. One was a fisheries treaty that resolved the long-standing dispute on the West Coast. (Shortly afterward, by a decision of the International Court of Justice that both sides accepted, the boundary dispute that had plagued the Atlantic fisheries on the East Coast was settled.) The other agreement concerned the modernization of the North American Aerospace Defense (NORAD) surveillance system in the far north. Ottawa agreed to pay about 12 percent of the estimated $7 billion needed to overhaul NORAD, including a new radar warning system to replace the aging Distant Early Warning (DEW) Line. Mulroney and Reagan agreed to postpone action on acid rain, airborne sulfur and nitrogen oxides, by appointing a panel of special envoys to report back before the next summit. The leaders also declared their intention to expand trade by removing the few remaining tariff barriers and agreed to resist the mounting protectionism on both sides of the border.

The key symbolic objective of the Shamrock Summit—to demonstrate the strength of Canadian-American friendship—was thus largely achieved. In no small measure it was helped by the excellent personal chemistry between the two leaders. The relationship between President Reagan and Prime Minister Mulroney stayed close and warm at their next two summits in Washington in March 1986 and in Ottawa in April 1987. Yet even the leaders' good intentions were not enough to solidify the new relationship. During their talks in Washington, divergent national interests reasserted themselves, especially over free trade and acid rain. Nor were the leaders able to come to an agreement on sovereignty over the Northwest Passage, which Canada claims are internal waters. For its part, the United States, which regards the passage as an international strait, has consistently rejected the Canadian claim. The Americans are concerned that by conceding Canada's position, they would implicitly recognize similar claims on other waterways by other coastal states. Thus, when a U.S. Coast Guard icebreaker traveled the passage without seeking permission from the Canadian government in the fall of 1985, the matter came to a head.

The Ottawa summit of last April was the most politically charged. Both leaders were in trouble at home, and wanted to emerge from the meeting with the best possible image. It was Reagan's first visit abroad since the Iran-contra revelations, and he was eager to demonstrate that he remained an effective player in foreign affairs. He succeeded in this endeavor: his speech to the Canadian Parliament was an accomplished performance, and his response to heckling by some members of the New Democratic Party (NDP) was smooth and witty. For Mulroney the summit was an occasion to improve his own sagging popularity. Two years after their landslide victory, the Progressive Conservatives were not doing well: a series of scandals in the cabinet and the prime minister's tendency to avoid contentious issues, or occasionally to reverse himself on them, had eroded the government's credibility and popularity. In the polls, the Progressive Conservatives fell behind both the Liberals and the New Democrats in popular support. Moreover, the opposition parties were effectively using the snail's pace of trade negotiations with the United States, the reluctance of the Reagan Administration to implement fully the recommendations of the special envoys regarding acid rain, and the Arctic sovereignty issue to discredit the government.

By early 1987 Reagan was evidently trying to help Mulroney as much as he could. In January Vice President George Bush was dispatched to Ottawa, where he received what he described as an "earful" of highly publicized Canadian complaints about the state of the relationship. At their April summit, Reagan went out of his way to praise Mulroney—even attributing to the prime minister the original idea of an economic accord between the two countries—but offered no real concessions. The two leaders promised to accelerate negotiations on free trade and Arctic sovereignty, but they did not go beyond that.

IV

From the outset, the Progressive Conservative government was committed to expanded trade with the United States. Prime Minister Mulroney very much identified himself with this objective; in many ways it has become his personal quest. It was not only because Mulroney genuinely likes the United States and was favorably impressed with the Reagan Administration. He also believed that closer economic bonds with Canada's powerful southern neighbor were indispensable to the country's future well-being. In a world economy increasingly composed of large trading blocs, a free trade agreement would give Canada unrestricted access to the largest and most technologically advanced national economy. Mulroney, moreover, was committed to a bilateral approach to trade negotiations: multilateral trade talks, he felt, would not stem the impact of American protectionism on the Canadian economy quickly enough.

While the Conservatives had a grand design, the specifics remained vague. It was only after a chief negotiator was appointed in November 1985 that the Canadian side started to address itself to the concrete issues. On the American side progress was also slow. Before the Reagan Administration could commit itself to the negotiating process it had to overcome the hurdle of Senate approval for "fast-track" negotiations, which promised that the final agreement would be either approved or rejected in toto without amendments. This was only obtained in April 1986, and with the narrowest margin, in the Senate Finance Committee. But the fast-track procedure requires that the negotiators submit an agreement to the Senate by October 1987. Considerable barriers still exist that could preclude reaching a trade agreement by the deadline. At the present stage of negotiations the major problems are the American demands for unrestricted flows of investment into Canada and Canada's insistence on a binding mechanism to resolve future disputes.

In Canada, public opinion polls indicate that the idea of a free trade agreement enjoys the support of a slight majority. Ultimately, of course, the accord will be judged on its substance. Yet even if the terms of the agreement are favorable for Canada, there are staunch opponents of closer economic ties with the United States who are unlikely to be won over. They include nationalists, labor union activists and those in business whose interests will likely suffer. Reinforcing this is a widespread concern among many Canadians that closer economic ties with the United States will culminate in a formal political union of the North American neighbors. It was precisely for this reason that when the last free trade agreement was put before the voters by Sir Wilfrid Laurier's Liberal government in 1911, it was roundly defeated.

Canada's federal system also poses a problem for Mulroney. The provinces have a constitutional role in economic development issues, and can argue that the federal government cannot take sole responsibility for negotiating an international agreement that might alter their economic structures. The federal government rejected the provinces' demands that they be given a seat at the negotiating table, although it keeps them informed of the progress of the talks. Nonetheless, there are still murmurs of apprehension from provincial premiers. Particularly in the two largest provinces, Ontario and Quebec, worries persist that a free trade agreement will cause severe economic dislocation as the branch-plant economy which has been nurtured behind tariff walls collapses under the weight of an influx of cheaper American goods.

Indeed, a select committee of the Ontario legislature has formally recommended that if Ottawa negotiates a free trade agreement that damages Ontario's economic interests, the provincial government should "veto" it. It should be noted that the provinces have no formal veto power over international agreements entered into by the federal government. But they can refuse to implement those provisions that impinge on their constitutional powers. Thus, the Mulroney government faces the embarrassing possibility that it may not be able to implement those portions of a trade accord that deal with nontariff barriers within provincial jurisdiction.

Finally, since the Progressive Conservative government initially did not clearly think through what it wanted in a trade agreement, Ottawa kept adding to a list of items that it considered nonnegotiable. These included social welfare programs, the 1965 Auto Pact, cultural protection policies, the taxation system, and the level of the Canadian dollar. As the list grew, the impression was conveyed that what Canada really wanted was to gain secure access to the huge American market without giving much in return.

Understandably, Washington has taken the position that if Canada wants unfettered access to the U.S. market, Ottawa will have to offer significant concessions too. As it happens, the items that the American negotiators are interested in overlap largely with those the Canadians consider nonnegotiable. This places Mulroney in a serious predicament. He cannot put more than 40 years of social welfare legislation, the Auto Pact or protection for Canadian culture on the negotiating table.

In his quest for a free trade agreement, Mulroney has not been helped by policy developments in the United States. Just days after Peter Murphy, the American negotiator, and Simon Reisman, his Canadian counterpart, launched the negotiations in May 1986, American protectionist interests rudely thrust themselves into the picture. With Reagan's approval, the United States imposed a 35-percent countervailing tariff on cedar shakes and shingles imported from Canada on the grounds that the American industry needed protection against subsidized Canadian producers. Mulroney was furious at the move—publicly calling it "bizarre"—and retaliated with minor tariffs on American books and computers. Nevertheless he rebuffed opposition calls to suspend the trade talks. In October 1986 the Mulroney government was embarrassed again by the threat of another punitive tariff imposed on Canadian softwood lumber exports. Although the dispute was eventually settled by a compromise, the episode added to bitterness in Canada.

In promoting free trade with Canada, Reagan also faces serious domestic constraints. It is unlikely that the protectionist mood of the present Congress will change substantially any time soon. Often it is not explicitly directed at Canada, but reflects a general annoyance with American trading partners, including Japan and Western Europe. The president remains personally committed to the process. After the 1986 Washington summit he made it explicit that he considers the conclusion of a trade agreement with Canada one of the top priorities of his Administration. Indeed, it seems to rank only second in importance to a U.S.-Soviet arms control pact. Yet as Reagan's term comes to a close, his ability to expend political capital on behalf of a free trade agreement with Canada is likely to decline. The narrow Senate vote over the "fast track" procedure and the president's consent to the imposition of tariffs on Canadian exports suggest that even firmer commitment on his part will be needed to overcome the protectionist interests so strongly entrenched in Congress.

These obstacles in the United States have had an evident effect on the Canadian prime minister. In the October 1986 "Speech from the Throne" outlining the government's intentions for the next year's parliamentary session, Mulroney carefully downplayed the free trade negotiations. After the lumber dispute he even mused aloud about the feasibility of an agreement with the United States. Nevertheless, the prime minister persisted in his efforts. When the pace of the negotiations visibly slowed in the spring of 1987, he pressed the issue with President Reagan, not only in Washington, but also during a special session at the Venice summit.

Mulroney has persevered because he knows that if a trade accord is not reached by October, or if it is rejected by Congress, he will be hard-pressed to explain the failure of the policy which was so central to the Progressive Conservative program. In such circumstances, he will have little political choice but to blame the United States for the failure. Such an explanation by Ottawa may in turn provoke anger in Washington. . . .

For Mulroney and the Conservatives, therefore, it is essential that a trade pact be concluded with the United States, and that it be on terms that can be readily embraced by a government seeking reelection. The obstacles to such an agreement are, as we have argued, formidable. Domestic political realities on both sides of the border are pushing the two governments further away from the spirit of goodwill and compromise so essential for trade liberalization.

Mulroney and Reagan face a historic opportunity to forge a new North American relationship that would not only stem the tide of nationalism on both sides of the border but would also help to push back the rising tide of protectionism globally. Brian Mulroney is deeply committed to bringing the two countries closer together, but he is not willing to pay any political price for it. And certainly neither of the two opposition parties will make the Americans a better offer.

As for Ronald Reagan, this will be the last chance to bring about such a historic change in North America. The price of an agreement with Canada for the United States is modest. Economically, both countries will benefit in the long run. And politically, this would involve the recognition by the Americans that Canadians, although the closest of allies and friends, are a different people, with their own distinct traditions and their own particular vision of the world.

Shortly before the Ottawa summit the U.S. ambassador to Canada, Thomas Niles, claimed that the state of Canadian-American relations was excellent. At one level, this is an appropriate characterization: there is an ongoing dialogue between the two governments, and it is being constantly expanded. Contentious issues are discussed with candor and an obvious willingness to mitigate differences. On the other hand, Mr. Niles' statement masks an important reality: nationalist sentiment on both sides of the border threatens to disrupt the relationship. Should the trade negotiations derail, these sentiments could become inflamed. And as electoral campaigns on both sides of the border heat up in the next year, there will be an even greater need for mutual understanding and restraint.

FREE TRADE—ANOTHER VIEW[5]

It is a commonly held view of Canadians that their country has been created and maintained in explicit defiance of the requirements of economic rationality as determined by the combined forces of North American geography and the continental marketplace. There is much to be said for this interpretation of Canadian history. But in fact there have always been some Canadians who have argued that if our pockets could only be kept full, our political, social and cultural identities could safely be left to take care of themselves. If we prospered economically, we would have the means with which to prosper politically, socially and culturally, as well. In the middle of the nineteenth century, for example, after the British had repealed the Corn Laws, and had moved in the direction of free trade at the expense of the system of colonial preferences that had previously given Canadian products an advantage in British markets, Canadian authorities were quick to pursue access to the US market as an alternative. One of the arguments that was mounted in support of the reciprocal free trade agreement that resulted in 1854 (confined though it was to natural products—fish, timber, coal and agricultural commodities notably among them) was that it would help to undermine the case for political annexation to the United States as a solution to Canada's economic problems. If Canadians could maintain their economic wealth, in short, full political amalgamation with the United States would seem neither necessary nor at-

[5]Reprint of a magazine article by Denis Stairs, professor of political science at Dalhousie University in Halifax. *International Perspectives* pp. 3–8, May/June '87. Reprinted by permission.

tractive. A policy of reciprocal free trade that many were later to oppose on the ground that it would eventually lead to the political integration of the two countries, was thus perceived at first as a necessary defence of Canada's independence.

Earlier Free Trade

The 1854 Reciprocity Treaty was abandoned at American request in 1866, and it is sometimes forgotten that in the early years of Confederation Canadian governments vigorously pursued its renewal. They failed, and the Prime Minister, Sir John A. Macdonald, mounted his so-called "National Policy" in 1879 almost as a second-best solution. At the beginning, moreover, he defended the policy partly on the ground that one of the principal advantages of the new structure of protective tariffs that it included was that it would lead the Americans eventually to the realization that reciprocal free trade with Canada was actually in their own best interest, and would therefore ultimately make possible a resurrection of the reciprocity agreement. Macdonald's adoption, therefore, of the view that free trade with the US would actually *threaten* Canada's independence (as well as the cherished Canadian connection with Great Britain) came only with his successful election campaign in 1891, at a time when the opposition Liberals were advocating the negotiation of an unrestricted reciprocity arrangement, and thereby made a particularly inviting target for political attack on nationalist grounds.

Even in 1911, when the Liberal government of Sir Wilfrid Laurier announced that a new reciprocity agreement had been successfully negotiated with the Americans, the opposition that ensued came first from interests that were vested more in economics than in politics. It was led, that is, by business leaders—mainly in central Canada—who feared that the new arrangement, which applied again only to natural products, would soon be extended to manufactured goods as well, and hence deprive them of their beloved protective tariffs. The electoral battle that ensued, being exposed to public view, was naturally fought on higher ground. The maintenance of the British Empire (widely viewed by Canadians as a force for good), and the survival, as one of its most important parts, of a Canada that was independent of the United States, were portrayed as the principal stakes at issue. But in retrospect, some of the architects of these high-blown arguments appear to have been transparently self-serving.

Even if the political arguments were inspired at their source more by economic advantage than by political conviction, however, they struck a responsive chord in the electorate. The Liberals were turfed out of office, and reciprocity was turfed out with them. The result thus reflected in large measure the more general and persistent Canadian fear that economic integration with the United States would soon be followed by political, social, and cultural integration as well.

It was this same preoccupation that caused Prime Minister Mackenzie King in 1948 to reject an ambitious proposal for a Canada-US customs union, which had been engineered by Canadian and American officials in negotiations over the previous winter.

Historically it is clear that Canadians in general have found it difficult to separate their economic relationship with the United States from their concern to preserve their autonomy and independence in other areas of public policy, and to protect what they have perceived—often only dimly—as distinctive features of their society. Canadian governments, moreover, have deployed a substantial array of policy instruments in their attempts to respond to these preoccupations. In so doing, they have had in some measure to defy the iron laws of economics and to resist the natural pull of continental economic forces.

Economics Dominant Consideration

Given this historical background, the surprising feature of the present debate in Canada is the intensity with which it has focused on the economic aspects of the issue, to the neglect of traditional concerns about its implications for the country's political, social and cultural life at home, and for the conduct of its foreign policy abroad. It would appear, in effect, that those who support the bilateral initiative are in pursuit of economic gains (for the first time in Canadian history) without serious reference to non-economic costs. Implicitly, therefore, and sometimes explicitly, too, they have accepted the primacy of economic over other values. Their ranks include not merely the Prime Minister and the governing political party, which seems almost completely to have abandoned its traditional nation-building role (or, at least, its conception of how that role can be most effectively played), but far more importantly, the technocrats and bureaucrats by which the government is most obviously advised, and those sectors of the academic, journalistic and business communities by which it is most heavily influenced.

This is not to say that non-economic arguments are never heard, for some of them obviously are. But this suggests that for the first time in Canadian history they are not being considered seriously, and on their merits, by those who are now responsible for the making of Canadian public policy. They are received, that is, not so much as considerations that must be carefully weighed in the balance and taken soberly into account, but as untutored expressions of the immature and the naive—as inconveniences emanating from a domestic political environment in which the exercise of reason is threatened by irrational myths and ignorant fears. That being so, they amount to obstacles against which tactical campaigns must be mounted, rather than concerns that a responsible public policy may need to reflect.

This is, of course, a sweeping assertion, and it is in the nature of such observations that they are to some extent impressionistic. But supporting evidence can nonetheless be found, and it may be useful to consider some of it here, beginning with the changes that have taken place over the last decade or so in official expressions of government opinions and policies.

"White Paper," 1972

For this purpose, the obvious point of departure is the special *White Paper* on Canadian-American relations, which was issued by the Department of External Affairs in the autumn of 1972 under the title "Canada-US Relations: Options for the Future." Almost entirely preoccupied with the question of continental "integration," the paper examined the problem from the military, political, economic and cultural points of view. Drawing attention to the pervasiveness of the American presence in almost every aspect of Canadian life, it identified three broad options for Canadian policy.

The first option was to try "to maintain more or less our present relationship with the United States with a minimum of policy adjustment." This was rejected—largely because there was "a risk," as the paper observed, "that, in pursuing a purely pragmatic course we may find ourselves drawn more closely into the US orbit."

The second option was to "move deliberately toward closer integration with the United States." This option, too, was rejected. The paper's authors, observing that a "free trade area or a customs union arrangement with the United States would, to all intents and purposes, be irreversible for Canada once embarked upon," noted that the idea had "been rejected in the past because it was judged to be inconsistent with Canada's desire to preserve a maximum degree of independence, not because it lacked economic sense in terms of Canadian living standards and the stability of the Canadian economy." Their own conclusion was that the "probable economic costs and benefits . . . would require careful calculation," but that the "more fundamental issues . . . [were] clearly political," and it was "a moot question whether [the] option, or any part of it, is politically tenable in the present or any foreseeable climate of Canadian public opinion."

The acceptable option, therefore, was the third. Ottawa wags called it the "ham in the sandwich." It was described as a "comprehensive, long-term strategy to develop and strengthen the Canadian economy and other aspects of our national life and in the process to reduce the present Canadian vulnerability." This was a little, perhaps, like having one's sandwich and eating it, too. It could be argued, after all, that to suggest that Canada should develop its economy while promoting its independence was to state the problem rather than the solution. But what in fact it meant was a strategy of diversification in economic activity abroad, of which the "contractual link" with the European Community was to become the chief example, combined with traditional nation-building policies in economic, cultural and other fields at home. The entire thrust of the paper reflected above all the view that the relationship with the United States could not reasonably be considered in economic terms alone, but also had to take into account an interlocking array of political, economic, social, cultural and foreign policy interests.

New Strategy for the '80s

This performance can be usefully contrasted with the discussion paper entitled, *Canadian Trade Policy for the 1980s*, issued by the Department of External Affairs eleven years later, in 1983. The paper was a sophisticated review of Canada's trading position in an increasingly competitive international environment.

While generally favoring a multilateral approach to trade liberalization—that is, an approach through the General Agreement on Tariffs and Trade—and while stopping short of advocating a policy of complete bilateral free trade with the United States, it suggested the negotiation of limited Canada-US free trade arrangements on a sector-by-sector basis. In rejecting bilateral free trade across the board, the paper made brief mention of the political sovereignty factor, but the issue was not further developed in the discussion, and the cultural aspects of the problem were not raised at all.

The Department's position—now reflective of settled Cabinet policy—was taken one step further in its December 1985 booklet entitled *Canadian Trade Negotiations: Introduction, Selected Documents, Further Reading*. The particular texts that are assembled in the collection are focused almost entirely on the economic objectives of the bilateral talks, and little attention is given to political or other issues. The booklet included a June 1985 departmental analysis in which there is a brief mention of "political sovereignty implications," but these are viewed in beneficial terms. A move toward freer trade, the authors argue, "should strengthen the economic fabric of the country; it should reduce regional differences on the conduct of trade policy; and it should reinforce a growing sense of national confidence." They go on to suggest that "a bilateral treaty could be a better guarantor of our sovereignty than the gradual uncontrolled drift toward integration now taking place. The possible adverse consequences can be managed by pursuing deliberate policies of strengthening cultural and other fields of endeavour which would bolster our national identity." In effect, the authors reach conclusions that are the precise antitheses of the arguments their predecessors advanced in 1972, and their position is, of course, echoed in a speech by the Secretary of State for External Affairs, Joe Clark, which is reprinted elsewhere in the volume under the title "Trade Negotiations and Cultural Industries."

In assessing these evolutions, it may be pertinent to note that by 1983 the Department of External Affairs had been amalgamated with the trade divisions of the old Department of Industry, Trade and Commerce. It is possible, therefore, that the change in the Department's policy can be explained in part by the change in its bureaucratic composition (as well as by the more obvious change in the country's political leadership). In fairness, too, it should be understood that the 1983 and 1985 publications were directed specifically to trade policy, and not to the analysis of Canada-US relations in general. The point, however, is that in 1972 it would have been thought totally inappropriate—and certainly unhelpful—to have analyzed the problem of Canada's trading relationship with the United States without also taking fully into account a variety of other political, social, cultural and foreign policy interests. In short, the policy problem would not have been conceived, much less resolved, in economic terms alone.

Fundamental Changes in Attitude

This may have the appearance of making too much of too little. Government position papers, after all, come and go—like academic enthusiasms—in easy accommodation of passing fads. But there are other indicators—apart from the fact of the negotiations themselves—to suggest that the change may be more deeply rooted than this interpretation would allow. Bilateral free trade with the United States has also been supported by the Economic Council of Canada, and by the Senate Committee On Foreign Affairs. It was one of the most central recommendations of the massive report of the Royal Commission on the Economic Union and Development Prospects for Canada (the "Macdonald Commission"), and the Commissioners found strong support for bilateral negotiations in the testimony of many of those who presented briefs at their public hearings. All of the provinces except Ontario have been broadly supportive of the free trade initiative, and even the Ontario government is cross-pressured by an economic constituency that is clearly divided on the issue. Business community organizations such as the Canadian Manufacturers' Association (until recently a strongly protectionist voice) and the Canadian Federation of Independent Business have also tended to favor the negotiations. In the press, there have been occasional expressions of caution and concern, but relatively little of the comment has focused on the non-economic aspects of the debate.

It could be argued, of course, that these indicators reflect only a temporary phenomenon, and that the pendulum will eventually swing the other way. But there are reasons for suggesting that this will not happen.

The first results from the obvious fact that, in spite of the various counter-measures that Canadian governments have deployed, the country has already become so closely integrated with the United States that the process appears now to be an irreversible force of history. Some 30 percent of Canada's GNP enters into foreign trade, and more than 75 percent of total Canadian exports go to the US market. Similarly, more than 70 percent of imports are purchased from American sources. The proportion has been increasing steadily, and in the manufacturing sector it has been encouraged in particular by the growth of intra-corporate exchange—that is, by trade between Canadian subsidiaries and their American parents. Tariff walls have been dropping in any case as a result of multilateral agreements negotiated through the GATT.

On the cultural side, it is true, there have been very substantial displays of indigenous Canadian prowess in the literary and performing arts, but this has been much less noticeable in the related, but more commercially-dependent, field of popular entertainment. The flood of American books, magazines, films and television programs—to say nothing of fashions and fads—continues unabated. In some areas, advances in communications technology have reached the point at which government regulation becomes managerially impossible even if regarded as socially desirable. The Liberal government's abandonment not long ago of the attempt to regulate the private use of devices for receiving satellite transmissions of American television programs provides an obvious case in point.

Reactions to the Changing Attitudes

These realities seem now to be producing two reactions, and they reinforce one another. The first is pragmatic. It is represented by the conclusions that the attempt by government authorities to resist the integrative process through the use of countervailing public policy instruments is ultimately futile because it is impracticable. It is better, in short, to align with the inevitable than to wage a war that cannot be won.

The second reaction is at once more subtle and more significant. It is reflected in the view that resistance is not merely ineffectual, but also to some extent improper or illegitimate. This is partly, of course, a matter of allowing the secular principles of

Western liberalism to take over, and to assert that it is not the proper function of government to attempt, in these areas at least, to inhibit or otherwise influence the spontaneous evolution of our political, social and cultural values. These are questions for individuals in society to determine, and not for governments to mold. But the argument may also reflect the pervasive success of the assimilative process itself, so that liberal postulates of this sort are being invoked, not because Canadian policymakers and "attentive publics" are more enthusiastic liberals now than they were before, but because they no longer see anything fundamentally worrying in what has been happening to their society. If this is true, it effectively means that Canada's cultural integration with the United States has passed the point of no return. It has ceased, that is, to be seen as a legitimate issue on the national agenda.

Economic Panic

If Canadians have given up on their founding national purpose, therefore, it may be partly because they no longer believe that continental integration can be resisted, and partly because they have lost the will to think that it should be resisted. But they may have given it up for a second reason, as well—economic panic. For, with some exceptions, Canadian economists and public administrators have become more and more concerned that, in an increasingly regionalized world, Canada has no other place to go. The negotiations of the "contractual link" with the European Community may have been a triumph of Canadian diplomacy, but it was a lamentable failure as an instrument of foreign economic policy. It has become increasingly difficult, in fact, to find overseas markets for Canada's manufactured goods, and exports of raw materials and natural resources (as any inhabitant of British Columbia will attest) are subject to unseemly ups and downs.

Having no easy access to either industrialized Europe or industrialized Asia, and having discovered that for the foreseeable future there is little prospect of solving the problem through trade with the so-called "Third World" (to say nothing of the NICs), it seems natural to turn to the United States as the only accessible market of sufficient size to encourage the exploitation of economies-of-scale, and hence the production of value-added goods at internationally competitive prices. That being so, there is a strong feeling in Ottawa and elsewhere that every effort should be made to ensure that Canada's access to the US market is not only expanded, but permanently secured, so that Canadian producers will be exempted from such future rounds of American protectionism as may eventually find unwelcome expression in Congress.

Economists are practitioners of the dismal science, and the alternative they describe is appropriately gloomy: a contracting Canadian economy, plagued with inefficient industries, rising prices, high levels of structural unemployment, and public services substantially reduced as a result of declining government revenues. Economic integration with the United States thus comes to be a virtue driven by necessity. And necessary virtues, unlike optional ones, are difficult to resist.

Shifts in Canadian Economy

A third reason for not expecting a return of the pendulum is the altered distribution of pertinent political forces *within* Canada in such a way as to make the change politically more acceptable. Historically, the lines of battle on the free trade questions have reflected the regional interests of different parts of the country, with the natural resource and agricultural economy of the West being in conflict with the industrial and manufacturing economy of central Canada. Now, however, the national economy as a whole has become more diversified and complex, and even within particular economic sectors there are differences of interest, and hence of opinion. The result is that support for the free trade option has become more general and the opposition more diffused. Ontario, at the manufacturing core, still hesitates but its position is ambiguous. It is not clear whether its reservations are genuinely and deeply held, or are only being expressed on one hand to test the waters, and on the other to establish bargaining leverage for concessions from the federal negotiating authorities. In any case, the government in Ottawa is in a position to pursue the initiative with much less fear than ever before that it will arouse significant concentrations of opposition within a particular part of the country. To put the point another way, the issue is now less likely than in earlier decades to generate cleavages that coincide with important provincial boundaries.

Fundamental Impact of Freer Trade

The central question remains: Does it really matter what the arguments for and against free trade are? The answer depends in part on the perspective and values of the analyst, and even then a "judgment call" is required. Individuals, therefore, who start from the same premises often reach different conclusions. It may be useful, nonetheless, to identify some of the more important of the non-economic concerns and to attempt in each case to assess the significance of the argument. For purposes of exposition it will be convenient to consider first the arguments that can be safely dismissed, and secondly the ones that thoughtful Canadians will want to take seriously into account.

There is no reason, first of all, to conclude that a bilateral free trade agreement would lead—even by slow degrees—to Canada's political integration with the United States in the formal, or institutional, sense of the term. That is, there is no reason to expect that it would eventually culminate in the unification of the two countries. For a variety of reasons, Canadians would vigorously resist any such development, and there is no cause to think that the Americans would press the case. In any event, both parties would have obtained most of what they wanted without this further step being required.

Second—and with qualifications to be discussed below—it seems unlikely that a bilateral free trade regime would have a significant impact on at least the *fundamentals* of Canada's political culture. This is partly because the two countries are driven, at the level of political philosophy, by the same basic values, and are organized politically on very similar premises. They are identical, that is, in their commitment to the liberal democratic state, as governed by representative political institutions. To the extent, moreover, that there are differences in their political styles and practices, these are deeply imbedded in their respective institutional arrangements, and it seems improbable that these will be dislodged.

Third, it seems unlikely that a bilateral free trade arrangement, in itself, will have a truly significant impact on Canadian cultural activities or popular entertainments. This is not because patterns of trade are unimportant as determinants of the cultural process, but because the citadel—if ever there was one—has already been taken. Pump-priming of indigenous cultural activities could still be maintained (although probably not without occasional American protest), but there is little reason to think that the influx of American "products" in cultural fields would be more overwhelming under free bilateral trade than it is now.

The argument, finally, that free trade will lead to an erosion of the amiable gentilities of Canadian society also seems not to be entirely persuasive, although here it is more difficult to be certain. It is, of course, a cliché of Canadian commentators to observe that theirs is a more ordered and restrained, and less ruthlessly competitive, community than the American; that Canada prefers industrious beavers to soaring eagles, "peace, order, and good government" to "life, liberty, and the pursuit of happiness," and the RCMP to Billy the Kid. The vitality of America is expressed in its creative accomplishments and in the exuberance of its economic life. Canadians are duller. But they can safely walk the streets of their cities at night.

These, obviously, are stereotypical images. It is hard to know what to make of them. But to the extent that they reflect a genuine contrast between the two societies, it is not clear that that contrast will be eroded, at least in the short run, by a slight expansion of continental trade.

Unwelcome Side Effects

There are other areas, however, in which the side effects of a comprehensive free trade agreement could be very substantial—and from the Canadian point of view not altogether welcome. Three possibilities—or *types* of possibility—come most obviously to mind.

The first of these is that a bilateral agreement will tend to reduce Canada's freedom of maneuver in a large number of areas of public policy that are not directly related to trade *per se*, and lead in time to a "harmonization" of Canadian policies with those of the United States. This will happen under the impact of two simultaneous political processes. On the Canadian side, the process will result from the fact that any policy within Canada that has the effect of increasing the costs of Canadian producers relative to those of the United States will be strongly resisted by the industries concerned. These will argue, in effect, that if they are to have a reasonable chance of surviving the powerful competition of their American rivals, they must have an even start at the

gate, and cannot be unfairly disadvantaged by government policy. This is a phenomenon that can be detected even now, but it
will intensify—and certainly it will be more difficult for governments to resist—if it is legitimized by an agreement founded on
the principle that all enterprises should have equal opportunity
in the marketplace. Where Canadian corporate taxes are higher
than the American, for example, Canadian producers can be expected to demand that they be appropriately reduced.

The same phenomenon can be expected to arise in relation
to regulatory controls. If, for example, Canadian labor codes,
safety requirements, product standards, or environmental regulations are in certain areas more stringent than the American,
and hence more expensive to implement, Canadian production
costs will be correspondingly higher, and Canadian firms will be
quick to demand relief. The consequence over time is almost certain to be a harmonization of Canadian policy with American in
a host of fields. In some areas, depending on one's point of view,
this may be seen as an advance. In others, it will not. But in either
event, the government's freedom of fiscal and regulatory maneuver will have been eroded. Even provincial government practices
will come in for critical examination. Indeed they already have,
as we saw in the softwood lumber dispute.

Constraints on Canadian policy can also be expected to result
from political forces generated on the American side of the border, although this time in the opposite direction. That is, American producers will object to any Canadian policy that has the
effect, not of increasing Canadian production costs, but of reducing them. The most obvious examples are government subsidies
and other incentives designed to promote regional and industrial
development (including the development of so-called "cultural
industries"). There is evidence already, however, of this argument being mounted against policies that in Canada have a much
wider social import—notably unemployment insurance, and other ingredients of the so-called social security "net." With a free
trade regime visibly in place, American industries that were feeling the pain of Canadian competition could be expected to cry
"Foul!" with even more than their present vigor.

In anticipation of such problems, Canadian negotiators will
obviously try to protect their future freedom of domestic maneuver by bargaining for specific exemptions from the general provisions of the treaty, and much will depend on the terms of the

eventual agreement. Even in the case of regional and industrial subsidies, moreover, the problem will presumably arise only in cases where part of the production is destined for the American market. Nonetheless, the potential implications for the autonomy of Canadian public policy are real and extensive, and it should come as no surprise to Americans if Canadians, in their public discussions, begin to take them seriously into account. Even now, there is a realization in some quarters that the negotiations with the United States have as much to do with "deregulation" as with trade *per se*. That, of course, gives them a significance which goes to the very heart of contemporary political debates in the Western world—debates bearing on the perennial question of the proper role in society of the state.

How We Would Look—to Them and to Us

There is a second group of considerations arising from the possible impact of a Canada-US free trade agreement on *perceptions* of Canada, both at home and abroad. In external affairs, for example, it is possible that the declaration of a Canada-US free trade area would persuade governments elsewhere in the world of what many of them suspect already—that for practical purposes Canada's interests in international politics are the same as those of the United States, and that Canadian foreign policy can be routinely expected to support the American cause. Impressions of this kind—even now a problem for the Canadian foreign service—could seriously limit Ottawa's freedom of diplomatic maneuver, and make it more difficult for its voice to be heard.

Within the United States itself, moreover, the creation of a free trade regime could lead to very similar expectations, with the result that Canadian deviations from American policy would be viewed as surprising acts of betrayal, and hence would be more vigorously resented than they are at present. Canadian governments, aware of these realities, might therefore become increasingly reluctant to adopt independent positions on international issues. This is already the case, for example, in relation to Latin America. While precise measurement in such matters is difficult, under free trade the problem could become worse. For Ottawa, moreover, the political consequences of this dilemma could be intensified were American policies to become especially unpopular in Canada—as they were, for example, during the Vietnam War. Federal authorities would then have the always difficult choice of irritating the Americans or irritating their constituents.

More importantly still, it seems probable that a public announcement that Canada and the United States had established a bilateral free trade area would have an enormous impact on Canadians' view of themselves. Psychologically, in effect, they would be "throwing in the towel" after more than 200 years of trying, against the opposition of overwhelming economic forces, to establish and maintain a political and social community clearly distinguishable from that of the United States. In other words, it would place Canadians, psychologically, inside the American "worldview," and in so doing it could well erode such slender will to meaningful national survival as they still possess. This does not mean that they would give up their formal sovereignty—for reasons already discussed, that would hardly be necessary. It means only that they might give up the attempt to *use* their sovereignty in significantly differentiated ways.

Accepting Another Ideology

The third serious possibility, closely related to the other two, is that the implementation of a free trade agreement would have the effect, very broadly, of changing the prevailing "public philosophy" in Canada in such a way as to make it very similar to that of the United States. This is partly a matter of "deregulation," and of the particular version of modern liberalism that deregulation represents. But, more broadly, it refers to the way in which the role of the state in society is conceived, and the priority that is given to economic over other values. Sweeping assertions on matters of this kind are rarely more than half-true, but one way of illustrating the difference is to observe that in the United States there is a general assumption in economic matters that labor should move to where the jobs are, while in Canada the expectation is that the jobs will move to where the labor is (and that the government will take remedial action if they do not). This is an economically inefficient principle, but it has always been argued in Canada, nonetheless, that it is a socially, culturally, and politically desirable foundation upon which to base public policy. It has been regarded, in effect, as a conception dictated by the kind of country Canada is, by the way in which its population is geographically distributed, and by the history and environment that its inhabitants have experienced. While there may be a strong argument in economics for saying that Cape Breton, for example, should be allowed to turn into a nearly-deserted national park, it is (Canadians have traditionally held) insufficient as a foundation for public policy precisely because it comes from economics alone and neglects other community values. If a free trade agreement, by exposing Canadians to both the philosophy and the reality of American economic competition, alters these assumptions, it will have transformed the character of the country itself.

One's view of these issues is thus ultimately a matter of political, as well as economic choice. Canadians will need to make that choice with the greatest care. Perhaps Americans will understand if the choosing proves difficult, and if it seems to complicate unreasonably the negotiations that have so recently begun.

NEO-PROTECTIONISM: DÉJA VU ALL OVER AGAIN[6]

I'm delighted to have this opportunity to address the Americas Society. I admire your commitment to increased understanding and communication among all people in our hemisphere, and with all people of the world.

The timing of this gathering could not be better, just two days after your congressional elections. I'm anxious to learn more about the new Congress, and the impact it will have on relations between our countries.

And in light of recent political developments, I'm eager to express Canadian concerns about the apparent shift in the historic U.S. commitment to expanded world trade.

Over the years, our trade relationship grew and prospered with only a few minor hiccups along the way. It's ironic that since bilateral free trade talks between our countries got underway, we have seen the opening of a pandora's box of trade irritants.

First let's put these differences in perspective: our countries enjoy the largest trading relationship the world has ever seen.

[6]Excerpt of a speech delivered to the Americas Society by David Peterson, Premier of Ontario, on November 6, 1986.

Canada is by far your biggest trading partner. This year, the value of trade in goods and services between us will approach $150 billion.

In fact, other than Canada as a whole, the province of Ontario is your biggest customer—bigger than Japan.

It's obvious that the best thing either of our countries has going for us in trade is the business we do with each other. Both of us suffer trade deficits with every industrialized country outside North America.

It's clear that rapid technological advances will continue to alter the way all of us do business.

Neither of us can afford to ignore the challenges and opportunities of an expanding and more competitive global market.

In Ontario, the thrust of our public policies is to build competitiveness in international markets, where we face the same challenges as you.

But there is no question that the United States will always be our most important trading partner.

It is now just over a year since Canada's federal government proposed negotiations to work out a bilateral trade agreement between our countries.

Obviously, we're anxious to secure and enhance our access to the U.S. market. Certainly, we're determined that any trade agreement must provide mutual improvements in job opportunities and living standards.

But we also recognize that when it comes to strengthening our ability to produce and compete, a bilateral agreement can at most be only part of our effort. There are many other approaches that both of us must consider.

There is one option that I believe we must both reject—a frantic stampede into a new and dangerous round of protectionism.

We are all aware of the consequences incurred when the international trading system collapsed after the adoption of such measures as the Smoot-Hawley Tariff of 1930, and the British Tariff of 1932.

The sudden surge of protectionism snapped a golden age of trade, cutting down assembly lines and creating souplines, closing banks and foreclosing farms.

The foundations of those protectionist trade walls bear a remarkable resemblance to trends we see today, more than a half-century later.

The trade wars of the 20's and 30's were sparked by slow growth in demand for traditional goods and services; a sudden spread of technological knowledge which narrowed competitive gaps between nations; an abrupt decline in the need for raw materials; and rapid shifts in the balance of market power.

The similarities to today's conditions remind me of the words of a great philosopher, Yogi Berra: "It's déjà vu all over again."

Americans can be proud of your post-war efforts to ensure an era of stability and predictability in international trade.

I'm certainly proud of Canada's role.

Both of us helped to usher in this century's second golden age of trade. And both of us benefited—along with the rest of the industrialized world.

It's hard to see how a new round of protectionist measures can help the United States any more than in the 1930's, when Hoovervilles ringed Washington.

As a wise person once observed: "Perhaps if we listened to history, it would stop repeating itself."

We seem to be witnessing the birth of a new strain of protectionist fever—a new-protectionism that attempts to disguise a provocative offense as a justified defense.

The neo-protectionists claim to be only responding to the unfair trade practices of others. What they are really saying is: Do unto others before they get a chance to do unto you. They assume that if some U.S. industries are finding it difficult to compete, it must be because other countries are acting unfairly.

In the past few months, neo-protectionism has spawned high U.S. contervail tariffs on a wide range of Canadian products, including hogs and pork, fish and raspberries.

It has threatened the access of a number of goods, from steel to uranium, from cement to telecommunications equipment.

Ironically, in the six months since Canada and the United States formally initiated free trade talks, U.S. countervail and legislative protectionist actions has affected roughly three-quarters of a billion dollars in trade with Canada.

Since 1980, similar actions or threats have affected about $4.5 billion in trade with us.

These actions have harmed Americans as well as Canadians.

An example of blatantly unjustified actions against Canada was the U.S. Commerce Department's preliminary determination, under considerable industry and political pressure, to apply a 15 percent countervail surcharge against softwood lumber from Canada.

I cannot overemphasize the importance of this issue to Canada, and what serious damage it can do to our relationship.

The Commerce Department is almost literally missing the forest for the trees. The lumber determination was legally flawed, and politically motivated. In 1983 the U.S. Commerce Department ruled there was no basis for countervail. In the three years that have passed, the only thing that has changed is the U.S. political climate.

Domestic political considerations took the place of sound trade considerations.

Officials of the Canadian federal and provincial governments are meeting today in Washington with Commerce Secretary Malcolm Baldridge to protest the lumber tariff in the strongest possible terms.

Ontario fully supports the Canadian federal government's determination to fight this case with every legal means at our disposal.

Many Americans opposed the action, including the National Lumber and Building Material Dealers Association, the National Association of Home Builders, the Lumber Association of Southern California, several U.S. senators, and a number of U.S. newspapers.

The U.S. Federal Trade Commission said a surcharge is not justified.

Because of our economic links, actions directed at Canada's economy cause enormous harm—to both of us. They add to the costs of materials for many U.S. manufacturers, and reduce the buying power of your best customer.

The surcharge would raise the cost of the average American home by $1,000. The National Association of Home Builders has estimated that for every $1,000 cost increase, more than 300,000 American families would be priced out of the housing market.

A study conducted by Wharton Econometrics estimates that the surcharge will eliminate four American jobs for every one it creates. That will do away with more than 13,000 U.S. jobs in less than four years.

Quite simply, beggar-thy-neighbour policies lead to beggar-thyself results.

The lumber issue could also damage the reputation the United States has earned as a fair trader. U.S. spokesmen described bilateral trade talks as an opportunity to demonstrate a model for the world. Is this the model they want to display?

As a friend and neighbour, I'd like to offer an observer's view: the United States can wipe away its trade deficit only if it concentrates on opening foreign markets to American goods, rather than closing American markets to foreign goods.

One of the most disturbing aspects of the trade actions against Canada is the fact that U.S. officials have made it clear they will not drop their methods of trade retaliation—such as the countervail clause that was used against Canadian lumber—even if a bilateral trade deal is struck.

Just a week ago today, Trade Ambassador Clayton Yeutter reiterated that position.

Mr. Yeutter has also charged that Canadian exporters benefit from differences in our political system, and our approach to economic development.

Just as we must steer clear of extreme protectionism, we must also avoid taking free trade to an extreme. Some may see a contradiction between those two themes. But I believe they are inextricably linked.

Free trade will achieve nothing for either of us if it prevents us from acting on legitimate regional or sectoral development needs. And it will work against us if it is based on an unrealistic assumption that our economies are identical.

In trade policy it is clear that we need a balanced approach— one based on diversity, flexibility, global co-operation, and fairness.

First, both of our countries must maintain the ability to preserve our unique values, and our unique ways of solving our own problems.

If government programs help our industries to become more competitive, that could benefit all of us. If Canadians earn more money, they can buy more U.S. goods—and vice versa.

We have to distinguish between protectionism to shelter inefficient industries, and legitimate economic development efforts to bolster efficient ones.

We have to find ways to ensure that both our countries can pursue technological innovations, without imposing on each other approaches for which we are not suited.

Rather than try to prevent the development of new technologies, we should work out an approach that will encourage growth within a framework based on fairness. Otherwise, all of North America will fall behind.

Second, we must leave undisturbed those areas in which we have already developed a flexible approach. A good example of that is the automotive products trade agreement—the Auto Pact.

Since Canada and the United States entered into that agreement 20 years ago, automotive trade between our countries has leapt from $1.2 billion, to $42 billion.

In some years you have enjoyed surpluses, in some years we have. But over the course of the agreement, auto trade has flowed equally between our countries.

In my view, the Auto Pact has been as successful as it has because it's based on neither protectionism nor unfettered free trade. Rather, it's a managed trade approach that is by and large fair to both countries.

Third, we must seek growth on a global basis. The new Gatt round that got underway recently in Geneva must be dedicated to international growth, by the fairest and most effective means possible.

While Canada and the United States have a great deal to gain from maintaining and expanding our unique trading relationship, the price for doing so cannot be exclusion from the rest of the world.

Canadians do not want to see the return of fortress America. The establishment of fortress North America holds as little appeal.

Our closest links will continue to be southward, but our vision must be worldwide.

Fourth, and finally, Canadians cannot be expected to enter into an agreement that does not include relief from the threat of countervail actions such as the recent softwood lumber surcharge.

If any agreement is to be viable, it must include a fair method for settling disputes, as an alternative to countervail.

If Canadians see no hope of relief from the policies characterized by the recent tariff on softwood lumber, then the value of any trade agreement has to be questioned.

We can grow together, even if we sometimes take different paths. I'm hopeful that we can avoid the trade wars that led to hardship for so many, and resume our mission of prosperity for all.

BIBLIOGRAPHY

An asterisk (*) preceding a reference indicates that the article or part of it has been reprinted in this book.

BOOKS AND PAMPHLETS

Corden, W. M. Theory of protection. Oxford University Press. '71.

Culbertson, John M. Curing the trade disease. Ballinger. '87.

Hufbauer, Gary. Trade protection in the United States: thirty-one case studies. Institute of International Economics. '86.

*International Encyclopedia of the Social Sciences. MacMillan/The Free Press. '68.

*Keynes, John Maynard. Essays in persuasion. MacMillan and Co., London. '31.

Lawrence, Robert A. and Litan, Robert E. Saving free trade: a pragmatic approach. Brookings. '86.

Shutt, H. D. The myth of free trade. Basil Blackwell. '85.

*Smith, Adam. The wealth of nations. 1776.

PERIODICALS

A new protectionism rises. Hein, John. Across the Board. 20:22–30. Ap. '83.

Twelve protectionist traps. Levinson, Marc. Across the Board. 22:24–8. S. '85.

Free trade is called best for all. Lapham, Edward. Automotive News. 6. S. 6, '82.

Congress debates protectionist policy. Aviation Week & Space Technology. 118:123+. My. 30, '83.

The invisible hand: how free trade is choking the life out of America, by Jay I. Olnek; book review of. Donlan, Thomas G. Barron's. 62:51. Jl. 5, '82.

Trade wars: protectionism rears its ugly head. Boland, John C. Barron's. 62:22+. S. 27, '82.

No-win trade war: retaliation inevitably makes it a losing proposition (editorial). Bleiberg, Robert M. Barron's 65:11. Jl. 22, '85.

A national coalition for trade. Samuels, Michael A. Business America. 7: inside front cover. Mr. 19, '84.

A case for free trade. Baldridge, Malcolm. Business America. 7: inside front cover. N. 26, '84.

Free trade area agreement eases barriers to U.S.-Israeli commerce. Keim, Kathleen. Business America. 8:2-7. Je. 24, '85.

President Reagan discusses trade, competitiveness in State of Union (January 27, 1987). Business America. 10:16. F. 2, '87.

Japan and the United States: mutual obligations, mutual benefits (speech excerpt). Smart, Bruce. Business America. 10:10. Ag. 31, '87.

The momentum builds for protectionism. Business Week. 44-5. O. 4, '82.

Trade talks that could snap the frayed U.S.-Japanese ties. Business Week. 64. O. 4, '82.

The U.S. can no longer afford free trade. Givens, William L. Business Week. 15. N. 22, '82.

The new politics of U.S. protectionism. Business Week. 38-9. D. 27, '82.

Protectionism can damage recovery. Wolf, Martin. Business Week. 20. Mr. 28, '83.

Faith in free trade has not waned (Business Week/Harris poll). Business Week. 16. My. 30, '83.

An antiprotectionist backlash is gathering strength on the Hill. France, Boyd. Business Week. 40. S. 17, '84.

The latest handshake on free trade looks firm—for now (Canada-U.S.). Javetski, Bill and Terry, Edith. Business Week. 46-7. Ap. 1, '85.

Protectionism isn't such a dirty word anymore. Mervosk, Edward and Jonas, Norman. Business Week. 95-6. O. 7, '85.

Blind faith in free trade doesn't pay. Kuttner, Robert. Business Week. 22. O. 14, '85.

We don't need protectionism to close the trade gap. Feldstein, Martin S. Business Week. 30. S. 15, '86.

*U.S.-Japan trade friction: creating a new relationship. Prestowitz, Claude V., Jr. California Management Review. 29:9-19. Winter '87.

The United States–Israel free trade area agreement: a model for Canada? Jansen, Gordon W. V. The Canadian Business Review. 12:24-7. Aut. '85.

Failure of protectionism: a study of the steel industry. Canto, Victor A., Eastin, Richard V., and Laffer, Arthur B. The Columbia Journal of World Business. 17:43-57. Winter '82.

*Protectionism: a threat to our prosperity. Wallis, W. Allen. Department of State Bulletin. Mr. '85.

*Protectionism and U.S.-Japan trade. Wolfowitz, Paul D. Department of State Bulletin. Jl. '85.

*Myth of free trade. Tyler, Gus. Dissent. 35:212-218. Spring '88.

Protection from protectionists. The Economist. 284:18. Jl. 31, '82.

Is free trade dead? The Economist. 285:75-93. D. 25, '82.

Free trade at the summit (Williamsburg, Va.). The Economist. 287:13-14. Je. 4, '83.

Trade: no free lunch. The Economist. 291:26. Ap. 7, '84.

Protectionism threatens profits. The Economist. 294:67. Ja. 26, '85.

How protectionists score own goals (mainly hurts a country's own exporters). The Economist. 295:69. My. 25, '85.

The slings and arrows of outrageous protectionism. The Economist. 296:71-2. S. 14, '85.

Routing protectionists. The Economist. 300:15-16. Ag. 9, '86.

Soaked by protectionists (consumers pay price of protectionism). The Economist. 300:15-16. S. 13, '86.

Free trade or fair. The Economist. 303:18. Ap. 25, '87.

Beyond free trade. Reich, Robert B. Foreign Affairs. 61:773-804. Spring '83.

Double or nothing: open trade and competitive industry. Zysman, John and Cohen, Stephen S. Foreign Affairs. 61:1113-39. Summer '83.

*Japan problem. van Wolferen, Karel G. Foreign Affairs. 65:288-303. Winter '86/'87.

*A turning point in U.S.-Canadian relations. Bromke, Adam and Nossal, Kim. Foreign Affairs. 66:150-169. Fall '87.

*Truth in trading. Gordon, Bernard K. Foreign Policy. 61:94-108. Winter '85-'86.

How to foil protectionism (aiding healthy industries). Guzzardi, Walter, Jr. Fortune. 107:76-82+. Mr. 21, '83.

Free-trade politics. Fortune. 110:8. O. 1, '84.

The new case for protectionism (strategic high-tech policy). Nasar, Sylvia. Fortune. 112:33-4+. S. 16, '85.

Protectionism: down but not out. Reilly, Ann. Fortune. 112:23. O. 28, '85.

Protectionism in disguise (pro-competitive laws that are little more than old-fashioned trade barriers). Dowd, Ann Reilly. Fortune. 114:99+. D. 8, '86.

Protectionism can't protect jobs. McFadden, Michael. Fortune. 115:121+. My. 11, '87.

Doorstop for free trade. Nevin, John J. Harvard Business Review. 61:88-95. Mr.-Ap. '83.

*The folly of free trade. Culbertson, John M. Harvard Business Review. 64:122-8. S.-O. '86.

Why protectionism doesn't pay. Lawrence, Robert Z. and Litan, Robert E. Harvard Business Review. 65:60-7. My.-Je. '87.

Asking for protection is asking for trouble. Levinson, Marc. Harvard Business Review. 65:42-4+. Jl.-Ag. '87.

Protectionist paranoia. Kinsley, Michael. Inc. 5:14+. F. '83.

Protectionism: a dangerous web to spin. Evans, Michael K. Industry Week. 218:78. Ag. 8, '83.

Free trade and the facts of life. Tippett, W. Paul. Industry Week. 219:10. O. 3, '83.

History sheds light on trade debate. Scott, Peter L. Industry Week. 235:14. O. 5, '87.

*Free trade—another view. Denis Stairs. International Perspectives. pp. 3–8. My./Je. '87.

A reconsideration of the protectionism debate: Keynes and import controls. Willoughby, John A. Journal of Economic Issues. 16:555–61. Je. '82.

The myth of free trade: patterns of protectionism since 1945, by Harry Shutt; book review of. Dietz, James L. Journal of Economic Issues. 20:904–6. S. '86.

The cases for and against open trade. Andres, William A. Management Review. 74:53–4. N. '85.

The assault on international trade (adaptation of address). Weidenbaum, Murray L. National Review. 36:29+. D. 28, '84.

Free trade is no free lunch. Hawkins, William R. National Review. 39:38–9. Ag. 28, '87.

Protectionist peril. Kantor, Seth. Nation's Business. 71:28–30. Ja. '83.

Open season on consumers. Eason, Henry. Nation's Business. 72:78. Jl. '84.

Trade law's squeeze on protectionism. Eason, Henry. Nation's Business. 72:43–4. D. '84.

Protectionism: the fight goes on. Nation's Business. 74:12. Je. '86.

Protectionism is not the answer (editorial). Nation's Business. 74:72. S. '86.

Cutting the cost of free trade (proposing international trade negotiations). Blum, Albert A. The New Leader. 69:12–14. Jl. 14–28, '86.

A rising tide of protectionism. Pauly, David. Newsweek. 101:26–8+. My. 30, '83.

Upsurge in protectionism. Alexander, Charles P. Time. 121:66. My. 9, '83.

Has trade protection revitalized domestic industries? United States. Congress. Budget Office. N. '86. Supt. of Docs. Washington, D.C. 20402

Is world on brink of trade war? Doan, Michael. U.S. News & World Report. 94:57–8. Mr. 14, '83.

New protectionism to fit the times. Bork, Robert H., Jr. U.S. News & World Report. 102:44–5. Ap. 6, '87.

Free trade and economic development (address, April 19, 1984). Harriss, C. Lowell. Vital Speeches of the Day. 50:741–5. O. 1, '84.

Trade wars (address, May 7, 1985), Wilson, John Oliver. Vital Speeches of the Day. 51:517-19. Je. 15, '85.

Guidance from a classic: the centennial of Henry George's Protection or free trade (address, November 13, 1986). Harriss, C. Lowell. Vital Speeches of the Day. 53:171-3. Ja. 1, '87.

*Neo-protectionism: déja vu all over again. Peterson, David. Vital Speeches of the Day. 53:230-232. F. 1, '87.

*Beyond protectionism. World Policy Journal. 3:157-181. Winter '85-'86.

The protectionism cloud. World Press Review. 30:41-2. N. '83.

*Protectionism: why not? Strange, Susan. World Today. 41:148-50. Ag./S. '85.

SYSTEMATIC THEOLOGY
ETHICS

SYSTEMATIC THEOLOGY

ETHICS

JAMES WM. MCCLENDON, JR.

ABINGDON PRESS
Nashville

ETHICS: SYSTEMATIC THEOLOGY, VOLUME I

Copyright © 1986 by Abingdon Press

Third Printing 1988

Library of Congress Cataloging-in-Publication Data

McClendon, James William
   Ethics: systematic theology.
   Bibliography: p.
   Includes index.
   1. Christian ethics. 2. Social ethics.
   3. Theology, doctrinal. I. Title
BJ1251.M46   1986   241'.046   85-30627

ISBN 0-687-12016-0

pbk.: alk. paper

An early version of Chapter One appeared as "What Is a baptist Theology" in *The American Baptist Quarterly*, I/1. The poetry quotation in Chapter Three is taken from "For the Time Being, A Christmas Oratorio," in *W. H. Auden: Collected Poems*, by W. H. Auden, edited by Mendelson, Random House.

Scripture quotations noted NEB are from the New English Bible. Copyright © the Delegates of the Oxford University Press and the Syndics of the Cambridge University Press 1961, 1970. Reprinted by permission.

Scripture quotations noted RSV are from the Revised Standard Version of the Bible, copyrighted 1946, 1952, © 1971, 1973 by the Division of Christian Education of the National Council of the Churches of Christ in the U. S. A. and used by permission.

Scripture quotations noted TEV are from the Good News Bible, the Bible in Today's English Version. Copyright © American Bible Society 1976. Used by permission.

Scripture quotations noted ASV are from the American Standard Version of the Bible.

Other Scripture quotations are the author's translation, or are from the Authorized or King James Version of the Bible.

Scripture portions italicized are the author's emphases.

Double quotes (" ") are used for all quotations except for quotes within quotes (" ' ' ") and 'scare' quotes.

MANUFACTURED BY THE PARTHENON PRESS AT
NASHVILLE, TENNESSEE, UNITED STATES OF AMERICA

TO NANCEY

Preface

Nineteen seventy-four, I believe, was the year I read John Yoder's *Politics of Jesus*. I was then a professor in the Church Divinity School of the Pacific, a Baptist from the South teaching in an Episcopal seminary in an ecumenical setting, the Graduate Theological Union in Berkeley. I am still there, but that book changed my life. In it I discovered, or rediscovered, my own profound roots in the Anabaptist (or as I now prefer to write it, baptist) vision. Subsequently, in 1976–77 I spent a year at the University of Notre Dame. In the stimulating center of Christian exchange that it was then, I could teach with Yoder and with Stanley Hauerwas and Robert Wilken and David Burrell and Joe Blenkinsopp and others in whose work changes were underway. It became clear to me that while other traditions, Reformed and Catholic and Lutheran and Anglican, had enjoyed a rich development, my own had not, or not enough. So in about 1980 I resolved to write (and Abingdon guided by its Academic Editor Pierce Ellis agreed to publish) a 3-volume systematic theology "in light of the baptist vision," the whole to appear in the order I, Ethics; II, Doctrine; III, Fundamental or Philosophical Questions. This is the *Ethics*.

Any systematic theology, or ethics of any sort, presupposes human community, but theology and ethics in the perspective attempted here is especially bound to recognize consensus based on conversation. So in 1981, on another leave from CDSP, I set out to visit twenty-five centers of current 'baptist' thought and life, from Walla Walla College in Washington to the Interdenominational Theological Center in Atlanta, from Fort Worth, Texas, to Elkhart, Indiana, laying my plans before scholars and students in many places and asking their counsel. I have come this far now, but readers who see where I've gone wrong or how I can do the job better from here on in are asked to write and tell me. I may not answer every letter, but I promise to read each one and think.

Not that I have found universal consent so far! Some have thought my basis mistaken: they said I should start from Calvin, not Anabaptism; others have urged me not to be identified with any particular standpoint, indicating as they did so the catholicity of the drafts I had to show. Each had a point, and I believe I really listened to all, but I have come out here. There is indeed this 'free church' or 'believers' church' or *baptist* style of Christian thought that is widely displayed but only haltingly voiced. Not until it has sounded its own note can there be full and fair conversation in our times between it and other voices, other styles in the one kingdom of Christ.

Thus I may disappoint some critics, as well as disappointing others for other reasons. Here is an ethics that jumps some hard philosophical questions—why be moral and what is the good and how define justice? Nor does it answer questions a proper tract for our times might address—what to do about population control and nuclear proliferation and the high divorce rate and still other life and death issues. So some will think it needlessly narrow, while others may (narrowly?) complain that I have not hewed to their rules of denomination or party or sex or class. Thus women are conscious of new roles in the world, and understandably want those roles acknowledged. I have responded to this awareness, in the biographical chapters and in other passages as well, but I have not always conformed to the linguistic revisionism some feminists demand, having my own ideas about what is 'inclusive' and 'exclusive' language in theology. Likewise, conservative biblicists, if they will read with care, will discover that their legitimate concerns are not ignored here, but on the other hand they will not find these concerns treated in just the old familiar ways, either. Rather, like the "scribe which is instructed unto the kingdom," I have brought forth things new and old from the store of treasure (cf. Matt. 13:52). And still other interest groups may find my response to their concerns unsuitable. I have not been all things to all men—and women.

Another feature deserves mention and may even draw down some reproach—here there are no footnotes or back-of-the-book notes. Weary of reading books with my finger in two places at once, I resolved either to say it in the text or not to say it. Instead, social science style parentheses such as (McClendon, 1978) refer to the bibliography, which though long is as short as honesty permits. For the bibliography indicates only my immediate debts to a vast literature, much of which though consulted goes unmentioned. Also, some important books (e.g., James Gustafson's volume 2, which is listed, and Sabina Lovibond's impressive *Realism and Imagination in Ethics*, which is not) came too late to be of use this time.

There are debts, as well, to those I have talked with and learned from over a lifetime—my former teachers, my old and new students, and (happy case) my students who have become my teachers. Among these friends, a special debt is owed those who have read drafts and given me written responses. These include Robert Adams, Eugene Bianchi, Thomas Breidenthal, Dale Brown, Wesley Brown, Frederick Borsch, William Countryman, John Coleman, John Dillenberger, Donald Durnbaugh, Thomas Drain, Kenneth Eakins, Eldon Ernst, William Estep, Daniel Ellsberg, Wayne Floyd, Michael Goldberg, Clifford Green, Clinton Gardiner, David Hackett, Stanley Hauerwas, Glenn Hinson, Fred Horton, Thorwald Lorenzen, Howard Loewen, Guy Lytle, John McEntyre, Charles McCoy, Wallace Matson, Brigid Merriman, Ramsey Michaels, Donn Morgan, Ched Myers, John Noonan, Wayne Pipkin, Paul Ramsey, Deotis Roberts, Don Saliers, Charles Scriven, Ronald Sider, Archie Smith, James M. Smith, Theophus Smith, Glen Stassen, Claude Stewart, Willard Swartley, Charles W. Taylor, William Spohn, John Toews, Dixon Sutherland, Terrence Tilley, Paul van Buren, Robert Wilken, Claude Welch, Ralph Wood, John Yoder. It looks almost like a Christmas card list, yet there is probably someone else whom I have unkindly—but unintentionally—omitted here.

My creditors include others, too—the typists and word processors and editors who have straightened me out time and again; my own CDSP and the Association of Theological Schools, who with money have provided free time for the work; my family and dear friends who have encouraged my work, and most of all my best friend and loyal wife Nancey

Murphy McClendon, who has done all the above and more, making substantive suggestions (especially in connection with Chapters Nine and Twelve), reading, advising, suggesting, encouraging, and more. To her and to all, and always to a gracious, providing God, thanks, and here it is.

A last first word: this is not a volume on which to practice speed reading. As my little history of its writing shows, it has only slowly come to be. Readers are urged, even begged, to read slowly, too.

James Wm. McClendon, Jr.
Kensington, California
Thanksgiving Day, 1985

Contents

PROSPECT

ONE   WHAT IS THEOLOGY?
1. Why baptists Have Produced So
   Little Theology 20
2. The Quest for the baptist Vision 27
3. Matter and Method in Theology 35
4. Why Ethics Comes First 41

TWO   WHAT IS ETHICS?
1. Recent Christian Ethics 48
2. From Decision to Story 56
3. Three Strands of Christian Ethics ... 62
4. How Some Ethicists Go About
   Their Work 67

Part I: THE SPHERE OF THE ORGANIC

THREE   BODY ETHICS
1. Black Religion as Embodied
   Ethics 79
2. The Focus of Body Ethics 84
3. The Morality of the Body 90
4. Embodied Virtues 104

FOUR   SARAH AND JONATHAN EDWARDS
1. The Story in Brief 111
2. An Episode for Further
   Investigation 118
3. The Convergence of Theory
   and Life 126

FIVE   EROS—TOWARD AN ETHIC
       OF SEXUAL LOVE
       1. The Myth of Romantic Love 133
       2. The Freudian Corrective 139
       3. The Romance of Orthodoxy 143

PART II: THE SPHERE OF THE COMMUNAL

SIX   SOCIAL ETHICS
      1. The Forms of Social Life 160
      2. The Community of the
         Ten Commandments 177
      3. Why the Social Strand
         Cannot Stand Alone 184

SEVEN   DIETRICH BONHOEFFER
        1. Bonhoeffer the Theologian-
           in-the-making 188
        2. The Theologian Becomes
           a Christian 192
        3. The Christian Becomes
           a Conspirator 199
        4. The Tragedy of Dietrich
           Bonhoeffer 205

EIGHT   THE POLITICS OF FORGIVENESS
        1. An Ethics for Disciples
           in Community 212
        2. The Politics of Forgiveness 219
        3. The Church in the World 230

PART III: THE SPHERE OF THE ANASTATIC

NINE   RESURRECTION ETHICS
       1. What Has the Resurrection
          to Do with Morality? 244
       2. Why the Resurrection Strand
          Cannot Stand Alone 259
       3. How the Strands Work Together
          in Christian Morality 266

TEN   DOROTHY DAY
        1. Natural Unhappiness 278
        2. The Search for Ultimacy 283
        3. Thy Kingdom Come 288

ELEVEN   A FUTURE FOR PEACE?
        1. Is Jesus a Pacifist? 300
        2. Mindset and the Myths of War 308
        3. The Peaceable Kingdom 318

RETROSPECT

TWELVE   WHY NARRATIVE ETHICS?
        1. The Defense of Narrative Ethics ... 329
        2. The Ethics of
           Propositional Principles 334
        3. The Ethics of Values 347

BIBLIOGRAPHY 357

INDEX OF NAMES AND SUBJECTS 375

INDEX OF SCRIPTURE REFERENCES........................383

PROSPECT

In Jesus Christ we have faith in the incarnate, crucified, and risen God. In the incarnation we learn of the love of God for His creation; in the crucifixion we learn of the judgment of God upon all flesh; and in the resurrection we learn of God's will for a new world. There could be no greater error than to tear these elements apart; for each of them comprises the whole.

Dietrich Bonhoeffer, *Ethics*

A threefold cord is not quickly broken.

Ecclesiastes 4:12 RSV

What Is Theology?

Theology means struggle. It may begin as Bonhoeffer said in silence, but when the silence is broken, a battle begins. This seems regrettable; in matters of great import, the human heart yearns ceaselessly for secure truth, and it is easy for us to believe that unchallenged beliefs are self-evident truths. A little reflection, however, will show that this is not so; in fact we very often have believed without doubt or contradiction what turn out to be mere falsehoods. It is small enough comfort to know that other people do the same. Thus when we set out upon Christian theology or ethics we must be reconciled to the fact that here as elsewhere hard truth is not available without hard struggles.

The struggle begins with the humble fact that the church is not the world. This means that Christians face an interior struggle, inasmuch as the line between church and world passes right through each Christian heart. It nevertheless means that the standpoint, basic point of view, the theology of the church is not the standpoint, basic point of view, theology of the world. The church's story will not interpret the world to the world's satisfaction. Hence there is a *temptation* (no weaker word will do) for the church to deny her "counter, original, spare, strange" starting point in Abraham and Jesus and to give instead a self-account or theology that will seem true to the world on the world's own present terms. Surely, it will be said, the salvation of the world must rest on some better foundation than tales about an ancient nomad and stories of a

Jewish healer? The strength of this worldly appeal lies in its claim to the universal—an appeal which faith must also make somehow. Its vice is that in its approach to universal truth it abandons the truth available to Christians, which is that the church is not the world, her story not the world's accepted story, her theology not the world's theology. If we yield this point, conspiring to conceal the difference between church and world, we may in the short run entice the world, but we will do so only by betraying the church.

A second humble fact is that Christianity itself is not one congruent whole. If the world is divided, so is the church. Who can quote such a great unity passage as Ephesians 4:5, "One Lord, one faith, one baptism," without being reminded of the historical reality: A thousand warring sects, schism and heresy, division and excommunication, all justified in the name of the aforesaid one Lord. And if someone sees in this variety and struggle no great scandal but instead a healthy living diversity of religion; or if someone claims to see here and there in the diversity some true Christian essence now and again appearing; or if someone claims by whatever means to discern amidst the variety some true path of historic faithfulness, some True Church, with other paths relegated to heterodoxy; or if someone sees the great variety of ways grouped according to a few main types, each bearing witness to a part of the Christian truth but no type witnessing to all the truth—in any case, the main difficulty remains. A divided Christianity yields divided theologies. Friedrich Schleiermacher (1768–1834), whose systematic approach to theology entitles him to the role of father of modern theology, argued that any given theology must represent and refer to the doctrine of some particular Christian body at some particular time. (It fell to successors more modern but less theological than Schleiermacher to abstract from church to individual, making theology mere organized subjectivity.) He said that since there was in his day no "systematic connection" between Catholic and Protestant doctrine, a theology could not be Christian in general, but must in the West be either Catholic or Protestant (Schleiermacher, 1835/1928:§19).

Some might hope that Schleiermacher was wrong, or that theology today has overcome denominational barriers in its work. Yet the facts now (and then) are even more complex than he said. For example, there is Eastern Orthodoxy, maintaining a traditional life nearly two millennia old, with a rich theology of image and mystery remote from the understanding of the West. There is the Anglican tradition, claiming to be both Catholic and Protestant. And there are the younger churches in mission lands, propagated or cross-bred from earlier communions in fertile cultural environments that make in each case their own living contribution to their theologies. Arthur Piepkorn in his massive four-volume survey of religious bodies (1977–79) counted more than 500 "bodies" or denominations of Christians in the United States and Canada alone!

Yet of these 500 bodies nearly 100, according to Piepkorn, are "Churches with origins in the Radical Reformation," while almost 300 more are Holiness and Pentecostal, Evangelical and Fundamentalist bodies—many of which have roots in the same radical soil. This may underline the schismatic tendency of these strains of church life, but it also underlines the difficulty of the theological task—shall there be in each theological generation nearly 400 different American theologies for these alone? Surely, though, what Schleiermacher had in mind by distinct "churches" was more nearly akin to Piepkorn's broad divisions, such as "Lutheran Churches," "Reformed and Presbyterian Churches," and (of special interest here) "the Churches of the Radical Reformation." A Christian theology, we may say provisionally, must have a community of reference that cannot without confusion be subsumed under some more general ecclesial type; it must be Orthodox or Protestant or Catholic or the like. Historical scholarship since Schleiermacher's day has made it certain that the Christian bodies of the Radical Reformation do in fact constitute such a distinctive type. At the center of the Radical Reformation (a term made familiar by George H. Williams [1957; 1962]) are the *Wiedertäufer* (Anabaptists, that is, those who it was said "illegitimately repeated" baptism), or, as they preferred to say, brethren, or *Täufer* (in English, simply baptists). My project will be especially related to this baptist focus, as I will call it, of Christian life. Others have with reason named this community of reference the "Free Church" (Littell, 1957; Westin, 1954), or the "Believers' Church" (Durnbaugh, 1968; Garrett, 1969); yet "baptist" (or the more prejudicial term "anabaptist") has history in its favor, and I propose staying with it. Yet the quest should also be of great interest to those who do not see themselves as direct heirs of the baptist vision, for if this vision is even a part of the light reflected from Christ's face, we all want to know the quality of that reflected light, inasmuch as we want to see finally that one face.

These historical discoveries about the early baptists have not been easily achieved. From the sixteenth century until the present, fierce controversy has swirled around the Radical Reformers and their successors. (So fierce that some of the successors, such as Baptists, long preferred whenever possible to dissociate themselves from their Radical forebears [Hudson, 1953], though Glen Stassen [1962] has shown that the claim for Baptist independence from Anabaptists is historically mistaken.) Who were the Radicals? What did they do and believe? What were their origins? What were their just deserts? These battles still rage, and some of them must be engaged below. A preliminary observation, however, may find general consent: Their contemporaries regarded the Anabaptists as *dangerous*. This is an undisputed fact. They were seen as a danger to society, to politics, to the religious fabric of Europe. Yet they were by and large nonviolent, that is, pacifists, and individually they were widely regarded as men and women of good character. What, then, was the danger? From today's perspective perhaps we cannot say. If we cannot, it may be a measure of the difference between the late Middle Ages and our times, and hence of the difference the original Radicals did make despite their short life tenure.

Yet the question should not be too quickly abandoned. For if we can penetrate their times, seeing that which was central to them but noxious to the religious and political authorities, picking out the hinges on which their story turned, we may be able to see the ways in which our story is like or unlike theirs, and the ways in which a theology in light of the baptist vision must have a distinctive (dangerous?) shape and scope. Before pursuing the vision further, though, it will be helpful to say a few things about theology itself.

1. Why baptists Have Produced So Little Theology

Such a community of reference may not seem promising, for the sharers of the Radical vision have produced little that deserves the name theology. One of the necessary tasks of

theology in a baptist mode must be to give an adequate
explanation for the scarcity of baptist theologies, and to show
how the scarcity may be overcome.

That there are few baptist theologies of merit will be granted
by most observers. One task of the present chapter will be to
indicate my predecessors in this work, but that is not a
daunting duty. Some have supposed that there are so few
because baptists have been in the main poor, and alienated
from society, and indeed that may be a partial explanation.
Like any science, theology presupposes social leisure. Yet on
British and American soil some baptists have flourished
economically and socially—without producing a theological
literature proportionate to that of their Reformed, or Catholic,
or Lutheran, or even Methodist counterparts. In America,
Walter Rauschenbusch (1861-1918) alone has attained cosmopolitan stature—and significantly, his starting point was
ethics.

a. *What theology is*—In explaining this theological lack it will
be convenient to have a relatively open notion of what
"theology" comprises, for definitions of theology have been
proposed that implicitly or even explicitly exclude any but
their own. Thus Karl Rahner, by way of definition, says that
"theology is a science which presupposes faith (grace of faith)
and the Church (magisterium, Scripture, Tradition)" (1965)—
hardly reassuring to the heirs of Anabaptism. At the other
extreme, it is possible to use the word "theology" so loosely
that whoever has any beliefs, or any religious beliefs, may be
said to have a 'theology.' In that case "*Everybody* has won, and
all must have prizes," but the attempt to understand theology
as a determinative body of knowledge has been abandoned.
Clearly what is wanted is a definition of theology that avoids
both extremes—one that will define theology neither as, in
effect, "our theology—or whatever is sufficiently like ours to
count," nor as "whatever is religiously believed." The
judicious mean, however, is not easily discovered. For
example, the etymological definition so tiresomely proffered
beginning students—that theology is a "*logos* of *theos*," ideas
or discourse about God—commits both faults: it narrowly
discriminates against polytheistic and atheistic theologies (and
there are some), while at the same time it admits mere
occasional or random ideas. Anyone who nevertheless feels

imprisoned by the etymology of the term might ask if penitentiaries are places of meditative reflection, if economics is the science of cooking and housecleaning, and if all revolutions restore some original state of affairs—all these being definitions in a like manner based on etymology.

Terms change, and no definition should be an intellectual straitjacket. In describing a new approach to a task what is wanted is a standing definition of that task that is close enough to the traditional idea to make sense of earlier practice, one that in this case provides some help in understanding the activity in which most of those called theologians have engaged, yet one that is neither loaded in favor of some newly chosen doctrinal or methodological way, nor so restrictive that creative development is foreclosed by the very definition. It must not, in other words, be a definition of good theology or the best theology (best in the definer's view), but it must enable us successfully to distinguish any and all *theology* from other enterprises.

Many of us have some intuitive idea of what a theology must be, regardless of formal definitions. We know that a theology represents something deeply self-involving for its adherents. Thus atheistic (or polytheistic) theologians are attending to something or other that in its importance plays for them a role in some ways like that of God. It is recognized, too, that even mystical theologies are not mere effusions of feeling, but are attempts systematically to connect mystical experience with what is and is not there in the world—or beyond it. Theology, we might say, has its objective pole, as well as its subjective one; it deals with matters of supreme importance, but seeks to do so in an orderly, even a scientific way.

Here it will help to introduce the useful term "conviction." We readily distinguish our convictions from our opinions. Opinions are the stuff of debate and discussion. We acquire opinions quickly and shed them just as quickly. They may require thought, but they require no commitment. Convictions, on the other hand, are less readily expressed but more tenaciously held. It may take a long time to discover my own convictions, but when I do, I have discovered . . . myself. They are the gutsy beliefs that I live out—or in failing to live them out, I betray myself. "We are," said Willem F. Zuurdeeg, "our convictions" (1958:58). Yet, as Zuurdeeg has shown, convictions for that very reason are not mere blind instincts;

they are our persuasions, the beliefs we embody with some reason, guiding all our thought, shaping our lives. Consider this definition:

Conviction. "A persistent belief such that if X (a person or a community) has a conviction, it will not be easily relinquished, and it cannot be relinquished without making X a significantly different person (or community) than before" (McClendon and Smith, 1975:7, 91-94).

Two features of this definition deserve further comment. The first is that convictions may be shared, held by communities that are formed by them as individuals are. And the second is that the beliefs that form human beings are not restricted in topic: One may be formed by convictions about God and neighbor, another by convictions about guns, girls, and gold. Which is to say that convictional differences may be ultimate differences.

Now we are in position to offer a definition of theology:

Theology. The discovery, understanding, and transformation of the convictions of a convictional community, including the discovery and critical revision of their relation to one another *and to whatever else there is.*

In a sense, the entire project represented here will constitute an explication of this definition, so it will not be possible immediately to explore all its ramifications. Note, however, that the definition seeks to fulfill the requirements of precision and neutrality laid down above. It fits the work of historic exemplars; thus John of Damascus may be seen as engaged throughout his Christian writings in the "discovery, understanding, and transformation" of the convictions of the eighth-century Orthodox church, and Schleiermacher of the nineteenth-century Evangelical church, and David Tracy of the contemporary Roman Catholic church, and so on. This is not all they do, but it is one thing they believe they must do. In "discovery" and "understanding" (or "interpretation," a synonym I will use throughout) the definition points to what theologians do in homage to what is handed on to them, but in "transformation" it points to what is necessarily creative in their task. Theology is thus both a descriptive discipline and a normative one.

Yet the definition does not aim to favor this or that kind of theology. It does not favor the subjective pole (represented by "convictions") at the expense of the objective (represented by "whatever else there is"), or vice versa. Nor does it restrict the implied subject and implied object of theology in a way that would exclude by definition any main contemporary approaches (Tracy, 1975:ch. 2; 1981:ch. 1).

Some may object that in its bare neutrality this definition fails even to tell us that theology's communities of reference must be religious ones. But "religious," like "religion," is a notoriously sticky word, whose various uses often carry unwanted theological freight. And if it is objected that the definition as it stands would apply to Marxist theoretics just as well, I answer that to the extent the definition fits, the label is appropriate. (Nor need we object if Marxists or others reciprocally refer to our theology as "Christian theoretics" [McClendon and Smith, 1975:ch. 1; 191f.].)

On the other hand, this definition is not entirely formal or empty. While postponing full discussion, we may note that it emphasizes the _pluralistic_ character of theology (it is necessarily done in many rival camps), its _narrative_ and _historical_ functions (discovering the actual convictions of a given community in their setting in the ongoing community story), its _rational_ or perhaps even scientific nature (concern with logical relations and the relation of convictions to _what there is_), and its praxis-related or _self-involving_ character (see the preceding discussion on the nature of convictions). Theology is to be distinguished from ideology by the former's stronger drive to truth; theology is held to be necessarily critical and self-critical. Yet it must be distinguished from the descriptive sciences because of theology's drive to self-involvement. One needn't, for example, be a criminal to teach criminology (though it might conceivably help); on the other hand it makes no sense to think of a theologian who has no convictions at all. All these points must be further elaborated before the present chapter is ended. Yet the definition does not say whether theology must be biblical, or Christ-centered, or have an organizing principle—all elements I will with appropriate qualifications affirm, but no part of the definition, any more than by _definition_ theology must be Christian!

b. _The poverty explained_—With a notion of theology staked out in a preliminary way, we may again ask why the communities here labelled 'baptist' have produced so little of it. A cultural explanation has already been suggested: These communities have been preoccupied with the harsh struggle to survive and have not had the leisure for theological reflection. The Reformation baptists, for example, were literally driven out of most of Europe including Britain. Most of their leaders were soon dead; their literary production was sharply limited to instruction for the faithful, to polemic and apologetic confessions, and (significantly enough) to historical narratives. But there were other difficult circumstances as well.

In America, for example, two historic and all-absorbing struggles set the limits of reflection. In the eighteenth and early nineteenth centuries, baptists and others were formed, indeed for the most part created, by the revival awakenings, which set an indelible imprint upon their piety (Goen, 1962). These awakenings ran head on into a theology, mediated by Puritanism, that had been shaped by the magisterial Reformers, especially Calvin, not by the Radical heritage. Now there appeared to baptists and others a contradiction between the human means required by the revivals and the *sola gratia* of strict Calvinism. Does God's election discourage human effort, or legitimate it? Is grace "particular" (only for some) or "general" (intended for all)? These dilemmas set the agenda for theological reflection both inside and outside the baptist camp, and set it on terms defined by the Calvinist-Arminian polarity, not on terms suggested by earlier Anabaptist motifs.

Then, from the later nineteenth century to the present, a second dilemma, almost unrelated to the first, appeared and dominated others' (and once again, baptists') intellectual energies. This was the struggle over Scripture, occasioned by the development of post-Enlightenment critical methods and historical knowledge, fomented by the Fundamentalist movement, and exacerbated by the perceived link between the battle over the Bible and other Modernist-Fundamentalist cruxes (Alley, 1970; Lindsell, 1976; Gaustad, 1980). In this struggle, Modernists accused Fundamentalists of idolatry, and Fundamentalists accused Modernists of unbelief—each being at least partially right in its harsh judgment of the other, while neither seemed able to find a foothold above the battle from which to see what stake baptists or others had in the outcome of the struggle.

Other momentous issues stirred baptists in the centuries now under review: revolution, slavery, war, Enlightened thought, the hunger for salvation in alienated lives, global missionary openings and closings, economic hardship and excess accumulation, the role of the sexes and of the family, depth psychology, and still more. It may seem idle to say that an earlier baptist ethos and doctrine might have afforded a theological perspective upon these issues that the Calvinist-Arminian and the Modernist-Fundamentalist polarities did not provide. Yet the fact remains that for baptists these matrices had no issue in theological fruitfulness of the sort that others in similar critical epochs of church history have experienced.

More to the point, authentic baptist convictions do exist—they have survived the turbulent centuries we call the modern age and remain, to some degree shaping the lives of millions. Thus the theological question remains: Why have others' agendas prevailed? Why have these convictions not given birth to theologies richly Christian because richly baptist? Why are the several baptist communities of today so often prey to ideologies of the political left and (more often now in America) right, or to theologies whose provenance is Constantinian, not primitive-Christian? If some Calvinist (or Arminian, or Modernist, or Fundamentalist) thinks those are biased questions, there is still the original puzzle, the poverty of baptist theologies, to be explained (Swartley, 1984).

It will not do to blame a harsh environment (harsh though it has been), or others' preoccupation with creeds and catechisms (preoccupied though they be) for the baptist default. The truth, I believe, is this: The baptists in all their variety and disunity failed to see in their own heritage, their own way of using Scripture, their own communal practices and patterns, *their own guiding vision,* a resource for theology unlike the prevailing scholasticism round about them. Some were attracted to current fashions and tried theologizing in those fashions. The results were seldom good, and the consequence was further distrust of theology in baptist ranks: Theology was seen as arrogant (facing God), as imperialistic (toward plain Christians), and in any case, as irrelevant. Yet the basic failure was baptists' distrust of their own vision, their common life, their very gospel; whereas it might have been the resource for their theology, and theology in turn the means of exploring that gospel, revitalizing that life, focusing that vision. Failing in this, baptists became the victim of ideologies left and right—and thereby became less themselves, spiritually impoverishing both themselves and their Christian neighbors in other churches.

This brings us back to the hard fact that theology is hard work, struggle. If we have not done well we must admit it—and struggle on. Yet it will help immensely to see what needs to be done. The claim here is that we need (1) to find and focus upon that *theological center,* the vision around which our contructive work can be done. Honoring the past (but not too much!) we must trust God to lead us into the future (and not too late!). (2) We need to do this by acknowledging the rich resources for theology in the *narrative common life* of that vision. And (3) we need to seize the appropriate point of departure for reflection upon this narrative and common life in *theological ethics.* The three following sections of this chapter will address these three themes in turn.

2. The Quest for the baptist Vision

The churches that historians might justly call 'baptist' are characterized by no authoritative creed; no single set of doctrines marks them off from all others; no finespun theory particularizes their way of life; no private 'revelation' separates them from other Christians. Recognition of these indisputable facts has led some to suppose that there could be no baptist theology, no clear or definite expression of the *thought* that gives shape to the common life of this tribe of Israel, none that bonds this connection together so as to distinguish it among all God's children. Yet the supposition, as we have seen, has done damage to the integrity of baptist life (and has thereby damaged all Christians, who suffer when any one suffers); it has permitted alien thought forms to supplant the baptist vision, which is at the true center of this way of life.

By such a vision, I do not mean some end result of theoretical reflection, remote from the daily life of a rather plain people. Nor do I mean a detachable baptist Ideal—what baptists ought to be (but of course are not). Instead, by a vision I mean the guiding stimulus by which a people (or as here, a combination of peoples) shape their life and thought as that people or that combination; I mean by it the continually emerging theme and tonic structure of their common life. The vision is thus already present, waiting to be recognized and employed; it must not seem a stranger to those who share in baptist life or to their sympathetic observers. Yet once acknowledged for what it is, it should serve as the touchstone by which authentic baptist life is discovered and described, and also as the organizing principle around which a genuine baptist theology can take shape.

The existence of such a vision is not an altogether strange idea. In an ecumenical era, many thinkers have been led to search out the distinctive spirit (in contrast to the common elements) that animates Catholicism and Protestantism (Adam, 1937; R. M. Brown, 1961). In a like quest, partly polemic but partly irenic as well, some have sought the distinctive vision of those here called baptists (e.g., Mullins, 1908; Durnbaugh, 1968). These inquirers have found a number of persistent marks of the heirs of the Radicals. Consider such a list.

(1) Biblicism, understood not as one or another theory of inspiration, but as humble acceptance of the authority of Scripture for both faith and practice. (Related themes are restitution and restoration.)

(2) Mission (or evangelism), understood not as an attempt to control history for the ends we believe to be good, but as the responsibility to witness to Christ—and accept the suffering that witness entails.

(3) Liberty, or soul competency, understood not as the overthrow of all oppressive authority, but as the God-given freedom to respond to God without the intervention of the state or other powers. (Related themes are intentional community, voluntarism, separation of church and state.)

(4) Discipleship, understood neither as a vocation for the few nor an esoteric discipline for adepts, but as life transformed into service by the lordship of Jesus Christ. (Signified by believer's baptism; a related theme is the regenerate or believers' church.)

(5) Community, understood not as privileged access to God or to sacred status, but as sharing together in a storied life of obedient service to and with Christ. (Signified by the Lord's supper.)

Yet even so short and perhaps incomplete an inventory of convictional features raises the question, What is the vision that unites, organizes, guides these disparate elements into one set? For example, can any one feature be understood to evoke or determine all the others? To phrase the question differently: While many Christians have embraced (or at least acknowledged) some of these elements just listed, is there a governing vision that, once seen, is seen to require them all?

A more technical way to put the question is to ask whether any one feature of Christian life listed here can provide a genuine organizing principle for a baptist theology. It may appear that the first item on the list, *biblicism*, does provide such a principle, and Donovan Smucker once argued that the unique contribution of the early Anabaptists was just the recovery of the theology of the Bible. The Anabaptists, he said, were willing to follow the logic of Protestantism consistently; among the Reformers they alone fully submitted to biblical authority (1945). This is a compelling proposal, and we must reconsider it in the end. Yet as it stands, it is defective. There is logic in the baptist vision—but what separated the Anabaptists from their persecutors was not merely the courage to draw an inference! Certainly, too, there is a profound relation to biblical authority in the baptist vision, yet biblical authority being, like the authority of Christ, in some sense the common property of all Christians, this brings to the fore complex Christian problems of tradition, hermeneutics, and history that cannot be resolved merely by appeals to the Bible as such.

I know of no full scale attempt to find in *mission* or evangelism the organizing vision sought here (but see Loewen in Swartley, 1984); each of the other three features listed, however, has been singled out by some.

The theme of *liberty* or freedom was the focus of enduring interest in the baptist movement by German theologian-philosopher Ernst Troeltsch (1865–1923). In his *Social Teaching of the Christian Churches* (1912a) and again in *Protestantism and Progress* (1912b), he traced Anabaptist motifs in English and American free churches, noting in the latter book that they expressed three basic Christian principles: (1) the separation of church and state; (2) voluntarism as the form of the church itself; and (3) individual liberty of conscience over against the state. Troeltsch's libertarian interpretation provided a watershed in the development of nonpolemical historical study of the Radical Reformers, but his formulation of their heritage comes closer to providing a political theory than a theological organizing vision of the sort we want now. What Troeltsch saw politically, Edgar Young Mullins (1860–1928) had conceived in religious terms in his groundbreaking *Axioms of Religion* (1908). Yet Mullins' motto of "soul competency" was framed too much in terms of the rugged individualism of pre–New Deal America to do justice to the shared discipleship earlier baptists had embraced. It may be noted here that the theme of liberty also implies the rejection of violence as the basis of community, yet such rejection remains largely unfinished business among baptists (see Chapter Eleven).

Discipleship was central to the understanding of the movement in Harold S. Bender (1897–1962), a Mennonite historian. His view, epitomized in a classic essay, "The Anabaptist Vision," is that the key to that vision is discipleship. "The great word of the Anabaptists was not 'faith' as it was with the reformers, but 'following' (*Nachfolge Christi*)." Bender went on to develop the vision under three headings, "Christianity as discipleship; . . . the church as a brotherhood; and . . . a new ethic of love and nonresistance," showing the interdependence of the three (1944:42f.). Discipleship came to the fore again in the thought of German Protestant Dietrich Bonhoeffer (1906–1945), whose book *The Cost of Discipleship* (1937/1963)—in German, *Nachfolge*—introduced this theme in the midst of the Nazi crisis. But Bonhoeffer's life story, as we will see in a later chapter, revealed the theological tragedy of costly commitment not knitted to other baptist themes as well. Others have proposed the lordship of Jesus Christ as the organizing theme. Indeed it is implied in discipleship and each of the other distinguishing marks listed. But as one defining mark of every sort of Christianity, it does not *by itself* distinguish the baptist way.

Community was the focus of the interpretation of the baptist movement in Methodist Franklin H. Littell's significant *Anabaptist View of the Church* (1952). Littell suggested that for working purposes Anabaptists be defined as "Those in the radical Reformation who gathered and disciplined a 'true church' (*rechte Kirche*) upon the apostolic pattern as they understood it" (1952:xvii). Most important to Littell's view was the sense of *history* that he believed had formed the Anabaptists: They were Christians who accepted a primitivist philosophy of history and applied it to the "fall of the church." In primitivism, history moves from Eden's perfection, to a fall, to a partial restitution, to God's final restoration. For the Anabaptists, said Littell, the "fall" was the Constantinian marriage of church and state, while beginnings of restitution had occurred in their own communities. This emphasis upon restitution, however, was rejected as merely marginal to Anabaptist thought by Robert Friedmann, who argued moreover that whatever is valuable in this theme could better be subsumed under the Harold Bender "vision" of obedient discipleship (Friedmann, 1959). Yet Littell's conjoining of history and community, as we shall see, comes close to the mark.

These four proposals in recent scholarship, some made by historians and philosophers, others by theologians, have each some merit, but none has shown itself able to meet all difficulties or persuade all theorists. I will now make another attempt to show how these marks of the Radical Reformation draw together. It, too, may be inadequate. It is important to remember, in assessing it, that another test of its adequacy will be the capacity of the vision not only to generate a theology but also to give form or shape to a shared life in Christ Jesus. If the shared life of the communities of the vision (the 'baptists') consists in what they suffer and do and feel and live out, the theological task of discovering and unfolding their vision will find its true meaning only in the arena of that life itself. That is the hard test my proposal—or any other—must survive.

In this spirit, consider the following suggestion: The role of Scripture is indeed the clue. But the term "biblicism" (Smucker, 1945) has the sound of one side of a weary old controversy. Rather, say that Scripture in this vision effects a link between the church of the apostles and our own. So the vision can be expressed as a hermeneutical motto, which is shared awareness of *the present Christian community as the primitive community and the eschatological community*. In other words, the church now is the primitive church and the church on the day of judgment is the church now; the obedience and liberty of the followers of Jesus of Nazareth is *our* liberty, *our* obedience.

This is not meant as a denial of the facts of history, nor a rejection of their significance; it *is* a claim for the historic significance of this present time in the life of the church and therefore by implication of every other present time in her life. So this interpretation is not a rejection of biblical studies in favor of naïve biblicism; rather, it is a justification *for* intense biblical study by every intelligible means, since the biblical story has present, not mere antiquarian, relevance. Positively, this understanding of the vision appropriates Littell's version without committing itself to literal eras of "fall" and datable periods of "restitution"—the present church, like the New Testament community of disciples, is often errant or fallen, often restored. This interpretation can also include Bender's version of the vision without confining its scope to an inward-looking community of disciples-in-waiting. The true church today is mission-oriented as was the apostolic church—according to the vision, it *is* the apostolic church. And (with more caution) this interpretation can accept Troeltsch's account of the power of the obedient minority to transform history, but without finding history's meaning, with Troeltsch, merely in the social by-products of the church's witness. Finally, it can accept Mullins' theme of soul competency as the heart of baptist liberty, knowing that it will be protected from his excess of individualism by the Christocentric solidarity of the New Testament.

This version of the vision endorses the positive content of Smucker's "biblicism": the church, as the apostolic community, reads (in community) the apostolic writings, the New Testament, and with the primitive church lives also under the guidance of the Old. The Bible is in this sense the church's book: we are the people of that book. But by shifting the emphasis from mere biblicism to a vision that shows *how* the church sees itself as that people, we avoid any dogmatic bibliolatry which could substitute attention to the book for participation in the life. That shift seems small; the consequences, though, are momentous.

To clarify the sense in which "the church now *is* the primitive church," consider two parallel assertions. The first appears in Catholic eucharistic doctrine. There the bread (and wine) upon the altar, when consecrated, *is* the body (and blood) of Christ. Not "represents" or "symbolizes," but *is*. No lesser word will do. In the force of that "is" lies the power, the distinctive emphasis, of the Catholic doctrine. Note well that the Catholic assertion, while it cannot be proved true in any straightforward way, cannot be falsified by any obvious means, either (cf. MacKinnon, 1970, on this point). For if we remark to the intelligent Catholic that the bread is still bread, can be analyzed in a laboratory as bread, etc., he will not quarrel with us. "Yes, it is, as you say, still bread, but . . ." Now just such a claim is made by the baptist vision. The church now *is* the primitive church; *we* are Jesus' followers; the commands are addressed directly to *us*. And no rejoinder about the date of Jesus' earthly ministry versus today's date can refute that claim. (A misunderstanding may be avoided by contrasting the present sense of "the church now is the apostolic church" with a possible Catholic sense of those very words. The latter requires some notion of *succession* and therefore of legitimate *development*. But successionism is close to heresy in baptist eyes though embraced by a few, and development conveys a claim to inevitable progress more at home in nineteenth-century liberalism than in the thought world of the New Testament. The baptist "is" in "this is that" is therefore neither developmental nor successionist, but mystical and immediate; it might be better understood by the artist and poet than by the metaphysician and dogmatist.)

The second parallel assertion is found throughout the Bible. In Acts 2, Simon Peter, preaching on the day of Pentecost, refers to a passage in the prophet Joel: "And it shall come to pass afterward, that I will pour out my Spirit upon all flesh: and your sons and your daughters shall prophesy" (2:28 ASV). Peter applies this passage to the events occurring as he speaks, saying *"this is that* which hath been spoken through the prophet Joel" (Acts 2:16 ASV); that is, the events of Pentecost are the events of the prophetic message. We have the now-familiar pattern again: This *is* that. And once again the historian's judgment that the Joel passage refers to entirely different events, perhaps in the prophet's own day, cannot falsify Peter's claim. For we are here in the presence of a regular motif in biblical literature in which language about one set of events and circumstances is applied under divine guidance to another set of events and circumstances. Thus scholar and poet Davie Napier can say of the Old Testament prophetic mind that

we have in the Old Testament no past which has not already been appropriated in the present, and so appropriated as to *be* in the present, to *live* in the present. [The past] *was* past, but it now *is*. . . . The event lives in faith. . . . As such, it is . . . not so much . . . merely memorialized as reexperienced—created and lived again.

(Napier, 1962:906)

Napier is speaking in the first instance of the role of Moses in later Old Testament prophecy, but his theme is drawn from the whole Bible: this is what in a later setting I will call the baptist vision. It is on one side a reading strategy for the church confronting Scripture; on the other, a way—properly, *the* way—of Christian existence.

For my claim in brief is that just such an awareness of the Bible and especially of the New Testament setting in the present situation is characteristic of the baptist vision wherever we find it; further, that this understanding of the vision is sufficiently encompassing and sufficiently distinctive to enable us to interpret the baptist way of life by it; that this sense of the vision adequately incorporates the other senses reviewed above; and that the vision so understood is *a necessary and sufficient organizing principle for a (baptist) theology.*

This is a claim, not a proof, not even an argument. It requires testing, both theological and historical. When tested historically, the interpretation, if valid, should shed light upon many phases of at least the baptist movement. It should for example help make sense of the conviction of those not very mystical nineteenth-century American Restorationists ('Campbellites') that theirs were in fact "New Testament churches." It should make sense as well of the indubitably mystical nineteenth- and twentieth-century black Baptist sense of identity with the children of Israel suffering in Egyptian bondage. More generally, the vision should show how a people's identity is construed via narratives that are historically set in another time and place but display redemptive power here and now. All this is agenda for further historical work, and so, while important, is not the immediate task.

On the other hand, this understanding of the baptist vision invites theological testing of a sort that is the very business at hand. In this test, the vision must yield power to organize the convictions of the present sharers of the vision, as well as the narrative life in which these are imbedded. And who are these sharers? Well, it is not easy to say. There is no single, distinct body of people called "believers' church," or "baptists." Instead there are Disciples of Christ and Churches of Christ, Mennonites, Plymouth Brethren, Adventists, Russian Evangelicals, perhaps Quakers, certainly black Baptists (who often go by other names), the (Anderson, Indiana) Church of God, Southern and British and European and American Baptists, the Church of the Brethren, perhaps some Methodists, Assemblies of God, assorted intentional communities not organized as churches, missionary affiliates of all the above, and, as pointed out in an earlier section, hundreds of other bodies even in the United States and Canada.

Do all these share the vision? Consider again our initial list of baptist distinctives, modified now in light of the present discussion: first of all the awareness of the *biblical* story as our story, but also of *mission* as responsibility for costly witness, of *liberty* as the freedom to obey God without state help or hindrance, of *discipleship* as life transformed into obedience to Jesus' lordship, and of *community* as daily sharing in the vision. Will it not appear that some of these named communities have some of these, and more rarely, most of them, but that few exhibit all? Yet thereby our theological task is set. For that task is not complete when we have discovered those convictions by which the church supposes she lives, or even when we have framed those by which we hope she might truly live. Rather, theology is the mirror in which today's church is confronted with her potential convictions, the mirror which asks if in this set she recognizes herself not as she is but as she must be. Thus theologian and church are necessary partners in an ongoing dialogue.

3. *Matter and Method in Theology*

In this way even baptists *can* have a theology! But should they? It makes little sense to think of convinced men and women living a life based upon their shared convictions, yet engaging in no reflection upon them. Still, it might be possible merely to think about them in an ad hoc manner. Why not cope with convictions when and as they arise to view, in contexts of Bible study, pastoral care, and daily life? Most Christians do this, and for many it seems to suffice. For some seminary students it would be a vast relief to be freed from the burden imposed by systematic studies. Would it also be more coherent with the baptist way?

Certainly such an 'anti-intellectual' note has recurred from earliest times in Christian life. The Anabaptists, a case in point, were dubious about theology; it was their persecutors, whether Catholics or Protestants, who called themselves "theologians." Yet the virtual elimination of generations of early Radical Reformation leaders by persecution, imprisonment, and execution hardly made theoretical reflection convenient (Bender, 1959:705). Hence the antitheological attitude may have been in more than one sense thrust upon the early baptists. Similarly, later 'anti-intellectualism,' when not due to proud resentment, may reflect only theology's failure to undertake the task mandated here.

Yet the temptation to resort to invective rather than argument, a temptation felt both by those who oppose and those who espouse real theological work, suggests that something is at issue here that will not be reduced to rational argument. Perhaps the best we can do now is simply to indicate the broad method that would be followed in theology as defined above, work in which it is understood as the theoretic of our common convictions, the web in which they adhere and breathe together. Then we can leave each to discover his or her own vocation in the matter.

(a. *Theology is pluralistic*—Here we may disagree profoundly with Karl Rahner, who sees the task of theology as attempting to conform ever more closely to 'the true theology'—to theology as God knows it ought to be (1970). If, however, theology is a science of convictions, and if human convictions differ as much as people do, that image of theology is partly misleading. To be true, our theologies must represent us as we are, as well as representing God as God. That fact introduces a necessary, not a sinful, pluralism into the theological task. God, having created the human variety we represent, *wants* us to theologize in varied ways. This does not introduce a laissez-faire subjectivism into theology, however, because theology is always the theology of the community, not just of the individual Christian, and because theology is the very means by which those of one community encounter those of other communities (or of none) for mutual witness and critical correction. Theology provides the *loggia* (as in a Renaissance Italian city) or the gallery (as attached to a U.S. Southern house) along which dwellers in the household of faith can walk into the give and take of humane dialogue. Without theology there can be no such dialogue on equal terms.

But the believers' conversation is not just with outsiders, as may be seen by the following display of baptist variety:

Century	baptist Theoretician	Dominant Context
16th	Swiss Brethren	Catholic views of sacrament and society; Zwinglian evangelicalism
	Menno Simons	The debacle of Münster
17th	Roger Williams	Puritan models and assumptions
18th	John Gill	Strict Calvinism in Restoration England
	Isaac Backus	New England's struggle for religious liberty
	John Leland	Scottish moral philosophy; American political ideals
19th	Thomas and Alexander Campbell	Locke; the Scottish Enlightenment; the American frontier
	Sytse Hoekstra Bzn	Kant and Liberalism; Dutch Mennonite culture
	Rufus Lewis Perry	African models of cult and culture; emancipation experience
20th	Augustus H. Strong and William N. Clarke	The Modernist-Fundamentalist controversy
	Walter Rauschenbusch	Urban industrialization and poverty
	E. Y. Mullins	Schleiermacher and James

Differing contexts, methods, and assumptions have provided lively disagreement even among those who in some measure share the baptist vision. Among these conversation partners, special honor must be given the few who have attempted the *systematic* task. These include Gill (1767–70), J. L. Dagg (1858–59), Clarke (1894), Strong (1886), Rauschenbusch (1917), Mullins (1920), D. C. MacIntosh (1919), W. T. Conner (1936; 1945), J. C. Wenger (1954), Gordon Kaufman (1968), Carl F. H. Henry (1976–83), Dale Moody (1981), and perhaps a few more. Two features stand out here. One is how short the list is; the other is the relative neglect of systematic ethics. Nevertheless, it is a substantive tradition, deserving careful attention from any theology that would reflect on the plurality of the baptist vision.

b. *Theology is narrative-based*—A review of the baptist theologians listed above will show that along with the variety of contexts on which they draw, there are at least two common features: emphasis on the Bible, and emphasis on experience. After the Enlightenment, though, it seemed difficult to relate these without diminishing one or the other; this was expressed in the struggles over both Calvinism and Modernism. Now, however, the recovery of the primacy of narrative in theology, while not solving all the difficulties, may show more clearly how experience and Bible are related to one another. For though it is sometimes suppressed, theology necessarily has a narrative dimension (McClendon, 1974; Goldberg, 1982; cf. Tilley, 1985). Now the baptist vision reminds us that the narrative the Bible reflects, the story of Israel, of Jesus, and of the church, is intimately related to the narrative we ourselves live. Thus that vision functions as a hermeneutic that relates our experience to the Scriptures, showing how the two are joined (cf. Kelsey, 1975).

In post-Enlightenment Christianity the Bible was made a touchstone of many 'orthodoxies,' but in practice the Bible never fitted neatly into the assigned niches. To make it with Catholics into "the church's book," reading the Bible as a (perhaps primary) illustrative document of a known institution, has not always worked. Nor has the Protestant device, by which the Bible was read as evidence of the truth of an extrinsic principle such as *sola fide*, been adequate. Even when misunderstood, the Bible remained bigger than the niches to which it was relegated. For it requires that we be hearers of the Word, listening for what it asks us, not bringing *our* questions to find the Bible's answers, but prepared to have our current questions discredited or revised by its own. Scripture confronts its readers with another world and asks if it will not become our world; with another hope than our own hopes, and thus teaches us to ask, "What wait I for?" (Psalm 39:7). In at least that sense, the Bible is the Book of a story that claims to be our real story (cf. H. R. Niebuhr, 1941:ch. 2).

By bringing the idea of "experience" under the heading of narrative, we may clear up a confusion that has beset theology since Schleiermacher. "Experience" is a systematically ambiguous word, referring now to evanescent, private, inward feeling, and again to matters of communal and public knowledge. If, however, we see that the experience that matters for Christian life is not mere flashes of feeling, but is what we have lived through and lived out in company with one another, the experience that constitutes our share in the Christ story, then the confusion dissolves. Experience in that sense is the enduring or timely aspect of our lives in relation to God and one another; as plot and character in some setting, it is the stuff of narrative. Every theology is linked to some narrative; successful theology, knowing this, discovers and renovates its own narrative base.

Thus in Christian theology we are directed not only to Scripture, but to a rich variety of material—practices, stories, hymns, and history—as well as to confessions of faith (Lumpkin, 1959; Loewen, 1985; Parker, 1982) and theological essays. Happily, this material is for baptists richly available. A striking example is the *Ausbund*, said to be the oldest hymnal in current use in any church, preserving texts from the first two decades of Anabaptist life. Other hymnals show baptist life at other illuminating moments in the history. *Martyrs Mirror* and the *GeschichtBuch* are Mennonite and Hutterian chronicles respectively, from the seventeenth and sixteenth centuries. More recent historians following William Warren Sweet (1881–1959) have made just the approach to religious life in America that is here required (cf. Mathews, 1977). Currently black history is recovering the story of blackness in America in its relation to God and neighbor (cf. Raboteau, 1978; and within, Chapter Three), and the actual role of women in all the above is at last being noted more honestly (within, Chapters Four and Ten). What is wanted is exactly the theological appropriation of such rich materials.

c. *Theology is rational*—Some have called theology a "science," and in one ancient sense of the word, that is correct. Perhaps it is less misleading, though, to speak of it as a "discipline" (as are the natural sciences, as is art, as are law and medicine also) and to insist only that each display a rationality appropriate to its own *metier*. A part of theology's rationality is its sense of connection and interdependence with other disciplines—with the social sciences (whose sphere is properly discovery of the way things are in the human world), the humanities (whose sphere is that of understanding and interpretation), and philosophy (whose sphere, like that of poets and artists, is creative transformation of human awareness). Another aspect of theology's rationality is its control of its own internal organization, and its grasp of the logical and contingent relations obtaining among the subdisciplines that make up theology in the most general sense (Lonergan, 1972). In the eighteenth and nineteenth centuries such matters were studied in an organized way in theological departments and schools under the somewhat forbidding title, "theological encyclopedia" (cf. Schleiermacher, 1830/ 1966). While recognizing the relevance of these, we must limit ourselves here merely to noting the rational and creative dimension of the systematic theologian's proper task. Mathematics suggests one model: the transformation of an equation leaves everything the same, yet creates possibilities the original formula had not suggested. So it is in theology; the theologian receives the heritage and by transforming it creates new possibilities for the shape of shared convictions. In this task the sources are not only those philosophical and aesthetic models that imagination may invoke, but are in another sense the very life of the theologian-in-community and the theologian-in-dialogue.

d. *Theology is self-involving*—The last paragraph leads directly to the self-involving nature of the theological task. It is not to be denied here that a Christian may engage in Muslim theology, or a Jew in Christian theology. Yet these are exceptions whose function is in part to prove the rule that in convictional work, self-involvement is natural and appropriate, while disengagement requires to be explained case by case. One's own story may not be disconnected from the common story; the theologian's proposals require testing at every stage by participation in the common life. Meanwhile the baptist theologian, by the very nature of those shared convictions, must not be remote from the challenge of pluralistic engagement with other Christian communities, and with other ways of life in the wide world: the definitive themes of evangelism and of service demand that this be so. It was no providential mischance that saw Jesus' ministry begin in "Galilee of the Gentiles," that cultural mingling ground of the near East; no accident, either, that found the apostle to the Gentiles, Paul, one who moved easily in several cultures, Jewish and Gentile, Roman and Greek.

In one sense, the multiplicity of the data and the nature of the task simply require that the theologian in obedience to that task shall be free, and this for the communities' sake even more than for the theologians'. In another sense, the 'authority' to which every theological worker must bow the knee

is single and all-commanding, the authority of truth, and with
it is coupled the moral demand of courageous personal
truthfulness. Truthfulness, though, must be self-enforced; it is
a skill to acquire; thus it cannot be the gift of a denominational
cattle prod, or cultural brainwashing however well-intended,
or of less subtle persecution "for the cause of conscience"
(Williams, 1644), either by foe or 'friend.' And for anyone who
wonders if the pattern of authority (Ramm, 1957; cf. Harrison,
1959) has been rightly grasped by this theologian or any other,
there is the encouragement of Balthasar Hubmaier's motto—
"Truth is immortal"; I may sometimes fail and I shall indeed
die; the truth is God's and will not.

4. Why Ethics Comes First

Systematic Christian theology, as a segment of the whole
'encyclopedia' of Christian studies, is often treated in three
parts: *'foundations'* (also called prolegomena or philosophical
theology or fundamental theology or apologetics); Christian
doctrine (or historical theology, sometimes but misleadingly
called 'theology proper'); and Christian *ethics* (also called
moral theology or theological ethics). Often, too, it is
supposed that these three parts should be presented in that
order: 'foundations' providing the grounding or basis for all
that is to follow, doctrine showing what must be believed and
taught, and ethics discovering the conduct or decisions that
"flow from" the given doctrines. None of the baptist
predecessors listed above followed this scheme exactly, but
some, for example Strong, have implied it by moving from
philosophical theology to doctrine, leaving the implication
that ethics followed in their train. The suggestion is that
'foundations'-doctrine-ethics is the *logical* order.

I will argue that it is not. In the first place, no part of
systematic theology stands quite independent; each presupposes the other parts. This is true of philosophical theology as
well, a point as clear to Schleiermacher as it was to Barth
(Schleiermacher, 1835/1928:§32-33; Barth, 1936:I/1). Perhaps
more persuasive to some than this citation of authorities is the
argument, from the philosophical side, that the modern dream
from Descartes and Locke onwards of philosophy as an
ultimate intellectual umpire, telling ethics and religion what

can and cannot be validly believed, is increasingly seen to be empty. At least Richard Rorty has so argued in an important book (1979). In this case, if there are serious questions to be treated under 'foundations,' these must have a different relation to doctrine and to ethics than that of a philosophical licensing agency that will allow or disallow religious belief and conduct. Finally, there is the pedagogical consideration: When the study of systematic theology is understood as preparation for ministry, there is little reason to initiate students into it via that part of systematic theology most abstruse, most remote from daily life, and therefore least congenial. Many students, starting there, quit as soon as they can!

Should we begin, then, with doctrine or with ethics? When Friedrich Schleiermacher, whose *Glaubenslehre* remains the paragon in systematic theology, considered this question, he noted that either one would do—he might just as well have begun with ethics as doctrine (1835/1928:§26). There was, he felt, no logical reason to treat Christian doctrinal convictions prior to Christian moral convictions. His choice, however, had fateful consequences. Though he lived to his sixty-sixth year, Schleiermacher's Christian ethics was never completed; the work we inherit is based on students' lecture notes. Yet this consequence is all too typical of theological scholarship, which as I have heard Ron Sider say, is forever leaving ethics till last, and then leaving it out. Note that what is argued for here is the chronological priority of ethics, not its logical priority (none has that), not the reduction of all else to ethics. Is it not worth considering, finally, how different might have been the history of Christianity if after the accession of the Emperor Constantine the church's leaders had met at Nicaea, not to anathematize others' inadequate Christological metaphysics, but to devise a strategy by which the church might remain the church in light of the fateful political shift—to secure Christian social ethics before refining Christian dogma?

A story may give focus to the concern expressed here. It involves Origen (185–254), greatest of ancient Bible scholars, literary critic, preacher, and author of the oldest systematic theology on record, the *First Principles* (c. 225). For various reasons, Origen was obliged to leave his teaching place in Alexandria and start afresh in Caesarea in Palestine (c. 233). Here he accepted as pupil one Gregory, later to be called "Thaumaturgus," meaning wonder-worker, who was to become a famous bishop. When Origen received Gregory, however, he was a young scholar looking forward to a brilliant career in law. The encounter with Origen changed his life.

Gregory tells us about this in his *Panegyric,* an address in praise of Origen. Since we know of Origen as a learned scholar, we might have expected Gregory's eulogy to focus on his teacher's erudition. Instead, he tells how Origen in accepting Gregory and his brother as students first *made friends* with these young men—and did it as if it were a valuable achievement on Origen's side to have such friends. Gregory felt himself a Jonathan embraced by this academic David (1 Sam. 18:1; *Pan.* vi).

Then followed the course of instruction, in which rhetoric—sheer verbal skill—was minimized, but the student was instead asked to think what the words *meant.* This training required introspection: In Gregory's reminiscence one can picture the ancient doctor of the psyche at work: "penetrating into us more deeply, and probing what is most inward in us, he put us to the question, and made propositions to us, and listened to us in our replies" (*Pan.* vi). So the teacher fished for the souls of his nominally Christian students, seeking to precipitate that transformation of life by which Origen himself, they noted, already lived. It was not merely theories about morality that Origen sought, but its very practice; he "stimulated us by the deeds he did more than by the doctrines he taught" (*Pan.* ix). From there the instruction led on into all writers in philosophy, to the old poets, and finally to Origen's own specialty, sacred Scripture. Origen taught these students that no topic was undiscussable, no question forbidden, no opinion too daunting, no one school of Grecian philosophy exclusively to be owned. Supremely, he taught them that piety and scholarship were partners, not rivals.

If we recall that Origen had been chief teacher in the catechetical school at Alexandria, the earliest Christian 'theological seminary' we know about, it appears we have here a clue to the character of Christian theology at the time of its beginning. Alexandria's School was not at heart the home of flighty speculation in philosophy. It was no "university of antiquity." It was rather a training ground for Christianity, where spiritual and moral instruction necessarily took first place since only upon such a basis could the further reaches of Christian knowledge ever be understood. Not only in the hands of Origen, but of his predecessors Pantaenus and Clement of Alexandria, it was "a school for training in virtue," whose goal was to form the lives of its students "in light of the ideal set forth in the Scriptures and imaged in Christ" (Robert Wilken, 1984:19).

So ethics, and the morality that ethics is about, lay at the very heart of theology in the oldest seminary of them all. This was expressed in the role of the teacher as a model and in his approach, in friendship, to the student. It was expressed in the expectation that the student would be *converted* to a new way of life, and finally as well in the ordering of the curriculum (Wilken, 1984:15-30). But it is the last of these that is our immediate concern. In ancient Alexandrian theology, the place where theology impinged upon the *life* of its practition-ers—namely, ethics or the study of virtue—was the starting line for the entire course.

It is worth inquiring why, despite the well-known practical tendency of American Christianity, ethics here has been so often detached from systematic theology. How is it that D. C. MacIntosh, a Canadian Baptist teaching at Yale, could produce a systematic treatise, *Theology as an Empirical Science* (1919), that in some ways foreshadows the present project, yet never betray any obligation to deal with Christian morality, although we know that MacIntosh was a deeply moral man who wrote a book against war? Whereas Menno Simons, in his *Foundation of Christian Doctrine* (1539/1956), had so interwoven ethics and doctrine that the seam between the two cannot be found. What happened to the baptist vision in the interval between these two? The answer, I believe, lay partly in the turn in eighteenth-century American colleges to "moral philosophy" as an independent rational discipline, which took ethics away from Bible and theology; partly in the preoccupation of systematic theologians with the Calvinist-Arminian and Modernist-Fundamentalist controversies mentioned earlier, and partly with the subsequent development, within the social sciences, of "social ethics," which was itself a response to the demise of the older moral philosophy (Ahlstrom, 1961; Sloan, 1979).

Yet if moral theology (ethics) is indeed proper to systematic theology as such, what is its relation to doctrine and to philosophical theology? If we jettison the so far unworkable proposal that moral theology is a series of deductions from doctrine (cf. Carney, 1978), and the unsatisfying one that ethics, doctrine, and 'foundations' simply deal with different subject matter, we have still the possibility that these three reflect three logical levels of penetration into the data of theology. All three, on this view, have the same subject—the convictions of the community in relation to all else; and all have the same object or goal—to provide a faithful yet transformative account of those convictions that cohere in a living community (McClendon and Smith, 1975:103). So all three have a common task—they properly constitute one system, one theology. Yet there is a difference in the insight each requires. On this view, we begin by finding the shape of the common life in the body of Christ, which is for Christians partly a matter of self-discovery, as Gregory learned from Origen. That is ethics. We continue with the investigation of the common and public teaching that sanctions and supports that common life by displaying its doctrinal height and breadth and depth. That is doctrine. And we end by discovering those apologetic and speculative positions that such life and such teaching call forth. That is philosophical theology or apologetics. Yet like the rest, the last-named of these, as Origen so clearly saw (*De Prin.* pref. i), is without value except as it leads back to the new that comes in Christ.

* * * * *

Theology's struggle is a hard one because we are divided both within and without. My sense of the new that has come to me in Christ Jesus necessarily conflicts with "another law at war with the law of my mind" (Rom. 7:23 RSV). I learn it is one thing to find the truth, another to live it. Meantime, however valiantly we struggle toward the truth that Christ has held out toward us, we cannot fail to be aware of others who in the name of the same Christ reach out toward other truths that cancel, challenge, contradict our own. Or so it seems. Such brotherly and sisterly adversaries provoke still another hard struggle. Yet has not past experience shown for this fight two constitutive rules that can guide us? One is what James M. Smith and I have called "the principle of fallibility." Simply put, it is that "*even one's most cherished and tenaciously held convictions might be false and are in principle always subject to rejection, reformulation, improvement, or reformation*" (McClendon and Smith, 1975:118). If that seems too harsh a rule to bear, here are two consolations that go with it: one is that of course the principle applies also to itself. And the other is that happily, it applies to our adversaries as well!

The other rule to guide our twofold combat in theology comes from old Roger Williams (1603?–1683) of Rhode Island, briefly a Baptist, long a baptist. As well as any American Christian who has lived, Williams knew both these battles, the one within and the other with his fellows. Himself a Cambridge University product, he spoke scornfully, even at the height of his own career, of those who arrogated to themselves alone, on the basis of such education, the title "scholar"—a term he felt belonged properly to "all believers and saints, who are frequently in the testament of Christ styled disciples or scholars of Christ Jesus, and only they as believers. And this title is so much theirs that both men and women, believing, were called 'scholars' "(Williams, 1652b:169). In that vein, Williams went on to express the second constitutive rule for theology in its struggles: *"It is the command of Christ Jesus to his scholars to try all things: and liberty of trying what a friend, yea what an (esteemed) enemy presents hath ever (in point of Christianity) proved one especial means of attaining to the truth of Christ"* (Williams, 1652a:29).

So we struggle in ourselves and with one another, "trying all things" (cf. 1 Thess. 5:21), never losing sight of the distant yet just visible goal, that unity of the faith that Ephesians calls "the measure of the stature of the fulness of Christ," and also full humanity (4:13).

What Is Ethics?

In beginning any study, it is helpful to know the meaning of the most fundamental terms employed, the present state of work in the field, and any distinctive approach to be employed by the author. To place the remaining chapters in this way is the business of this one. Placing will involve all three of the aspects just indicated, terms, present state, and my own approach, for as we will shortly see, these are intertwined with one another. As to basic terms, this is a study of Christian ethics. Now ethics and morals are related as theory and practice; thus "ethics" is the study (or systematization) of morals, while "morals" (or "morality") means the actual conduct of people viewed with concern for right and wrong, good and evil, virtue and vice. Thus "ethics" will generally (though not always) be used here of *theories* of morality, that is, of conduct or a way of life; accordingly "Christian ethics" will refer to theories of the Christian way of life. These words can be used in other ways; this will be my way.

These definitions are deliberately broad, and thereby I have violated the limits of ethics set by some theorists. A strong modern tendency is to focus exclusively upon the role of the human will in morality, and to say, correspondingly, that ethics consists of the study of the choosing *will* as it makes decisions. On this narrow view, morality consists just in making decisions, and ethics in saying how decisions are made, or how they ought to be made. Over against the modern focus on decisions as the essence of morality I will emphasize

47

instead the story-formed or narrative shape of the shared life of the Christian church. I hope to make good the claim for this broader understanding on grounds acceptable to any Christian, but I think there is a special compatibility between this emphasis and the "baptist vision" described in Chapter One.

To describe ethics, like all theology, as a struggle or contest (Chapter One) is particularly apt, for moral ground is, almost by definition, contested ground. As Aristotle put it, ethics is a subject in which much fluctuation of opinion is possible (*Eth. Nic.* 1094b). Or, in the language of the previous chapter, moral convictions are matters about which men and women cannot readily be persuaded to abandon their present views or to adopt new ones. In a contest, though, we ought to be fair to other entrants. Many names of other ethicists will appear in the pages to come. Here it will suffice to mention two who typify today's Protestant and Catholic ethics, J. Philip Wogaman and Timothy E. O'Connell. From these, we can learn something of the opposition we face, for they represent two sorts of decisionism. The plan for the chapter then is (1) to examine the ethics of Wogaman the Protestant and O'Connell the Catholic, (2) to evaluate critically the decisionism they share, (3) to show a contrasting, biblical ethics consisting of three necessary interwoven strands or elements, and (4) to illustrate these three strands by noting an ethicist who has founded his work in each of the three—in order, Francis Wayland, Stanley Hauerwas, and John Howard Yoder. This three-stranded structure will then be unfolded in the body of the book, consisting in three parts, of three chapters each. Each part will contain a theoretical, a biographical, and an applicatory chapter. Finally, a chapter on the theory of narrative ethics and its justification will conclude this volume.

1.   Recent Christian Ethics

a. *A Protestant ethicist*—J. Philip Wogaman, Dean of Wesley Theological Seminary, published in 1976 *A Christian Method of Moral Judgment*, a book that brought together many of the characteristic features of recent Protestant ethical thought. Clearly written and sharply focused, Wogaman's book (together with O'Connell's Roman Catholic text) sets the stage for what follows here. The central feature of the moral life, as

Wogaman declares in his first chapter, is our immediate ability to choose, or decide, by an act of the will, together with our uncertainty about *what* to choose. This latter dilemma is seen as a feature of human nature itself: "there is less immediacy to our knowledge of the factual world than there is immediacy to our will" (1976:4). We often do not know what is best. Yet choose we do. Thus "moral commitment and ethical uncertainty," taken together, sum up the moral life. Wogaman's is not just the Aristotelean point, mentioned above, about ethics as a realm in which more than one opinion is possible. Rather it is the more unsettling claim that the world a moral man confronts is *always* morally ambiguous. We might say an 'uncertainty principle' dominates Wogaman's ethics. Or, in Pincoffs' phrase, here is "quandary ethics," indeed! (Pincoffs, 1971).

Given the dilemma of committed Christian wills unable surely to discover the good to which they are committed, the problem Wogaman's ethics addresses, and his formal thesis, can quickly be stated. The problem he confronts is how to make appropriate moral judgments in such a climate of necessary uncertainty. Various recent Protestant thinkers (Wogaman singles out Joseph Fletcher, John Bennett, Paul Ramsey, and Walter G. Muelder) have offered partial solutions to this predicament, but Wogaman thinks none has been altogether satisfactory, and his own proposal will go beyond these to form "a *Christian* method of moral judgment."

This method itself depends upon the concept of *presumption*, a term used in the same sense as in "the presumption of innocence" in courts of law, with its corresponding "burden of proof." By setting out a series of moral "presumptions," Wogaman would teach us how to make Christian moral judgments. Thus, for example, the "four positive presumptions of Christian faith" are "(i) the goodness of created existence, (ii) the value of individual life, (iii) the unity of the human family in God, and (iv) the equality of persons in God" (1976:104), while the "negative presumptions" are the "human finitude" and "human sinfulness" that together entail the necessity of doing evil in this world. From these positive and negative presumptions it follows, for example, that should we wish to take human life, or to treat persons unequally, the burden of proof is on us to show why in this case we must do so. Although this will come out more clearly later, it is worth emphasizing that taking human life, etc., is by no means forbidden in Wogaman's ethics. Rather one must be prepared with reasons to show why in a particular case the burden of proof *can* be borne and the presumption (e.g., against killing someone) overturned—a very different requirement. Yet even here, something is forbidden and inflexible: there can for Wogaman be no relaxation of the requirement that one must have *good reasons* for such 'counterpresumptuous' acts.

But we get ahead of the story. Besides "positive" and "negative" presumptions, there are three other sorts: "polar presumptions" (which, like Aristotle's mean, warn us against an all or nothing approach in certain realms of life, such as the realm of freedom and responsibility—each requires the other); also "presumptions of human authority" (to whom must we defer, when it comes to moral judgments?); and "ideological presumptions" (in one chapter Wogaman claims that liberal democracy and perhaps welfare capitalism are to be presumed the best ideologies for Christian social thinking). Wogaman believes that "the moral life largely consists of the attempt to build one's whole life-style around faithfulness to such presumptions." But that is for him a half-truth. For to speak of presumptions is to imply exceptions. At law, the presumption of innocence implies the possibility of guilt. So beyond the initial statement of his presumptions, Wogaman's energies, the real drive of his book, are devoted to showing when and where and how the Christian *may* find exceptions to the guidelines laid down by the presumptions themselves. Thus "peace" and "faithfulness in marriage" and "truthtelling" may all sooner or later become dubious, and "some kinds of exceptions may be advisable," though the exceptions themselves will be subject to the criterion of gaining "more good . . . by making an exception than by remaining truthful" to the original presumption (1976:49-51). So the upshot of Wogaman's decisionism is the belief that we *can* weigh and measure the consequences of our action—a belief, it might seem to some, sadly inconsistent with the original uncertainty principle of his ethics.

What makes this 'consequentialism' even more like modern utilitarianism—and in my judgment, even less like New Testament ethics—is its bold insistence that the method of presumption will frequently enough lead us to do evil: to do it that good may come. Before we can exclaim with the apostle Paul "God forbid" (μὴ γένοιτο, Rom. 6:1f.), however, we should in fairness hear Wogaman's argument for his position. He admits, to begin, that the "earliest" Christian writings, that is, those of the New Testament, were strongly "perfectionist," a term he uses to characterize those who reject the doctrine of doing "necessary evil" as part of the Christian life (Wogaman, 1976:117). From the later patristic writers on, however, he says that there were those whose interpretation of the fall of man from Eden's innocence entailed the necessity of Christians' sometimes doing evil "if even greater evils are to be prevented." And this view is the "majority report" of most Christians throughout history.

My own view is that, however important majority reports may be, we ought to be exceptionally careful about taking sides against the New Testament, especially if the theological argument that leads us to do so leans heavily on the Constantinian era and region of church history (Europe from 300 to 1900?) and on philosophical utilitarianism. To be sure, Wogaman does have a powerful argument on his side: the ubiquitous presence of evil in the world. If so much is done that is evil, must not God intend Christians to do it, too? (A nice logical exercise that will be left to the reader is to ask the sense of "necessary" in "necessary evil." Does it mean "prescribed," or "ordained," even "entailed"? Or just "existing," "widespread," or "common"?) On the other hand, Wogaman senses the difficulty in his view. This is shown by the space he devotes to controverting those baptists and others who hold, with John Howard Yoder, that while it will indeed be necessary for Christians to *suffer* evil, there is no Christian reason to *do* evil. In fact, Yoder and other "Christian perfectionists" are singled out in the book as Wogaman's chief opponents.

To be sure we might ask, What of the case where worse consequences come from right than from wrong? We must raise that issue when we discuss Yoder's ethics. Meanwhile, let us summarize Wogaman's stance as so far presented. It is this: The Christian life can be indicated by a series of (positive, negative, etc.) presumptions, all of which will have exceptions, and morality consists in making the judgments that sort out the exceptional cases. Taking the consequences of these judgments into account inevitably requires Christians to do evil "that good may come." Now we can add a final step: Making such judgments links together Christian ethics and the doctrine of creation. The Christians' way of being responsible is to take charge of the whole world, when and as they can, and to direct the course of history. Thus "creation" is probably the most important doctrine as far as ethical method is concerned, for this doctrine, Wogaman believes, leads directly to the necessity for Christians to use the world's ways (the only ones there are) in order to accomplish, sometimes through evil means, God's purposes (1976:62-70; 185-93).

Now we have the full picture. To express it rather differently in summary, Wogaman's surface thesis is that Christian ethics requires placing the burden of proof in moral judgments against any action that would stray from the "presumptions" of Christian morality. So stated, it is a thesis about how to form judgments for future action. But what we might call his deep theses are three: (1) that the content of Christian ethics can be well expressed in a few *propositions* about persons, evil, ideology, and the like; (2) that the stuff of Christian morality, its essence, consists in making *decisions* in light of these propositions; and (3) that these decisions while inevitably involving us in doing evil "that good may come," fulfill the Christian responsibility to *organize the world*. To speak a bit too sharply, it seems that in Wogaman's ethics the kingdom of God has become the kingdoms of this world, rather than the other way around—and that without benefit of eschatology!

b. *A Catholic ethicist*—Whatever weakness we may sense in Wogaman's position, it nevertheless has the virtue of representing well the present Protestant (especially American Protestant) standpoint. Until recently, it might not have been possible to find so representative a Catholic work in our era, since rapid changes are currently taking place in Catholic moral theology. Happily, there has lately appeared Catholic seminary professor Timothy E. O'Connell's *Principles for a Catholic Morality* (1978), incorporating the recent developments. As Charles Curran says in the book's foreword, "O'Connell combines the strength of the manualist tradition [Curran is referring to the traditional post-Tridentine Catholic manuals]—clarity, order, and precision—with the content of the new approaches."

These are indeed O'Connell's traits. He names the kinds of sources on which Catholic moral theology must depend: human wisdom (significantly first), insights from the sciences, history or tradition, Scripture, and dogmatic theology. His book is divided into the two main parts, dealing with subjective morality (the human person, the *subject* who makes moral judgments) and objective morality (the moral *world*, which gives objective content to morality). A survey of these two will prepare us for a critical estimate of O'Connell's approach.

The first main section, "The Moral Person" (1978:Part II), takes three consecutive steps. The first is to report on the manual tradition of Catholic ethics with regard to the self, human action, free will and its impediments, mortal versus venial sin, and the means by which the latter may be distinguished. The second step is to set forth recent (and especially European) developments in Catholic ethical thinking, claiming that in all important respects the new theology (J. Fuchs, B. Haering, *et al.*) incorporates, while improving on the vital features of, the manual tradition. Briefly put, the new tradition views one's life not as so many isolated acts but as a continuous whole, marked by a "fundamental stance" toward God or the world—a stance that may sometimes be altered (or confirmed) by a "fundamental option" or choice that significantly indicates one's basic orientation. A "positive" fundamental option is called a conversion, while a "negative" fundamental option is equivalent to falling into, or continuing in, mortal sin. A main difference in the manuals and the new understanding is that in the former, mortal sin is chiefly determined by the "matter" (for example, is this adultery? is it murder?), while in the new, the whole drift of a particular life must be considered, and not single acts alone. Thus trivial sins may be 'mortal' ones, and 'grave' sins may (in a given life) finally be insignificant because no fundamental option is then and there involved.

And finally, O'Connell's third step is to claim that since God's grace is everywhere, these same (step two) standards apply to all people everywhere, quite apart from any hearing of the gospel of Christ. Thus *anyone's* life may express a negative fundamental stance (and by the doctrine of original sin, everyone's does), but thanks to ubiquitous grace, anyone may exercise a positive fundamental option, and many do: "whosoever says 'yes' from the depths of his being to anything, says 'yes' to everything. . . . In the deepest sense of the word, they have been saved" (1978:105f.). "Saved," in this case, without the gospel, without faith in Christ, without discipleship, without the way of the cross! Here moral universality has been purchased for Christian ethics, but at the expense of the ("spare, strange") particularity that comes from Jesus of Nazareth and his Way. Thus in a (carefully qualified) sense, O'Connell's subjective ethics comes down to following conscience (1978:88-93), for after all, the doctrine of incarnation teaches that Jesus' great achievement was merely and fully to be *human:* Christian ethics is therefore "a human task seeking human wisdom about the human conduct of human affairs" (1978:40).

Thus when we turn to the second main part of O'Connell's text, "The Moral World" (1978:Part III), we are well prepared to learn that the objective moral world of Christians consists not in the new that has broken upon them in Christ Jesus (cf. 2 Cor. 5:17; Gal. 6:15), nor even in the ordered ongoing world of the Catholic Church, with its traditions and customs, its dynamism and its destiny—but in the ubiquitous law of nature, the natural law. Morality is certainly not just our conscience; it is not (at another extreme) merely the arbitrary commandments of God; but it is *the way things are,* as that reflects God's own nature apprehended by intelligent human reason. In this way morality has objective status, and the various kinds of human law—in Scripture, in the gospel's "law of the Spirit," and in the laws of civil community—can be interpreted as ways of realizing or fulfilling the law of nature (1978:chs.12, 18).

So it is essential to be clear about what O'Connell means by natural law itself. Of two traditions of natural law, that of the Stoics (and Ulpian), which emphasized the inexorable, given content of the moral order, and that of Cicero (and Isidore of Seville), which viewed natural law as essentially the human capacity to think reasonably about moral matters, O'Connell favors the latter. This 'law' is real or objective, but it is flexible, historical, based on changing human experience and its capacity to think things out. In O'Connell's formula, natural law is "real, experiential, consequential, historical, and proportional" (1978:144).

To concede so much to human reasoning, however, makes it doubly important to show how "objective" law is different from "subjective" conscience. O'Connell's answer to this question lies in his terms "consequential" and "proportional." He means by the former that "what makes things right or wrong is precisely and solely the fact that they truly help or hurt the human persons that inhabit this world" (1978:144). In other words, the test of what natural law teaches about human conduct is "precisely and solely" the *consequences* of that conduct. And by "proportional," O'Connell means that, since in this world we cannot merely do good and avoid evil, we must be prepared to do evil "that good may come of it"—but in doing so, we must do what results in the greatest good and the least evil (1978:152f.). Shades of Wogaman! And once again, shades of utilitarianism, with its twin principles of "the greatest good for the greatest number," together with a prudential calculus, the "proportion," for reckoning what that good is, case by case. For this reckoning is exactly what, according to O'Connell, the natural law comes to. It is not a law that ever requires us simply to *do* this or that or the other. For there are, as with Wogaman, always the exceptions, always the hard cases—and then once more we may be required to do evil that good may come. It begins to seem a theme of recent Christian ethics!

In sum, the picture of Catholic ethics presented by O'Connell is one full of unresolved—and perhaps unresolvable—tension. On the one hand there is the dominant decisionism of our age, treating the moral life as consisting primarily in prudent judgments. Even more explicitly than in Wogaman's book, these judgments, though it is said they reflect "natural law," come down for O'Connell to a kind of utilitarianism: doing good or evil as required that more good may come. As in Wogaman's ethics, Jesus' own story plays only a small role here (O'Connell, 1978:40, 215f., note 7; cf. Wogaman, 1976:117-31). Neither of these writers finds a way to make Jesus of Nazareth fully relevant to our so different times.

On the other hand, there are in the O'Connell text some profound if subordinated themes that might, if developed, have overcome its dominant decisionism. His discussion of fundamental stance might unfold into a genuine narrative moral theology. There is a short chapter on character and the Christian life that goes well with this latent theme (1978:ch. 10). There are passing remarks that cohere with the great Edwardsean vision of the moral life as consent to being. And the attention to law as an ethical theme might have been, but is not, developed into a distinctively Christian social ethic. Thus O'Connell's book, poised between a rich tradition and the dominant idols of the age, offers much that is trendy, but much that is full of promise, as well.

2. From Decision to Story

a. *Decisionism*—What's wrong with decisions as the substance of morality? Certainly in other realms decision making
is given high billing. Doctors decide, and lawyers, and
merchant chiefs. Why not the moral self? Is not "the hour of
decision" all-important? What can morality consist in, if *not* in
decisions? That we find these questions natural, even
unanswerable, may say more about our times, our *Zeitgeist*,
than about Christian ethics. The dawn of our era in the North
European Renaissance brought a strong new emphasis upon
the *will* in human nature. This emphasis was, to be sure, as old
as the Hebrew prophets, but for the men and women of the
Renaissance the will arose with a strange fascination, like a
malevolent beast from the abyss. Marlowe's Doctor Faustus is
a character in whom not knowledge but the lust for it is
revealed as ruinous. Shakespeare, in *Julius Caesar*, paints
portraits of men in whom the will to power or its fatal converse
shapes destiny. For the Elizabethans, 'ambition' was a vice, for
beneath it lay a power they could little understand but knew to
dread—the unruly human will. And it is at least worth noting
that *Lady* Macbeth is perhaps Shakespeare's purest incarnation of this chaotic force.

Little wonder, then, that when the eighteenth century
sought to impose order on the world it had inherited from the
Renaissance, the moral government of the human will would
be seen as the chief task of the Enlightened intellect. Thus
Immanuel Kant (1724–1804), master philosopher of the
Enlightenment, found the locus of morality to be the direction
of the transcendent human will in accordance with the
categorical imperative, and held that in a world of radical evil
the only truly good thing was a good will. And to shorten a
complex story, when William James (1842–1910) sought the
vital nerve by which he himself might be roused from
impotence to vibrant action, the ganglion of selfhood that he
seized was precisely the self-direction of the will by an act of
will. Dangerous will, purely good will, impotent will—the
history of moral philosophy for five centuries parallels the
changing concept of the human will.

All that remained for recent ethicists was to localize those
primal acts of will in *decisions*, and to say that *morality consists in*

decision making. The perfect expression of this last stage may be found in Jean-Paul Sartre (1905–1980), the French existentialist, for whom true morality consisted not in deciding this or that, but purely and merely in deciding. Decide, and you have acted morally, while not to decide is—bad faith (1943/1957:47-72).

The two chief sorts of decisionism, however, come from the eighteenth century. One is *utilitarianism,* whose distinctive creator was an English student of law, Jeremy Bentham (1748–1832). He presented two fundamental doctrines. One is the principle of utility or welfare or pleasure: We act in order to attain the perceived good, and that good, according to Bentham, is our own *happiness* (hedonism), though this may be conceived in more than one way by utilitarians. The other is the hedonic *calculus:* Human pleasure in any given set of circumstances may be quantified and calculated by summing up the pleasure to be realized by each in any proposed action. Suppose that I am deliberating whether to take my little niece, Erica, to the circus. I apply the calculus: To her very great pleasure, assign +5 units. To my own mild inconvenience, −2. To the relief her mother will feel in getting the little brat off her hands for the afternoon, +3. To expense of tickets and refreshments, estimated at $38, assign −4. To benefit to the circus of two extra patrons, +1. Slight risk of harm to self or to niece, −1. The net value is +2, so a utilitarian (happily, we presume) takes his niece to the circus. And the utilitarian claim is that such a decisionist calculus will be the guide to life (Alston, 1967).

At the other end of the spectrum of decisionism stands the moral philosophy of Immanuel Kant. Here the question will be not, What *good* may I achieve, but, What is *right* in itself? To find the right and to act on it from the motive of a purely good will is to walk the path of moral duty. For example, I must not lie. Confronted with temptation to do so, I sense the categorical imperative as the claim upon my will. I ought to tell the truth for truth's sake. With that pure motive, without self-interest, I decide to tell the truth; morality has prevailed. These two schemes, the consequentialist and the deontological, seem to differ at almost every point; what interests us now, though, is what they have in common: morality as deciding.

To see how this decisionist emphasis captured Christian ethics, still another development must be recognized. The same centuries that saw the growth of the emphasis upon the will in human nature brought also an intense interiorization of Christian life. Puritanism, pietism, revivalism—all emphasized the inner struggles of the soul. Krister Stendahl, a Lutheran scholar, has shown in an important essay, "The Apostle Paul and the Introspective Conscience of the West" (1976), how little this interiorization is biblical and how much it is due to Augustine and Luther. We misread Romans 7, Stendahl argues, if we fail to see that Paul was a Christian (and Jew) of robust conscience, whose concern in that famous chapter was with the place of the law since Messiah has come—and *not* with the (Lutheran) role of conscience in leading sinners to the gospel. It was through Augustine, not Paul, that the introspective interpretation of justification by faith was first sounded, and it was through Luther, an Augustinian monk deeply enmeshed in the practice of penance, that this introspective conscience became the standard hermeneutic by which, says Stendahl, *we* read the whole New Testament—and misread Paul. He goes on to claim that the introspective approach, once it has entered the stream of history, is inescapable. We cannot like Paul be men and women of robust conscience; our questions must be Augustine's and Luther's, for we live in the modern West.

However that may be, see how the emphases upon will and inwardness converge in the concept of deciding. Originally "decide" and its Latin original meant "to cut off"—to end a battle by a 'decisive' victory, or to settle a lawsuit with an award to one of the contestants. Hence the word implied (1) a struggle, and (2) its termination. Then the same word was applied to an interior 'battle' in which the mind wavers until one 'side' of the mind overcomes the other—as in the uncertainty of a lover torn between two loves. So "decision" comes to mean the end of an *inner* contest. Unquestionably, such inner struggle is a recurrent feature of human life. But in modern Christianity, the new exaltation of the will, together with the interiorization of the Christian life, made it seem that such struggles are not part but the whole of morality—as if being continually divided against itself were the soul's main business, as if a self divided were the normal moral status of the Christian life. My point is not to deny that such "sick souls" (Wm. James) exist, but to ask whether their perpetual sickness is the moral norm of the Christian life.

Some recent ethicists, at any rate, have entered a strong dissent. Dietrich Bonhoeffer, with perhaps typical German abruptness, argued that the very idea of ethics as *our* knowing good and evil is the sign and consequence of the fall away from our primal unity with God. This fall is represented in the Eden story as the eating of forbidden fruit. Its effect is that we usurp the place of God ("you will be like God, knowing good and evil" Gen. 3:5 RSV); we take to ourselves the divine role of choosing and become the source of moral decisions rather than the objects of God's choice for us. To know good and evil, to be *ethicists*, to choose—these are the marks of our *fallen* creaturehood (Bonhoeffer, 1949/1965:17-20). And on the other hand, in Christ's redemption, the single-minded one (James 1:8) is freed from that spurious 'knowledge.' "Not fettered by principles, but bound by love for God, he has been set free from the conflicts of ethical decisions" (1949/1965:68). Perhaps this seems one-sided, but it does point to a Christian morality other than decisionism.

For the present argument is not that no Christian ever need decide: there are perplexities, there is surely temptation; our minds are sometimes divided. It is only to claim that decisionism with its entailed voluntarism and interiorization cannot be an adequate or full account of the moral life. As clearly as anywhere, this can be seen in the great sheep and goats judgment parable of Matthew 25. There, when the righteous are summoned to inherit the kingdom, they are startled by the recital of their deeds of love and mercy. So far from having been deliberate and calculated acts of moral decision, their conduct, insofar as it reflected their destiny, seems to have been constituted by deeds that unconsciously registered their character and their faith: "Lord, when saw we thee hungry, and fed thee? or athirst, and gave thee drink?" (25:37 ASV). The King's judgment is based, not on their deliberate decisions if any, but on their unreckoned generosity, their uncalculating love, their 'aimless' faithfulness.

b. *The Bunyan narrative*—But the Christian alternative to decisionism may better be represented by a life story than by a parable. Consider a writer who stands in a truly borderline position between the medieval world and our own, John

Bunyan (1628–1688), the Bedford tinker, roisterer, convert, baptist preacher, and prisoner for the sake of conscience. In Bunyan we find a theologian (Greaves, 1969) who embodies the psychology of Western introspection, but who has retained or recovered an outlook sufficiently biblical to save him from subjective decisionism.

Bunyan's two best known works (among fifty or more) are his autobiography, *Grace Abounding* (1666), and his allegorical novel, *The Pilgrim's Progress*, completed in 1684. These should be read together, not only because together they establish his reputation as the earliest master of English narrative prose, but because they show the inside and the outside of Bunyan's storied conception of the Christian life.

There is indeed an inner side to the Christian story. *Grace Abounding* is the account of a conversion almost purely Augustinian and Lutheran in its onset of guilt, its struggles, its accession of grace, and its continuing dynamic of struggle and relapse and renewed grace. At its outset, Bunyan acknowledges the inevitable judgment of the world: This will be called the tale of an unsound mind. Indeed, what keeps it from being just that is the outcome—the richly redemptive life that issues from the struggle. The symbolic outer sins that are the counters in this fierce spiritual battle—swearing, dancing, bell-ringing—are, like Augustine's stolen pears, the tokens of titanic inner struggles.

After he relates being driven to agonies of conscience over whether he should, at an inner urging he later recognized as Satanic, drop his food while he sat at table and rush away to pray, Bunyan goes on to tell of a morning when,

. . . as I did lie in my bed, I was, as at other times, most fiercely assaulted with this temptation to sell and part with Christ; the wicked suggestion still running in my mind, Sell him, sell him, sell him, sell him, as fast as a man could speak; against which also, in my mind, as at other times, I answered, No, no, not for thousands, thousands, at least twenty times together. But at last, after much striving, even until I was almost out of breath, I felt this thought pass through my heart, Let him go, if he will! And I thought also, that I felt my heart freely consent thereto. Oh, the diligence of Satan! Oh, the desperateness of man's heart! (1666/1969:§139)

What saves these agonies from bathos, gives them an almost biblical flavor, distinguishing them from Kantian writhings after pure conscience and Benthamite calculation of the pains and pleasures of taking little Erica to the circus, is I believe twofold: On the one hand, Bunyan's interiority is made vivid by being linked to a whole life story which we learn as we read *Grace Abounding;* on the other, the struggles are directly linked to the central issue, to the question of his life-changing conversion and union with Christ.

This double linkage becomes explicit in *Pilgrim's Progress.* In its two parts, the Christian life is unfolded in a journey of pilgrims from the City of Destruction to the Celestial City. The allegory is at once (1) realistic, earthy narrative of an imaginary journey, (2) the symbolic representation of the life journey of any Christian pilgrim, and (3) a recall of the link between that life journey and the Scripture story. In the weaving together of these three, the symbols (characters with names like Pliable and Mr. Worldlywiseman, a county fair called Vanity, companions named Faithful and Mr. Greatheart, a wicket gate, a burden, a cross) together form links between interiority and realism and biblical story, making of these one vision (cf. Chapter One, above).

But again Bunyan's own dialogue may better convey the flavor. Bunyan tells how as Christian advances toward the heavenly city he is met along the way by two men who have turned back in terror. They describe the scene that lies ahead.

CHR.   But what have you seen? said Christian.
MEN.   Seen! Why the valley itself, which is as dark as pitch; we also saw there the hobgoblins, satyrs, and dragons of the pit; we heard also in that valley a continual howling and yelling, as of a people under unutterable misery, who there sat about in affliction and irons; and over that valley hangs the discouraging clouds of confusion; death also doth always spread his wings over it. In a word it is every whit dreadful, being utterly without order.
CHR.   Then said Christian, I perceive not yet, by what you have said, but that this is my way to the desired haven.
MEN.   Be it thy way; we will not choose it for ours. So they parted, and Christian went on his way, but still with his sword drawn in his hand, for fear lest he should be assaulted.
                                                    (1684/1969:129)

And the journey goes on. Bunyan's own life story, here so fleetingly indicated, seems to me to represent well the true place of decisions in the moral life. They are not everything there. Some decisions are spurious—the devil's word, Bunyan said. And others are evanescent, as O'Connell has also recognized, being no part of a Christian's fundamental stance. But what of that one great decision, when the pilgrim stands at the foot of the cross, and the burden of sin rolls away to disappear into the empty tomb (1684/1969:113)? That decision, Bunyan would be the first to say, is in no straightforward way one's own, for the 'I' that might have decided is the 'I' that ever refused the way, the truth, the life, whereas the 'I' that is created in that decisive moment is, as Bonhoeffer also saw, God's election, not our own. So Bunyan's narratives point us away from moral decisionism, but toward a Christian life where vision and community and hope converge in the disciples' way. As Valiant, one of Christian's companions, sings in *Pilgrim's Progress:*

> Hobgoblin nor foul fiend
> Can daunt his spirit;
> He knows he at the end
> Shall life inherit.
> Then fancies fly away,
> He'll fear not what men say,
> He'll labour night and day
> To be a pilgrim.
>   (1684/1969:299)

3.   *Three Strands of Christian Ethics*

So far the work of this chapter has been mainly negative. I have argued that decisionism in whatever form, situationist or 'presumptive,' Kantian or utilitarian, Protestant or Catholic, provides an insufficient and thus misleading account of the moral life of Christians. But the argument is incomplete unless it can be shown in what that moral life does consist. To point to this is the business of this section. Christians are a people formed by their shared convictions. As participants in a common story, they are bound together by convictions, moral convictions, about God and neighbor, about self and community, about where they have been and whither they are bound. Christian ethics must display the grammar of these convictions, or, to change the metaphor, must reveal the structure of the shared Christian story, if it is to offer critical insight about the moral life. It must provide moral theologians, at every level of skill, with analytical concepts by which to discover, interpret, and transform the convictions that shape their Christian story (cf. Chapter One on convictions).

One way to bungle this task is to make the substance of Christian morality too simple. My first, best teacher of ethics, Thomas Buford Maston (1897–), wrote a book nearly twenty years ago, surveying the ethical teaching of the Bible. At the end, he summarized his conclusions. One of these was that "the biblical ethic is so deep and broad, as is true of the Christian life in general, that it cannot be described adequately by the use of any one term." Maston recites a number of popular mottoes (biblical ethics as "covenant," or "koinonia," or "love," or "will of God," or "kingdom," or "eschatological," or "perfectionist," or "disciples'," or "Holy Spirit," or "holiness," or "cross" ethics), only to reject each as incomplete (1967:286). More generally, attempts in Christian ethics to found everything upon some *one* principle, whether duty, or law, or love, or hope, have proved disappointing, not only to Maston, but to most laborers in the field.

Another strategy has been to provide a typology of historic sorts of Christian morality: H. Richard Niebuhr attempted this twice, first in *Christ and Culture* (1951), and later in *The Responsible Self* (1963). But aside from the sharp critiques that Niebuhr's earlier typology has justly evoked (Yoder, 1964; Scriven, 1985; cf. McClendon, 1978), there is the deeper question of what themes all biblical and Christian ethics must have in common. In other words, what must Christian ethics be to be *ethics* (Williams, 1972), and what must it be to be *Christian* (Gustafson, 1975)?

Many writers have detected a threefold complexity in Christian morality. For some (e.g., Kierkegaard, 1845/1940), three elements were represented as three stages on life's way, for others (e.g., Rauschenbusch, 1968:32) as three dimensions of the kingdom, for others still (e.g., H. R. Niebuhr, 1963) as three kinds of symbol by which the human animal shapes his conduct. For Karl Barth, ethics is related to the three great doctrines, creation, reconciliation, redemption, that organize his *Church Dogmatics* (1936–69). And there are still other triads. Are these various threes just identical? I think not. Have they anything to do with the divine Trinity? At least not in every case, though inevitably someone will try to make out a fit. What they do confirm is that there is an inherent complexity in Christian moral life not safely to be disregarded by those who want to get the story straight.

Let me offer, then, my own analysis of the complexity. Adapting an image from the philosopher Wittgenstein (1953:§67), consider a rope with (at least) three strands. Such a rope has no single strand that *is* the rope, or around which the others are formed—and there is no central, invisible core, either. The whole rope is nothing but the strands, yet none of them alone can do what the rope does. My proposal is that biblical morality be viewed as such a multistranded rope. So my task now is to identify all the strands (but only the strands) that work together to constitute the Christian moral life. As in other such efforts, the test of success will be the adequacy of the resultant account to the Christian moral life itself.

A good beginning place is the biblical story of the sacrifice or binding of Isaac told in Genesis 22. Many cultural and theological themes flow through this story—as we may imagine that many themes were internalized by that ancient pluralist, the patriarch Abraham. This complexity works to our advantage, though, in displaying within this story all three strands of biblical morality. Suppose we take up the story at the time when the young man, carrying firewood, and the old man, carrying fire and a knife, are seen toiling laboriously up the mountain. Why are they ascending? So that the old man can kill the younger one. Here the characters and perhaps the reader are engaged by the first strand. Kill the boy? Kill his son? But this is horrible! Surely the ethics of the human body itself will cry out in protest? But the march is not halted, and we may remember that in our psychic depths there is another voice than the voice of protest, namely the voice of paternal jealousy, of oedipal rage, that cries out in unconscious assent, "Go. It is delightful, virile, to kill one's son, one's only son!" There is between the generations a rivalry, an estrangement, a 'generation gap,' however it be construed. So there exist at this first level of morality conflicting signals. Strand one here asks a question it cannot answer: Shall Abraham and Isaac continue, or not?

Yet in the story Abraham's purpose is not merely to kill, but truly to sacrifice, his son, and that by God's own command (Gen. 22:2). Now for "sacrifice" and for "command" the first strand will no longer be adequate. For these concepts, we must reckon with culture, with community and its practices, with custom and law, in brief, with strand two. Indeed, we here encounter a complex of cultures, for Abraham was an emigrant and an immigrant, a truly transcultural figure. So the point of the story as it was first told may have been this: we Hebrews also practice sacrifice, but our God does not permit the sacrifice of a child (cf. Lev. 20:2-5; etc.)—though an earlier strand two (the ethic of Ur of the Chaldees?) had permitted that.

How, then, is strand two redesigned, and how in the story is the tension of strand one between generational love and strife resolved? That is answered in the climax: Abraham's knife is stayed by a voice from heaven, "Abraham, Abraham!" (22:11). The angelic voice brings resolution by introducing *a new element:* the old practice is forbidden, the old command annulled. Here is a ram for the sacrifice. This angel voice is the voice of God intervening to introduce a new state of affairs, a new human order, and this morally revisionary element in the story, here and more generally in Scripture, is what I will here and after call strand three. So now our thesis can be stated: All three of these strands are necessary to a truly biblical, a truly Christian morality; we cannot understand the moral life God gives, the life we are to share, without encompassing all three of them.

There is of course far more to say about this story than can be covered here (cf. Spiegel, 1967), even if we limit ourselves to the literature of ethics alone. Kierkegaard, for example, holds that the story's point is that God can command anything he likes, even something evidently immoral, and faith's task is merely to obey. Faith is taking God's orders, period. God can suspend ethics ("a teleological suspension of the ethical"), and in this story he does so for a while as a test of faith (1843/1952). Favoring Kierkegaard's reading is the strong emphasis in the present biblical text upon Abraham's obedience to God's command (22:15; cf. 1 Sam. 15:22). But is it so evident that obedience is 'beyond' morality? In our terms, for Abraham to obey God is exactly to participate in a certain way *in the second strand* of biblical morality. This obedience might seem baffling in strand-one terms, or in one aspect of strand one, but it is perfectly at home among the practices of strand two.

Another kind of objection comes from those who believe they know already the 'answer' to which the story points ("human sacrifice is wrong"—note the propositional form of the summary), and who are morally offended because in the story other possibilities are even treated as viable. But these critics make the mistake of splitting off the revisionary third strand from its roots in the other two. That is tantamount to disregarding human nature (strand one), and the received culture (strand two), whereas the story shows its biblical power exactly by regarding each of these, showing how by the grace of God they are transcended in the strand-three element of the story itself ("Do not lay your hand on the lad," 22:12 RSV). And for those who think such a call to transcendence belongs merely to antiquity and is hardly necessary any longer, let today's relation of parents and children or today's customs of human sacrifice—in war, in business, in the attitude to the unborn—be well considered. My claim, though, is not that this ancient tale solves all our moral problems, but that it displays a three-stranded breadth that is constitutive of the biblical style in morality.

This is to say, in other words, that we Christians find ourselves with three necessary ways of talking about morality, correlated with the fact that we are (1) part of the natural order, organic beings, bodies in an organic continuum, God's *natural* creation; but also (2) part of a social world that is constituted first by the corporate nature of Christian existence, the church, and thereby by our share in human society, God's *social* creation, as well; and (3) part of an *eschatological* realm, the kingdom of God, the "new world" (καινὴ κτίσις) established by God's resurrection of Jesus of Nazareth from the dead. I will call these three respectively the *body*, the *social*, and the *resurrection* strands or spheres of Christian ethics (cf. McClendon, 1978).

These three represent three ways, moreover, in which we have to do with God: (1) as creatures, embodied selves in an environment, we respond to our Creator; (2) as social persons, members of a society, we interact with our neighbors but also with God the Social Person who covenants, legislates, commands, governs, and reconciles; (3) as witnesses to the resurrection of Jesus Christ from the dead we live in the presence of One who makes all things new by his Spirit. In motto, then, God is for us the God of Adam, the God of the old and the new Moses, and the God of the risen Jesus Christ. And finally, the three strands also point to three ways in which Christians experience the moral world itself: (1) as the world of the embodied self in its organic continuity with all nature; (2) as the world of custom, covenant, law, practice, and social roles in which we find ourselves; (3) as the new world in formation, revised and under revision by the Spirit and power of the risen Christ.

The three parts of the book will offer a more exact explication of each of these strands. Here at the outset it is important to note carefully the integral character of the three: Each without the other two is not only partial but defective in itself, so that Christian moral thought has often gone astray by neglecting one or more of the strands. Thus Gnosticism neglected the first or body strand, Protestant individualism the social strand, and Catholic legalism has often gone wrong, not by emphasizing law, but by neglecting the revisionary resurrection strand. And again, we may detect moral heresy by finding some who base everything on just one strand: Christian hedonism (popular again today) on the first alone, for example, or situation ethics perhaps on the third, whereas the moral strength of Scripture's story lies in the integrity of the three. By way of a final illustration, once again left to the reader to develop, consider the correlation with these strands of the narrative of the temptations of Jesus in the Synoptic Gospels: (1) to turn stones to bread for the body; (2) to rule over society by serving Satan; (3) to risk all in an eschatological leap (Matt. 4:1-11 and parallels).

4. How Some Ethicists Go About Their Work

Still, someone may wonder, granting all the above, how are these three strands to be used in moral decision making? What is the outcome? Such a question cannot be answered, and indeed misses the point of what has preceded. Yet that the question will arise for many shows how strong a hold the voluntarist or decisionist picture has upon us. If an alternative picture is to appear, it must come from all the following chapters. For the present the best thing will be to end by showing how three moralists (each, as it happens, a sharer of the baptist vision) have gone about their work. By selecting one who starts with each of the three strands, we can begin to see the way three-stranded ethical analysis functions. This should serve as an aid in understanding what ethics is about if it is not about deciding.

a. *Francis Wayland*—The choice of Francis Wayland (1796–1865) as a representative strand-one ethicist is doubly useful:

He can both show us how such a grounding may be important in itself, and give us some idea of the nineteenth-century heritage of today's Christian ethics. Throughout that century, it was customary in America's colleges for the culmination of the curriculum to be a course in "moral philosophy." Usually it was taught by the college's clergyman-president. Wayland fulfilled this role at Brown University in Providence, Rhode Island, from 1827 to 1855, and his text, *Moral Science* (first edition, 1835) became the most popular work of its times in Christian ethics. De Tocqueville noted the primacy of ethics in American Christianity; courses in colleges such as Brown provided a main vehicle for that primacy.

It is worth noting at the outset the strong and persistent individualism in Francis Wayland's work. He followed the eighteenth-century practice of treating ethics as a branch of philosophy, not theology. Bible and gospel are not formally presupposed; instead, morality is simply ingredient to human nature, and more precisely, for Wayland, this is *individual* human nature. Individualism is implicit in the very terms he makes central: conscience, intention, discernment, impulse, passion, appetite, self-love, feeling, and virtue—the last construed as right action by the individual (Wayland, 1865:84-86).

Wayland, however, gave a characteristic shape to these elements. As the moral life begins, we find ourselves in such and such relations to God and to our neighbors. But to be aware of these relations—of being God's creature, or our neighbor's neighbor—is at once to be aware of an obligation to feel and act in appropriate ways (toward God, awe and obedience are appropriate; toward the neighbor, justice), and to be aware of an impulse to carry out the felt obligation. This sense of obligation, with its corresponding impulse to act, is what is meant by *conscience*. So conscience for Wayland is a faculty or feeling lying at the very center of the moral life (1865:45-83). (In making conscience central, Wayland was working in conscious opposition to William Paley's early utilitarianism, and in the footsteps of Joseph Butler.) So obligations arising from personal relations of various sorts are the stuff of morality, and conscience more or less correctly senses these obligations, and more or less effectively impels us to act upon them. Contingently, God has so ordered the world that to obey enlightened conscience makes for pleasure; to disobey it makes for pain. Thus the 'truth' in utilitarianism is acknowledged, while its 'error' is rejected: one must do right for conscience' sake, and not as utilitarians suppose for the sake of the anticipated happiness.

Conscience in our fallen state, however, is an imperfect faculty. Although its impulse is always to do right and not wrong, the impulse may not be felt, or not very strongly felt. Worse still, fallen conscience may fail even to discern what is right. The divine remedies for these failures are (1) natural religion, which teaches mankind about the evil consequences that follow upon wrong actions, and (2) revealed religion, the morality taught by God in the New Testament (1865:118-36). These do not supplant conscience; rather they progressively enable it to discover its duty. To the spelling out of these duties, Wayland devoted the balance of his text, never abandoning his original strong emphasis upon conscience and its demands.

While this form of first-strand emphasis already moves down the road toward decisionism, and while it falls far short of the biblical vision I hope to display in my own strand-one account in Chapters Three through Five, its emphasis on conscience does point to an august and irreplaceable element in the moral life. Conscience is fallible and it is finite, but it occupies a vital role in our moral development. The truly grave weakness of Wayland's ethics, however, is its inability to come to terms with the full dimensions of strands two and three. To be sure, conscience (strand one) worked for Wayland by perceiving existing social relations (our strand two). But he seems never to conceive that, as Reinhold Niebuhr was later to point out, the morality of groups may be something *sui generis*, of its own kind, and not just the morality of individual relations multiplied. And (far worse for a baptist theorist) Wayland seems grandly indifferent to the radical revision of morality entailed by the resurrection: for him, the New Testament ethic is merely the revelation of abiding human moral duties; morally speaking, an enlightened Stoic might have believed the same.

b. *Stanley Hauerwas*—Hauerwas (1940–) is preeminent among the moral theologians who are today in rebellion against decisionism and look to older traditions in moral philosophy (Aristotle, Aquinas, Edwards) while employing analytical philosophical techniques and a rich sense of social solidarity to construct a new understanding. An heir of the work of both of the Niebuhrs and of his own teacher James Gustafson, Hauerwas has benefited from Protestant training and from several years in a Catholic working context, but he has increasingly been captivated by the baptist vision in theological ethics (1981:6). He will serve as our illustration of work primarily grounded in strand two, the social strand of Christian morality.

This is not to say that Hauerwas has ignored decisionism. Instead, he argued in his doctoral dissertation that "situation-ists" and "contextualists" (two kinds of decisionist), while rightly maintaining the self-involvement implied in moral acts, had not seen the concept of the human self required by their own views. The self that acts, if it is moral, must be a self *capable* of action. But such action, as Aristotle and Aquinas knew, is inseparable from forms of human community—in particular, from shared forms of language and shared community convictions. And the notion of a responsible choice-maker or agent is tied to those continuities of selfhood that we call character. So the idea of moral choice, Hauerwas could argue, was meaningless apart from the sort of formed character in community that made 'free action' a logical possibility (1975:chs. 1–2; cf. McClendon, 1974:ch. 1). This set the stage for the central concerns of Hauerwas' subsequent work, which was to be occupied with the themes of virtue, character, and community in the context of the biblical narrative.

In developing these ideas, Hauerwas was attracted early to the work of British philosopher Iris Murdoch, whose important "Vision and Choice in Morality" (1946) had brought back into current discussion the Platonic theme of the contemplation of the good. But Hauerwas went beyond Murdoch in arguing that the vision that shapes the moral life of Christians is not only timeless contemplation of beauty or goodness, but a *narrative* vision, a sense of the continuing Christian story in which present-day Christians must participate (along with Jesus and the first disciples) if they are to develop character conformable to Christian faith (Hauerwas, 1974:ch. 2).

These themes come together in a programmatic essay in which Hauerwas draws a parallel between Christian ethics and the fable-novel by Richard Adams, *Watership Down* (1972). The rabbits in Adams' tale live in various warrens whose ways of life are shaped by the varied stories of rabbitdom that each warren remembers and retells (Hauerwas, 1981:ch. 1). Hauerwas is saying that the stories Christians remember and identify themselves with and repeat are formative not so much of discrete 'decisions' as of distinctively Christian ways of life, while these ways constitute community members as the people that they are. Jesus, for a prime example, does not merely teach the way—he *is* the way of life—and because of his solidarity with his community, the story Jesus lived out and bequeaths is not an individual but a *social* ethic. The moral distinctiveness of Christianity therefore lies in the inseparability of Jesus and the kingdom: he "is the *autobasileia*—the Kingdom in person" (1981:45; cf. 1983:ch. 5).

Since Hauerwas' work is still in progress it is difficult to make any definitive judgment on it as a whole. The most that I will attempt here is to point out some of its main themes and tendencies. In his most fully integrated work to this point, the textbooklike *Peaceable Kingdom* (1983), some of these tendencies are prominent. There is the theme of relativism: the admission (or assertion) that Hauerwas knows of no general or value-free standpoint from which to do ethics. There is no ethics in general; only ethics qualified by some adjective (e.g., Christian, liberal secular, etc.). Hauerwas believes that this fact does not subvert truth, but rightly forces any question about the 'truth' of morality into prior questions about the truthfulness, that is, the character, of the questioner (cf. Chapter Twelve, within). There are the themes of narrative and the centrality of Jesus in the formative master story of Christians, themes we have already touched upon. And then there is the theme, quite central for Hauerwas, of "the Servant Community," the church as the touchstone of Christian social ethics. This centrality has led some to characterize this ethics as "sectarian," but that term may easily be misunderstood if it connotes dogmatic narrowness of vision. The church is just that community in whose narrative shape people can discover who they are meant to be. Thus, disciplined by the church's casuistry, formed by its "spirituality of peaceableness," they can engage in the human quest for freedom and justice, equality and liberty, without losing sight of the point or end of the quest: the kingdom whose servants they are (1983:ch. 6).

Thus Hauerwas shapes a notion of Christian community at once conservative in its retention of the past and radical in its adamant challenge to the unstoried blandness (and the mortal terrors) of late-twentieth-century liberal individualism. He successfully moves across the line that separates the first from the second strands of Christian ethics. His work defends the moral uniqueness of the way of Jesus without surrendering its claim to truthfulness. Yet Hauerwas depends upon insights that he is just beginning to incorporate (see, e.g., 1983:87-91) into his work, namely those of strand three. For more about these we must turn to the writing of John Howard Yoder, as Hauerwas himself is inclined to do (Hauerwas, 1974:ch. 11).

There is, however, a further instructive comparison between Hauerwas and our strand-one exemplar, Francis Wayland. Both had been popular and successful teachers when they wrote. But a century separates them, and in that time there has been a great shift in the audience for Christian ethics in America. Wayland's tone is magisterial, displaying confidence that his "application of these self-evident principles" will meet with success. His audience, judging by his effectiveness in his day, was inclined to accept his personal link of learning and piety and "duty" much as he assumed. Hauerwas' convictions are quite possibly more profoundly biblical than Wayland's were, but in most of his writing he deliberately adopts the standpoint of one who seeks the truth of the Christian way from a position at the margins of that way—the standpoint of the half-Christian. An illustration of this rhetorical stance is Hauerwas' "Medicine as a Tragic Profession" (1977:ch. 14)—an essay originally given as an address to a doctors' convention. Built into the ethics of modern medical practice, Hauerwas there suggests, is the assumption that science can remedy all our ills. But, taken with the finitude and error that limit all human knowledge, this assumption yields a tragic state of affairs. Medicine "must necessarily fail," for the patient will sooner or later sicken and die (1977:202); thus the medical profession is in profound need of a moral community that can teach it how to sustain tragedy.

The "Medicine" essay does not go on to explore the ways in which Christianity may form such community, and in that sense it takes its stand, as said above, at the margins of faith. Thereby it shows how good ethical analysis can be good apologetics; it also shows how Hauerwas indirectly but effectively approaches as central the strand-two questions of Christian community.

c. *John Howard Yoder*—Yoder (1927–) is the *bête noir* of contemporary moral theology, especially of mainline Protestant ethics. Though his extensive work remains at this writing mostly unpublished, and though much of his teaching has been in a small midwestern Mennonite seminary, yet as we have seen, the influential Wogaman singles out Yoder among all his contemporaries for refutation. Again, Protestant James Gustafson says that "all constructive theology in the Christian tradition needs to be defined [over against this Yoderian] radical option" with its focus on discipleship to Jesus (Gustafson, 1981:75). While showing briefly what it is in Yoder's work that arouses such anxiety in these mainline hearts, I will also present him as a representative strand-three moral thinker, thus completing our sample.

Yoder published in 1972 a book, *The Politics of Jesus*, that epitomizes his ethical thrust. Contemporary ethicists, he charges, have proceeded on the assumption that for one reason or another Jesus of Nazareth is irrelevant to social ethics. Jesus as such is merely a "simple figure" from the past, or he mistakenly believed the world would soon end, or he was preoccupied with "religion" and the individual. Or (at the other end of the spectrum) Jesus was infinitely far above us and our human concerns, relativizing them all. Or again, times have changed; Christians now are responsible for the world as Jesus and the disciples were not. In any case, today's task is to reconstruct ethics on this side of the great chasm that is supposed to separate us from him (1972:ch. 1). Yoder challenges all this by insisting that it is out of touch with modern New Testament scholarship—he cites Bartsch and Brandon, Bultmann and Betz, F. C. Baur and M. Barth and a score of others to prove his point (1972:pass.).

The real Jesus was the eschatological Jesus. His mission was the inauguration of a new social order not comprehended by the old aeon; his message was "the kingdom coming"; his method was—the way of the cross, for his followers and for himself. Thus the ethics of Jesus was grounded and founded in eschatology, but that made him, not irrelevant, but immediately relevant to the prevailing social structures of his own day and equally relevant to those of our own. (How else explain that the authorities found it necessary to eliminate him?) Today's disciples are called to follow the way of nonviolent love (the way of the cross) in obedience to Jesus Christ as surely as were those of the first century. Such following will seem unrealistic from the standpoint of today's Constantinian 'Christendom,' but from the standpoint of "the original revolution," it is "the creation of a distinct community with its own deviant set of values and its coherent way of incarnating them." The church's business is first of all to be that 'deviant' community, that is, to be the church (1971a:28).

Yoder's opponents have complained that this picture of the church's task abandons responsibility for society. In assessing this charge, it is helpful to remember that Yoder is the scion of old-line Mennonites, and within that community has some-times been perceived as a troublemaker exactly because he has been so deeply committed *to* responsible social action. Yoder is no passive quietist. Rather, what is at issue here is what kind of social action is most truly responsible. Are Christians obliged, as Wogaman thinks, to try to run the world? Or are they, as Yoder thinks, to make their social witness in and to a world that is still (even though temporarily) under alien control? Is democracy, as Wogaman thinks Christians must "presume," the best form of government for anyone anytime, or is that, as Yoder believes, a Constantinian question for which there can be no New Testament answer? (Yoder, 1984:155). Yoder's view is deeply influenced by his eschatology—by a doctrine of two aeons, the old and the new, and by the idea of a Messianic community, the believers' church, that inhabits the new aeon while still confronting the old (1972:chs. 7–8). (Thus he grounds his ethics in strand three but immediately relates it to an ever being revised strand two, taking a less lively interest in strand one.)

As for the Wogaman claim that Christians must sometimes do evil because worse consequences would at those times come of doing good, Yoder simply denies that *Christians* have been charged with making the world come out right. Instead, we are commissioned to obedience, faithfulness to the Master, and it is God not we who must bear final responsibility for the strategy of dealing with the world by the way of the cross rather than by the ways of violence and its power (1972:110-14).

The obvious theological criticism of Yoder is that his ethics can have no room for tradition. The standpoint of the Radical Reformation (cf. Chapter One, above) seems to some to imply a denial of the value of church history. Yet that criticism somehow misses the mark; Yoder's doctoral training at Basel was in church history; he is a historian both by training and by disposition. It would be more accurate to say that he rejects the dominant developmental *view* of church history and tradition which holds that whatever 'the whole church' (really, European Christianity) has by now adopted must have been God's own plan. Clearly, Yoder's ethics is deeply critical of modern Christianity and its culture, yet his criticisms are themselves historical ones, depending strongly on the baptist vision of certain sixteenth-century Reformers as well as on biblical insights. But the fuller defence in this book of the viewpoint John Howard Yoder represents must come in what follows, especially in Part Three.

* * * * *

Indeed something like that could be said of this entire chapter. To some, the chapter may have seemed unfair. The decisionists are presented, but their case is not fully argued. Even the case against them is given only in outline. The three strands of the Christian narrative are limned in, and representative workers in each strand are named, yet many questions remain about these as well. The aim, though, has been to introduce, not to conclude. The best argument against decisionism will be, not to deny its partial truth, but to show a broader picture than it can of how that truth fits into the full picture of Christian ethics. These introductory pages on the three strands and their story could only begin to provide such an account. The task of the rest of the volume is to provide it more fully.

PART I

THE SPHERE
OF THE ORGANIC

Because God is not only infinitely greater and more excellent than all other being, but he is the head of the universal system of existence; the foundation and fountain of all being and all beauty; from whom all is perfectly derived, and on whom all is most absolutely and perfectly dependent; of whom, and through whom, and to whom is all being and all perfection; and whose being and beauty are, as it were, the sum and comprehension of all existence and excellence: much more than the sun is the fountain and summary comprehension of all the light and brightness of the day.

Jonathan Edwards, *The Nature of True Virtue*

All things counter, original, spare, strange;
*   Whatever is fickle, freckled (who knows how?)*
*   With swift, slow; sweet, sour; adazzle, dim;*
He fathers-forth whose beauty is past change:
*   Praise Him.*

Gerard Manley Hopkins, *Pied Beauty*

T H R E E

Body Ethics

All of us are conscious of compelling drives, needs, and functions that we locate in our bodily or organic existence. The moral problem, for Christians as for others, is what to make of these indications. Are they to be heard as the voice of God or as the temptations of the devil? Are they to be balanced with the claims of Christian community and divine revelation, or are they to be strictly subordinated to these claims? And even if we can cope with these questions, how are the organic signals themselves to be interpreted when they seemingly counter one another? For example, how is the voice of 'conscience' to be assessed when it cries out against other claims our bodies make? Or how is the sense of shame or guilt to be weighed against the sense of rational judgment? This chapter will seek to give a coherent account of the dimension of the Christian moral life in which such questions arise. In doing so, it may begin to provide an answer to the questions themselves.

There is a blindness upon Christian morality in connection with this strand, and it is this blindness, rather than any logical priority (for each of the strands presupposes the other two) that justifies our treating first what may else be overlooked. We Christians are too accustomed to believe that ethics has nothing to do with our bodies, their environment, our mutual needs, our delights and horrors, our organic selfhood in its context. Why this is so is a long story; part of the trouble has been a persistent misinterpretation of what Paul says about σάρξ (flesh). The body has been treated as the very enemy of

78

Christian ethics and the enemy of spiritual religion. There is a long history of ascetic dualism in both Catholic and Protestant thought that makes it very difficult to hear what the Bible has to say on the creaturely side of its message (Miles, 1981). As a consequence, part of the task of ethics in this strand is simply to show that our creaturely existence is morally legitimate, that "if a body meet a body," whether coming through the rye or coming through the pages of Christian ethical reflection, there is so far no cause for tears, but rather for natural delight. Meanwhile, from another source comes another sort of blindness. The eighteenth and nineteenth centuries saw a deification of Nature. To live according to one's nature—self-fulfillment—was often taken by Enlightened thinkers to be not merely a valued part, but the sum total of morality. And this ethic of "human potential" has even found its way inside the church and its practice of pastoral care. So the present chapter confronts a genuine problem of rethinking the morality of bodily creaturehood.

1. Black Religion as Embodied Ethics

Our attempt to locate and sense this strand of Christian ethics will be better aimed if we can relate it to the true story of a Christian community. I propose as a test case a significant baptist development, the history of black Christianity in America. The vivid evidence of the organic strand in this community of witness may lend realism to our sense of the strands, while reference to such a community will serve as a check on the theory to be developed following it.

We should recognize a danger in using this material in this way, the danger that a stereotype of black people as emotional or less rational than others may be perpetuated. I believe the stereotype is viciously false, but I risk its reappearance in order to seek the strength of the Christian reality present in Afro-American Christian life. And for once, even the stereotype may ironically serve a purpose by marking the path to the reality it conceals—the reality of a profound Christian presence. If this reality has remained unexamined, even unnoticed, by white Christians, perhaps the reason is that what white historian Donald G. Mathews says of black and white southern evangelicals in their formative period remains true today: "Most whites never achieved the religious maturity of their black fellow Christians" (1977:186).

Why the black church has been so often Methodist, Pentecostal, and Baptist, and so in present language broadly baptist, is frequently discussed without adequate answer, and something more will shortly be said in explanation. For the present it suffices to note that the origin of the black church in America cannot readily be dated. Blacks were present as indentured servants in the English colonies from 1619 on ("before the *Mayflower*"), but were from early on treated as slaves and as fit only for slavery. Their presence in white Christian worship services was sporadic—sometimes encouraged, sometimes forbidden. The first separate black church did not appear until 1773–75 (the Baptist church at Silver Bluff, South Carolina, across the Savannah River from Georgia [Raboteau, 1978:139]), and the first black general Christian bodies (denominations) did not appear in the North until Reconstruction. Yet when these bodies were finally formed in the South as well, they already represented a style of Christian life as distinctive and integral as that of any Christian people in history, with a unique way of worship and song, an established practice of mission and evangelism, a coherent sense of congregational life and ministry, and a distinctive ethic. Even today these facts are not generally known.

For the unfolding of this 250 years' achievement prior to 1865 often eludes the historian. Of the three general theories of black church origins—(1) borrowing from whites, (2) African survivals given a Christian overlay, and (3) indigenous development under conditions of slavery—each has some truth, and perhaps circumstances varied from place to place (Raboteau, 1978; Mathews, 1977:ch. 5). For present purposes, it is not necessary to settle the debate, but to point out what the debaters agree upon: that the form of black American Christian life, with its roots in both African traditional religion and in Christian history, has been distinctive, and remains so even to the present.

Without rehearsing that history here, it may be possible to recall some features that make it morally significant. Black religion has been *embodied* religion. That is, it has not been mere emotional compensation or an appeal to an otherworldly hope or to a spiritual existence apart from bodily life (which is not to say that it lacked the elements of the spiritual, the eschatological, or the compensatory). The issue of embodiment has been fought out over the interpretation of the spirituals, those sounding documents of slave religion. Some have seen the spirituals as primarily otherworldly, while others have read them as a code for slave rebellion and escape; "Steal away to Jesus" will easily bear both interpretations (Cone, 1972). But as LeRoy Moore, James Cone, and others have shown, the power of meaning in the spirituals lies exactly in their ambiguity: like all great poetry they mean more than any one interpretation can show. "Steal Away" *is* about secret slave meetings and the road to Canada; it is also about death and a final meeting with the Lord; but neither of these contravenes another message: The Christian beset by troubles can encounter the Lord now, here in this present embodied life, and can thus be redeemed from indignity and self-hatred and the curse of ongoing sorrow (McClendon, 1974:80-82).

Another way to put this is to say that black Christianity was and is *life-affirming*. This is less surprising, for "life-affirming" is one of the terms most used to characterize the tribal religions of West Africa, whence most slaves had been seized (Genovese, 1974:213). The spirituals, in text and even more in music, radiate this affirmation:

> You got a right, I got a right
> We all got a right to the tree of life.

This "right" is no product of constitutions and courtrooms, but (as the spiritual's evocation of the primal garden scene in Genesis 2:9 implies) is that elemental justice to which law itself must finally appeal.

Implicit in the mere possession of bodily life is its correlate, liberty. The evidence shows that the theme of life-affirmation was never absent from black Christian slaves. They were not given to suicide. Instead, there was the claim of freedom as an inherent right and somehow as a present possession as well.

> Before I'd be a slave, I'd be buried in my grave
> And go home to my Lord, and be free.

If, as some surmise (*per contra*, Lovell, 1972), this song originated after emancipation, it shows how ex-slaves reflected on the meaning of this deliverance: liberation was only what was implicit in the whole story. In the past dozen years, a new

"Black Theology" has appeared, appropriating the liberation theme and making it the center of a reinterpretation of black religion (see Wilmore and Cone, 1979). Liberation will engage us in the third strand of Christian ethics (Chapter Nine); here we may just note that the Liberation form of Black Theology has been criticized for its omission of other central black themes, such as the crucial importance of conversion experience (e.g., C. Cone, 1975; Moyd, 1979). Surely, if true, this is a startling neglect. Perhaps the omission can be explained, however, by noting what Albert J. Raboteau has called "the tangible, or 'sensuous' nature of the slaves' conversion experience" (1978:269). The former slaves interviewed in the documentary *God Struck Me Dead* tell stories of conversions that possess a pictorial, imaginal quality significantly different from white narratives of the same epoch. Consider this example:

Then, like a flash, the power of God struck me. It seemed like something struck me in the top of my head and then went out through the toes of my feet. I jumped . . . (Rawick, 1972:45)

Embodied religion, indeed, this! Yet for our purposes it may speak more eloquently than a library of theories. For here we meet the profound *theme of presence*—the presence of God to souls and of souls to God and one another. Here in the black conversion experience the data of African traditional religion assume new importance. In the African world view surveyed by John S. Mbiti (1969) and interpreted for westerners by John V. Taylor (1963), there is a primal vision of God and world and selves closer to biblical understanding than to the Cartesian world of Enlightened Christians. In the African view there is a wholeness, an interrelatedness, a participation by every part of the world in the whole. A tribe, or a family, or a man or woman can find peace only by such participation. In such a world it is possible to believe, indeed natural to believe, that one being is *possessed* by another, higher being—hence the fertile possibilities of witchcraft, the immoral appropriation of these powers for selfish gain; but hence also the possibility of an appropriate harmony with the cosmic totality—of possession by the Spirit of holiness (Mitchell, 1975:136-53).

Consider now the fact that in America the first numerically significant adherence of blacks to Christian faith occurred in

Virginia and the Carolinas in connection with the evangelical awakening of the late eighteenth century (Mathews, 1977:192ff.). Here was no catechetical instruction of the sort earlier offered slaves by Anglican masters on their plantations ("What is your duty?" "To obey my master."). Rather in the revivals whites and blacks alike were implored by hot-hearted preachers to forsake their sins and be converted to Christ and be filled with God's own Spirit. Is it not likely that the greater success of Baptists and Methodists in evangelization of blacks lay in the congruence of the conversion experience they made central with the concept of possession for which the African mind had made preparation? (Mathews, 1977:196). Were there not in the camp meetings and revivals the very elements W. E. B. DuBois was later to say were the essentials of black religion: "the Preacher, the Music, and the Frenzy"? (DuBois, 1902/1965:338). And does this central "frenzy" not point back once again to the deep strand of Christian life now under examination: true Christianity is never less than embodied religion, a religion of the body, in all its relations, all its presence to God and brother and sister and neighbor, all its world involvement, all its vulnerability to a cross—or to an 'owner's' lash?

This brings up a final aspect: black Christianity, because it is embodied religion and does not evade the task of presence, is uniquely *open to the depth of human suffering*. To be human is to suffer, but there are differences in the way men and women plumb the depths of suffering. Certainly there is no meaningful quantification of 400 years of black anguish, born of slavery and its long entail in American life, so as to measure it against Chinese or Armenian or Hebrew-Jewish suffering. Rather the claim to be made is qualitative: There is in the black experience a unique but in some degree communicable sense of the significance of what is suffered. "Were you there," asks the spiritual, "when they crucified my Lord?" And the implicit answer of the singers is, Yes, we were there. Blacks learned in their understanding of the Jesus story to see that what they endured was not meaningless, but that by each son and daughter of them it could be said, "In my flesh *I complete what is lacking in Christ's afflictions* for the sake of his body, that is, the church, of which I became a minister" (Col. 1:24-25a RSV). So we encounter two necessary aspects of the black gospel: that it is irreducibly narrative in form, and that, as has been earlier implied (Chapter One), in it the baptist vision appears again—the story *now* echoes the story *then, is* the story then. According to that gospel, Jesus' story is the story of each and every black slave who ever lived. And thus there sings out the message of the spiritual:

> Nobody knows de trouble I see,
> Nobody knows *but Jesus.*

And we are back again in the world of the New Testament, the world of the Psalms, the world of the wide biblical vision itself.

2. The Focus of Body Ethics

a. *Dietrich Bonhoeffer and 'the natural'*—It is one thing to remind ourselves of a story, even a true story that works as a parable, but it is another to say how that story yields insight for our theory about morality. So it may be worthwhile here to remind ourselves of some valid if limited attempts in modern Christian ethics to come to terms with the organic dimension which we also seek. We turn first to the posthumous *Ethics* of German Evangelical theologian Dietrich Bonhoeffer (1906–1945).

Two motives can always be detected in Bonhoeffer's ethical writing. One is evangelistic—to present Christianity in a mode intelligible to interested outsiders. The other is pastoral—to protect Christ's flock from the poison gases of ideology, in his case, Nazi ideology. Both these motives can be seen in the *Ethics*. In one of its segments, Bonhoeffer introduced the concepts of the "penultimate" and the "natural" 1949/1965: ch. 4). Justification (always the great gospel word for Lutherans) is the "last word" of God to the human situation. But that there is a last word of God implies that there is some other that is not the last. So there is also a *penultimate* realm in which God and his creatures are involved together. This is not a claim about the periods before and after 30 C.E., but about the history of each of us in the eyes of God. By each a way must be traversed; Luther had his time as a monk; Paul his life as a Pharisee. There is preparation as well as ultimacy, and so there must be an ethic of preparation. Thus there will be for the wise pastor a time to declare to prospective pilgrims of the Christian way God's forgiveness—and a time not yet to declare it.

(Bonhoeffer would later cite his own unwillingness to give his warders in the Tegel prison the 'Christian' comfort they pathetically sought from him.) There will be a time to proclaim God's judgment—and a time merely to express human sympathy with those trapped in sin. The Christian must be taught to traverse the penultimate as well as to be faced with ultimacy. Thus there is opened for Bonhoeffer a legitimate worldly realm that is not yet the realm of redemption achieved. This is the sphere of the *natural*. It is in this sphere that "the hungry man needs bread and the homeless man needs a roof; the dispossessed need justice and the lonely need fellowship; the undisciplined need order and the slave needs freedom" (1949/1965:137). The natural, as Bonhoeffer used the term, is not the creaturely merely, but the creaturely after the Fall; precisely, it is "that which, after the Fall, is directed towards the coming of Christ," while "the unnatural is that which, after the Fall, closes its doors against the coming of Christ" (1949/1965:144). To give bread to the hungry who have need is to prepare the way for the ultimate; to 'eliminate' the 'unfit' (as in the Nazi practice of euthanasia) is unnaturally to close the door upon Christ's way.

Two questions must be raised about Bonhoeffer's unfinished account. One is whether it tends to subordinate and thus to derogate the embodied needs of human selfhood. Would it have been adequate to the cry for freedom of black slaves—or the slaves in Hitler's infamous camps—to assign those cries to a preliminary (or "penultimate") moral realm? Are not such cries the very stuff of moral ultimacy? And this question only makes more vivid another: has Bonhoeffer not remained complacent in these pages toward the old division between a realm in the Christian's life that is properly Christ's and a realm that is not—between "gospel" and "law," to use the classic Lutheran terms? For this division has not stood the test of modern biblical exegesis, far less the test of radical discipleship advocated here. Nevertheless, we can learn more from Bonhoeffer than from any other modern ethicist at this point. He shows us the organic sphere as created by the Word that speaks to us in Christ; he shows us the fallenness of our lives in this sphere as a fallenness in hope of the redemption Christ promises; he shows organic goodness as a 'penulti-macy' that necessarily looks toward the ultimate.

b. *Neo-orthodox and Process alternatives*—This may appear more clearly if we consider two alternative ways of dealing with the organic strand in twentieth-century ethics, each of which emphasizes only one of the two motifs Bonhoeffer so brilliantly combined. The dominant Protestant ethical systems of our century have taken their clue from the genius nineteenth-century Danish philosopher-theologian Søren Kierkegaard (1813–1855), and have shaped this part of ethics within the limits of the human and psychological investigations that formed a part of his writing. Thus Paul Tillich's *Courage to Be* (1952) takes the fundamental human weakness to be anxiety in the face of the "meaninglessness" of the world. And Reinhold Niebuhr, in his influential *Nature and Destiny of Man* (1941–43), interprets the nature of the fallen creature as arising from its "inevitable but not necessary" plunge into either pride or sensuality—each being a means of evading the anxiety that is given to using our creation as beings at once bodily and spiritual. Note the point of view implicit in both these theologians: Both assume that the Christian gospel is to be understood from the side of creation by examining (1) the *human* phenomenon—and so not all of organic or inorganic nature; (2) the human phenomenon on its *mental* rather than on its bodily side—psychology, not biology; (3) the mental in its *pathological* rather than its healthy functioning—anxiety and despair, not for example caring and delight, are taken as first clues to man's moral nature. One may locate these choices in the personal history of Niebuhr and Tillich themselves—both were tense, unsettled men; both were involved in one way or another with Freudian psychoanalysis and its view of the human condition. Or one may locate their choices with respect to their times, the grievous history of the mid-twentieth century, with its global alienation, its genocidal wars, its death camps, its outrage and moral nihilism. In any case one might trace the choices to their source in Kierkegaard, whose well-known life history made it seem natural for him to choose angst as the sign of human nature. Yet this last overlooks one telling point about Kierkegaard himself—despite his own neurotic personal history, his program of thought about human nature was far more comprehensive than the study of anxiety and despair alone. For example, in *Either/Or* (1834/ 1944), Kierkegaard devoted the entire first volume to an account of the "aesthetic" mode of existence, in which taste, sensation, and the desire of the moment as a way of life were lovingly described in far more detail than would have been necessary for the sake of mere contrast with the second, "ethical" volume. And in *Stages on Life's Way* (1845/1940), Kierkegaard presents the aesthetic, the ethical, and the religious as steps in a pilgrimage that corresponds to a broader vision of Christian life than mere pathological studies of anxiety and despair. My point is that insofar as Tillich and Reinhold Niebuhr concentrated on the pathological, they presented a view of the organic strand of Christian ethics more determined by their own somber outlook than by the full spectrum of Christian thought, even by Christian thought as it is represented in their complex Danish mentor.

Another kind of motif is found in a Christian ethics that seeks to comprehend human existence by finding its place within the entire cosmos. Since Hiroshima and Nagasaki, 1945, mankind has had the capacity to decimate, and now to destroy, life on this planet with its weapons. This threat gives urgent relevance to thinkers who seek a global or even cosmic scale for the understanding of the moral situation. Their focus is not upon the sick human psyche but upon the world-process itself. Chief among these are the Process theologians, not only the (mainly Protestant) disciples of A. N. Whitehead (1861–1947) but others, such as the Jesuit scientist-philosopher Pierre Teilhard de Chardin (1881–1955), whose concepts focus upon a vast timestream older than history and wider than human concerns. In the Teilhardian vision, the human story is subordinated to the progress of the "biosphere" and "noosphere"—collocations of life and thought beyond the reach of any single moral self to comprehend, much less deflect. In the Whiteheadian tradition, similarly, a metaphysic of nature is produced in which feeling or emotion is assigned not only to human selves, but also to the elemental entities of the world—to one-celled animals, but also to such "enduring individuals" as electrons and protons, and even to the "occasions" (i.e., events) of which the latter are representative. Once this technical metaphysical picture of an emotional universe is accepted, it becomes possible to grade or assign values to various entities, from molecules to Maoris, on the basis of their capacity for "enjoyment," and thereby to reckon the appropriate relation of things to one another in a universe in which nothing is entirely without selfhood.

There seem to be two main objections to these enlarged foci
for Christian ethics. The first is that as the scope of moral
awareness is widened in process perspective, it becomes
proportionately more difficult to justify the taking up of any
particular moral standpoint from which judgment might be
exercised. In a competitive world, why is our own species to be
preferred over ants, or trees, or for that matter over rocks or
oil? As John Cobb and David Griffin themselves say, "working
out an ecological ethic will be a gigantic undertaking" from a
process perspective (1976:79). The other objection is that
whatever their framers intend, there is in these speculative
schemes a reversal of the order of moral knowledge as it is
given in Christian experience. From necessarily vague
speculative hypotheses about the biosphere, the character of
enduring entities, or the emotional fabric of molecules and
spider mites, conclusions are reached concerning those
matters that are as near to us as our own consciences and loves
and loyalties. Yet it is of these, and not the speculation, that we
can be morally certain.

There is also a special difficulty in any ecological ethics that
seeks to ground its doctrine in our knowledge of nature. This is
that the issues ecological morality confronts are most often
ones that involve not natural but social conflicts: It is
governments, multinational corporations, the attitude of racial
groups and interest groups and nations, that the environ-
mentalists confront again and again. So these conflicts cannot
fairly be resolved in terms of nature alone.

Nevertheless, there is something strongly compelling about
an ecological understanding of our organic selfhood. The
tilling and keeping of the garden (Gen. 2:15) is a winsome
image, whether it is the garden of the vast cosmos, or the
planet earth, or the little plot of ground outside a theologian's
study door that is the point of application of the ancient story.
What focus can be found that, without falling into the
difficulties just noted, will preserve our sense of the cosmic
whole as the range of moral concern, while grappling as well
with the intimate self-knowledge that Kierkegaard and his
followers pursued? Concretely, what focus will do justice to
Christian stories such as that of the black church—or to the
whole Christian story, of which theirs is so poignant a part?
The proposal here is that Christian ethics focus first on the
embodied selfhood of the human species, seeking to understand

our bodily nature both as the consequence of the natural history of *homo sapiens* (that is our link to the environment to its far limits) *and* as the locus of an interiority of shame, delight, guilt, and virtue rooted in the narrative tradition that is ours. To keep these two concerns, the natural environment and our native moral equipment, in a single theological frame is the challenge.

Another way of stating the issue we confront here is to borrow the old Christian image of moral vision—the standpoint or capacity for discernment made possible only by taking up a distinctive way of life (Hauerwas, 1974:ch. 2). In this image, the perils to the truthful living of the Christian life can be indicated as distortions of wide and single sight. On the one hand there is the danger that comes from double vision: an appeal to the moral authority of nature or history, or experience, or 'the Holy Spirit,' as if one or more of these had a claim upon the Christian other than the claim of Jesus Christ as Lord, rivalling Christ's lordship or correcting it. John Howard Yoder has argued that H. R. Niebuhr fell prey to this peril by assigning a separate revelatory role to the Holy Spirit in history, thereby diminishing the claim of Jesus Christ upon our lives (Yoder, 1972:103; 1976). Whether this be so or not, it is certain that some Protestant thinkers have rejected the old idea of natural law—a 'law' or moral knowledge available to any rational mind—just because it would introduce such double vision into the moral life. The opposite danger is that we shall embrace a moral Christocentrism so narrow that it cannot see the organic strand of Christian ethics at all. (The consequence of that narrowing will be a severe moral relativism that cannot even make contact with the everyday of common Christian life and thought.) In these terms, the ethical problem is to avoid both double vision and narrow vision. Or to change the image, it is to take seriously the 'fallenness' of the world and our own duplicity, while taking more seriously still the redemption of the world in Christ, and our own new nature (cf. Eph. 2:1-10).

c. *The present focus*—The solution, however, is already at hand in the concept of embodied selfhood. Christians do not live two lives, one life as Christians and another as embodied selves and parts of the organic universe. Our life as Christians *is* our life as organic constituents of the crust of this planet. We cannot be Christians in soul while remaining pagans in body; rather baptism is the baptism of our bodies; in the Lord's supper we feed body and soul alike and at once; it is with physical, fleshly ears that we hear—the word of God. To be sure, we are tempted not to see ourselves and our world in this way; thus Paul can scold the Corinthian Christians for their merely 'soulish' (ψυχικός) outlook (1 Cor. 2:14), and can warn in Romans against the desire of our 'lower natures' (σάρξ— Rom. 8:5), but these sins and temptations are just that; departures from the Christian way. The 'lower nature' is not our embodied selfhood, but a false image of that selfhood, a disguise we must learn to penetrate and discard. The Christian community in its health is not a disembodied fellowship but a bodily one—it was this same Paul whose writing first gave us "body" (σῶμα) as a metaphor of our solidarity with one another in Christ (1 Cor. 12:12ff.). To be sure, the world is not Christian; there is fallenness and rebellion and ruin enough here. But the eyes through which we Christians see the world are redeemed eyes; it is exactly through these eyes that we must be trained to look if we would see without double or narrow vision. To say that the way Jesus sees the organic world is normative for our seeing may be too cryptic for clarity, but if it reminds us that Christians have no moral Lord save Christ, it is beyond question a good motto. The Word became flesh (John 1:14); that he did so encourages us to seek the way of Christ in a life truly organic, truly God's; fully created, fully Christ's.

> He is the Life.
> Love him in the World of the Flesh;
> And at your marriage all its occasions shall dance for joy.
>   W. H. Auden, For the Time Being

3. The Morality of the Body

Perhaps modern alienation from biblical ways of thought has been inevitable, given the changed world of thought in which we live. For the Bible does not so much emphasize embodied selfhood as assume it, and the assumption it made is no longer self-evident. What is still clear in Scripture from beginning to end, though, is that believers "live and move and have our being" (cf. Acts 17:28) in ongoing relation to God. God creates, God sustains, God redeems, God renews, God judges; he is the absolute context, the everlasting environment (Psalm 139) of life. That that is the biblical standpoint cannot be gainsaid. So perhaps our latter day difficulty can be described this way: we simply do not believe that the God we know will have to do with *things*. Yet this biblical materialism is the very fiber of which the first strand of Christian ethics is formed. To make this standpoint concrete is the immediate task.

Consider then the hypothesis that (1) our embodied selves are equipped *by their Creator* with certain characteristic drives, or impulses, or instincts, such as the drives to sex and aggression; (2) that we are furnished as well with certain related, determinate needs, such as the needs for food and air, but also the needs for companionship and prayer; and (3) that in the adventure of meeting (or seeking to meet) these needs and coping (or seeking to cope) with these drives, our selves come to be equipped with a range of feelings and may develop relevant powers of judgment which we may well call moral feelings and moral judgment, constituting the moral equipment of the body. Certainly Christians do not exclusively possess these drives, needs, and capacities; evidently others do also. Nor are Christians devoid or exempt, by virtue of Christ's grace, from any such drives or needs or embodied capacities. Yet, as suggested in the last section, the *way* in which we participate in the common lot is a Christian way; our share in the created order is marked by our share in Christ—who on earth also possessed these native drives, natural needs, and nascent resources of the body.

a. *The instincts and morality*—So there can be no surrender of Christian ethics to those who in Manichaean dualist fashion regard the body's drives or instincts as the enemy of morality—or even its mere material base, being neither good nor evil. "God saw everything that he had made, and behold, it was very good," not least "man in our image, and after our likeness" (Gen. 1:31, 26). Granted that human nature is fallen and sinful; we here take up the standpoint of that same nature redeemed into Christian discipleship, reconciled to its created environment.

Because the human drives of sex and aggression are ones we share with other animals, two separable questions, sometimes confused, appear here. The first is whether our animal natures are evil just because they are animal (cf. Dillard, 1974). There has been a widespread but shameful depreciation of our fellow creatures the beasts. Thus in our modern vocabulary, the beasts are "beastly" while we hope to act "humanely"; "bestial" behavior is by our definition morally depraved behavior. Mary Midgley, in a valuable book *Beast and Man: The Roots of Human Nature* (1978) has shown how Western philosophers and theologians have erroneously but typically used "the beast" as a horrible example of all that is evil in human nature, whereas actual studies of animal behavior instead reveal something much more like ingrained morality: The mating, nesting, offspring-rearing, food-gathering, and social instincts of various species vary enormously, but they are alike in exhibiting patterns of behavior in which senseless violence and vandalism have no place (1978:ch. 2). (The appearance of occasional 'lawless' bears or bison or elephants no more contradicts Midgley's generalization than the birth of a legless child contradicts the fact that man is a biped.) Thus to speak of ourselves as animals should not be to depreciate the human species, but at best to call attention to the given instinctual patterns of behavior in terms of which organic (or any other) morality can alone exist.

Why do people form families?Why do they take care of their homes and quarrel over boundaries? Why do they own property? Why do they talk so much, and dance, and sing? Why do children play, and for that matter adults too? (Midgley, 1978:56)

What Midgley calls open instincts (those that may be fulfilled by many kinds of behavior) provide the first answer to these questions, thereby showing that embodied instinct must form the background of human morality for Christians as well.

The other question is whether there are in human nature purely evil instincts. Robert Ardrey among others has argued (1961) that we are descended in evolution from "killer apes," and that therefore murder and war are natural to man, while Ashley Montagu and others have replied (1976) that cooperation and peaceful ways are our biological heritage. In order to think about this, we may have to examine more closely the human moral structure as it presents itself today. For among our animal qualities there is indeed some distinctive human quality to be recognized, though it seems not to reside in any single feature of our animate life. Various 'distinctive' features have indeed been proposed—the possession of morality, or culture, or the use of tools, or language, or large brain size—but each seems distinctive only in degrees of quality or quantity, not as an absolute difference. The evidence is that other animals do use tools, do 'speak,' do as we have noted display a kind of 'morality.' It is as though the Creator had playfully determined to make ourselves of the very stuff of all organic creation so that no aspect of our embodied selfhood could be cast aside as inhuman. In the Genesis stories of creation, the only clear difference in the human animal, man, is this: this creature is *addressed* by the Creator (Gen. 1:28-30; 2:16f.; cf. Barth, 1958a:III/1).

Yet the various differences of degree and detail do add up to a remarkably distinctive species. For one thing, there is indeed a vandal perversity in some human conduct that calls for special explanation (Ardrey, 1971; Harned, 1977:ch. 4). Among the animals, only man generates evil (Genesis 3). Second, however, human conduct is not nearly so limited by instinct as that of other species. While man's physical equipment is generalized so that we may not be as swift as one animal or as strong as another or as agile as a third, still our brain capacity together with our flexible instinctual patterns permit a range of geographic habitat and growth in culture not open to more fixed species. For example, though our species has aggressive instincts, it is not necessary to the life of the species that these be fulfilled by killing (Montagu, 1976). And third, not only does the human species display culture; it is not found apart from culture. The use of tools and fire, the appearance of social structures such as tribes and families (as opposed to mere bands or droves of individuals), and supremely, the use of language fit in with the generalized heredity and cranial structure just described to make of man a distinctly cultural and not just a biological species.

That is to say that what distinguishes us as human is not merely brain size or the thumb's hinge or the fluidity of instinct: it is also the content of our culture. An illustration drawn from anthropologist Peter J. Wilson may underline this thesis. Wilson distinguishes *two* kinds of distinctively human bonding: the primary bond, that between a mother and her infant, which because of the prolonged and relatively helpless infancy period of five to six years is exceptionally intense for both infant and mother, and the pair bond, between mate and mate, which in the absence of estrus is for our species also intense, inasmuch as mating is a continuing possibility not limited to seasons of 'heat.' Now the possibility of these two kinds of bonds linking a single human female both to offspring and to mate creates a situation which does not in the same way apply to any other species—namely, the possibility of *a third kind of bond* arising between the adult male and the offspring of the female. This third bond is that of fatherhood. Since the father is not organically related to the offspring save by the brief act of conception, the fulfillment of this possibility is of a different kind than either pairing or primary bonds. To admit this third bond is to admit the possibility of its extension, and so to introduce into the species the idea of kinship.

For if fatherhood can be an ongoing (and not just genetic) bond, so can brother and sisterhood be, and all other forms of kinship as extensions of these. "The outstanding feature of human kinship is that it unites both sexes and all generations by focusing them on reproduction and in this way creates both individualized relationships and a generalized possibility for the formation of groups" (Wilson, 1980:61). Wilson does not deny that in some nonhuman species an instinctual role is played by the male parent after conception; the speciality of human fatherhood, however, is that it depends not upon instinct, but upon the action of the female, who by admitting the male to the pair bond makes possible a father-kinship bond to the offspring. Hence it is the implied promises of the female, at once to male and to child, that are the primal element in culture itself—thus the (deliberately) ambiguous title of Wilson's book, *Man the Promising Primate*. Since the female cannot simultaneously meet the needs of both her bond-partners, the possibility of kinship for each depends on her 'promise,' which thus lies at the basis of culture.

"God made the countryside; the city is the work of the hand of man," says a Latin epigram, suggesting that though nature including the human body may be God's work, culture is ineluctably our own addition. Yet we can see now that this is dubious on anthropological grounds as well as on biblical. Peter Wilson's argument merely gives rational coherence to the general paleontological testimony: human culture is as old as humanity itself. Where *homo* has evolved, culture has been present already, and Wilson's account gives biological footing to this evidence from ancient rocks. God is as truly the creator of culture as of nature. In the language of Genesis, Adam and Eve in the garden were not beasts, but were already, culturally, man (Gen. 1:26). The doctrine of creation, then, will be as truly presupposed by the social as by the body strand of Christian ethics, and these strands require one another; for neither can be fully explained in isolation.

Our question about 'evil instincts' led on into the cultural complexity of human nature, and so to the doctrine that the phenomenon of 'original' or basic sin in human nature is connected not simply to bestial or animal drives of sex or aggression, but to the historic and variable forms of human culture. (Though full discussion of the doctrine of sin must await another volume, this cultural or institutional structure of sin will be addressed directly in Chapter Six, while the sex drive will be considered in Chapter Five, and the aggressive drive in Chapter Eleven.) The present task, however, is to show the organic relation of these drives to other features of our human morality, and first to the role of need.

b. *The needs of embodied selves*—The concept of needs must be clearly distinguished from two others with which it is liable to be confused, goods and rights. It is not my intention here to seek to clarify the concept, more Hellenic than biblical, of "the good," yet almost everyone will agree that it is good to have one's needs met, as does the Gospel parable that relates "I was hungry and you gave me food, I was thirsty and you gave me drink, I was a stranger and you welcomed me, I was naked and you clothed me" (Matt. 24:35f.). In a very loose sense, meeting needs *is* Christian morality. On the other hand, many today have sought to bring everything here under the heading of rights. However, the notion that there are 'human rights,' to which persons *qua* persons are entitled, confuses the idea of social rights (those that arise within a particular social structure) with the idea of basic human needs. The best picture of human rights is as a metaphor, sometimes politically (because rhetorically) effective, but not addressed to the more basic moral issues we are concerned with here.

While the meeting of a need is in itself a good, we cannot conclude from that alone that it is fitting to meet any particular need at any given time. Nor is the question of who is to meet the need, and how and where, settled by the very need itself. Biblical narratives often make their (moral) point by trading on this fact. Consider the role of sexual need in the story of David and his warrior, Uriah the Hittite (2 Samuel 11). During the spring of a certain year, the season when kings, we are pointedly told, go forth to battle (v. 1) David's troops go off to war, while he remains indolent at home. The king sees a beautiful woman, inquires about her, sends for her, lies with her, and as it happens, gets her pregnant. Now what is to be done about this unsuitable pregnancy of a woman whose husband is away fighting with the army? Well, kings have extraordinary resources. David sends for the warrior husband and arranges for him to be in town overnight. Surely he will go home to his wife—and thereby be duped into accepting a father's role opposite his freshly pregnant spouse? But Uriah (because he suspects something?) refuses, pleading the common lot of comrades at arms—a lot David in his royal leisure has openly neglected. "The ark and Israel and Judah dwell in booths," says Uriah, "and my lord Joab and the servants of my lord are camping in the open field; shall I then go to my house, to eat and to drink, and to lie with my wife?" (v. 11 RSV). Thereby, we know, he seals his doom by inviting his own murder, accomplished through the message he will bear as he returns to the front.

Now in all this story, sexual need is front and center, though in the spare biblical style it has hardly been mentioned. The idle king's need for a woman and the sunbathing Bathsheba's need for a man set the plot in action. Uriah's need for the domestic comfort his wife can give is the pretext for David's 'generosity': "Go down to your house, and wash your feet" (v. 8). And Uriah's deliberate refusal is made more strange by the presumed need of an army wife for leave time with her soldier; would it not offend any warrior's woman to remain unvisited during his time in town? Yet the power of the story rests exactly upon the reader's awareness that needs alone do not create their own justification: David has sinned in indulging his need and playing upon Uriah's; Bathsheba is hardly innocent, though her position is a difficult one. Uriah has acted honorably (yet fatally) in checking his own need, even though he thereby deprives his wife of fulfilling her (supposed) need as well. The general view is that the existence of needs is not to be denied; they form a central ingredient in the biblical narratives here and elsewhere; but they are quite literally only part of the story.

This imbedding of needs (as well as drives and capacities) in a narrative ground makes it understandable that there is in Scripture no list of needs in general; and our own attempts to catalog our needs must remain faithful to this biblical reticence: "your Father knows what you need before you ask him" (Matt. 6:8 RSV), so the Christian goal in prayer may be not to fulfill known wants, but to discover our actual needs from him who alone truly knows them.

One modern writer whose discussion of needs also displays this reticence is Simone Weil. She has suggested a list of "needs of the soul" that treats hunger as a paradigmatic human need and claims that these are like it, not that one could not literally survive without one or more of them, but that without them "we fall little by little into a state resembling death" (1952:7). Her list of soul needs includes: *order, liberty, obedience, responsibility, equality, hierarchism, honor, punishment, freedom of opinion, security, risk, private property, collective property, truth* (1952:xiii). There are striking omissions here: Besides presupposing the means of life already mentioned, her list neglects such obvious needs as love and affection, and it includes strongly traditional elements such as order, hierarchy, and honor, perhaps unusual in a thinker disciplined by Marxism. A strong feature is the pairing: If one moves freedom of opinion (which of course includes *false* opinion) alongside truth, the list readily falls into natural pairs—order-liberty, obedience-responsibility, and so on. This emphasizes the central theme that no need can be considered in isolation from others. Had she included *life* (and the means of life) in her list, it might well have been paired with *death* (cf. Eccles. 3:2) and its means as well, open to abuse though such a 'need' might seem. A different list might have paired love and freedom, and one might profitably construct still other need lists.

But Weil's discussion must not lead us to suppose that from needs, any more than from 'rights,' one can deduce an entire morality. We have seen two reasons for this: one is that needs provide an incomplete account of bodily morality itself (there are, for example, the capacities, still to be discussed); the other that, contrary to Weil's claim, needs often fail to tell us who must meet that need. Thus one cannot from a need for death deduce a duty of (or right to) euthanasia, or from the need for life, a condemnation of abortion. Induced abortion and euthanasia are social practices rather than parts of our organic heritage, and it is as (dubious) social practices (strand two) that euthanasia and abortion must be assessed. Admittedly, in the sheep and goats parable, some are condemned because they have not met needs of hunger, thirst, aid to prisoners, and the rest. But the further explanation is that the needy are *brethren* of the Son of Man, the King, while the hearers are his *subjects*, so that those social relationships constitute the premises for their daily conduct. If we reckon that everyone is in some sense the King's sister or brother, that he is by Christian account brother to all flesh, then a license for charity appears that transforms everything *for his followers*. So the needs are not everything, but they are fundaments. I think that much of the power of Liberation Theology's defense of the privileged status "in God's eyes" of the poor is an appeal to this fundament. For "the poor" are exactly those whose elemental *needs* are flagrantly denied fulfillment, and who have in that degree a *prima facie* moral claim upon us all.

c. *Our natural moral equipment*—Concerning conscience (and its rational function of moral judgment) and even more concerning such moral phenomena as blame, shame, and guilt, Christian opinion tends to swing between two poles. Either these human capacities are reckoned to be authoritative by right (as in the recurrent teaching that it is always wrong to 'disobey' conscience), or in reaction against that extreme, they are demoted, and exactly because of their embodied or genetic origin are treated as part of the problem morality must resolve (as in the Freudian designation of conscience as parental superego). The task here is to form a just view of this equipment, neither overlooking the human frailty every bit of it exemplifies, nor discarding its moral powers in yet another version of the Gnostic derogation of the body. In a summary chapter presenting the organic strand, none of these can receive full treatment; instead, I will illustrate the point of view by attending first to two clusters of moral emotions, that of which delight and horror are a part, and that focused upon blame, shame, and guilt. Then we can build on these in seeking a biblical viewpoint toward conscience and (moral) judgment.

i. *Delight and horror*—Many ethicists have noted an elementary moral polarity—pleasure and pain, the attractive and the repulsive, or in the ultimate subjectivism of the emotivists, "pro" and "con" feelings (Stevenson, 1944). While psychological accounts have dealt with these as polar opposites, it was a theologian, Rudolph Otto, who in his seminal work, *The Idea of the Holy* (1923) showed a profound connection between the two. The holy, or in Otto's term the numinous, is on its experiential side that which at once attracts and repels us, the *mysterium tremendum et fascinans*. Moses, seeing a bush that burns and is not consumed, is irresistibly drawn *to* that numinous object—but is warned *not* to tread the ground with sandalled feet (Exod. 3:1-5). Simon Peter, awed by uncanny filling of the boat with fish, falls at Jesus' knees, but begs him to depart—"for I am a sinful man, O Lord" (Luke 5:8). This 'sin' is not consciousness of fault or failing, but a more primitive awareness of the mutual repulsion that separates the 'clean' from the 'unclean,' the unholy from the holy (cf. Otto, 1923:chs. 10–11). So it is, too, with the horror with which from Cain onward mankind has trembled at and fled from its own acts of violence—fleeing from the "blood [that] crieth unto me [JHWH] from the ground" (Gen. 4:10).

But are delight and horror *moral* emotions, or are these sensations more akin to nausea or to thirst—urges to action (or contemplation) that are at best *premoral*? In answering, we must be careful not to descend to merely verbal debate; our question asks us to think, What is morality? These feelings alone do not normally carry full moral weight for us. Yet that sometimes they do so seems undeniable. Thus Herbert McCabe (1969) points out that when the moralities of social structure and tradition—our strand two—seem to have failed, such feelings as horror at the grisly burning of children in a guerilla war may be morality's final resort. And similarly, Bernard Williams suggests that the genuine *shock* felt by members of the Hernando Cortez expedition, themselves a "morally unpretentious collection of bravos," upon discovering what was done in the Aztec temples of human sacrifice in sixteenth-century Mexico, may be a sign, not of intolerance, but of their own humanity (1972:24f.). Perhaps when we investigate such elementary reactions we are close to the borderland of three worlds, the religious with its concepts of the *fascinans* and the taboo (Otto), the aesthetic, with its concepts of the beautiful and the ugly, and the ethical, with its perceptions of good and evil. This can be expressed by saying with the sages that beauty is holy, or goodness sacred—or by saying that morality is (in the first of its three strands) aesthetic (cf. Temple, 1934:chs. 6–7).

ii. *Shame, blame, and guilt*—Perhaps there is no human emotion that is not related to morality, but some emotions are certainly characteristically moral. Pity and resentment, sympathy and aversion, indignation and love are part of a larger spectrum of human feelings that by turns motivate, inform, distort, or define the moral lives of the individuals who experience them. Yet there has been a tendency in post-Reformation Christianity to narrow this wide spectrum down to love and guilt, or perhaps only to guilt. So a part of the present task is to remind ourselves of the whole of which these are only a part, and to see the whole spectrum of emotions as morally relevant.

Guilt, for example, begins to take on more natural proportions when it is seen, not as the singular tutor of Christian morality, but as partner to shame and as the ripe seed of its more childish ancestor, blame. Our task is complicated here by the inability of many to distinguish objective from subjective guilt. In English (and in Hebrew and Greek as well) the objective sense is prior: in the history of our languages, "guilt" was first the wrongful act itself (!), then liability or responsibility for that act, and only last the remorse associated (whether justly or not) with the liability. Since the Enlightenment, however, a popular world view has dismissed objective guilt or liability, and a crude but widespread misunderstanding of psychoanalysis (and pastoral care) sees its task as the evaporation of subjective guilt. Thus objective guilt is treated as a fiction, subjective guilt as a disease, and the proper role of each is discarded.

A helpful corrective here is discerning the role of guilt in contrast to the roles of shame and blame. Shame roughly speaking is a sense of deficiency or worthlessness. When we compare what we seem to be with what we think we might have been a loss of face or presence can arise, a dejection that takes all the wind from our sails. A man without shoes in a society that strongly values shoe wearing may have *no* guilt, but he is liable to feel profound shame when he sees his bare feet in company. And the uncovering of areas of the body more sensitive than feet is even more likely to produce shame. Bonhoeffer believed the root of this deficiency pertained to the creature's awareness of estrangement from the Creator. Thus the nakedness felt by our first parents ("And they knew that they were naked; and they sewed fig-leaves together, and made themselves aprons," Gen. 3:7*b* ASV) is intended by the writer to symbolize the lonely exposure alienated man and woman feel when they have abandoned God; that exposure is the elemental shame, capable of attaching itself afresh to situations that repeat for us the primitive sense of deficiency and loss (Bonhoeffer, 1978:20-23). So the gospel remedy for shame must be a restoration of the divine presence (Rom. 1:16; 2 Tim. 1:12 ASV).

To blame is to hold another responsible, but behind that (strand two) act of judgment there often lies a powerful (strand one) feeling—the spontaneous feeling of resentment and pride that appears when we encounter in others conduct that offends us. At the age of the grade school child, such spontaneous blaming is as natural, and as necessary to maturity, as the loss of milk teeth. Children at play and work experience repeatedly the elemental social bond that comes in blaming others and in being blamed; doing so, they enjoy the sort of moral community that when extended will form the laws and practices of strand two. Psychoanalysts might add that blame is closely allied to temptation: We feel that hot flush of blame aimed at another only when the fault encountered is one to which we ourselves are tempted, and the psychodynamic function of blaming is to reprove in another the behavior that might well have proved too attractive to resist in ourselves (Fingarette, 1973:ch. 3).

Thus in a sense moral development beyond blaming, if it is genuine freedom not to blame and not mere feigned tolerance or mere apathy, is real progress in the moral life. But few if any of us outgrow all temptations, and to the extent we can be tempted, blaming remains a valuable resource of embodied selfhood. So continued blame in some areas of life is a sign that our lives are still in progress (A. Freud, 1966). It is noteworthy that Jesus, according to the Gospels, engaged in outspoken attacks on his rivals, the Pharisees, and against some of the behavior of his followers—supporting, on this theory, the suggestion that these represented some of his own not yet resolved temptations (see for example Mark 7:1-23; 12:38 and parallels; and especially Matthew 23).

Similar considerations apply to guilt. While shame is roughly for what we deem we are or are not, guilt (as the etymology makes plain) is for what we have done or left undone. So I may rightly be *ashamed* of having so few friends that are not white like me (for I wanted to think myself unprejudiced), but I will be *guilty* of overt acts of discriminatory racial pride. And obviously these two are related: one who *is* prejudiced will sometimes *act* prejudicially, other things being equal. Guilt is somewhat differently connected to blame, however; while blame 'protects' the integrity of oneself by attacking another, guilt has the courage to point the accusing finger at itself. Thus feelings of guilt reflect greater maturity than feelings of blame. The self that can appropriately acknowledge its own guiltiness is a self able to shoulder responsibility, acknowledging its share of fault for the misshapen past and accepting the task of reshaping the future—for unlike blame and shame, guilt can look forward as well as back. In biblical perspective as in modern psychoanalysis it is not the sense of guilt but unacknowledged or hidden guilt that is destructive of selfhood: "When I declared not my sin, my body wasted away through my groaning all day long" (Ps. 32:3 RSV).

What, then, of the modern sense that guilt is more a disease than a function of embodied selfhood? Here we must distinguish between pathological guilt and real guilt. For the pathological cases, therapy is as necessary and as appropriate for Christians as for others; it may permit half-formed wishes and destructive antagonisms to be brought to acknowledgment and so become available for forgiveness and healing. Real guilt, on the other hand, involves actual offenses against community, and calls for its own appropriate 'therapy' of confession, repentance, restitution or reparation, and restoration; thus it forms a vital part not only of strand one, but of strand two (Morris, 1976:98-108). In the happy case, the Christian's life journey is made in the context of a community of acceptance, reproach, and forgiveness (cf. Matthew 18) in which every onset of guilt (with all its false imaginings and deceptive stabs of conscience and callous missings of the mark) may be brought into a remembering and reconstitution shaped by the shared way of Jesus the Christ.

iii. *Conscience and moral judgment*—The ideas of guilt and of conscience are both more at home in modern than in biblical thought; "conscience" barely appears in the Old Testament, and in the New, its use is occasional and unsystematic. One cannot avoid the impression that the labor expended upon this concept by New Testament students owes more to post-Kantian forms of moral theology than to the New Testament itself (cf. Furnish, 1968:228f.). W. D. Davies reminds us that "conscience" was a term of Paul's opponents, not of Paul's own ethics. For as Davies says, Paul makes it clear (in 1 Cor. 4:4) "that conscience is not his ultimate court of appeal. This is Christ himself." Hence conscience stands in need of being "quickened by the Spirit and itself enlightened by Christ" (1962:675).

Because the concept of 'conscience' is so broad, most writers find it helpful to distinguish two or more senses of the term for the sake of clarity—O'Connell, for example, speaks of "conscience/1, conscience/2, and conscience/3" (1978:89). A less elaborate proposal is to distinguish conscience and moral judgment, using the former term for the felt urge to "do right and not wrong," an urge that in most of us is accompanied by the parental imprint upon the developing self. Thus we can agree in a trivial sense with those who say that conscience is always right (since analytically it is right to do right), but we can reserve to the moral judgment the finite—and fallible—capacity to say *what* is right and wrong here and now and thus to sit in judgment not only upon one's other bodily drives, but if necessary upon the contents of the parentally imprinted urge themselves. In that sense, moral judgment sits in judgment upon the tendencies of (inherited) 'conscience.' Because popular speech does not usually make such distinctions, it is not always easy to tell, when people claim to have "followed their conscience," whether they mean merely to say that they responded to an unreflective urge to do what they currently grasped as right, or mean to say instead that they exercised moral judgment, the educable (though still fallible) capacity for reflection, and were guided thereby. Each element, namely 'conscience' and 'moral judgment,' has a role to play in the moral life, but neither one (nor both together) guarantee success in human conduct; strand one itself provides a richer set of resources than these alone. Perhaps it is worth noting, though, that it is judgment, and not the mere conscientious urge, that is highlighted in the Wisdom tradition of the Old Testament and the New.

4. *Embodied Virtues*

Our summary of the organic structure of Christian morality, though spare, is now complete, and yet there has been no employment of a notion some would have held absolutely central, that of *virtue*. To be sure, "virtue" plays no large role in the biblical vocabulary, and some Protestant moralists have discounted it for this reason alone, while others have held that the very notion of virtue was in conflict with salvation *sola gratia*. For virtues require human effort and training. Yet these are indecisive reasons: the term "virtue" (ἀρετή; *virtus*) comes to us from Hellenistic and Latin thought, but so do "morality" and "ethics" and "theology" itself. It is true that virtue implies training—but so does prayer, so do ministry and mission. The reason for postponement here has rather been that virtue is an exceedingly complex moral notion (cf. MacIntyre, 1984; Meilaender, 1984). Christian writers and philosophers have meant very different things by it, so that it is necessary to show how virtue is related to the moral concepts already introduced if we are to be clear about it.

One way to think of the Christian virtues is as excellencies or skills enabling us to enjoy to the full or fulfill the elements of the embodied moral life presented in the preceding section— and to see vices as defects preventing or diminishing that enjoyment. Indeed, some virtues, such as hope, seem so basic to life that they might have been treated as themselves elements alongside need, delight, and the rest. To give virtue in this way an organic base would not counter the idea that virtues require training; rather moral development might be understood as building upon the organic foundations of life the skills required for its living, much as architecture assembles materials into habitable structures. Thus particular Christian virtues could be picked out by asking what sorts of development of *homo sapiens* could best fulfill the promise implied by the open *instincts* of our species, what traits could assure the meeting of those *needs* of the embodied self that Christians can identify in themselves and in others, what skills might enhance our natural *delights* and respect our natural *horrors*, what qualities could best respect our germinal character as creatures liable to *shame*, *blame*, and *guilt*, and what might develop our capacity for moral *judgment*.

Yet even to contemplate the manifold ways in which such a prescription for moral training could be fulfilled shows the need for more exact lines of direction. For example, shall we place Weil's need for hierarchy first, and above all send our children to Eastern prep schools? Or shall we focus on the element of *delight*, and seek for them the guidance of a sunbaked West Coast guru? Again, is the faith (to name a classic 'theological' virtue) that we want for ourselves and our own to be modeled on Eriksonian basic trust in the trustworthiness of life? (In that case, our elemental guilt might be sufficiently remedied by therapeutic self-acceptance.) Or is faith to be modeled on Lutheran *Anfechtung* and self-aban- donment to the mercy of Christ's shed blood *for me?* (Here will be a very different treatment of guilt—*simul justus et peccator*.) Or is faith to be commitment in a band of radical disciples of Jesus of Nazareth bound together in shared obedience? (On this baptist view, guilt has a communal locus and a collegial remedy—see Matthew 18.) The point is that these are real alternatives: it is not enough to assent to undifferentiated 'faith' or to any mere list of named but undefined virtues.

Such considerations have led some recent ethicists to a quite different understanding of virtue. They have argued that the coherence of the virtues in a definite moral character and way of life, exactly because it can be fulfilled in so many ways, requires the grounding of the virtues in the shared practices and commonly acknowledged goods of a particular 'tradi- tional' community (MacIntyre, 1984), or in a shared story, sufficiently truthful to form our characters in coherence with its truth (Hauerwas, 1981:136). Thus these writers argue that even to say what is meant by a particular virtue, for example, courage, we have to specify a narrative background against which that virtue appears. The courage of Jesus is not the courage of Achilles, for Jesus was neither violent nor deceptive, yet both are marks of the courage of Homer's hero. Nonviolence is a gospel virtue, but in heroic society it was merely a cowardly vice. And this certainly seems a compelling argument.

Yet we have been saying that there are basic human needs and qualities, not just Christian or Hellenic or Chinese ones. Are there then no recognizably *human* virtues? What appears to be the case here is that "virtue" will have to bear more than one sense (MacIntyre, 1984:ch. 16). On the one hand, for example, almost everyone will recognize that life is a good that is sustained by hope—so hope is for that reason a very basic or general virtue. On the other, hope is not for long effectual unless it has some particular content, unless there is something to hope *for* or hope *in* (Rom. 8:24f.). Thus Christian hope has a particular *telos* or direction as a part of the way of life of the storied community centered on Jesus Christ. So we seem to find two sorts of hope, two kinds of virtue called hope, and in crisis situations the two may even conflict with one another—as they do for Jesus in the Gethsemane story. (And of course other communities may have still other 'hopes'.)

To epitomize several of these points, and to bring the threads of the chapter together at the close, let us attend to a particular Christian virtue, not as it happens hope, but rather *presence*. By presence is meant quite simply the quality of *being there* for and with the other. Exactly because it is not on the classic lists of virtues, it may be easier to approach without preconceptions. We remember that God's presence with us is one of the great gifts of the gospel, associated with the incarnation of the Word, the giving of the Spirit, and the return of the Lord; we recall that in Christian history his presence is celebrated in every eucharistic meal, invoked at every baptism, and claimed anew at every gathering of disciples. What we want now, however, is to understand presence as a dimension of the Christian life. Clearly *being there* is for us a function of our embodied existence; it is only by metaphor or analogy that we can speak of a disembodied presence. Still, that very analogy is important, for if a Paul whose bodily presence is judged "weak" (2 Cor. 10:10) can, though absent in body, be "present in spirit" to judge a flagrant case of misconduct (1 Cor. 5:3f.), so can we, though bodily present, *fail* to be there for those who need us. One thinks of an estranged couple sitting at a table for two and staring moodily past one another; they are there bodily, but neither is *present* for the other. Presence is being one's self for someone else; it is refusing the temptation to withdraw mentally and emotionally; but it is also on occasion putting our own body's weight and shape alongside the neighbor, the friend, the lover in need.

But is presence, even in this extended sense, really a virtue, or is it like left-handedness or curiosity, merely somebody's quality or distinguishing feature? Earlier in this chapter the black church was set forth as displaying the quality of presence. When black slaves had no other earthly resource, they knew how to be present to and for one another, and knew that Another was present for them as well. (Not that they were always virtuously where they should have been—or what does the spiritual mean when it laments, "Couldn't hear nobody pray"?) To characterize this presence as a virtue is to say that it is a strength or skill, developed by training and practice, which is a substantive part of (the Christian) life. (I do not forget that not all blacks, nor all slaves, were Christians.) This strength meets the needs, fulfills the goals, carries the meaning of Christian living. Dilsey, in Faulkner's *Sound and the Fury*, paradigmatically displays this virtue in the novel. It is no accident that Dilsey, who is the ultimate moral resource of her white 'family,' finds her own resource in faithful participation in the black church.

Presence has its ghostly imitations. Thus there is stage presence, the actor's simulacrum of the reality, and there is a politician's or a salesman's 'presence' that is as artificial as stage scenery—the assumption of a virtue not possessed. Presence has also its 'perverse'—the name some give to a distorted yet still potent caricature of any virtue. Perhaps the perverse of presence is *nosiness*, butting into others' lives and homes and attention. But the counterfeit here is rarely confused by recipients with the good coin! The contrary of presence is not absence (which as we have seen may paradoxically have some of the force of presence in a given case) but avoidance or alienation. Throughout most of *The Scarlet Letter* Dimmesdale avoids Hester, thereby showing us by its default what the virtue of presence would be. But the primal defection from presence is found in the experience of shame. In genuine presence I am with another and she or he with me, and there is a wholeness in the shared act or fact of our being there. But shame is a failed wholeness. Thus face to face with another, but ashamed, we sense a loss of presence. The black Christian community, in slavery, stripped of its clothing, shorn of its family life, confronted with arrogance, deprived of honor as the world grants honor, nevertheless discovered in its roots and in the face of the present Christ its own presence, and was *un*ashamed—and its heritage of presence is a treasure held as in escrow for the whole church, waiting to be released to rightful claimants.

From presence as from any true virtue there is a path leading to other virtues as well. Thus we can better understand the *agape* love that led Martin Luther King's followers to *confront* their oppressors in the streets of Birmingham and Selma, rather than to flee from them (or led Clarence Jordan's Koinonia Community to *remain* in Georgia when the dynamite sticks began to explode their weathered buildings) if we interpret their action not as a "protest" but as a presence, a being there, and a being there for those who themselves shamelessly denied or opposed their neighbor's presence (McClendon, 1974). And for another example, we can better understand the urgency of the idea of *truth* in the Christian Restorationism of Alexander Campbell and his nineteenth-century followers (or the *witness* of the seventeenth-century Quaker followers of George Fox) if we see that the appeal to truth and to witness required the full *presence* of the witnesses to that truth—even their presence to and for churches and denominations and civil authorities that sought to eject them. They could not, *could* not just go away and leave the others alone as they were asked to do and still be true to this virtue. Presence is one of the profound forms of Christian witness. There is a Catholic religious order whose members live inside South American prisons and jails in order to be present to and for the prisoners—the ministry of presence.

If now we ask whether presence as understood here can best be comprehended in terms of the organic or the social (strand one or strand two), there is no simple answer. Expressing embodiment, meeting the human needs of companionship and adventure, the obverse of shame, presence is deeply rooted in our organic natures. Yet every instance of presence that we have cited has appeared as a part of the Christian story with its aims and practices, social structure and community order—that is, as part of the fabric of the Christian social strand. The presence we have met is a temporal presence, not a timeless one. To see this, though, is to recognize that the virtues are strand-encompassing phenomena—which is no cause for surprise if we acknowledge that though often easy to identify (for we know well enough when a brother or sister has *been there* for us), the virtues are complex structures of the moral life, not its mere elements but its products, not the bare data of Christian existence, but its evolved ripe fruit.

In that case, we can understand that this ripeness will take quite different forms in different communities. This does not rule out the possibility of importantly overlapping concepts of virtue (and of particular virtues) in different settings—Hellenistic presence is not Christian presence, and yet they have something in common, not least that they are (rival) ways of realizing the organic root of each. And to refer again to the conflicting concepts of virtue mentioned earlier, that these *can* conflict is a sign of hope for the Christian moral witness in the world: it means that there is a penultimate basis for understanding the uniquely Christian forms of faith, or courage, or presence.

Christian presence cannot be accounted for in organic terms alone—and yet it lays claim upon us exactly because it fulfills elements of our bodily selfhood: our existence as creatures bound to our environment, needing the support of our fellows, involved in a psychic structure that cries out for realization in such a way as *this*. Which is to say once again that the moral life is not complete except in the union of its several strands.

Sarah and
Jonathan Edwards

The reader who has had to struggle with the preceding chapter may come with a sigh of relief to one that sets out, by way of development of those ideas, simply to present the story of a life. Relief may admittedly be short-lived if it is discovered that the life is to be that of Jonathan Edwards (1703–58), whose name is associated by many with hell-fire preaching, and by the better informed with abstruse discussions of predestination, original sin, and freedom of the will. To be sure, of these subjects—sin and its hell, God's grace, human freedom and destiny—none is without deep intrinsic interest, and each will engage us here, albeit briefly. Yet the present chapter is about Edwards the man, and in particular about his life with Sarah Pierpont Edwards (1710–58), the woman he loved. For that reason her name stands deliberately first in the chapter title: *Sarah* and Jonathan. It is certain that more will be said about him than her; we know more. Yet it is him in relation to her, his life with her—and therefore finally Sarah who is the focus of the present chapter. If in turn the key to her life should somehow turn out to be Jonathan's, then we shall have learned something about both, and more about our main topic, the morality of life in the body.

This chapter, like two that come later, can be seen as an experiment with an idea first presented in my work on "biography as theology." The content of Christian faith, or for that matter any faith that must be lived out, not just thought out, is best expressed in the shared lives of its believers;

without such lives, that faith is dead. These lives in their integrity and compelling power do not just illustrate, but test and verify (or by their absence or failure falsify) the set of religious convictions that they embody. Now the time has come to examine this thesis not in relation to doctrine, as in my earlier work, but as suggested there, in relation to ethical theory: the shape of the common life of Christians (McClendon, 1971, 1974). Sarah and Jonathan Edwards offer distinct advantages for testing out the ethical theory so far advanced here: theirs was a richly *embodied* life together, rich in erotic passion, rich in mutual love, 'rich' too in the pain and death that are part of life itself. These were two lives aware of their own embodied nature, two that emphasized the necessary connection between religious thought and feeling and actual daily conduct—Sarah in her autobiography, and Jonathan both in his and all his writing. Edwards scholarship in our century has traveled a long way: from the hell-fire caricatures of the Puritans referred to above, to studies that made Edwards seem a disembodied intellect (Sydney Ahlstrom justly called him "America's greatest speculative theologian"), to work that sought to bring together his (and perforce her) triumphs and catastrophes, their friendships and enmities, along with Edwardsean thought, into one whole life. If the present chapter is to add anything to this, it will be its emphasis upon one central and explicitly erotic friendship, that of Sarah and Jonathan, contributing to our sense of the whole life they shared.

1. *The Story in Brief*

Jonathan Edwards was born October 5, 1703, significantly near the beginning of the century we call "the Age of Reason." He was born in a rural village, East Windsor, Connecticut, significantly remote from the intellectual centers of Europe, and a long day's horseback ride even from colonial New Haven. He was the son, and on his mother's side the grandson, of New England clergy, a child of Puritanism, but of that sort of nonseparatist Puritanism that still thought itself to be only the advance guard of all English-speaking Christendom—a son of Reformed, but definitely of mainline, Christianity. He was the fifth child and the only boy among eleven siblings.

What would life be for a lad with a mother, ten sisters, and a preacher for a father? Jonathan turned early to nature, perhaps as an escape from the intense sociality of home; he turned also to books. He turned as well to God, built with his boy playmates a "booth in the swamp" for prayer, and prayed alone long hours. He would discount those prayers, later. By age seventeen, or earlier, he was displaying original powers in what was then called "natural philosophy," what we would call scientific reasoning. His youthful scientific work, drawings and all, has been preserved in manuscript form (Edwards, 1980).

Meanwhile, in coastal and somewhat more refined New Haven, a daughter was born (January 10, 1710) to another Congregationalist clergyman, James Pierpont, and his wife Mary Hooker, she the granddaughter of the inimitable Thomas Hooker, first generation American, Puritan preacher, founder of Hartford. They named their baby Sarah, Hebrew for "princess," and even from the beginning she stunned everyone with her beauty and charm, to which before long were added the well-known Hooker and Pierpont skills of sociability.

Jonathan, the introvert boy genius, and Sarah, the extravert belle of the little college town, met when he was almost twenty-one. Having graduated, he had worked briefly as a minister and had returned to tutor younger students at little Yale, while she, a possibly precocious but noticeably nubile thirteen-year-old, was still in her parents' home on "Quality Row" in New Haven. It is remarkable, Elisabeth Dodds tells us, that these two survived their courtship, so different from one another were this "improbable couple"—he tall, gangling, bookish, inept; she "a vibrant brunette, with erect posture and burnished manners" (Dodds, 1971:11f.).

By the way, when it comes to biographical facts in this and the remaining biographical chapters, I will not cite the sources each time, save for direct quotations or to buttress a disputed position. In this chapter I will normally depend upon the resourceful Mrs. Dodds, and upon the documented early biographies by Samuel Hopkins (1765) and Sereno Edwards Dwight (Edwards, 1830:Vol. I) and the standard modern one by Ola E. Winslow (1940), guided all the while by Nancy Manspeaker's indispensible bibliographical notes (1981).

To continue, Sarah and Jonathan did nevertheless survive the courtship, and judging from one of its souvenirs, a little pen-picture of Sarah that Jonathan wrote on the flyleaf of his Greek grammar soon after they met, he at least was deeply in love: "They say there is a young lady in [New Haven] . . . ." (Edwards, 1962:56). Jonathan later said that he had then "sunk in religion; my mind being diverted . . . by some affairs that greatly perplexed and distracted my mind" (Hopkins, 1765:33). Could those "affairs" have been his meetings with Sarah, and the unexpected arousal that a passionate young Christian could experience so soon after his "hopeful conversion"? Or was it college tasks that disturbed him so? They courted by the fire in her parents' home, and on hikes on the beaches and through the woods. They talked books and nature, religion, and—no doubt—love. Evidently she found him awkward but loveable, while he found her gorgeous, but was afraid to say so. Four years later (1727), he having accepted a call to be assistant pastor of his grandfather Stoddard's big church in frontier Northampton, Massachusetts, Sarah and Jonathan were wed in New Haven. By then, she was seventeen. Thus the newlyweds set out for their first great common venture, a new home and a new calling in the West.

The Northampton years were tumultuous. Solomon Stoddard, Jonathan's grandfather, had become pastor of the church there when the town was a village and he a young ministerial graduate (1672). Town, church, and pastor had grown up together, and together they had faced the problems of how faith was to survive as wealth, drawn from the rich agricultural lands of the Connecticut Valley, increased, while Protestant piety became not a fresh new discovery of one generation, but the inherited possession of another. Stoddard himself was a shrewd investor and had prospered as the town prospered. The church's most difficult question had been how to attract members among the flourishing younger generation: Stoddard had answered this in terms of the Half Way Covenant, an ecclesiastical rule New England churches had adopted the year he had finished his Harvard A.M. (1662). By it, the infant-baptized children of members were to be considered already half-members of the church without professing any saving faith of their own; they could vote in town and parish matters, and since 1704 Stoddard had encouraged such folk to come to communion as well. It would, he said, be a "converting" ordinance, that is, a means toward their ultimate conversion.

By 1727, this half-way (older Puritans might have thought half-baked) scheme had gained one marvelous American argument in its favor: it had worked. Concretely, the church Jonathan and Sarah now joined had experienced repeated seasons of revival under Stoddard's regime; it had apparently flourished. And now it welcomed the new apprentice minister and his bride, providing for them a large field of labor. That the Half Way Covenant was a ticking time bomb, waiting to explode in Northampton, was in no way evident to the newcomers, and certainly not to old Solomon.

The married life of a young couple took its course. The first year a baby was born, a girl, whom they named for her mother. There is a comic touch here: New England superstition held that a baby's day of birth disclosed its day of conception—and little Sarah was born on Sunday, a day when Christians, and ministers in particular, were supposed to be worshiping and *resting!* The joke gets richer: Of the eleven children Sarah Edwards bore, no fewer than six were born on the Sabbath, and a seventh missed by only half an hour. Blessed day of rest! In any case, after they settled, in connubial union, to their work in Northampton in the summer of '27, there had been a halcyon period, he busy daily about the labors of visiting, study, and sermons, she busy with child-rearing (a new one arriving as on schedule every two years) and the special leader's role of a pastor's wife; both busy about household tasks, splitting wood, milking cows, acquiring furniture, making their house a home. In 1729, Solomon Stoddard died and the honeymoon period was over; Jonathan Edwards was elected pastor of the church.

At the start the young pastor and his younger wife were lionized. He was an excellent preacher; she was an inimitable teacher, mother, and hostess—and beautiful to boot. He was invited to distant, cosmopolitan Boston to preach a "publick lecture" at the age of twenty-seven: Harvard was paying its sceptical respects to Yale's pulpit prodigy. (The sermon-lecture, "God Glorified in Man's Dependence" was his first blow struck in the coming New England theological battle over revivals and the reaction to them.) Three years later, the divine light most evidently shone upon Northampton's First Church:

a revival broke out there in late 1734, continuing through spring and summer. The Edwardses were elated. God had blessed their faith in him with ripe fruitage in ministry. The Edwards study was filled with inquirers; the days were not long enough for their tasks in God's vineyard.

Even now, however, the storm was gathering. The revivals, in Northampton and elsewhere, attracted not only admirers but critics. Ultimately the battle would break friendships, split churches, even create several new denominations such as the Separatist Baptists and the Unitarians. Although at first there was little opposition in Northampton, where after all religion was flourishing again, scepticism appeared there, too. One overburdened church member, Joseph Hawley, Sr., afflicted by the chief emotional ill of eighteenth-century New England, 'melancholy,' committed suicide, slashing his throat. Elsewhere, emotional excesses marred the revival spirit. Jonathan worked incessantly in his parish, seeking to help his flock separate the wheat of revival from the chaff of mere natural excitement. Meanwhile, he patiently wrote to friends in Boston and abroad, describing the local events with the eye of a scientist, relating them to one another with a historian's discernment, interpreting them by Scripture light as a master theologian. He described the townspeople of Northampton, related individual narratives of apparent conversions (he never pretended to be able to see what God alone can), generalized upon the phenomena, noted exceptions, recorded observable consequences in the character and conduct of the converts, all with a care for the data worthy of generations of sociologists yet to be born (Edwards, 1737).

Next the Calvinist evangelist, George Whitefield, came to the colonies, preaching in all the major population centers and many other places. He reached Northampton, where Sarah was his hostess, in 1740, and straightway the Great Awakening broke out in the Connecticut Valley. Event followed event, fast and furious. Jonathan preached his "Sinners in the Hands of an Angry God" to spectacular results. Sarah provided counsel and offered her earnest prayers for young ministers such as Samuel Hopkins, who came to study with Jonathan—and she nursed her children through an epidemic of measles. James Davenport, a minister half ecstatic half berserk, went preaching from town to town, disaster following in his wake. In the midst of all this, one cold winter week Sarah collapsed (January, 1742)—her symptoms could have been diagnosed as spiritual crisis or alternatively as a nervous collapse—but recovered to a new serenity. More babies were born in the Edwards home on the old biennial schedule. The older Edwards girls were wooed, won, and wed, and sadly one daughter, Jerusha, died of the tuberculosis she contracted from her heroic but dying fiancé, David Brainerd, whom the Edwardses had given a temporary home.

Meanwhile, Jonathan preached his way through a definitive study of true religion, to be published four years later as the *Religious Affections* (1746). Strengthened by the revivals, by his successes in the pulpit, and by this study of Scripture, Jonathan now found courage to revolt against the spirit of his grandfather and the Half Way Covenant: henceforth, his pastoral practice would be to present candidates for church membership only when they professed true, that is converted, religion—a new heart evidenced by a new life. The Stoddard innovation, he had decided, was a spiritual failure. In socially climbing Northampton, however, this was not to be a welcome move. And then, in 1748, Colonel John Stoddard, the Edwards' staunchest friend in Northampton and a pillar in town and church, died; the way was open for Jonathan's opponents to bring him down (Miller, 1956:ch. 6).

When it came, the controversy erupted not over the root question of a regenerate church membership, nor even over the touchy one of Jonathan's handling of a problem of church discipline for some young people caught with a 'dirty' book. It was expressly over the formal question of who was to be admitted to the sacrament of communion. Was this, as Stoddard had come to hold, an ordinance for those who just might someday be converted, or was it as Edwards (with most of historic Christianity) was now persuaded, for those who were already Christians? And what was, who was, a 'Christian'? The church fractured over the question; the voting majority, led by Joseph Hawley, Jr., the sick son of the man who had once slashed his own throat, demanded Jonathan's resignation. Sarah, distressed, watched her circle of friends diminish. Jonathan sought to reason and to teach, but it was too late. Refused the privilege of explaining his view to the congregation, voted down in church meeting on an issue where he was sure he was in the right, his departure openly sought by many, he consented to be guided by a council to be drawn from sister churches. He lost there by one vote. Joseph Hawley, dogged by guilt, wrote years later to admit he had manipulated the outcome. Now, however, there was no further recourse. Twenty-three years of the Edwards' ministry in Northampton were ended—a shame as well as a tragedy in a land where lifelong pastorates were common enough.

They could have gone to Scotland or to England, where fame beckoned; Boston and New Haven were not open, however. In the end, they moved again to the frontier, this time to Stockbridge, Massachusetts—site of an Indian school and mission. It was the fringe of two worlds, the red and the white, unknown and known. He would be a missionary, she homemaker and once again advisor to women and men who sought her strength and wisdom. He settled down in this lonely outpost to minister and teach and to write books that thanks to their sheer intellectual power and original grasp of Christian theology are still in print: *The Freedom of the Will; The Nature of True Virtue; The End for Which God Created the World; Original Sin.* More Edwards children married and moved away; mission duties plucked incessantly at the parents' lives; Jonathan, never vigorous, and Sarah, mother of eleven, began visibly to age.

Then, after six years, destiny spoke—or seemed to speak. The College of New Jersey, future Princeton, needed a president. Would Jonathan Edwards be available? He would consider it. He prayed, and consulted his friends as a church council. He explained, to all who would listen, why he was hardly a suitable candidate for the presidency he clearly wanted so much. The council listened gravely, conferred with one another, told him he should accept. Touched in heart, "America's greatest speculative theologian" burst into tears.

The rest is anticlimactic. Jonathan went on ahead to Princeton in January, 1758, to get the college work lined up and to prepare the way for his family. Sarah would follow with the others. He was fifty-four years old. In February, as a precaution, he was inoculated for smallpox by a trusted physician, using the newly discovered vaccine. He was duly inaugurated as president. Then the expected vaccine fever set in, but it was too much for his frail system to resist. He weakened, rallied briefly, then died. Sarah came now to Princeton, but from this time on hers would be a lonely bed. Exhausted by events, worn by grief, harried by the duties death brings, she contracted dysentery. In six months, at the age of forty-seven, she was dead.

On his deathbed, Jonathan's last coherent words had been a message to Sarah. "Tell her," he dictated to his daughter, "that the uncommon union, which has so long subsisted between us, has been of such a nature, as I trust is spiritual, and therefore will continue forever" (Hopkins, 1765:80).

2. An Episode for Further Investigation

What did Jonathan Edwards mean in sending word to his wife that their union was "uncommon"? Was it that? And how was a union "spiritual" that had issued in eleven offspring? Of one thing we may be sure: Jonathan Edwards was not using his last words carelessly. The "major artist and chief American philosopher" (Miller, 1949:225) had not yet discarded his palette. His message to her had—all his words had—an exact meaning, Lockean in their empirical force, uncoded, that is there for us to recover if we will attend. Our business now is to discover if we can, both in his terms and in hers, the consistency of this "uncommon" and "spiritual" union that was at the same time unquestionably an erotic bond. Something greater than curiosity is at stake here. Jonathan Edwards is said to be a theologian of the heart and of the affections; to discover the kind of love that was central between these two may provide an exact clue to his strand-one based theological ethics—a bonus not to be disdained.

a. *Sarah's own narrative*—Our search could not go far, I think, but for the survival of a narrative written by Sarah, one of the few things that came from her hand to us. This was an autobiography, not in the sense of providing an account of external events or spanning a lifetime, but in the sense that in it she sought to discover and disclose her own deepest selfhood (for this sense of "autobiography," cf. Shea, 1968:207). I have already mentioned a "collapse" Sarah experienced in January, 1742, at the height of the Awakening in Northampton. The circumstances were these. Jonathan was about to leave on another of his many preaching trips. Two events that preceded his departure stood out vividly in Sarah's memory later: One was that she had felt "low in grace," but had been reassured in prayer that help would be forthcoming in God's own time and way. The other was that "Mr. Edwards" had found fault with her—she had shown, he said, some want of prudence—in her latest conversation with their family enemy in neighboring Hadley, the Reverend Mr. Williams. Sarah's distress focused neither upon the annoying Williamses nor upon the (apparently gentle) reproach from Jonathan, but upon herself: She did not like the fact that her husband and lover's criticism could upset her so, for that seemed to imply in her a lack of full reliance upon God only. She linked this excessive sensitivity to her too great desire to please everyone in the town, thus avoiding all criticism there, also. Now these two memories, that of being "low in grace," and that of cringing at slight criticism, seemed linked: They could be summed up as "uneasiness" within. Sarah's subsequent thoughts swung between the sweetness of the love of God and her privilege, through Jesus, to call God "Father"—thoughts that she found made her sometimes weak and faint. Sometimes these were accompanied by a corresponding sense of her own unworthiness. Still, the two ills that had recently preyed most on her mind—the town's mistreatment of her and Jonathan's censure—persisted as well, but now they seemed trivial by comparison to her "sweet and lively sense of divine things." Something was about to happen.

The time came for Jonathan to leave, and Samuel Buell, an attractive young Edwards protegé, arrived to stay in the Edwards household and conduct daily services in the church. Sarah braced herself afresh: What if Buell were to enjoy ministerial success in Northampton that overshadowed her pastor husband's work? She prayed for an accepting attitude, and thought she had been granted it. Indeed, she had, and in an extraordinary degree! After the second Buell service, there was excitement in the congregation, and many lingered inside the church. Rapturous feelings of "love to the souls of men" swept over Sarah; her bodily strength was overcome by these feelings. Thereafter, Buell's presence and conversation back at the Edwards' home tended to drive her into fresh heavenly raptures. She fainted, grew weak, and on one occasion "leaped unconsciously" from her chair as Buell read aloud a "melting hymn" about the loveliness of Christ. Household members had to help her to bed. Thursday night—two days after Buell's arrival, and eight after Jonathan's criticism had

jarred her so—was "the sweetest night I ever had in my life."
She lay half awake all night, drifting between the sense of
Christ's love for all, her love to Christ, and the glow of his love,
like "a pencil of sweet light," coming down into her heart.
Now, she realized, no criticism from town or from Jonathan
could touch her, and she was entirely willing that even the
reprehensible Williams of Hadley, who happened to be the
next scheduled pulpit visitor in Jonathan's absence, should be
the instrument of God in conversions there, willing that even
he should be more successful than her husband. Vanquished,
she felt, were "self-love," and "private, selfish interest";
God's glory was everything.

During all this inner turmoil, life in church and town went
on its regular if excited way. "Mrs. P—" let it be known she
was afraid that Sarah would die while Jonathan was away, and
then (she went on, dramatically) Mr. Edwards would believe
the people had killed his wife. This anxiety was dutifully and
promptly reported to Sarah, who responded tactfully. Still her
inner raptures continued unabated, for more than a week, and
with them the awareness of "a love to all mankind." Now the
Holy Spirit, "the Comforter," filled Sarah's attention; she
fainted once again. She recalled an old fantasy: what if
everything her family had were to be burned in a house fire,
and they were all turned out naked? Now, though, it seemed
she could accept this, resigning all cheerfully to God. And then
the extraordinary two weeks ended, and Jonathan returned
home, his own fresh triumphs of grace in another town
glowing in his memory.

How was it when the two lovers met again? There was his
reproach and her resentment to be acknowledged, certainly.
There was his trip to report. Most important of all, there were
her extraordinary adventures of the spirit that he had not been
there to witness. And was there as well the lovers' question,
whether spoken or implied: After all this, how is it between
us? In any case we know that Jonathan then did a very wise
thing: Hearing what had happened, he had Sarah sit down
with him and tell the whole story of her experience. After that,
he persuaded her to write it out in full, with the consequence
that these events of Sarah's life, never to be repeated with such
intensity, became a part of her record and ours (cf. Edwards,
1830:I, ch. 14; 1743:331-41; original ms. still unpublished).

b. *Varieties of interpretation*—To be sure, what can be made of the record depends greatly upon the tools of interpretation. Giving Sarah's own emphases first place, we might note that in her eyes the focus was to be placed not upon the weaknesses, the fainting spells, nor even upon the raptures of "the sweetest night I ever had," though she conscientiously notes without much comment these psychic and physical states. Rather from beginning to end her attention turns to herself in relation to God and neighbor: first the sensitivity to criticism, the sense of being "low in [God's] grace," and then the "love to all mankind," issuing from freshly realized love to the triune God of biblical religion—these are for Sarah the hinges on which everything turned. Buell, and Williams, and the obnoxious "Mrs. P—" (could there be a better pseudonym?) represent the neighbor; by natural standards they are objects of rivalry or enmity, but in Sarah's estimate of the episode, they became now objects of the grace of Christ, and she the channel of that grace.

Yet hers is not the only interpretation, and autobiography is a notoriously precarious task. What would a psychologist say? Happily, William James, the American father of that science, took particular interest in Mrs. Edwards' narrative. James in the *Varieties* explains the character he calls "saintliness," with its sense of the presence of the "Ideal power," its immense personal freedom, its shift of the emotional center toward harmonious affections, in terms of two elementary forces: impulses to action, and the inhibitions holding back, each at work in us all. Many of us experience brief moments in which impulses overcome all inhibitions: A mother whose baby is threatened, a soldier whose comrades charge into battle, each loses normal fears and inhibitions for the time. The saints, such as Sarah Edwards, are those in whom the impulses more permanently overcome the inhibitions, thus leading to lives of unusual devotion, heroic boldness, love that spills over even to enemies. James quotes at length from Sarah's narrative, treating her numinous night as a paradigm instance of that "sense of Presence" he thinks so typical of the saintly state. Later he returns to it as he seeks to illustrate the second characteristic of saintliness, its love to all, even enemies—"a level of emotion so unifying, so obliterative of differences . . . that even enmity may . . . fail to inhibit the friendlier interest aroused" (James, 1902/1958:219-24). Despite his capacity to classify and generalize, we may feel today that James' explanations leave something to be desired; let us look further.

Elisabeth Dodds provides a rather different analysis of Sarah's journey "to the breaking point and back"—her chapter title for the episode. For Dodds, the story is that of an illness with a favorable outcome. Sarah "went to pieces." The symptoms are those any woman, frustrated by the cares of a household, may experience; the explanation is that Sarah left alone at home passed into a manic period and "thought she was passing through a period of religious ecstasy." This hardly helps, but Dodds does add two valuable interpretive motifs that James omits: she notes the significance of the role of Samuel Buell (though she hardly goes beyond Sarah's recognition of Buell as a *ministerial* rival to her husband), and she recognizes the importance, throughout the episode, of Sarah's relation to the absent Jonathan: "without Jonathan near to steady her, Sarah cracked"—a touching note, since Dodds points out early on that it was Jonathan who depended on Sarah in many matters related to life at home (1971:100).

Have we any late-twentieth-century insight to add? Quite possibly there is a psycho-sexual dimension present in Sarah's autobiography. The tension between her and her husband and lover Jonathan, unresolved though diminished as he departs, stands in the background. Young Buell comes to take her husband's place, and she fears his arrival. As to impropriety of behavior between these two, there is no hint of this—and, had it existed in that fishbowl of a parsonage, there surely would have been talk. Buell may even have been unaware of his role in the drama (although we know that George Whitefield was not insensible to Sarah's feminine charms during his visit to that same house fifteen months earlier). Yet at another more elemental level may not Sarah's fainting in Buell's presence have been a "bodily weakness," as she called it, that bespoke sexual surrender at the approach of this young ram visiting Jonathan's flock in his absence? And in that light can we read an erotic coloration in the rest of Sarah's account? Not only in the fantasies in which she fled her house, stripped naked, but also in those scenes where she envisioned the heavenly life to come "with a ravishing sense of the unspeakable joys of the upper world," or lay in her "sweetest night" penetrated to the heart by Christ's beams of love? Yet this language implies, I think, no unseemly eroticism, but is rather the sublimation of primary process itself by a grace that suffused her soul and body alike. Or cannot the God who takes flesh invest his Spirit in mortals whose bodily makeup is among other things psycho-sexual?

Which brings us to the analysis Jonathan offered—he, who has been called "a pre-Freud Freudian" (Slosson, 1920), also thought long and hard about Sarah's narrative and its meaning. His first occasion to interpret these events came in the next of the series of narrative 'treatises' that in the war against the antirevivalists Edwards was firing like rockets from his study. *Some Thoughts Concerning the Revival*, written in the fall following Sarah's January crisis, appeared in Boston in March of the next year (Edwards, 1972:65). It was to be the last argument of its kind from his pen; hereafter he would choose other intellectual weapons. The book told again what had been happening in the awakened churches, but told it this time with an eye to the scornful objections of Boston rationalist Charles Chauncy and his sort. The test of the revivals, Edwards agreed with his critics, was their ripe fruit in Christ-like conduct. But it made no sense to say "we will wait to see the outcome"; the outcome was already here—not transports and ecstasies, for they were no certain evidences one way or another, and not excesses and indiscretions, which were regrettable—but the "strange alteration almost all over New England" in personal piety and social morality (Edwards, 1743:326).

And then, as if playing a trump card, Jonathan gave his sceptical readers the story of Sarah, utterly authentic, deeply Christian. Not that he would reveal her identity; through the account, she is simply "the person." Save for that protection, though, she is presented as revealingly as she had disclosed herself in the account she wrote for him; he suppresses, one judges from Dwight's version, only the references that Sarah had made to others, to Buell and Jonathan himself and the Reverend Williams and "Mrs. P—." Yet that made a telling change. For the story now seems curiously psychologized. With psychic and bodily states carefully noted, likely in Sarah's very words, and giving full credit to her emphases upon love to God and "mankind," the account still seems painfully clinical. What Edwards does furnish that Dwight does not is more clinical history: this crisis was not for Sarah a unique occurrence; it was one of several experiences continuing from long before anyone ever heard of the present Awakening, and its results remained to the present. Still, in understanding the events themselves, *Some Thoughts* hardly takes us beyond its forceful polemical point against the Boston rationalists.

Ten years later, though, again without naming Sarah or anyone else, Jonathan Edwards offered an analysis of true religion that connected Sarah's experience with his own deepest thoughts about love. *The Nature of True Virtue* showed how his thinking about love had unfolded subsequent to the Northampton tumult. Its formal theme was virtue, a term then synonymous with human goodness, with morality itself. Yet what "virtue" principally consists in (as even Edwards' intellectual opponents, "the more considerable Deists," must allow) is *love*. The term "love," however, requires that some distinctions be made. It is not this or that loving act or deed that constitutes true virtue, but a settled disposition to act lovingly; moreover it is not love toward one or another object of special favor that counts (could he have been thinking of the partisanship of those who drove him out of his church?), but "a disposition to benevolence towards being in general." And finally, it is not love that takes its rise in something lovable (love of complacence, in Edwards' archaic term) but love that is like the love of the Godhead, its motive self-giving, consent to the other, propensity to union, that alone filled the bill.

Here, then, were the distinctions on which Edwards could build a definition of Christian love: It was grace-love before it was delight-love ("benevolent" before "complacent"); it was not limited or partial (not "secondary"); it was steady ("dispositional," not episodic); it united those who loved in this way to God and to God's creatures (it was "consent," not "dissent"). Or, to quote a famous defining paragraph from *The Nature of True Virtue*:

True virtue most essentially consists in *benevolence to being in general*. Or perhaps, to speak more accurately, it is that consent, propensity, and union of heart to being in general, which is immediately exercised in a general good will. (Edwards, 1765/1960:3)

And that was true love—God's love to people, and the love God imparted *to* people when he gave "truly gracious religious affections"—when he saved them by his grace.

Not that there were not other 'loves'—other 'virtue' and 'beauty' as well. Edwards spoke of "particular" beauty, by which a thing appears beautiful only within a limited sphere or connection, as there might be a few musical notes, harmonious in themselves, but discordant in the whole composition. Corresponding to this in the moral sphere was that affection that was limited to a "private system" but that set itself against the whole of God's universe; by failing to consent to the whole, the private system (whether a band of pirates or a refractory Northampton congregation?) displayed a lack of that general consent that was the very nature of true love. This was a philosophically vital point, too; it gave Edwards a way to account for the *natural* beauty and virtue and love and conscience that other philosophers of the day celebrated (Fiering, 1981), while maintaining that what others were talking about remained at best a mere shadow of the true beauty, true love proclaimed, for example, in 1 Corinthians 13. "Charity . . . [that is, true love] seeketh not her own" (13:5): that makes charity the opposite of a selfish spirit (Edwards, 1852:lect. 8).

Now at last he had offered an account of love and of human goodness that made sense of the whole of Sarah's 'conversion.' His theory explained that which she had not liked in herself at the beginning of those two turbulent weeks, namely her confined dependence upon Jonathan's (and the town's) approval. To seek approval was not wrong, but it reflected only secondary virtue, the shadow love of a tight little private system there at home. It had needed replacement. Jonathan gave a name, as well, to the redeeming power that had reached down, then, into her life, shaking her, both body and soul. That had been the true beauty; it had been divine benevolence; it had been the love of God in Christ. And he gave a name, an explicit definition, to Sarah's new or renewed disposition that could overcome the old: What God had given her was love understood as cordial consent, her capacity to say yes to God and to all that was God's, not excluding Samuel Buell, and Mr. Williams, and even Mrs. P—.

And not least, Jonathan's theory provided a way to talk about her love for him and his for her. Lover's love confronts two possibilities: It can be an enclosed, bounded love that at bottom is mutual selfishness. Some who speak of love seem only to know about this kind. Or on the other hand it can be a love that while perfectly definite in its aim and perfectly delightful in experience (containing quite possibly a sizable amount of Edwardsean "complacence") is nevertheless continuous with unbounded (as Edwards said, with "general") love, love to being, love to God, love to all there is. As part of God's redemptive gift, moreover, this is "spiritual" love—and so far "uncommon," too—even when it is the love of erotic lovers such as this husband and this wife. In these terms, what Sarah had noticed in herself at the beginning of the two weeks was a bounded love that left her in conflict with her own ideals. She had valued excessively, she said, the "good opinion" of her husband, and had disliked that very excess exactly because she felt it sprang, not from God's love, but from love of self. But what she was enjoying at the end of the two weeks, and what was appropriately accompanied by her ecstasy, was unbounded love, spiritual love, and hence one that left her no longer fretful about the good opinion of the town, or about a lover's bark of displeasure over a trifle. In these terms Sarah's 'conversion' was, if truly gracious, a turn from secondary virtue (or bounded love) to true virtue (or the love of God).

3. *The Convergence of Theory and Life*

One vital link in Jonathan's interpretation of Sarah's crucial episode has so far been omitted. He had written out (perhaps for her) an account of his own similar experience. Jonathan's spiritual autobiography differed in one respect from his understanding of Sarah's: his conversion at age nineteen (shortly before he met her) was a new departure in his life, totally different from the mere 'natural' piety of his childhood prayers (Hopkins, 1765:24f., 28f.), while her childhood religious affections, he believed, were truly gracious from age five or six onward. Though he remained cautious as always about the limits of human knowledge in these matters, he thought that her crisis at age thirty-two was only "a vastly higher degree" of a work of grace begun much earlier (Edwards, 1743:335). So as he saw it their stories differed. More noteworthy, however, are the experiential parallels: the sweet sense of the beauty of God, the complete and unqualified commitment of life that each was freed to make as a consequence of the divine presence, the awareness of inner corruption and unworthiness not as a prelude to the sense of grace but as its consequence, the overflowing delight in God and gospel. Her account in every report of it is social, speaking of "love to all mankind" in a way that his does not; yet this perhaps reflects only different personalities, for the overall impression is of two who have breathed together the breath of the same Spirit.

a. *God's love in a harsh world*—If my surmise that Jonathan's sense of truly spiritual (albeit uncommon) love is a link that holds his life and thought together, it should be evident in those circumstances of his life in which his projects and purposes may run against our own. One such circumstance is that this gentle scholar and pastor did preach imprecatory (so-called "hell-fire") sermons, the best known being "Sinners in the Hands of an Angry God," which had no remarkable effect in Northampton, but when preached in neighboring Enfield church in June of 1741 made a historic impression on the hearers. How does such preaching comport with a theologian whose keys to God's character are said to be "beauty" and "love"?

Two things may strike the student of "Sinners" (Edwards, 1830:VII, 163-77) with special force today: its straightforward, unstrained tone, and its fascinating power over readers two and a half centuries later. The imagery of terror (the text is Deuteronomy 32:35, "their foot shall slide in due time") seems to come from one who was perfectly acquainted with the terror of which he spoke, one who had probed in the dark shadows of his own mind and found there a horror that most would have preferred to leave unexamined, whereas he had the courage to examine it with steady and unaverted gaze. The other striking observation is that the terror seems to preoccupy a later generation that denies it believes in any hell, but is curiously drawn, even while it professes disbelief, to attend the words of a preacher who described *his* hell without such denial. To be more direct, my attention is caught by those today whose hidden project may be the covert exploration of these dark recesses. Is their project aided (even while concealed) by the spectacle of a theorist of love who dared speak so bluntly of what he called "this awful subject"?

Dorothy Day, whose life story will appear in a later chapter, spoke of the love of God as a "harsh and dreadful love" (Miller, 1973:8f.) Perhaps some, in understanding that love, gain heights that enable them to see more clearly than the rest of us the horror, the terror, of love's alternative: love rejected. It comes out as hatred of self, of one another, and of God. Hell, indeed! Yet what the rest of us may not see very clearly, and may in our anxiety even forcefully deny, we nevertheless somehow prehend, and that harsh awareness rises with fresh force in our own century as we sense some all too human alternatives to divine love—the genocidal massacres, warfare and torture, mass starvation of populations, all of which seem to be the harvest of our own advanced century. Jonathan Edwards' imprecatory sermons, however we may deplore them, make that much clear.

The irony of that decade of the 1740s was that what he could truly depict only upon the eschatological screen of imminent judgment was actually being lived out, historically experienced, in the courtly minuet of life in Northampton, where he was in process of being dismissed by his congregation. As we have seen, the formal ground of the rupture between pastor and majority was the question of qualifications for communion. Beneath that formal issue, though, lay a material one that James Carse has decisively shown to be Edwards' demand for "visible saints" or evident Christians (Carse, 1967:ch. 8). Was a church of Christ to consist of two sorts of people—on the one hand those who are visibly Christian, and on the other those who are not? A true church and a false church, all within Christ's church? (Edwards, 1741:286f.) That, scripturally speaking, was ridiculous, but it was what Northampton's church practice under Stoddard had come to. If that were their theory (and Edwards could show them, if they cared to listen, that it was), then their only possible virtue was secondary virtue, their only love, the love of a "private system" that stopped at the cliquish walls of First Church. But a "private system," one which was in its foundation and essence closed, was (by all the logic there was) closed to the *general* system. Which meant in a word that it was hell. All God had to do was let a single foot slip, and such a system would, though too late, be seen for the essentially private Gehenna that it was. No wonder there was urgent need to display that peril in a way that would command attention. No wonder, too, that the prophet of love who brought that message was without honor in his own church.

b. *Love as consent and the problems of theology*—If love understood as cordial and general consent to being is Jonathan Edwards' organizing principle or key, it ought not only afford insight into his life with Sarah and his work as preacher, but also into those large intellectual tasks to which he devoted his time after the move from Northampton to Stockbridge. To unfold this line of argument, though, is clearly beyond the limits of the present chapter and book. James Gustafson has touched upon the centrality of love in Edwards' theology in noting that for him as for Augustine, Calvin, and Schleiermacher, affectivity is an indispensible element of true religion (Gustafson, 1981:163-76). And the New England theology (those thinkers starting with Hopkins and Joseph Bellamy who followed Edwards) recognized the centrality of love, which they defined as "disinterested benevolence" (Ahlstrom, 1972:408). Yet both of these miss the Edwardsean focus by their undue subjectivity, as do those interpreters who concentrate too much upon Edwards' "sense of the heart." For him, love is inconceivable without an object; when in *True Virtue* he turns to benevolence as theologically prior in true love (grace-love prior to delight-love in defense of the primacy of grace), he cannot establish it without positing being, God's own being and thence created being, as the necessary object or target of benevolence; hence love is necessarily for Edwards a relational term, a transitive verb, not a bare sentiment or affect (cf. DeLattre, 1968:18).

Those who have written about the theoretical treatises produced during the Edwards' Stockbridge period have usually spoken of Jonathan's intention to combat "Arminianism"—his label for the defect he saw in a contemporary theology that would finally banish God from an Enlightened universe. This was indeed his intention, but Jonathan Edwards would fight no intellectual battles without a strategic master plan by which they could be conducted. We can best discover the plan he had then by noting first *The End for Which God Created the World*, written as a companion "dissertation" to *True Virtue*. In the latter he unfolded the nature of divine and human love. In the other, he displayed that divine love at work toward its end or goal. Why did God create any world at all, seeing there was already so much primary beauty in the triune God's own being? Edwards' answer was, "God's glory," but this misstates what he said unless we add, "God's glory *emanating*"—not just remaining in God, but journeying out to the creature, its goal forever being to give itself away. The divine wisdom, goodness, and joy (the three things in which God's glory consists) were not to be hoarded, but imparted, so that the "union" (was it not an uncommon and spiritual one?) of the creature with God is to be "an infinitely perfect" union. "If by reason of the strictness of the union of a man and his family" (but Edwards has just noted that the biblical example, Ephesians 5:25ff., is not just any family, but *husband and wife*), "if . . . their interest may be looked upon as one, how much more so is the interest of Christ and his church—whose first union in heaven is unspeakably more perfect and exalted" (Edwards, 1830:III, 87).

Two substantial obstacles, Edwards knew, stood in the way of the positive program of the "dissertations." One was that people should fail to see what God was doing because they erroneously made the divine love mission to the world impossibly difficult. This move was made, he believed, by those who took too exalted a view of the human will, understanding it as a sort of absolute inner sovereign that would overshadow divinity itself. Against that portentous doctrine of the will, he wrote the treatise on *Freedom of the Will* (ed. Ramsey, 1754/1957). The other obstacle was the antithesis of the first; it was that people should be tempted to underestimate the human plight, supposing no grace-given salvation necessary. Against that, he wrote *Original Sin* (ed. Holbrook, 1758/1970). In a way, these two works came down to the same thing: correcting the presumptuous substitution of another story for the biblical story of God's good intention, of human fault and blame, and of the gracious rescue in Christ. Yet that presumption, with the errors it entailed, could finally be refuted only by the proper telling of the true story itself in all its contemporary power. Jonathan proposed to do just that—to undertake, as he wrote in October, 1757, to the Princeton trustees, "a great work, which I call a *History of the Work of Redemption*, a body of divinity in an entire new method, being thrown into the form of a history . . ." (Edwards, 1962:411). Yet America's great narrative theologian was not permitted the time to complete that work. We can be sure that had he done so, its theme would again have been the gift of a universe that moved merely by consent of being to being, that is, moved by love.

*   *   *   *   *

Jonathan and Sarah were lovers. As lovers may, they shared a life full of hard knocks, failure, and loss: children succumbed, others' loyalty failed them, changing times seemed to leave these two at the margins of our history. Yet this love story is not a sad one. For at its center glows a love that was truly gracious and truly human, too. As earthy, human love it sufficed to draw together two young people and hold them there, issuing along the way in eleven offspring. As the fabric of their common life, thinking and talking together, confronting enemies and friends in town and church, their love sustained them through life's vicissitudes. As transformative power, God's gracious gift, love drew them heavenward in a union at once spiritual and uncommon.

Interestingly, Jonathan Edwards' ethics displays, as we have seen in brief, three corresponding elements. At root it is 'aesthetic'—a strand-one ethic of beauty and consent. Yet his skill was to display (though sometimes, necessarily, as "secondary virtue") a politics that fitted his ethics, and could give strand-two account of social structures, including the very ones that brought him down. Meantime, in the turbulence of the Awakening he developed an ethic of conversion. Only God can give the new sense of the heart—"gracious and holy affections" that "have their exercise and fruit in Christian practice" (Edwards, 1746:383). So more than most we will examine here he plumbed the depths of Christian morality, just as in his life with Sarah he sounded the deeps of Christian love.

Eros —
Toward an Ethic
of Sexual Love

One of the themes of Denis de Rougemont's classic study, *Love in the Western World*, is that genuine romantic love shrinks from physical sexual expression. The act of love is a 'sin,' not in his view according to Christian doctrine, but according to the tradition of high romance. "The starting point of both *Lancelot* and *Tristan* is a sin against courtly love—the physical possession [by the hero] of a real woman, and hence a 'profanation' of love." (Rougemont, 1939/1983:126). It will be of some help to us in understanding how Rougemont's thesis is meant if we have a sense of this romantic tradition with its curiously antiphysical understanding of sexual love and eros. Such an understanding will be a useful prelude to our proper inquiry, which is to discover a characteristically Christian (and so not characteristically romantic) view of eros. Some Christians have always known that erotic love and its acts of love constitute as such no sin. Yet there is widespread misunderstanding at this point. So the task will be to show *how* as God's good gift sexual love is ingredient to the Christian morality of the body. In other words I must show, against considerable weight of tradition and stereotypical belief, the place of eros in Christian morality, and in the course of doing so also show why this place has been denied and how its truth may be recovered. Along the way we will again encounter Edwardsean insights.

132

It is, I think, no accident that some readers will have turned first to this chapter on sexual love. This is not only because of the telling fact that the very term "morality" is in popular use synonymous with "sexual morality," or merely because readers crave a bit of titillation in the otherwise dreary pages of a volume of theology. Mainly, it is because there is widespread confusion about eros. We are sure (pretty sure) of some wrong ways of thinking about its drives and needs, but we are not as sure of the right way as in other realms of life, and we want some guidance—yet not too much guidance, either—in a confusing venture. What is to be made of the demanding erotic signals that are no small part of the drives and needs of embodied selfhood? And what of the equally present but often chaotic feelings and judgments: feelings that include some shame and blame and guilt but that include also brave eros itself in all its spectacular variety, and judgments that in their apparent diversity nevertheless owe so much to their context in our own puzzled century? It will be evident from previous chapters that the sort of overall guidance or reassurance about eros that we wish for cannot come from first-strand considerations alone; for that reason if no other this chapter is bound to disappoint. Yet it may be worth noting that the writer shares with concerned readers a common sense of need here. So while the chapter cannot answer every, or even most, of our questions about Christian sexual morality, yet its more limited aim of a Christian understanding of eros may take us a significant step toward the moral self-understanding we want.

1. The Myth of Romantic Love

The sphere of sexual love is one in which most Christians are closely connected with the dominant thought patterns of the culture in which they live—a good thing, if the only alternative were isolation from the cares and sorrows of the rest of the world, but a circumstance requiring that we attend critically to that environment. How is this to be done? For love, in its inwardness and secrecy, the most reliable common access has always been by the way of literature; for a century now this avenue has been supplemented and sometimes supplanted by the insights of Freudian psychology. So it behooves us to listen to each of these in turn.

Let us return to the classic work of de Rougemont. He paints with broad brush strokes, his overall claim being that a distinct myth of love traveled from the medieval heretical Catholic movement, the Cathari ("pure ones") via the twelfth-century court bards, to the written verse romance of the star-crossed lovers Tristan and Iseult (or Isolde), and from these poems into modern romantic literature. The myth had as its distinguishing feature an ascetic note. This feature was deliberately (albeit covertly) opposed to the Christian or orthodox ideal of sexual love that finds its fulfillment in the marriage bed. Central to this "heretical" ascetic note was the renunciation of marriage because of its vulgar physical basis; it was the mere indulgence of lust. Courtly love, by contrast, was never a love for one's spouse, was seldom to be consummated, and reached its height only in an unfulfillable eros or desire considered valuable for its own sake—and ultimately in the tragic consummation of death for the lovers. Such erotic longing, intrinsically valuable exactly because it could not be fulfilled, cannot be comprehended as the offspring of straightforward animal sexual desire. It must rather be understood as the transposition into love story terms of a theme of suffering and yearning originally religious and mystical: hence the significance of Rougemont's attention to Manichaeism and the Cathari (Rougemont, 1939/1983:15-150).

Several twelfth-century poems tell the Tristan story. Tristan, an orphan, becomes the adopted son of King Mark of Cornwall. He shows martial prowess early, and is in due course entrusted by Mark with the task of bringing the king's chosen bride, Princess Iseult, from Ireland to Cornwall. On the homeward voyage, escort and princess "by mistake" drink a love potion intended for Iseult and Mark at the forthcoming wedding. Tristan and Iseult fall under its magical spell; now their doom is sealed. They make love—their 'sin' against courtly love—but Tristan is still bound to deliver her to King Mark, which he does. Nevertheless, after the royal wedding sexual adventures in the castle in Cornwall ensue, culminating in the flight of the romantic pair into the Forest of Morrois; there they live for three years a life "harsh and hard." At the end the love potion wears off; they 'repent' of their affair; Iseult returns to Mark. Secretly the lovers plot reunion, but they are found out. Following a trial by ordeal for Iseult, and a mistaken marriage to another woman for Tristan, they once more seek one another out; but death intervenes for them both, and the story ends. Rougemont points out that by the canons of mere sexual (and knightly) adventure, it should have ended much sooner. Why, he asks, does Tristan not early on challenge Mark's right to Iseult? Why does he later contract a loveless marriage? These and a dozen other questions can only be answered by discovering within the tale the disguised myth its tellers have inherited: the need for love understood as yearning, and for death as passionate fulfillment, is stronger than the need for love understood as consummation and for marital sex (1939/1983:35-46).

Rougemont's larger claim is that the *passion* of love, understood as deprivation and yearning, is the dominant theme not only of *Tristan* but also of love in the Western world to the present. I accept the claim; let me illustrate it with the plot of a popular romance from the 1960s, Erich Segal's *Love Story* (1970). Panned by critics as banal and without literary merit, *Love Story* at first glance appears to have abandoned the romantic tradition outright. Its hero and heroine do get married and yet the story continues; they carry on a 'courtship' in fairly explicit sexual terms; otherwise the plot seems almost nonexistent: Harvard boy meets Radcliffe girl; they marry and move to New York; she contracts leukemia and dies.

Neither this nor what I take to be the novel's authentic report of Cambridge, Massachusetts, 1960s youth lingo and mating habits would seem to explain its popular success. What does? Note some further details: Oliver Barrett IV (Tristan?) has a powerful opponent in the person of his father, Oliver Barrett III (King Mark?), himself a Harvard alumnus. Oliver IV plays varsity hockey ('martial' prowess?). Like Tristan and Iseult, Oliver and Jennifer Cavilleri sharply distinguish physical sex from 'being in love.' Sexual adventures in the dormitory (the castle?) culminate in their civil marriage (for they like Tristan and Iseult are indifferent to the church's claims). Immediately after marriage, they enter upon *three years* of shared student poverty (their time in the Forest of Morrois?). This period ends in the 'going back' to the world of Oliver's father (a New York job for Oliver-Tristan), yet they avoid procreation (though not copulation) until the novel's climax, at which time Jenny-Iseult's fatal illness is discovered.

Allowing a few adjustments from mid-twelfth to mid-twentieth century, and a considerably larger adjustment from the poetic powers of Thomas of Britain to those of Erich Segal, we can reckon that the myth has survived very nearly intact. Perhaps the point at which the parallel comes nearest to failing is in the claim of de Rougemont that the intercourse that sets the romance of Tristan in action is a "profanation" of courtly love. Yet it can be argued that the sexual encounters of Jennifer and Oliver even here fit the mythic pattern, the evidence being the pains which Oliver as narrator takes in describing his attitude prior to their first sexual congress in Jenny's room and in relating the later amatory activity in his own. The sexual behavior of these two, author and narrator would have us believe, is to be distinguished from all superficially similar acts. This alone is real love. Oliver refuses, for example, to admit to his roommate Ray Stratton that he is "making it" with Jenny, for to treat what he does with Jenny as "making it" would, we might say, be a *profanation*.

Love Story is hardly the nadir of recent romantic literature; supermarket racks are filled with worse. At the other end of the spectrum, though, lies the justly celebrated work of John Updike (1932–), whose novels, short stories, poetry, and critical essays have won praise from critics and common readers alike. Does the Tristan myth survive in the work of this modern master? The first clear evidence comes from *Marry Me*, a relatively early Updike work. In the book, Jerry and Sally are in love, and are having an affair. There is a complication—each is married to another, and the two married couples are 'friends' in the same small suburban Connecticut town. This tangled familial setting, together with Updike's use of realistic detail, gives the story verisimilitude. Yet woven through it are hints that the author is deliberately repeating, in this disguise, the old myth of Tristan and Iseult. Images from the medieval romantic tradition ("magic mirror," "an idyllic day," "My poor brave lady," "princess married to an ogre," "knight to rescue,") recur throughout the book. Sally is, thanks exactly to her marriage and children, the "unattainable lady" whom Jerry must endlessly pursue. Unable to break the spell, even after the secret affair is confessed to both spouses, Jerry goes away to St. Croix in the Virgin Islands, and there, as the book ends, he fantasizes "a dimension in which he did go, as was right, at that party, or the next, and stand, timid and exultant, above the downcast eyes of her gracious, sorrowing face, and say to Sally, *Marry me*" (Updike, 1976:303).

On the other hand, *Marry Me* carries more than one antidote to the myth it repeats. There is Ruth, Jerry's Unitarian, no-nonsense wife, whose own affair with Richard, Sally's husband, is sensibly terminated, and who believes in the practicalities of sex and marriage (she is a more skillful lover than Sally) rather than in high romance. And there is Updike's device of juxtaposing Jerry's romantic dream of suffering love with the insufferable jargon in which Jerry and Sally talk to one another: *"Your hair is so soft, Jerry./I washed it last night. For you./For me?/It was full of sand from the beach, and I thought to myself . . . ."* (1976:278). All this at book's length, as though Updike were saying to us, Here is our received myth of love. Can we really abide in it—or even abide it? It is instructive to learn that at the time he was working on *Marry Me*, Updike was also writing a long critical study of the work of Denis de Rougemont, in which the modern author both challenges and concedes the power of de Rougemont's analysis (Updike, 1966; cf. J. Campbell, 1980-81).

This ambiguous stance toward the myth is even more pronounced in Updike's next major work, the novel *Couples*. (Though published long before *Marry Me*, *Couples* was written just after it.) Also set in the early sixties in suburban New England, *Couples* seems to discard altogether the Tristan and Iseult myth that the other book half scorned, half embraced. *Couples'* hero, Piet Hanema, is married to Angela as the novel begins and despite his frequent lecheries remains committed to marriage, at least, at novel's end, and the remaining characters, middle-aged New England business and professional people, appear in pairs as uniformly as Noah's animals entering the ark. To be sure, the interest of the novel is no more in marital sex than was Thomas of Britain's *Tristan*. The couples in *Couples* are married only to permit the author to establish the dull, rejected legitimacy against which the illegitimate spice of their relentless adulteries may be displayed. So while the explicit *Tristan* plot seems missing from *Couples*, its constituent motifs, as in a cubist painting, are still present. Piet's affair with his latest love object, Foxy (whose very name suggests that nothing other than animal sexuality constitutes her attractiveness) is no unrealizable ideal—instead, at novel's end, she is about to move away with Piet. The unattainable woman is rather Angela, who as Piet's lawful wife is his to possess, so that her inaccessibility as his lover seems to lie in her simple goodness, and not in cruel circumstance or physical shortcomings. So the *Tristan* plot *appears* to be abandoned, but its separated motifs remain, as if Updike were asking us, as sharers in the romantic tradition, Now what do we couples do with these shards of love that lie about us still? (J. Campbell, 1980-81). At novel's end, we are told that the new couple, Piet and Foxy, will move to another town where we must assume they will repeat the endless and aimless couplings the novel has just displayed.

What these samples of the recent literature illustrate, though in rather different ways, is the continuing power of the old romantic love myth in its primal form: the attractiveness of love understood as yearning desire, the banality or triviality of ordinary sexual intercourse (contrasted with its enormous symbolic importance in exceptional cases), and finally the necessity of suffering and ultimate loss: death as the culmination of romance. True love can't last. Updike's work, appealing to a somewhat different audience, makes a related point clear: the persistence of these elements of the mythic story even when its original narrative line is explicitly rejected. Piet Hanema, in contrast to his wife Angela, professes Christian belief, but it makes no difference to his sexual behavior; his life is dominated by love understood according to another sort of story than the Christian one. The enormous power of the romantic myth shows itself here, too, for we are bound to acknowledge the real life quality of Updike's characters. Though we dismiss Segal's, despite the occasional realistic details, as an escapist fiction, Updike's novel is more difficult to ignore simply because it tells us the truth, at least some of the truth, about ourselves, namely that we remain 'romantic' despite everything.

This brings up the question whether these writers about romantic love write as they do because it represents the way many of us experience life, or whether we Westerners experience typical romantic feelings in real life (for example, falling in love as if we had drunk a magic potion) because we have been provided with this (mythic) story. Common sense suggests the former, yet there is more reason to agree with de Rougemont: what we have to do with in romantic love is a very powerful *myth* that, for those under its influence, creates like a drug the very hunger it purports to assuage (1939/1983:141f.). The myth, the story, creates the experience of love in those who know the story, rather than the other way around. If however there *is* a good argument for the primacy of sexual instinct over our (culturally determined) narratives, it must be that of Freud and his followers, so we had better hear from them next.

2. *The Freudian Corrective*

Toward the end of his life, Sigmund Freud (1856–1939) sought more and more to simplify and unify the rather complex psychological theories he had produced in the course of his discovery of psychoanalysis. At the same time, he tried to relate these newly unified theories to the besetting problems of twentieth-century life: widespread discontent with common life in the West, the rise of totalitarianism, and the threat of annihilating war. Over the years his theory of the instincts, the most elemental of life's drives, had gone through several revisions. By the time he wrote what was perhaps the greatest of his synthesizing works, *Civilization and Its Discontents*, Freud had concluded that there were two elemental instincts—one, libido or eros, functioning to perpetuate life, the other, aggression or destruction, functioning to end it. Of these two, eros was the greater; indeed "civilization is a process in the service of Eros, whose purpose is to combine single human individuals, and after that families, then races, peoples and nations, into one great unity, the unity of mankind" (1930/1962:69). Freud went on to express wonderment that this unifying drive should indeed be present in all life. Before the present chapter is done we may have cause to address the same essentially theological wonderment and to seek a Christian answer.

However, for Freud, a nonobservant Viennese Jew, the more urgent question had long been the relation of eros to the elemental physiological facts. At one early stage he had even sketched out a scheme for relating the flow of charged neurons in the nervous system to these elemental drives (1895/1954)—an attempt ultimately abandoned. His characteristic work on sex and love, however, was carried through in connection with the development of psychoanalytic technique, as we can see today from the summary in the *Introductory Lectures* he gave at the University of Vienna during the second decade of this century (1917/1973:lects. 20f.).

Freud the lecturer was never a dogmatist. His method was to lay the often unwelcome evidence on which he had based his theories before his audience of medical students, asking these "ladies and gentlemen" to draw their own conclusions. Thus the lecture dealing with "The Sexual Life of Human Beings" begins with the question of what "sexual" is supposed to convey. An unsatisfactory, because too limited, answer is offered: The sexual has to do with reproduction, or with its means of achievement. But this definition, Freud points out, will exclude two very important classes of people: deviants, whose aim and object in sex differ from the genital-reproductive sexual norm, and, even more important, children, who have not yet the power of reproduction, but who are nevertheless sexual beings. The definition also omits the evidence provided by a third class, Freud's neurotic patients, whose symptoms recapitulate the sexual poly-morphy of childhood, as does the deviants' behavior. By these steps Freud leads his listeners to consider his own hypothesis: What we call genital sexual behavior is but a special (though of course an important) case of a much more diffuse, lifelong, and ubiquitous drive, the erotic or libidinal impulse, which is also present in phenomena as diverse as the intense pleasure taken in sucking by a newborn infant, in the attachment of children to parents and of siblings to one another, and even in the austere pleasures of friendship, as well as in the everyday (but nongenital) eroticism of a lovers' kiss. That there are differences in these phenomena, Freud never denies; indeed his task is to understand the differences, but this is to be done by discovering the continuities. Homosexuality and hetero-sexuality, the love of kin and the love that generates new kin, base 'depraved' love and elevated 'spiritual' love—all these have a common erotic root, experienced already in the oral pleasure of the sucking babe.

This, then, is the famous Freudian reductionism applied to love. What shall we make of it? First, one should note that Freud's thinking is remarkably open to whatever facts are available, even the facts that may be ignored as trivial or rejected because they shock or offend. While today psychoan-alytic doctrine in various dilutions is a commonplace of counselors and even of preachers of the gospel, in earlier decades of our century (as even now in some settings) it would have given offense not only because of its conclusions but even because of its data. Second, Freud himself did not draw amoral or immoral conclusions from his own work. He remained to the end of his life devoted to the cause of lawful, civilized conduct, and was on the best evidence an irreproachably loyal and decent husband and father.

On all these points Freud seems from our present standpoint beyond serious criticism. If he is to be criticized for present purposes, it is rather from the opposite point of view: that his reductionism is not sufficiently thoroughgoing. In the lecture on sex, for example, Freud drew on three kinds of evidence for his broadened definition of eroticism, a definition crucial to his theory. These were the experience of deviants, that of infants, and that of neurotics. But the first might have been discounted by Freud's moralizing opponents, and the second was admittedly a matter of interpretation. The real key, then, was the evidence provided by Freud's patients, complaining of crippling neurotic symptoms. And from these patients the evidence he drew was *a story*—the deep and sometimes almost inextricably hidden story of their own lives. Thus the sense he made of their bewildering symptoms—compulsions, fetishes, phobias, 'hysterical' weaknesses and incapacities, 'irrational' habits and attitudes—was just the sense that a story can make of the otherwise disconnected happenings that compose it. His was a story-formed therapy, a story-formed account of sex and aggression and their many permutations. And when in time an overall theory of the love-instinct finally took shape, first in the *Three Essays* (1905b) and in summary in the *Introductory Lectures* (1917/1973), it was a theory born of his narrative reconstruction of these lives in distress.

A second but like consideration in understanding what Freud was up to is this: In formulating the later, general theories, Freud, who had from his boyhood on immersed himself in the classics of European literature and art, drew upon the poets and dramatists not merely for the illustration but also for the formulation of his theory. The Oedipus myth of Sophocles' play and the Hamlet theme of Shakespeare's were for Freud meter stick and laboratory balance in developing the theory of childhood's forgotten sexuality. *Eros* was not only the label for the libido of 'neuronal cathexes,' but the name of a

Greek god whose myths might be employed to draw out and analyze the story of love. Freud the 'reductionist' has his stories of love as much as did Thomas of Britain or John Updike; he is a *narrative* psychologist. And more profound than either of these uses of story, since it is basic to both, is the mythic self-understanding of Enlightenment civilization embodied in Freud, the narrative he had inherited not from the poets and playwrights but from Hume and Feuerbach, of a human world long oppressed by its persistent religious illusion, but needing to break that bond in the name of "education to reality" (1927/1964:81).

Carol Gilligan, whose study of the psychological development of girls as it differs from that of boys challenged the work of Lawrence Kohlberg (Gilligan, 1982), subsequently criticized Sigmund Freud's failure to be sufficiently attentive to the characteristic interests of women in the case studies from which he developed his theory of love. Using Freud's report of the Dora case (Freud, 1905a) as evidence, Gilligan surmised that Freud had paid insufficient attention to certain clues imbedded in what Dora was telling him about herself. This is in fact the repetition of a reproach Freud had brought against himself in connection with his report of this case. In retrospect, he wrote that "the fault in my technique lay in . . . [my] failure to discover in time and to inform the patient that her homosexual love for Frau K. was the strongest unconscious current in her mental life." And to this Freud had appended a further thought: one of Dora's dreams had concealed "the magnanimity with which she forgave the treachery of [Frau K.]." After quoting these Freudian ruminations, Carol Gilligan suggested that the real story, the one "*not* heard in the analysis," was "a story of loyalty and love" (1984:84).

We find ourselves caring about this little conflict between the living and the dead psychologist, between the female and the male theoretician, because it reminds us of an interest shared with Carol Gilligan and with feminists generally: that women's stories be truly heard and truly told. In this case it is an interest shared by Freud as well, who was persistently interested in the "asymmetry" of male and female development and the light it shed on the deep understanding of human nature (Freud, 1933/1965:lect. 33). There is a further value of the disagreement for us now, however. This lies in its testimony to the conflict between story and story: the way in which in the Dora case "the elucidation of one story of love led another to become progressively obscured" (Gilligan, 1984:86). At the level of discovering what went on for patients like Dora that is important enough. But what if an obscuring story, shared by Freud and his critical followers alike, affects not merely that patient, or every psychiatric patient, but all of us?

That brings us back to the more general question that has arisen for us about love in the West. We began with the claim (de Rougemont) that our Western understanding of love is dominated by a mythic narrative of romance, which interprets love as uncontrollable magic, infinite yearning, the road to tragic death. We saw that view, or its broken remains, retaining power even today, as reflected in recent literature. For relief, we then turned to the psychoanalytic picture of love. Here love can indeed be seen reduced to organic libidinal drive, but the reduction turns out to be shorthand for *another* cluster of narratives—the stories of the developing sexual child, of the oedipal struggle, of the emancipated or illusion-free individual or the sexually liberated society—stories that carry their own substantial interpretive freight into the understanding of love. Thus stories of love can collide, and can obscure one another from view. We exist as in a tournament of narratives; nowhere is there a story-free 'love' to be discovered; our Christian hope lies rather in finding the banner of those true stories of love that will set us free from the less true and from the false.

3. *The Romance of Orthodoxy*

a. *The Augustinian version*—Finding our Christian way here may not be as easy as the image of the fluttering banners may suggest. There is some question whether the banners of an authentically Christian view of sexual love have ever been properly hoisted; if they have, they may have been hidden from view by other, less attractive ensigns. While we cannot set this right all at once in this place, we can at least hope to see what has gone wrong.

There can be no coming to terms with the Christian view of sexual love that does not sooner or later encounter the views of Augustine of Hippo (354–430), and no understanding of

Augustine that does not constantly turn back to his remarkable life story (P. Brown, 1969). Born into a Christian household in North Africa, Augustine was trained for a career as a rhetorician—a sort of literature professor and philosopher combined. Education for this career introduced him to the Manichaeans, whose part Christian, part Gnostic movement we have noted above. Manichaean dualism and asceticism (matter is evil, spirit is good) appealed both to the intellect of the orator in him and to the moral nature of a youth struggling just then to come to terms with his sexual drive. He became a Manichee. He settled with a woman, and was already a father at nineteen though, his wife not being of the right class, it was not a 'proper' marriage. In a few years the little family journeyed to Italy for Augustine to seek his fortune as a rhetorician. There he became a neoplatonist (another step within the dualist frame), made friends, and attained success. Strongly influenced by Monica, his mother, he sent away his faithful mistress preparatory to a socially suitable marriage, only to find that the long habit of sex drove him now to an interim arrangement with another woman. Then, under the influence of Ambrose, Bishop of Milan, he was inwardly converted (while reading the text, "not in chambering and wantonness"—Romans 13:13f.), and at the age of thirty-three he was baptized a Catholic Christian.

Before long he had been ordained a priest, had established a monastery back in North Africa, and, recognized for his brilliance, had been made bishop of Hippo Regius, second port city of Africa. His oratory, his writing, and his political adroitness soon made this now celibate monk-bishop the intellectual master of the Western Catholic Church. His views on sex would modify the attitudes of Christian Europe for more than a thousand years. What were those views?

Two themes appear, tied together by the often puzzling Augustinian term *concupiscentia carnis*—which we may translate "the longing of the flesh" only if we remember that "flesh" here, as in Paul, may mean a disturbance of mind or soul rather than of the biological self. The first theme, evident in the *Confessions* Augustine wrote more than a decade after his conversion, reflected a view that had become common enough in the ascetic morality of earlier church Fathers: sex is a descent from the high level of spirituality. A Christian, a true Christian, will long for that splendid estate that is God's and the angels' and was perhaps Adam's and Eve's before their sin: In that state, *concupiscentia* has no power over human beings. Augustine at this level of his thought even regretted the necessity of eating and drinking, for whenever he ate and drank, the temptation, the lustful longing to do so for sheer pleasure, not for nourishment, once again arose (*Conf.* 10:44). How glad he was to be free of the similar temptation of marriage! While technically, *concupiscentia* is an evil or trauma, not a sin, its inevitable association with sin in fallen beings leaves that only a technicality. Peter Brown associates this stage of Augustine's thought with the "ascetic paradigm" of Manichaeism and of the ancient world (Brown, 1983:5f.). Had it been Augustine's only level of thinking about sex, perhaps he would have remained intellectually a Manichaean or neoplatonist.

In the complex mind of the African bishop, however, another theme on another level also appears. What Brown calls the "social paradigm" of sin (Brown, 1983:11) dominates Augustine's discussion of sex in Book 14 of the *City of God*. The old Manichaean dualism with its hierarchy of value from spiritual at one end to material at the other is here abandoned: the incarnation has abolished such thinking. The Word became *flesh*. Now sexual capacity is recognized in Adam and Eve before their fall; a sexual nature is original equipment for human beings. *Concupiscentia* is here as in the other paradigm a mark of fallen human life, but now it is more a symptom than an ill. Fallen man is unable to control his sexual organs at will. The shame we associate with these involuntary phenomena gives evidence of psychically disordered human selves after the fall. Moreover it is exact evidence, for just as the human will in sin has closed itself against God, so in an altogether fitting punishment human flesh erratically closes itself against its owner's intentions. Since sin is a social disorder, the breaking of relations with God, it follows that sex, the most social of human attributes, should be fitly thrown into disorder as punishment for the primal sin.

Yet over against that disorder, at this second level of his thinking, Augustine counterposes in Book 22 of *City of God* a note of hope: the resurrection will be in and of the body, including the body's sexual distinctiveness. And this anticipation casts its happy promise back over present life, enabling Augustine to celebrate also the propagation of the generations in this age as God's blessing and gift. Had this second theme alone predominated, Augustine might have been a kind of earnest Pelagian (rather than the mortal enemy of all Pelagian moral optimism). Instead, both themes together form a paradoxical Christian stance toward sex.

As Margaret Miles has pointed out (1979; 1981:ch. 3), Augustine did not pass decisively from one of these themes to the other but from time to time fluctuated between their contrary outlooks upon sex. From the former there would flow the subsequent exaltation of celibacy in clerical and monastic ranks as a 'higher' state. From the latter would flow the developing Catholic view of sacramental marriage with its close limits upon lawful sex within marriage. And from both together would come the seriousness—but serious discomfort—with which Christianity in the West has looked upon sex ever since. For example, Martin Luther in the sixteenth century could view Christian life in general, and its sexual life in particular, as *simul justus et peccator*, at once righteous and sinful (Meilaender, 1984:ch. 5). And Reinhold Niebuhr in the twentieth century, in this regard once again heir of both Augustine and Luther, could say that the sexual act, while not sinful as such, was always accompanied by sin since it was inevitably tinged with either sensuality, self-love, or both (R. Niebuhr, 1941–43:I, ch. 8).

b. *Another version*—The rival stories of love offered by romance and by psychoanalysis can be tested in part by their social consequences. Measured by that test, the romantic myth fails to provide a plot true to our lives, as Segal's book, negatively, and Updike's, positively, served to illustrate. But the Freudian account also fails, to the extent that its harvest has been the production of the therapeutic society, where social control of love passed to a professional class—a society where confessors were supplanted by therapists (Foucault, 1980). Another test of either story is its capacity to include the truth of the other. By this standard, psychoanalysis wins, since it is more nearly possible for us to give a Freudian account of romantic love than a romantic account of psychoanalysis. But by these same standards, the dominant Christian story of love in its Augustinian version fails also, since its consequence has been the low esteem even in Christian ranks of the kind of marriage it sought to sanctify, and since it has been easier to give a romantic *or* a psychoanalytic account of Christian love than vice versa— witness the content of modern literature. Yet this is a qualified claim; it speaks only of "the dominant Christian story." Is it possible that the dominant story about sexual love is not the true story? An heir of the Radical Reformers must always be open to this methodological suspicion. Let us test it now.

The Christian story in its primal form tells of a God who (unlike gods of human fabrication) is the very Ground of Adventure, the Weaver of society's Web, the Holy Source of nature in its concreteness—the one and only God, who, when time began, began to be God for a world that in its orderly constitution finally came by his will and choice to include also—ourselves. We human beings, having our natural frame and basis, with our own (it seemed our own) penchant for community, and (it seemed) our own hankerings after adventure, found ourselves, before long, in trouble. Our very adventurousness led us astray; our drive to cohesion fostered monstrous imperial alternatives to the adventure and the sociality of the Way God had intended, while our continuity with nature became an excuse to despise ourselves and whatever was the cause of us. We sin. In his loving concern, God set among us, by every means infinite wisdom could propose, the foundations of a new human society; in his patience he sent messengers to recall the people of his Way to their way; in the first bright glimmers of opportunity he sent—himself, incognito, without splendor and fanfare, the Maker amid the things made, the fundamental Web as if a single fiber, the Ground of Adventure risking everything in this adventure. His purpose—sheer love; his means—pure faith; his promise—unquenchable hope. In that love he lived a life of love; by that faith he died a faithful death; from that death he rose to fructify hope for the people of his Way, newly gathered, newly equipped. The rest of the story is still his—yet it can also be ours, yours.

That is the fundamental love story of Christian faith, or rather a brief allusion to that story whose telling in full must exhaust all skill and consume all words (see John 21:25). To outsiders the story is sure to count as a myth among myths, but to us it is no myth, but our only way of telling the whole truth. Now what has this to say to us about our topic of sexual love? How does that even come into the Christian story?

i. *Help from Jonathan Edwards*—The sharpest difficulties will be felt here, I think, by those who, following uncritically the example of Anders Nygren (1932/1969), have come to believe the Christian gospel to be associated with one Greek word for love, ἀγάπη, in perfect contrast to neoplatonic mysticism associated with another Greek word for love, ἔρως. Nygren certainly had a legitimate point to make: The prevenience of God in our salvation must not be compromised by a sense of Christian love that in Pelagian fashion has Christians climbing up to God by virtue of their own loving desire for him, as if that desire were either their own original contribution to the salvific effort, or as if such desire for God, if good, could be anything but God's good gift. Quite apart from Greek words, the point is for us unexceptionable.

The trouble comes when we fasten that point to a terminological distinction in a way Nygren himself would not have wished us to do (see Philip Watson in Nygren, 1932/1969:xvi). For the agape-eros distinction is one of which the Greek Bible knows nothing. The Old Testament uses Hebrew *ahavah* and Greek ἀγάπη (and the corresponding verbs) for human sexual love as well as for other kinds: for example, these two are the regular words for sexual love in the Song of Solomon (2:4, 5, 7; 3:5, 10; 5:8; etc.). It is true that the New Testament writers avoid (or neglect) ἔρως and ἐράω—but they also largely neglect φιλέω, "befriend," with the result that their vocabulary, rather like that of modern English and modern German speakers, has only a single wide-ranging word (for them, ἀγάπη, for us, love or *Liebe*), which consequently bears many shades of meaning. Perhaps we users of English should envy languages where there exist a variety of shaded senses reflecting the many sides of our "love," but on the other hand, perhaps they should envy us the flexibility of our term—us, and the New Testament with its flexible and encompassing ἀγάπη (cf. Outka, 1972).

I do not mean to say that we should make no distinctions, linguistic or other, in speaking of divine and human love. On the contrary, such distinctions are sometimes essential. We have already noted the distinction between love that responds with gratitude and delight to God's prevenient grace, as opposed to that love (or ἔρως, if you please) that yearns and climbs in a mystical religion of which as said before the New Testament's gospel knows nothing. And earlier on in the chapter, via de Rougemont, we have noted a possible link between that sort of mysticism and the romantic yearning of Tristan and all his successors. The point now is merely that these alien loves are alike called by the same name—love. We must and we can make the distinction between them and Christian love, but we make it in other ways than terminologically.

Still other distinctions are indispensable. Two of these, associated in the previous chapter with Jonathan Edwards, are so central to our present task that I note them here. First is the distinction between love that loves with no other motive than its own intent to be loving, versus the love that loves on the basis of the preexisting loveliness of its target. Edwards called these respectively the "love of benevolence" and the "love of complacence" (1765/1960:6), yet since "benevolence" and "complacence" have each acquired new meanings in the meantime, we will do better to call these, as suggested there, *grace-love* and *delight-love* respectively. Clearly God's love, in purposing to create and in rescuing us from our sins, is all of the former sort, grace-love. We did not merit salvation; creation was not 'there' to deserve being created. On the other hand, our resultant gratitude for salvation received, and God's resultant pleasure in creation achieved ("And God saw that it was good"—three times in Genesis 1) are instances of delight-love. A little reflection will reveal that both grace-love and delight-love can serve as models for erotic love. Both the love that consents to give itself to the lover (we might say, just for love's sake) and the love that consentingly attaches itself to the lover (because he or she is so eminently lovable and lovely) are characteristic of erotic love, as Jonathan and Sarah Edwards the lovers well knew.

A second Edwardsean distinction that is equally necessary, however, is between what Jonathan Edwards calls general and particular (1765/1960:18-23). While general love can attend to particulars (and is thus not a mere diffuse cloud of divine or human good will), particular or private love can by definition never reach out beyond its private sphere to the whole; it necessarily has as its target only a limited range of possibilities. Edwards' example of such private love (or virtue) is a band of rebels, pirates, or brigands, who are bound in loyalty to one another, perhaps, yet who are murderously against all not of their band (1765/1960:52f.). Let us name this the distinction between *unbounded love* (love which is at least in principle unlimited) and *bound love* (limited to members of a certain party, sect, or band of confederates). Edwards used this distinction to show the difference between true virtue or free love for all that is, which he believed characterized both God and those who were God's consenting collaborators in being, over against the "secondary" or apparent virtue of those who (like the pirates) had a form of loyalty, obedience, or consent that was strictly bounded so that they could not (while remaining pirates) transcend its limited loyalty.

If love is understood with these qualifications of its motive (grace versus delight) and its scope (unbounded versus bound) it should be possible to get along well enough without the misleading traditional distinction of agape and eros, despite its theological repute. (The truth is, there is some eros *in* agape, so that attempts to separate these two were necessarily flawed.) We can readily see that once the Creator's prevenient love has done its work, the love with which God thereafter loves the world, while always unbounded or free in scope, is a love that by way of motive will combine grace with delight; or for a higher example still, the love of the eternal Father for his eternal Son is a love that (as grace) is self-giving, but that is extended (as delight) to one in whom the Father is well pleased (cf. Mark 1:11).

ii. *The analogy of love*—All these terminological points should make more sense, however, if we can see them at work in the actual shaping of our erotic lives in response to the great love story that is claimed as the Christian model. Of course to provide such accounts must be an ongoing, rather than a once-for-all, task of Christian life and creative artistry. Yet we may call attention to certain characteristic features of our model and ask how they can be recaptured in our love life.

"From that death he rose." The resurrection may seem to some the least likely prospect for analogical guidance toward Christian eros. It turns out, on the contrary, to be indispensable. While the romantic myth moves from love to death, the Christian master story moves (through death) to newfound life—in the body. The risen Christ conveys hope that transforms our present life, and erotic love at its best will turn upon episodes of transformation. Rosemary Haughton, in *The Transformation of Man* (1980) tells the story of two lonely and almost loveless though otherwise decent people, a man and a woman, who meet, become friends, in time become lovers. In the process, they become for one another and for themselves new people. Haughton wants us to see that there is in this erotic encounter a power of transformation that, because it changes everything for them, is analog and sign of the *transformation* that awaits us each in the salvation Christ offers: their falling in love is not irrelevant to anyone's 'falling' into Christ's Way. Here the marks of love do not seem to be fruitless yearning and tragic death, but the opening of selves to one another and to themselves as sign (and perhaps as part?) of their opening to God.

"He died a faithful death." Unless the role of faithful, costly, and redemptive suffering in Christian love is ingredient to erotic love also, our analogy breaks down at its center. It does not break down; while the romantic myth exults in deprivation and ultimate loss, the Christian experience of love has its own tale of a different sort of costly suffering, and though that may sometimes issue in loss that seems irreparable, the assurance of the gospel is that suffering that remains loyal to the faithfulness of the Master is destined to be redemptive (Romans 8).

Among the novels that celebrate erotic love from this standpoint, a striking example is Robert Louis Stevenson's *Catriona*, first published about a century ago, and written during the Indian summer of Stevenson's final settlement upon Samoa (1890–94). The setting of the novel is Scotland in the troubled days just after the nationalist 'rising' of 1745. The grey-eyed Catriona, daughter of a Highland clan, is unforgettable from the first time David Balfour, the narrator and fumbling hero, encounters her in the narrow streets of Edinburgh. Though Stevenson's language is strictly governed by the conventions of the last century, the novel's erotic interest is unmistakable and powerful. For us now its value lies in the section where the growing love of Catriona and David develops under circumstances that oblige them, Scottish exiles in Holland, to live together disguised as sister and brother. There are rich proto-Freudian overtones in this section: the amorous engagement of the two 'siblings,' the struggle between Catriona's father and her suitor for her possession, the power of her jealousy (focused on the innocent Barbara Grant) to deflect eros. Less noticeable are surviving remnants of the romantic myth: one fragment of this is perhaps the 'circumstances' that prevent an immediate union of the two lovers, so that their love must be tested during an unacknowledged courtship as they share living quarters.

But most prominent in this section is a strongly Christian theme: the power of love to persist despite the obstacles of character in the lovers themselves—their foolish pride, their vagrant jealousy. Forgiveness and patience, humility and trust, slowly begin to flourish in each, and this flourishing releases the full power of the eros in which these demands upon the character of each were first evoked. At one stage of the sojourn in Holland, the two young people, temporarily penniless and alone among strangers, are forced to walk by night the road from Rotterdam to Leyden. The intimacy of the cold, lonely walk frees them to speak of their friendship—and Catriona's jealousy flares again. She demands that David never again mention her (imagined) rival, "Miss Grant"; he gives her a little lecture on fairmindedness and reasonableness; they separate and trudge on side by side in silence, their hearts "burning with enmity," but "the darkness and the cold, and the silence, which only the cocks sometimes interrupted, or sometimes the farmyard dogs, had pretty soon brought down our pride to the dust; and for my own particular, I would have jumped at any decent opening for speech" (1893/1952:439f.). The chance for reconciliation does come when it rains, and he can offer her a cloak. She accepts; patience melts a little of the rancor of pride away from two selves, and the would-be lovers walk on together in the dripping rain.

In *Catriona*, too, we can find material for a response to Freud's tart suggestion that since love implies preference, its very nature works against the Christian command to "love thy neighbor as thyself" (Freud, 1930/1961:56f.). Indeed, Catriona's jealousy arises while her own love relation with David is insecure, and David in turn fears and hates James More, the father, in that same stage of the affair. In this regard the "preference" of each does exclude love directed toward others. But when they begin to realize that their own love for one another is *unbounded*, James More can be forgiven, and the lovers, now married, choose Barbara Grant to give her name to their daughter. "Preference" conflicts with love's unboundedness only as long as preferential love remains itself bound, mere "secondary virtue" in Edwards' term.

This brings us to a last distinctively Christian note: strand-one love and strand-two marriage are not in *Catriona* set into opposition; rather the one is the completion of the other. The final scene of the novel is a retrospective passage in which David the narrator, snug in the company of his wife and their children, for whom the story has been told, sets that story into the wider narrative of their children's lives, of Scotland's people, and (in the final paragraph) of heaven and earth itself:

For the life of man upon this world of ours is a funny business. They talk of the angels weeping; but I think they must more often be holding their sides, as they look on; and there was one thing I determined to do when I began this long story, and that was to tell out everything as it befell. (Stevenson, 1893/1952:507)

Love, seen from heaven's vantage, is not tragic but comic—part of the good news.

"In that love he lived a life of love." Something is lacking in our account here. While the Christian love story acknowledges physical love, body joined to body in erotic union, it has yet fully to find a way from its master story to the celebration of that union. We may even look with a certain longing to the erotic art of India where heaven and earth meet in such evident sexuality, though we find we cannot impose that strangeness upon our own understanding. Perhaps the contingent fact that Christianity was launched into a world in which sexual gods dominated Greek and Roman imagination, with the consequent Christian need to steer clear of even the imagery of divine Venus, led to a justifiable caution that is even yet not overcome, so that we leave to one side for the most part also the imagery of the Hebrew Bible about JHWH the divine lover of his people. The evidence of this failure is the absence from literature of any full-scale celebration of erotic marriage in Christian dress.

At the same time, the doctrine of the life of our Lord Jesus, a life fully and truly human, opens possibilities here for a new Christian sense of the life of the senses. Yet that is to speak of the possibilities of the future, not the gains of the present age. For sexual love is one place where "vision" is no metaphor but plain fact. It is in seeing, along with hearing, smelling, touching, that love discovers its object and thereby finds its goal. Iris Murdoch has spoken of the "attention" which is at once the artist's skill and the lover's: In attending, in learning faithfully to look, we take the journey from the illusions of love to the reality of loving (Murdoch, 1970:84). Perhaps love must begin with illusions, for without them we might never break through the preoccupation with self that so fiercely grips us. But love can grow only when we pass through or beyond the illusion to the reality it had presented in disguise. And once again the logos becomes flesh in this adjusted sense, a sense having its own proper earthly and human integrity: the idea becomes flesh; love finds itself in its object.

iii. *A resumé*—Some things have been said or implied about the Christian understanding of sexual love that may now be pulled together in summary fashion. In doing so, matters may be made a little clearer than they have been to this point. I will arrange these under a threefold heading: love as feeling, as virtue, and as gift.

Love is a feeling. Doubtless we do not know what we say when we assign "feelings" to God, but to distinguish God's pity, mercy, forgiveness, and delight as he looks toward our human condition as if these aspects of God's nature were without feeling—pure good will, or mere taking thought for us—would be, not to raise God above ourselves, but to lower him beneath. Feeling, if it be God's feeling, is itself divine, and love of whatever degree in some way mirrors or echoes that feelingness in divinity. Yet neither in God nor in ourselves are feelings mere random whims or bare impulses: Every account of love that we sought found that feelings operate according to the pattern of a story—which story, of course, being the very issue at stake. The task that arises here, then, is to discover that narrative base from which the love we feel can be compre-hended and brought into the service of our redeemed selfhood. Yet to acknowledge this need of a story of love as we have done is to find that our strand one, the strand of the body in its organic setting, is in need of the other strands where that story can take full shape: for us, no love without community; no love without resurrection. And these points I think have been evident in what is said above.

Love is a virtue. Perhaps love always begins as a feeling, but certainly it must be continued as a virtue if it is to continue indeed. Feelings come and go; virtue is skill and strength that persist, an aspect of character. This has been a chapter not about marriage but about love, yet the 'practice' (a term to be defined in the next chapter) of marriage makes little sense for Christians without the virtue of love. This, then, is the sense in which even sexual love can be commanded, as wedding sermons have often assumed: Feelings are beyond our command, but we may be able to uncover or recover existing feelings, though only by dint of the hard work and obedience that are a part (yet only a part) of love.

To emphasize the necessity for the other strands is also to point out why things have not been said in this chapter that readers will have looked for in vain: little or nothing has been said about who is to love whom, under what circumstances, with what consequences, and so on. But this is simply to repeat from another angle the necessary emphasis upon the contribution of the several strands to our moral thinking: It is to repeat as a criticism what has already been asserted as a presupposition. We cannot simply extract our morality of life together from the fact of our organic drives, needs, and capacities. As it happens, the next section will not closely address these particular questions, either, though it will, I hope, unfold the method by which they may be approached. To attempt to answer here every question of Christian morality, however, seems both to neglect the existence of other, excellent books where such matters are addressed, and to presume near-infinite patience in the reader. I have been trying to avoid both the neglect and the presumption. That we see the necessary status of love as virtue as well as feeling is enough gain now: It necessarily opens the way to these other considerations. We will require the others before we can see the biblical (and baptist) vision come to flower in the mode of erotic love.

Love is a gift. This is where we are led by the previous conclusions. It is God's gift, the gift that (to the wonderment of Sigmund Freud) is ever present, breaking down our so carefully enacted barriers of race and class and caste, melting our resistance to the ongoing of the generations, overcoming (while life shall last) our destructive and self-destructive urges, welding us together in a unity that (if God's love be true) death itself cannot destroy. As gift it returns to the giver; God *is* love, and to the extent that we love (who would narrow the sense of the term here?), to that extent we abide in God, and he in us (cf. 1 John 3:16).

PART II

THE SPHERE OF THE COMMUNAL

Extra ecclesiam nulla salus.

Cyprian of Carthage

Doops spoke again. "Do you forgive me?" . . .

"Who you think we are? God?" he answered impatiently. . . .

"But we have to start with each other first," Doops said, a sound of entreaty, a sound of testimony.

Doops continued to sit with his hands holding his knees, his chin resting on them, his eyes averted. A warm, ghostly breeze was moving in from the coast, ruffling the cypress branches lightly. A random cloud, retiring inland, moved beneath the moon, dimming the light in the marsh like a rheostat.

Model T spoke softly but commandingly out of the darkness. "We forgive you."

Will D. Campbell, The Glad River

And forgive us our debts, as we forgive our debtors.

Matthew 6:12

Social Ethics

The moral life of Christians is a life in society. Whether this life is, at one extreme, the frugal interchange of coenobitic monks bound by a vow of silence, or at another the immersion in world citizenship of an 'anonymous' Christian such as a Dag Hammarskjøld, it remains typical of Christian existence, under God, to be formed by the social structures of church and of society at large. The task of this chapter is to give a preliminary account of Christian moral life as it grapples with and is formed by this social engagement. In this task, there are two chief dangers. The first and more obvious is that in attending to the social ethic we shall lose sight of the other strands our analysis reveals. The Christian life is one life, to be lived in solidarity with Christ and fellow Christians, under the guidance of the Spirit of God. If we analyze this way of life into its several strands, it is only for the better understanding of that necessary unity. The analysis must not lead us to think that we have three lives, or three moral lives, or that our moral life falls into three separate, if connected, compartments—a more complex Jim Crow coach. Thus, as we begin now to examine the social strand of Christian morality we must still keep before us the picture, already drawn, of embodied selfhood with its drives, needs, and capacities, and we must also anticipate the account still to come of the resurrected newness of the Christian way.

The other danger, though, is greater. This is that we shall fail to distinguish sociality itself, confusing it for example with mere organic multiplicity. Many cells in a tissue, many fledglings together in a nest, are not yet a society. What, then, constitutes the distinctively social, and what is the ethic that thereby arises for Christians? That is the new question.

It is noteworthy that the Bible seems to furnish no general social theoretic. The New Testament apparently provides no blueprint for society, and Christian attempts, from Roman antiquity to latest Puritanism and Liberation Theology, to translate Old Testament theocracy into a pattern for the world at large have had grievous consequences for both the Christian and the world. (One of the deep insights of the Radical Reformers, the baptists of the sixteenth century, was that Old Testament government was *not* to be invoked in this simplistic fashion as a modern model [Rideman, 1545/1970:104ff.; Marpeck, 1544/1978:555ff.; Menno Simons, 1552/1956:518f.].) But if not a Puritan theocracy, what is the social model to be? Or, to rephrase the question, can *any* general account of social relations be offered that will first (and primarily) do justice to the biblical and baptist vision, while at the same time offering insight into the life of the people of God in the most varied circumstances of their social and political life—some in the capitalist West, others in the Marxist East, and yet more in the inchoate Third World—in which tomorrow's Christianity is now being formed anew? Difficult though it may be to provide such an account, it must be attempted, for we are constituted as social beings, and this means not merely that we are many, or that solitude is rare in human experience; it means that there is a cultural function of human life as such; man displays *structural forms* that govern life even in its solitude and shape human relations even in the limiting case where only "two walk together" (cf. Amos 3:3). How shall we interpret this constitutive fact?

This chapter will consist of three parts. The first will begin with a hint about how the mysterious biblical concepts of principalities and powers are to be received. Then it will offer another way of understanding social structures and their relation to morality, based upon the concepts of *games* and *practices*. It will be found desirable to bring these two parallel analyses—that of games and practices and that of principalities and powers—together, for each supplements the insight offered by the other. Then the second part of the chapter will apply these mated concepts to the interpretation of a particular pattern of biblical community, that to which the Ten Commandments are addressed. I will attempt to show the moral dimension of that community in a way that throws proleptic light upon our own communities and on Christian social morality. The chapter will close by pointing out the dependence of the social strand upon another still to be examined—the resurrection strand.

1. The Forms of Social Life

Alasdair MacIntyre begins his important study in moral philosophy, *After Virtue* (1984), with what he calls "a disquieting suggestion." What, he asks, if the moral words and language that we all use today had fallen into grave disorder, so that we now possess merely the fragments of a morality, with vital parts that might give meaning to the rest unaccountably missing? MacIntyre believes that this has actually happened: "We possess indeed simulacra of morality, we continue to use many of the key expressions. But we have—very largely, if not entirely—lost our comprehension, both theoretical and practical, of morality" (1984:2). He even assigns a date to this great catastrophe. It happened, he thinks, in the seventeenth and eighteenth centuries, when the prevailing moral scheme of the Middle Ages was renounced by thinking people, while no adequate substitute was found. If we can understand what has happened, however, we may be able to carry out a rescue operation, even "after virtue," that is, after the virtues have been discarded in modern thought.

However it may otherwise be with MacIntyre's thesis, it certainly provides a helpful clue to understanding the point of view of those writers who developed the main lines of the biblical heritage of social thought, and first of all that of the biblical authors or editors themselves. For these have an even more inclusive idea of a moral catastrophe that has enveloped human life. From Augustine of Hippo to Reinhold Niebuhr heavy use has been made by social thinkers of the concepts of the fall and original sin. This had the advantage of showing clearly the inevitable participation of each of us in the disorder of the world while providing a universal historical (or mythic) explanation of that participation. But these traditional concepts failed the test of sound *biblical* exegesis (see critical commentaries on Genesis 3 and Romans 5), while at the same time they were inclined to an overly pessimistic account of human nature—one that made little room for the life of redeemed discipleship celebrated in the New Testament. Thus R. Niebuhr, for example, can allow for redemption from the curse of the fall only "beyond history" (1941–43:II, 90ff.). Niebuhr is too grimly "realistic" in his assessment of the revolutionary possibilities of Christian community; his realism overlooks the new life in Christ.

More recent biblical thinkers such as Jacques Ellul and John Howard Yoder have invested in an alternative concept, that of the *principalities and powers*. This is an authentic recovery of a concept that had been lost to view in the course of Christian history, for the "principalities and powers" of Scripture had been identified altogether with the angels and demons of the medieval world view, and had been relegated to obscurity when the angels and demons ceased to function for modern thought save as comic figures or as Christmas card decorations. In biblical perspective, however, the principalities and powers, developed from the concepts of the alien gods of Old Testament understanding, served as constant reminders of the structured world of power and authority that stood over against the kingdom of Christ. Defeated by Christ's cross and his resurrection, these powers were perceived as lingering on, beaten yet dangerous still, lurking at the margins of life. Like the angry beasts of *Pilgrim's Progress* they might but for God's grace devour the unwary pilgrim on his journey.

Contemporary ethics, however, had better not rely too exclusively on the "principalities and powers" concept in forming its social theoretic. For just as the characteristic images of Constantinian social theory such as John Locke's contract theory of society, or Thomas Aquinas' hierarchical construction of the universe, or even Augustine's image of the *peregrinus* (as Peter Brown translates, "resident stranger") may too readily lend themselves to Constantinian contentment with the powers that be, so the biblical and baptist image of social forces as principalities and powers may if left to itself too readily turn Christian social theory into a shunning of this present world in the interest of an unworldly purity. Moreover, just like the doctrine of original sin, the concept of

the powers as disordered and fallen creatures of God
necessarily raises a prior question: What is the original or
created *order* of which this disorder is a distorted reflection?
Christians, in contrast with Manichaeans, cannot be content
with an ultimate dualism of good and evil; the disobedient
powers force us to ask, What would their obedience be like?

a. *The concept of a practice*—My first suggestion for understanding social order and value is therefore to be made partly
by way of the concepts of *games* and *practices*. Alasdair
MacIntyre has recently followed this approach exclusively,
showing how the virtues of common life depend upon the
existence of common human social practices, and these in turn
upon a narrative understanding of life. He has developed a
notion of practice best exemplified by such phenomena as the
practice of law or the practice of medicine, with all the
complexity these embody. While MacIntyre's account is
attractive, I will approach the topic differently, exploring first
the concept of a *game* as an intrinsically valuable social activity.
(This is compatible with MacIntyre's development, for he
offers such games as football and chess as the readiest
illustrations, outside the professions, of practices.) From
games we can proceed to more serious practices, and finally
relate these to the biblical principalities and powers.

i. *Games*—There is a special risk here: the focus on games
may be seen as a dilettante and superficial account of genuine
life and death social concerns. Indeed, no "theology of play" is
intended. In the short run, however, the risk of misunderstanding will simply have to be taken, with the preliminary
assurance that it is not my design to reduce to leisure time
activities such Christian social concerns as the welfare of the
worker, the fate of the family, and the quest for lasting peace.
The final result, though, will be the best evidence for this.
One difficulty is that though all of us have played games,
there is no widely accepted theoretical consensus as to what a
game is. (Indeed, the great Wittgenstein used "game" as the
very paradigm of an indefinable family term [1953:§66f.]—a
view he made famous, though it rested, I believe, upon
confusion between "play" and "game," two distinct concepts
though only one word in German.) My first task must
therefore be to say (*pace* Wittgenstein) what a game is. I begin

with the definition offered by Bernard Suits in his entertaining book *The Grasshopper: Games, Life, and Utopia*.

> To play a game is to engage in activity directed towards bringing about a specific state of affairs, using only means permitted by rules, where the rules prohibit more efficient in favor of less efficient means, and where such rules are accepted just because they make possible such activity. (1978:34)

Suits clarifies the definition (or allows his protagonist, the Grasshopper, to clarify it) by distinguishing the chief elements of game-playing contained in it. These are four in number: the *end* or goal of the game (for example, getting a ball into certain holes in the ground), the *means* allowed (hitting the ball with a stick), the *rules* (the player with fewest stick-strokes wins), and "one more element, namely, the attitude of game players qua game players . . . the attitude [of intending to play that game] without which it is not possible to play a game" (Suits, 1978:35). Suits calls this the *lusory* (from Latin *ludus*, game) *attitude*.

A little reflection will show, as Suits allows the characters in *The Grasshopper* to discover, that each of these four is a strictly necessary element. That a game must have a goal logically prior to the goal of winning (as Suits puts it, a *prelusory goal*) seems evident; how else would we know what constituted winning a race, for example, unless crossing some finish line were designated as the goal of the racers? Next, that strictly limited means are to be employed seems to be accepted by every gameplayer—else I might win the race by cutting across the track's infield, or might reduce my golf score by carrying the ball right up to the green rather than hitting it there stroke by stroke. From these two, the third necessity, that of rules, becomes evident. The rules are not arbitrary additions we might very well discard in actual play: It is exactly the rules that constitute tennis as tennis, or bridge as bridge, and without them we would have no notion which game we were playing. Suits puts it strongly: "It is impossible to win a game and at the same time to break one of its rules" (1978:20f.), though of course the rules themselves may provide the possibility of particular violations (e.g., off sides) with penalties attached thereto (five yards). To disregard the *constitutive* rules, however (say by trying to win by crossing the goal line over and over again before the game begins) is not a way to win at football, nor does it incur a penalty; it simply shows failure to understand what the rules are, that is, what constitutes the game itself.

This brings us to the fourth essential element, the 'lusory' attitude required of players—namely intending to play the game. Without this, an Olympic class runner who just happens to jog along the course of a neighborhood footrace might be supposed to have 'won' the race—but this will not do if the Olympic speedster wasn't even in the race. By noting that the rules of any game do specify both its goal (for example, putting the ball through the hoop more times than your opponents do) and its permitted means (for example, dribbling or passing to others on your team, but not running with the ball) we might reduce the essentials of any game to two, constitutive rules and lusory attitude, but no further reduction is possible: As Suits succinctly puts it, playing a game is the *voluntary* attempt to overcome *unnecessary* obstacles (1978:41). Here "unnecessary" means "called for not by the goal itself, but only by the rules," and "voluntary" points to the players' lusory attitudes.

A final check on the game definition itself may be provided by testing its capacity to delimit three common sorts of nonplayers, namely, triflers, spoilsports, and cheats. Consider Aunt Lucy, who doesn't really want to play checkers, but who to oblige bored nephew Billy sits down at the board and takes a turn moving the pieces on the squares. She is not playing, though, she is *trifling* with the red and black disks, and her (definitional) failure to play is an exemplary though unattractive lack of the lusory attitude. Or consider burly Ben, dumb but eager to look athletic, who runs round and round with the ball after being tagged repeatedly; his *spoilsport* behavior breaks up a neighborhood touch football game whose procedures he simply ignores. Finally, naughty Nell doesn't count her strokes in the sandtrap until at last she chips to the green; she is, alas, a *cheat* whether anyone else knows it or not, though she appears to be playing golf by the rules. In Suits' neat summary, "triflers recognize rules but not goals, cheats recognize goals but not rules, players recognize both rules and goals and spoilsports recognize neither" (1978:47). So the definition works to show why these fraudulent players are not actual ones, thereby passing one test of a good definition.

Other theorists have produced other philosophical definitions, and have labored to relate games to and distinguish
them from other human pursuits such as work, leisure, sport,
mimetic activity, and still more. It is not part of the plan here to
defend the Grasshopper definition of games save by com-
mending the book, which does defend it. Rather I will
stipulatively adopt Suits' notion of game as one that reminds
us of some characteristic features of games we all know about,
for this should open the way to grasping the sense of social
practices, which is the real aim of this section.

Before moving on, however, two features of games, one of
them not explicit in the definition, must be made clear.
Remember that the rules, as Suits says, are accepted "just
because they make possible such activity" (1978:34) and that
the lusory attitude lays it down that only those intending to
play the game are players. Together these two imply or at least
suggest a third point: games are ends, never (merely) means.
This definitional point is intuitively evident for amateurs;
anyone who plays tennis must intend—not merely to get
exercise, or meet pretty girls or handsome boys, or be accepted
into the tennis club, but—to play tennis. Of course professional tennis players generally intend also to make a living at
tennis, but that cannot be their only intention; they must
intend set by set and match by match to play the game itself
with its goals, means, and rules. Therefore athletes who throw
a game or even narrow the margin of their win for pay have
given up the lusory attitude and have made their game a fraud.
Also, the distinction between "just playing" and "playing to
win" (or coming as close as possible to winning) is a phony
one; *playing* is playing to win; there can be no intelligible
contrast between those who play 'for the game's sake' and
those who merely want victory. As said above, those who do
not play to *win* are not players; they are triflers; while those
who do not *play* to win are cheats. We will meet this logical
necessity afresh when we come to consider practices as
self-justifying or intrinsically valuable (rather than merely
instrumental) human activities. In this regard, games,
whether amateur or professional, will afford us a useful logical
model.

The other aspect of games that needs to be drawn out is their
social character. *The Grasshopper's* definition suppresses this
feature in order to allow for limiting cases such as solitaire, or

solo golf, or ocean racing against one's own best time. These exceptions, however, prove the rule by calling attention to their own exceptional nature. Most games require partners, opponents, or both. Perhaps the most interesting point Suits makes in this regard is to show that his ends-means-rules-attitude definition embraces cooperative as well as contested games. Thus the point of one kind of table tennis may be to keep the celluloid ball in action on the table, rather than forcing the other player to miss a stroke. Still better examples are found in the childhood games of "playing house" and "playing cops and robbers," where cooperative imaginal activity is required of each player exactly in order to keep the game going along its dramatic (and ideally interminable) way. These cooperative games do not have as their end, like poker, the bringing about of some terminal state of affairs (e.g., all the money in the possession of one player); instead they aim at permitting roles to be played as colorfully and effectively as possible (Suits, 1978:ch. 9). This sort of "open game" introduces the further idea of role-playing, and suggests (Suits, 1978:chs. 10–13) that it is not merely children who find role-playing deeply satisfying for its own sake.

ii. *Practices*—With the concept of games before us, we are prepared to go on to the concept of a social *practice*, and to discover how the latter makes possible the discrimination of a distinctively social strand in the moral life of Christians. The worth of this part of our inquiry rests simply upon its ability to show the structures of biblical social morality in ways that are clearer or more revealing than alternative theoretical approaches (such as the old liberal approach through a search for biblical *values*, or the recent Marxian and Liberationist analysis of biblical *ideology* and *praxis*, to name a couple of others). In other words, attention to *practices* will be validated (if at all) just by the better sense we can thereby make of law and gospel, of Israel and the church.

Alasdair MacIntyre has defined a practice as follows:

Practice. Any coherent and complex form of socially established cooperative human activity through which goods internal to that form of activity are realized in the course of trying to achieve those standards of excellence which are appropriate to, and partially definitive of, that form of activity, with the result that human powers to achieve excellence, and human conceptions of the ends and goods involved, are systematically extended. (1984:175)

Marriage and the practice of medicine are in this sense practices, and so according to MacIntyre are chess and the game of football; architecture is, but bricklaying is not. (The latter is rather a skill that finds its point only in connection with some practice.) Thoughtful Christians will see that prayer, being properly communal, may constitute a practice, though merely "saying a prayer," even in company, does not.

If we compare practices as defined above with games, we see some striking similarities. (1) Both are end-means activities; the intentional end that games pursue is their prelusory goal, for example dramatic role-fulfillment in such a game as "cops and robbers," or crossing a designated finish line in a race; while practices likewise pursue their own internal goals—perhaps domesticity and child-rearing in the practice of marriage, health in the practice of medicine, and habitable space in the practice of architecture. (2) But not just any way of attaining these goals will do either for games or practices. Thus the gamesmith must create games whose means are neither too hard nor too easy and obvious, while similarly, real-life practices must develop means of reaching their goals that are sufficiently stable and sufficiently flexible to permit the growth of the practice and the human life it invests. Medicine, for example, must be teachable to qualified beginners, yet able to change over the years with changing needs and knowledge. (3) On the other hand, both games and practices must have means sufficiently definite at any time to permit formulable rules of practice, "those standards of excellence," as MacIntyre says, "which are appropriate to, and partially definitive of, that form of activity." (Though the rules may sometimes be unwritten, and even unformulated.) And finally, (4) no one will be said to be marrying, or practicing medicine or architecture (any more than one will be said to play a game) who does not *intend* to achieve its goals by such recognizable, in other words rule-describable, means. Thus just as it is possible to pick out as nonplayers those who wander into the ball park and engage in some vaguely athletic activity or other, so must it be possible to distinguish quack doctors, and bogus architects, and invalid marriages from the real thing. Possible, even if not always easy.

But there seems to be something wrong with all these comparisons. For if it were possible to reach the goals of marriage, medicine, or architecture without following the rules of a practice (as in fact one *can* merely cross a finish line without running in a race) would there be any reason not to do so? What if we could all have health without doctors, merely by wishing it, or what if Kubla Khan could have a stately pleasure dome in Xanadu merely by his dreamlike decree, without architectural design or construction of any sort by anyone? Or what about family love without anyone's taking the costly path of marriage? In the game case, we would say the 'runner' had not really won because he had not run the *race*. What of these other practices? Surely (we may think), no one would object on moral grounds to health by fiat, or for that matter to the providential abolition of disease? Yet, on the other hand, an entirely effortless world would seem to omit something that is valuable in itself even apart from the usual goals of the practices just mentioned—namely the value of the practices themselves. Unlike games, the 'obstacles' in a (nongame) practice may be set by circumstances alone. Life, we say, is worth living, and part of what we mean is that the struggles entailed by such a world as this are worthwhile independent of the ultimate rest that will come when all is over. Yet the kind of struggle we have in mind here may be, not difficulty for difficulty's sake, but exercises that are part and parcel of practices such as those just described.

Perhaps any perplexity we sense at this point comes from a false attempt to separate practices from the organic world in which they are set—as if to separate strand two from strand one. If we acknowledge that biologically members of our species must grow, mate, reproduce, encounter threats to life and opportunities for delight, enjoying their drives, needs, and capacities in a given environment, and must sooner or later mature, age, and die, then it is clear that the sort of limitation of means that a gamesmith may have to invent (rough versus fairways versus greens) is, often enough, provided gratis for human moral practices by the natural environment; our own Maker seems to have underlined our intuitive sense that just as recreation is *re*-creative, the practices of human life, by their participation in the ongoing creation of a provisional and still untidy world, are valuable in and of themselves (cf. Bushnell, 1864).

Let us linger for a moment with this notion of intrinsic value, with the claim that practices are worth pursuing in and of themselves, for this will lead us on into the full claim being made here about the social morality of practices. MacIntyre distinguishes between goods externally attached to a practice—say the practice of playing chess—and those internally attached to it. External goods are such as may be related to a practice by mere happenstance: I offer my niece candy, which she loves, if she will play chess with me, and more candy whenever she wins. But this provides only an external relation between candy and chess. If on the other hand the niece learns to play and begins to play well, she may discover the pleasure and satisfaction of chess itself; if so, she has found "goods internal to that form of activity . . . realized in the course of trying to achieve those standards of excellence . . . appropriate to, and partially definitive of, that form of activity." In a word, she has become a chess player (MacIntyre, 1984:175f.).

This brings us to the next important concern, the relation of virtues to practices. In Chapter Three we met the question whether some general human virtues, understood as skills for living, might be merely the enhancement of our organic psychological and physical equipment, and thus pretty much the same for all organically similar people. The answer offered there, however, was that our skills for living are imbedded in the several stories of which we are a part and so cannot be understood apart from these stories. For example, love seems inseparable from human life as such (for everyone loves something) but love is always by its very grammar love *of* something; thus as we saw in Chapter Five it is being imbedded in a particular human situation or story that defines it as *this* love. Now we can say more clearly how that is so; many virtues have their home in connection with particular practices whose pursuit evokes exactly those virtues. For example, if we are members of a community one of whose practices is Christian witness or evangelism, it will be plain to us that the virtue of presence, first discussed in Chapter Three, is required by that practice—in MacIntyre's words, is "appropriate to, and partially definitive of, that form of activity," while the 'perversions' of and vices contrary to presence (e.g., nosiness) will be condemned in part just because they defeat the practice of evangelism. For one who will not be present to and for the neighbor cannot effectively witness to that neighbor, even though witness consists in a good deal more than presence alone.

Or, to draw an illustration from another realm, if the practice in question is one of the arts, say painting, we can see that the flourishing of that art, while dependent on a number of related factors—the existence of a community that will nurture art and artists, the development of a tradition of painting in which this practice can make its contribution, the vocation and dedication of particular men or women as 'practitioners'—all these depend in turn upon the inculcation in the artists and their audience of a particular set of skills or capacities, the artistic virtues. These skills have to do with color and form and line, with material and its application, with knowing the way an art tradition may be developed, with the eye and back and arm and brush hand of the artist, and also with patience and human insight and verve and self-control. Now someone may object that this illegitimately mixes 'artistic' virtues with 'moral' ones, but the point of the illustration is to show that when we properly understand morality in relation to practices, such distinctions are not easily made. For example, how do we distinguish Rembrandt's patience (surely a moral virtue) from the training of his arm and back muscles to endure the painter's fatigue and to support palette and brush to the end of the day?

Finally, there may turn out to be virtues that are evoked by *every* practice (MacIntyre thinks this is true of justice, courage, and honesty—1984:178), or, to substitute a more cautious thesis, it may turn out that the practices inherent *in a particular culture* or narrative tradition may have requirements for common virtues that will sustain and enhance them. This would explain, for example, why the 'cardinal' virtues of medieval Christianity came to be recognized as such—and also why the New Testament thematizes distinctive skills for the Christian life. (On the question whether there are universal 'values' or criteria for every human life, regardless of the story it is living out, see McClendon and Smith, 1975:162-71, and see Chapter Twelve within.)

iii. *Narrative and virtue*—This brings up the relation of MacIntyre's practices to the narrative form of the moral life. *After Virtue* argues at chapter's length that the Aristotelean concept of virtue requires a concept of the human self "whose unity resides in . . . a narrative which links birth to life to death as narrative beginning to middle to end" (1982:191). The concepts of action, intelligible action, the identity of the self, narrative, history, and tradition fit together and require one another for their own intelligibility. Rather than repeat MacIntyre's argument, let us consider a parallel account of the matter.

What must human beings be like in order to participate in moral practices, and what must be the quality of human actions that makes possible such participation? The answer seems obvious: If practices are cooperative human activities that are internally linked to certain virtues, and if practices require of participants characteristic intentions (illustrated by the lusory attitude of intending to play the game), then the lives of those who do engage in these practices must have at least enough continuity and coherence to permit the *formation* of those virtues and *sustaining* of those intentions—in a word, their lives must take a narrative form. Virtues cannot be mere episodes; practical intentions cannot be mere whims; the practices of morality require the coherence of a singular story, the story of our lives. Here we meet again, as in Chapter Two, the contrast with forms of ethics that center upon episodic decision and arbitrary choice, and as before our concern is not to deny the role that such episodes may play in life's drama; rather it is to insist that there must *be* a drama, a story, if the reversals and decisive turns that occupy decisionists are even to be recognized as real reversals and actual turns. Yet some modern philosophers (Sartre; the emotivists) have sought to make episodes of decision the whole of morality, and in this they have been much imitated by Christian ethicists. It must now be clear, though, that if the morality these describe is any morality at all, it cannot be a *social* morality, for social morality embodies practices, and practices require virtues and intentions—in brief, the development of human character—that can only appear in lives displaying a narrative coherence.

Now what is true in this regard of the social atoms, ourselves, is all the more true of the social whole, a society or community. There is no single form of social whole to be designated "society." The wide variety of practices would have made that unlikely, for differing practices will require differing institutions for their embodiment. Nomads will have no architecture; warring clans will lack the sophisticated practices of peace. What *is* indispensable for making any society (or culture or community) *one* society is that it shall have a narrative tradition whose function is to provide a setting for the several practices of that society, a web that unites them in a single meaning. The discomfort we felt earlier with Suits' (nevertheless correct) claim that games are intrinsically valuable activities can now be identified and interpreted. That a game is "only a game" distinguishes it from (otherwise gamelike) practices whose fuller meaning is found in their relation to the ongoing story of which they are parts. (Games, too, seem more valuable when they are given the wider context of a pennant race or a tournament—even though these too are 'only a game.') Society may take many forms, but it *must* be narrative to be a society. The stories a people tell, the memories and traditions they share, the history that they receive and modify by their own lives and pass on to their children—these are the carriers of social value.

And what if a people has no story? In Richard Adams' *Watership Down* (1972) each warren displays traits that correspond to the way each remembers the traditional story of rabbithood. Then Adams introduces a warren that has lost its narratives. Moreover, members do not seem to miss having a story, and they resent the authentic rabbit stories visitors tell them. It is indeed possible for a community to lose its story—and with it the traditional rabbit traits and skills for living well. It turns out that these are only an easy food supply for a farmer. We need not agree with Hauerwas' contention that the storyless warren is a parable of Western liberal democratic society ("it allowed each rabbit to do as he pleased") in order to see that his claim that a society must have a narrative structure is not empirical but *conceptual*—it must have that, he is saying, if it is to be a human society (Hauerwas, 1981:18-21).

All these elements may be conveniently gathered up by reflecting briefly upon *friendship* as that practice is available to today's Christians (cf. Meilaender, 1981). Most of us are conscious of being and of having friends. It may not have occurred to us that the network of our friends constituted either a game or a MacIntyrian practice, yet we may test our definitions against such a possible network. Certainly the end or goal of the practice of friendship is internally related to the practice itself: One who 'has friends' merely in order to gain social or financial advantage has missed the point of the practice of friendship. It may be objected that friendship, unlike the practices we have just discussed, functions without rules, but this view will not stand up to reflection. For example, loyalty is part of friendship, so that being a friend rules out disloyalty to the friend. And finally, friendship is a practice for which standards of excellence both exist and may be extended, with the development enhancing those virtues of friendship such as patience, sympathy, and fidelity, while at the same time enlarging the practice itself. Thus, Aristotle's pagan concept held that friends must be moral equals (*Eth. Nic.* 1157*a*), whereas Jesus in John's Gospel accepts his followers, who are evidently not his equals, in the role of friends (John 15:15). Whether there is growth from Aristotle's concept to Jesus', or whether I have grown if I pass from one to the other, is of course a matter that itself requires moral judgment.

b. *Powerful practices*—In this we may be reminded of the generally optimistic and progressive ring of MacIntyre's overall account of practices, and that is just what must now be examined. MacIntyre grants that in the development of a practice there are "sequences of decline as well as of progress" (1984:177), and he warns us, as a wary university professor might, that *institutions* (the structures that house practices, as universities house education and hospitals, medicine) *corrupt practices:* "The ideals and the creativity of the practice are always vulnerable to the acquisitiveness of the institution" (1984:181), so that in his vocabulary practices seem all good though vulnerable, while institutions seem only a necessary evil. Now if the words are so defined, it might appear natural to identify institutions alone with the New Testament's ominous principalities and powers. But my suspicion is that the "institutions versus practices" distinction is not a viable one (instead some practices, for example, hospital operation, *are* institutionalized; they are given by law or custom a formal status that fixes their place in the social structure), and thus *the principalities and powers are none other than the social structures we may also identify as (MacIntyrian) practices.*

I have already said that modern biblical scholarship has recovered these seemingly exotic entities, the *powers* (ἐξουσίαι or δυνάμεις) from the scrap heap of discarded antiques. It may help to note now in outline the contents thus recovered. *First,* in the Near East, power was inevitably associated with gods, and gods were linked with particular nations, that is to say, with *politics* and *society*. There was no clear distinction in the Israelite mind between the Egyptians or the Canaanites on the one hand and their respective gods on the other (Hengel, 1973/1977:7-13). *Second*, the existence of *alien deities*, powers other than God's own power, created a theological dilemma. Israel typically resolved that dilemma in one of three ways (Caird, 1956:1f.): by syncretism—the Canaanite El was said to be really JHWH; or by suppression—the prophets condemned idolatry; or by subordination—in many psalms, for example, JHWH is said to preside over the council of gods (Pss. 39:1; 89:6f.; 104:4; 98:10; and especially 82), so they become his (not always subservient!) staff or retinue. *Third*, in the New Testament the powers retain their status subordinate to God, and also their political role: they are God's creatures (Col. 1:15-17), fallen and rebellious (Eph. 2:1ff.; Gal. 4:1-11), and may be identical with empire and its lords (Rom. 13:1-4; Berkhof, 1953/1962:13-28).

Fourth, the mission of Jesus is understood both in Epistles and Gospels as conflict with and conquest of these powers. This point is so crucial for us that it must be expanded: In the Epistles the narrative of Christ's conflict with and conquest of the powers is typically represented in summary, proclamatory form, as for example, in Colossians 2:15 RSV: "He disarmed the principalities and powers [τὰς ἀρχὰς καὶ τὰς ἐξουσίας] and made a public example of them, triumphing over them in him." In the Gospels, however, these conflicts take the form of a story, indeed, they are *the* story, and the opponents are no longer called "the principalities and powers"; rather, they are the human overlords of state and temple, the Herods and Caiaphases and Pilates, or they are the demonic forces that sponsor illness, madness, and temptation, namely the demons and Satan. These can be cast as actors in the drama—while abstractions such as "headship," "authority," and "power" cannot. Note further that the contra-power that Jesus (and through him, God's Spirit) mounts against these is nothing less than the whole course of his obedient life, with its successive moments of proclamation, healing, instruction, the gathering of a redemptive community, and costly submission to the way of the cross and its death and resurrection. Therefore it is at a decisive moment in *that* story that the Lucan Jesus says, "I saw Satan fall like lightning from heaven" (10:18 RSV).

Fifth, in the New Testament period (and this is a development well prepared for in the Old) the historical circumstances of Jews and *a fortiori* of Jewish Christians is such that writers can apply this critical tool of social assessment not only to 'powers' that interrupt and threaten their own society (as the prophets had earlier criticized heathen idols), but also to the structures of the Jewish state and religious establishment, including priesthood, temple, and synagogue, as well as to the 'protecting' but crucifying Roman superstate (Revelation 13). Even that solid citizen, the apostle Paul, applies the scornful codeword ἐξουσία to Rome, albeit cautiously (Rom. 13:1-4; cf. Hengel, 1973/1977:ch. 6). Even more startling, Paul carries this institutional criticism home to his own most precious Pharisaic center, the law (Torah) itself (Caird, 1956:ch. 2; Stendahl, 1976).

The summary is not complete, but we can already raise a crucial question: are we able to use this powerful biblical social criticism in the understanding and assessment of our own world of powerful practice-incorporating structures? At one level, the answer seems easy. We will apply them to the governmental practices of the United States and the Soviet Union (ἀρχεξουσίαι, indeed!). We will also apply them to the institutionalized practices of General Motors and the Pentagon, of the bureaucracy and the labor unions, of the school system and the police, of mass communications and scientific technology, of smart New York and San Francisco society and Mencken's boobocracy, of the world of marriage and the world of sport, of the co-op and the country club, of patriarchy and of feminism, of our network of friends and of our own political parties. But shall we apply them also to the practices of the institutionalized Christian church, as Paul did to the law? To answer this requires that we complete the summary of the biblical doctrine of the powers.

Sixth, then, wherever Christ's victory is proclaimed, the corrupted reign of the powers is challenged, and yet the powers remain in being. They are neither destroyed nor abolished, but dethroned. So in the time between the resurrection and the final coming of Christ, they remain in an ambiguous state, and thus they delimit and define the social morality of Jesus' followers, who will have to encounter in the form of these powers crosses of their own. To them, the disciple must witness concerning the reversal of power achieved in Christ's resurrection; that is, make plain that these civil, military, economic, traditional, cultural, social, yes, *religious* and other structures are not themselves the end and meaning of life (Eph. 2:15; 3:9f.; 4:17-24; Berkhof, 1953/1962:39-41; Yoder, 1972:142-50; Wink, 1984:Part 3). Finally, *seventh*, there is the hint in the New Testament and especially in the Pauline Epistles that the final destiny of *all* the powers conquered by the cross will be not their abolition but their full restoration. See Ephesians 3:10 and especially 1:10 "to sum up [ἀνακεφαλαιώσασθαι] *all things* in Christ."

So the task of Christians confronting a world of *powerful practices* (as we may now call them) requires almost infinite adjustments, distinctions, and gradations. Just as the pastoral ministry to people must respect the variety of their circumstances (Paul would be "all things to all men," 1 Cor. 9:19-23), so Christian engagement of the powerful practices must attend to their variety. Whereas Constantinian Christianity in both its Catholic and Protestant forms has too readily confused the city of God with the earthly city, mistaking Augustine's resident alien for the mayor of the town, on the other hand 'sectarian' Christianity has sometimes mistakenly withdrawn into pietist enclaves that disregarded God's magnificent creature, the powerful practice, and the divine intentions for each. These dual errors (not exactly twin since one is a giant, the other a starveling) must be avoided by a new sensitivity to the point of practices as well as to their power. No one should, on Christian grounds, abandon hope in the costly work of witness to the structures of society, or indulge in a nonselective antipathy to whatever any government anywhere proposes. Glen Stassen has reminded me that the latter is a special temptation of today's Christian left—perhaps as a consequence of Reinhold Niebuhr's dictum that "group relations can never be as ethical as . . . individual relations"—the doctrine that society is necessarily immoral (1932:83).

At the same time, it is vital *not* to imagine that when some rulers become church members, the conversion of the great power over which those rulers preside has already taken place. For in the case of the Roman Empire that naïveté was exceedingly costly to the ongoing economy of the kingdom of God, as the post-Constantinian wedlock of church and empire again and again proved. Whereas Constantinian ethical theory has equated the many powers, as "orders of society" or "mandates," making the state paradigmatic for all the rest, the New Testament does *not* equate these. Marriage is a power in one way, the free market in another, the military in a third (Yoder, 1979). The Christian's dynamic and varied stance in facing each of these is already foreshadowed by the complex mission and ministry of Jesus, and by Christ's requirement of intelligible obedience from those who follow him. It is enough here to see that Christian obedience is challenged by a world of power as surely as it is framed in a world of nature. Therefore the faithful Christian "community will not ask whether to enter or to escape the realm of power"; rather it must ask, "What kinds of power are in conformity with the victory of the Lamb?" (Yoder, 1979:28).

2. *The Community of the Ten Commandments*

If powerful practices imbedded in a narrative foundation constitute the matrix of biblical social morality, it should be possible to sense this by examining the force of such a classic moral passage as the giving of the law at Sinai (Exod. 20:1-17; cf. Deut. 5:6-21). This section will test that thesis by examining the Exodus passage. As the reader will soon see, there is no attempt here to penetrate the maze of Pentateuchal investigation that scholarship has burrowed out: It appears that despite two centuries' investigation, there is no undisputed idea who the earliest readers of Exodus were (Childs, 1979:161-79). I will be content to treat as "the community that received the law at Sinai" that people represented by Exodus itself—Israel in Exodus—without further inquiry. The points that can thus be made would *mutatis mutandis* apply to any later communities who take themselves to be addressed in Exodus 2 by JHWH God.

The Ten Commandments seem not to have fared well in recent Christianity. Though the giving of the law at Sinai remains as a colorful part of the story Christians tell, there seems to be a sense that the Ten Words belong to the past, though it is uncertain whether "the past" means Judaism (a view that must seem ironic to contemporary Jews), or pre-Reformation times (yet Catholics seem to have the same difficulties with the Commandments that Protestants do), or perhaps only the previous century, when Francis Wayland, for example, could still treat "the law of Moses" as "revealed religion" and make it a mainstay of his argument against slavery (Wayland, 1865:208-23). If our difficulty with the law is in part a misunderstanding of its role in the community of its origin, a first task must be to see that role clearly. Law is a phenomenon not unique to any single people, and the Decalogue is only a part of biblical law—the rabbis counted altogether 613 commandments (*mitzvoth*), 365 negative and 248 positive ones in the Hebrew Bible. Yet the unique biblical role of the Ten (for example, Jesus in the Gospels simply refers to them as "*the* commandments"—Mark 10:19 and parallels) makes them a focus for our understanding of law in ethics (Harrelson, 1962).

To point out this unique role is quite different from claiming that the Ten Words are universal moral prescriptions; certainly that is not the way they are represented in Exodus. As the story of the making of the covenant is told in Exodus 19, JHWH through Moses treats with encamped Israel rather as a near Eastern monarch might deal with a people who have fallen into his power: He provides that they may enter into peoplehood, becoming "a kingdom of priests and a holy nation" (v. 6 RSV) not on the basis of their prior virtues or obedience, but on the basis of his redemption of this people from Egyptian bond servitude. There is, so to speak, a 'gospel' note in the covenant. "I bore you on eagles' wings and brought you to myself" (v. 4). At the climax of the account God indicates the provisions of this new peoplehood, beginning with the Ten Words: "And God spoke all these words, saying" (20:1). Here, by the way, is fresh evidence of the insufficiency of the second strand of biblical ethics. Neither law nor community exists on its own or *sui generis;* rather the existence of law and community springs from the anastatic intervention of God ("on eagles' wings"). The thunder on Sinai is to the discerning reader a clue signalling (strand-three) intervention.

Now, to the law itself. Structurally, Exodus 20:2-17 (cf. Deut. 5:6-21) may be seen as ten 'words' (i.e., utterances), of which eight are negative and two positive, in the following pattern: no, no, no, do this, do this, no, no, no, no, no. (In fact, because of the complexity of commandments Two and Ten—following the Jewish enumeration—there are not ten but thirteen injunctions, eleven being no's, but I will not pursue that complication here.) The predominance of negatives will not offend us, for we have seen how rules function to define practices by limiting the means of their accomplishment, and we know that limitation requires negation. For a clue to the whole, look first, though, at the two positive commandments, Four ("Remember the sabbath day") and Five ("Honor your father and your mother"). These two might be said to give the community *time*, Four providing the *cultural* time of an articulated succession of weeks and of weekly consecration, and Five, the *biological* time of the long succession of generations in Israel. By this double rhythm, the rhythm of memory and the rhythm of hope, it is declared that Israel shall live (Martin Buber, 1944/1946:132).

Here we meet a principle vital to interpreting all the commandments. Exactly because the Ten Words condense all biblical law, each must be read as implying whatever expansion its provenance requires (cf. Calvin, 1559/1960:II/viii). Thus with the Sabbath the whole calendar of Jewish festivals around the year is brought to mind, and with honor to father and mother all the ties of the kinship system. The Sabbath was said to be for remembering and for rest. In Exodus, this memory looks back to creation (God rested on creation's seventh day); in Deuteronomy it looks to Israel's Egyptian slavery (in which there had been no rest day) and to the divine deliverance from that ceaseless toil. So the people who keep this commandment will celebrate their liberation and their creaturehood as they remember God the Creator who is also God the Liberator. Doing so, they will show that time is for Israel no bare succession, but means recapitulation as well. (Here is a primal form of what I have called the baptist vision: the Sabbath *is* the divine rest-day of Genesis 2:2f.; it *is* the freed slaves' Exodus from bond labor.) Commandment Five, on the other hand, looks forward to future time: in requiring honor toward parents, it is addressed primarily to the young. Thus Five boldly places in the tender hands of each new generation the possibility of the survival of Israelite culture (cf. Deut. 6:1-8).

Before exploring the practices (and power) invoked in these two, let us briefly note the role of the remaining Words. Commandments One, Two, and Three look to the covenant people's new relation to JHWH, while Six through Ten refer to their new relations to one another. As Buber says "If the first

part deals with the *God* of the Community and the second
[Four and Five] with the *time*, the one-after-another of the
Community, the third is devoted to the *space*, the with-one-
another of the Community" (1944/1946:133). In other words,
Commandments One, Two, and Three lay it down that God
alone and not alien gods shall be worshiped: That is made
explicit in One; alien forms of worship are forbidden by Two
("graven images"); and alien religious practices are excluded
by Three ("name in vain"—probably originally an exclusion of
magic from JHWH-worship). Then Six through Nine forbid
those social ruptures—murder, adultery, theft, and false
witness (i.e., perjury)—that would destroy a people's solidarity with one another. That leaves Ten, which has become a
general extension of the preceding Words to the lawkeeper's
very intention as well (cf. Morris, 1976:ch. 1).

So it appears that each Commandment (except perhaps the
first and the last) has its place in connection with a *powerful
practice* in the community of Israel. As a guide to morality each
will remind its hearers of a particular existing moral 'game' and
will provide a line of direction for life in that 'game.' (Only the
first and last are 'metacommandments' indicating more
general directions for the entire realm of conduct—One
relating everything to the one God JHWH, and Ten insisting
that every commandment be carried out wholeheartedly.) For
an example, honoring a father (Five) makes no sense except in
a community where there *are* fathers, where, that is to say, a
kinship system makes fathers (and other relatives) socially
visible (cf. Chapter Three pp. 93-95). So to issue the Commandment is both to presuppose a practice and to show a way
of conduct with regard to that practice.

Some have categorized the ethics of the law as an ethics of
mere obedience to divine commands—an obedience ethics
(see essays in Helm, 1981). Yet the Decalogue's social morality,
we now see, cannot consist in obedience alone, for the very
concept of obedience depends upon a common life that
includes (in the case of Five) a kinship *practice*. But if there is
such a practice, its value lies in its capacity to evoke virtues and
seek goods internal to itself—including, but not limited to,
parental honor and filial obedience. Moreover, the command
does not merely designate the practice; it also indicates a line of
direction with respect to it. Concern for parental honor, for
example, has been contrasted with a kinship policy that would

simply neglect or cast off aging kin whose child-rearing days are past. Such characteristics have led still others to seek greater generality for biblical ethics by summing up the point of the commandments under some motto such as "be humane." But such summaries fail to tell us the contents of humaneness; when abstracted from the practices, these 'universalizations' become empty. (Chapter Eight will indicate that this applies to Jesus' love command and to the Golden Rule as well.)

Now if as I suppose the Decalogue originated in the earliest period of Israel's life, our knowledge of the related original practices is necessarily limited. The earliest use of Three ("name in vain") may have been to forbid magical employment of the sacred name of JHWH as a means to control the world (such magic, by the way, probably lies historically behind all forms of modern swearing—whether legal oaths or profane curses; the oath-taker invokes magic as a substitute for his or her own integrity.) Thus Three, while not simply forbidding the practice of magic, places it outside the realm of JHWH's service—banishing it (and all its successors!) to the place to which "other gods" have been consigned in the first commandment. For another example, some today are shocked to learn that Six only forbade "unsanctioned killing" such as murder of fellow Israelites, but not in the first instance killing people or killing in general. What is important to see, though, is that Six rejected violence in connection with the widest and most inclusive of the practices available to Israel, the practice of constituting a people. Compare MacIntyre's observation that "the creation and sustaining of human communities—of households, cities, nations—is generally taken to be a practice in the sense in which I have defined it" (1981:175). Going beyond the division of tribe or kinship groups, this practice declared *every* Israelite a citizen, whose life was therefore protected and entitled to the regard of all. So those Jews and Christians who today use Six as a motto for a still more inclusive human brother-and-sisterhood or community and thus by it are forbidden all killing are not wrong. But it is important that we see how that wider application grows from the original practice.

As a start toward understanding the moral role of the Commandments, then, consider the suggestions of the following table:

Commandment		Powerful Practice	
One	no other gods	metacommand (see text)	
Two	no graven images	art—and worship	
Three	no oaths	magic—and worship	
Four	remember the Sabbath	calendric time-keeping— and production of goods and services	positive; inculcates virtue of memory
Five	honor parents	kinship	positive; inculcates virtue of hope
Six	no murder	sustaining the community of Israel	
Seven	no adultery	marriage	
Eight	no stealing	stewardship of property	
Nine	no 'false witness'	law courts	
Ten	no coveting	metacommand (see text)	

Historical biblical study must correct and complete whatever has merit in these hints. For to construe the Ten Words in
this way makes possible an understanding of law that is not
"legalistic," but which demands of lawkeepers the recovery of
the narrative structure of Israel's faith. It must seem a mistaken
construal only from modern viewpoints that wish to reduce
ethics to "imprincipled decisions" or the like. That we are on
the biblical track, though, is further evidenced by the word
torah itself. We often translate it, "law," yet it comes from a
root meaning "to give a direction," "to point the way." In the
Bible, it means first a particular oracle showing God's direction
for conduct, and finally it comes to mean the entire Pentateuch
(cf. Neh. 8:1). So the Torah, the law, is the Way—and the chief
Hebrew word for sin, *chatah*, means not as we might say to
"break" the law, but literally, to "miss the way."

On this Way, God, too, is a traveler. When his people ask for
his name, his essence, he answers, JHWH—that is, "I will be
what I will be," or more freely, "You will come to know me
only as you follow me" (cf. Exod. 3:14 RSV NOTE). He is God the
Companion. Preoccupied with God the Creative Source
(strand one) or God the Pioneer who breaks ground with *new*

law (strand three), we may miss this central social note. The community of Israel has among its lively participants also—God the Partner. In its practices, he, too, is involved. By entering into these powerful practices (in accordance with the constituent rules, as just explained), the sons and daughters of Israel would do moral business with one another, but they would also do business with God and he with them. He himself participates in sacrifices, engages in battles, monitors politics, gives direction to family life, checks the balances used in commerce, comforts the naked, the helpless, and the stranger, encamps on Mount Zion (cf. Wicker, 1975:71-106). In a word, God is a *member* of the community—not of course a member just like other members, but in his own way—so that life in the social strand is necessarily a life of intercourse with this One.

If this 'anthropomorphism' strains our biblical faith, consider a related though more theoretical question: Whence come the particular powerful practices to which the law is (necessarily) attached? Clearly, the law forbidding adultery (and by implication, other sorts of sexual license) can have meaning only in a culture that practices marriage. But "Practice marriage!" is *not* one of the Commandments. And so with the other institutions and practices to which the law is internal. What then is the status of these institutions and practices? Is it right or moral to have them? Some have taken the extreme view that practices cannot be evaluated save from the standpoint of the practices themselves—whatever that may mean (Phillips and Mounce, 1970:26f.). But this view-point seems to come from the old mistake of confining morality to a single strand—in this case, strand two. God, as the Creator of culture as well as of nature, is the Creator of all the powerful practices. Yet the chosen people, Israel, do not engage in every possible practice. Why some, and not others? Why, in particular, these? Our answer must refer in part to the earthly origin of these practices in the organic strand with its needs, drives, and capacities. But we must refer as well to the *story* in which these practices (of worship, art, the rhythm of time, kinship, and the rest) arise and take their place—to the story of Israel, and behind that, as Genesis 1–11 shows, to the story of all the earth—and to the role of JHWH in each of these stories. In these human ways, out of these drives and needs, the practices did arise, but they arose already subject to abuse

or corruption. (We meet again the doctrine of the "powers.")
Confronting this crisis of human and institutional corruption,
the establishment of the community Israel represents a
redemptive move by God ("you shall be to me a kingdom of
priests") designed to free Israel and finally all of us from our
missings of the way, and to do so through this community, via
this story, by means of these particular laws. The Decalogue
acknowledges the *power* of the practices by laying down crucial
rules of limitation that show the (redeemed) people how they
may live with these practices yet not be tyrannized by them.
But their final protection lies not in the law (which can itself
become a powerful tyrant) but in God who gives it. If we dare
believe that, though, perhaps we can believe also the
consequent claim—that in this story, God indeed is with us,
not only our Commander, but our Leader on the way.

3.   Why the Social Strand Cannot Stand Alone

A quick review of this chapter may be helpful at this stage.
Struck by the tendency, in Old Testament and in New, to treat
the loci of power as demonic or rebellious "gods" or
"powers," we asked what the creative intent for such
turbulent social structures might originally have been. A
hypothesis was tried: gamelike human 'practices,' complex
and developing shared activities such as art or education or
marriage, have values internal to themselves; and such
practices, when united by a narrative bond, provide the very
stuff or matrix of social morality. Such a theory must be tested
by its capacity to make moral sense of the God-given
communities of law and gospel. We found that we could
understand one such community in these terms. *Quod erat
demonstrandum.*

Two elements, however, are lacking in the argument. On
the biblical side, our treatment of the Exodus community to
whom the Decalogue is addressed, while accurate in its own
terms, does not yet truly foreshadow the new that comes in
Christ. What is missing is eschatology, the sense of an ending
and of unheard-of ultimacy that marks every book of the New
Testament as well as much of the Old. This omission is
deliberate, since this chapter presents a mere strand-two
account of biblical morality. This account is true, but is not

the whole truth. The Exodus narrative of the Ten Commandments also looks or leans beyond its temporal sphere to the
prophetic and apocalyptic, in general, to the anastatic word.

At the same time, there is another, theoretical defect in the
chapter. This can be expressed in a question: What is to keep
communities of character and virtue, of laws and powerful
practices, from the sin of moral smugness, arrogance, pride?
Certainly that is a charge that Christians have made against
Jews, and often against one another, and (though perhaps not
quite so often) even against themselves. To be sure, all these
communities will count arrogance evil, smugness a sin;
perhaps pride will be named the sin of sins. Yet will they not be
guilty of it just the same, and guilty *just because* of the striving
for moral excellence just portrayed? Leaving Jews aside as able
to face their own difficulties for themselves, are not Christians,
and not least Christians whose social morality takes the
Decalogue seriously, liable to this fatal flaw of moral smugness
or self-righteousness? The apostle Paul, whose insight here
has not been surpassed, saw that to have his own righteousness as a source of moral or religious boasting was simply
self-defeating (Phil. 3:9; cf. Eph. 2:9)—the more one had to
boast of, morally speaking, the lower one's confidence ought
to be. It almost made it seem that (contrary to all moral reason)
one ought to "continue in sin, that grace may abound" (Rom.
6:1 RSV). And it certainly forced the Torah, the law, which Paul
had to acknowledge as in itself "holy, and just, and good"
(Rom. 7:12) into the alien role of a 'fallen' power or institution,
itself not the redeemer but in need of redemption.

The way out of the paradox for Paul, however, did not lie in
rational resolution, but in a faith that, turning away from self
as a ground of salvation, looked instead to Christ and only
Christ—"that I may know him and the power of his
resurrection, and may share his sufferings, becoming like him
in his death" (Phil. 3:10 RSV). As I understand this, it means
that Paul escaped the paradox of self-righteousness, that is,
the crazy maelstrom of self-contemplating moral stultification,
whenever it threatened, by throwing his life afresh into the
way of the cross, a way that necessarily "leaves self behind"
and follows Jesus. But this new way was open to Paul only
because he had a new way of seeing Jesus Christ, thanks to
Christ's resurrection from the dead (cf. 2 Cor. 5:16f.).

What is true of Paul here is true of apostolic Christianity in all its forms. We have noted Paul's case because he so eloquently expresses the difficulty and its resolution: "Who will deliver me from this body of death? Thanks be to God through Jesus Christ our Lord!" (Rom. 7:24f. RSV). But on this point—concerning what we are calling the resurrection strand of Christian life—the whole New Testament is on the side of Paul.

Yet this anastatic or eschatological element of biblical common life has been suppressed in this chapter so far in order to give a purely "social" account. Thus the two missing features are actually one. When we turn to the resurrection or newness that Christians find in Christ, we come to the very aspect of Christian morality that (by apostolic testimony) heals and banishes the self-righteousness of the isolated social strand.

Note clearly that it is *not* being said that God comes in strand three while strand two is merely human morality. That is not the sense of the strands. God as God is present to us in every strand, every dimension of our existence—as nature's Numen, as society's Web, as the resurrection's adventurous Ground (McClendon, 1981:198-204). Rather, if we seek to live out our moral lives in less than this three-stranded, God-given way, as by omitting the reality of Christ incarnate, or Christ crucified, or Christ risen from the dead, we fall into self-defeating forms of the Christian moral life (cf. Bonhoeffer, 1949/1965:130f.).

Yet this chapter's role has been to sketch a strand that has its own proper claim upon us—the social strand—and to show how a necessary dimension of Christian life is engagement in particular and given social structures. I have done little to apply this to Christian social life today; in part that will be done in the two following chapters. I have sought to show the beauty and elegance of social structures in their own formal standing as God's powerful creatures, and to recall the Way taken by a people whose lives were engaged both in the structures of the law and in the rebellious but divinely vanquished structures of the world.

Dietrich Bonhoeffer

The other prisoners are conspirators—apprehended, convicted, sentenced to death by a desperate regime. Canaris, Oster, Sack, others, enemies of the state, according to the state's law and the state's courts. Naked as an emblem of their shame, pale from prison darkness, they stand silent in line, awaiting their turn at the gaunt gallows that rises over their heads. Among them, also naked, also condemned, stands Pastor Bonhoeffer, age thirty-nine. His hapless presence there to be hanged on this April morning in 1945 shapes the question: What is Dietrich Bonhoeffer doing among these doomed 'public enemies'? Why is he there?

The previous chapter has described the structure of Christian social ethics in terms of Christian community and its relation to *powerful practices*. "Practices" there meant those rule-governed human activities, such as the practices of architecture, or law, or the military profession, or of marriage, property ownership, or worship. On one side, practices as there defined can best be understood on the analogy of games—and indeed some games are so complex and self-involving that they have grown to be practices: baseball, and possibly warfare, are examples. But on the other side, practices display power, and here the biblical image evoked was that of the *principalities and powers*, such as Jewish law or Roman *imperium*—or the German *Reich*. On a biblical analysis these acquire a life and energy of their own so that they require for their subjugation nothing less than the redemptive work of Christ.

Attending to both their structure and their power, we saw these powerful practices as constitutive of human sociality. In their creatureliness and in their capacity for good or for evil, they present a constant challenge to Christian existence. It was also implied in Chapter Six (and will be shown in Chapter Eight) that such practices, with all their risk and promise, constitute the moral life of Christians in community as well. The church is a society that embodies powerful practices; among these are the practice of evangelism and the practice of worship. The church also fitfully embodies the ministry or practice of peacemaking. These insights are now to be employed in unfolding the theological meaning of the life of Dietrich Bonhoeffer. We are to see how engagement in certain practices, those of the church and those of a modern society, worked out for one distinguished Christian participant in our times.

Such a chapter cannot very well unfold a story that required Bonhoeffer's principal biographer, Eberhard Bethge, more than eight hundred pages of close-packed German text to tell (Bethge, 1967). For clarity I will concentrate upon three crucial episodes: the events or circumstances in which Bonhoeffer became first, a pastor-theologian, second (and only second!) in his own words, "a Christian," and third, a conspirator in assassination. At the end I will assess the tragedy with which his life closed, seeking to relate this to all the preceding episodes. As before, I will cite biographical sources only when I am aware of departing from the standard account, in this case as it is found in Bethge (1970).

1.   Bonhoeffer the Theologian-in-the-making

In the summer term of 1933 in the University of Berlin a young *Privatdozent*, or lecturer, stood up in a lecture hall to begin a course in Christology. Though he was so near its beginning, this would turn out to be the high point of his tragically interrupted academic career. He stood in the hall where the great Schleiermacher had taught. He was a beginner in the faculty of the university where his own father had long been head of the medical department of psychiatry. He taught where nine years before, at the age of eighteen, he himself had entered as a student in theology. He was beginning this Christology lecture just six months after Adolf Hitler had, quite legally, become Chancellor of Germany. Bonhoeffer had previously given university lectures on Genesis 1–3 in which he had said in effect that the world belonged to Jesus Christ, was created by Christ, and therefore (it was implied) the world was not created by nor did it belong to the new mystique of blood and soil, of nation and *Volk*. Three months before this course's beginning, he had given a radio talk in Berlin on "The Leadership Principle"—clearly political in implication—and been cut off the air before he had finished. Therefore every word he spoke now would be politically measured (was it treason?), theologically measured (was it genuinely Lutheran or Reformed?), personally measured by his student friends there in the hall (was this their Dietrich?).

He opened the notes and read the first sentence: "Teaching about Christ begins in silence" (Bonhoeffer, 1978:27). He looked, one of his students said later, like a student himself. "But then what he had to say so gripped us all that we were no longer there to listen to this very young man, but we were there because of what he had to say" (Bethge, 1970:164). Happily, though, what he had to say and what he was were close together; how close, we can better see if we understand how he had come to be in the theological classroom at all, how he had become a theologian.

Dietrich Bonhoeffer was born (February 4, 1906) in Breslau, the sixth (and his twin sister the seventh) of eight children of Dr. Karl Bonhoeffer and his wife Paula, she born a von Hase. The families of these two had for centuries been distinguished middle-class Swabian, Thuringian, and Prussian members of society: goldsmiths, doctors, clergymen, councilors of state. The von Hases tended to conservatism in politics, and many were ministers of religion or soldiers; on the Bonhoeffer side there were more liberal politicians, one forebear having actually read Karl Marx! On both sides, as anecdotal evidence shows, there had appeared sometimes a stubborn streak; convinced, they stuck to their convictions.

Now the tone in Dietrich's own family home was urbane, 'cultural' in a way foreign to the experience of most contemporary Americans, but with only perfunctory religious observance. Respect for parents, orderly customs of family life, the love of the rich literary and artistic heritage of Europe, all shaped daily life. They were, of course, Protestant, at least in name. When Dietrich was six the family had moved to Berlin as Father Karl assumed his new university post. The year 1914 had brought war, and for Germany hard years followed: rationing, deaths in nearly every family (Dietrich had lost a brother), and ultimate defeat, with the abdication of the Kaiser, an idealistic Weimar republic, and the economic inflations and political crises of a defeated empire. Thus Dietrich's adolescent years were those of the Youth Movement, which featured wandering youth in the countryside, girls in long loose-fitting dresses, with guitars and folksongs, while Berlin, "the liveliest city in the world," inevitably put its own worldly, sophisticated mark on those who grew up there. The Bonhoeffers and their friends were just as likely to be singing Beethoven or Brahms as folksongs, with Dietrich, by now an accomplished pianist, playing the accompaniment in either case. Parties and school examinations and games and serious conversation with adults, learning and friends and family life: it was an exhilarating childhood and youth. For Dietrich, at least, the hilarity took. One may judge that before anything else, he learned the skills of this sociality—to be a Bonhoeffer, a member of his own family, in its place in society.

But something else took as well. From rather early on, he announced to his sceptical 'scientific' brothers and sisters and his somewhat bemused parents that he intended to become a theologian—unlike brother Karl-Friedrich, who was to be a superb physicist, or Klaus, a lawyer. Too little is known about Dietrich's youth to know quite why he made that choice for ministry and stuck to it with Bonhoeffer stubbornness. Biographers mention a pious Moravian nurse in the family; others speculate upon his rebellion against his older brothers, or upon the influence of his mother's practical piety. What is known is Dietrich's own brilliant university record. By the time of his licentiate or doctorate (1927) he was marked in Berlin as the bright hope of the University's liberal faculty of theology—this despite (or perhaps even partly because?) he rebelled against his teachers' theological stance, looking for guidance to their rival and nemesis, the young Karl Barth, whose writings were by now breaking the glacial calm of late-liberal orthodoxy, and looking also beyond Barth to Rome, whose majestic integrity caught Dietrich's sharp boyish eye on a visit at eighteen. Bonhoeffer had in the German fashion spent a year at another university, Tübingen, a later semester in Rome as a culture-tourist, and a still later year abroad, at Union Theological Seminary in New York. He had argued theology with his brilliant polymath professor, Adolf von Harnack, and would spend a working year in Barcelona as assistant pastor of a German-speaking congregation.

Bonhoeffer's early theological productions, however rebellious in principle, were still caught up in the thought forms of von Harnack's Berlin liberalism. His dissertation under Reinhold Seeberg, *The Communion of Saints* (1930/1962), was guided by some of the same motifs that were soon to stir H. Richard Niebuhr and his pupils across the Atlantic: The church is to be understood in sociological terms as a human community. At the same time, the church is to be understood in theological terms as the body of Christ. Neither cancels the other; Troeltsch is right, but so is Barth. And Bonhoeffer's customary second thesis, *Act and Being* (1931/1962), took issue with current idealist philosophy, arguing that neither in its neo-Kantian or its neo-Hegelian forms could philosophy come to terms with the notion of a God truly transcendent; such a conception must wait upon theology, upon revelation. Now the groundwork was laid; Bonhoeffer was ready for Christology. And as we have seen, the Christology took on flesh in the 1933 Berlin lectures: Christ is not the remote, unattainable end point of the scientific historian's search for the "Jesus of history"; Jesus Christ, the *risen* Christ, is immediately known to the church today. Whenever the Word of God is preached in the church, whenever the sacraments of baptism and Lord's supper are administered, Christ is present. And Christ is also (and just as truly) present in the *Gemeinde*—that is, in the congregation, the local here and now fellowship of Christians one with another. And Christ, this present Christ, is God; the old creeds tell the truth (Bonhoeffer, 1978). It was rich orthodoxy, passionately crafted in the face of current heresies by a modern theological master in the making.

But politics would not wait for a new theology to be worked through. The academic year of Bonhoeffer's ascendance as a theologian (1932–33) was the year of Hitler's accession to power. On April 1, 1933, Hitler proclaimed a national boycott of Jewish shops in Germany. Brown-shirted gangs roamed the streets, beating up Jews and other victims. The immediate problem for Christians was the infection of the church itself with Nazis and Nazi sympathizers in the clergy. These 'German Christians' favored bringing the Nazi anti-Semitic exclusiveness within the church itself, thus making it "racially pure." Bonhoeffer, with his older colleague Pastor Martin Niemoeller and others, met the challenge first with the preacher's age-old weapons: lectures, pamphlets, a "Pastor's Emergency League." It made little difference. By October of fateful 1933, Bonhoeffer had accepted a call to a German congregation in London; it would be for him a vantage point from which to watch, to think, and to make loyal friends in the Anglo-American world in preparation for the gathering storm.

What do you do if you are a Christian theologian and have come to believe that your own country—the country you and your ancestors have loved and served—is slipping into the control of men who are about to commit massive evil? What if, moreover, you have been taught to respect the old Constantinian accommodation—*Reichskirche* and *Reich*—as history's inevitable fixtures? Studying the writings and the actions of 1933–35, we can say that Bonhoeffer's immediate answer was threefold. First, he was driven (with Barth, with Luther before him) back upon Scripture. This was to have a radical impact in the days ahead. Second, he turned to the fledgling ecumenical movement, seeking to seal a bond between world Christianity and the German Confessing Church (the attempted restructuring of Protestant Christianity that had been the response to Hitler's takeover) that would make it impossible for Christians to remain Hitler supporters. This effort, though, was ultimately ineffective. And third, Dietrich Bonhoeffer made plans to go to India, where he would be able to learn from Gandhi the techniques of inwardness, community, and nonviolence, closely linked to the Sermon on the Mount, that were by now capturing his interest. But events overtook the young pastor; he never reached India—a failure, as we will see, with serious consequences.

2. *The Theologian Becomes a Christian*

"Bonhoeffer," says the redoubtable Eberhard Bethge, "always greatly disliked stories of conversion told by pietists for purposes of edification" (Bethge, 1970:156). Indeed, like his neurologically oriented psychiatrist father, Dietrich disliked most references to the inner self (cf. Green, 1981). It is therefore not a little ironic that Bethge is able to chart an indisputable transformative change in his subject, displayed in the hard documentary evidence of Dietrich's own writing. And that change, as Bonhoeffer himself put it, meant "becoming a Christian" (Bethge, 1970:154f.).

Grasping this event must take us back a bit in our story. The time can be fixed around the beginning of Bonhoeffer's work in the church, and as a university lecturer in Berlin, just following the visit of 1930–31 to America. That visit ("my first impressions abroad") had shown him something about America, but it had shown him a good deal more about himself. He had spent considerable time with a French Reformed student, Jean Lasserre—who was a pacifist. Also, impatient with the white mainline churches in New York City, he had found with the help of a black fellow student, Frank Fisher, a church home away from home in the Abyssinian Baptist Church, located in Harlem. Here Dietrich had taught a Sunday school class, had met church families and been entertained in their humble homes, and had discovered an authenticity for which he evidently hungered. Is it altogether coincidental that it was after visiting this Afro-American church for nearly a year, and after making friends with the deeply committed Lasserre, that he was ready explicitly to own his inherited Christian faith? However that may be, "it was then," at the time of the first impressions abroad, Bonhoeffer wrote to his friend Bethge in a rare autobiographical comment, "that I turned from phraseology to reality" (Bonhoeffer, 1972a:275; for another view, Kelley, 1984).

Remember that we are seeking in this chapter an answer to the question, how is it that Pastor Bonhoeffer came to be involved in a conspiracy against Hitler? We require not merely the circumstances of his involvement (his acquaintances, friends, and family, and his usefulness to the quixotic cause represented by the plot) but the deep springs of his action; springs we did not find in his theological career as such. Can we find them here in the turn to being a Christian? Before we can say, though, we must see what this turn meant in Dietrich Bonhoeffer's life. What kind of Christian? In what sense, "Christian"?

Bethge, after listing some habitual patterns in the new Dietrich's life—churchgoing, oral confession as a practice, biblical meditation—speaks in answering this question of a fresh focus for Bonhoeffer's thinking, soon to be spelled out in *The Cost of Discipleship*. The Sermon on the Mount will henceforth be regarded as central and to be acted out, no longer merely as a 'law' to quicken conscience; moreover, Dietrich's piety will now begin to seem "too fervent" for some; and he will begin taking a stand for Christian pacifism (Bethge, 1970:254). At the heart of everything in this new ordering of life lies the image of discipleship. *Nachfolge*, for Bonhoeffer as he began the new shaping of life, was the image of life abandoned in costly commitment to the way of the Crucified One.

Concrete evidence of the new convictions is found in 1934 correspondence between Bonhoeffer and Reinhold Niebuhr, back at Union Theological Seminary where he had spent that significant year. In light of the political crisis in Germany, he told Niebuhr, he was now thinking of taking his long-delayed trip to India; there he could meet Gandhi and learn from him how the Confessing Church might engage in resistance to Hitler in obedience to the Sermon on the Mount. Niebuhr warned him against this: Gandhi was "an ethical liberal"; moreover, Nazi Germany was not a place where Gandhian methods would work. The Germans were not open to moral suasion as were the British in India. "Organized passive resistance would end in utter failure." Bonhoeffer, though, was not deterred by this exchange with the great "realist." This was not because he doubted Niebuhr's assessment of the high cost of opposing Hitler with nonviolent methods; indeed he believed him, and was prepared to suffer physically. But he had also come to believe that being a Christian meant nothing less than committing one's life to the dominance of Jesus Christ in political life, also—which meant that now pacifism was "a matter of course." This would not be expressed by entering the political arena as such. Rather, the church as church—the Confessing Church—was to be the community that would by its nonviolent action "speak 'for the dumb,' the innocent victims of Nazi criminality" (Rasmussen, 1970:167-70; regretfully Rasmussen leaves this almost out of account in his interpretation, relegating it to an appendix).

Bonhoeffer did not get to India to listen there to the voice of Gandhi, or to learn Gandhian techniques of nonviolent group action. But the conviction remained, to be expressed in *The Cost of Discipleship* (1937/1963), and even sooner in a sermon he delivered at an ecumenical conference at Fanø, Denmark, in the summer of 1934: "For the members of the ecumenical church . . . cannot take up arms against Christ himself—yet this is what they do if they take up arms against one another!" Christ has forbidden war; Christians may not disobey (Bonhoeffer, 1970:285f.).

The term as a London pastor was ended, not by the intended visit to India, but by a call to return to Germany as pastor-in-charge (professor, president, chaplain, and business manager in one) of a Confessing Church seminary or school of practical ministry for ordinands, eventually to be located at Finkenwalde (in present-day Poland). Here, in the founding of this school, was at last a chance to *act*, and to act in concert with fellow Christians: to build up the church of God. It is remarkable that several commentators (e.g., Gill, 1971:125f.) have treated this seminary phase as a time of "withdrawal" in Bonhoeffer's life. A study of the record shows almost the contrary. At least, during the so-called 'withdrawn' period (i.e., between April, 1935 and March, 1940) Dietrich Bonhoeffer managed to publish a stream of articles and books, found an intentional community alongside the seminary, continue lectures at Berlin until dismissed, attend two official ecumenical meetings and make one Scandinavian junket *with* his student body, get himself banned from Berlin, carry on (but eventually break off) at least one love affair, make initial contact with the Hitler conspirators, take an abortive trip to New York, and meet his obligations of teaching his seminarians term by term as well. The truth seems to be that this was a period of intense activity, most of it richly communal, in which the newly self-discovered Christian was rethinking his theology in Sermon on the Mount focus, testing his ideas about community living at Finkenwalde (and the other training sites chosen for the nearly illegal seminary), and continuing the fight to make the Confessing Church of Barmen the Christian Church of Protestant Germany. The ideas that he sought to live out in company with other Christian Germans in this period are central to the correct understanding of Bonhoeffer's entire life and its tragic end; they are not marginal, not 'withdrawn.'

And what were those ideas? There was, foremost, the idea of *obedience*. The title Bonhoeffer gave to the big book he completed during the Finkenwalde period was *Nachfolge*; its English translation was fittingly titled *The Cost of Discipleship*.

Bonhoeffer wanted to say that discipleship *is* costly, and that its cost begins with obedience. Hence the attention in the seminary training to the Sermon on the Mount as a pattern for obedient action; hence the focus upon a disciplined routine of meditation and prayer during the seminary day; hence the pungent Bonhoeffer saying that tied to the old Lutheran free grace a fresh Lutheran concept of costly obedience: "The only man [*Mensch*] who has the right to say that he is justified by grace alone is the man who has left all to follow Christ" (Bonhoeffer, 1937/1963:55).

To be a Christian meant a costly "I follow after"; that entailed obedience; it also entailed a communal discipline in which disciples watched over, corrected, and cared for one another. At the seminary each student 'brother' was encouraged to choose a fellow student to whom he would privately confess his sins in preparation for the common eucharist—a plan that, with some hitches, worked. The surprise came when it was discovered that Bonhoeffer the leader also intended to be one of the 'brothers,' choosing one—it turned out to be Bethge—to hear his own confession. (For this and other practices Bonhoeffer, who had little contact at this time with Catholic communities, was indebted to the Anglican monasteries he had visited while in England.) Some of the failings in community harmony could thus be handled by the discipline of self-searching, confession, and God's forgiveness. But more stubborn ruptures of community discipline were to be treated by the methods of Matthew 18 (which we find at the center of baptist structures also)—always aiming at repentance and reconciliation (1937/1963:323-30).

It is in this light, I believe, that we are to understand Bonhoeffer's passionate effort during this period to bring order and discipline to the Confessing Church as a whole. The Nazis, through a combination of state decrees and church politics, had achieved what many (including Bonhoeffer) had indeed yearned for: a single German Protestant Church, headed by a Reichsbishop. But the new structure was expressly anti-Jewish, and the church was subservient to the state. So at the Synod of Barmen (May, 1934), while Bonhoeffer had been still in London, Niemoeller, Barth, and others had adopted a "confession" that defined an alternative church, obedient to Christ alone as Lord. The Confessing

Church had its own troubles, however. How far should one compromise with an ever encroaching state? And how was such a question even to be decided? For Bonhoeffer in 1935–39, the answer, just as in the little Finkenwalde brotherhood, lay in collective discipline, to which each must submit as if to Christ himself. In the struggle with the 'German Christians' and their Nazi state, there could be no uncommitted bystanders (Bonhoeffer, 1972b:75-96).

So *Nachfolge* meant obedience to Christ for each disciple, and it meant communal discipline (under Christ) for the whole community. But as we have seen, this brought the practices of *Nachfolge*, the practices of true discipleship, into conflict with the power of the state and its apparatus. For Hitler was just then promising the German people that by remilitarization and self-aggrandizement they could restore the former glory of defeated Germany. As these lines are being written (1984) the American people have just returned to presidential office a leader who has promised them safety based on unequaled military power. Whatever the differences, this phenomenon, so warmly endorsed by many American pastors, should make it easier for Americans now to understand Germans half a century ago, and to appreciate the difficulty of a church polity that dared challenge the express national will.

Bonhoeffer, however, accepted such opposition as the reality of the church's way under Christ. To be a Christian was not to withdraw into inwardness that would never run head on into the world's opposition. Those who 'follow after' are a city set on a hill (Matt. 5:14). "Hence," Bonhoeffer wrote in *The Cost of Discipleship*,

there is a certain 'political' character involved in the idea of sanctification and it is this character which provides the only basis for the Church's political ethic. The world is the world and the Church the Church, and yet the Word of God must go forth from the Church into all the world, proclaiming that the earth is the Lord's and all that therein is. Herein lies the 'political' character of the Church. (1937/1963:314)

Certainly the church's proclaiming that "the earth is the Lord's" (Ps. 24:1) would not seem a very bold or daring 'political' act even in Nazi Germany. Yet two aspects of this paragraph must be noted very carefully. The first is that already in these Finkenwalde days, being a Christian, a

Nachfolge, meant 'political' conflict. Only there were still the qualifying quotation marks; it was still 'political,' not just political. The other is that the claim for the Lord of the *whole* earth is in its way as total a claim as Hitler would ever make. The question still remained how that claim would be understood by Bonhoeffer himself in the course of the days ahead.

Those familiar with the Radical tradition will note that in *Nachfolge* Bonhoeffer had grasped a word central to Anabaptists and their spiritual heirs. Although as a scholar and theologian he knew next to nothing of that other heritage, he had certainly touched its living growing edge when in New York he had attended the Abyssinian Baptist Church. Still, it was pretty clearly independent Bible study, rather than this or other contacts, that brought him to his view. The baptist vision is more often caught from the Scriptures than taught by a tradition. Yet this brings up afresh the key question of nonviolence and Bonhoeffer's stance with regard to it.

Discussing Matthew 5:38-42 in the section on "Revenge" in his *Nachfolge*, Bonhoeffer took up the topic, facing all the doubting sceptical questions that arose in his own mind and, we can imagine, in his students'. The church, unlike old Israel, is not to be a national community, he notes. Thus it is not assigned the military role that Israel once assumed. On the other hand, obedience to Jesus' way of nonviolence is not merely addressed to individuals as individuals, with an exception for larger groups, or for the Christian office-holder (as the Reformers had taught). The New Testament, says Bonhoeffer, knows nothing of such a distinction. Rather all Christians are to take the way of the nonresistant cross: "The only way to overcome evil is to let it run itself to a standstill because it does not find the resistance it is looking for." And a little further on, "There is no deed on earth so outrageous as to justify a different attitude" (1937/1963:157-59). But just a little later, Bonhoeffer would be saying something like this in private:

If I were walking down the Kurfürstendamm and saw a racing car striking some pedestrians and imperiling more, I would not consider I had done my whole Christian duty if I at once began to comfort the victims. It would be as much my responsibility as anyone's *to stop that car.* (Gill, 225; cf. Zimmerman, 1973:82, 157)

These sayings, the one sort in his book, the other in conversations with friends, seem to point in contrary directions:

the latter toward conspiracy plots, assassinations, the recapture of government by "good people"; the former toward a very different kind of 'political' strategy. But concretely, what was that different strategy to have been?

3. The Christian Becomes a Conspirator

We do not know what the strategy would have been, because under repression by the state the Confessing Church, torn by inner dissension, failed. Many of its members compromised with the Nazis; the Church Struggle subsided into a stalemate or truce. When war came in 1939 the Finkenwalde seminarians were drafted (some, who had heard Bonhoeffer's pacifist teaching and quite possibly believed he was right, died as German soldiers fighting in Poland); in 1940 the secret seminaries were closed by the Gestapo. The close fellowship of teacher and students, Bonhoeffer's little 'church,' virtually ceased to exist. In a few more months, the German armies under Hitler had defeated France, occupied the Low Countries, Denmark, and Norway, threatened England with invasion, and reigned supreme in Western Europe. By force of arms Hitler had won a decisive political victory. Putative internal revolts against him, some of which had been haltingly considered from the time he attained power, faded. The newly triumphant *Wehrmacht* generals (upon whom the anti-Hitler plotters in Germany ever staked their hopes) could not quarrel with success at arms. Victory spread its proud feathers over the German people. *Sieg heil!*

By this time, however, Dietrich Bonhoeffer was already at work for the German army's military intelligence bureau, the *Abwehr*, as a spy; indeed, he was a double agent, also employed, under cover of this office, in a plot to overthrow Hitler, if need be by assassination, and to replace the German government. Here we reach a crux in the interpretation of Bonhoeffer's life. How has it come about that the devoted young pastor who as recently as mid-March had been still an (extralegal) teacher of theology in a seminary focused upon *Nachfolge*, discipleship, is by August of that same year making arrangements to go to work for the *Abwehr*—and to join the plot against the head of state, Adolf Hitler? What could have occurred to make this timetable possible? Interpreters of

Bonhoeffer who approached the story twenty years afterward, from their own 1960s standpoint, the theology of secularity and the ethics of situationism, provided an answer that has been so widely accepted that we must consider it. Their theory was that Bonhoeffer at last had his eyes opened; reality was not in the stuffy little world of the church; it was out there in the big world of men and politics, of statecraft and war. Already and always a situationist in ethics, say these theorists, he now became under pressure of events a secularist as well; he engaged in the plot, and then later in the prison letters wrote out a theory to match his actions. In effect, there was in 1939 or 1940 a second Bonhoeffer 'conversion'; the Christian became a worldly humanist. This is, with variation in detail, the explanation adopted by Ronald Gregor Smith (1967:9-21), by Theodore Gill (1971), and by situationist contributors to a recent collection of Bonhoeffer studies as well (Klassen, ed., 1981). Meanwhile Clifford Green (1972) and Wayne Floyd (1984), as well as Bethge (1970 and subsequently), have presented a less flamboyant account of Bonhoeffer's transition from subversive seminaries to subversive statecraft. On this latter view Bonhoeffer was never the 'withdrawn' pietist, and on the other hand never became the model death-of-God secularist. They say there is a consistency in Bonhoeffer from student days to prison writings. So it seems the doctors disagree, and we must make our own way through the factual evidence.

About some of the facts there can be little dispute. All through the London and the Finkenwalde periods (1933–40) and after, Bonhoeffer remained in close touch with his extended family, linked through the Berlin home of his parents. The entire family was pro-German but anti-Hitler. So far from being anti-Semitic, they were through Dietrich's sister Sabine intermarried with Gerhard Leibholz, Jewish in ancestry though Lutheran by profession. Equally far from accepting Hitler's program of chauvinistic international bullying, they maintained personal contacts in France, England, and the United States. The family were neither Marxist-socialist nor strictly democratic; their political leanings were mainly conservative but traditional. And as earlier noted, save for sister Susanne's theologian husband Walter Dress and of course Dietrich, the family had little religious interest. Dietrich remained at the center of this family; still a bachelor at thirty-four, he continued to have his own room in the parents' Marienburger Allee residence. So it was through this aristocratic Bonhoeffer family, and particularly through his brother-in-law Hans von Dohnanyi, that he already knew about the resistance to Hitler, such as it was, just as the others knew about his covert church activities. When Dietrich came home from the closing of the last seminary session on March 15, 1940, he found his brother-in-law Hans closeted with Oster, Hassell, and Beck, three of the conspirators, discussing a secret peace proposal—one that presumed Hitler's overthrow and the installation of a conservative new German government. This was the circle into which, in the following months, Bonhoeffer was decisively drawn.

At this point it is necessary to say a word about the conspiracy against Hitler. It was never a very large or very well organized movement. Partly this was because of the considerable skill of Hitler's internal security forces, particularly the SS with its Gestapo section, in suppressing dissent. Even without joining the conspiracy, Bonhoeffer, for example, had found himself dismissed from his teaching post, forbidden to publish, banned from residing in Berlin, and required to report periodically to the police. All the more were known political dissidents forced, even earlier in the Hitler period, to flee or be confined in the dread concentration camps. There remained free a few politicians such as Karl Goerdeler, a sometime mayor of Leipzig, and a few patriots such as Dohnanyi and Josef Müller, both lawyers. The remainder of the conspirators were drawn from what they all conceived to be the necessary focus of a revolt, namely the officer corps of the German army. High *Wehrmacht* leaders had played a key role in Hitler's rise to power, but between the demonic politician and these old soldiers there remained a latent tension that might be fanned into active revolt. And in fact plans for a *Putsch* or takeover had germinated among them all through the 1930s, coming to a head from time to time in various abortive schemes. Typical of these had been the plot of July, 1938: the highly respected General Ludwig Beck, recently retired Chief of Staff of the army, and his successor, General Franz Halder, agreed that a general war at this time would be disastrous for Germany. So they arranged with their fellow generals that should Hitler order the threatened invasion of Czechoslovakia, they would seize Hitler and try him before one of his own People's Courts on the charge of incompetence, based on that very order. But they reckoned without Hitler's political finesse: Before the invasion materialized, British Prime Minister Chamberlain and France's Daladier had met at Munich to guarantee Hitler the Czech territory he wanted; Czechoslovakia collapsed, and the Beck-Halder plot lacked the spark plug event upon which it had been premised, for no invasion order was now forthcoming.

Such was the long history of high-level resistance to Hitler's hegemony all through his twelve years in office. The plots always depended upon a generals' revolt; the generals, though many disliked and some despised Hitler, were at best reluctant participants in each projected coup, and Hitler's political finesse, cunning, and apparent good luck held out until the very end. Interestingly, another of the earlier plots had proposed a nonviolent strike by the generals: they would, it was planned, simply resign *en masse* upon orders for a Czech invasion, leaving Hitler with no means to carry out his plan (Shirer, 1960:368). The one attempt that finally gained more than a modicum of 'success'—in that a bomb actually exploded in Hitler's presence, followed by a few desultory staff orders in Berlin and elsewhere to seize the reins of power—was nevertheless abortive like all the rest; by the end of that day, July 20, 1944, its effective leader, the brave Colonel von Stauffenberg, would lie shot to death by a firing squad, General Beck, the nominal leader, would have mortally wounded himself, Hitler would have regained full power, and the arrest orders would have been issued that ultimately led to the execution of nearly five thousand implicated officers and others, including within the year Pastor Dietrich Bonhoeffer, who by then had already been arrested and jailed.

This long-simmering and ever ineffectual military conspiracy was what Pastor Bonhoeffer joined in 1940. It is not my aim here to judge the moral worth of his action so much as to attempt to understand it. What he did is partly to be understood in terms of opportunity: His family were involved; he shared their horror of Hitler; how then should he not be involved as well? Partly, too, he is to be understood in terms of an exigency today's American reader may not readily grasp: Bonhoeffer faced the likelihood of being called up with his age-group in the military draft. There was no category of conscientious objectors. And conscientious protest, he saw clearly enough, was meaningless save as the expression of a community of conviction—yet *such a community did not exist* in 1939–40 Germany. Its nearest candidate, the Confessing Church, was as militaristic as the rest of Germany on that point. All this had come out in a letter Dietrich had already written his English friend Bishop Bell in March, 1939: "I am thinking of leaving Germany sometime. The main reason is the compulsory military service." Dietrich went on to explain to Bell that to refuse this service would actually be a cause of scandal to the Confessing Church. Noting that on his view "the worst thing of all" was the required military oath (in *Cost of Discipleship* he had written that "for the Christian . . . any oath which makes an unconditional demand on him will for him be a lie"), he summed the matter up:

So I am rather puzzled in this situation, and perhaps even more because I feel it is really only on Christian grounds that I find it difficult to do military service under the present conditions, *and yet there are only very few friends who would approve of my attitude.* (Bethge, 1970:541, Bonhoeffer's italics; Bonhoeffer, 1937/1963:154)

Here, then, we have a significant, though not yet complete, explanation of his entry into the *Abwehr* spy job: it was not only a way to seek the end of the war and to oppose Hitler; it was a way to remain in Germany and yet avoid the draft. For him this was not a "principled" but a here-and-now stand; perhaps in other circumstances, he said, but not in these, he would be willing to serve in the army. Surely the most important element in this way of avoiding military service, however, is the one Bonhoeffer himself underlined for George Bell: no significant community existed that would have supported his open refusal of the draft call. Whereas the *Abwehr* alternative, with its double-agent role, was indeed supported by the only functioning community of which he could still feel a part, his family with its network of allies and friends.

But does the passage just quoted lead us toward another reading of Bonhoeffer's life? Was he, though not a principled decisionist, nevertheless a situational decisionist, ever wavering on the razor's edge of options, choices, cost-benefit analyses, arbitrary leaps of the will to be determined by immediate circumstances alone? The best clue here will be what he said in the one major writing undertaken at this time

(1940 on), the *Ethics*. In Chapters Two and Three I have offered
the beginnings of a reading of the *Ethics* that points away from
decisionism. While the only adequate test of this reading
would be the examination of the whole work, until rather
recently there was some reason to believe such a summary
reading was impossible. The scattered production of this
work, published only after the war, undertaken in quiet
intervals between his international travels for the *Abwehr*,
written on many kinds of paper in several places as opportunity arose, together with remarks by Bethge (in Bonhoeffer,
1949/1965:11-15) led many to suppose that the existing *Ethics* is
only a melange of false starts and overlaps, fragmentary both
in conception and execution. But more recent detective work
on the manuscripts by Clifford Green (1985) has shown that in
fact our existing text can and must be rearranged to display the
very outline, and much of the content, that Bonhoeffer
projected from 1940 on.

What follows from Green's work is that we do after all have
access to the moral mind of the young pastor during the very
crisis in question—the moment of his abandonment of hope in
the Confessing Church (or rather the moment of its sinking
under his steadfast feet), and of his laying hold of the only
remaining fellowship in which he might make a stand, namely
the family Bonhoeffer. What we find in the *Ethics'* connected
argument is that Bonhoeffer continued to found everything in
Christian ethics upon Christ and church: "Christ the center,"
with due allowance for the way Christ's witness had impinged
upon Western culture, with acknowledgment of the role
"good people" who were not like himself Christians (his
family?) might play as Christ's allies, and with flashes even of
brilliance in his argument that the "natural" order leads to and
culminates in Christ, while what is "unnatural," and is on that
account condemned, is precisely that which "closes its doors
against the coming of Christ" (Bonhoeffer, 1949/1965:144).
Thus Nazi 'euthanasia,' or suicide as an arrogation of God's
own choice by ourselves, like abortion, torture, and slavery, is
an example of the "unnatural"; such acts do not lead to nor do
they prepare anyone for the coming of Christ; whereas
meeting of human need is "natural" just because it does do
that. The church is not destined to occupy a limited (far less a
withdrawn) sphere in human life. Its one and only task is to
witness to Christ, but to Christ as the Lord of all life.

In other words, so far from having abandoned the centrality of Christ and church during these spy years, Bonhoeffer affirmed these in the *Ethics* with new vigor. This makes vivid the tragedy his life exhibits. Even while his contemporary writing affirmed the superiority of Christ over all life, he served a plot whose goal was just the replacement of Hitler with another government, and a conservative, even an elitist, government, at that. Moreover, the means adopted was assassination—though as his friends pointed out when he offered himself as the assassin, Bonhoeffer didn't know which was the business end of a gun. In fact, as the outcome shows, the plot required skills of violence and deception and political craftiness that were beyond the whole company of inept, or hesitant, or even woolyheaded conspirators with whom he then linked his destiny. Their immediate goal, the removal of Hitler from power in some way, was so far unexceptionable, as every thoughtful Christian would now agree. Hitler was the demon genius of a government that, even while Bonhoeffer made his political move, was forming the Jews of Europe into ghettoes, concentration camps, annihilation camps. Ultimately six million, more than half the Jews in Europe, would perish in this terror (Dawidowicz, 1975). That the means chosen was not only inconsistent with Bonhoeffer's long formed Christian convictions, but was ineffectual as well, seems only to heighten the sense of tragedy that hangs over the entire story.

4. The Tragedy of Dietrich Bonhoeffer

That Bonhoeffer's own story is essentially a tragic one seems to find agreement from nearly every point of view. What remains at issue is understanding the kind of tragedy that it was. There is the view, already implied, that it was a tragedy of too little too late. If only he had turned to politics in 1933, as Hitler came to power and Bonhoeffer with prescience saw the evil that rise entailed. If only he had not wasted time with those precious seminarians. Or (an alternative view) if only he had stuck by his nonviolent convictions and stayed out of the plot, how much more would have come from his leadership after the war. Or (third alternative) there *were* no options—he was caught by fate, did nobly what he felt he had to do, and was a tragic victim of essentially tragic times. This last comes closest to my own view, but it requires some filling out to convey its full impact.

Bonhoeffer, on my interpretation of the facts, was a man unusually gifted in the acquisition and employment of strand-two moral skills—the skills of society (cf. Green, 1972). He came from a sociable family, and was a member of a highly socialized, albeit politically reactionary, people, the Germans. But he was not merely the bearer of social traditions or memories. In his conversion (enter, at least briefly, strand three) he moved, in his words, "from phraseology to reality" to become a real Christian. Here he discovered a new way of life, personal but profoundly communal. Perhaps this 'way' was divined partly at Abyssinian Baptist Church in New York; in any case it came ultimately from the Bible. He set out, in the Finkenwalde experiment, to share its life with his students, and even founded a community house where seminary graduates might prolong the impact of the disciples' way. It was not a withdrawn or inward turned community, but was profoundly evangelical and outward looking. One vital element, to be sure, was lacking: He had three times projected a trip to India, where he had hoped to learn much from Mohandas Gandhi including the discipline and techniques of *satyagraha*, nonviolence. This discipline and these techniques might have made a massive difference in the events that followed. But this of course must remain speculation now. In any case, he found in the seminary and in the wider, concentric circles of Confessing Church and Ecumenical Church a sphere in which the goals, practices, and skills of the kingdom of Christ could be worked out in common. He had brought *Nachfolge* into reality, however briefly.

But when the communities, small and large, whose practices he shaped and shared crumbled under government pressure, he no longer had any resource for *Christian* resistance. Instead, he turned to the time-honored practices and skills of his family, and to the 'practice' (if it was that) of the *Putsch*, for which neither he nor his family and friends had sufficient skills of any sort. So the *Putsch* failed, the participants were destroyed, and the raging Hitler regime moved on to its fateful end as though nothing had happened. If the conspirators made any difference at all to the outcome of that regime, perhaps they only prolonged it by giving Hitler's propaganda a new excuse: Past failures could now be blamed on the traitor generals; with their elimination, German arms could be expected to prevail at last.

My thesis, then, is that Bonhoeffer's grisly death was part and parcel of the tragic dimension of his life, and that in turn but an element in the greater tragedy of the Christian community of Germany. Put in the briefest terms, it was that they had no effective strand-two moral structure in the church that was adequate to the crucial need of church and German people alike (to say nothing of the need of Jewish people; to say nothing of the world's people). No structures, no practices, no skills of political life existed that were capable of resisting, christianly resisting, the totalitarianism of the times. The tragedy is the more intense because of all Christians in Germany Dietrich Bonhoeffer was perhaps the one who came nearest to displaying exactly those skills and to developing exactly those practices. But it is a shared tragedy, for he could not in any case have met the need alone. And finally it is an instructive tragedy, for there is considerable evidence that the Christian church in the world, not least in America, faces again at the end of our century the same qualities of intrusive government, ideological warfare, and coopted religion that so readily deceived the Germans half a century ago.

Bonhoeffer was arrested (on a charge related to the *Abwehr*'s struggle with a rival secret agency, the Gestapo!) more than a year before the attempted *Putsch* of July, 1944, and was kept alive for nearly a year after that event for questioning related to it. During these two years in prison he had plenty of time to think about the past he had lived through, and to speculate on the future, as well. Much of his tentative writing from this prison period is well known; a few sentences from it were seized by the 1960s theologians in the interest of their own program, as noted above, while in Germany extreme Lutheran conservatives seized rather on his known loyalty to the Confessing Church as a weapon in their battle for reactionary Protestantism. In either case, the only adequate response has been to attend to the full context and content of his life and work: in it the strength and loveliness of his discipleship shine forth through and beyond the tragedy of his times. It is in such a context, for example, that we must read about "religionless Christianity." For Bonhoeffer this expression did not mean the abandonment of prayer, or faith, or common worship, all of which he retained to the very end. It meant rather abandoning at last the flawed ideal of a Constantinian church in a Constantinian society (Bonhoeffer, 1972a:282ff., 380ff.)—for these had proved their insufficiency in the era of Adolf Hitler.

*   *   *   *   *

The Lutheran Churches in America remember in their calendar of saints' days Dietrich Bonhoeffer, "theologian and martyr." He was a martyr, that is, a witness, to the truth, and he died faithful to Jesus Christ. His last known words were spoken to a friend at Schönberg, the prison to which he had been transported just before the end. There, when the SS came to take him away, he sent a hasty message by way of a fellow prisoner to his English friend Bishop George Bell, affirming his belief in the Church Universal, and he said as well, "This is the end—for me, the beginning of life." Then they led him away to be transported toward the waiting gallows.

The Politics
of Forgiveness

Christian social ethics, we have seen in the two preceding chapters, is ethics engaged by the structures of social or political life—its practices and institutions—but also by its mass movements and migrations, its wars and upheavals. It responds, in one way or another, to these drumbeats of social or political destiny. Whatever we may have thought of the response Dietrich Bonhoeffer made to the drumbeats of his epoch and the events of his history, we have surely learned one thing from him: Engagement such as his involves an intense inner journey that must display its own distinctive moral features. Bonhoeffer was reticent about the details of that journey, but one cannot read his writings without discovering its existence. So far our theoretical account has offered a way of thinking about social ethics (strand two) as well as a way of thinking about the inwardness of the moral life (aspects of strand one). But has it shown how these two are to be connected? If not, the theory is in this respect defective.

This defect would seem, however, to be a predicament all too common in twentieth-century Christian life. On the one hand, many Christians are aware of some inner dynamic of blame, shame, and guilt, and their churches may provide religious therapy or 'counseling' to minister to such symptoms of the soul. On the other hand, the same Christians are often offered by their churches a social ethic that takes no account of the embodied selfhood of each of us, with its drives, needs, and capacities. Instead, it may offer prescriptions for social ills grandly defined—idealistic remedies for "racism, sexism, classism" (or, in another current version of social morality, nostalgic remedies for "weak-kneed churches" confronting a "godless society"). Yet these diagnoses and these remedies seem alike untouched by any awareness of the needs of our souls, just as the pastoral remedies churches offer seem to be untouched by any sense of societal structure and its bearing on our lives (Archie Smith, 1982).

The pathos of Bonhoeffer's own story lay in bringing together the needs of the soul and the needs of society in a single life, and the instrument he so unerringly grasped in response, and then so helplessly relinquished, was the political life of church and congregation. That instrument must become the key to the present chapter.

An interesting project, though not one to be carried out here, might be to go back to the beginnings of our moral theology in seventeenth-century England (the time of the Caroline divines and the rise of the Puritan movement within the Church of England; the time, also, when the English language began to replace Latin in theological writing there and in America). At that time, it would appear, this schism between the ethics of interiority and the ethics of society first appears (Wood, 1952, 1967). Here, also, might be found the circumstances in which Christian morality became more and more preoccupied with a mission to the individual that concentrated upon solitary conscience and its problems, accompanied by a mission to society concentrated upon public and legal righteousness, with no organic links between the two.

My claim is that for Christians the connecting link between body ethics and social ethics, between the moral self and the morals of society, is to be found in the body of Christ that is the gathered church. The place where conscience comes to light in a baptist ethic is not in solitary or Kierkegaardian introspection, nor is it in the social concerns of individual private citizens who happen to be Christian as well (not even in their widely held and in that sense "common" concerns). Rather the link is found in congregational reflection, discernment, discipline, and action, whose model is nearer to the Wesleyan class meeting or the Anabaptist *Gemeinde* than to the denominational social action lobby agency or the mass membership churches of today's suburban society. It is such gathered sharing (so goes my thesis) that issues in directives for the pilgrimage of each *and* issues in a shared witness to the outside world. This explains why, although conscience and judgment could be introduced along with guilt and blame and shame as strand-one *phenomena* of the moral life, these could not be adequately discussed there as *functions* of the moral life. For as we have seen, this functioning requires for Christians also strand two, where conscience and judgment can be evoked in the communal setting of the faithful congregation and its common life.

The place of this chapter, then, will be to explore further the shape of the gathered church as the integral and necessary form of the moral life of Christians. Since, in Chapter Six, I have laid down a brief account of the way in which social structure in general entails social morality, and have illustrated that account by reference to the community that received the Ten Commandments, it will be highly appropriate now to see how similar moral structures constitute community for Christians as well. A convenient beginning can be made by considering the community for whom the Gospel of Matthew was first written. This Gospel's author or redactor deliberately sought to relate Christian community to the community of the Law, to Israel and Torah. Perhaps partly for this reason Matthew, with its Sermon on the Mount (chs. 5–7) and its account of the discipline of forgiveness (ch. 18), has played a large role in the baptist movement, which is our touchstone. Matthew is no mere partisan traditional choice, however. For it is "a well-known fact," says Krister Stendahl, "that the spiritual and religious atmosphere of this gospel is most nearly akin to post-apostolic Christianity" generally (1968:30). Thus, to understand Matthew is to get a handhold upon the social morality of much of early Christianity. Lest anyone nevertheless believe that this Gospel is in some important way atypical of the primitive Jesus movement, I will sometimes substantiate my main points by reference to the Pauline communities, about which there is even more abundant evidence (Meeks, 1983).

The arrangement of the chapter will be threefold. First, I will present the Matthean (and in general, the early Christian) concepts of *discipleship* and *community*, showing their relation to one another and to the community for which Matthew was written, and their bearing on our communities. Second, I will show how the understanding of *law* and *forgiveness* in these sources occupied a place in the disciple community, and will explore the concept of forgiveness as a crucial element of the social life of Christians. Third, I will treat the Christian understanding of *the church in the world*, showing that it is no afterthought or contingent historical circumstance that puts the church in relation to its wider environment. Rather, Christian conduct, guided by the Great Commission, must be distinctively engaged in such worldly presence—a point as vital to the risen Jesus Christ of Matthew's Gospel (cf. Matt. 28:19-20) as to latter day social activists.

1. An Ethics for Disciples in Community

a. *Who were the disciples?*—Who, really, were "the disciples" Matthew's Gospel tells about? Preeminently, this Gospel portrays the men and women Jesus summoned to follow him in the days of his flesh. In another sense, though, "the disciples" were the later generation readers for whom the Gospel was written. (This dual identification will be further developed in Chapter Twelve.) I am following the informed guess that these readers were in fact members of a mixed, but increasingly non-Jewish, Christian community in Syria, perhaps in Antioch, in the years 80–85 (cf. Hamerton-Kelly, 1976). So while the setting of the Gospel is early first-century Palestine, with Jesus and Peter, James, John, and company as its chief actors, readers would realize that the stories Matthew told were also their own later stories: The call to fishermen to leave their nets perhaps called into question the occupations of these later Syrian disciples; Simon's "You are the Christ" made him also the spokesman for these second and third generation Christians; the debates with Pharisees, the question about temple tax, the temptations to greed and lust and violence that the Master encountered along the way—all these corresponded, we may reckon, to Syrian debates, Syrian questions, Syrian temptations. The setting was bygone Galilee and Judea, but the impact was contemporary Syrian, here and now. In our terms, the 'baptist vision' was at work; "this" was "that"; and it was this doubleness that gave these tales their power. Matthew the writer had turned the telescope around, put its large end to his reader's eye, made the immediacy of Christian life in Syria seem as distant as Palestine in the days of Christ's flesh, and, by replacing their own story with the true story of Jesus and Peter and Judas and Herod, had given the readers perspective from which to judge both stories aright. Our own task is to turn the telescope back again for a moment, so that, from what is said to them in their Gospel, we can form an idea of these Syrian Christians and their church.

These readers, then, knew themselves to be *disciples* (μαθηταί). "Come, follow me" (19:21) is the Matthean Jesus' characteristic phrase. Jack Dean Kingsbury has shown how Matthew uses "with" (μετά) as a term of art to distinguish those who in this sense follow Jesus: it is just the inner circle, the twelve or eleven, Mary, tax collectors and sinners, who are said to be "with Jesus." The crowds, even when they surround Jesus, are not "with" him in this way of speaking. Thus it is Matthew who has Jesus saying, "He who is not *with me* is against me" (12:30 RSV; Kingsbury, 1977:80).

At the very least, then, Matthean discipleship implies the willing participation of each follower. Matthew recalls a community, and addresses a church, of intentional or voluntary participants. His is not, like the 'Christian' faction in present-day Lebanon, a hereditary or ethnic community, nor is it, like some current American religiosity, a civil religion. Wayne A. Meeks has picked up the threads of an old discussion by noting that the household (οἶκος) was often a basic unit in the narration of the story of the earlier, Pauline missionary developments. Whole households were converted (Acts 10, 16), baptized (see also 1 Cor. 1:16), and sometimes as such commended for Christian service (1 Cor. 16:15f.). Meeks surmises that in such group conversions, "not everyone who went along with the new practices would do so with the *same* understanding or inner participation" (1983:77). It is a case of modern practice shaping exegesis, however, if we extrapolate from Meeks' cautious inference to the unwarranted conclusion that some members perhaps had no faith at all, and were helpless infants or hapless slaves. For as Meeks correctly notes, Paul's letter to Philemon makes it clear that "not every member of a household always became a Christian when its head did," in Paul's understanding of the matter (1983:76). Whatever lapses may have occurred then or later, Paul's doctrine was in this regard consonant with Matthew's.

Discipleship meant following Jesus, each disciple a follower, each follower "with Jesus," if and only if a disciple. In the Troeltschian sense, then, the church Matthew addresses is sectarian, composed of men and women of whatever age who have freely obeyed the "follow me" of Christ. Some are Jews, more, we think, Gentiles; all are united by their shared solidarity with Jesus: "For where two or three are gathered in my name, there am I in the midst of them" (18:20 RSV).

Solidarity is expressed in *obedience*. Whenever in the Gospel Jesus' calls to follow are met with a willing response, Jack Suggs has pointed out, there ensues a fresh commissioning. Those who will follow are blessed, given a new name or a new role or a new task, and finally are empowered by Jesus to fulfill that task (cf. 5:1-20; 16:17-19; 28:18-20; Suggs, 1970:120-27). Of great interest for us here are the typical tasks disciples are given in the three passages just listed: (1) to fulfill (with Jesus) the law (every jot and tittle of it!); (2) to administer discipline and forgiveness; (3) to carry this "teaching" to all the Gentiles so that they, too, may become $\mu\alpha\theta\eta\tau\alpha\iota$, disciples. These three are logically related: The disciples in community are to be the 'treasurers,' the wise stewards, of the law (5:20; cf. 13:52); therefore their practice of discipline must exist as a means of exercising such stewardship (16:17-19; cf. 18:15-20); finally, their full mission is to share this stewardship with all, everywhere—the church in the world (28:18-20).

Discipleship meant such obedience; it also meant *solidarity with one another*. Matthew would have his Syrian readers understand that by voluntarily linking their lives to Jesus, they have linked them to each other as well. These ties override the existing links of kinship and of household (12:46-50; 10:34-39). Members are not ranked as "fathers" or "rabbis"—such titles are forbidden (20:25-28; 23:8-12), and the Matthean church seems to know nothing of the prestigious hierarchy that would spring up later and elsewhere. They are brothers and sisters, or they are one another's servants. All this is eloquently expressed in their simple meal of recollection, in which they 'significantly' share the body of their Master. As they do so, they renew their own unity, acknowledging the forgiveness of each, and they renew their common hope, eating bread and sharing a cup "until that day" (25:26-29).

b. *The covenant meal*—Perhaps it is inevitable that any rite that has come to be so widely used by such diverse communities, pre-Christian, Christian, and post-Christian, should have amalgamated to itself various meanings and purposes. Already this was true of the Passover meal that (according to Matthew 26) formed the basis of the Last Supper. It may be helpful, then, to note afresh the elegant simplicity of the First Gospel, which devotes in the Aland Greek text a scant ninety-five words (26:26-30) to the account of that foundation. Central to the rite Matthew describes are two acts of sharing by Jesus: one of bread, the other of a cup (of wine). The principal words are simply these performative acts of sharing: "Take, eat. . . . Drink of it, all of you" (vv. 26-27). For each act a single interpretation is furnished: for the bread, "This is my body" (v. 26); for the cup, "this is my blood of the covenant, shed for many unto forgiveness of sins" (v. 28). Thereby two notes are sounded, the solidaristic ("my body," "my blood," "covenant") and the redemptive ("unto forgiveness of sins").

It is the first, the solidaristic, that is uppermost for us here, so let us consider its three governing images: body, blood, and covenant. Theological doctrine has concentrated on the first and second of these, body and blood, understood mystically, or philosophically, or in some combination, but never to the satisfaction of all interpreters. Perhaps theological ethics does well, then, if it concentrates on the third, reading not "this is my *blood* (of the covenant)," but with a better exegesis: "This is *my* blood-of-the-covenant"; that is, "This rite we share tonight in the upper room is *my* reaffirmation of JHWH God's ancient pledge, linking us to it and thereby to the ancient solidarity of God-and-Israel, and [as the reader knows with foreboding] linking it also to the ultimate blood-sacrifice, that of the Servant who will witness to God's truth, even on a Roman cross, on the morrow." In that case, the primary new union expressed in our passage is the solidarity of Master and disciples, with these being linked by the meal itself to their wider Jewish tradition.

In this light, what of the other images? What will "this is my body" mean? Our best exegesis is already in the New Testament, in the very place where we find the oldest account of the Thanksgiving Meal itself, 1 Corinthians 10 through 12. Here the widespread perception of the ancient world, that sharing a meal is communion (κοινωνία) with the one who either as host or as *numen* presides over the meal (10:14-22), is linked (10:16) with the powerful metaphor of the gathered church constituting the body of Christ (ch. 12). Set between these two pictures (in sociological style we might call them respectively the contaminative and the organic) is Paul's recounting of the Lord's supper tradition he had received and already delivered to the Corinthians, including the words of Jesus over the (already broken) bread: "This is my body which is for you" (11:24 RSV). In such a context, the ideas to which we are naturally led are those of group solidarity, of an identity that includes rather than excludes, that inclusion being the incorporation of the lives of the gathered disciples not only into their crucified and risen Lord, but also into one another.

Now if we permit "body" in 1 Corinthians 10 and 12 to shape our understanding of that image as it is used in the intervening Lord's supper account in chapter 11, if, that is, we allow the notions of communion and sharing and organic oneness in the gathered disciple band to form our understanding of "this is my body" in 11:26, what follows? This, I think: At the fundament of missionary, gentile Christianity, there is a rite not magical, nor even (in many usual senses of the term) "sacramental"—but moral and ethical first of all; that is, aimed at the shaping of the common life of Christian community. This is the rite, and the emphasis, that Matthew's church also would find, a generation or so later, in its own passion narrative in Matthew 26.

Here we see an exact way in which the 'religious' life of Christians is inseparable from their moral formation. It is a way that escapes the sweep of standard modern ethical theory. For it is not that the act of communion in the Lord's supper provides the church with motives for good behavior as emotivists might concede, or that this act changes the balance of utilitarian goods for its communicants. Rather the meal is part and parcel of a *practice* (Chapter Six) which we might roughly name the practice of *establishing and maintaining Christian community*. The 'rules' for the meal are among the constitutive rules for that practice. Among those rules are ones that link the conduct of participants to their participation in the meal. In Matthew, this is presented in narrative form. Jesus, the presiding communicant, goes out to the Mount of Olives, leading his followers on a *via crucis* they must follow if they are to follow him. In the long run, they do, but in the short run, he alone takes that path of witness, faithfulness, and death. By the logic of the story we see the consonance between what he does and what at the meal he enacted.

This comes clearest if we imagine the contrary—Jesus slips out of town after the meal, escapes, becomes a well-known intellectual leader in another country, and lives to a ripe old age. In that case, though, it is not only the ending that is changed; the meal is different, too. Now for Jesus to say, "this is *my* shed-blood-of-the-covenant," must be read as ironic, or empty. Paul makes this point not by narrative, but by argument: If when you assemble, you ignore one another, each going ahead with his own meal, some hungry, others overindulging, then the meal you have just eaten is not the Lord's supper after all (1 Cor. 11:20f.). For the point of that meal is solidarity in the kingdom; those who ignore this have missed the first lesson of Christian social ethics, and lost sight of the meaning of the rite. If its meaning has to do with the conduct of Christians at the meal itself, it also has to do with their conduct in the daily fellowship, and in their relation to the wider society as well, as the surrounding chapters (10 and 12) of 1 Corinthians bring out.

In giving the Matthean and Pauline interpretations of the supper, I have said nothing about two central elements of its significance. There is for one its thrust into the future. "I tell you," says Jesus, "I shall not drink again of this fruit of the vine until that day when I drink it new with you in my Father's kingdom" (Matt. 26:29 RSV). Thus Matthew allots nearly a fourth of his account to this eschatological saying. And Paul's spare account also concludes, "For as often as you eat this bread and drink the cup, you proclaim the Lord's death *until he comes*" (1 Cor. 11:26 RSV). The omission here simply underlines my omission so far of the third, eschatological strand; it brings out the demand to press on to strand three.

The other element is one inherited from the Jewish Passover—the eucharistic or thanksgiving note. While I have emphasized the quality of remembrance (explicit in Paul, implicit in the Matthean narrative structure), I have passed over the central note of awed gratitude in that remembrance (cf. McClendon and Smith, 1975:74-77). As the other omission, when supplied, points on to strand three, this one looks back to strand one, where embodied selfhood with its affective focus gives shape to the moral life of Christians. The more general lesson to be learned from noting these two inalienable

elements of the supper is that, though privatistic understandings of communion might focus exclusively on gratitude or other
attitudes, and though a liberation-oriented sacramental meal
might focus exclusively on God's coming kingdom and its
demands, each would be in that way false to the supper itself,
just as a Lord's supper that focused exclusively on the social
dimension would be untrue to full-sphered Christian morality.

   c. *Community formation as powerful practice*—To speak of
one-sided or false versions of the ritual meal brings us to the
power of the practice of Christian community formation and
maintenance, and hence of the imbedded practice of the
memorial meal. It may be helpful at this point to recall the
outlook on the powers summarized in Chapter Six: their links
with religion and politics, their ambiguous standing with
respect to the one God JHWH, their conflict with Jesus and his
decisive victory over them, their identification, not only with
pagan empires and persecutors of the faithful, but also with
the sacred structures of Jewish and Christian life, and finally,
Christians' call to exercise discerning selectivity toward
particular powers. Too much emphasis can hardly be laid on
this theme of discrimination. Governments are not all as
wicked as they can be, though all are in some degree powerful.
Not all churches, nor all religious rites, are beneficent, and
they are powers, too. If, recalling Chapter Six, we discard the
mythical (and unbiblical) idea that all the powers 'fell' in some
timeless prehistoric catastrophe, then we are free to inquire,
instead, about the actual history of a particular power: the
degree to which its politics and claims are functions of the
creative and redemptive power of God in Christ, and the
degree to which these are corruptions (as MacIntyre might
say, mere simulacra) of that power.
   What then of the powerful practice of Christian community,
with its imbedded symbolic elements of baptism and Lord's
supper? So far we have seen a practice as a way of giving social
shape to Christian life. As a practice, we know it must have its
end and its lawlike means, and it must exist only by way of the
intentional participation of 'the players,' its members. Their
goal-directed participation will evoke the excellences of the
practice itself, and enhance its progress. But in keeping with
what has just been said, we must also understand our
churchly practice as an existing *power*. To do so will remind us,

not merely that practices as powers may undergo "sequences of decline as well as progress" (MacIntyre, 1984:177) (a qualifier compatible with unblemished optimism about any human practice!), but also that this powerful practice, like others, may rebel, 'fall,' lash out at the reign of the Lamb, and persecute the saints. To think of the church as a practice reminds us of all the inspiring things the New Testament says about it: built on rock (Matt. 16:18), the body of Christ (1 Cor. 12:12f. and parallels), temple of the Spirit (1 Cor. 6:19), God's own assembly (1 Cor. 1:2), destined to be holy and without blemish (Eph. 5:27). Yet to think of it as a power should also remind us of other (inspired, though less inspiring) utterances also in our New Testament: the church Christ died for is, alas, one he may spew out of his mouth (Rev. 3:16). To see the church as a set of *powerful practices* is to turn from dogmatic blindness to the historical realities of church. Not every 'church' is a font of Christian practice and faith, nor is every liturgy life-breathing, though it be called Lord's supper or eucharist most holy. That nevertheless many are, even in sparse spiritual times, is a matter of divine gift and promise (Matt. 16:18). This brings us to a final point: Even corrupted powers *may* be redeemed. Telling the difference between what is and is not redeemable will concern us in the next section.

2. The Politics of Forgiveness

a. *Forgiveness and law*—Forgiveness is our theme, but there can be no forgiveness unless there is something to forgive, some offense against some requirement or rule or law. So we must first seek some clarity about the sense in which the Christians of the New Testament, and particularly those of the Matthean church, were a community of lawkeepers. The inquiry here goes against the widespread, if unspoken, understanding that Jesus abolished the law and that early Christianity, led by Paul, opposed it, for we have seen (Chapter Six) that this cannot literally be the case in a community of shared practices, for a practice is according to a rule, even when rules are never made explicit. Since many Christians today suppose they have come to terms with the Pauline injunctions, we will concentrate upon the apparently more alien Matthean community.

For Matthew's church the lawlike pattern was tied closely to an understanding of Jewish law. Yet even this must be qualified. Since they did not reside in the land of Israel, where alone, according to traditional understanding, the law had been fully in effect, and since Jerusalem and its temple had been destroyed, there was disagreement at this time, even among non-Christian Jews, about how the law was to be kept in the new situation. Moreover, the Syrian church's understanding of Jesus, transmitted in their own Gospel, represented the Master in a complex way: On the one hand, not a jot or tittle would pass from the law, he had said, "until all is accomplished" (5:18), and his behavior in the narrative shows him respecting the legally flexible Pharisaic tradition (23:23), even while challenging its current representatives. Yet on the other hand, Jesus here shows a surprisingly cavalier freedom with respect to some Pharisaic regulations (cf. 15:1-20). And, hardest of all to grasp, in the very context where the law is reinforced in his teaching, there appear a set of six 'antitheses' that sometimes merely amend, but sometimes seem even to abrogate or cancel Mosaic legislation. Sorting out these complicated, not to say paradoxical, moral signals must indeed have produced "kingdom scribes" in the Matthean community (cf. 13:51).

For simplicity, we can reduce the problems Matthew raises for us here to four: (1) How is the strong affirmation of the law to be reconciled with its paradoxical 'repeal' in some cases (5:18, 31f., etc.)? (2) More generally, how is the authority of Jesus to be reconciled with the authority of Torah? (3) What is the role, in a lawkeeping community, of such ideas as the higher righteousness, the law of love, the gospel of the kingdom, the will of God, or, in Matthew's term, being "perfect, as your heavenly Father is"? (4) What agency is to adjudicate and administer the law to the congregation? Recovering Matthew's answer to these questions should disclose the moral structure of the Syrian church he wrote for, and begin to disclose the politics of forgiveness in Christian community. The role of forgiveness is the goal of our inquiry, but to see it in context, we must find how it worked for a community shaped by law.

The second of our four questions, about authority, provides the best approach to all. In an elegant analysis of the First Gospel's teaching, Jack Suggs has shown that its deep rooting in Israel's wisdom tradition made it inevitable for Matthew to interpret Jesus in terms of the divine Wisdom. In brief, God's Son, Jesus, *was* Sophia, Wisdom, and since Wisdom was the source of Torah itself, when Jesus spoke, it was Wisdom-Torah who was speaking. Hence the authority of Jesus and that of Torah need not be further reconciled, for it is at bottom one authority (Suggs, 1970:114f., and ch. 2). To see this, however, is to see the answer to our first question as well. The antitheses of the Sermon on the Mount are of two sorts (Kingsbury, 1977:82-86): Some of them deepen or intensify the law's demand; others change or correct it. Broadening the Sixth Commandment to forbid murderous hate as well as hateful murder is the first sort of antithesis; not only the awful deed, but its crescendo of angry preparation, is forbidden to disciples (Matt. 5:21f.). Abolishing the provisions that the law had made for retribution (see Exod. 21:23-25) is of the second sort: Nonresistance, not the vendetta, now becomes the law of the kingdom (5:38-42). Each of the antitheses can be understood in one or the other of these ways, though opinions may differ on which is which. Is love to enemies (5:44) simply the radical restatement of Leviticus 19:18 ("love your neighbor as yourself"), or does it go beyond its bounds altogether? Or what about divorce? Mosaic legislation had restrained but in the end permitted it—for males at least (Deut. 24:1-4). With one exception, Jesus here forbids it. But Jesus (in 19:8) explains that the Mosaic permission was "for your hardness of heart," thus arguing that his new law regarding marriage is more in line with the original *practice* as the practice coheres with the Mosaic story.

And this is our clue to the whole. Where the typical or Matthean first-century community of Christians will be continuing a practice of the Mosaic community, albeit with revised goals or directions (e.g., new understandings of kinship and of marriage) the Messianic law will be revisionary. Where the community is to take up what will seem to be a radically different stance with regard to a former practice (e.g., full abandonment of violence) the legal revision may amount to abolition of the relevant law—by the authoritative Law-giver. Where laws are understood as the rules for practices, and practices as the substance of an ongoing story, the necessity for their firmness and their flexibility are alike evident.

This brings us to our third question. How are we to understand having "righteousness greater than . . .," or "doing the will of God," being "perfect," that is, "whole-hearted," keeping the "love commandment," and the like, in this Christian community? To answer this, we need to recall that the central function of Matthew is to tell a true story, the story of God's own Son who preaches and demonstrates a Way so costly that it issues in his suffering and death and resurrection. If we compare this Way and story with the Way and story of Torah as epitomized in the Ten Commandments, we find not so much contrast as continuity. As the biblical story becomes (for Jesus' followers) the Christian story, some practices (and hence some rules or laws) change, but the reason is that Jesus sees where the story must go, and therefore gives new overall direction to the Way. This is most clearly expressed in his own beginning and life and mysterious end. So there is a need for signals to the reader not to read the familiar commandments in the light of what they had known of the old story alone. Rather, the reader must look for a *new sense* of where the story is going and must find that sense in Jesus' own way, which the reader is now summoned to live out afresh (Goldberg, 1985).

That defines the role of "will of God," and "perfect," and the others. These are not meant idealistically to abrogate the law with its cases and qualifications and nuances. Rather they are meant to show the direction—the redefined direction—of the law. To be "perfect" is not to be flawless; it is rather to take Jesus' way, the way of the ripe or full-grown kingdom now at hand. The best illustrations of this are the summing up of all the law in terms of love to God and neighbor (22:36-40), or the Golden Rule (7:12). As a *substitute* for law or rules, such summaries are pitifully inadequate. (The Golden Rule, for example, *if taken alone*, would work as well for a band of sadomasochists as for a community of disciples.) But as showing how to take all the rest—the direction of Torah—these summaries have an important role. Certainly that role is not to set up an impossible standard for disciples, for in that case all else that Matthew says with rabbinic care would be wasted.

How, then (our fourth question) *was* such a way practically possible? How, in a 'sectarian' community that was distinct from the state and its powers of enforcement, as well as from

Jewish legal procedures, could an entire community, even of committed disciples, be kept on the track? In terms of technique, the answer lay in a never-ending congregational *conversation*—a conversation that may now engage only two or three, but again will involve the gathered ἐκκλησία itself. When a brother or sister believes another is sinning, a procedure is invoked that at its simplest involves a private rebuke, confession, and forgiveness (18:15, 21f.), and at its most elaborate, a full-scale congregational review of the matter in the presence of the offender (18:17). This procedure is not to be seen as equivalent to the excluding or shunning practiced by some modern sectarians. Its genius lies rather in the confidence it places in the church's ongoing conversation as a means of pastoral guidance. There is, to be sure, the limiting case of expulsion when the church must admit its failure for the time being. But that expulsion puts the offender in the class of those Jesus especially befriended—Gentiles and tax collectors. Such a process will, of course, make law in the same sense that civil courts make law—by its decisions. So it is here that the often abused notion of "decision" comes into its own, not as the private willful optings of moral individuals, but as the guiding limits set from time to time by the brothers and sisters in the course of their ongoing conversation. It is the dynamics of that conversation that protect the wholehearted-ness of discipleship from a legalism that is only its perversion.

The word "conversation" rightly points to the informal, almost casual nature of congregational interchange. Yet there underlies the ongoing community conversation something akin to judicial process. It is important to examine this underlying structural element, for only with it will we understand how Christian community is a *politics* of forgive-ness. Note first that forgiveness and punishment have something in common. What is it to punish (as opposed to mistreating, assaulting, or injuring) another? Among many widely held theories of punishment, the formulation of the distinguished legal philosopher Herbert Morris (1976) com-mends itself. Imagine, says Morris, a community bound together by common goods (such as individual freedom and safety) in which each member assumes certain burdens (such as not infringing on the freedom and safety of the others). In such a community, what is to be done in the case of one who does discard his own burden by stealing, breaking the peace, or otherwise taking others' goods away from them? Morris' answer is that he be punished according to a rule that will both specify the punishment and limit its extent. For a rule-breaker is one who unbalances the community, threatens its existence, while just deprivation laid upon such a one constitutes the restoration of the disturbed balance and threatened existence, achieving this by taking away some limited good or privilege that the offender had enjoyed. Thus he has a burden (the punishment) to take the place of the burden he had unfairly discarded, and the community balance is righted (Morris, 1976:31-45). (Morris further claims that offenders have a "right to punishment," that is, a right to be treated according to the rules of such a system, and that this right is part and parcel of a fundamental right to be treated as a person in society rather than as a mere manipulable object or a candidate for 'therapy' [Morris, 1976:46-57], but we cannot pursue that interesting argument here.) However, he makes an important qualification. The equilibrium of a society may be restored in yet another way.

Forgiveness—with its legal analogue of a pardon—while not the righting of an unfair distribution by making one pay his debt is, nevertheless, a restoring of the equilibrium by cancelling the debt (Morris, 1976:34). It is just the belief that its frequent use will increase violations that disqualifies pardon as the usual remedy for offenses. While we must remember this danger, my suggestion is that *Christian community is exactly one in which forgiveness not punishment is the norm.* Not unlike a just practice of punishment, such forgiveness has as its goal the restoration of a rupture in the community. Forgiveness is the healing of a broken church. As such, it is intimately linked with salvation itself—with atonement, with Christ's presence, with the goal of the common life in the body of Christ. Its great beauty is that, unlike most systems of punishment in the world we know, forgiveness really works, really achieves its goals.

b. *The anatomy of forgiveness*—To see why this is so, it will be necessary to think a little more carefully about the nature of forgiveness itself. To forgive, says a common definition, is to grant pardon without harboring resentment. This points to two elements, one formal, socially structured, judicial—the granting of pardon; the other affective, attitudinal, inward—the cessation of ongoing resentment. The *act* of forgiveness is at home in strand two; it is a transaction; the *attitude* belongs to strand one. Forgiveness, to be itself, requires both.

Consider first the inward, strand-one element, for it will show us well why the other must exist also. Joseph Butler, in his sermon "Upon Resentment" (1729/1970:72-79), has shown how natural and appropriate the feeling of resentment is upon our receiving any real (or supposed) injury. Resentment, Butler says, is God's good gift, protecting us in an injurious world from greater harms and inciting us to secure a justice we might otherwise be too placid or too compassionate to enforce. But like any of God's gifts, resentment is subject to abuse; thus Butler immediately follows his discussion of it with his sermon on forgiveness. We are meant to resent mistreatment of others or of ourselves, but resentment must come to an end, and how that will happen is the present question. For most of us, there is nothing that sticks more persistently in memory than rankling resentment of old wrongs. Forgiveness is never easy.

This brings up the recurrent belief that forgiving means forgetting. And indeed, Scripture says that God tells Israel he "will remember your sins no more" (Isa. 43:25 NEB). Yet this cannot be understood with literal simplicity, for in the following verse (26) the forgiving God recounts those very forgiven sins Israel has committed. In this passage, then, to forget must mean to cease to harbor resentment, must mean *to hold their sins against them no longer*. Indeed, it might be more truly said of forgiveness that it is a special kind of remembrance. One who forgives knows the other's offense to be offense; forgiveness takes its rise, begins, as Butler has shown, from natural resentment, else there is nothing to forgive. Then the forgiving one takes that offense up into his or her own life, makes the other's story part of his or her own story, and by owning it destroys its power to divide forgiver and forgiven. In this sense, to forgive is truly to love one's offending neighbor *as oneself*. Forgiving is not forgetting, for we can repress the memory and still be at enmity with one another; for Christians, forgiving is rather remembering under the aspect of membership in the body of Christ: it is knowing that he who is our body and we, forgiven and forgiver, are all one.

In this sense, to forgive is to learn a new and truer story about myself by discovering how fully my life is bound up with those whose sins are also sins against myself. Horace Bushnell, pastor to a congregation of New England business folk, tells of an older man who took in a partner, befriended, aided, and trusted him. Then the younger betrayed that trust, used the partnership for crooked schemes, nearly ruined it and both the partners. So the generous one lost his business and all that he had. Yet with Yankee industry (we may suppose) he recovered, and after some time was again prospering. The other, however, went his way from disaster to disaster. The first certainly did not forget the second—the very name brought up bitter memories, and he would cross the street rather than meet him face to face. Yet this honest man believed he should forgive, and said he did forgive. Then there came a time when it was said the younger was destitute, and his family suffering. The first saw it as an opportunity to express forgiveness—anonymously, he sent money. Next the child of the younger was in trouble with the law, and the older went to intercede; forgiveness seemed to require it. Finally, dangerous illness struck the other's home. There was no one else, and the first, remembering he said he forgave, went and built the fire, washed the dishes, laundered, nursed, risking infection, while his former partner sat helpless by and wept. But now, Bushnell asks, where is the reluctance, the enmity, that made the other's name hateful? All gone, melted in the caring work of forgiveness. "You have taken his sin upon you in the cost you have borne for his sake" (Bushnell, 1874/1965:317-19).

This may or may not be a true story (I suspect it is a disguised account of events in Bushnell's own life). But there is in any event something that rings true about it. Do we not know cases where two whose lives are intertwined have hurt and been hurt, and yet the injured one has taken the hurt in such a way that atonement, at-one-ment, has been achieved between them and their lives are made closer than if there had been no offense and no costly work of forgiveness? Attitudinally speaking, forgiveness is this: one takes another's life up into one's own, making the offender a part of one's own story in such a way that the cost of doing so overcomes the power of the injury, healing it in a new bond of union between them.

Here, though, we must pass from attitude to act—and not just the acts of reconciliation and mercy Bushnell has told us about, but (in that story) the older partner's act of forgiveness that preceded all of these, his "I do forgive him." In the happy case, this act is two-sided, the one saying in effect "I forgive"; the other in effect, "I accept forgiveness." But even where the response from the one forgiven is muted or absent, the act of forgiveness, by reaching out as in a transaction to the other, is yet a real act if real consequences flow from it. This is the act that is formalized in the Disciples' Prayer taught in the Sermon on the Mount. "Forgive us our debts *as we forgive*" (Matt. 6:12)—the "as we forgive" is not the report of some prior state of mind in the worshiper; it is not an attitude avowed; it is the performative act of the disciple *granting* pardon to those who have offended. And this is done in the very moment of seeking pardon for one's own unpayable debts owed to God. When Matthew's church prayed this prayer, they would know themselves to be granting forgiveness, whether of uncollectable debts, or of untruthful words, or of injury at the hands of family members long gone, or of enmity from a world acknowledged to be against them. In saying the words, these disciples did not merely tell about pardon, they extended it to their debtors, in the eyes and under the authority of God, and were bound thereafter to live accordingly.

With these perhaps familiar but often neglected points about forgiveness as act and attitude before us, we may read with fresh eyes the process of Matthew 18. The crucial paragraph (vv. 15-20) is set in a wider context of Jesus' teaching about sin, temptation, and forgiveness in community. The preceding passages deal with relations with those struggling with temptation, and with the joy in recovering the one stray sheep in a flock of a hundred, while those just after it give the saying about how often to forgive (seventy times seven) and relate the parable of the fate of the *un*merciful servant. In such a setting, we may expect that a paragraph beginning "If your brother sins . . ." (v. 15 RSV) will certainly have something to do with forgiveness. In fact, the first instruction is "go and tell him his fault,"—a procedure whose happy outcome would be reconciliation: "you have gained your brother." We remember that if there is no resentment, 'forgiveness' is meaningless. Clearly the Matthean process respects this fact. A private conference can bring out whatever resentment there is on either side; it can also resolve misunderstanding and achieve harmony. Perhaps there will turn out to have been nothing to forgive. If on the other hand the resentment is deserved, such a conference provides maximal privacy for acknowledgment of the offender's fault and the crucial assurance of forgiveness by the other.

If, however, the resolution is not so easily achieved in private meeting, the process points to a step-by-step enlargement of the number of those involved. Conflict management in the Matthean church was at once rule governed and creative, since the "one or two others along with you" (v. 16) may have their own insight into the fresh formation of discipleship that the situation requires. And finally, as we have noted, the task may need to involve the entire fellowship, and even a formal meeting for its resolution. Even here, the goal is that each shall "hear" all, and the dynamic of the meeting is still toward forgiveness, as the question of verse 21 brings out. Even the refusal to "listen to the church" at this last stage is not without recourse: the erring one is now reckoned in the outsider state again, but that is the very state in which the traditional author of our Gospel had been when he first heard the good news (Matt. 9:9); it is a hopeful one.

So far, our evocation of a New Testament politics of forgiveness has been confined to the Matthean model, so that some may wonder if the picture of community social structure we have called up can also pass the Pauline checkpoint. Turning back a generation or so to the churches established by Paul the missionary, what sort of common life and social control do we find there? Were the Pauline communities informed by 'law,' and did that law shape itself around a focus of forgiveness? While there have been many approaches to Pauline ethics (Furnish, 1968: Appendix) a good beginning for us may be the conclusions of Wayne Meeks' discussion of these churches' "governance." "In the letters," Meeks summarizes, "the norms of the Pauline communities are only rarely stated as rules." We may surmise the reason: Paul was too busy defending his churches (e.g., in Galatia) against the arbitrary imposition of old rules to find rhetorical room to acknowledge the new. But Meeks then goes on to say that nevertheless, "there were rules," though some of them were quite general (e.g., no πορνεία), and though all were qualified by Paul's free interpretation and by the flexibility of decision required in applying them.

The impression is one of great fluidity, of a complex, multipolar, open-ended process of mutual discipline. Perhaps this fluid structure . . . marked the end of the time when "the Law" shaped the limits of God's people and the beginning of the new age that would yield to his Kingdom. (Meeks, 1983:138f.)

Yet as we have just seen, it was a combination of fluidity (or complexity) of structure and a Messianic awareness that marked the Matthean community as well. And (disregarding for the moment the Messianic consciousness) "fluidity" must be the mark of any community with living law—law, that is, that is interpreted, applied, and adjudicated case by case in a community where some kind of ongoing reconciliation is a communal goal.

c. *Summary*—For our purposes, two lessons arise from this rich evidence. The first is that the practice of community establishment and maintenance was at the center of the social ethic of earliest Christianity; if its Apostolic Writings speak authoritatively to us, it is such community practice that they require. This practice was for them no mere social convenience; the risen Christ was at the center of their meetings; their assemblies were his "body"; their nourishment was his proffered selfhood. Just such a practice of community is the social norm for Christian existence. So the second lesson is part of the first: For us, too, a central skill for this community maintenance is forgiveness of one another, based upon and empowered by our own forgiveness from God through Jesus Christ. *"As a community"* (we may paraphrase, struggling to retain in English the lost force of the New Testament's plural imperatives) *"be merciful*, with tender hearts *forgiving* one another as God in Christ forgave you"* (Eph. 4:32). This central skill determines the character of the community, just as the imperatives of the Decalogue had pointed a direction with regard to community practices. It is exactly this skill of forgiveness that is the divine gift enabling disciple communities to cope with the looming power of their own practice of community, otherwise so oppressive, so centripetally destructive. Without forgiveness, the social power of a closed circle may crush its members, soil itself, and sour its social world. Examples of such soured communitarianism litter the pages of every honest church history. But with forgiveness controlling everything, the closed circle is opened, the forgiven forgivers' practice of community is redeemed and becomes positively redemptive; thus this powerful practice renders obedience to the law of the Lord Jesus.

3. The Church in the World

If we explore here the relation of such a church to the world in which it lives, it is not likely that much that is genuinely new will appear, for the theme has been opened from the earliest New Testament writings (1 Thessalonians?) to the most recent pronouncements of church and ecumenical agencies. Indeed, the church-world relation is intrinsic to Christian existence: The line between the church and the world still passes through the heart of every believer, and we may now add, through the heart of every churchly practice as well. What we can hope to do is to remind ourselves of the old arguments, and add to them present evidence, and in their light see afresh the relation between these two.

a. *Three models: Niebuhr, Barth, Hauerwas*—In the social strand, three models or paradigms for understanding church-world relations dominate most discussion, at least implicitly: We may for convenience call these the (H. R.) Niebuhrian, the Barthian, and the Hauerwasian; all others can be seen as some adaptation or combination of these three. In brief, the paradigm offered by the younger Niebuhr brother may be called *interactional:* "Christ" is one entity in the world, represented by all that is truly his; "culture" is another entity, represented by all else, and the question to be answered is, What has the one to do with the other—Christ with Caesar, Athens with Jerusalem? The Niebuhrian answer is found in an Aristotelean golden mean, where extremes are the rejection of "culture" by "Christ" (minimal interaction, an extreme imputed by Niebuhr to our own baptist heritage!) and identification ("the Christ *of* culture," attributed to liberal culture-Protestantism), and where the happiest form of the happy mean is an interaction called "transformation": "Christ" transforming "culture," not vice versa. Niebuhr presented his argument via a sociological typology, using these three and two other, intermediate types to display, he believed, the full range of historic Christian possibilities (H. R. Niebuhr, 1951).

But the typology, by its definitions and its choice of examples, is rigged so as to make the Aristotlean answer emerge at the end. Thus, the overall Niebuhrian picture of Christ and culture has captivated us too easily. Still, we will find here no reason to reject its imbedded theme of church-world interaction. That the Niebuhrian paradigm is often misleading, however, must also be acknowledged. A telling clue is that those who embrace it have so often been led to contrast the "responsibility" of their own culture-based outlook with the "withdrawal" (and implied *ir*responsibility) of baptist groups. We met these themes in Wogaman as early as Chapter Two. But to display the radical heritage as "withdrawn" over against Catholics or Protestants as "responsible," besides begging many questions of historical fact, fails to reckon with the character of either the world or the church as these have been developed in the present pages. The world (or "culture") has appeared for us not as one smooth global unity, but as an indefinite congeries of powerful practices, spread over time and space, so that any number of these practices may impinge upon believers in a variety of ways, while our witness to them will necessarily take a corresponding variety of forms. Conscientious withdrawal from the practice of warfare may be coupled with conscientious engagement in practices of peacemaking or education, economics or the arts. "Culture" is not (as H. R. Niebuhr would too often have it) monolithic; "the world" is itself divided. Meanwhile, "the church" is exactly the realm in which responsibility to Jesus Christ is the hallmark of discipleship, so in it the call to be "responsible" can only be defined in terms of his Lordship over all, not by some worldly measurement. The greater temptation for today's disciples may be to feel "responsible" to the world as worldlings perceive it while "withdrawing" from the absolute claim of Jesus Christ's lordship.

The Barthian and Hauerwasian theses display variations on the theme of interaction. For Barth, the key term is *exemplarity* (Barth, 1958b:IV/2, ¶67; cf. the earlier Barth, 1946/1960). The task of Christian community is to be an example and foretaste of what God in Christ intends for all human community. By shaping its law (the rules that structure its liturgy, service, and common life) according to the "christologico-ecclesiological concept," that is, the principle of Christ's headship, the church provides this model for the world, and even though the world and its laws are evil, by their very nature unable to acknowledge Christ as King, the church's witness will be effectual, for the world is not wholly evil: "They also are in the hand of God and have not escaped his judgment and grace" (Barth, 1958b:IV/2, 724; Barth, 1946/1960). Barth goes on in the fine print to show some of the gifts church community may have to offer civil community: its order or structure based upon service, its foundation in mutual trust, its involvement of *all* members, its emphasis upon absolute brotherhood, its fluidity as "living," that is, flexible, law. We might say that on this paradigm the church's role in society's transformation is primarily the social example of its common (internal) life—a city set on a hill.

Somewhat different is the Hauerwasian theme of *interpretation*. "The world," he rightly notes, is not just there, available for observation; that there *is* a world, a realm that knows not God and is disobedient to him, is a truth discernible only from the standpoint of church—that is, the standpoint from which "people faithfully carry out the task of being a witness to the reality of God's Kingdom" (1981:109). That this is so evokes in Hauerwas thoughts of relativism, the theoretical impossibility of finding any truth really true. But Hauerwas believes there is no theoretical defeating of relativism; instead, it is just the church that is the community that will enable us to comprehend the "splintered and tribal existence" of the world we live in (1981:92). In other words, the standpoint of church community and only that enables Christians to see the world for what it is, and thus to make their moral way through its disorder. Certainly there is more to Hauerwas' understanding of church-world relations than this interpretive theme, just as there is more to Barth's than exemplarity. I have introduced these, however, with Niebuhr's more comprehensive (but more vague) category of interaction, because the three together cover the bases of current strand-two thinking pretty well. Now let us compare them to our touchstone Matthean community understood as a community of shared powerful practices, and draw some conclusions.

b. *The Matthean model*—One thing that leaps out, in our inspection of the church for whom the Gospel according to Matthew was written, is that it was so fully a church in the world. None of the early Christian communities followed the well-known example of the Essenes, who had withdrawn to the Dead Sea and lived a separated existence; none took the route of later monasticism. Instead, these Christians selectively but deliberately remained a part of the wider world, both on Jewish and on Gentile soil. Therefore, the practices in which their lives were engaged were often enough the practices of the older world that surrounded them. In Syria, these would have been the practices of a polyglot and pluralistic Near East, overlaid with dominant Hellenism and (by this time) with Roman hegemony. Therefore the form taken by the gospel as 'new law' was in large measure set by an encounter with an alien but very present world. Laws, by our account, are rules guiding a community's engagement in practices, and for Syrian Christians (as for earlier Palestinian ones) the practices that involved them included those of a government and an economic structure in a society at odds with the kingdom of Christ. Here lay the point of turning the other cheek, of refusing any kind of oath, of settling lawsuits by reckless generosity, and of being a generous, even an imprudent, lender (5:33-42). Here, too, lay the root of total refusal to engage in ways of violence—the pacifism of this Gospel. Behind these refusals and selective ways of participating (no to war and all violence, a yes and a no to some economic practices, yes both to marriage and to single chastity) lay a deeper motive—the Christians' engagement in evangelism or witness, the overriding practice that shaped participation in all other social practices. For Matthew, the central task of this witness was *discipling* (μαθητεύσατε), forming lives in accordance with the gospel story, whose elements were *going* (hence, withdrawal was impossible), *baptizing* (entailing full communal commitment by each to the Way), and *teaching* (and thus the formation of a church culture that would stand creatively over against the world's culture by imparting its own) (28:19f.). So engagement with the world was not optional or accidental, but lay at the heart of obedient discipleship.

On this communal journey, two sorts of foes confronted them. One was without, the other within. The external foe (in Pauline terms, the "principalities and powers") is given narrative shape in the Gospel story of a confrontation that leads to a public execution. The powers of the land exact the cross, and Jesus' and the disciples' responses to it are presented intertwined. In bearing the cross alone, he redeems the disciples' lives from their own failure; only thus do they

become followers of the Way; the power of outmoded institutions and their practices is symbolically torn only by the
event of Calvary (27:51). Thus readers, identifying with the
disciples, know that they, too, must confront the powers
afresh (16:24), but with Christ's help will overcome them.

Alongside this outer foe lurks an inner one. Syrian readers
would perhaps find themselves, like their Gospel proxies,
understanding but failing to act (25:45), succumbing to the
seduction of wealth (13:22), despising other brothers and
sisters (18:10), becoming status-seekers (23:8-12), unwilling to
forgive (18:21-35), nourishing inward, evil thoughts (15:19)
(Kingsbury, 1977:91f.). Their very 'powerful practice' of
community formation, in other words, might transform them
into Matthew's (stereotypical) Pharisees. Yet they could know
also the forgiveness of Christ's blood-of-the-covenant, and
could use the process of Matthew 18 to guide one another's
conduct. Matthean Christianity, we might conclude, was not
'perfectionist' if that means lacking a sense of their own
shortcomings, but they knew themselves summoned to a
mature way of life, and to wholehearted sharing in it.

c. *Today's church in the world*—What does all this add to our
modern Niebuhr-Barth-Hauerwas summary of church-world
interaction? Perhaps a stronger sense than these provided of
the dynamic *clash* of Christ and power, of disciples and their
adversary world, and of Christ's assured final victory. For
some, that may suggest turning to the insights of today's
Liberation Theology. But that will be to look on to the
resurrection strand, where our account can be completed.
Perhaps, for present purposes, a clearer vision of the way the
concrete practices overflow into engagement with society is
our best contribution.

Our example must still be the Christian practice of
community building. Those who have learned to deal with
brothers and sisters within the community will not find it
difficult to adapt to new contexts outside the community both
the forgiveness process and the sort of action that wipes clean
the slate. Indeed "forgive us our debts as we forgive" (Matt.
6:12) seems already unrestricted in range. And had not Jesus
on the cross, by one tradition, been praying forgiveness for his
executioners even as they did the deed (Luke 23:24)? So both
the process of life together and its guiding theme of

forgiveness seem suited to be means of community witness. Disciples will share in the common life and practices of the church. They will also share other commonalities with other neighbors, and in those settings Christian ways can overflow into the wider society. Taken to the full, the analogy will be both to individuals within a society, and to the relation of communities, nations even, to one another, modeled upon Christian interchurch or ecumenical relations.

Here is an opportunity for obedience some heirs of the baptist vision have yet to take with full seriousness. Captured by a confessionalism more appropriate to the seventeenth than to a later century, these persist in a kind of vicious sectarianism that draws ever more tightly the lines of 'fellowship,' ever more narrowly those of cooperation, and therefore ever more faintly the lines of influence upon their fellow Christians and upon the world. Happily that is not true of all. For the strong evidence of the New Testament is that the conversation guiding life within the meeting congregation was carried on also beyond its borders. Letters and visits engaged the church at Corinth, about which we happen to know the most, and the visitors were by no means screened for uniformity of teaching (1 Cor. 1:12f.; 3:1-9). Yet there was indeed among the churches a concern for concert and unity, and the chief means for resolving outstanding conflict was the familiar one of meeting and talking things over (Meeks, 1983:113)—compare the technique of Acts 15, for example, and the Pauline parallels, with that of Matthew 18.

These are for today's Christians, East and West, in rich lands and poor ones, vital issues now, for our capacity to be reconciled one to another as the people of God may be the best foretaste we can offer a divided and struggling world of the overcoming of its own deadly divisions. For those who believe that world empire and imperial church structure are now alike inadequate to the reconciling of these respective differences, there is hope in the less rigid, more pluriform, and yet not impotent unities that Christian fellowship via correspondence, visits, and conferences across party lines may offer in our day. The real ecumenism takes place, finally, at the grass roots of neighbor congregations, not in world-class councils.

This does not rule out the role of Christian appeals to the environing societies themselves. While we have found no reason to believe in any "natural law," standing outside the

law of Christ, as a universal basis for such appeals (cf. Chapter
Two, above), and while no single social model (capitalist,
Marxist, or other) has here been found to have any claim upon
Christian thought save in terms of the powerful practices it
sponsors or inhibits, some of the features Christians may need
to urge upon any social order, East or West, are worth noting
down. Christians know that their own life engages body,
mind, and spirit, and thus they will seek an environment
consonant with the health of all three: For bodily life we
require some minimal *stability*, that is, an economic, political,
and social order sufficiently stable to foster life in a family
setting, decent health for ourselves as well as our neighbors,
enough prosperity to permit all of these. Synonyms for
stability are justice, well-being, and peace. For the life of the
mind, Christians need an order possessing some measure of
integrity. This means society not propped chiefly upon lies; it
means opportunity for education that nurtures openness of
mind, critical examination of current beliefs, coherent or
integral ways of thought for each consistent with the item next
to follow, full spiritual liberty. Thus for the life of the spirit we
require *liberty*. This will be preeminently what we have come
to call 'religious' liberty. It is the acknowledgment that society
and its practices, though they are paraded as gods, are not
God; for God alone is God, and social structures must retain a
corresponding modesty about their writ and competence. To
these three one other feature must be added: *plurality*. For
Christians this demand is a function of the biblical doctrine of
election and the knowledge of the world's dividedness, but it
may be advocated in terms outsiders will accept as due to the
variety in human life within every social boundary. Within the
human race, the varieties of racial grouping, national entities,
tribes, clans, families, classes, trade and work groups, religions, cities, countrysides, all facing one another in diversity,
may serve to determine policies of acceptance, freedom,
inclusiveness, and cooperation for common ends in contrast to
that Babel-like drive to towering unity which has marked the
great empires and the totalitarianisms in our era. Our social
impulses to unity are strongly rooted in human nature; the
Christian concern must be that neither these impulses nor the
drive to conquest, blighted as both are by sin, shall overturn
the contingent stabilities, integrities, liberties, and pluralities
human history has contingently achieved.

Our only care must be that such appeals by lobbying, education, and the like not be allowed to erode the distinctive Christian social witness conveyed by example more than precept. The disciples who join in a public protest witness, and who thereby show that reproach is the first step toward forgiveness; the disciple who investigates, criticizes, proposes reconstruction of the current penal system, guided by the forgiveness model learned in Christian community; the disciples who, victims as Jesus was a victim, bear the long weight of Soviet or other prison camps and transform their punishment into redemption by the alchemy of forgiveness—these vivify as can no theory the application of Christian common life to social structure. Perhaps, then, a single example can now focus and interpret these reflections.

Will Campbell, in his evocative biographical-autobiographical story of a life with his older brother, *Brother to a Dragonfly*, tells how he grew up in south Mississippi, the son of poor dirt farmers, but always aimed toward the 'preacher' image they perceived as fitting. So his maturing was a growing to discover the length and breadth and depth of that imposed yet elusive ideal. He went with family encouragement to the 'best' religious schools, ending at Yale Divinity School, and took up the career of a Baptist Southern liberal—as he envisioned it, a kind of prophetic chaplain to church and society. Called to Ole Miss as university chaplain, he espoused racial integration in the fifties; employed next by the National Council of Churches, he aided civil rights work and workers. God and national law were handily allied for him in this struggle, though curiously, Will's own white Southern 'redneck' people had now become the enemy.

The turning point came when one Jonathan Daniels, a gentle white divinity student working for the summer at black voter registration in Lowndes County, Alabama, was shotgunned to death by an enraged white deputy sheriff named Thomas Coleman. The news flash of this outrage drove preacher Will to frustrating phone calls to the Department of Justice, the American Civil Liberties Union, and a concerned lawyer friend.

I had talked of the death of my friend as being a travesty of justice, as a complete breakdown of law and order, as a violation of Federal and State law. I had used words like redneck, backwoods, woolhat, cracker, Kluxer, ignoramus and many others. I had studied sociology, psychology, and social ethics and was speaking and thinking in these concepts. I had also studied New Testament theology.

That last sentence, ironic in intent, sets the stage for the scene that followed, as Will's Christian assessment of the slaying was challenged by a highly sceptical but theologically acute friend, P. D. East. In the course of a long and somewhat boozy evening, East demanded to know whether Christian teaching held that God regarded both slayer and victim as sinners (as they put it, whether both were "bastards"), and whether on Will's view God now loved one of those "bastards" more than the other.

He leaned his face closer to mine, patting first his own knee and then mine, holding the other hand aloft in oath-taking fashion.
"Which one of these two bastards does God love the most? Does he love that little dead bastard Jonathan the most? Or does He love that living bastard Thomas the most?
Suddenly everything became clear. . . .

The transformation Will Campbell then experienced in that summer night was nothing less than the discovery of the overflow of the gospel of forgiveness and its application to his own situation. Perversely, P. D. East was right. Forgiven, one could forgive even Thomas Coleman.

Loved. And if loved, forgiven. And if forgiven, reconciled. Yet sitting there in his own jail cell, the blood of two of his and my brothers on his hands. (Campbell, 1979:221f.)

Will Campbell found his ministry wrenched around toward reconciling mission to his own Southern white outcasts—the "Kluxers, woolhats, rednecks" he had been seeing only as the enemy. In the sequel, he became something of a legend among socially concerned Southern Christians, a kind of saint in a wool hat, himself.

But when my own seminary students in Berkeley were asked to read this story, some of them, I found, regarded it as a story of Campbell's loss of vision. "Once a racist, always a racist," was the reaction of one to the passage just quoted. They wished that Will, like themselves, were willing simply to condemn whites for racism and fight on for black victory. There is here, I think, a fundamental fork in Christian understanding. Certainly (as Will Campbell knows well enough) my student and his kin have deep reason for intransigence. Certainly forgiveness that is not preceded by resentment and reproach is empty forgiveness. And certainly the world's wrongs (and my Christian brother's wronging me) remain grievous sins.

Yet I think Will Campbell, without denying any of those truths, has found a deeper one, nearer the gospel, nearer the disciples' Way. If that is a depth gained only at personal cost and by way of conversion, does that make it any stranger to the gospel? But if it comes in so costly a way even into the Christian camp, how will it fare among the Gentiles and the tax-gatherers? If this is our social ethic, must we not ask with the disciples (though in another context than theirs), "Who then can be saved?" Though then, also, we must hear Jesus' answer: "With men this is impossible, but with God all things are possible" (Matt. 19:25f. RSV).

* * * * *

We have in this chapter sought a connecting link between body ethics (strand one) and social ethics (strand two) for Christians, and have found that link in the self-involving common practices that draw the disciples of Jesus Christ into solidaristic union in their obedient following of him. Such a practice is that of establishing and maintaining Christian community, with its involved symbolic meal, the Lord's supper. Community maintenance presumes rules, that is, laws, whether spoken or unspoken, by which the practices function, and these in turn give occasion for the ongoing process of community guidance, focused upon Christ's forgiveness of us and our forgiveness of one another. This process is necessarily internal to the Christian community. But the call to evangelize and the demand for public Christian witness point to the overflow of the Christian Way into action toward and with and for the neighbor, as well. The church is in the world, not as an added requirement of Christian duty, but by the very nature of what church and world mean in gospel perspective. Very simply put, Christian ethics makes central the cross that the world will be sure to provide for the members of Jesus' community. The question for Christian ethics is not whether there is such a cross, but rather how the spirit and deeds of forgiveness shall engage those other spirits, still in prison. Yet the full account of this engagement requires the introducton of our third strand.

PART III

THE SPHERE
OF THE ANASTATIC

When anyone is united to Christ, there is a new world; the old order has gone, and a new order has already begun.

2 Corinthians 5:17 NEB

Swords and spears were forged into and used as pruning hooks and saws and other useful tools. There were no muskets, swords, or pikes—not a single weapon made for fighting was to be found at all . . . . They took no revenge.

The Oldest Chronicle of the Hutterian Brethren

Resurrection Ethics

To sum up from a new angle of vision our study of the previous two strands, we can say that together these answered one question only to present us with another. The question answered was this: What explains the moral particularity of our human life? How is it, in other words, that we do well to spend our lives in such and such places, engaged in such and such tasks—and not in other life engagements that appear equally worthwhile? Concretely, when many households in my city are hungry and lonely and in need of my protection, what validates my bringing groceries home exactly to *my* family, staying with them, providing them first of all with my care? Logically, to be sure, it is impossible for me to be with all families—I am not God—and dividing my time among as many families as possible (in the manner of a Mormon patriarch extraordinary), while perhaps not unimaginable for some, is nevertheless self-defeating; playing parent to all would make one effectively parent to none. Still, the question has relevance, for we Christians do respect marriage and kinship as well as singleness, do give special preference to our own families, do settle into particular work and ministry, do discriminate in every dimension of life. The analysis of the bodily and social strands offered a clear account of two legitimate sorts of discrimination: the sort occasioned by our drives, needs, and capacities as embodied selves, and the sort arising from our story-formed participation in certain social structures. Exactly because as Christians we are creatures with such and such earthly and heavenly needs, and exactly because we are part of the Messianic story at such and such a time and place in the story, with such and such companions, communities, practices, and tasks, involving such and such duties and skills—for exactly these good reasons we become the men and women that we are, acquiring in the bargain the responsibilities that we have and the characters with which we meet these responsibilities. Particularity is the name of human existence, and for Christians there is morally speaking no shame in it.

Yet the solution seems too pat, the answer too neat. The picture of human existence that arises is too conservative, and even self-serving, to match the Way of the Master or to fit the venturesome matrix of creation in Christ. It comports too well with the comfortable wasteland of that numerous tribe, the half-Christians, busy about their little cares and wants, unquestioningly accepting the hand fate has dealt them, conformed to the mores of their own society or the fashions of this present age. Of course that is not what the analysis of strands one and two intended, and there is much in each of the strands that conflicts with this snug, smug picture of the moral life. But the question does arise whether taken alone, this is their tendency. To say that is only to repeat in a fresh way what was said first in Chapter Two—that these two strands yearn for a third, that they do not by themselves, or even added together, constitute true Christian morality. Thus from them we can infer the existence of another strand as surely as astronomers could from the orbits of the known planets infer the existence of one still unobserved. And the third, resurrection strand is no tiny Pluto, no minor planet in Christian ethics. Or, to put the hunger of the bodily and social strands in a fresh way: when we have learned about them and the Christian story to which they point, we are left to ask, why *this* story among all earth's possibilities? And how do we know to take the story itself in *this* way? Why, for example, should we read the Old Testament in the light of the New, and not vice versa, as might a liberal rabbi? Or why even read it *as* a (true) story, and not, as did the Enlightenment philosophers, as Timeless Truth or myth (Frei, 1974)?

Christians find the answer to these questions preeminently in the resurrection of Jesus Christ from death, and thus it is to the moral impact of that resurrection, puzzling to many, that we must turn if we are to grasp the third strand of Christian ethics.

1.   What Has the Resurrection to Do with Morality?

It was Walter Rauschenbusch (1861–1918), a professor at the Rochester Theological Seminary (and probably the outstanding baptist theologian of our century), who more clearly than any other saw the place of all three strands of Christian ethics. It is thus appropriate to turn to Rauschenbusch's writing to find how, in his search for a theology adequate to the new Social Gospel, he laid hold of the crucial third strand.

a. *Rauschenbush's theology as model*—In the last full year of his life Rauschenbusch was invited to give at Yale Divinity School the lectures that became his best-known book, *A Theology for the Social Gospel* (1917). Their thesis was that, in light of the growing social consciousness of the Christian churches, a readjustment in doctrinal theology was necessary, and most of the lectures were devoted to concrete proposals for such readjustments. Toward the end, Rauschenbusch came to treat the ticklish theme of last things—eschatology, which he understood to mean the church's teaching about human destiny. Much of the inherited eschatology of Christianity, Rauschenbusch pointed out, was not native to Christianity at all, but was borrowed from neighboring cultures in the ancient world. Its various ideas did not fit together very well—hence the awkwardness of many eschatological schemes in present-day Christianity. Christians were entitled, indeed obliged, to scan this material, asking of each element among the various judgments, millennia, etc., whether it came authentically from the God-consciousness of the prophets, the apostles, and Jesus himself, and whether or not it made a constructive contribution to the growing awareness of the kingdom of God in social Christianity. By making such a survey, Rauschenbusch was able to present the main elements of classical eschatology in perspective. He also showed some emphases that a reconstructed doctrinal system would have to include, although he did not go on to detailed positive construction (1917:ch. 18).

In the process, Rauschenbusch showed himself capable of deft historical handling of the material (he was professor of church history at Rochester), and he developed a social criticism of the history of Christian doctrine, along Marxian-Feuerbachian lines, that today's Liberation theologians, with their own Marxian dimension, might study with profit. For example, he was able to show that the discarding of the doctrine of purgatory by the Protestant Reformers, while not altogether satisfactory on purely doctrinal grounds, was historically inevitable because of purgatory's link to indulgences and thence to the vast economic system of the medieval European church: The Reformers meant to challenge that system, and purgatory was expendable on biblical grounds—a case of doctrinal change springing from, and also contributing to, social change. Similar points could be made regarding assorted eschatological elements of the biblical history as well; Rauschenbusch was particularly critical of modern premillennialism, the literalistic reading of the books of Daniel and the Revelation of John, because it failed to take into account the social situation of the ancient writers (1917:221f.).

Moreover, Rauschenbusch was able to do what some political theologies find difficult. He applied the Marxian critical technique to his own Social Gospel. He did this in a positive sense: In an age when democratization of society was the password, it was all the more appropriate that Christian doctrine, whose roots lay in the vision of equality and justice proclaimed by the prophets, should be further democratized. Thus the millenary hope of a 'thousand-year' time of peace and harmony on earth, while antisocial in the hands of contemporary premillennialists, nevertheless deserved a place in the eschatology of the Social Gospel. With similar arguments, Rauschenbusch went on to reaffirm convictions he had nurtured throughout his career: (1) the vital interest of Christianity in the future development of the entire human race (no minor stipulation for a 'sectarian' theologian); (2) the sense of God's involvement with all of human history; (3) the need for a shift from a catastrophic to a developmental idea of the changes mandated by the kingdom of God (a gradualist view that, alas, closed Rauschenbusch's eyes to the radical eschatology in Jesus' outlook); and thus (4) the consequent rejection of any "final" consummation of the kingdom; (5) the willingness to recognize the rule of superpersonal forces (cf. "principalities and powers") at work in history; and (6) a realistic note—the recognition of powerful evil, and the inevitable conflict with evil, in the growth of the kingdom of God (1917:223-27; cf. his earliest book, ed. Stackhouse, 1968).

246 Ethics: Systematic Theology, Volume I

Despite his great insight, Rauschenbusch was naturally unable to stand on his own shoulders and anticipate criticisms of his work that seem fairly obvious several generations later. His classic liberal commitment to continuity made it seem evident to him, as it had to his mentor Albrecht Ritschl (1822–1889), that unbroken development was the story of every earthly (and heavenly) thing; there are no gaps in the universe; thus he was unable to digest the recent news from German New Testament scholarship (Johannes Weiss and Albert Schweitzer) about Jesus' own apocalyptic expectations, and he was unduly sure that progress, not catastrophe, marked the course of human history in general—all of these being views that seem far less obvious to late-twentieth-century Christians. And, at a deeper level of theological method, Rauschenbusch was unable to shake free of the assumption that the mere need for a doctrinal belief is somehow its justification—a principle which, if applied to another sphere of life, would put every dreamy-eyed youth in a sports car, or at least astride a horse: "If wishes were horses . . . ." The fatal omission in Rauschenbusch's eschatology for the Social Gospel, however, is his failure to make any reference to the moral relevance of the resurrection of Jesus from the dead, a doctrine to which he gives more casual than convinced assent in *A Theology for the Social Gospel* (1917:228). Yet we can understand this outcome if we consider that the resurrection is a *dis*continuous event in history, while Rauschenbusch's mind was fascinated by continuity.

Yet the resurrection event is in fact the turning point of all Christian thought, the cardinal matter of the New Testament, the entering wedge of a gospel that is not mere moralism or mere sentiment. As Rauschenbusch well knew, the belief in a bodily resurrection at the last day was a common idea of first-century Judaism, though not one that could claim universal assent. When Jesus predicted his own resurrection, the disciples would naturally have understood him to mean he would be raised *at the last day*. What took them by surprise, and in doing so constituted the founding event of primitive Christianity, was that on that first-day morning, Jesus' resurrection had already occurred! An eschatological hope had become a present reality, though the world had not come to an end (J. A. T. Robinson, 1962). Other eschatological events—the millennium, the general resurrection, the last judgment—

must remain necessarily faint and uncertain just because they are still future, but this eschatological event had in fact happened; as such, it could not fail to be central for Christian morality.

In fact Rauschenbusch's eschatological social ethic becomes much clearer if it is related to a new aeon that begins with the resurrection. Yet his given contribution cannot be neglected. His interpretation of 'last things' as a doctrine of present significance for the moral life of Christians, his deep sense of the newness of the present and its opportunity, and the centrality of hope in his life work (beset as it was by frequent discouragement), with his capacity to turn his anastatic insights into concrete social doctrine, mean that this Social Gospel is still inescapable for any who would hope to make today's ethics Christian (Gustafson, 1975).

b. *The difference made by the resurrection*—It is important that we see exactly why the *resurrection* of Jesus is pivotal, not only for doctrine, but for the Christian moral life. I will here assume what the New Testament evidently assumes throughout— that the bodily resurrection of Jesus Christ on the first Easter is an actual, though 'eschatological,' event; therefore it is not on the one hand to be identified with mere resuscitations of 'dead' bodies (that is, those presumed dead who are later, even amazingly, revived, only to die again in due course); nor is the resurrection to be identified with other events, which are rather its consequences (the transformed faith of the disciples, the birth of the Christian church) or its immediate evidences (the appearances, the empty tomb). It is an event *sui generis*, occurring in history yet defying the current canons of the study of history (R. R. Niebuhr, 1957); it is, in the full sense of the words, an act of God. If it did not happen, Christian faith is false and the Christian life lives out a lie; since it did happen, all our standards of judgment, and we ourselves, are profoundly called into question, but Christ is fully alive, and there is hope also for us who can wonder, doubt—and believe.

Viewed in this way, the resurrection is central not only for doctrine but also for ethics; it is the *sine qua non* of the Christian life itself. The claim that life is to be lived in *this* way—in the Christian way—depends upon Christ's rightful lordship, his right to the mastery of our lives. According to the New Testament, the divine act in which that claim is established is

the ἀνάστασις ἐκ νεκρῶν—the resurrection from the dead of
Jesus Christ (cf. Acts 5:31; 10:40-42; 13:33; 17:31). As Paul puts
it, probably quoting an earlier confession, Jesus Christ has
been "designated Son of God in power according to the Spirit
of holiness *by his resurrection from the dead*" (Rom. 1:4 RSV). This
designation establishes his rightful rank *vis-à-vis* both God and
God's people (Phil. 2:9-11).

Here we are touching not some second order theological
reflection, or even *one* New Testament theology, but the
common stem of all New Testament conviction. The resurrection is as fundamental to the primitive Jewish Christianity of
the book of James (cf. 2:1; 5:8) as it is to the sophisticated
meditations of the Fourth Gospel. Nevertheless, the New
Testament did elaborate the conviction theologically over a
period of time, and a reminder of this development in its
ethical mode may help us to grasp the full significance of the
resurrection event. This reminder contains three propositions.
The resurrection is:

i. *The vindication of justice*—It is not in any sense the first
appearance of God's justice. Long before Jesus' day, *tsedeqah*,
justice or righteousness, referred in the Old Testament to the
state of harmony and peace enjoyed by those who fulfilled the
relationships that the community provided (Achtemeier,
1962:80). But as we saw in our discussion of the social strand,
there is a preliminary question which that strand itself cannot
answer—by what *moral* right does this (moral) community
even exist? What is the 'justicing' (G. M. Hopkins) of its
justice, the justification of its morality? This is not a
comparative question about the relative righteousness of Israel
and her neighbors, or of the communities of law and gospel; it
is a general question about the righteousness or justice, the
tsedeqah, of a moral community as such. Why be moral?

Paul in Romans means to answer that question for his
Christian readers by reference to the vindicating act of God
focused upon the death and resurrection of Jesus Christ, "who
was put to death for our trespasses *and raised for our
justification*" (4:25 RSV). In the biblical pattern, that divine act
corresponds to the voice that calls "Abraham, Abraham," in
the story of the binding of Isaac (and, not incidentally, raises
Isaac the son from a sacrificial slaying—Genesis 22:11). The
resurrection corresponds to the word of the waiting father that

changes the whole story for the prodigal son ("Bring quickly the best robe, and put it on him"—Luke 15:22 RSV). It corresponds to JHWH's calling "out of the mountain" and saying, "I bore you on eagles' wings and brought you to myself. Now, therefore . . . you shall be my own possession"—to the constitution of the people of Israel (Exod. 19:3f. RSV).

In all these analogies, God (or the father in the parable) speaks only a word, and everything is changed. How is it that in what Christians take to be the supreme instance of divine intervention, God's word has changed into a deed—the mysterious eschatological event of ἀνάστασις? But words are themselves deeds—acts of speech, speech-acts (McClendon and Smith, 1975:ch. 3). And there is hence no loss of beautiful symmetry when God's supreme word is no mere command, but a divine self-giving, a word that is God's life-imparting self in action.

The resurrection is the acted word in which God identified his own immortal life, once and for all, with the life, the life story, of Jesus of Nazareth. In this event-that-is-God's Word, this enacted word, this historic sign, Christians 'hear' the vindication of the story of Jesus, of his way. In this event, Jesus' way is designated henceforth to constitute God's own way for his people. Thus the resurrection is the reestablishment of the community of the Israel of God (Gal. 6:16) on a new basis, vindicating the justice of God in the older establishment, and promising that very justice, through Christ, to all the world (M. Barth, 1964). It is also:

ii. *A new way of construing the world*—"He is the beginning, the first-born from the dead" (Col. 1:18 RSV). That is, in the death and resurrection of Jesus Christ, a new kind of time, end-time, has begun; in Christ a "new creation" (2 Cor. 5:17) has come to pass. Yet the new creation does not simply replace the old as today replaces yesterday; the old epoch lingers, and disciples live between two 'times,' participating in the new epoch even while they confront the old, and thus await the final consummation, when the old will vanish at last (Cullmann, 1962).

Since Rauschenbusch's day, most biblical scholars have come to believe that eschatology is not marginal but central for the New Testament outlook (Fiorenza, 1976). By beginning with the one eschatological event that the first Christians could not ignore—Christ's resurrection—we are brought face to face with that outlook: Ethics must reckon with the epoch that the resurrection has inaugurated. The problem is how to adapt our own ethical thought to this exotic, if inescapable, material. We can safely follow Rauschenbusch in recognizing that the very variety of New Testament eschatologies, from the expectation of the end "in this generation" (Mark 9:1; 13:30) to its cautious postponement for a little while (Rev. 6:9-11), frees us from the jigsaw puzzle task of making each utterance fit a single, unified picture of history and its consummation. The New Testament presents no such picture. But we cannot (without evading the entire New Testament canon) fail to ask what difference it makes to our ethics if it is the case that we, too, live between the times.

Let us confront once more a perennial problem. It is often said that expectation of the end gave primitive Christians an indifference to the responsibilities of the real world which we, who know that they were wrong, must reject. Never mind, for the moment, whether they *were* wrong about their world—is it so apparent to anyone in the late twentieth century that our own world will not perish, abruptly perish? Perhaps, if they were wrong about themselves, they are nevertheless oddly right about us? How would this understanding work out? As an example, consider the 'extreme' language of Paul in 1 Corinthians 7:29-31 (RSV). "The appointed time (i.e., the time between the times, the time before the final end) "has grown very short" (so Paul believes). What follows? "From now on, let those who have wives live as though they had none, and those who mourn" (or "rejoice") as if they did not, "and those who buy as though they had no goods," and in general, "those who deal with the world as though they had no dealings with it." The five times repeated ὡς μή ("as if not") delineates a strategy for dealing with a vanishing epoch: in effect to treat its institutions and practices as the frail creatures that they are—since the σχῆμα, the social structure, of that epoch "is passing away."

This is not new doctrine; one can find its moral equivalent in the wisdom literature and the psalms (e.g., Pss. 127:1f.; 146:3f.; Ecclesiastes pass.). What is new is the powerful reinforcement the ὡς μή attitude receives from the eschatological sensibility of the New Testament. These texts do not advocate withdrawal or asceticism in the ordinary sense of the terms. Paul does not seek to abolish marriage (and to him marriage presumes sex and procreation), or weddings and their rejoicing, or funerals with their mourning, or the practices of the economic order. He only forbids *staking one's life* upon these—in present terms, he forbids an irrevocable and exclusive immersion in the second or social strand of first-century morality, because (and just to the extent that) that strand has congealed in the old aeon. For, as he concludes the ὡς μή passage, "the σχῆμα of this world is passing away," so that absolute dependence on it is simply foolhardy. Clearly, this is not asceticism in the sense of a discipline for training the stubborn will by withholding from it the good; neither is it otherworldliness in the sense of resignation from present reality in favor of a better life by and by. Paul requires neither social flight nor inward detachment, but a tough-minded facing of the historical reality; investing in given societal practices only the moral capital that their published balance sheets will justify when they are examined in resurrection light (cf. Georgi, 1976:183).

A modern parallel to Paul's view may be found in the social teaching of the contemporary French sociologist, legal philosopher, and theologian Jacques Ellul (1912-). Ellul begins his analysis of modern society with a consideration of the concept of *technique*. While his definition of this ubiquitous notion is never clear in any one passage, his illustrations of it are plain enough. Take the case of nuclear weaponry. Once these weapons are invented, Ellul says, it is not a question for technological society whether they will be used; the questions turn only on their *efficient* use, on their rational deployment and use in pursuit of the technological ends of those who control them. *That* nuclear weapons will be used is from the point of view of "technique" unchallengeable; they exist, that is the fact, and the facts determine everything. Ellul makes similar analyses of technique across the range of modern life: economics, social organization, the state, education, propaganda, sports, medicine, etc. In every field, technique is the absolute dictator from whose "necessary" grasp there is no escape (Ellul, 1964). It may help us understand his claim if we see it as composed of two separable theses, though Ellul's point is that modern society does not separate them. There is the thesis that technical skills provide handy means for the *quantification* of social life (data banks, weapons arsenals, course requirements, surgical options, etc.); and there is the thesis that social 'decisions' shall be governed by this quantified data alone. It is the union of these two which gives Ellul's analysis its (rightly) chilling tone.

Enter now, however, Ellul the prophetic biblical theologian, who announces that though that is how things really are, the Christian cannot be governed by those depressing alien powers. In Christ the Christian is set free from the "order of necessity." Thus on the theme of inevitable violence in the conduct of human affairs, Ellul writes "I hold that in every situation of injustice and oppression, the Christian—who cannot deal with it by violence—must make himself completely a part of it as *representative of the victims* . . . . He lends his intelligence, his influence, his hands, and his face to the faceless mass that has no hands and no influence" (1969:151-52). Ellul thus provides an example of the capacity of present-day Christian thought, in the light of the risen Christ, both to make a realistic assessment of the world and to respond to it in a clear-eyed but redemptive way, although, for American readers at least, his work is best approached through friendly but critical interpretation (D. Gill, 1984).

To return to the present point: Did the primitive Christians, expecting the early end of the αἰών (world or age), simply govern their lives by what we know today to be a mistake? After all, their world did not end. *But did it not?* Not, perhaps, as they expected. But then, biblical writers' future historical expectations are never in this sense accurate—as the surprising first coming of the Messiah well illustrates. Were the early Christians not right? Jerusalem fell, Hellenism perished, Rome was sacked, antiquity itself expired, and the Christian church that survived these terrible events found itself living in a 'modern' world that we call the Middle Ages, which in its turn has now vanished. Was that ancient world not ended? And were those Christians who by resurrection light foresaw its end wrong to treat it as after all a contingent realm? No more than we are wrong to regard our own technological-nuclear age—and the very earth it threatens—as a set of fragile contingencies that may not last long. Finally, then, the resurrection is:

iii. *A transformation of human life*—It is not only that the resurrection of Jesus Christ from the dead is the vindication of the justice of God and hence our "acquittal by resurrection" (M. Barth, 1964)—the first and proper concern of the anastatic strand of Christian ethics; it is not only that *and* the consequent re-vision of the social structures, seen now in resurrection light—and hence the power to construe in a new and liberating way the social strand of Christian ethics; it is both of the above and another still—the transformation of life in the body itself, here and now, and thus a revolution in the bodily ethics of strand one. "I am the resurrection *and the life*," says the Fourth Gospel's Jesus at the tomb of Lazarus (11:25 RSV). "Christ Jesus," says 2 Timothy, "abolished death and brought *life* and immortality to light through the gospel" (1:10 RSV). What kind of "life" is understood in these pronouncements? The central idea is best seen, though in an exaggerated and heretical form, in the doctrine held by Paul's wayward flock at Corinth. Some there said that "there is no resurrection of the dead" (1 Cor. 15:12 RSV). Biblical scholars point out that these were not sceptical twentieth-century rationalists who believed too little; they were credulous first-century fanatics who believed too much. What others would have called baptism and new birth, they apparently called "resurrection"; thus they had no reason to look for a future resurrection in the end time; the fullness of eternity was theirs *now:* "Already you are filled!" Paul sarcastically chides them (4:8) (J. M. Robinson, 1981:14-16). They abolished the tension of what Paul taught as the Christian life in favor of a competitive ladder-climb into spiritual excellence; on that individualistic path the stern conditions imposed on Paul and other Christians by life in the body (our strand one) could simply be shrugged off (1 Cor. 4:8-13): It was easy to be 'perfect.' With disdain for the bodily strand went disdain for the social strand also: For these Corinthians, it no longer mattered where you were in society or community or in what circumstances your Christian vocation had begun, or in general what your *story* was (7:17-24), or how your conduct now might affect your fellow Christians' stories (6:9-20); everything was eschatological.

Now the interest for us in this is not the evidence it provides of crypto-gnosticism at Corinth (J. M. Robinson, 1981); rather it is the fact that the fanatics' views were so close to Paul's that he could not simply dismiss them! Indeed, on the positive side, they were correct: There *was* in baptism identification with Christ's resurrection (Rom. 6:4f.); there *was* a higher

Christian gnosis or wisdom (1 Cor. 1:20–2:3); the law was in a certain sense *not* necessary (1 Cor. 6:9-20). What Paul had to do was to set opposite each of these truths a corrective, further truth: We are still in the body with its humbling limitations (4:8-13); Christ is risen, but we await the general resurrection (15:12-58); individual liberty and gifts must be harmonized into solidarity in rule-shaped community (chs. 12–14); baptism and the eucharistic meal are not magical sacraments but corporate ethical practices (chs. 10–11). Paul does not deny the ecstatic claim of the resurrection upon Christian morality; he seeks to place that claim in a fully biblical frame of body and social ethics. How could he deny it—his own Christian life had begun in a conversion or commissioning whose center was the bright appearance and voice of the risen Lord—a fact his readers knew so well that he barely mentions it in 1 Corinthians (15:8).

The battle Paul fought and won was to *keep conversion*, understood not as a mere change of religious or doctrinal allegiance but as the transformation of the human self in all its spheres or strands, *squarely in the center* of the Christian Way. Many since Paul's day have sought to evade this consequence by limiting the transformation experience to a few exceptional individuals, or shunting it to Christian groups said to be marginal or socially dispossessed (heretics, dissenters, baptists, pentecostals), or subordinating transformation to the orderly rhythms of an organized church life with formalized 'initiation rites' and 'confirmations' and 'ordinations' and 'consecrations.' Yet the hot breath of the Spirit blows, the liberating air of the resurrection rushes in, the rumor of the new that comes in Christ breaks the old molds of convention time and time again, not merely in the so-called marginal churches and social strata (though perhaps especially there) but within the high structures of ecclesiastical convention and Christian social control as well.

Just as the second strand of Christian ethics declares that our lives find their meaning through our share in Christ's story, and as the first strand declares that the life so lived is a life in the body with its earthy basis, so the resurrection strand makes it inescapably clear that the story is to be marked with incalculable surprises, and that our lives belong to Christ just in terms of the surprise endings and turns that mark the resurrection Way. In Christian perspective, everybody (and every community?) needs at least one such transforming conversion. For it is in these transformations, be they evolutionary or cataclysmic, singular or cumulative, that the resurrection of Jesus Christ lays its power upon the life of the believer. Since the individual side of this claim is made most explicit in the sign of Christian baptism, it is to the moral nature of baptism that we now turn.

c. *Baptism as the inception of resurrection morality*—Those who attend to baptism mainly as it is practiced in the Christian world today may well suspect the integrity of a section linking baptism and ethics, for the present rite seems most often sentimental, or magical, or merely perfunctory. Yet according to the sources, in the apostolic church it was not so, and we must try to understand the moral significance of baptism as it appeared there, and only then inquire about the moral significance (and the morality!) of current practices.

John's baptism, in which Christian baptism was grounded, was an eschatological rite—that is, it admitted its candidates to the number of those who avowedly awaited the coming Messianic Day John foretold (Mark 1:1-8 and parallels). Such a hopeful stance, however, required concrete μετάνοια ("repentance" or "conversion"—neither word alone seems an adequate translation) on the part of each candidate, and the baptism was administered with reference to this profound life-change, giving dramatic visibility in the waters of the Jordan River to the candidate's turnabout (Mark 1:5). At the same time, John's baptism was a prayer for (εἰς) forgiveness of the sin that repentant converts confessed, and the rite was practiced without distinction upon both Jews and Gentiles (unlike Jewish proselyte baptism, which was for Gentile converts only)—all who came forward were baptized; among these sinners one day there came also Jesus of Nazareth!

Primitive Christian baptism retained and developed each of these ideas: The eschatological community of the baptized becomes now the community of the risen Lord awaiting his final return; the association with the candidate's μετάνοια and God's forgiveness is deepened by its link with the redemption achieved by Jesus of Nazareth. There are, however, some new notes in the Christian sign: the baptism of Jesus provides the narrative prototype for the baptism of each disciple, and baptism is now "into Jesus' name" (Acts 19:5), or later, into the triune name (Matt. 28:19). And finally, in a series of striking metaphors the New Testament writers associate baptism with the Holy Spirit and the new life that comes to each disciple of Christ; these 'metaphors of salvation' are so forceful that they will give rise later on, in the patristic era, to interpretations of baptism as "mystery" or "sacrament" (neither term is used of baptism in the New Testament) effectual prior to and apart from faith (a view opposed as late as Tertullian, *De Bapt.*, xviii).

The question of how baptism 'works' can only be dealt with adequately in connection with a full discussion of the prophetic and remembering signs in Scripture and church and their relation to grace, faith, and God's word (bibliography in Beasley-Murray, 1962; Wainwright, 1980:482-84; cf. also McClendon, 1966 and 1967); for the present the point is to note the richness of the New Testament metaphors. Baptism is a putting on (like a garment) of Christ (Gal. 3:27); it "saves" as "an appeal to God for a clear conscience, through the resurrection of Jesus Christ" (1 Pet. 3:21 RSV; cf. Kittel, 1964:II, 688); it is incorporation into the divine unities which faith embraces (Eph. 4:5); it is the counterpart of the Spirit's overwhelming, pentecostal presence (Acts 1:5ff.); it is a bath to wash away sins (Acts 22:16); the acquiring of a new name (1 Cor. 1:12-15 with Acts 19:5 and Matt. 28:19); and the burial of the believer, who having been put to death with Christ is both buried with him and, rising again, anticipates the believers' resurrection while celebrating Christ's accomplished one (Rom. 6:4-11; Col. 2:12).

The moral significance of these dramatically enacted metaphors is threefold. First, baptism points to, refers to, the life-story of Jesus himself. His baptism had been his commitment and ordination to the cause of the kingdom of God, his first deliberate step on that way. Confessing his sin, the sinless one had declared his identification with sinners, and set out on the way of redemption. Now in his or her own baptism, each believer claims that story, appropriates it, accepts Jesus' story as this believer's identity-narrative. Second, however, baptism focuses the candidate's own life-story: as a brother or sister takes this step the narrative of his or her own life is brought out of obscurity, laid before God in repentance and faith, and decisively turned into God's new path in the company of the community. In baptism, one's own conversion is acknowledged and oriented. Third, these two narratives, Christ's and the candidate's, are brought by baptism into connection with one another in the company of all the saints. When one is baptized, the reference is both to Jesus' story and to one's own story—and these are in baptism confessed to be *one* story. Thus the identification with Jesus as the incarnate, obedient, crucified, and risen one is not merely legal or mystical; it is a *narrative* identification (just as in the resurrection, Jesus' identification with God consists in a narrative linking of his life with the life of God—Rom. 1:4). Here, then, the baptist vision is at work: "this is that"—our baptisms recapitulate and so claim his resurrection in our own lives afresh.

What, then, can the life of the baptized community be but a sharing in the eschatological freedom of the risen Lord? Hence the New Testament language that describes the situation of the baptized displays a daring intensity and exaltation. A single example must suffice: in three Pauline Epistles, passages appear linking baptism with the breakdown in Christ of the classic social and natural barriers that separate Greeks from Jews, slaves from free men, and males from females—all the baptized are one (or one body) in Christ (Gal. 3:27f.; 1 Cor. 12:12f.; Col. 3:9-11). Probably the rhythmic saying behind these passages ("neither . . . neither . . . neither") was a baptismal formula, older than that of Matthew 28:19f., declaring with performative force the character of the realm into which the baptized were accepted (Betz, 1979:181-201; Lohse, 1971:136-53). This was a new era in time, inaugurated by Jesus' resurrection, in which the ordinary distinctions of creation (male-female) and of society (Greek-Jew; slave-free) were superseded because unity in the body of Christ took their place.

Certainly these were Paul's own convictions. His ministry to the Gentiles constituted an assault on the Jew-Gentile barrier. Onesimus the slave is remanded to Philemon the owner—but as a beloved brother "both in the flesh and in the Lord"—and not as a slave (Philem. 15-17 RSV). And Paul's own practice of ministry, though of course it lacks the careful arrangements about bishops, elders, deacons, and the like that later, less gifted missionaries would fret over, accepts the shared ministry of women who lead in worship, preach, and even have suitable costume prescribed for these functions (1 Cor. 11:2-16; on textual and literary grounds, I take the gagging of women in 14:33b-36 as a later insertion). Paul also assigns equal value and responsibility to women and men, both in marriage and in singleness (Scroggs, 1972).

Robin Scroggs, in an important essay, has shown that it is easy to underestimate the radical stance of Paul (and of earliest Christianity more generally) regarding women and men because his words have become stale through familiarity: "if any one is in Christ, he is [or there is] *a new creation*; the old has passed away, behold, *the new has come*" (2 Cor. 5:17 RSV). When we read Paul through the lens of the deutero-Pauline letters and of traditional later Christianity, we fail to see how socially radical the original message was. In the body of Christ, pagan (and Jewish) social arrangements were dissolved. The one thing Paul was not willing to do in his defense of the equal value of all in the one body was to obliterate the factual male-female (and other) distinctions that were being revalued. (In this regard, says Scroggs, the Gnostics wanted to go further, and we shall have to explore that Gnostic urge below.) In present terms, Paul was not willing to *reduce* Christian ethics to the third strand by denying the contributions of nature and of storied community to the Christian situation—he was not willing to reject strands one and two in order to capitalize the resurrection strand. On the contrary, the New Testament more generally, expanding its baptismal teaching from the primitive resurrection core, often invokes the first committed step, which is baptism, as a basis on which also to require the virtues (and forbid the vices) that accompanied the full scope of Christian practice (Col. 3:1–4:6; perhaps 1 Peter). They used baptism exactly to summon converts to a socially accountable newness of life.

Now where are *we* in the story? What of the moral status of today's baptism? In the Protestant and Catholic churches of the Constantinian compromise, baptism has become (usually) infant baptism, so that what was the decisive first step of discipleship has been reduced instead to a mere religious mining-claim staked out on the territory of babes in arms. Liturgically, this practice is "always . . . an abnormality" (Dix, 1946:38), but theologically it has found a host of defenders and defenses. Christian ethics, however, must deplore the intrinsic failure of infant baptism: It becomes a rite neither responsive on the candidate's part or responsible on the administrator's. Meanwhile, the churches of the baptist vision have mostly responded to the same societal pressures that generated the Constantinian practice, making of the great death-and-resurrection remembering sign a mere cultural symbol, administered in young childhood to every child who displays (often sincere) religious feeling, and who seeks (as would be normal in childhood's latency period) to emulate admired older persons and to rival other children of the church. So in baptist churches baptism is admittedly responsive; still it often fails to be responsible. The recovery of New Testament baptism is surely the business of the whole church, but exactly because of the baptist vision it is in a special sense the *unaccomplished* business of the sharers of that vision; meanwhile, moral theology must have the courage to tell the truth about the radical sign both to Constantinians and to baptists.

Perhaps a beginning might be made if every church were to teach its people that New Testament baptism was neither a benign welcome to human existence, nor a rite of passage to adolescence, nor a viaticum offering safe conduct to an afterlife, but rather was the commissioning of those who by resurrection light took up the way of Jesus of Nazareth—the way of the cross—when they did in fact take it up! If the teaching church dared make that difference known, the learning church, that is, we ourselves, might ask with new meaning: "What is to keep me from being baptized?" (Acts 8:36 TEV).

2. Why the Resurrection Strand Cannot Stand Alone

a. *Contextualism*—Resurrection ethics is necessary, though for Christians it is not sufficient. That has been claimed; now we must see how it is so, and the best way of seeing will be to give a particular example of insufficiency. One of the best-known Christians ethicists in America is Paul L. Lehmann (1906–), now retired from Union Theological Seminary in New York. His work reflects a development from mid-century Protestant neo-orthodoxy, through the flowering of 'contextual' or 'situation' ethics, to the appearance in the 1960s of (North) American Liberation Theology with its distinctive emphases. Lehmann's stance through these changes, however, has been a firm commitment to what is here called the third strand of Christian ethics. From first to last, his ethics is eschatological. That worthy commitment, together with what I judge to be his failure to incorporate the other strands, will illustrate the claim that the resurrection strand cannot stand alone today any more than it could in the Gnosticism of ancient times.

It should not be supposed that this presentation of Lehmann is meant to diminish the importance of his work. On the contrary, he is chosen here exactly because the considerable care and skill with which he proceeds clearly brings out the significance of his stance; he is the best of his kind. For Lehmann, the starting point of ethics is revelation; however, this does not mean primary reference to the biblical response to Christ's life-death-resurrection; rather it means attention to what God is doing *now* in the world "to make (and keep) human life human." In Lehmann's basic *Ethics in a Christian Context* (1963), the Christian community (*koinonia*) is said to be important because it is the "foretaste and sign" of this divine activity. But history cannot fully contain the revelation of the triune God: "the ethical reality of the second Adam [Christ] points intrinsically toward the ethical reality of the second Advent." Christ will come again with power and glory—this will be "the final and radical transvaluation of the whole created and historical order" (Lehmann, 1963:122). This anticipated consummation casts its light backward upon every present ethical decision. So Christian conduct *cannot* be generalized or expressed in terms of law or rules; instead, doing the will of God means responding to what God is doing, "bereft of every prudential calculation, every motivational concern" (1963:123), as the Christian aims at a 'maturity' that has no need for a community of character or virtue (strand two), far less for the drives and needs of embodied selfhood (strand one).

How does this ethical eschatology work out in practice? A first answer is provided in the 1963 volume. There Lehmann gives a series of examples or 'situations' in which contextual ethics shows its divergence from an ethic of "principles" or an "absolutist" ethics (1963:128-45). Concretely, he presents four cases (a small enough number for a 380-page volume), one of which is never quite stated. In each case, a dilemma or problem is produced, and the easy but unsatisfactory solution of the "absolutist" is considered, followed by Lehmann's contextualist answer. The four are the sale of a (used?) car, the case of a woman dying of cancer, the "difficult and delicate" area of sexual experience (in which no answer is ever explicitly presented), and the question of participation in a war. What is striking is that in each of these cases, Lehmann fudges his answer, and in each the fudge is systematically connected with his reliance upon a purely anastatic ethics.

Take the case of the car sale. The problem Lehmann raises is how much (or what) the seller must tell the buyer. Contrary "absolutist" answers are proposed: either full disclosure, or say nothing at all (caveat emptor). One might expect that a "contextual" answer would discuss the need for the seller to adapt his disclosure to the capacity of the buyer to understand the information provided (since a dishonest seller sometimes uses only facts in order to do the dirty work), or the likely temptation of the seller to misrepresent the car in his own immediate interest. But Lehmann does not discuss these. Instead he says that the contextualist answer consists in "the living word"—that word which "holds the concrete situation together," that is, "makes it possible for human beings to be open *for* one another and *to* one another." When such verbal intimacy occurs, seller and buyer "are linked to each other as human beings," so that "they do not merely transact business." And it is "this *human* factor in the interrelationships of men which is the definitely *ethical* factor"—that is, in this intimacy, God is acting to make and keep human life human (1963:129f.).

Certainly it is a warm, satisfying, humane (if not a distinctively Christian) moment when a seller and buyer of a car evoke one another's human sympathies; we might suppose the situation has acquired pastoral, even fatherly or friendlike qualities. Who can quarrel if that happens? But note the fudge: This openness, Lehmann says, permits human beings to be open for and to one another—that is, *to tell the truth* about the car sale. But what being truthful here consists in has to do with the further question: What constitutes honest disclosure? Has the odometer gone around 100,000 once? Has there been a crash that has warped the frame? Is this the original paint, or a cheap cover-up job? Humane warmth or friendliness that skips over such questions is just what gives used car salesmen a bad name; therefore a humaneness that evokes such warmth still has to confront the question of what constitutes truthfulness appropriate to the practice of salesmanship. Warmth cannot take the place of truth.

Yet this is not a special fudge for a special case; something like it comes through in *every* case that Lehmann presents. The problem in his dying patient case is whether to lie when the patient asks if she will recover. What does telling the truth consist in here, asks Lehmann? "Absolutists" might divide, he suggests, between counseling a therapeutic lie and telling the harsh but honest truth; Lehmann, however, recommends talking with the patient about reliance on Jesus Christ "when in the next days and weeks the going gets hard." This seems a credible procedure as presented, but it either amounts to avoiding the patient's question (on one interpretation of the pastoral solution Lehmann offers) or telling the honest truth indirectly (is that what "when the going gets hard" means?). So as before, the fudge consists either in avoiding the problem of practice that Lehmann himself has raised, or in answering it in so roundabout a way that its problematic nature is obscured. That there is a problem arises from the fact that in life-or-death situations, either Christians have a commitment to being truthful with one another or they do not; to put it in strand-two terms, either the practice of Christian friendship evokes the virtue of honesty here or it does not, and to say which is to say something important about the Christian moral life. Yet Lehmann will not say. He produces the same kind of fudge again when on the question of participation in war he rejects both the nonviolent and the just war positions in favor of (what can only be a *principle* of) *ambiguity* (1963:140-44).

The one exception to the fudging policy may be the "sexual experience" case—the one he never concretizes into a particular story or experience. Here the dilemma seems to be, Shall I have sexual intercourse apart from (or prior to an intended) marriage? Now there is no fudge, because Lehmann frankly favors "sexual nonconformity," which in the United States in 1963 would still, though marginally, have meant, as Lehmann gingerly puts it, that "the sexual act is loosed from the marriage criterion" and instead is "anchored . . . under conditions of trust and fulfillment" (1963:137). This is finally forthright, and thus no fudge, but like the fudged cases, it achieves its result by abstracting both from the human structures of the social strand (where "trust" might indeed have found the communal practices capable of evoking and sustaining it over an extended period of time) and also from the organic data of the bodily strand (notably from the link, unmentioned by Lehmann, between copulation and procreation; that is, the link between the sexual drive he fleetingly recognizes and the babies he leaves out altogether).

In all these cases, the common element is the systematic identification of the ethical moment in Christian life with an 'eschatological' (or at least ecstatic) event or choice or charismatic act or word—the *evoked trust* of the car buyer, the *inspired* pastoral word to the patient, the *choice* of going (or not going) to war, the *"running of the risk"* of sexual *"nonconformity."* Or rather, it is the identification of these free-floating moments, together with the systematic refusal to link them back to the moral elements of the bodily and social strands, that constitutes the consistent, but consistently flawed, element in Lehmann's ethics.

It must be clear from what has been said before that the criticism of Lehmann here is addressed neither to his Christian particularism (his understanding of norms that apply to Christians alone), nor to his third-strand basis (a basis also occupied, as we saw in Chapter Two, by John Howard Yoder). Rather it is addressed to his failure to provide an 'incarnation' in ongoing lived experience for the ecstatic choices and moments of an eschatological ethics. And this is ironic, since it seems just parallel to the criticism he so frequently (and with some justice) aims at baptist and other experiential types—our failure to bring individual salvation experience into concrete relation with ongoing Christian living (1963:57f.; 155f.). Is sauce for the goose not sauce for the gander? However, there is another chapter in Lehmann's theological development, in which he does seem to give way to the urge to make concrete identification between moments of "transfiguration" and enduring historical patterns. But this can best be discussed under the heading of Liberation Theology.

b. *A Liberation Theology*—It would be inappropriate here to turn aside for a general or schematic survey of the many varieties of theological ethics that shelter under the umbrella of "Liberation Theology." That survey might include as well the German movement called "Political Theology," with its deeper roots in Marxian, Hegelian, Enlightenment, and

French revolutionary thought, and the contribution these have made to the South American theological scene. More-over, appreciation of the special South American situation would also require the assessment of a historical heritage vastly different from that of the rest of the world. The intellectual history of South America includes no Protestant Reformation, no Puritan revolution, no Scottish Enlighten-ment, no 'American' revolution (the Bolivar episodes had a quite different function than the events of 1776). It is thus a stranger to the sweeping cultural, religious, and political changes these 'northern' factors have induced. Instead, the South American heritage is the state-and-church policies of the Conquistadores, and behind these, the Constantinian culture of late medieval southern Europe. On the other hand, in North America "Liberation Theology" has served as a motto-name for the most widely varied ideological and cultural move-ments, including some of the legitimate liberal-Protestant heirs of the Social Gospel—and some of their more conserva-tive counterparts as well. So what is said here cannot be fairly taken as a critique of all Liberation theologians, except in the degree to which they share the methods and commitments of the later Paul Lehmann—as some do!

Lehmann's Liberation (or Revolution) Theology can best be seen as a development of his earlier contextual ethics. Just as in the earlier work, mundane morality is discounted in favor of what we have here called the "ethical moment"—the moment when the car seller and buyer 'become human' for one another and are then open to the truth, or the moment when the sexual subject decides to "risk unconventionality," or when the draftee decides to go (or not go) to war, and thus each participates via that moment in "the ethical"—so in the later political theology there is a moment of transfiguration, when politics is lifted above the mundane, and God's action to make human life human is revealed. If we can find what Lehmann considers to be the political moment of transfiguration, we will be at the ethical center of his Liberation Theology. Then we will be able to ask afresh about the viability of this almost purely anastatic approach.

The idea of transfiguration comes from the numinous event depicted in Mark 9:2-8 and parallels, in which "after six [or eight] days," Jesus with three followers ascends a high mountain and is "transfigured" before them, his garments becoming intensely white "as no fuller on earth could bleach them." Elijah and Moses then appear, and discuss with Jesus "His departure [i.e., the cross], which he was to accomplish at Jerusalem" (Luke 9:31 RSV). Lehmann argues that the settings of this account in the Gospels, together with the language used, are the evangelists' way of showing this event as a meaningful commentary upon the political dimension of Jesus' ministry: Jesus as the preacher of human liberation has challenged the Palestinian authorities, both Roman and Jewish; he is effectively allied with the Zealots. Yet the transfiguration shows that Jesus' revolution will transcend the Zealots' position, or rather transfigure it; and this transfiguration is realized in the subsequent events in Jerusalem. Lehmann notes that Jesus deliberately avoids violence to the end—but there is more to be said about that (1975:ch. 7).

Thus the transfiguration, as a pointer, provides the clue to political theology today: *Revolutions* are "what God is doing to keep human life human"; like the transfiguration, they are signs of "a divinely appointed new and freeing and fulfilling human order" (1975:127). Revolutions are the *Transfiguration of Politics*. And within revolutions, the moment of truth is reached (Lehmann does not shrink from revolutionary logic here) in the eruption of *violence*. Violence is not good in itself, but in biblical perspective its "human and operational meaning" is changed; it becomes the apocalyptic moment in which God's will is realized for and by revolutionaries (1975:259, 262).

Since we will discuss the Christian morality of violence, nonviolence, and peace in Chapter Eleven, let it suffice here to point out that Lehmann is not, like James Cone, justifying violence as a "lesser evil" (Cone, 1969:145), nor is he like Jacques Ellul acknowledging that violence is a necessary feature of the world—to be necessarily opposed by Christians (Ellul, 1969:129f.); rather he is *celebrating* revolutionary violence as the apocalyptic ethical moment of Christian politics—a view which may find no adequate antecedent in Christian history later than the Crusades of the Middle Ages.

It must be noted, however, that even a romantic celebration of revolutionary violence compels its author to enter the concrete strand of social ethics, taking a stand on the worldly issues that confront the Christian in this age. For Lehmann, this is expressed by a series of biographical and historical

sketches of modern revolutionary leaders, from Marx to Che
Guevara, including (somewhat oddly) the consistently nonviolent Martin Luther King, Jr. (Lehmann, 1975:110-228). Yet
these biographies do not answer the questions that haunt
Lehmann's ethical project from beginning to end. His
frequently quoted motto is that the goal of social ethics is "to
make human life human." But what is the nature of the human
nature that God creates and intends to redeem (since God's
purpose is to make human life *human*)? And what is the
structure of human society such that a Christian community
(κοινωνία) can provide the context of ethical reflection? With
these root questions unanswered, in line with his general
indifference to strands one and two, Lehmann's ethics
remains radically incomplete.

3. How the Strands Work Together in Christian Morality

If we are to improve upon Lehmann's example, two tasks
remain in this chapter: We must show, even if only in outline
or by example, how the resurrection strand turns back upon
and fulfills the hunger of the bodily strand; and we must show
how it fulfills the structure and satisfies the hunger of the
social strand of Christian ethics. Since in a larger sense these
are the tasks of this entire chapter with the two that follow it, it
will be appropriate to meet the demand here simply by an
illustrative argument and a historic example.

a. *John Cobb's return to the bodily strand*—An illustrious
example of a moral theology based in the third strand that
returns to incorporate the first is found in the theological ethics
of Process theologian John B. Cobb, Jr. (1925–) (McClendon,
1978:73-75). Regrettably, there is a terminological hiatus that
we must cope with in order to present Cobb's view: he uses the
words "moral" and "ethical," not as in the present work to
refer to the Christian life in all its dimensions, but in a nar-
rower way to refer only to the (strand-two?) realm in which we
make moral "decisions" on principle, shouldering responsibility and (often) incurring guilt in the bargain (Cobb, 1973:ch. 8;
1976:9f.). For this reason, Cobb's narrow "ethical" realm is one
we should all wish to escape, if only we could.

Cobb thinks we can. There is another realm, and this, the realm of "spiritual existence," is just what Christianity provides (though not Christianity only, there are other paths, other religions). The human psyche, Cobb believes, may be organized or structured in any one of a variety of ways. In one very primitive way, emotion provides the center, or "structure," of our existence. But without discarding emotion, human beings may be organized instead around reasoning; their "structure of existence" is now said to be "rational." Perhaps this is best represented by ancient Greek civilization at its Socratic flower. The Hebrew prophets, on the other hand, centered everything on the human will, which subordinated feeling and thinking to itself in the way of life Cobb calls "prophetic existence." Thus the different human civilizations (Cobb gives many other examples—1967:chs. 3–7) actually represent different psychological structures, even different 'varieties' of *homo sapiens*. Of these several kinds of selfhood, the prophetic or "ethical," focusing upon the will, might have seemed the highest possible, but it encounters special problems; these are sharply expressed in the strictures against "Pharisaism" in the Gospels. Its chief glory is to have been the structure from which a still higher sort of existence was born: from prophetic (or "Pharisaic") existence there emerged the kind of selfhood exhibited by Jesus of Nazareth and by Paul (cf. Romans 7). In the latter, the self as *will* is no longer dominant, but a new spiritual self appears that can use the will as its agent, just as at an earlier stage of mankind, will used intellect (and at a still earlier stage, intellect used emotion). In the stage occupied by Jesus, the self is not identified primarily as intellect or as will, but as *spirit*, so Cobb calls this stage "spiritual existence" (1975b).

Jesus' "structure of existence" was spiritual—a fact that requires Cobb's full Christology fully to explicate (1975a:ch. 8). Briefly, we can say that the divine power of creativity and Jesus of Nazareth's human life story were present together in such a manner that Jesus was liberated to take the way of the kingdom of love without being hindered by "Pharisaic" legalism and guilt. (In our terms, he had transcended strand two.) In the resurrection, Jesus' liberation was transmitted to his followers, notably Paul, giving them ground for hope that enabled them to share in the new structure of existence. Thus in our turn we, too, are permitted to share in spiritual existence.

One feature of Cobb's account of spiritual existence (or, as it might be named here, strand-three-centered Christianity) is central for us: The resurrection appearances made possible for the disciples a new awareness of God's nearness. This nearness was the phenomenon of the Spirit. God at Pentecost came to be known as empowering Presence, just as earlier, through the teaching of the earthly Jesus, God had come to be known as the heavenly Father. But this new gift of the Spirit opened for the disciples a new quality of life—a freedom from repression or suppression of the psychic forces that constitute the human personality. So there was in early Christianity a return to the archaic contents of the self (the return of strand one!) that Cobb believes had marked a much earlier stage of human existence, but had almost been lost in the development of civilization and religion. This "return of the repressed" was evidenced in early Christian experience. There was "a sense of release and refreshment, the possibility of feeling whole and at peace" (Cobb, 1967:118). The overt sign of this recovery was paranormal phenomena—visions, miracles of healing, ecstatic behavior such as speaking in tongues—constituting a new version of life in the body.

There was, of course, the danger that such an archaic reversion would mean the loss of prophetic (i.e., strand-two) existence. But for the young Christian community, this did not happen. Instead, the early Christians retained the high "ethical" quality Jesus had inherited from the prophets, but added to it the resurrection elan *and* renewal of psychic-bodily existence; that is, to strand two they added the morality granted by strands three and one, all in a new key that Cobb, as we have noted, calls "spiritual existence" (1967:ch. 10).

To this lively account we have to add two sobering notes, one from Cobb, one of our own. Cobb regretfully adds that historic Christianity did not retain the full, adventurous stage of "spiritual existence" as exemplified by primitive Christianity. Paul certainly attained the new level, and others did so as well (Cobb, 1975a:ch. 6). But in the main, the level of "spiritual existence" reached by Christians over the centuries has been closer to Pharisaism or prophetic existence—a self-conscious ethical state that is keen on Niebuhrian "total responsibility," with the attendant moral liabilities of pride and guilt, but without the freedom and openness of Jesus of Nazareth. That attainment remains a project for Christianity's future (Cobb, 1975b:109; 1975a:chs.12, 13, 16; 1976).

To this caution, we add our own. Cobb's splendid breadth (perhaps greater than any other theologian discussed in this volume save Jonathan Edwards) nevertheless retains a curious blind spot regarding the structures of the social strand. His references to these strand-two structures seem to make them necessarily self-defeating. For example, he offers the illustration of a woman whose self-identity is tied to her desires for a home and family. Then she gains freedom by "disidentifying" herself from that role (Cobb, 1977:5). Will she now have a new role, say as a disciple of Jesus Christ? No, on Cobb's view, her task is to become *free from all roles*—though free to pursue any. But is a self shorn of all roles a philosophically coherent idea? Is it not very like the old substantial monadic self that Cobb as a Whiteheadian rightly rejects? To put the objection more generally: Cobb's resurrection ethics would more nearly fulfill its own role if it found a central place for the structured life of the Christian church, with its practices, its virtues, and its (ongoing) story in which redeemed men and women could find new lives, new identities—and new roles.

b. *Koinonia at Schleitheim*—Therefore let us note, finally, a chapter in Christian history (Blanke, 1961; Estep, 1975) in which a radical believers' community did find a way to develop resurrection ethics into a second-strand social fabric. Conventional church history, when it adverts to the sixteenth-century baptist movement, has typically recited the tragedy at Muenster. Indeed Muenster, like Jonestown, Guyana (1978), shows how the baptist vision can be perverted, just as the Crusades, the Inquisition, the Thirty Years' War, and the Salem witchcraft trials show how the Catholic and Protestant traditions can be perverted. But an earlier and more authentic picture of baptists—perhaps the very earliest communal picture—comes not from Muenster but from the gathering of radical Christians on a mountainside near Schleitheim, a Swiss-Austrian border town, in February, 1527.

Here was the situation: In the preceding decade, a religious and theological tsunami had raced across Europe. Luther at Wittenberg and Zwingli at Zürich were set afloat by this wave, but so were Capito and Bucer at Strasbourg, Hubmaier at Waldshut, Oecolampadius at Basel, and a host of others across the continent. In the wider upheaval there were some—Grebel, Blaurock, Manz, Hubmaier, Sattler, Denck, Haetzer, and more—who realized that the old European foundations were undermined. The return of some of them to believer's baptism was only a symptom of the new vision they hoped would replace the old, doomed pattern of religious life. Losing Christendom, they had found—Jesus Christ.

At first, the radicals had not been clear about the scope of their own movement. Were they, like Carlstadt at Wittenberg, to be mere goads for the conservatives? Or was there, as seemed possible to the "Swiss Brethren" at Zürich in '25, or to Sattler at Strasbourg in '26, to be a development of reform everywhere into the baptist vision—a total Christian revolution? Regretfully, by 1527 the banishment of Michael Sattler from Strasbourg and the execution by drowning of Felix Manz in Zürich had hardened the options. Disputations, formal theological debates which the radicals would continue to seek, had failed to move magisterial Reformers such as Luther and Zwingli. The latter displayed as strong an inclination to fall back on civil authority to enforce religious belief and practice as had the Old Church. Reformation Europe seemed as blindly committed as was Catholic Europe to *cuius regio, eius religio*. In these circumstances, some of the radicals (Denck, Haetzer) favored the accommodation dubbed "spiritualism": Since outward forms did not matter, the state church could without offense compel whatever practices it pleased. Indeed, some antinomians went even further: both conformity and immorality were matters of indifference; only the heart mattered.

In the circumstances of early 1527, the radical baptists of South Germany, Switzerland, and Austria were perplexed. Both magisterial conformity and spiritualism came down to the same thing—submitting the word of God to the power of the princes or prelates in each place. Should the radicals also submit? Or if not, what alternative was viable? Would theirs be an evanescent sixteenth-century idea, froth churned by the religious tsunami only to drift insubstantially away, or would they perforce (and sadly) become a 'sectarian' community—would the baptists, too, have a 'church'? Facing this unwelcome question, Michael Sattler and others adopted a method that was to have historic consequences—the *dialogue of those concerned*. They called a meeting for dialogue and decision, beginning on a day in February, near centrally located but quiet Schleitheim.

We have no first-hand report of that meeting; we do have the resultant documents—the 'constitution' of seven articles, the 'discipline,' and the covering letter—that summarized their work (Lumpkin, 1959:22-35; Estep, 1976:ch. 11; Yoder, 1973:ch. 2). From these we can infer the process of the Schleitheim meeting: (1) Participants met as equals; as a security measure, no names appear on the resultant documents, so the references are only to "brothers and sisters" (explicitly thus), to "sons and daughters of God," to "members of God." (2) In the dialogue, those who had favored the state-church compromise in one version or another gave way to those who reluctantly favored a separate, radical church; Yoder remarks that, perhaps uniquely in Reformation history, minds were changed in the course of a discussion! The baptist movement acquired at Schleitheim a free church ecclesiology and thereby survived to the present time. Their belief in communitarian discipline, Arnold Snyder has shown, was closely related to the earlier Benedictine tradition in which Michael Sattler had been formed. But Snyder hardly explores an element he notes is missing from the Benedictine pattern: the sense of eschatology already at hand (Snyder, 1984; cf. Haughton, 1980:ch. 7). (3) The tone of the meeting was dominated by the (quite realistic) sense of danger from the authorities, but also by this sense of eschatology already breaking in—by the ethics of the resurrection. Baptism, says a Schleitheim document, is for "all those who desire *to walk in the resurrection of Jesus Christ*" (Yoder, 1973:36; cf. Bender, 1961:96ff.). (4) Most important for present purposes, the dialogue process gave concrete expression to the *koinonia*-love that guided the conference, and that *koinonia*-love shaped the anastatic ethics of the movement into a social structure fitted for the "resurrection walk" to which they were committed.

The last idea can be expanded. Κοινωνία had been a central term for the community spirit of early Christianity. (Paul Lehmann's failure to develop this crucial insight, which he had correctly grasped (1963:45-56), is perhaps *the* false turn in his ethics.) Based on a stem meaning "shared" or "common," κοινωνία and cognates had been used by Paul, for example, of the *community* of believers with Christ (1 Cor. 1:9), of the *participation* that sacrificial meals implied in those who ate them (1 Cor. 10:18), of the *communion* in the blood and body of Christ in the eucharist (1 Cor. 10:16), of the church's *share* in

the contribution to poor Jewish believers (2 Cor. 8:4; 9:13), of
Titus' *partnership* in Christian service (2 Cor. 8:23), and of the
fellowship of the Holy Spirit (2 Cor. 13:14)—that is, the fact that
all the community shared in the indwelling Spirit. Κοινωνία
is used by the authors of Acts and 1 John as a general word for
the continuing *common love* of the apostolic church—for one
another, and for God (Acts 2:42; 1 John 1:3, 7). I believe it is the
most inclusive New Testament term for love, gathering up the
sense of the other words; in any case it is the characteristic term
for the new, shared love of those whose lives are remade by
the resurrection of Christ. It is *the* word for love in the anastatic
strand.

Michael Sattler and the "brothers and sisters" at Schleitheim
did not employ any Greek terms in what they composed there;
indeed, only once did they cite Scripture by chapter and verse
in the documents. But the *idea* of κοινωνία runs through their
texts. The key German term, as Yoder (1973:48, note 31) has
shown, is *Vereinigung,* translated "union," "reconciliation,"
"atonement," "fellowship." The conferees have been *reconciled* to Jesus Christ. This enables them to *join* in issuing the
Schleitheim articles, through a dialogue in which they have
been *united* in mind concerning baptism, ban, and bread,
concerning separation from evil (remember the incipient
antinomian sentiment), concerning shepherds of the church,
the sword of the world, and the swearing of the state's
oath—the Seven Articles. One senses at work in the drafted
document a theologian (though not a scholastic one) who
knew the power of words and had a poet's sensitivity to the
shadings of meaning a single word could bear. Doubtless that
poet-theologian was Michael Sattler himself. Like a great bell,
Vereinigung, κοινωνία, peals again and again through the
document, tocsin of the unity of sisters and brothers, herald of
the baptist way in the world there being reborn.

It remains only to point out that the content of the Articles
was the setting forth of a simple but effective structure for
church life understood as a *way* of life, focusing on just those
points that the old Constantinianism of the Roman South and
the new Constantinianism of the Reformed and Lutheran
North had made impossible. Ethically, this structure of
Schleitheim set the conditions for the free church, and if
Troeltsch is right about the larger scene, it was determinative
for the later free state and the Bill of Rights as well (1912*a*:II,

810-12). But these points go beyond the present argument, which is simply that a resurrection ethic contains a dynamic power to turn back into the social strand the energies of the resurrection of Jesus Christ from the dead. Schleitheim witnesses to the truth of that argument. These brothers and sisters loved life in the body as well, though most of them were not long to enjoy it. Their circumstances gave them little freedom to work out that side of their ethic—it is for us to supply their want, as they have supplied ours.

*   *   *   *   *

It is time to survey the ground gained in this chapter. The resurrection of Jesus Christ from death is at the center of Christian morality, providing a new ground, a new outlook, a new dynamism for followers of the Way. That this was true of the earliest disciples is the testimony of all the New Testament writings; that it must be true of today's disciples as well is the demand of any ethics that would be authentically Christian. As with the other strands, it is possible for theorists to distort, or overinflate, or suppress the resurrection strand; but that these moves are false to Christian morality itself is seen by the outcome of such moves. And in two classic instances, the ethics of contemporary moral theologian John Cobb and the moral achievement of sixteenth-century reformers with Michael Sattler, we have seen the power of the resurrection strand to reach out to a revitalization of other strands as well.

This means that for the Christian, life in the body cannot be understood in the way that it is for those untouched by the new that comes in Christ. For us, the embodied life is once again incarnation—the sharing of life in the flesh in continuity with all flesh, indeed with the organic world itself. Hence on one side of Christian experience there is the common lot of embodied selves in nature and in history, with all the sorrows, fears, and hopes to which flesh is heir. But on the other side, all this life is transplanted, rooted in new ground, by the resurrection of Jesus the Lord. It may be, as John Cobb says, that there is in this new life a "return of the repressed," so that Christians in every age have fresh contact with the psychic depths of their own being. The experience of pentecostal Christians in many churches seems to bear this out. The deeper truth, however, is that all of our life is changed by resurrection newness: Our delights now are tinted by the color of his presence, our guilt is redeemed from futility by his sharing it, our blame grows into the task of judging all things human in the light of his cross, and our attitude of forgiveness is shaped by one who lives to guarantee that we too, are forgiven (cf. Rom. 4:25–5:2).

As it is with the first strand, so it is with the second. Withdrawal can be no general strategy for Christian existence—this Way is not a way for escape into isolated community, but a way of witness by an engaged community. Now as in biblical days Christians live in interaction with the surrounding society of the 'principalities and powers,' engaging in many (though not all) of the practices of that society. Yet in resurrection light this becomes engagement with a difference. New Testament Christians often continued to serve as slaves—but they saw themselves as voluntarily doing so, so that the practice of slavery was transformed and ultimately abolished among Christians. Christians freed from Constantinian presuppositions may now and again be able to serve as leaders of cities, states, even nations—but not in every such capacity, since for them the practice of leadership is transformed into a way of service en route to a cross, not a way of power (Mark 10:42-45 and parallels). American Christians, like those in other lands, participate in our society's practice of marriage. But for us, the end is different (for example, marriage and procreation are said to be 'saving' relationships), and the partners have a full equality granted by Christ, whose liberation of marriage partners by his resurrection precedes and exceeds any liberation current mores can conceive. Thus the practice of marriage is transformed, and acquires a stability and permanence in Christian community that divorce laws cannot alter. And similarly with all the common practices: Military service may be no longer open to the followers of one who was crucified by soldiers, but peace-making service is (Chapter Eleven); homemaking is no longer governed by the competitive race for prestige in the suburbs, but is a skill nurtured for the sake of hospitality (Hauerwas, 1981); earning, buying, and selling are no longer for the sake of our own support (since we have a heavenly Father to provide for us), but are now to enable Christians to provide as good stewards for others' needs; suits in court are normally replaced by each voluntarily making room for the other; work is either work in some kingdom task, valuable in its own right, or it becomes instrumental 'tentmaking' to preserve the good name of the Christian witness.

In general, then, the policy of Christians facing the practices of their wider social context must fall into one of two patterns: Either they must for Christ's sake refuse to engage in those practices (and accept as the way of the cross the consequences of such refusal), or they must nonresistingly submit to them—yet submit for Christian reasons, with Christian intentions, by Christian means. But in the latter case the practice is for them thereby transformed, while in the former, it is Christian faith to believe that our very nonresistant refusal will mean the transformation of the oppressing powers, though only by way of the cross—and the resurrection. On the other hand, the central tasks of Christian social life are exactly those fit to be informed by resurrection ethics—the worship, evangelism, service, and mission of the church either live by resurrection light, or they do not deserve to live.

Dorothy Day

Some time during the winter of 1953–54, an FBI agent called on Dorothy Day at the *Catholic Worker* office in New York. His object, he said, was to seek information on a young friend of Miss Day's whose conscientious objector status was under scrutiny by the Bureau. How long had she known so-and-so? How did he describe his views on pacifism? Was he willing to defend himself? Ever willing to turn an interrogation into a dialogue, Dorothy Day responded with questions of her own about Christians and violence that must somehow have aroused Agent Daly's ire, for (as she told the story in the January, 1954, *Catholic Worker*) he suddenly jerked back his coat, exposed a revolver butt, and said, "I believe in defending myself!" the while patting the weapon—bravely, she said.

"I could not but think," Day went on as she concluded the little story in her column, "how brave a man, himself with his gun against us unarmed women and children hereabouts."

The incident found its way into Bureau files, where other similar (and therefore 'derogatory') information about Dorothy Day and the Catholic Worker Movement was accumulating during that era of Senator Joseph McCarthy and FBI director J. Edgar Hoover. Indeed, Hoover himself wrote the summary character sketch in her file. Dorothy Day, he said, was "a very erratic and irresponsible person." And he warned his agents to have nothing more to do with her, lest there be "further unfavorable comments regarding the Bureau" (R. Ellsberg, *Catholic Worker*, May and June, 1979;

Roberts, 1984:144f.). Most of the motifs that make up Dorothy Day's life are sounded in this little vignette from the 1950s. There is her playful, teasing way with a man, a way many had found provocative, even sexy. There is her capacity to turn the everyday—in this case, a routine inquiry—into drama, almost into a parable of the kingdom, for her readers. There is the lingering aroma of radicalism in this big, grey-haired woman in her late fifties, sitting in a shabby newspaper office, being questioned (and lectured) by the emissary of earth's strongest government, a government that nonetheless feared she might be dangerously seditious. And there is the puzzling disjunction between her consistent witness on the American scene during a half century of work, and the nevertheless quite understandable Hoover judgment that she was "erratic."

It is the business of this chapter to make sense of these diverse elements, to show how they fit together or come apart in the life story of Dorothy Day. Coming after one on the ethics of the resurrection, this chapter will turn on the thesis that her life can only be understood in its wholeness if seen in resurrection light. She lived by responding to the coming age as though it were (as Jesus said) already at hand; only by recognizing it for the eschatological life in time that it truly is can we make sense of Day's "erratic" life. "Her passion," as William D. Miller put it, "was a primal one. It was to end time because her longing was for eternity" (Miller, 1982:p. x).

Miller, by the way, is the author of the standard biography (1982) that will, with Dorothy Day's own published writing, be my ordinary source of information here except when otherwise noted. There is a crucial turn or conversion in this life (Statnick, 1983), as in the others examined, so my plan is to show first, her childhood and youth as preparation for what was to follow; second, a downward spiral that was partly unknown until Miller's revelatory book appeared; and third, her conversion and the discovery of the vocation that made Dorothy Day the conscience of her church, perhaps even the harbinger of its future, and in any case made her a focus of radical Christianity in the twentieth century. Some may be surprised at the choice of a devout Catholic as a biographical element in this baptist approach to Christian ethics; they should remember, though, that historically many have come to more or less baptist styles of thought and life while institutionally Catholic (and Day did this, as we shall see, complete with believer's baptism). Perhaps they should remember as well that on this way of thinking, no ecclesiastical definitions can cage God's truth.

1. *Natural Unhappiness*

Dorothy Day's was no "cradle Christianity," if there be such a thing. Her parents, John I. and Grace Satterlee Day, were 'Congregationalist' and 'Episcopalian,' respectively, but neither went to church, or provided religious training for their five children of any more formative sort than "Now I lay me . . . ." Moral convention, not passionate conversion, shaped this middle-class American household. Dorothy, the third child and first daughter, was born November 8, 1897, in Brooklyn, New York. Her father, John, was a race track journalist; he was taciturn, good at his craft, a dominant and 'responsible,' though hardly a companionable husband and father. His roots were in the established white citizenry of the upper South; skeptical and alienated, he hated, without understanding them, these Southern kinfolk he had abandoned. John Day drank, apparently to excess. Grace, the mother, was in many ways John's opposite: compliant, sociable, a graceful daughter of New York's Hudson River valley. She loved pretty clothes, good things, and the sort of life she could never afford, married to John. Conformity was Grace's household deity, though daughter Dorothy would not grow up to serve at its shrine. Liking her mother more, Dorothy was in many ways more like her father.

a. *California sojourn*—When Dorothy was six, the family moved to the San Francisco Bay area so that her father could take a job as sports editor of a city newspaper. Soon after their arrival, and while they were living in a rented furnished house in Berkeley, Dorothy's memory was stamped with poignant childhood happenings. One of these was 'working' in the garden, making dolls of the calla lilies and roses that grew there so plentifully, playing with dirt, listening to a brook, smelling the ubiquitous Berkeley geraniums. She would in her lifetime often be going to ground in ways that could evoke those memories. Another memory, though, was equally sensory and poignant: one rainy Sunday afternoon she and her sister Della climbed into the attic and found a Bible, which Dorothy, playing teacher, sat at a desk and read aloud. It was not its contents that she later recalled, but that she had known somehow that this was a holy book, the holy Word.

In Oakland, their next home, the Days lived next door to a family named Reed. The Reeds invited Dorothy to attend their Methodist Sunday school and church; they also liked to sing hymns, family style. Dorothy was impressed; under this influence she quickly became pious, though in a smug way, she thought later, and was alternately afraid of God and death and eternity. "I believed and yet was afraid of nothingness." *What* she believed was less clear, yet the memory, like that of the Bible in the attic, lingered even after a split with the Reeds brought an end to the Sunday school episode. The trouble was that Mrs. Reed had overheard eight-year-old Dorothy using 'bad' language in a fight with her brother, and had decided that she was unsuitable company for her own children (Day, 1938:20f.; 1952:19f.). So much for evangelism.

Bad language was not far removed from the shame that Dorothy learned to associate with another mysterious realm— that of sex. Little boys could be strangely attractive, and at least one of them wanted to "play house" with Dorothy in a sheltered recess in an Oakland field covered with big thistle plants. "House" was an attractive idea, but there was something wrong about it, Dorothy knew. Later she recalled refusing this ardent playmate. Still, there must have been a power in that memory that persisted, to be recalled so many years later.

The salient memory from Oakland days, though, was the earthquake, *the* earthquake of 1906. Dorothy was at home in bed, naturally enough, at 5:13 on an April morning. She was awakened by a deep rumbling sound; then the shock waves reached the house, tossing the ground and the house back and forth, and splashing the water in the household tower tank out back onto the house roof. Dorothy in her brass bed was inexplicably left alone while her parents snatched up the other children and ran outside. The bed skated to and fro, but Dorothy was unhurt and unafraid. Later, the memory of the earthquake coalesced with two others—one in which mother Grace fainted on the floor one night and father John had to carry her back to bed; the other, Dorothy's remembered fear of God, who became for her a great noise that grew louder and louder as she drifted off to sleep, those Oakland nights.

Certainly the earthquake was the voice of God for the Day family plans. Although Oakland was not destroyed, John Day's newspaper plant in San Francisco burned, and a few days after the quake he sold out and with his family boarded a train bound for a new home in Chicago.

b. *Chicago days*—So Chicago was to be Dorothy's home from eight until sixteen. It would be the place where the earlier epiphanies—of religion and of sex—would be encountered on a bigger scale, and where a new one, the misery of urban poverty and the class struggle, would become explicit alongside these other two. Poverty began with first-hand experience. John Day had no money; the job he hoped to get did not materialize, and instead he sat down at home with a nineteenth-century typewriter, a pack of cigarettes, and often enough, a glass of whiskey, to write an adventure novel. The novel never panned out, though he did sell a few short pieces. Grace Day was left to manage and to cope. So the family's residences were cheap, grim flats; food was spartan; their clothing was sewn by Grace—without a sewing machine. Dorothy, ashamed of dwelling above a saloon, would walk with the friends from her new school to within a block of her house, then bid them goodbye and turn in to the doorway of a prettier building she let her companions believe was her place.

John Day at last got a job, and gradually, the Days got their feet on the ground again. They moved to a better flat, north of the Loop, near Lincoln Park. But Dorothy did not lose her newly acquired sense of the stigma of poverty. After baby John was born, the fourteen-year-old sister was assigned the job of airing him with long walks in a baby carriage. She would go through the park, then west through slum districts where she could "watch the slatternly women and the unkempt children" of poverty, and could dream of someday doing something herself "toward making 'a new earth wherein justice dwelleth' " (Day, 1938:35). Before she finished high school, she would read Jack London's essays of social protest; later such thoughts of social concern would make her an atheistic Marxist, and later still, a Christian. For now, they just made her sad and lonely. The loneliness was persistent through her girlhood, although Dorothy's days were full enough of school and housework and reading, and she did not lack for companionship: her mother and younger sister Della as well as two older brothers and the baby at home.

Besides, now there was church. The rector of the neighborhood Episcopal church on Cottage Grove Avenue had enlisted
the Days soon after their arrival, and shortly all the children
attended, the boys becoming acolytes in due course. Dorothy
liked the Psalms and the old prayerbook prayers, as well as the
Benedictus and Te Deum. And when the family moved, there
was another Episcopal church on Fullerton Avenue, and
before long she was a "baptized and confirmed" communicant. She even read Wesley's sermons, and some "essays on
Jonathan Edwards"—one wonders which—though neither
reading was standard confirmation class fare for age fourteen!
The Episcopal phase ended before she completed high school;
Dorothy decided that "it was really better for the soul to bask
in the sun" rather than go to church services (Miller, 1982:28).

Two things did stick. One was a lifelong love of the
traditional liturgy, the 'common prayer' of the Western
church. The other was the discovery that the "holy book"
encountered first in the Berkeley attic had content as well as
mana. In high school, the journalist's daughter found her
favorite subjects were English, Latin, and Greek. In the course
of learning Greek (taught after school to a volunteer class by
Mr. Matheson, the Latin teacher), she discovered the Greek
New Testament, bought a copy for a dime in a used book store,
and studiously translated it. We are not told how far she got,
but if she began at the beginning, after only four chapters she
would have reached Jesus' Sermon on the Mount (Matthew
5–7). Once again, seed sown.

She also read, in school or more likely out, Algernon Charles
Swinburne's lyrical epic poem, *Tristram of Lyonesse*: "Love, that
is first and last of all things made . . . ." So she was fully
exposed to the old Western myth of love and death, of passion
unto death (Chapter Five, above), and that in the version of
Swinburne, whose sensual verse and anti-Christian stance
may have had something to do with her own rising scepticism.
It is even more likely that the poem's retelling of the romance
of Tristan (Tristram) and Iseult gave shape to her erotic
fantasies. Dorothy Day has been more frank than many an
autobiographer (though as we shall see, not quite frank
enough) to tell us about her loves: the rejected playmate under
the Oakland thistles, the blond boy in the Episcopal choir, and
then the stunning neighborhood musician, Armand Hand,
who conducted summer band concerts in Lincoln Park.

Nothing came of these early passions save within herself—her targets survived all unconscious of Cupid's darts. And her energies were duly diverted into the wonder of holding, petting, and caring for little John, a task that a weary Grace was glad to pass on to Dorothy and Della. Yet the tide of erotic energy did not recede, but as we will see, rose even higher.

c. *The University of Illinois*—These preparatory motifs (religious hunger, sexual passion, social concern) were held in suspense, though, during her brief college career, or rather two of them were. Sustained only by a $300 scholarship, Dorothy at sixteen entered the University of Illinois at Urbana, three hours' train ride from Chicago. As a student, she was desperately poor, often to the point of doing without food or heat. Perhaps her own need helped to focus her reading on the socialist and protest writers of her day as well as on her enduring favorites, the Russian novelists such as Turgenev, Tolstoy, Dostoevski. Her social consciousness kept her from making friends among the well-to-do students, with their sororities, their football games, and their silly chatter (silly, that is, to alienated and therefore sullen Dorothy). And her alienation from the church, which by now she had learned to think of as "smug" and full of hypocrites, in turn kept her from associating with the campus Y, where she might have found both friends and a job commensurate with her skills. As it was, she washed dishes, kept house for poorly paid faculty families, and sank further into gloom deepened by cold and hunger. Her studies were neglected; the high school honors student actually failed a course. On the other hand, she read avidly and widely on her own. With all else, she was, rather to her surprise, homesick. And certainly there were still no boyfriends to notice her.

The one bright spot was her interest in writing. It got her into a club, the Scribblers, and there she met her only college friends, Rayna and Raphe. But what friends! These two were engaged to each other, Jewish, sophisticated—and socially aware. They befriended Dorothy in such a way that the three became almost an innocent *ménage à trois*. They talked the days and nights away, went to hear the visiting campus speakers—Rose Pastor Stokes the feminist and Scott Nearing, both Socialists, but also John Masefield, Edgar Lee Masters, Vachel Lindsay the poets—listened to music, puzzled together over the eternal questions of adolescence. World War I was being fought, but America had not entered, and perhaps they agreed a Socialist could not take sides in capitalist warfare. 'Raphe' was Samson Raphaelson, later the writer of movie scripts, and Rayna was beautiful, unforgettable Rayna Simons, daughter of the wealthy Chicago broker; she was to figure in the personal lives both of Raphe and of Vincent Sheean, and was to die, a flaming Communist, in Moscow in 1927. But in 1915, she was preeminently Dorothy's rich and generous friend and sponsor, turning two otherwise bad Urbana years into good ones for Dorothy Day.

2. *The Search for Ultimacy*

When Dorothy Day came home at age eighteen to Chicago it was June, 1916. She had had enough of college; she wanted real doing, not irrelevant learning. She was never thereafter to place much value on formal schooling for herself or anyone else. Besides, her family were moving back to New York City where she was born, and she wanted to go, too. New York ought to provide a job, and independence, and being on the side of the poor, and—life! And so it did, though in ways she had not foreseen.

a. *The power of eros*—The job, and enlistment in the cause of social justice, came through Mike Gold, young Jewish editor of the *Call,* a small Socialist paper. She marched into the paper's busy workroom with an idea for a story about frugal existence in New York, life on $5 a week. He hired her. They would be good friends (though never lovers) as over the years Gold became one of New York's better-known leftist editors. The *Call* was a morning paper, and so the day's work for reporters ended between 2 and 3 A.M. Mike the editor with Dorothy and two or three others would then go for pancakes and coffee to Child's Restaurant on lower Park Row and sit there, smoking and solving the world's problems, perhaps till dawn. Dorothy was hungry for romance, but Mike Gold wasn't the one.

Another New York acquaintance who would become a lifelong friend was Peggy Baird, a young artist. Her view of sex was earthy and 'honest.' One night, according to biographer William Miller, the two women had a long talk about it while Peggy sketched the nude Dorothy's rather satisfying figure

curled up on Peggy's apartment sofa. Dorothy had not found
the physical approaches of men at all thrilling, she admitted.
Peggy replied that she simply needed to be awakened to such
pleasure. But Dorothy wanted something more than gratifica-
tion. She said she did not oppose sex "out of bounds," but it
had to be high drama or nothing. Perhaps she remembered
Swinburne's Tristram, with his heroic blood battles, his love
lyrics, and his suicidal but undying passion for Iseult. In any
case, she remembered those themes: that was the kind of love
she wanted.

The men Dorothy met, though, had a different approach.
The next year she met Floyd Dell, assistant editor of *The
Masses*, the brilliant publication that was linking social with
literary radicalism in America, and began to work for him on
its staff. Once they went on a picnic in New Jersey, and the talk
turned, as it often did, to sex. Dell advocated "the new
morality"—a girl, he said, should have sex with the first one
who aroused the tingle of desire. By that standard, Dorothy
reasoned, she should have given herself at fourteen to
Armand Hand the bandmaster. Anyway, she told Dell,
intellectual approaches to seduction were old stuff to her. Dell
was not to be Dorothy's Tristram. A better candidate might
have been Eugene O'Neill, the playwright, whom she met a
little later in Greenwich Village. To him, virginal Dorothy Day
was fresh and fascinating, and he was getting over a failed
romance when he met her. But again, they became friends, not
lovers. She tucked him into his bed, drunk, after late nights in
the Hell Hole, a local bar, and he loved drunkenly to recite
Francis Thompson's poem, *The Hound of Heaven*—about a God
who is not elusive but pursues us men and women until we are
finally his. Dorothy never told tipsy Gene O'Neill how deeply
that poem affected her. Meanwhile, sex and eros remained in
her life an unresolved though present tension.

b. *A socialist millennium?*—Day's life, of course, was no
endless round of parties and partners. She was a working
journalist, writing and editing as she took a series of jobs
connected with the spectrum of left wing causes. One of her
early 'features' was an article on the birth control movement,
which she supported. Then there were the political movements: the Socialists, 'parliamentary' in technique and given
to ideological hair-splitting; the IWW, Industrial Workers of

the World, committed to social change via direct action such as strikes, so that its leaders in those early days of the labor movement incurred severe penalties for their activity; supremely the Communists, who believed in a violent but brief revolution to bring in the new order when the time was ripe. And on the fringe, unorganized, were the anarchists, some open to violence, some not, whose 'program' would abolish even Socialist government. Most of these movements had in common at least two Marxian assumptions: (1) that the basic cause of human troubles is economic, namely unjust ownership and distribution of goods; and (2) that 'salvation,' the righting of the wrongs, must be here and now, in this world—not, as Marxists thought religion would have it, in the sweet by and by. Closest at first to the IWW, Dorothy befriended them all. Though never a cell-group, card-carrying Communist, she was not just a liberal "sympathizer," either; later in life she freely spoke of herself as an "ex-Communist," and therefore as one who knew whereof she spoke (cf. Day, 1938:146). Indeed, it is only as we see how strongly this not very political woman had identified with that earlier cause that we can make full sense of her later, intensely loyal Catholicism.

Perhaps the emotional high point of Day's involvement came rather early in her career as a Marxist. In Russia, early in 1917, a *soviet* or workers' council had called for strikes against the government. Rioting and insurrections of soldiers (still engaged in the long World War) ensued, until on March 15, Tsar Nicholas abdicated, leaving Russia in the hands of a moderate government that proclaimed a general amnesty and broad civil liberties, while deferring other matters to a proposed general assembly to be elected by universal suffrage. This was the "February Revolution," upon news of which Russian emigrés, many of whom had suffered under the Tsar's autocracy, arranged to meet for a mass celebration of Russian liberation in New York's Madison Square Garden on the evening of March 21. Dorothy attended, with Mike Gold and other *Call* staffers. She "felt the exultation, the joyous sense of victory of the masses." A high point was the singing of what Dorothy believed to be "the Russian workman's hymn, *Ei Uchnjem*"—actually the familiar Volga Boatman's Song—which the *Call*'s enthusiastic reporters took to be a signal that "like the flow of the river is the progress of human events" (Miller, 1982:65). Of course not even the politically knowledgeable that night could have foretold the actual harvest of the Russian Revolution: Bolsheviks following Mensheviks, the "dictatorship of the proletariat," the massive evil of the Gulag system, the almost century-long persecution of faithful Christians. What a penetrating observer might have seen even that night, though, was that Dorothy Day was caught up in a false eschatology, one that would seek peace by the way of violence, justice by way of forced chaos. So she later believed, anyway. Then, however, she could only contrast the joy of the Russian revolutionaries with the "war-mad" audience at a rally in Madison Square Garden two nights later, when they gathered to promote American entry into the World War (Day, 1938:73f.).

Dorothy's socialist convictions sometimes involved her in protests and demonstrations of a more direct sort. In the spring of 1917, and again in the fall, she went along on demonstrations to Washington, D.C. The first time she was covering a peace protest by Columbia University students; the second, in company with artist friend Peggy, was a demonstration ostensibly for women's suffrage—though Dorothy went, she said, simply to protest 'the System' in general. This time, she was arrested with the other picketers, suffered for the first time the indignities of jail, and served more than two weeks of a thirty-day prison sentence before the group received a presidential pardon. Jail, however, did not only provide indignity; it offered her as well unaccustomed isolation and leisure for reading the Bible, the only book available. On the whole, this experience was productive for the youthful Day, giving rise to questions prompted partly by the Bible reading: Was personal conversion necessary before any revolution could be successful? Was the secular struggle for causes, even worthy ones, enough to fulfill one's life?

During the last days of her jailing, after taking part in a hunger strike to protest conditions at Occoquan Prison, Day and her fellow protesters were transferred to Washington's city jail. This, like other American jails, was racially as well as sexually segregated, but from a distance Dorothy was able to watch the black women prisoners at work and play. They had games, and dancing to the music of singing and clapping. On Saturday, these same women scrubbed and primped, ready for the next day's church services—the one occasion when they caught sight of a man. There were two services, both jammed. "The men and women were separated, but I saw sex and felt it at its crudest and was ashamed that I should be stirred by it" (Day, 1952:83). So there was still that issue of eros, but at the moment no opportunities arose.

c. *Into the depths*—The opportunity came soon. Back in New York, Dorothy Day realized that she was discontent. In a few months, she and young sister Della had agreed to enter nurses' training in Brooklyn. After all, there was a war on, and a nursing shortage, and she wanted to do something meaningful. Yet as so often happens in real life, a turn to the good coincided with a turn to evil—and evil wilfully chosen. Shortly after beginning hospital residence, she met there Lionel Moise (pronounced Moe-ees), a bent-nosed, tough-talking actor who had taken a menial job in the hospital to recover from a drinking bout (striking that the men in her life, like her father, all had a weakness for alcohol?). It was, as Dorothy wrote in *The Eleventh Virgin*, "a fatal passion."

But was that not just what she had been looking for? Was that not what Tristram and Iseult had contracted when they drank the love potion on the voyage of the Swallow?

> And they saw dark, though still the unsunken sun
> Far through fine rain shot fire into the south;
> And their four lips became one burning mouth.
> (Swinburne, 1904:42)

Sought or not, the passion blazed. Lionel and Dorothy made clear to one another just how matters stood. He told her he wanted to have an affair and move on; she told him she intended to have and keep him no matter what. She was strong. With her mother's uneasy consent, Dorothy moved into Moise's apartment; eagerly she there surrendered her virginity to him. Shortly, they quarreled; he was jealous, and could not accept her easy way with other men, could not befriend her friends. He locked her out of his apartment; she returned, and so it went for a few months until, in May, 1919, Dorothy found herself pregnant. Eventually she told him, and they conferred, she the birth-control advocate and he the casual lover. An abortion, they decided, was indicated.

She found a woman doctor; the procedure was accomplished in the doctor's home. It involved scraping the womb with an instrument; labor thus induced aborted the destroyed fetus in a few painful hours. That night, Dorothy realized

Moise was gone for good. She wrote about this abortion a year later in her semiautobiographical novel, *The Eleventh Virgin* (1924). Yet in her postconversion autobiographies, *From Union Square to Rome* (1938) and *The Long Loneliness* (1952), she artfully skipped over the critical Moise episode, and even in old age was unwilling to affirm, though she was sometimes too truthful to deny, what had taken place. When it had happened, though, her dominant feeling seems to have been not guilt (for neither home nor church had taught her anything on this topic) but shame, and it is (strand-one) shame that suffuses the account of the abortion in the autobiographical novel.

Moise was gone, yet Dorothy was not done. Despairing, she apparently attempted suicide, Iseult-like, with a gas jet, but failed in the attempt. More calculatingly, she married another, older man, Barkeley Tobey, man-about-town and womanizer, and traveled with him in Europe for a year, writing *The Eleventh Virgin* during part of that time. And finally, after quitting Tobey, she followed Lionel Moise to Chicago, where while pursuing him vainly, she worked as (among other things) a secretary to Robert Minor, editor of *Liberator*, and as an artist's model. It was bad time, spent in vain pursuit of better. Happily, Dorothy Day did not succeed in recapturing Lionel Moise, and after two fitful and inconclusive Chicago years (1921–23), she traveled with her sister to New Orleans, to begin there a new chapter of her life.

3. *Thy Kingdom Come*

We are about to hear of conversion, a turnabout that makes a life over again. As is so often the case, a change in scene (in this case, the change from Chicago to New Orleans) goes along with and even seems to make possible a change in life. We are one thing to the old associates; we may be something else to the new—and to ourselves. Dorothy in New Orleans is no longer focused in quite the same way; her orientation has subtly shifted. Looking back on events, she later thought one cause of the shift had been the companionship, back in Chicago, of two young women who like Dorothy were having romantic troubles. "Blanche," as she calls her, Dorothy's roommate in the winter of 1922–23, was Catholic. She had been in love, however, with a young man who was a Mason—one whom Catholics were forbidden to marry. "Bee," the landlord's daughter, had likewise been in love and Catholic. Bee's worry had been that she might not be able to refrain from "premarital intimacy" with her young man. Both women had confided in Dorothy as a wiser and more experienced woman. Yet what struck her then and later was that they had a church whose structure and rules gave some order to their lives, while she in her own perplexities had nothing.

In New Orleans the following winter, everything appeared outwardly very much the same. On arrival, Dorothy and Della found a cheap place to stay in the French Quarter, and Dorothy, ever resourceful when it came to jobs, talked her way into one on the *Item* by proposing a series of articles on the life of a New Orleans taxi dancer—herself to be the taxi dancer. So she got a job in a dance hall, and wrote about her difficulties with the heavy-footed, heavy-handed men who came to pay for a dance and company. In some ways, though, life was changing. There were no more mad flings in pursuit of Moise or his surrogate. For the first time in years, she was back in touch with her sister Della—a fact doubtless reassuring to mother Grace back in New York. And there was church: Dorothy now regularly attended services at the French Quarter's Catholic cathedral. This provided a symbolic focus for her new self-understanding. She went, and prayed, and came away, taking no active part, yet finding a new contentment in the practice.

a. *"Natural happiness"*—Soon events changed her life once again. Her novel was published, that spring of 1924. It was not much of a book—"just one more adolescent novel," *The New York Times* reviewer wrote—but Hollywood bought the movie rights, so Dorothy had a check for $2,500, and as Louisiana's warm spring surrounded her, she joyfully decided she could go home to New York. A year later, she was back in touch with old friends there, and had made new ones; she had bought a little beach cottage on Staten Island where she could enjoy her newfound 'wealth', and—she had taken up with a man who there became her live-in lover. This "common law husband," as she would later call him, was Forster (pronounced Foster) Batterham, scion of an Asheville, North Carolina, family with literary connections. He was an anarchist, a gentleman of leisure (mainly, he fished), and one who "didn't believe in marriage" because he opposed all institutions. Batterham liked to come to the Staten Island cottage, spend a few days fishing offshore, and then drift away again. Yet in one way he figures vitally in Dorothy Day's story: By the following summer (1926) she was pregnant again, and in March, 1927, gave birth to a daughter whose father was Forster Batterham.

The birth of Teresa Tamar was part of an inseparable chain of linked events, for it brought into full awareness Dorothy's conviction that her daughter must be given the context of religion and church that she herself had not had; Tamar must be baptized Catholic. And that necessity would lead on to Dorothy's own significant baptism, and to the expulsion of Tamar's father Forster. The actual sequence of these events just named, as Dorothy tells it twice over in her autobiographies, is a complex tangle of her own fears and hopes for a new order of life, of timid negotiations with a kindly but superstitious nun from a nearby convent, of complications caused by Batterham's status as lover and Dorothy's as in some sense still married to the odd Barkeley Tobey, and of the climactic day of Tamar's infant baptism (even Forster Batterham providing a fish fry for that grand social event). Six months later Dorothy would present herself to her new church's minister for her own rite of (believer's) baptism.

Why the Catholic and not her old Episcopal Church? Dorothy's answer was simple: the Catholic Church was the church of the immigrant, the church of the poor. It was bad enough to be leaving her Communist friends; at least she could identify with the Catholic poor. She had come to believe, also, that it was the true church descended from the apostles. Perhaps, too, it represented for her the reality of Eastern Orthodoxy, as she knew it from her Russian novels. And Catholic ritual—the earthy signs of water, and oil, and wine, and salt—spoke to her of that going to ground that was a motif at least as old in her life as the childhood house in Berkeley, with its garden of callas and roses and geraniums, and its nearby brook. She had come home.

There is another reason, I think, why she turned to this "church of the poor," and not to Pentecostal, say, or Baptist churches, or to the synagogue. It was all she knew. In the great cities, New York, Chicago, even New Orleans, most of her friends were Marxist, or they were Jewish. She felt very close to Jewish life in New York, but her Jewish friends were all secular. Religiously, Catholicism was there, like Everest, to be ascended.

It did present difficulties, though. Besides the negotiations the rite for Tamar had required, there was the awkward matter of the baby's father living with Dorothy. In effect, Catholic teaching as Dorothy encountered it said to her, If you want to be Catholic, give up your child's father. Forster, who loved Dorothy in his way and was more loyal to her than any man she had known, perceived her 'religion' as a threat, one he hoped would vanish, given time. And she loved him, too. Forster, and the Staten Island cottage, and the salt and sand and spray of the shore, and Tamar the baby, and friendly immigrant neighbors, belonged together in a sensate bond that Dorothy, thinking back on it a quarter of a century later, would call "natural happiness" (Day, 1952:111). "Natural" here was a theological term meaning "not supernatural"; it was to her thinking nature without grace. Yet that category may have been too stark for the good that was then growing in her life. One wonders, indeed, if the story might not have been a better one—better for Tamar, for Forster, better even for Dorothy—if he had been allowed to remain with the two of them, anarchism and all.

Yet that is not the way it went. In December, 1927, an "explosion" occurred between Dorothy and Forster, and he left. When he next returned to the cottage, she refused to let him in. Their life together, she said, was over. The next day, as if that settled it, a tense, intense Dorothy Day received her church's baptism ("conditional," it was carefully said) in nearby Tottenville, and the day after that, she first communicated as a Roman Catholic. These things seemed to her as she went through with them merely tasks to be completed. So there she was, without friends beside her, "grimly, coldly, making acts of faith, and certainly with no consolation whatever" (Day, 1952:148). She had doubts, she felt herself a hypocrite; perhaps she was the betrayer of her former commitments. Where, now, was the ultimacy she longed for? Where was that kingdom Jesus spoke of, in the Sermon on the Mount?

b. *The Catholic Worker*—As it happened, the kingdom was indeed at hand, and in ways Dorothy Day had hardly dreamed. Her baptism was in December, 1927. In the five years that followed, she cared for her daughter and worked to support the two of them, mainly with writing jobs. There was an interlude in Hollywood as a paid script writer (though, in Hollywood's breezy way, she never got to write a script); there was another interval in Mexico, and still another with her parents, by then living near Hialeah race track in Florida. Then, in December, 1932, friends directed to Dorothy's New York East Side apartment a stranger with a thick foreign accent who introduced himself as Peter Maurin and announced that he intended to become her teacher. In that meeting, the Catholic Worker Movement, we might say, was issued its first summons to appear (Miller, 1973).

. In some ways, Dorothy never liked Peter Maurin. He was earnest and pedantic, insensitive to the niceties of personal relations, and indifferent to the custom of daily (or weekly!) baths. Twenty years older than she, he was one of twenty-three children of a French peasant family. He had taken vows as a Christian Brother, had served as a draftee in the French army, and had then become a teacher, deeply interested in European Catholic social thought. Inspired in part by the papal encyclicals, he had for a time belonged to a Catholic and democratic political action group named *Sillon*, "The Furrow." Maurin next emigrated to Canada, and wandered about, there and in the United States working as a day laborer, turning over in his mind the ideas that had engaged him, and developing the pithy, short-phrased speaking style of a debater on a public square. Above all, he loved to talk. And this was the man Dorothy Day accepted, almost upon meeting, as the prophet who would show her what her own vocation was to be. A drifter, aged fifty-five, utterly without worldly goods, the 'teacher' enrolled his first student, Dorothy Day.

Maurin's teaching was often expressed in simple and memorable mottoes he then assembled into "easy essays" (Maurin, 1961). One of the mottoes was "cult, culture, and cultivation." In more conventional terms, this meant that three aspects of social existence—religion, education, and agriculture—were indispensable to the good life, and should therefore be interconnected in building the new social and economic order that so many were dreaming of in those days (Ellis, 1981). Two of these elements, religion and cultivation of the soil, were right in tune with Dorothy's disposition and her new selfhood. The third, education or 'culture,' was congenial, too, especially when Peter explained that it meant dialogue "for clarification of thought"; it also meant that a newspaper would be necessary to disseminate ideas. Dorothy liked newspapers. And it seemed there was need as well for houses of hospitality, eventually one in every Catholic parish as a place where the rich could encounter the poor and concerned minds could meet.

With Dorothy, to think was to act. She quickly raised the $57 she found the printer wanted for the first issue of an eight-page tabloid paper, and began writing copy for it. It would be called *The Catholic Worker*: "Worker," to rival the Communist *Daily Worker* and to declare identification with the laboring class; "Catholic" to assure readers that one could be radical though Catholic (a dubious proposition at that time in America). On May Day, 1933, Dorothy Day went out with a younger Worker, Joe Bennett, into Union Square, and sold the first 1¢ copies of their paper. The Depression was at its nadir; many were unemployed and standing about; Communists had earlier that afternoon filled the Square for a march, and the *Catholic Worker* was in its element. So the movement was underway. Her own apartment, expanded, became the first House of Hospitality and the paper's office; Dorothy, without rank or title, effectively ran both. Concerned acquaintances came to help, and some stayed on to live there. Soup was served; discussion groups were formed; people sensed that something was happening of radical importance for American Christianity.

c. *Putting on Christ*—When does a conversion happen? If we simply look at the outward course of events, Day's life made its turn in 1923, when she left Chicago (and the hopeless pursuit of Moise) to take up her own life anew (Statnik, 1983). If we look at ecclesiastical rites, it happened when she excluded Batterham and became a Catholic. If we see conversion as vocation (cf. Mark 8:34f.), it happened when, meeting Maurin, she began the *Catholic Worker* and opened her home to the poor. And wherever we place the fulcrum of fundamental option or choice, there is a sense in which Day's conversion must have comprehended all these renunciations and commitments. Yet there is still another element.

Starting in about 1940, Dorothy Day became involved in the retreat movement, more exactly in that part of it led by two Catholic clergymen, Pacifique Roy and John Hugo, who in turn were guided by the Canadian Jesuit, Onesimus Lacouture. Spiritual retreats are an old technique by which those caught up in the daily round, even the daily round of church activity, may come away for a season to hear Christian truth lifted up and explained, to examine themselves in its light, and to pray. Often all but the leader submit themselves to a rule of silence during the period of the retreat in order to concentrate their attention.

What distinguished Lacouture retreats (sometimes called rather grandly The Retreat) was a strong 'evangelical' note that gave them the doctrinal flavor of a series of revival sermons in the Edwardsean tradition (and evoked considerable Catholic theological criticism): There would be a profound emphasis, sometimes lasting eight days, upon the sinfulness of sin; there would be a strong distinction between "nature" (comprising our fallen selfhood, and tending to issue in sin) and "supernature" (God's lifegiving and lifechanging grace); finally, there would be a summons to live according to 'supernature,' issuing in a maximal rather than a minimal Christianity. One must live according to the Sermon on the Mount; with Paul, one must "put on" Christ. Dorothy's advisor, Father John Hugo, seems to have assumed that many of his Catholic retreatants believed in a 'least effort' version of Christianity: "Avoid mortal sin and you will be safe." He countered this in the retreats with a barrage of appeals, based partly on common sense, partly on Scripture. Shall I pound my mother with a hammer, so long as I am careful not actually to kill her? Does Jesus in the Sermon on the Mount discuss how one may steal without actually committing mortal sin? Doesn't he rather call his followers to perfection—and is that not the regular New Testament teaching? (Hugo, 1944:ch. 4; see also 1984, and n.d.). Two things here especially appealed to Dorothy Day. One was the retreats' insistence that holiness was for all Christians, not just clergy and members of religious orders. It answered those who told her that if she wanted to be so devoted to Jesus, she ought to join a 'religious' community. The other was the retreats' interiorization of the Christian way; it provided an ordered way for the mind and soul as well as for outward social relations.

So this strenuous call to a Christian life with inward content, God-given and all-consuming, fell like sparks onto the dry tinder of Dorothy Day's soul. Shaken and moved by the retreat she attended near Pittsburgh in the summer of 1943, Dorothy resolved to take a year's leave from the *Worker*, making of it a time for the renewal of her own inner life. Those who knew her about that time saw a change in her person, as well. Not only did she speak often of the retreats and their significance (see *Catholic Worker*, July-August, 1943), but something about her—Miller calls it her brassiness—altered as well; she stopped smoking and gave up the little drinking she did; her speech became in a new way gentle. So there was an inner dimension to Dorothy Day's conversion as well. Yet the remarkable thing, that which gave unity to her life and made Hoover's complaint that she was "erratic" false though understandable, was also coming most clearly into focus about this time.

d. *The gospel of peace*—We can readily see why J. Edgar Hoover and his FBI agents would have found Dorothy's stance puzzling. On the one hand she was certainly "radical" in the sense of believing that fundamental social and economic changes were in order in 1950s America—she would say the same in our day. That seemed to class her with the dreaded Communists. On the other hand, she had a kind but firm "no" for Communism of the Marxist sort: Private property was not itself evil; there should be no armed revolution; there should be no class war or any other war. What Hoover and company had no category to describe—probably because they had seen so few examples—was radical *Christianity*, a Christianity that in obedience to Jesus Christ would be consistently nonviolent, refusing violence on the side of revolution, but also refusing it on the side of establishment and oppression.

In fact, the Christian church has always included disciples of Jesus committed to nonviolence. In the first three Christian centuries, these were the usual sort of Christian. After that, the coopting of Christianity by the Roman Empire produced an enduring change, so that in our much later century many Christians, when they pray for 'peace,' simply mean they hope that the governing authority, backed by military force and of course always prepared to fight, doesn't run into any opposition. Any other sort of peace, they feel, would be unpatriotic. The Catholic Church Dorothy Day had joined often spoke out officially for peace (a fact she could use to good advantage in the *Worker*), but what was often if not always implied was a peace achieved by fighting 'just' wars or crusades, that is, only wars that were conducted under particular limits, rules, and conditions, and for particular goals. John Yoder has called this position "the pacifism of

Christian cosmopolitanism." The pastor and the sheriff in a small town, Yoder points out, are interested in amicable settlement of disputes between the inhabitants of the town—including but not limited to those involving church members. If necessary, though, the sheriff will 'settle' disputes another way. If we stretch this picture to the global scale, we represent the 'pacifism' of many popes and of the World Council of Churches—the world is their parish (Yoder, 1971b:ch. 1).

It was Day's misfortune or fortune not to have been nurtured on this 'just war pacifism.' Instead, she read the Greek New Testament in high school, with Jesus' Sermon on the Mount ("love your enemies") front and center in it. Nobody explained to her that the word "peace" in the Christian liturgies she attended through her years of intermittent and later regular churchgoing did not mean *peace*. Instead, the first fairly competent social theorist she encountered in her new life, Peter Maurin, just happened to be a radical Catholic who was in full rebellion against the militarism of his French youth. When she met more sophisticated historians, they told her (correctly) that the early church was indeed pacifist. Pacifism fit in, too, with views she had held at least since 1917 on other grounds. The *Catholic Worker* was therefore committed from the first to the pacifism of Jesus, and never wavered. To 1950s Americans, engaged at home and abroad with what they saw as a cold and sometimes a hot war against Communism, this might easily have seemed "erratic and irresponsible."

Yet to describe Day's pacifism only as the contingent consequence of some life experiences seems not yet to do it justice as part of her. This commitment was not just a happenstance reading of Christian moral teaching; it lay right at the center of the new love that had come into her life in Christ Jesus. Of course, the newness contradicted much to which the world, even the good people of the world, even some of her good friends, subscribed. To be a pacifist put her at odds with many. But it put her in the center of obedience to Jesus Christ, and that was now what mattered. "Heaven," she jotted down after a 1940 retreat, "can begin here." The saying was from Catherine of Siena (Miller, 1982:336; Day, 1960:121), but the thought was now Dorothy's own. John Hugo taught her in the retreats she attended a little later that at baptism, a seed of new life is planted, and the business of being a Christian is to nurture that seed so that the new life grows. Dorothy had always loved nurture and growth. Here was the new living thing that God had given her, the Christ life within. How should she not nurture it with all her strength?

Pacifism is fairly easy in times of peace. In the *Worker's* first decade, though, America went to war. It was a popular war, thanks to Nazi fanaticism and to the December 7, 1941, Japanese attack on Pearl Harbor that triggered American entry. The war's popularity heightened the crisis of the Catholic Worker Movement. "We Continue Our Christian Pacifist Stand," ran the following month's *Worker* headline. The country was officially at war at last, Dorothy's story went on, but "We will print the words of Christ who is with us always, even to the end of the world. 'Love your enemies, do good to those who hate you.' "

The truth was that war sentiment had already decimated the Movement. In June, 1940, while America's war effort had been confined to lend-lease to its allies and a food embargo of Europe, Day had written the Worker Houses around the country, in an editorial titled "Our Stand," that the Sermon on the Mount was the Worker standard. The consequence was mass defections. Worker houses eventually shrank from thirty to eleven in number. Notable among the defectors was John Cogley, later distinguished religious journalist for *Commonweal* and *The New York Times*, but who in 1940 had been the editor of the Chicago version of the *Catholic Worker*. Cogley stood by the historic just war theory and volunteered for the army. Dorothy, while she accepted his conscientious exit, and remained Cogley's friend, maintained the lonely vigil for Christian pacifism: As war news flooded in from Europe, from Africa, Asia, and the Pacific, she wrote:

I have been and still am a Christian Pacifist, opposing class war, race war, civil war, and international war. [I]f conscription comes for women, I will not register, and if this breaking of the law means [I must], I shall consider myself privileged to go to jail, where one can be quite sure of not doing one's own will.

"Not doing one's own will" meant taking the way of the cross, following Jesus, who had put "denying self" at the center of the gospel. That did not fit the American Way very well, or even the way of most young Catholic Workers, who deserted the Houses in droves then. By those standards, hers was indeed an 'erratic' way. Yet it did fit, she believed, the new age that had dawned first in Christ, and now in her life. Her consistent obedience to that newness, an *eschaton* not merely awaited but already here, gave a grand coherence to her life.

* * * * *

There is more to tell about Dorothy Day. She survived for half a century of Worker life (she died quietly in a New York Worker House, November 29, 1980, at the age of eighty-three). The Movement did surmount the war, and the FBI and other hurdles, including Dorothy's old age and partial retirement in the sixties, and her puzzled rejection of the updated thinking of some younger Catholics who became her associates but believed the church itself ought to change in unaccustomed ways. The Catholic Worker Movement is alive and well today (cf. Ellis, 1978). One of many Houses of Hospitality at this writing is located in Oakland, California, not far from the neighborhood where Dorothy's brass bed skated on the floor in the earthquake, and where she once heard another rumbling sound, too—the ever louder voice of God, coming nearer and nearer. In the Worker House now, there is a low-cost food store, and rooms for unexpected guests, and a basement room with cast off furniture where the Catholic liturgy is sometimes said and sung.

That liturgy has changed, now, as has Dorothy's adopted church. In fact, she changed it a good deal herself. Though she did not much like some of the consequences of Vatican II, being in many ways an old-fashioned Catholic, one of the Council's effects was opening the Catholic Church to the influence of radical lives like hers. Among American laity who have influenced those changes, hers just may be the most influential life of all, so far (cf. Piehl, 1982:244). More significant still, she incorporates, for those with eyes to see, elements of the vision that has guided disciples of Jesus in every land and age and congregation: a deep love of creation, a hunger for "new heavens *and a new earth*," and a willingness to shape her life according to the new that was disclosed to her. In words she liked, partly for their antiquity but also for their theme, her life says to us, *Pax vobiscum*, "peace be with you all."

A Future
for Peace?

Now we do have a fight on our hands. It is only a theological fight, but in many ways these are the worst sort, since, being about convictions (see Chapter One), they go to the deeps of our selfhood, and since as we shall see theological fights have been known to turn into bloody ones—crusades and holy wars. It is surely ironic that the present theological battle is about peace. Love and forgiveness, the foci of the two previous applied chapters, are controversial, too, but it is peace that has divided Christian thought into sharply opposed camps!

Many Christians, of course, do not realize that such a clash of convictions is underway among us. As long as their country or class or clan is at peace, they prefer peace. When it goes to war, however, they find ways to support the war, either as a necessary evil or as a God-given crusade against others' evil. What the New Testament says about peace then becomes an "impossible ideal," or is neglected. Anyhow, war and peace are matters for nations to work out, not church folk, and the latter must accept what national leaders do—for they know best.

There is a fragment of wisdom in these attitudes, and yet they overlook the existence of a sharp division within Christian thought itself. Are Christians free to engage in their nations' (or classes', or clans') warfare? While most have answered with a qualified yes, Dorothy Day, as we saw, answered no, and so have some significant baptist thinkers through the centuries—and not only the Anabaptists. This chapter will therefore explore the matter, paying particular attention (1) to the standpoint of Jesus, (2) to the nature of the arguments *against* pacifism, and (3) to the possibilities of peace*making* in the kingdom of God. (Attending to these theological issues, it will necessarily omit many other relevant ethical matters about war and peace, violence and nonviolence.) The challenge as I see it is to discuss this crux of applied ethics without slipping off either into dreamy irrelevance or cynical despair. Finally, if it can deal fairly with this topic, this chapter should be a good test of all that has gone before. Will the three strands help? Will the baptist vision?

1. Is Jesus a Pacifist?

Both sides in the dispute over Christians and war are in some sense peaceloving; they agree that peace is in general a human good and a divine gift; they agree that it is not the only good or gift; both can support their views by argument and by appeal to one stream or another of Christian tradition; both find some warrant for their views in the rich diversity of the Old Testament. The real place of division for those who accept its authority must therefore be the New Testament, especially if it is read as witnessing to the demand of the incarnate, crucified, and risen Jesus Christ. We may differ even with him—some Christians (using the word now as historians do) have even consciously done so and still do—yet the question whether Jesus is a 'pacifist' and would have his followers be, or not, is at least an intelligible one that should be resolved. By the ethical standards followed here, it should be resolved first. At least for sharers of the baptist vision, there can be no higher concern.

a. *The evidence of history*—Perhaps the greatest obstacle to objectivity in examining the New Testament is the temptation to separate these documents from the history in which they first appeared. Once that move has been made, all sorts of mischief follow. Let us then approach the New Testament retrospectively, from the direction of late antiquity, a period better externally documented than is the century of the Epistles and Gospels. It is well established, to begin, that by medieval times Christianity did not renounce violence and war. This was the age of the Crusades, of knightly combat, of Christian wars against the barbarians. Yet even in this post-Constantinian age, in which one side (or both sides!) fought under the banner of the cross, one remarkable fact appears—clergy were forbidden to engage in bloodshed. Canon law codified an ancient rule: the minister of the Crucified One cannot be a killer of any sort. Even though killing in war was not necessarily a "sin," a priest could not do it. As late as the trial of Michael Sattler in sixteenth-century South Germany, the authorities had a difficult time in seating a court, because potential judges, being either priests or candidates for the priesthood, refused to serve. Participating in a capital case was forbidden to the former, and would disqualify the latter from ordination (Yoder, 1973:66f.). Why this old rule? The best explanation seems to be that canon law retained for clergy the regular practice of all Christians before Constantine. What was once the common practice was still applied to monks and priests.

For the best evidence we have is that until the year 170, no church member could serve in the army, or engage in violence, for that was not legitimate Christian conduct (Bainton, 1960:67). One of Celsus' reproaches of Christianity was that Christians by refusing to fight were disloyal to the Emperor. And Origen in his celebrated reply to Celsus (written about 250) had to acknowledge the truth of the reproach (*Cont. Cels.* 8:68). Even after 170, the evidence is that military service was rare until the time of Constantine (312). So the 'pacifism' (a word we have still to define here) practiced by early Christians, lasting into the fourth century and (in the relic of canon law) for at least sixteen centuries more, leads us to approach the New Testament writings with the expectation that this unusual practice may have its roots there and in the authority of Jesus.

b. *The evidence of the New Testament*—Our goal is to discover whether Jesus Christ by word and deed has forbidden his followers to fight. The question has been answered both ways by quoting isolated texts: "not . . . peace, but a sword" (Matt. 10:34), or "Put your sword into its sheath" (John 18:11). This is not to be my approach. Rather, I intend to inquire about the character and demand of Christ as revealed in the New Testament, read as the many-sided narrative of his incarnate life (though certainly I will not disregard questions of historical fact). To see this, a step by step approach will prove helpful.

i. *MacGregor*—Consider first G. H. C. MacGregor's reading of
the Gospels. MacGregor, a Glasgow professor and exegete,
wrote *The New Testament Basis of Pacifism* (rev. ed., 1954), which
held that both the teaching of Jesus (the Golden Rule, complete
love of God, unfailing love of the neighbor) and his life
(culminating in acceptance of the cross), as these are presented
in the four Gospels, are clearly on the side of peace not war. This
is because Jesus pointed to a way in human relations based on
God's own nature, namely the love of enemies. Certainly in
Matthew 5 the acceptance of injury, forbearance toward *personal*
enemies, nonresistance, is Jesus' own way ("If anyone strikes
you on the right cheek . . . "—Matt. 5:39). Patiently, MacGregor deals with attempts to water down or defuse these piercing
moral teachings of the Sermon on the Mount, concluding that
while Jesus neither abrogates society's law (which of course uses
civil force), nor explicitly rejects all use of force in human affairs,
his own teaching and example have a different aim: "The moral
order can be vindicated, not by forcible restraint and punishment of the evil-doer, but only . . . by the power of truth and
goodness and self-sacrificing love" (MacGregor, 1954:39).

Now so far it may appear that MacGregor's interpretation of
Jesus goes aground on the shoals of a shallow repetition of
selected texts, a method already rejected. In fact, though, he
has only begun. For next he marshalls evidence and argument
from New Testament scholars Hans Windisch, C. H. Dodd,
and C. J. Cadoux to make three substantial historical points:
(1) The kingdom Jesus proclaimed must have been understood
by his hearers as a proposal for a communal and Jewish
institution—a reordering of the Jewish state on new principles
(on this point, cf. Lohfink, 1984:ch. 1). (2) Thus his teaching
was not, as in the stereotype of Adolf von Harnack, merely
"religious" and "inward"; rather the teaching about love of
enemies and accepting suffering was addressed also to
outward questions of public policy. And (3) Jesus' actual
temptation—the one he rejected in reality as well as in the
'temptation' stories (Matt. 3:1ff. and parallels)—was to engage
in a Messianic war to restore Israel (MacGregor, 1954:ch. 4).
MacGregor's Jesus, then, was a fully political figure who went
to the cross partly because of opposition to his public policy of
love to enemies, partly in exemplification of its total demand,
because "the same principles which forbade rebellion against
Rome also forbade violent resistance to his enemies on Jesus'

own part. . . . Because Jesus was *not* a Barabbas, he went to the Cross" (MacGregor, 1954:48f.).

While this is only a partial report of MacGregor's extended and forceful exposition of the New Testament's pacifism (for another, more recent survey, cf. Klassen, 1984), it unearths a contemporary objection we must consider: Was not Jesus actually a Zealot and revolutionary, a sort of first-century Che Guevara? Does the New Testament conceal (though not quite effectively) this dark truth?

ii. *Brandon and Pixley*—This is the view of British historian of religions S. G. F. Brandon, who argued the case in two books a generation ago. An erudite if unconventional scholar, Brandon acknowledges that our only extensive sources concerning Jesus' political career, trial, and execution, the four Gospels, represent Jesus as an innocently accused and nonviolent leader. However, this is merely their ingenious twisting of their own data. Their motives are patent: Mark wanted to show Rome that it had no reason to fear an insurrection by the Christians; Matthew was concerned lest his Christian readers might join in a suicidal struggle against Rome and meet the fate of destroyed Jerusalem; Luke and John sought to show Hellenistic readers that the crucifixion was Jewish, not a Gentile crime. Yet the reality is different; Jesus was in fact a Zealot, a member of the guerilla party that sought the violent overthrow of Roman rule; with Barabbas he led an uprising in Jerusalem; he was apprehended, convicted of this crime, and executed. The evidence for all this is in the Gospels themselves, though concealed there (Brandon, 1958:chs. 5–7; cf. his 1967).

While Brandon's reconstruction, since it depends heavily upon the supposition that the Gospels hide this central truth about Jesus, can have little appeal to most readers of this chapter, a related account may. This holds that Jesus, while not actually a Zealot, led a parallel revolutionary movement. The Zealots, it will be remembered, were one of several rival Jewish political groups in occupied first-century Palestine; in today's term, the Zealots were 'terrorists.' Other parties favored collaboration with the occupying conquerors (the Sadducee party), or a withdrawn alternative community (the Essenes at the Dead Sea), or scrupulous law-keeping as the source of renewed national life (the Pharisees). On the view now to be considered, Jesus' political involvement came nearest to that of the Zealots, and he was indeed executed (though mistakenly) as one of them.

One representative of this position, George Pixley, a Liberation theologian in Mexico, offers a Marxist analysis of first-century Palestine: The social struggle in Jesus' day as in earlier Israel lay between village autonomy and city-based economic oppression; by now, however, Rome controlled the cities, while local tyranny was exercised by the Jerusalem Temple authorities. The 'Temple economy' of currency exchange, village taxation, and commerce, in league with Roman military and political power, was the instrument by which the upper class in Palestine dominated the other classes.

Jesus, like the Zealots, rebelled against this oppression. But his strategy differed. According to the Synoptic Gospels, Jesus' strategy was to build a popular base in Galilee by teaching and attracting followers, then to confront the local elite, the "Asiatic class system" centered in Jerusalem, whereas the Zealots had concentrated upon the Roman rule. Jesus' attack on the Temple's banking and commercial practices (Luke 19:45) was to be the focus of this confrontation. (His intention was not to go to Jerusalem to die; that is a "theological reading overlaid on the narrative.") But it was of course risky work, and when the confrontation came he was executed by Jewish and Roman collusion because his egalitarian community of followers threatened the beneficiaries of the class system, the Pharisees as well as the Sadducees and the Romans (Pixley, 1983:386f.). So Pixley's Jesus dies as he had lived, nonviolent just as the Gospels report; yet with nonviolence as a tactic not a principle. Sooner or later, had he lived, he would have had to confront the Roman army, and that might have required another tactic. In any case, liberationist Pixley believes, the Jesus movement failed and died out in Palestine, though such lessons of failure are of great importance for the people of Latin America if they are one day to establish, as Pixley believes they will, "a just society" (1983:392f.).

iii. *Scofield*—George Pixley's view in some ways comes closer than others to the biblical narrative view I will soon present, but first it will be instructive to note a sharply contrasted reading of the Jesus of the Gospels. This is the radical "dispensationalism" represented by Cyrus Ingerson Scofield (1843–1921), father of Dallas Theological Seminary, whose

Scofield Reference Bible (1917) popularized the views of an earlier British dispensationalist, John Nelson Darby (1800–1882). Scofield (and his associated editors) conveyed their theology to millions by means of titles and marginal notes, including some sixty-seven doctrinal "summaries," inserted into the King James Version. The "pattern for the ages" (Ahlstrom, 1972:809-12) that they found in the Bible embodied a complex premillennial eschatology, yet the pattern was "simplified" into a scheme of sevens (seven dispensations, seven judgments, seven—plus one—covenants, and more) well suited to the experience of a certain traveler to St. Ives.

Scofield's Jesus, like MacGregor's, Brandon's, and Pixley's, is forthrightly political. The kingdom of Heaven (to be distinguished from the kingdom of God) is the earthly institution Jesus proposed to set up. But the Jews rejected Jesus' offer, whereupon he made a pivotal (if 'temporary') reversal of field, offering instead a salvation for individuals that would be only loosely related to the original "kingdom of heaven" once proposed. This arrangement is to last until the end of the age, when Christ's Second Advent will finally inaugurate the establishment of the postponed kingdom on earth (Scofield, 1917:notes on Matt. 3:2; 11:20; 13:1; Acts 1:11). But the Sermon on the Mount (and with it Jesus' central teaching on nonviolence) is law for *that* kingdom, and its requirements apply directly only to that coming time; hence it is not in that sense applicable to the present age. Therefore peace as Scripture teaches it may now consist in peace between individuals and God, or in an (Augustinian) "inner peace," but the present age will be characterized by wars. While wars are the mark of an unconverted age, at least no hint in Scofield warns the reader against taking part in them, although of course it remains true that "the poor in spirit, rather than the proud, are blessed" (notes on Matt. 5:2; 10:34; 24:3).

Scofield's Jesus, making an abrupt midstream change of direction, promulgating a gospel (the kingdom of heaven) and a law (the Sermon on the Mount) that do not directly engage today's disciples, and divulging a mysterious sevenfold apocalyptic, may surprise those who know the dispensational school only at second hand or not at all. Yet my portrayal serves two purposes: it may give a clue to the moral character of today's Fundamentalism; at the same time it may point to a remarkable consensus: Jesus' original proclamation, all our diverse authorities agree, was powerfully social or political; they also agree that it was intensely eschatological. (When we add our own emphasis upon organic selfhood, we will have met again three essential strands of Christian ethics.)

iv. *Another view*—What comes last is at hand now. That is the eschatological claim that is indispensable in Jesus' own gospel (Mark 1:15 and parallels; cf. for what follows McClendon, 1981; Hauerwas, 1983:ch. 5; Yoder, 1972). Albert Schweitzer was correct in finding that the quest of the historical Jesus led to an eschatological figure, though understandably neither he nor his contemporaries found it possible to fit this strange Jesus into the assumptions of late-nineteenth-century liberal Protestantism (1906/1968:chs. 19f.). Did Jesus really believe the world was about to end? Perhaps, though the evidence for that is unclear. What he certainly taught and acted upon was that the end of the age was even nearer than that; God's Movement (Clarence Jordan) was already breaking in upon Jesus' own generation. So one must hear the Good News, and thereafter act accordingly.

His own action is to be understood in these terms. Like John the Baptizer, though evidently with greater skill and impact, he set about forming an 'eschatological' community, that is, a network of followers willing to shape their lives in accordance with the inbreaking new, and centered in personal allegiance to himself. The style of his teaching was fitted to this content; it consisted partly in pointed and pithy sayings, partly in deeds that served like the old prophetic signs as fodder for subsequent rumination, partly in parables that (in John Dominic Crossan's language) "subvert worlds." Such parables call into question the moral world in which the hearer exists—just what Jesus had to do if he was to invite his hearers to enter a new world, a new moral order, with him (cf. Crossan, 1975:59). Through such teaching, he began to form a community marked both by its life of shared practices, and by an openness to outsiders: Jesus "ate with sinners" (Mark 2:16 and parallels).

In our century, we have learned again that Jesus' impact consisted in what he did at least as much as in what he said. Here the "mighty signs" play a crucial role (cf. Mark 6:2, 5). For while it is no longer disputed since Weiss and Schweitzer that his proclamation was eschatological in content as well as form, and while our writers all agree that his program was communitarian and (at least in that sense) political, there has been a continuing neglect of the healing miracles and the nature-signs reported in the Gospels. Yet without these signs we are likely (with the followers of Scofield) to turn the imminent kingdom into an always expected but never arriving Godot, or we are likely (with Liberation Theology) to concentrate upon an immanent political struggle more akin to first-century Zealotry than to Jesus; in short, if we omit the organic or body strand of Jesus' ministry with its healings and mighty signs we may miss the point of his claim about the time and misunderstand his community formation as well. (Even if only briefly, it must be pointed out that the mighty 'nature' signs, for example the feeding of the five thousand [Mark 6:32-44 and parallels]; and the stilling of the storm [Mark 4:35-41 and parallels] have close connection with the 'signs' of baptism and Last Supper, and so once again, as do the healing and nature signs, these rites disclose the present power of God in Jesus' ministry.)

How, then, are the final events in Jerusalem to be interpreted? Here the narrative gathers together with nearly unbearable suspense. Surely the inbreaking of the new age will succor one who loved even his enemies (Luke 13:34f. and parallels)? Surely the solidarity of community will sustain its leader and Lord (Mark 14:27 and parallels)? Surely, if all else fail, a mighty sign from God will intervene to turn back the powers that crush him (Mark 14:35 and parallels)? None of these things do happen, as each Gospel writer in his own way is at pains to show us. Jesus is faithful to his Father's nonviolent way of the coming age, even though (as Pixley almost admits) nonviolence was evidently *not* an expedient tactic. Jesus is tried alone, condemned alone, dies miserably alone, while the disciples each and all show us what disciples must not be (Mark 14:50). No mighty sign intervenes. He is returned to earth's womb, the tomb. Yet just as the hearer or reader of the gospel story gives up, God does intervene. The body is renewed, raised; the disciples are regathered; the new age—despite an apparently hopeless impasse—is begun.

A revealing aspect of Pixley's account (reading it in narrative terms rather than his chosen Marxist-sociological ones) is that it throws light from a present liberation story, in his case, the (often violent) Latin American one, back on the Jesus story. By that method, though, Pixley is unable to see how Jesus could cope with Rome without violence (Pixley, 1983:389ff.). But other liberation stories are available in our century. For example there is the Gandhian one that renounced violence in favor of *ahimsa*. It is noteworthy, as Daniel Ellsberg once pointed out to me, that the Gandhian strategy was two-pronged. On the one hand, civil disobedience in face of oppression. On the other, the breaking of unhealthy dependence upon the oppressors by the building of an alternative community—epitomized for Mohandas Gandhi by the spinning wheel, tool of cottage industry. And Gandhi repeatedly said, "In the centre of the programme is the spinning wheel" (Gandhi, 1951:100, et pass.); that is, in the strategy of nonviolent liberation, the economic (and social) skills of alternative community are not marginal but essential. Now, what if at the center of Jesus' gospel program lay, not the revolt of a more sophisticated Che Guevara, but the community building of a more astute Gandhi—and behind that, the sense of power and destiny of the kingdom of God? That might explain as Pixley's analysis cannot why the nonviolence movement is alive today, even, as it happens, on Palestinian soil (Kennedy, 1984).

This, then, is the sense in which Jesus is a pacifist: He evokes and guides a program of nonviolent action that transforms human conduct for its sharers. The core of that program lies in the Sermon on the Mount (Matthew 5–7; cf. Luke 6:20-49). It is inwardly but also outwardly oriented; its theme is the love of enemies; its focus, in light of God's mighty signs and the inbreaking of the end, is the building of a community that can survive the dying of an old age while with its Lord it anticipates the new.

2. Mindset and the Myths of War

The New Testament's teaching about the practice and requirement of Jesus on peace and nonviolence seems clear enough. Although some have supposed that the Epistles offer a different approach than the Gospels, William Klassen has (most recently) provided a survey of the crucial passages, showing the centrality of peace and the love of enemies throughout the New Testament (1984). The puzzling thing is that the entire age of the New Testament appears on first examination to be in this regard a lost island of doctrine, its peacemaking bearings unmappable from the standpoint either of the Old Testament, where God himself is portrayed as a Warrior, or of later Christian history, where 'just' wars, crusades, and 'righteous' revolutions fill most of Christian history. This section must take seriously these apparent contradictions of known New Testament teaching.

It must be acknowledged at the outset that war has a tremendous if tragic human appeal. Thus Othello, correctly sensing that Desdemona's alleged inconstancy is his own ruin, bids farewell to what had made life bearable:

> Farewell the plumed troop and the big wars
> That makes ambition virtue! O, farewell!
> Farewell the neighing steed, and the shrill trump,
> The spirit-stirring drum, th' ear-piercing fife,
> The royal banner, and all quality,
> Pride, pomp, and circumstance of glorious war!
> And, O you mortal engines, whose rude throats
> Th' immortal Jove's dread clamors counterfeit,
> Farewell! Othello's occupation's gone!
>
> (*Othello*, Act III, scene 3)

It is clear that there is a power here that attracts Christian minds as well as others!

a. *Romans*—A crucial passage in the argument of those who legitimate (some) Christian warmaking is a paragraph in Paul's Epistle to the Romans (13:1-7). The interpretation of this passage (and its parallels in 1 Peter 2 and 1 Timothy 2) illustrates well the diversity of Christians' mindset about war, for with a little historical imagination we can envision two very different standpoints toward it. First, the historical situation in which the Romans passage was written: Roman Christians, who will in just seven years face the first general persecution (under Nero in 64) and who are therefore bound to regard the state as a potential if not yet an actual dangerous enemy, are reminded by the Apostle of Jesus' requirement to love one's enemies—to "overcome evil with good" (12:21f.). Immediately, Paul gives these saints some helpful ways to love their imperial enemy: Remember that God created him; consider the good God thereby intended; have respect for the enemy and give him his due (13:1-7). (Naturally Paul does not *call* the Roman state "the enemy"; to do so would be particularly dangerous in a document sent into the capital city itself, into the jaws of the Roman wolf.) Still, the point would not be lost. Such submission, he goes on, is part of self-sacrificial love on the part of those in positions of social inferiority (see 13:8). The warning, by the way, may have made a historic difference, for while we have record of Christians persecuted and martyred in Rome in those days—including perhaps Paul and Peter themselves—there is no record of the sort of rising there that Jews in Jerusalem would soon attempt against Rome (70 C.E.).

Now come forward in time nearly three centuries. Constantine, skillful soldier and crafty politician but no exegete, has made himself sole master of an often divided empire. He has done this in part by proffering an alliance to the Christian movement, by now rapidly growing. Imagine that Constantine or his advisors come across this passage in the library of their adopted church. Now the context in which Paul had written of suffering love and submission to enemies (12:20f.; 13:8-10) will be irrelevant: what use has the empire for such ideas? Constantine certainly has no intention to submit to *his* enemies. But abstracted from its context, the doctrine of submission to the emperor can be very useful indeed. So the paragraph can be read now in a new way—as teaching some special and unique authority assigned by God to empires (and other powers), which constitute one of the orders of creation or the like. Whatever the exact story then, that new reading was to become the standard doctrinal exegesis of the passage in the West, authorizing Christians now to do things that the first readers, far from being urged to *do*, had instead been asked if need be to suffer. With Constantine, then, an ironic historical shift has taken place.

Still, the supporters of (some) Christian warmaking might fairly argue, the situation since Constantine *is* changed. Christians in many places are a dominant majority; government nowadays is often 'Christian' government; it must act responsibly; responsibility requires that force shall meet force; obedience to that responsible government may entail military service, that is, entail Christians making war. An interesting argument, but one that contains a suppressed premise we had better examine, since it alone provides the link with our passage. The premise is this: The legitimate authority of the empire or of the state in general (Rom. 13:1-7 as read after Constantine) may require Christians to disobey God. How so?

Whereas the state on its authority tells me as a soldier, sailor, or flier (or as a supporting civilian) to be prepared to kill, God in the Decalogue says, "You shall not kill" (Commandment Six, Exod. 20:13). To which the answer will be, "Killing in war is not for Christians disobedience to God; as an exception, it is permitted." Where in the New Testament is it permitted? "In Romans 13"! Thus we come full circle in the argument, or rather we have been reminded by it of the conceptual shift between two readings.

The best argument I know for reading Romans 13 in the pacifist or peacemaker's way (as I would say, in Paul's and the Roman Christians' way, not in Constantine's and modern ethics') is found in the book of Jean Lasserre, *War and the Gospel* (1962). (This is the very Jean Lasserre, by the way, who as a student made an impact on young Dietrich Bonhoeffer—see Chapter Seven.) Lasserre was a pacifist who saw our passage in a non-Constantinian way. Yet, as a French Reformed pastor he had a Calvinist's high regard for government. He did not deny to it forceful authority. The one thing that government, however, may not do is to require the Christian to kill, for this calls into question the Christian's obedience to God—Commandment Six. This commandment, he believes, was explicitly extended by Jesus to forbid all killing of human beings, not just certain kinds of killing. Hence, anyone who argues that war is sanctioned (because the commandment "Thou shalt not kill" can be narrowly construed) must in good logic argue equally that rape, polygamy, and prostitution are sanctioned—because the relevant commandment says only "Thou shalt not commit *adultery*" (Lasserre, 1962:162, 170; cf. Chapter Six, above)!

While that argument ad hominem has force, in fact the Sixth Commandment's range is not narrow but broad even from the outset. Although some have believed that it meant only "no murder," Brevard Childs, in his commentary on Exodus, summarizes the evidence to the contrary. The Hebrew verb *ratsach*, to kill, is used elsewhere in the Old Testament of manslaughter as well as murder. The original point of Commandment Six is to forbid killing that would provoke blood vengeance—suggesting the theme that killing leads to killing (Childs, 1974:419-23). In general, it is unsanctioned killing of any sort that is forbidden by the commandment; thus Lassere (and Calvin before him) were not wrong to construe it broadly.

But as Lasserre sees, the real clincher for Christians is that Jesus, who in the Sermon on the Mount removes the permissive sanctions that for Jews had hedged divorce and oath-taking, also points to another way with regard to killing: Don't even nurse a grudge or taunt an enemy; be reconciled to your enemies; love them, don't hate them (Matt. 5:21-26, 38-48). Lasserre thinks this teaching forbids capital punishment as well, and he may be right, but our present argument need only note that since Jesus was in the Sermon indicating a way of life for his *band* of followers, it applied to group actions as truly as to individual. The disciples could not follow the Zealot way as a band while taking Jesus' way as individuals. As he taught, so he lived: His way was fulfilled in a cross, not in a war. Thus Jesus' interpretation of "You shall not kill" is finally displayed by his cross.

With this understanding, Lasserre's seems to me a flawless argument against the would-be warmaker's way of using Romans 13. Yet experience teaches that this will not settle the argument for those not already persuaded. So the significance of Romans 13 remains at issue, at least in the West, simply because we have moved from the mind of the Apostle to another mind.

b. *A conflict of narratives*—What is beginning to emerge is that the problem of Christian involvement in war is not one of rationality and clear thinking (on one side) versus muddled minds and irrationality (on the other). If this had been the case, thinkers with the rational powers of Paul Ramsey (1961) and John Howard Yoder (1971*b*) would long since have resolved the divisive issue at least to one another's satisfaction, leaving the rest of us to catch up to them when we could. This resolution has not occurred. Neither, though, is the conflict simply one of antithetical Christian convictions, with convinced Christian pacifists on one side and convinced Christian warriors on the other, awaiting that modern Thomas Aquinas who could resolve the doctrinal conflict. For many Christians, the conflict is rather an internal one: On the one hand, they are persuaded that Jesus practiced peace and requires them to do so; on the other, they equally believe that in this world much is necessary that conflicts with that first requirement, and one of those necessities is that sometimes Christians must make war, not peace. Except that he was not himself any longer constrained by Jesus' own way, this was the final position of Reinhold Niebuhr, and it is a powerful even if a paradoxical one (R. Niebuhr, 1939).

Others have sought an explanation of this agonizing division between peacemakers and their adversaries not in terms of mistakes in logic or differences in Christian conviction, but in psychological categories. Sigmund Freud, as noted in Chapter Three, posited two basic human drives, life (or eros) and death (thanatos); the former generates sex, reproduction, survival, while the latter yields destruction, self-destruction, war (Freud, 1920; 1933). This is particularly apt, as many have noted, in the era of hydrogen weapons whose deadliness exceeds the experience of all alive. And there are still other psychological theories.

Partly because it seems to point a way toward constructive action, I am more attracted to a 'narrative' explanation of persistent but diverse Christian attitudes to war and peace. Our lives are shaped by many stories: the ones we heard at our parents' knee as children; the stories we tell ourselves about ourselves (Hauerwas, 1977:ch. 5); the stories of our American (or African, or South Asian, or Soviet) culture; supremely for Christians (and "supremely" here is intended as a definition of "Christian") the story of Jesus with its prologue in Israel and its sequel in the historic church. By these stories our lives are shaped; their narrative logic controls our use of rationality; they are the stuff of our convictions. If, then, we find our own convictions in discord, the indication is that we have not gotten our own stories straight (Goldberg, 1985); we have missed their proper priority or we have muddled their actual content. When earlier in this volume we examined eros, it was possible to find a single story, the romantic myth, that had dominated thought about love in the West to the present. But no single myth in a like way dominates Western thought about war. James Aho (1981) finds that the myths of war (stories warring peoples tell themselves and others about what they are doing and why) are essentially religious; they have to do with deep feelings about nomos (order) and chaos. War is fought in order to protect or restore nomos when it is threatened by cosmic chaos. Behind this account stand the theories of Peter Berger, who identifies religion with protection against anomie (chaos) (1967). But this struggle, Aho shows, takes many forms in the war mythologies of world religions (including Catholicism and Protestantism), and in each case there are ambiguities within the myths themselves, since in war often both sides (by their myth) are fighting "against chaos," that is, employing a 'lesser evil' against ultimate evil; moreover, war as the cure for chaos creates the chaos of war. Thus paradoxically—or mythically— the aim of war is always said by some to be "peace"!

To give the myths of war a Christian overlay as Americans have liked doing involves bringing in Jesus. Edward Linenthal in his exploration of the mythology of American warfare (1980) shows that though many biblical images, both Hebraic and millenarian, have been employed here, the only surviving image by the time of Viet Nam was that of blood atonement (1980:90). As Ira Chernus interprets this,

In every war, the [American] nation has believed that its blood sacrifices would sow the seeds of a new world in which liberty would be given to all. And the individual soldier would find redemption through blood, for his red badge was less a badge of courage than of Christ-likeness. (Chernus, 1984:3)

Thus the war myth takes up into itself the very story that had appeared to overturn it, making of the professionally violent soldier a Jesus on his cross!

I said that the narrative analysis was an optimistic one. Now we are in position to see why. If war stories can capture or subvert the Jesus story, it can happen the other way around as well. (This occurred in one memorable epoch, the New Testament days and just after, when apostolic writers used martial imagery to depict not military but spiritual battle [e.g., Eph. 6:10-20].) A first sign of this renewed possibility in our generation may be the work of poets and novelists. Since World War I, war poetry worth reading has in the main been peace poetry, and war novels are not celebrations but subversions of war. John McEntyre has shown this for a series of novels from Tolstoy's *War and Peace* (1864/1869) to Heller's *Catch-22* (1964). Not only are war authors such as Faulkner and T. H. White personally antiwar; the controlling imagery of their novels begins to shape a new public myth: war as folly and chaos, not wisdom and order (McEntyre, 1981).

An interesting exercise, though regretfully one beyond the limits of this chapter, would be to explore the 'logic' of the chief Christian defenders of war in similar narrative terms. I take it there are three leading defenses: (1) war as crusade to destroy absolute evil; (2) "just" (i.e., "justifiable") war in defense of existing social and political arrangements; and (3) revolution against class oppression. The task not now undertaken would be to discover the implicit narrative beneath each of these, comparing and contrasting them with the Jesus story.

c. *The Old Testament and war*—Those who believe that Christian warmaking is sometimes appropriate rely on their understanding of classic 'prooftexts' such as Romans 13, but as we have seen, discussion of the meaning of these typically falls back, sooner or later, on the teaching of the Old Testament. Next it is too quickly said that Commandment Six does not bar Christians from all kinds of killing; it is also said that God in the Old Testament positively commanded wars. Chapter and verse are cited for this claim (Boettner, 1942). How is the peacemaker to respond to this? Has God changed? Is the Old Testament wrong? The difficulties that confront warmaking when it reads the New Testament seem to confront peacemaking when it reads the Old. To be sure, a reading strategy that treats every verse of Scripture on a flat level of teaching authority potentially confronts more problems than this one. There are many other Old Testament practices one never hears praised by Christians today. If wars are based on precedent, why not polygamy? The patriarchs practiced it; why not we? And surely this reading strategy will never charge interest on a loan? The Old Testament forbids that. Nor can it reject slavery, for "they had slaves in the Bible." In another day, that argument was often heard.

Surely what is needed here is a more consistent reading strategy (cf. Swartley, 1983). Long ago, Anabaptist leader Pilgram Marpeck pointed out that the Old Testament is "yesterday," the New Testament, "today," while in the next century after Marpeck, Roger Williams insisted, against theocratic Puritans, that all the "types" of the Old Testament were fulfilled in Christ, so that only as they are shaped by that fulfillment do the types and models of the Old Testament have authority over contemporary saints (on Marpeck, see Klassen, 1968; on Williams, see Miller, 1953:ch. 4). Since however, the question of war is, for Westerners at least, the most grave of these issues the Bible raises, and since Marpeck and Williams cannot settle them in our terms, I will suggest another approach to the Old Testament's teaching on war. If not as a document whose sentences are to be selected and read on demand but always independently of one another (the simplist militarist *and* simplist pacifist strategy), how are we to read the collection we call the Old Testament on this subject?

We might do well to begin where there is general agreement the books of the Old Testament focus—on the Exodus. This was the formative and creative event in Israel's social history; along with creation itself, it was the event remembered on every Sabbath day; the prophets look back to it as the definitive theological event. Now Millard Lind, in *Yahweh Is a Warrior* (1980) has shown that the treatment of the Exodus event in the oldest components of the Pentateuch understands it to have been a "holy war." This is an exact term. In other ancient nations the holy war was a formal, almost a ritual, practice of military rampage. These nations believed that their deities went into battle with them, wielding sword and spear and shield (cf. Gottwald, 1976). By treating the Exodus as their prototypical holy war, however, the Hebrew writers made a radical new departure. The formative event in Israel's history was not an invasion, it was a flight. It was withdrawal—the very strategy that militant ethicists warn baptists against! God defended Israel at the Red Sea; therefore Israel did not need to defend herself.

Moreover, the human hero of this event, the one who came nearest to representing God's way and will, was not a great king or a great warrior, but Moses, a prophet whose only weapon was a staff, and who as a prophet was not even eloquent. We remember that a little later there was Joshua, who was a war leader, but Joshua had no successor in Israel, while prophecy became the hallmark of Israel. The question of leadership is very important here. Lind points out that God's failure to provide a war leader for the Exodus, saying instead "the LORD will fight for you, and you have only to be still" (Exod. 14:14 RSV), just fits the later refusal of God to provide a king for Israel like the kings of the other nations. When finally Samuel anoints Saul, it is a concession to the people's foolish demand, and is not the divine way (1 Samuel 8f.). This seems to have been the uniting theme of the military exploits of Israel. Their formative 'military' event was a withdrawal, accompanied by a natural disaster—the wind and waves falling upon the pursuing Egyptians—that God substituted for the military victories other nations have always looked to as their formative events. Subsequently, the people chose the way of military exploits, and heard the voice of God commanding them to those exploits, but in doing so characteristically forgot their origins, and the different pattern (trust in God, not in arms). The authors of Joshua and of Judges did remember these themes to some degree, however, for the prototypical victories that introduce each of these books—the fall of Jericho in Joshua and the victory of Deborah in Judges—hearken back to the Exodus in one way or another. At Jericho, it is the mysterious collapse of the walls, not force of arms, that defeats the city, and in Judges the prophet Deborah is not a warrior but one whose role reminds us of Moses at the Exodus (Joshua 2–6; Judges 5; Lind, 1980:ch. 4).

No claim is implied here about the peaceable nature of early or later generations of Israelites or Jews, although a study of the time of the patriarchs would admittedly show us a remarkably peaceable or nonviolent saga of early Hebrew life. Rather the present claim is that in the times of the Exodus and the occupation of Palestine, and located in the center of the most deadly human (and 'religious') practice that the ancient world knew, in the holy war, *God planted a seed of nonviolence*, a command, not to fight, but to trust. The times were cruel and bloody ones—rather like our own times and the times of Jesus of Nazareth in that regard. Nevertheless, there was then planted a seed of a new sort, that would in due course flower in the work of the later prophets (e.g., Isaiah 40–66), and would drop its own seed in turn upon Gentile nations, borne by the ministry of the Prince of Peace (Isa. 9:6; cf. Hershberger, 1953:ch. 2). The practice of holy war *as the Jews learned it at the Exodus* was a seed that would spring up, as time went by, into the work of a greater than Moses, a new Joshua (it is surely no accident that was Jesus' name, too), whose 'warfare' would be the struggle of a peaceable kingdom.

What is at issue here is not whether one side can take some sort of account of scriptural evidence; each can. The question is rather whether the larger biblical narrative is one about a God of War whose name (depending on the setting) may as easily be Mars as Jehovah, or whether it is about a God of Peace whose people is a different people, and whose earthly name is Christ Jesus. To recall the discussion by Berger, Aho, and Chernus, the question is whether the gift of God is chaos disguised as nomos, destruction disguised as a way into life, as the old myths of war allege; or whether God's gift is rather the true story of a peaceful Way of life that overcomes, with divine patience, even our bloodlust and our war myths. The issue, as we have seen, remains uncertain.

3. The Peaceable Kingdom

a. *Peace without eschatology?*—Is there a future for peace? Peace *on earth* (Luke 2:14), not merely in the abyss of eternity? For Christians, questions about lasting peace can never be separated from eschatology (that is, from the doctrine about what *comes last* but also about what *lasts* and is fundamental). Our eschatology and our attitude to peacemaking are two sides of a single coin. In an essay that he titled "Peace without Eschatology?" (1954) the young John Howard Yoder raised questions that are still pertinent today. Are some Christian efforts to build peace separated from biblical eschatology and therefore invalid? If so, what would a biblical eschatology contribute to the understanding of peacemaking? The title of Yoder's essay referred immediately to those 1930s pacifists who, believing in "the brotherhood of man," thought that world peace was just around the corner, requiring only popular sentiment to support international renunciation of war. The Hitler era dissolved those dreams. But more generally, by "peace without eschatology" Yoder meant the views of the "Constantinians," those who seemed to him to identify church and world, who did not recognize the kairos or strategic opportunity of Christians situated between the old aeon and the new (cf. Chapter Nine, above), and who therefore clung pathetically to the old aeon, though professing Christian allegiance. Exactly their failure to take Christian eschatology seriously enough caused these to miss the way of the peaceable kingdom. Two examples, opposite to one another, will illustrate Yoder's point here.

C. I. Scofield and his associated editors of the *Scofield Reference Bible* certainly cannot be faulted for want of an eschatological view; their charted pageant of kingdoms, judgments, and apocalyptic splendors is, however, pushed away to history's rim, leaving the present an age in which "wars and rumours of wars" (Matt. 24:6 KJV; Scofield, 1917, note on 24:3) persist unchecked. Pessimism about the present is coupled with hope for a "first resurrection" (other millenarians have called this "the rapture") that will translate dead and living saints right out of earth's penultimate terrors. So Scofield's view of the present age might fairly be called "eschatology without peace."

Doubtless of more interest to many readers is the somber view of Reinhold Niebuhr alluded to in Chapter Three, above. While Niebuhr's thought developed throughout his life, the decisive turn here had long been made when he produced on the eve of World War II the pamphlet, *Why the Christian Church Is Not Pacifist* (1939) and reissued it in his *Christianity and Power Politics* (1940). The basic lines of this shift had been foretold when Niebuhr resigned (1934) from the Fellowship of Reconciliation (R. Niebuhr, 1957) and wrote "The Relevance of an Impossible Ideal" as a chapter in *An Interpretation of Christian Ethics* (1934). A brief summary of the view developed in these and other works may be helpful. Two doctrinal positions dominate his thought: first, Niebuhr's view of original sin as a key to human nature (R. Niebuhr, 1941–43:I, ch. 9); second, his application of that view to social existence. Man (the species, and thus all its members) is sinful; this sinfulness inheres particularly in classes and in nations, for group egoism cannot be ameliorated by the tensions of conscience or the constraints of love (R. Niebuhr, 1932).

But the "pacifist" (i.e., such a liberal as Niebuhr himself before his switch) naïvely supposes that love can dissolve these anthropological and sociological facts of egoism and sin; such naïveté makes the pacifist in Niebuhr's view pathetically irrelevant to power politics in the real world, and becomes sinful when it falls (as it usually does) into self-righteous pride. There is another pacifism, not sinful, but still not directly relevant to the world, that of Jesus and those who today imitate him by withdrawal into suffering love. Yet in another sense, Jesus' love *is* relevant; as the symbol of human destiny it provides in Niebuhr's view a twofold criticism (Yoder, 1955) of the rest of the world: (1) As indiscriminate criticism, it condemns us all as sinners, driving us, like Luther's "law," to take refuge in the gospel of grace; and (2) as discriminate criticism, it guides us in making choices that (as justice, and employing coercion and force) nevertheless approximate the otherwise unreachable ideal of love. Thus wars such as the war against Hitler are neither loving nor are those waging them free from guilt, but their cause may be closer to love's ideal than is the cause of Hitler's forces. It is important to see that these elements of Niebuhr's view fit closely together: the

universal sinfulness and its sinful denial that characterize
personal and even more group interaction; the suffering love
of the message and way of Jesus that is therefore ineffectual
(save as criticism of the real moral struggle); the consoling
grace that as pardon is a kind of peace, even in a strife-torn
world—all form a seamless whole without recourse to any
future consummation. If Scofield's is eschatology without
peace, Reinhold Niebuhr's best offer is still peace (such as it is
in this world) without eschatology.

By demanding that pacifists choose between responsible
relevance and irresponsible (if perhaps innocent) irrelevance,
Niebuhr mounted a powerful critique of at least his own
former pacifism. Whether it refutes other sorts remains to
say—for Niebuhr's later position has not proved invulnerable
(Yoder, 1955; MacGregor, 1954). Disregarding smaller points, I
note two crucial but dubious elements in Niebuhr's complex
outlook. The first is his assumption that the nonresistant way
of Jesus is practically irrelevant in the world today, affording
only a criticism of other ways. For this seems also to deny Jesus
a viable place in his own moral world; he is made a religious,
but not a morally relevant figure. Niebuhr's realism is thereby
made greater than Jesus' realism, by Niebuhr's account. A
second dubious element is Niebuhr's rejection of the efficacy
of the Holy Spirit to make Christians Christ-like, his downplay
of the new birth as a real transformation of human life, and his
neglect of the resurrection in favor of an exclusive emphasis on
the cross (cf. R. Niebuhr, 1941–43:II; Yoder, 1955). These omissions seem to be the consequence of an excessive emphasis
upon the ubiquity and power of original sin, an overemphasis
that makes of Niebuhr's ethic a strategy for (discriminately)
sinful living in an (indiscriminately) sinful world, rather than a
strategy for transformed life in a world become new in Christ
Jesus (2 Cor. 5:17). As John Yoder put it, "this view, based on a
realistic analysis of the old aeon, knows nothing of the new"
(1954:77).

Nevertheless, peacemakers have much to learn from
Reinhold Niebuhr. Most of all they can begin to acquire with
Hauerwas (perhaps Reinhold Niebuhr's true successor) the
skill to interpret the world as world. Niebuhr's sense of
injustice and oppression evokes his proximate discriminations. Not every war is equally unjust, even though seen with
Christian eyes all may be unjust. Peacemakers can learn as

well from Niebuhr to see themselves as the world sees them, though they may not as readily as he accept that portrait as truthful. There is a corresponding lesson, by the way, to be learned from Scofield: that is, not necessarily to judge as the world judges. Fundamentalists have sometimes (less often, alas, in connection with peace) displayed the courage to hear the word of God in Scripture, and to care not a fig for the world's opposition. Both lessons carry weight.

I would cast my own lot, though, with the insights of John Howard Yoder on this topic. In his early but classic essay (1954) he had already pointed a line of direction that took seriously the eschatology of Jesus as a thought pattern for today's Christians. This is a viewpoint that requires of most of us at least an intellectual conversion. It requires that the world we thought so sane and self-evident, the world that Reinhold Niebuhr describes as reality with such canny insight and which C. I. Scofield views with such resignation, the world of power struggles and decisions, of self-made selves and of the powers that be, shall be seen for the shabby and pretentious cosmos that it is, while our eyes instead grow accustomed to the light of a new aeon, pupils adjusting to the dawning of the coming age in which Christ alone is Lord and we servants of his lordship and thus of one another. In this new life there are discriminations enough, forgiveness of sin enough, reality enough to satisfy the most ardent Niebuhrian, and there is plenty of peace work to be done as well.

b. *The practices of peace*—Many folk, including quite a few pacifists, dislike the word "pacifist." It is to be preferred, I suppose, to "militarist," but why must one choose? To be sure, the root meaning of the word is "peacemaker." "Blessed are the peacemakers," *Beati pacifici*, says Jesus in the Latin version of the Sermon on the Mount (Matt. 5:9). Still, a meaning is more than its root, and "pacifist" has not a winsome ring. Yoder has counted twenty-three (or is it twenty-four) kinds of pacifism, with some one of which most disciples could surely identify (1971b). Yet we will not forget that the line between church and world still bisects believers' hearts. So what I now wish to propose is not addressed exclusively to those with a true blue or 'pure' adherence to Jesus' way of peace. It does presuppose that both individuals and churches are better prepared now than at some other times to learn Jesus' way. Perhaps this is because of

Viet Nam, perhaps because of the Bomb, perhaps because of our long, disastrously violent century. Perhaps it is because of a new awareness that human life as a whole, perhaps life itself, is at risk in a way we had not sensed before. In any case, what I have is offered as a proposal for growth, not a counsel of 'perfection.'

This is not to neglect days ahead that may put peaceful obedience to Jesus on trial once more, or to deny that then as before those who do obey him may have to suffer and to die. This is happening now in some parts of the world; it can happen in our part. Indeed, the more popular nonviolence becomes here, the more dangerous a way it will be. The worldly conformity of most Christians has for a long time sheltered the nonconformity of an 'inconsequential' few; if the few were to become many, the shelter would likely vanish, and Christians might once again have to answer the interrogation of a more authoritarian modern Celsus (above, p. 301).

i. *Strand one*—For coherence' sake, I propose to relate the disciples' peacemaking to each of the three strands of Christian ethics. In the first of these, Christians as well as others are conscious of aggressive as well as erotic and hunger drives; some regard human beings as unique in our natural willingness to kill apart from the need to eat. (There seem to be cooperative drives as well, but I will stay with the hard case.) William James, in a brief essay, "The Moral Equivalent of War" (1910), has led the way in recognizing that "the war party" can deploy the virtues of courage, discipline, fidelity, and many more even while James' own "antimilitarist party" appeals instead to softness, ease, and a shorter work week as its arguments for peace. The peacemakers should recognize, James thinks, the strength of the war party's psychological insight, and should devise a moral equivalent that will require of citizens stress, effort, discipline, and sacrifice. James' own proposal is for a conscription of youth everywhere into national peace corps and the like whose struggle will be a "war against Nature"; this would take the place of killing, and would demand the hardihood and sacrifice now required of troops. While James' concrete proposal bespeaks too much of the nationalist (and masculinist) arrogance later writers have seen as the very evil to be cured, and in any case appears from our vantage ecologically heretical, his recognition of 'military' virtues and his call for their capture by the side of peace seems not far from the kingdom of

God: "Foxes have holes, and birds of the air have nests; but the Son of man has nowhere to lay his head" (Luke 9:58 RSV). Jesus' way indeed entails courage to face hardship.

Yet the slide from disciplined public works to the Corps of Engineers and from that to Othello's mortal engines with rude throats ready to clamor, from discipline to devastation, seems dangerously easy. Discipleship's virtues had better grow from minds conformed to that of their own purposeful Teacher. Stanley Hauerwas, whose book *The Peaceable Kingdom* lends its title to this section, has explored in it the required "habits" of mind. He recalls a well-known debate of the 1930s between Reinhold Niebuhr and his brother, H. Richard. The debate was ostensibly over the desirability of American military intervention in Manchuria as the Japanese invaded. Reinhold took the line we have already noted; his brother wrote instead on "The Grace of Doing Nothing." Hauerwas suggests that at the heart of H. Richard Niebuhr's "nothing" there is of necessity a spirituality, a peaceableness of mind, that is foundational for all deeds and practices of peace. Indeed, the surprising thing, he finds, is that not only H. Richard's national strategy of restraint, sometimes inaction, but also Reinhold's alternative strategy of "realism" called for an inner discipline. To be sure, the disciplines differed. Richard's was a "particular faith in a definite kind of God" that made sense "only if the world is in fact bounded and storied by a God who has the power to use our faithfulness and unfaithfulness that the kingdom of peace might be present among us." But Reinhold's "is a spirituality that demands patience and hope" also. Yet the latter's depends upon the conviction that the world is necessarily a tragedy; it is "an attempt to help train us to have souls able to keep up the struggle for justice through the inevitable and ambiguous means of coercion." While Hauerwas thinks as do I that disciples must finally side with H. Richard's political position (as expressed in the debate) in today's world, he sees the need for a spirituality more like Reinhold Niebuhr's to sustain that position (Hauerwas, 1983:138-41).

For us, two lessons emerge. The first is the centrality in Hauerwas' ethics as in Jesus' teaching of a selfhood sustained by shared (and by solitary) Christian worship. The other is that the form of the schooling, that is the form of our worship, must be suited to the practices that it is to sustain. Thus we come to strand two, with its demand for a community setting for peacemaking, and its recognition (Chapter Six) of the role of powerful practices in shaping any life.

ii. *Strand two*—It may surprise some that "peace" in the New Testament is sometimes a verb (εἰρηνεύω) rather than a noun; yet Jesus in Mark 9:50 commands inner discipline for each, coupled with cooperative "peacing," to use a word we do not have: "Have salt in yourselves, and practice peace [εἰρηνεύετε] with one another." Perhaps our next thought is that peace won't work, for others are always limiting our ability to act peaceably. In part, this reflects a failure of imagination, perhaps caused by prior failure to attend to ways of peace. Yet Harvard theoretician of nonviolence Gene Sharp has produced a 900-page account of *The Politics of Nonviolent Action* (1973) detailing events throughout history in which peaceable techniques have proved effective. These range all the way from simple noncooperation to the coercive nonviolence of strikes and boycotts; they include the economic boycott by colonists prior to the American Revolution, the acceptance of imprisonment by leaders (e.g., M. L. King, Jr.) as a means of mobilizing public opinion, also speeches, petitions, letters of opposition or support, public declarations by groups, the use of slogans, banners, leaflets, pamphlets, books, publication of newspapers and journals, songs and records on radio and television, deputations, mock awards, the wearing of symbols, protest disrobings, the destruction of one's own property, sit-downs and strikes, provision of sanctuary, collective disappearance, refusal to pay fees or fines, withdrawal of bank deposits, tax refusal, boycott of elections. . . . The list goes on, but these convey its flavor. Against tyrannies and violence ancient and modern such peaceable (though not amiable) methods, Sharp reminds us, have won concessions, changed policies, sometimes even stopped armies, and effected change.

Here one may wonder what authorizes one or another of these tactics for Christians, and (more consequentially) what things make for our peace (Luke 19:42). Are these strategies of nonviolence the road to peace or stepping stones to war? The answer seems to be that they may constitute either. The American colonists' boycott and 'tea-parties,' for example, led on to armed revolt, while Gandhi's nonviolent revolt issued peaceably in a free (though partitioned and often violent) India.

Perhaps the crucial difference lies in the intent that forms a nonviolent movement. In any case, nonviolent resistance is not to be equated with the complacent Allied and German militarism (and complacent Allied pacifism) that paved the way to Hitler's rise.

Our next demurrer may be to note that while nonviolent methods have sometimes worked, they have not seldom incurred violent reaction. This is true, and is the necessary acknowledgment that must separate Christians, conscious of a summons to the cross, from those who see peaceable encounter as a strategy of convenience or necessity from case to case. At the end of the road for a Christian stands the Master's cross on which the disciple may be required to suffer: The reconciliation Jesus was able to achieve required his life, "making peace (εἰρηνοποιήσας) by the blood of his cross" (Col.1:20 RSV). That cross must guide every Christian social practice, either as a pattern or as a limit. This raises the question whether we have the heart for such strenuous discipleship, or for the severe self-discipline to which Hauerwas summons us. At least we seem here to be on the trail of the moral or psychological equivalent of war desired by William James. But have we the élan?

iii. *Strand three*—It seems appropriate here to bring alongside one another two ultimates that have lurked just beneath the surface of the chapter to this point: nuclear weapons and Jesus' resurrection. For a secular mind, the weapons present an ultimate threat. Jonathan Schell has pictured this eloquently in the very title of his jeremiad: *The Fate of the Earth* (1982). Either the human race must renounce these terrible weapons, organize world government to control them, and survive, or all that is dear will surely be lost. Whatever Schell's theological and political sophistication or lack, his description of the nuclear threat is not exaggerated. We really face in this case one kind of ultimate, the power of something very near biocide—the destruction of all life on our globe. This fact may make Jesus' kind of pacifism a little more available to some. The ultimate threat of human destruction that lies in thermonuclear (and not 'merely' atomic) weapons is one that now hovers over every war everywhere. War may be a deepseated human drive, but its terminus is evidently universal death—possibly the lingering and horrible death of our living earth in a long nuclear 'winter.'

Given that fact, war becomes intolerable even to many who do not know Jesus and his Way. Is it possible that so long ago Jesus saw where human violence led and rejected it for a new way grounded in his own ultimate?

That other 'ultimate' is very different—the resurrection of Jesus Christ from the dead. His resurrection stakes out indelibly in history the claim of the One the Bible calls the God of peace (Heb. 13:20); it announces that while the worst man can do is bad indeed, it is immeasurably fainter, weaker than the best that God can do. It is an instructive exercise of mind to reconsider the story of Jesus that preceded that resurrection, and to remember how often in the narrative it seemed within the power of some earthly Pilate or Herod or Caesar to dash God's last, best Word to death before his earthly work was done. These lines happen to be written on the last day of Epiphany, the time when many Christians in the West remember again the story of Herod's soldiers, whose violence was set to destroy the boy babies of Bethlehem and with them that New Moses, the boy named Jesus (Matthew 2). The story is retold, albeit in legendary form, in order to say that in the history of Jesus earth's evil does not destroy heaven's hope. Some, though, will remember that at the end of the story there was a crucifixion, in which that very One was destroyed. Many, remembering, have been filled with violent rage, against Jews, or Romans, or the Moslem inhabitants of the Near East a thousand years later, and have set out on militant crusades to save God's world from others' wickedness. Now again there are the frightened, the angry, the militant. Once again they will set out with bombs to save us from bombs, with crusades, perhaps, to save us from soldiers, and with totalitarian politics to save us from ultimate death. It is better, I think, and truly in line with what has been said here, to let our actions for peace be altogether the practices of peace, and to take heart from the risen Christ still with us (Matt. 28:20), trusting, beyond all our faith and ethics, in

> the God of peace, that brought again from the dead our Lord
> Jesus, that great shepherd of the sheep,
>
> who can,
>
> through the blood of the everlasting covenant, make you perfect
> in every good work to do his will, working in you that which is
> well-pleasing in his sight, through Jesus Christ; to whom be
> glory for ever and ever. Amen.   (Heb. 13:20f.)

RETROSPECT

The stress on narrative is correlative to the claim that every ethic requires a qualifier. No ethic can be freed from its narrative, and thus communal, context. To the extent that practical reason seeks to avoid its inherent historical character, it relinquishes any power to enable us to order our lives in accordance with our true ends. We thus become alienated from ourselves; we lose the ability to locate the history of which we are a part.

Stanley Hauerwas, *The Peaceable Kingdom*

. . . The play's the thing
Wherein I'll catch the conscience of the king.

Hamlet, Act II, scene 2

Why Narrative
Ethics?

Why should ethics for Christians be narrative ethics—the
sort of ethics represented by this volume and by the work of
Stanley Hauerwas (1981, 1983) and John Howard Yoder (1972),
and indicated by that of Alasdair MacIntyre (1984)? In this
chapter I will address that question, arguing that a truly
Christian ethics *must* be a narrative ethics. This chapter, then,
is a theoretical defense of the book's method. It comes last
because I believe the best defense of this method is its actual
use. *Demonstravi ambulando.* But it may also be helpful now to
point out in overview what the preceding chapters have
demonstrated by their 'walk' through Christian ethics. Such a
retrospective glimpse may help to relate this work to others in
its field. Readers more experienced in ethics may even find this
the best beginning place. Others may be glad not to have to
confront it until the end.

The procedure I will follow is this: First, an explanation of
the sense in which this three-stranded ethics *is* narrative
ethics; second and third, a defense of this method against two
proposals to reduce narrative ethics to some other sort: to the
'propositional principles' of some philosophical ethics or to the
'values' of still others. Throughout, the general strategy will be
to show not that narrative ethics obliterates other kinds of
ethical interest, but that these other approaches presuppose

and require some narrative, and that their Christian use presupposes and requires the Christian narrative. For example, 'rights' (a class of values) can be seen to make Christian moral sense only because certain rights have a place within a particular story Christians live out.

Since this chapter comes as close as any in the book to dealing with more philosophical questions, it seems appropriate to indicate here the connection between theological ethics (or moral theology) and philosophical ethics (or moral philosophy). At one time, many thinking Christians believed, with Thomas Aquinas (1225–1274), that the distinction between theology and philosophy was as follows: Theology accepts as a given the revelation in Scripture, and proceeds from it, whereas philosophy renounces such dependence, seeking only the neutral truth available to unaided human reason. But that distinction is no longer viable. For better or worse, human reasoning infects all our intellectual work, even that which takes Scripture or revelation as 'data.' And philosophy, while it may indeed ignore or even renounce the biblical sources of knowledge, never really attains the neutrality some have claimed for it, because the philosopher is immersed in a world of convictions that must either be, or must clash with, the convictions Christians hold (McClendon and Smith, 1975). Thus the old line between theology (including theological ethics) and philosophy (including philosophical ethics) is now blurred. From time to time, the present work has intruded upon questions traditionally thought philosophical; that will happen even more in this chapter. If anyone disagrees with what is said, it will be fair to use philosophical arguments to express the disagreement, for such arguments are used here. But it will also be fair to base disagreements on convictional grounds, and that may take the argument in a theological direction, which is just the direction taken throughout this work.

1. The Defense of Narrative Ethics

Before comparing the narrative approach in ethics to other approaches, it will be helpful to say more exactly what is meant by characterizing the present work as narrative ethics. "Narrative" means many things to many people, and diverse opinions about narrative theology in general are in part a consequence of the variety of uses of that term. To some, "narrative" means primarily personal narrative—specifically, autobiography. But autobiography has plainly not been the concern of the present work. Others use the term to refer to still other kinds of literature religions have employed—myths, fables, parables, epics, wonder-tales, and more, as well as biography and autobiography. Certainly, a narrative ethics must be conscious of all the genres present in the literature it counts central (Goldberg, 1982:ch. 6), yet it need not give equal weight to all.

Several theorists have called fresh attention to a style of narrative they claim to be central to any hermeneutic or reading strategy that aims to understand the Bible on its own terms: namely, the Bible's "realistic" or "historylike" narrative content. These theorists—both literary critics such as Robert Alter (1981) and theologians such as Hans Frei (1974, 1975)—do not choose to engage in the modern critical debate about how well the Bible serves the needs of critical historians. Rather they call attention to the style of the biblical books, found both in the individual narratives that constitute a great portion of both Testaments, for instance the story of David and Bathsheba, or the stories of Jesus, and also in the overall story implied by the lesser stories. (For Christians, this greater story must include the whole account of Israel, of the kingdom Jesus proclaimed, and of the church that followed.) And what is it that constitutes such "realistic narrative" or gives it its distinctive quality? This is a hard question, requiring detailed analysis for its answer. But we may make a beginning by noting with Frei that these biblical narratives are marked, as are other "realistic" narratives (e.g., eighteenth-century English novels) by the convergence and interdependence of three related but separable elements: character, social setting, and circumstance or incident (1974:321). It takes all three, but it takes no more than these three. "The king died, and then the queen died" has only incident and social setting; it reflects the mortuary table of a monarchy, but it is not yet a story. But "the king died, and then the queen died *of grief*" (I owe the illustration to Frank Kermode) is germinal narrative, susceptible of realistic enlargement, because character, the delineation of a queen who is more than a statistic, has been added to the chronicle. And it is just these three that mark not only the fiction about which Henry James wrote so insightfully ("What is character but the determination of incident? What is incident but the illustration of character?"—James, 1884/1984:55) but also the kind of realistic narrative or history the Bible relates.

Now my suggestion is that what the literary critics refer to under the shorthand emblem of "character" is very close, close enough for our purposes, to what ethics must address in its first strand, the strand of embodied selfhood (Chapter Three). Ethics' emphasis is a bit different than the critics', they emphasizing the self that is embodied, we the embodiment of such a self; but their "character" is nothing without (real or fictive) embodiment, and our "body" is nothing without the actual self thus made incarnate. It is the self in its continuity that is "embodied"; and it is the continuities of selfhood that both ethicists (e.g., Hauerwas, 1981) and literary critics understand as "character." Next, consider that "social setting" is just the concern of strand two, presented here as the communal or social strand of Christian ethics (Chapter Six). And finally, in a world in which (as Christians are supposed to believe) all the circumstances of our lives are finally seen to be in the hand and under the eye of a providential God, the third element of realistic narrative, namely incident or circumstance, is adequately conceived only as God's action upon us—even when that action be the 'incident' of a cruel cross (Acts 2:22) or an unanticipated resurrection (Acts 2:24). So the third or resurrection strand is our distinctive term for what literary critics more neutrally refer to as circumstance or incident. There are some difficulties in this last identification. How can all circumstance be counted as God's own action? Students of philosophy will recognize this as the historic problems of free will and evil. Yet that we do face such problems is evidence enough that in crucial cases we indeed identify circumstance, even cruel circumstance, with the decisive hand of God (cf. Gen. 45:8; Acts 2:23). As H. Richard Niebuhr so eloquently summarizes it, Christian ethics is just this: "God is acting in all actions upon you. So respond to all actions upon you as to respond to his action" (1963:126). (See further Chapter Nine, above.)

Now the consequence of this is that the present volume's analysis of the moral life into three spheres or strands that are necessarily and indissolubly one is just matched by the narrative literary critics' three necessarily interrelated strands or elements of realistic narrative. And the upshot of the whole matter is that three-stranded biblical or Christian ethics as here presented is none other than the critical analysis of the moral life of those who share in a certain ongoing real story—a story whose link with its primitive past is established by *anamnesis* or memory, and whose link with its final end is fixed by the anticipation or hope of the sharers of the Way. It is important to recall that in this way of speaking, ethics itself is not a story and does not tell a story; rather it investigates, analyzes, criticizes a way of life, a morality, that is itself story-formed. Thus this three-stranded ethics is a narrative ethics, or a part of narrative theology (Chapter One) not because it sometimes tells illustrative stories (though it may do that), and not merely because it emphasizes the long continuities of the moral life expressed by "character" or by "virtue" or by "practices" or by "convictions" (though these come still nearer the mark), but *because its task is the discovery, understanding, and creative transformation of a shared and lived story, one whose focus is Jesus of Nazareth and the kingdom he proclaims—a story that on its moral side requires such discovery, such understanding, such transformation to be true to itself.* To be true, Christian theological ethics must know this story, must understand this story, must give a lead for the appropriation of this story; when it does so, it thereby constitutes itself a 'narrative' ethics.

Perhaps this point could be put differently, especially for those who have not worked through the preceding pages. Many have agreed that one main task of ethical thinking is self-knowledge or self-understanding. As Robert M. Adams put this to me in a letter (Sept. 20, 1984), "Only if we understand who we are and what sort of history we are involved in will we be able to make wise decisions and know which of the more general ethical principles apply to us and why." The focus on "decisions" and "principles" in modern ethics has distracted us, I believe, from this deeper, narrative basis of self-knowledge of which Adams speaks; the present work tries to restore the balance. There is always a story that is integral to such knowledge, and for Christians this is so in two ways. First, there must be a vital link between the Christ we know in worship and the Christ who lived and died and rose: The story now and the story then must be linked by the identity of the one risen Christ Jesus (cf. Bonhoeffer, 1978). The Lord of Christian morality is not a principle or an ideal goal or *telos*, but a person whose timely life confronts our stories with his own. Second, there is both a logical and a narrative link between the original church and the church now (to which we can add, "and the church that is to be"—Chapter One, above). In earlier chapters I call this link the baptist vision. And it, too, brings out the indispensability of narrative to morality. The shape of the linked story is the (moral) shape of the Christian life.

So we come to the question of (philosophical) justification of such an ethics from an exact standpoint: It is *this* ethics that must be justified; *this* narrative style that must be found valid. The defense we offer must be suited to the stronghold we would defend. For it would be ironic to offer, for example, a Kantian defense of utilitarianism—the 'defense,' if valid, might paradoxically constitute a refutation. Similarly, we cannot justify narrative Christian ethics by showing that on utilitarian, or deontological, or emotivist, or some other alien ground this ethics is valid; indeed, such procedures are bound to be in the worst sense reductionist. We can reckon that the overall strategy of the opponents of narrative ethics will be to show that to the extent that it is true at all, it rests on foundations other (and more elementary) than itself, while our counterstrategy must be to deny this and to show that each such reduction of narrative ethics to something less than itself is misleading or mistaken.

This is our strategy. It is a piecemeal strategy. It cannot show that narrative ethics defeats every argument against it. At best, it will consider those proposed reductions that are most powerful or most threatening; if it can meet these, it is fair to hope it will be able to meet less powerful ones as well. Two standard reductions (so they seem from this standpoint) are (1) the basing of ethics not upon narratives but upon *principles*, usually expressed in propositional form, and (2) the basing of ethics upon *values*. An example of the first is the proposition, advanced by some philosophers as logically fundamental, "It is right to act rationally." An example of the second is the claim, advanced by some Christians, that ethics is ultimately based upon *love*, or (to show how readily one strategy can turn into the other) that "It is always right (or always rational) to do the loving thing"—a propositional principle. Some, fearing that narrative ethics leads to irrationality, will claim that insofar as it is ethics, its content is reducible without remainder to such (nonnarrative) propositions or to such principles. The general difficulty with this move is that rather than make Christian ethics more secure, the reduction may instead make it more dubious. For there is a profound difficulty in the ethics of principles and values: namely, that their advocates have never been able to agree among themselves upon which principles, or which values, are the right ones. This may lead a speculative reader to wonder if in fact modern moral philosophy, instead of 'reforming' Christian ethics in all its narrative particularity, would not do better to acknowledge the narratives that underlie its own.

Stanley Hauerwas and David Burrell have sketched, in a few brilliant paragraphs, the way in which the "standard account" of Christian ethics, that is, the reductionist account, covertly depends upon its own narratives. Perhaps the basic story on which the standard account depends, they say, is the ancient tale of "humankind's quest for certainty in a world of contingency." This mythic pattern is explicated, however, in a variety of modern narratives. There is the tale told by August Comte, of mankind's journey from the method of religion, whose form is stories, through the method of philosophy, whose form is metaphysics, to the method of science, whose form is "exact methods." Again, there is the story told by Hegel, showing "how each of these ages supplanted the other as refinement in the progressive development of reason." Doubtless there are still other standard account stories. Yet the feature of them all, these critics say, is ironically to tell a story that shows why we no longer need stories: "stories are prescientific, according to the story legitimizing the age which calls itself scientific" (Hauerwas, 1977:25). Yet strangely the irony has not deterred the reductionists in their program.

2. The Ethics of Propositional Principles

While reduction of narrative to propositional principles and reduction to values have much in common, it will be convenient to take them up one at a time. First to the propositionalists. A narrative (they can say) is composed of a series of sentences; each sentence constitutes one or more propositions. Not all the propositions will be moral propositions, but some may be. To take an example, consider the proposition: "Self-sacrifice is the *summum bonum*." This, it may be claimed, is the moral principle that the Gospel narratives illustrate or exemplify. There are of course other things in the Gospels, but they provide only example or background or local color. Note that the narrative cannot do more than this, since (by the claim now being considered) principles must stand independent of this and all narratives.

a. *A speech-act analysis of the Gospels*—Such an argument contains several kinds of difficulties. Here I must point out a fundamental flaw in the theory of language presupposed by the argument. For some time, now, language theorists have had available the concept of speech-acts, an understanding of the way spoken and written discourse works in conveying meaning. This understanding calls into question the basic assumptions of the scheme just presented. According to speech-act theory (whose roots lie in Gottlob Frege and especially in J. L. Austin) the working of language is not reducible to a series of 'propositions' whose task is merely to 'predicate' x of y, and whose only virtue is to be 'true' and whose only vices are to be 'false' or 'meaningless.' Rather, the utterances of our tongue and pen are a series of *acts performed in the world* in which we live, employing the conventions of the language at our disposal (English, or Tagalog, or Chinese) in order to make a move in the human situation in which we along with others are engaged. While 'describing' and 'predicating' are indeed among those possible moves, they are as such neither normative nor uniquely privileged, nor is 'true or false' the only standard by which their felicity or 'happiness' (to use the technical term) is to be gauged. (For more on this theory of speech-acts in relation to religion see McClendon and Smith, 1975: ch. 3; Tilley, 1978; Searle, 1979; and the literature cited in these.) Such happiness will instead depend sometimes on the suitability of the linguistic forms employed, sometimes on the way things are in the world, sometimes on the suitability of that speaker or writer to issue it here and now and of the reader or listener to receive it ('uptake'), and normally on all three 'suitabilities.'

To be sure, there is a difficulty in applying this analysis to narratives, since there is as yet no generally accepted scheme for advancing from the analysis of a single speech-act to the analysis of longer texts composed of many speech-acts, and since the complexities of advancing from the case of a single speaker (or writer) to a collective or redactive authorship such as recent biblical study postulates, and of advancing from a single hearer (or reader) to a mass audience, perhaps remote in time from the writer as well, have not yet been resolved. I believe, though, that the sense of what language *does*, advanced by speech-act theory, may even at this stage of the work aid us with these interpretive difficulties. We shall have to keep firmly in mind the threefold connectedness of language (1) with its own rules, (2) with the world, and (3) with the social relationship of writer and readers to one another. While we may not yet know well enough how these elements are related in narrative discourse, we should be able, by attending to each of them, to expose the flaws in the reductionism noted above. For while my opponents must assume, in order for moral 'propositionalism' to work, that propositions can simply be abstracted from the text and treated as independent moral truths, the theory of speech-acts reveals that such moves involve an ongoing mistake.

A good area for testing this claim may be the Gospel reading strategy proposed in the recent work of Hans Frei (1922–). In two major constructive essays Frei has argued first (1974) that a disastrous mismove was made when Enlightenment biblical scholars gave up the centuries-old idea that the biblical narratives meant what they said, and substituted for that (once obvious) notion of meaning another—the reconstructed 'scientific history' to which the narratives were said to refer—or failing that, some other more ingenious 'meaning' located beneath the surface of the text, a 'spiritual' sense, or a 'religious' meaning, or a Christ-myth, or whatever. Even conservative scholars, Frei believes, by confusing the relation between meaning and reference, furthered this Enlightenment mistake (1974, pass.). Then, second, he claimed (1975) that a proper reading strategy would see the Gospel narratives as identity-documents, that is, as writings whose sense was to claim that the one present now in the church, the risen Lord Christ, is *none other than* the one told about in those very documents. Hence follows the centrality of the resurrection in all four Gospels, since that alone could explain this identity. If with the help of speech-act theory we can see that Frei's strategy is a valid one, we will at the same time see the mistake made by the nonnarrative propositionalists in treating the Gospels' meaning as just the expression of a moral principle.

i. *Primary force: identifying*—Speech-act theory, though still incomplete, can teach us the proper questions to ask of Frei's reading strategy. The primary question to be put to any act of utterance, any speech-act, is this: what in the world is it *doing?* Frei's suggestion is that *the Gospels* (each viewed for present purposes as one extended speech-act) *are identifying the one we call Jesus Christ*. Now the speech-act of identifying, like the acts of promoting, or assessing, or reporting, or any other possible speech-act, has its own proper conditions for felicity, aptness, or 'happiness.' What are these conditions? We may begin to answer by noting that very often, identifications employ either titles or proper names, and that "Jesus Christ" is precisely a combination of those two: the name "Jesus" and the title "Christ." But titles and proper names function only imperfectly as definitive identifications: for example, there are many Professors of Theology, and alas, more than one James McClendon in the world. An identification that cannot be faulted in any way (as philosophers say, a "definite description") is one that eliminates all ambiguity of reference; thus "Mount Everest" is only a proper name, but "the tallest mountain on earth above sea level" is a definite description, and to know that Everest is that mountain is to identify it unambiguously. There are many Walter Scotts, but only one Scott is "the author of *Waverly*"; many James McClendons, but only one who admits to being the author of this chapter. For some philosophers at least, definite descriptions of this sort have provided the model of successful identification.

Now what if, following Frei, we understand the Gospel of Mark as a document that works to *identify* the one whom in the church today we know as the risen Christ? Then the entire Gospel of Mark, treated as an extended speech-act, is a (putative) definite description: it says, to be brief, that Jesus Christ (so named and titled in 1:1) *is* the one who: was baptized by John, was tempted by Satan, healed and taught in Galilee, appointed twelve disciples, worked great signs, encountered enemies, ate and drank with sinners, fed the hungry, opened blind eyes, demanded self-abandoning discipleship, rejected hierarchy among his followers, went boldly to Jerusalem, was arrested, tried, crucified—and appeared again, risen. Now if offering this identification is what Mark is doing, some problems do arise, for Matthew, Luke, and John provide somewhat different definite descriptions. So far, though, this is no more problematic than that "James VI of Scotland" is one definite description, and "James I of England" another, of the *same* Stuart monarch. It will be a bit more problematic if there are conflicts in the two descriptions (as there might be from Scottish and English perspectives) but still this will not defeat identification any more than it defeats identification of Shakespeare to find that, despite earlier claims, many now believe he never wrote the play named *Two Noble Kinsmen*. Note, though, that treating the Gospels as identity-documents puts the literary point of the Gospels on a quite different footing than thinking of them as (inept) attempts at modern historiography or biography. For it remains unexceptionably true that Jesus Christ is the one *of whom it is told*, as Mark does tell us, that he was baptized by John, tempted by Satan, etc.

However, two further identity-claims must be noted before we move on. Jesus is not the only character in the Gospel stories—there are his family, there are the crowds and the authorities, and (of great present importance) there are his followers, *the disciples*. Discipleship in Mark is not in the main portrayed by the delineation of individual characters (though "the twelve" are given names, and though James, John, and especially Simon Peter are even allowed speaking roles); rather it is "the disciples" as a group who are rendered by the narrative. At the outset they seem most often mere foils, present to expose Jesus' casual or revolutionary attitude regarding gastronomic practice, available as servants to provide boats or make household arrangements, ready to ask naïve questions or listen to the Master's teaching. They are loyal if inept servants. But at the climax (8:27ff.) it is they who receive the crucial call to follow the way of the cross, and their dim-sighted following—they are amazed (10:24) or afraid (10:32) or arrogant (10:35ff.)—is contrasted with that of one Bartimaeus ("son of the unclean") whose journey from blindness to sight, from blind hope to eager following, shows what the others ought to have been but were not. At the time of the crucifixion, not merely Peter but all the disciples including the twelve "left him and fled" (14:50), and again it is not "the twelve," but lowly women disciples who are honored to witness the resurrection first and to bear the news to the others (16:7).

Now note a vital feature of the Gospels understood as identity-documents: whereas the identity of Jesus is at once that of the risen Christ present in the readers' church *and* the central figure in the Gospel, the identity of the "disciples" is by invitation the readers themselves as well as their originals in the story (cf. Chapter Eight, above). *We* are invited to become disciples, and thus to see ourselves figuring in this narrative. If we do, we will be neither Jesus nor his opponents; our natural identification is with these hapless servants, indefinite in number, who nevertheless are transformed by the good news. (cf. Thiemann, 1985:ch. 7).

Not only do the Gospels identify Jesus and identify his disciples—identities which in two different ways impinge upon the reader; the Gospels also identify a narrative world, *the coming kingdom.* This is so common a feature of other narratives as to require little expansion. Sinclair Lewis depicts the twentieth-century world of small-town U.S.A., Charles Dickens the world of nineteenth-century England. Some (e.g., Bultmann) have thought the gospel world a strange one, and have reasoned that we must abstract from that world to hear the gospel message (demythologization). In Frei's work, however, a different view is proposed: The gospel world is strange, but it is into that strange world that today's reader is invited to enter. It is a world of familiar objects, persons, events—rulers, hungry masses, contentious debaters, conservative religionists interacting in familiar ways. Yet into that world a kingdom is breaking, a Master is appearing, a summons to obedience is sounding. In that new world, God answers prayers, sometimes; goodness suffers, sometimes; faith is born, sometimes. Within the old world a new world appears. By rendering it, the writer invites readers to enter; upon entering, readers find the perplexing secrets of the strange new world their own, its Lord their Lord, its disciple role their task. Thus the three identities—Christ, kingdom, disciples—are inseparable, while the weld that joins them is the story, a story that renders kingdom and disciples and the character called Christ by deftly distinguishing each from the other two (Frei, 1975:chs. 9–13). In this way, in this sense, the story gives moral shape to our lives.

I have so far claimed that finding the morality of the Gospels by extracting some 'moral propositions' from them is a reduction based on an inadequate theory of language, and I have proposed as more adequate a speech-act theory. Such a theory underlies the reading strategy of Hans Frei. By treating the primary (cf. 'performative') force of these narratives as *identifying* Jesus Christ, his disciples, and his kingdom, better sense can be made of these documents on their own terms. We have yet to consider, however, their representative and affective dimensions.

ii. *Representative force and the relation to history*—By this time we can see why it is vital for Christian ethics that the biblical story shall be a true or real story as opposed to a false or fictional one. For if the Lord we worship is identical with (and not just something like) the Jesus of the Gospels, and if today's disciple community is in another sense or senses identical with (and not just historically descended from) the disciple community then, and if the kingdom the Gospels herald is the kingdom to which we are here and now summoned—if, in the New Testament's language, "God has made *this Jesus*, whom you crucified, both Lord and Messiah" (Acts 2:36 NEB)—then the story must be a true story both then and now, or our faith is in vain. Here, then, the critical question about the historicity of the Gospels arises after all, it seems, and it arises about all the New Testament documents which are in one way or another part of the story—the Epistles as well as the Gospels. Their linguistic role as identity-documents requires that they shall be veridical, factual, actual history as well, whereas there is nothing whatever about 'moral propositions,' the darlings of the reductionist view here under attack, to make the same requirement within their theory. And since such a demand is typically Christian (cf. Luke 1:1-4), the reductionist theory is thereby in default as an account of Christian morality.

Notice that this is not quite the same as the related demand that some or all of these stories shall be available to and verifiable by public historical investigation, and I take it that a main result of Frei's work will be to keep these separable demands (for truth and for verifiability) separated. On the one hand, he finds no difficulty in categorizing elements of the Gospel accounts as "stylized," more like tableaux, perhaps, than like historical accounts. As Jesus, according to the story, begins to preach the kingdom of God, Frei says that kingdom and Jesus have so far not been given separate identities by the synoptic evangelists; hence tales will be told which may begin to identify Jesus as a person, but which in the main only more generally identify him together with the kingdom he is bringing (1975:132). Then, as the story moves on to its climax in Jerusalem, "history-like" narrative takes over, permitting Jesus' own identity to move to center stage in the narrative. But at this point, says Frei, it is "generally agreed" that the narrative reflects "actual events with considerable (though not absolute) accuracy" (1975:132f.). Moreover, there are within the Gospels identity-claims, such as the claim that Jesus is the one who is totally obedient to God, which are beyond the reach of any possible historical investigation. So in Frei's view, the position seems to be this: The truthfulness of this story in the synoptics is achieved by a variety of means, from the "stylized" episodes of the early kingdom teaching to the historylike identification of the intentions and actions of Jesus by way of personal narrative about him at the Jerusalem terminus of his public career. *And these varied literary devices stand in just that relation to what actually happened that is required for making them genuine identity-documents.* Historical investigation of a public sort cannot in all the cases just cited (to say nothing of still others, such as the birth and infancy narratives of Matthew and Luke) be a court of last appeal as to their truth, for the reasons just explained, but where it is *relevant* to investigate historically, it is fitting to do so, provided this is understood to be a separate historical inquiry and not a substitute for investigating the meaning of the narratives themselves.

This should be enough to show that in Frei's view, the triangular relation of narrative to fact to historical inquiry is complex enough to admit of no simplistic account. Rather, at each point the relation of the three must be determined by the narrative's own structure and intent. A rather interesting logical point arises here: How "absolute" (to use Frei's term) must accuracy in a description be in order to constitute it an identification of the individual intended by the description? Fortunately, this point has been canvassed by philosophers interested in the theories of identity and description. The upshot seems to be that a (non-ostensive) proper name to which no definite description in fact applies is a name without application. (If for example we have the name "Aristotle" but cannot truly say either that Aristotle was the teacher of Alexander, *or* that he was the most famous student of Plato, *or* the author of the *Nicomachean Ethics, or* that any other proposed definite description applies, then there is finally no difference between such a vague 'Aristotle' and no Aristotle at all.) But John Searle, who nearly twenty years ago wrote the philosophical encyclopedia article summarizing the matter (Searle, 1967), was hard put to say when the number of correct descriptions is sufficient to constitute a "definite" or positive identification—even though some number, he reasoned, must be sufficient. My own belief is that it is not mere adding up of 'descriptions,' but the concept of the story itself which forms the missing element in Searle's discussion. That is, what is required to give us a real identification of Aristotle is exactly an account long and accurate enough evidently to count as Aristotle's own story—a story that we recognize by its characteristic convergence of character, incident, and social setting, as outlined above. To say how many facts a story must have in order to be one is to miss what makes a story a story; the test is rather whether we know a factual story when we hear one; quantification is an inapplicable requirement. What is required to identify the real Jesus is the same. Public historiography, if not biased against Christianity by its very presuppositions (as, sadly, many modern historiographic theories have been) could *in principle* defeat the Gospel identification by challenging its descriptions, though in fact none has decisively done so. Faith, on this view, is not immune to history; identity-documents are not indifferent to truthfulness in character, incident, and setting; instead, they involve those elements in ways appropriate to the primary task.

Gotthold Ephraim Lessing (1729–1781), the Enlightenment philosopher, thought he had discovered a "broad ditch" that separated the contingent truths of history from the necessary truth on which faith could be based (Lessing, 1957:55). But Lessing belonged to the Enlightenment, which sought to separate religion from its own narrative. When we restore the narrative aspect of the disciples' self-identity, and restore it as well for their kingdom and their Lord, we find that the broad ditch has been drained; no uncrossable barrier separates the Christian either from the truth of the story or from (relevant) historical inquiry.

We are criticizing propositional reductionism in ethics, and have just considered its inability to take account of the relation between the Gospel narratives' point (namely, identifying Jesus, disciples, and kingdom) and their representative force—a relation that for us is expressed by the Christian understanding that the gospel story must be a *true* story. My claim is that while a narrative understanding of Christian morality can make sense (though only complicated sense) of this relationship, moral propositionalism can make none, for on that view there is no reason even to ask about the historical truth of what is for propositionalists at best an illustrative and edifying or at worst an irrelevant tale—the gospel story. Moral propositionalists might reply here that they have no interest in stories *or* their truth; they can make perfect sense of general moral propositions such as "it is right to act rationally," or "self-sacrifice is the *summum bonum*" by means of *definitions*. By defining terms such as "rational" and "sacrifice" in these propositions, the propositionalist will hope to avoid the vagueness with which he is charged, and do it without recourse to stories. It seems enough of a response, however, to remember that if the speech-act theory is a good theory, it applies not only to narratives but also to the propositionalists' propositions and definitions. Every meaningful proposition and every meaningful definition is an utterance issued by somebody (or bodies), in such and such a language with its structure and conventions, and with such and such requirements for happy or felicitous performance. This means that the definitions (that are supposed to avoid the narrative world in which we exist) *must* partake of that world if they are to be successful definitions. To give a concrete example, nobody should be surprised if "self-sacrifice" or "love" turns out to have, in William James' homely phrase, a different "cash value" for seventeenth-century Puritan armies intent upon overturning royal authority than it would for sixteenth-century Swiss Brethren, full of the discovery of a new way of life within the body of Christ. If in either case definitions of "self-sacrifice" are developed, their meaning and force must depend upon the social world that is their context, and thus upon the imbedded narratives of that world. This is not to deny the value either of the motto-propositions or the clarifying definitions; it is only to say that they cannot constitute reductive substitutes for narratives. Without them, they will prove inapplicable, or meaningless.

iii. *Affective (emotive) force*—I have still to show that these same points apply in connection with the third sort of force or dimension that all speech-acts characteristically display, their affective (or emotive, or less exactly, their self-involving) force.

As before, we will discover that propositional reductionism in morality can give no adequate nonnarrative account of the emotive force of moral propositions. Here, though, the going will be a bit easier, for the ground has been well worked. The twentieth century has thoroughly explored the possibility of an emotivist ethics, canvassing the theory that moral propositions (or the moral significance of mixed propositions) have only an emotive meaning expressing someone's likes and dislikes, loves and preferences, intentions and renunciations (cf. Stevenson, 1944; Hare, 1952, 1963; Braithwaite, 1955). Among these theorists, it is R. B. Braithwaite who has attended most carefully to the relation of morality to stories, and we may well conclude this critique of propositional reductionism by noting what Braithwaite had to say on the subject and relating it to what has just been said here. Braithwaite's account of morality proper, which is related to Richard Hare's, is that the basic task of moral propositions is to express the (generalizable) intention of the speaker. Thus "I *ought* to give Barbara a book," if it is a *moral* utterance, means on analysis: "I *intend* to give Barbara a book, and to do so as part of a general policy of giving books to scholarship students (of whom Barbara is one)." Since intention is an affect or psychological state, Braithwaite's theory is an affective or emotive (more precisely, a conative) one; moreover it is purely emotive: here there is no other dimension of morality than the intentional.

Where, then, do stories come in? With religion. *Religious* moral speakers, according to Braithwaite, are those who link some story or stories, true or fictional, with this expression of moral intention. Thus a religious speaker may say "God is love," and this on analysis means (1) that the speaker intends to act lovingly, and (2) that the speaker's intention is "associated with" stories (true or otherwise; for Braithwaite's theory it doesn't matter) of God's loving action, or stories of Jesus, or. . . .

Will it not have to be said, then, that here at long last the propositional reductionist is on solid ground, for at least the affective dimension of speech-acts is seen, in Braithwaite's theory, to exist, and to exist in logical independence of (though possibly in psychological dependence upon) the stories we have so stressed here? Alas, the answer is no. It is true that Braithwaite's analysis claims that the propositional utterances of moral speakers express intentions that are logically independent of the stories these speakers connect with it. But the consequence is that the genuine difference in the lives of those who invoke different stories cannot be acknowledged by Braithwaitians as a moral difference. For example, Braithwaite says that both Christians and Buddhists subscribe to an "agapeistic" way of life—both intend to act lovingly. Therein their morality consists. The profound differences in these ways of life—differences that have engaged other sympathetic scholars throughout a lifetime of study (cf. Cobb, 1975a, 1982)—must be assigned by Braithwaite to 'mere' differences in story, not to a Buddhist morality significantly different from the Christian one. I do not think this is merely a question about how to use the words "moral" and "ethical," on which admittedly there are many opinions. Rather Braithwaite's emotivism, by its drive to universalizability, is uncomfortable with the very possibility of logical links between the summary propositions and the stories on which, I am claiming, these are founded.

Even if, however, someone were to make good logical sense of the emotivists' connection between stories and moral utterances of a general sort, emotivism still falls hopelessly short of the goal emotivists must aim for if it is to count as the reduction of narrative morality to moral propositions, for by speech-act theory, emotivists must also show how the primary and representative forces of their reductive propositions contain the moral substance of the narrative itself, and since emotivists are by definition unwilling to do this, and as I have argued above, other reductionists are unable to do it, the reduction must fail on every count.

On the other hand, it is fairly easy for us to pick out the main line of affective force that is part and parcel of a Gospel narrative viewed as an extended speech-act of identification. By way of explanation, this does not call for random selection of possible affective responses to the Gospel. Rather it calls for the discovery of those feelings, intentions, or other psychological acts or states (in teller and hearer, or in writer and reader) *without which* we would not say that the gospel had been happily proclaimed. These affects are often noted in the Gospels and are implied by that very name, good news. Joy is the feeling-tone of gospel proclamation and reception. Is joy moral? Perhaps not to every imprincipled mind. But to receptive hearers of the good tidings, it is the very shape of moral life. Linked to that joy, if it is authentic, must be the *intention* (here at least Braithwaite is near the target) to abide by the good news, the willingness to live within the new possibilities of the kingdom. Associated with both joy and willingness are other, related feelings—regret (for the sin that is now disclosed as sin), resolution (to faithfulness), love (for the Source of goodness and all that owes being to him), delight, reverence, hope, and more.

iv. *Summary*—It may be helpful here to summarize the perhaps forbiddingly technical argument of the preceding section. I am defending narrative ethics against the reductive claim that insofar as narrative ethics is ethics, it can without loss of content be reduced to nonnarrative propositions that express moral principles. In short, against the claim that narrative ethics needs no narrative. The defense like the reduction presumes that there are in fact Christian moral narratives, for example, the Gospels. It seeks to show how the Gospels do (if *not* by propositional principles) convey their moral teaching. They do so principally by identifying characters (Jesus and the disciples) and a realm or setting (the coming kingdom). These are united by a plot—the Gospel story. This story becomes moral demand, moral guidance, moral *telos* for readers just to the extent that we get the point of the story, recognize the one there called Christ as our Lord, and thus confess ourselves to be among the disciples in the kingdom. So to recognize, confess, be born into the kingdom is to take up the way of life called Christian; it *is* Christian morality. Speech-act analysis was useful in clarifying these points: it provided awareness of the Gospels as *doing* something (and not for example just symbolizing something)—namely, identifying Jesus, disciples, kingdom. It also offered an analysis of the three dimensions of that doing that showed us how the Gospels work, and it showed the corresponding threefold failure of principled propositions to undercut or supplant this work. From this, it follows that narrative ethics, which is the regular ethics of every story-formed Christian community, cannot be replaced by a reduced nonnarrative ethics of principles.

3. The Ethics of Values

My goal throughout has been to present the strongest current rivals to narrative ethics and consider the challenges they offer. The next claimant, *value*, is certainly a strong, albeit a somewhat obscure, rival. A little history may illuminate the matter. "Value" was introduced into nineteenth-century philosophy (originally from economics, interestingly enough) as a way of achieving two disparate, indeed conflicting, goals. One goal was to widen the scope of ethical reflection beyond that indicated by certain classical ethical terms such as "the good," "right," "duty." This widening was to be accomplished by introducing a "general theory of value" that would include "economics, ethics, aesthetics, jurisprudence, education, and perhaps even logic and epistemology" (Frankena, 1967:229; cf. Frondizi, 1963). The crucial thinkers here were Alexius Meinong and Christian von Ehrenfels, and, in the twentieth century, the Husserlians Max Scheler and Nicolai Hartmann. This aspect of the "value" movement spread to America around World War I, especially in the work of Wilbur M. Urban, John Dewey, and Ralph Barton Perry. The other perhaps conflicting goal of value theory was to distinguish "judgments of value" as firmly as possible from "judgments of fact," as had already been done in the tradition that extends from David Hume (1711–1776) to William Frankena himself (cf. his *Ethics*, 1963, s.v. "value"). (The main theological name in this latter series is that of Albrecht Ritschl [1822–1889], whose distinction of value-judgments was an apologetic strategy designed to keep Christian faith safe from the ravages of critical history.) These two goals had to conflict, inasmuch as the effort to broaden 'values' across the borders of sciences and disciplines clashes with the effort to keep values neatly fenced off from facts.

Now narrative ethics is obviously a continual transgression of this distinction of facts and values. Whereas many philosophical ethicists, following the British analyst G. E. Moore (1873–1958), spoke of "the naturalistic fallacy" (the belief that a 'value' could be derived from some natural or supernatural 'fact'), within the story-shaped world in which the present work is done there are neither value-free facts nor fact-free values. From our standpoint these are chimerical abstractions rather than useful distinctions.

The present section, however, is more closely related to the notion of "value" in recent popular thought. Here "one's values" has come to mean whatever is prized or given priority in an individual life, while "shared values" points to the same status for communal interests and commitments. And this in turn is closely related to the work of those philosophers who reject or abandon the attempt to bring 'values' under a single ethical theory such as hedonism ("the good is whatever gives pleasure"—cf. Hume, Bentham, Mill, and their followers) or the 'form' of the good (Plato) or power (Friedrich Nietzsche). Instead, the pluralistic theories hold "that there are a number of things which are good or good-making in themselves." Philosophers who take this view (among them, Aristotle, G. E. Moore, W. D. Ross, John Laird, Scheler, Hartmann, and Perry) differ among themselves as to what these are, but "all include two or more of the following: pleasure, knowledge, aesthetic experience, beauty, truth, virtue, harmony, love, friendship, justice, freedom, self-expression" (cf. Frankena, 1967:231). In the preceding chapters, some of these 'values' have appeared; in Christian thought they exhibit a distinctive narrative setting. Now Christians certainly have no copyright on any of these terms. So my aim will be not so much to show that they may have a temporary home in the Christian or some other narrative, but to show that apart from such a base these 'value-words' lose their moral force altogether. I will attempt, for one of the 'values' listed above, not indeed to show that it has no general or philosophical use in ethics, but to show that, so far from the narrative use depending on the narrative-free meaning, it is just the other way around—our old argument again. The 'value' I have chosen for this exercise is *truth*.

a. *What is truth?*—While no doubt we must allow for individual variations, the drive to truth is strong in the human species. It has often been pointed out, for example, that lying, one common form of untruth, depends for its very existence upon the practice of truth-telling including the expectation that truth will be told; if everyone lied always, lying would evidently be of no effect. However strong may be our motives to lie, these presuppose a still stronger motive to tell the truth, and lies even when frequent have to be reckoned as exceptions. It is naïve never to suspect others (or oneself) of the tendency to lie, but it is self-contradictory to suppose that lies are all we can meet. So even lies trade upon the drive to truth.

Remember that our present goal is to show that truth (our sample 'value') is in practice narrative-dependent, so that for Christians its status is closely linked with its role in the story upon which Scripture launches us—the story of Israel, of Jesus, and of the Christian community, the church. As a value, then, truth is neither the one value, or one of several independent values, to which the Christian story may without moral loss be reduced; rather the very nature of this story is what enables us to see what *we* mean by "truth," see what truth amounts to here.

This is indeed what our argument requires. Yet to put it this way probably awakens (and perhaps ought to awaken) the deepest sort of suspicions in us. For an impulse that most naturally rises is to make 'truth,' elevated to a status independent of our story and of all stories, the test of all of them. We think we want an ethics of belief that will test our own and every story by the standard of truth. This impulse is well displayed in the familiar relativist dilemma. The modern study of religions has shown us a human species attached to more ways of being religious than would have seemed likely to our ancestors, and has urged on us an understanding of these many paths of faith. Correspondingly, many have reached a point of despairing scepticism about religious truth of any sort in such a world. These concerns are well summarized in a letter addressed to me a few years ago by a thoughtful pastor. Thinking about the attitudes of his urban (and urbane) flock, he wrote:

The increasing concern that I hear expressed relates to the truth or veracity inherent in the various religious faiths of the world. How is the truth in each [to be] honored? Where is the truth in each? More particularly, in a conversation between a Jew and a Christian, or a Buddhist and a Christian [daily possibilities in their city setting], where is truth? Is one "right" and the other "wrong"? Or is truth merely relative? Certainly the entire missionary enterprise is in question. Why ask a neighbor to come to church? Or support missionaries overseas?

How does this concern square with the project of this chapter?

Note first that the *relativism* implicit in this congregation's discontent has its own problem of intellectual integrity. The difficulty is this: How is it that the relativist, one who tells us all truth is relative, can expect us to believe that relativism itself is *true*? Perhaps relativism must be relativized as only the view of a jaded and discouraged community which has lost confidence in its own way? For as a general theory it seems to ask us to believe (a) that it is (in general) true, and (b) that nothing is (in general) true—and both can't be the case. Such relativism thus of necessity contains the seed of its own destruction. So there is a short way to dispose of it, but some may fear that the way is too short; after all, the facts relativism depends upon are real facts: There *is* a variety of religions (or ideologies, or world views—the same arguments apply to all) in the world; the adherents of each *are* tempted to chauvinistic insularity; *none* self-evidently has a total claim to truth. The trouble seems to come only when we elevate these evident facts to a general theory of relativism.

There are two other ways to treat the facts on which relativism trades. One, which we may call *absolutism* (these names are variable in current discussion), holds that there is a single and absolutely true way (in religion, or in world view or whatever else human beings contest), and that either one of the known ways (Islam, let us say) has captured it, with all others in error, or (a more tolerant version of absolutism) that many or all ways participate in the one truth to some extent. What this second view gains in logical coherence, it loses, alas, in credibility. For in effect the truth has now been turned into an ideal that some, luckily, embrace while others, unluckily, cannot even understand that it is the ideal. Since holders of the second theory invariably put themselves in the lucky class, it seems a self-serving theory.

The third theory, here called *perspectivism* ("soft perspectivism" in McClendon and Smith, 1975), like mere relativism, acknowledges the great, contrary variety of human convictional communities, and acknowledges that the truth perceived in one is not easily translated into the truth of another community. Yet it does not theorize that there is no truth that is true. While recognizing that truth may be hard to get at, it is not dismayed. Meanwhile, perspectivism thinks it sees difficult but real ways to bring together discordant elements in the human fabric—a project about which relativism is totally pessimistic, and absolutism blithely optimistic. It is perspectivism, I think, which has attracted the most attention in recent philosophical and theological thought (e.g., Hacking, 1982) and it is my own favored view (McClendon and Smith, 1975).

How does perspectivism sustain its own (limited) optimism about reconciling warring human convictions? Let us pursue this interesting if apparently tangential question, with the deeper agenda being the hope that this will make fully clear the narrative-bound quality of the truth we seek. Remember that what we are looking for cannot be a simple, easy answer to the problems of pluralism, for if it were, we would doubtless soon be back with the unsatisfactory simplicities of either relativism or absolutism.

b. *Truth and truthfulness*—I wish to proceed by an example, and following Peter Slater (1978) will consider the story by Ken Kesey, *One Flew Over the Cuckoo's Nest* (1962), a novel, and then a play and film. Kesey's story is set in a mental hospital (the cuckoo's nest) somewhere in the Pacific Northwest. Randle Patrick McMurphy, war hero, criminal, loner, arrives as a patient in the ward run by Nurse Ratched. The plot of the story, narrated in the novel by another patient, Chief Bromden, is the struggle between Big Nurse (Ms. Ratched) and McMurphy for the minds and hearts of the patients in the ward. She represents the Combine—Chief Bromden's name for the system of society—shoving everyone in the world into appointed slots. As Chief Bromden writes,

Yes. This is what I know. The ward is a factory for the Combine. It's for fixing up mistakes made in the neighborhood and in the schools and in the churches, the hospital is. When a completed product goes back out into society, all fixed up good as new, *better* than new sometimes, it brings joy to the Big Nurse's heart; something that came in all twisted different is now a functioning, adjusted component, a credit to the whole outfit and a marvel to behold. Watch him sliding across the land with a welded grin, fitting into some nice little neighborhood where they're just now digging trenches along the street to lay pipes for city water. He's happy with it. He's adjusted to surroundings finally. (Kesey, 1962:40)

Clearly, Kesey's story asks us to identify with McMurphy, Bromden, and their allies against the Combine, that is, against the nurse, the doctors, and their 'health care' system. The power of the story lies in its ability to get us to do just that. Most of us laugh at McMurphy's dauntless combat with the authoritarian Big Nurse, and we rollick through an uproarious salmon-fishing trip with a pretty little hooker, a bewildered staff doctor, and ten crazies. McMurphy is what something in me would like to be—an existential hero saving the warded world from its confinement, setting it free even at the cost of his own being.

At this point, however, second thoughts set in. For one thing, if all of us really identify with McMurphy's side in the McMurphy-Big Nurse struggle, how is it that we still live in a world of confinement—of mental hospitals, juvenile halls, 'facilities' for the criminally insane, prisons, jails, and the like? Are we really ready to abolish these locked wards for the deviant human spirit? Or do we not cling to them as "necessary"? Remember, too, that by the chief's definition, they are only the extension of the dominant society outside, with its commuter lanes, clipped lawns, and office cubicles. Which do we favor? Is not the closer truth this: Kesey persuades me to identify with McMurphy and company only because my own self is divided. There is the self that rebels, but there is also the self that (in collusion with others) maintains the Combine. Kesey's art awakes one of these selves. Yet when the novel or the film is over, the other self returns, sustaining the Combine Kesey had caricatured.

Of course, part of the trouble is that Kesey is not fair to Nurse Ratched's institutional and therapeutic viewpoint, though there are in reality points in its favor and against McMurphy's. For example, McMurphy himself has no place in his scheme of things for Nurse Ratched, no compassion for her. Neither, so far as we can tell from the novel, has Kesey. We want a viewpoint, though, which sees more than either of these two can.

But see, now, how our task has changed. As we began the account of truth, it was easy to picture ourselves as its possessors or at least as its earnest seekers. We were the pursuers, truth was the elusive hare. Which theory, which religion is *true*? But in the parabolic pages of *Cuckoo's Nest* as read here, we may come to see matters differently. Our common task is not so much discovering a truth hiding among contrary viewpoints as it is coming to possess a selfhood that no longer evades and eludes the truth with which it is importunately confronted. Of course Nurse Ratched had such a need, in the story. But what about McMurphy? And finally, what about myself? Is this not my need, too? In that event, though, truth has become the relentless hound, and I am the evasive hare.

I think this is why Stanley Hauerwas is forever insisting that truth requires truthfulness: truth (i.e., correspondence, coherence, verisimilitude, what works, etc.) requires a truthful life (one that has found the honesty to confess its need and the trust to receive help in the project of overcoming self-deceit). And here we can see why the prior issues of an ethic of belief in our time may be not the evidence and warrants, the scientific or logical method, and the centrality of reliable data we had supposed were the whole story (cf. Harvey, 1967), important though these may be in due course—but issues of the believers' character, and of the self-deceit by which that character evades truth's claims, and of the story or stories that may enable us to escape our own self-deceit.

c. *Another summary*—Those last points need some clarification, but before seeking that, it may be helpful to summarize the development of the chapter's argument so far. I set out to say why Christian ethics must be narrative ethics. ("How is narrative ethics justifiable?" it was noted, leaves to other occasions the questions, how is Christian ethics of any sort, or ethics of any sort, justifiable?) The first step was to say what "narrative" means here. Then the strategy became the piecemeal one of considering two preemptive alternatives to narrative ethics: one from propositionalists, the other from value-theorists, two kinds of reductionists from our standpoint. The response to the former was to invoke a theory of language, speech-act theory, showing how it might treat the central Christian narrative, the gospel, as having the primary force of an *identity narrative*, and might do so without losing hold of these representative (cf. 'cognitive') and affective (cf. self-involving) elements that are with the primary force indispensable to meaning in all our utterance. Once this analysis of Christian narratives was in hand (with proper gratitude to Professor Frei), it was short work to show that propositional reduction (that is, finding *the* moral content of narrative in some proposition or propositions such as "self-sacrifice is the *summum bonum*") was, in the bad sense of the term, reductionist. Propositionalism had omitted the moral force of the narrative, which in the chosen example included (1) the *identity* of Christ in the church with the Jesus of the gospel story (as well as our identity with the disciples there, and the kingdom's identity then and now); but also, therefore, (2) the *actual content* of the Jesus story, so that what the story says *about* Jesus and disciples and kingdom matters, morally speaking; but finally also (3) the emotive (including particularly the *intentional*) force that the story conveys and the reader appropriately takes up, so that the truth of moral emotivism (cf. Braithwaite) is included in a narrative account, but cannot be substituted for it. Nor can *any* isolated propositions be so substituted; for all presuppose some narrative upon which, even when they have been abstracted, they continue to depend for their meaning. Hence propositional reductionism fails, and narrative ethics is so far vindicated.

The argument against value-theory reductionists took a somewhat different line. Value theory had two conflicting goals: to enforce the fact-value distinction in ethics, and to embrace a wider sphere than ethics (as traditionally conceived) in the realm of value. The present discussion, sympathetic to the latter goal, has in consistency (and in line with a broad tendency in recent philosophy as well) rejected the former, the fact-value distinction. Consequently, value-theory must not be construed so that it supplants the fact-laden narratives in which its values are grounded. These themes have been illustrated throughout the earlier chapters in the treatment of such 'values' (if that is a good name for them) as presence, love, forgiveness, rights, peace, and still others; the final illustration has been the exploration of "truth" in the preceding section.

d. *Truth, character, and narrative*—There seem to be two possible strategies for arguing the narrative basis of truth. One is to show its link with various human traditions, apart from which it becomes too vague a term to settle divisive issues. For that argument, see James Smith's and my *Understanding Religious Convictions* (McClendon and Smith, 1975:163-71), or for the argument in a different key, see the work of J. B. Metz (1980:chs. 5, 11, 12). The other, often employed by Hauerwas (cf. *Truthfulness and Tragedy*, 1977) and followed in this chapter is to show that truth as a value is ineffectual apart from truthfulness; that is, that the pursuit of true facts, true beliefs, or a true theory about Christian moral theology is internally stultified unless the pursuit recognizes the self-involvement of the pursuer's own (narrative) project. For one to recognize that, however, is to see how one's own character, and the community or communities that form it, and one's own liability to self-deceit are all engaged in what might otherwise, but very misleadingly, seem an ideal pursuit of disinterested truth. This was the point of introducing Kesey's *Cuckoo's Nest*.

So character (with its temptations to self-deceit) is logically implicated in the struggle for the value "truth." Still, not everyone will see and little has been explicitly said here about how character presupposes narrative. Perhaps this can best be displayed by noting the relation between character and roles. Everyone has one or more roles to play in life: husband or wife, daughter or son, teacher, employer, architect, tile-setter, jury member, parent, neighbor, committee member, friend. Bernard Williams (1972:51-58) and Bernard Suits (1978), each in his own way, have pointed out the moral dangers involved in either identifying oneself so completely with one's roles that there is no "I" left to take responsibility for that involvement ("I was only taking orders" is sometimes a bad moral defense) *or* of denying that one necessarily has roles—in Suits' image, refusing to play the game of life. So there are my several roles (in my own case, husband, father, teacher, church member, friend, citizen, author, etc.) and there is the self that assumes those roles, shifts from one to another as required, and is not merely to be identified with any one of them. Yet that 'self' may itself be a role. To put it differently, I am not more myself when wavering between the claims of friendship and those of professorship than when I am simply immersed in one or the other of those roles, even though it remains true that none of them in itself is I. Still, if I am a man of character, there must be a congruence between my several roles: the 'I' who grades papers must not be a stranger to the 'I' who preaches in the Sunday service, and neither must be alien to the 'I' who relaxes with friends on a boat deck. Now this congruence, reappearing in most or all of my roles, comes as close as can be to indicating what is meant by character—the persistent qualities of my selfhood. If we now revert to the idea of an 'I' who plays my several roles, then the necessary connectedness of that character (taken with incidents and setting as provided by the roles themselves) assures that my life has a narrative quality:

The roles are narrative (indeed, often dramatic); the 'I' who cannot be myself save by means of them is therefore narrative as well.

*   *   *   *   *

Two essential Christian convictions must round out the account. One is the conviction (call it the doctrine of the church, if you please) that my own story is inadequate, taken alone, and is hungry for another to complete it. That gives us the communitarian element in Christian ethics: My story must be linked with the story of a people. The other is the conviction (call it the doctrine of salvation) that *our* story is inadequate as well: The story of each and all is itself hungry for a greater story that overcomes our persistent self-deceit, redeems our common life, and provides a way for us to be a people among all earth's peoples without subtracting from the significance of others' peoplehood, their own stories, their lives. The unfolding of these and other doctrines indeed calls for a volume of its own (a call I hope to answer), but perhaps enough has been said here to show that Christian ethics, because its truth entails character, must find that truth in a community that is of necessity story-shaped, and to show that Christian morality involves us, *necessarily* involves us, in the story of God.

Bibliography

ACHTEMEIER, Elizabeth R.
  1962   "Righteousness in the OT," *Interpreter's Dictionary of the Bible*.
            Ed. G. A. Buttrick. 4 vols. New York: Abingdon Press.
ADAM, Karl
  1937   *The Spirit of Catholicism*. Trans. Don J. McCann. New York:
            MacMillan Publishing Co.
ADAMS, Richard
  1972   *Watership Down*. New York: Avon Books.
AHLSTROM, Sydney E.
  1961   "Theology in America," *The Shaping of American Religion*. Ed.
            James Ward Smith and A. Leland Jamison. Vol. 1. Princeton:
            Princeton University Press.
  1972   *A Religious History of the American People*. New Haven: Yale
            University Press.
AHO, James
  1981   *Religious Mythology and the Art of War*. Westport, Conn.:
            Greenwood Press.
ALLEY, Robert S.
  1970   *Revolt Against the Faithful*. Philadelphia: Lippincott.
ALSTON, William P.
  1967   "Pleasure," in *Encyclopedia of Philosophy*. Ed. Paul Edwards. 8
            vols. New York: Macmillan and Free Press.
ALTER, Robert
  1981   *The Art of Biblical Narrative*. New York: Basic Books.
ARDREY, Robert
  1961   *African Genesis*. New York: Atheneum.
ARISTOTLE
            Nicomachean Ethics, in *The Complete Works of Aristotle*. Ed.
            Jonathan Barnes. 2 vols. Bollingen Series 71.2. Princeton:
            Princeton University Press, 1984.
AUDEN, Wystan Hugh
  1945   *The Collected Poetry of W. H. Auden*. New York: Random House.

357

BAINTON, Roland H.
    1960   *Christian Attitudes Toward War and Peace.* New York: Abingdon
              Press.
BARTH, Karl
    1936–69   *Church Dogmatics* (4 vols.). Trans. G. T. Thomson, et al.
              Edinburgh: T. & T. Clark. Separate part-volumes, if referred to in
              the text, are cited below.
    1936   *The Doctrine of the Word of God* (*Church Dogmatics*, I/1). Trans. G. T.
              Thomson. Edinburgh: T. & T. Clark.
    1946/1960 "The Christian Community and the Civil Community," in
              Community, State, and Church. Ed. Will Herberg. Garden City,
              N. Y.: Anchor Doubleday.
    1958a   *The Doctrine of Creation* (*Church Dogmatics*, III/1). Trans.
              J. W. Edwards, et al. Edinburgh: T. & T. Clark.
    1958b   *The Doctrine of Reconciliation* (*Church Dogmatics*, IV/2). Trans.
              G. W. Bromiley. Edinburgh: T. & T. Clark.
BARTH, Markus
    1964   *Acquittal by Resurrection*, with Verne H. Fletcher. New York:
              Holt, Rinehart, & Winston.
BEASLEY-MURRAY, George R.
    1962   *Baptism in the New Testament.* London: Macmillan Publishers.
BENDER, Harold S.
    1944   "The Anabaptist Vision." Reprinted in Guy F. Hershberger, *The
              Recovery of the Anabaptist Vision.* Scottdale, Pa.: Herald Press,
              1957.
    1959   "Theology, Anabaptist," *Mennonite Encyclopedia.* Ed. Harold S.
              Bender, et al. 4 vols. Scottdale, Pa.: Herald Press.
    1961   "Walking in the Resurrection,"*Mennonite Quarterly Review* 35
              (April), pp. 96ff.
BERGER, Peter
    1967   *The Sacred Canopy.* Garden City, N. Y.: Doubleday & Co.
BERKHOF, Hendrik
    1953/1962 *Christ and the Powers.* Trans. John Howard Yoder. Scottdale, Pa.:
              Herald Press.
BETHGE, Eberhard
    1967   *Dietrich Bonhoeffer.* München: Chr. Kaiser Verlag.
    1970   *Dietrich Bonhoeffer.* Trans. of Bethge (1967) by Edwin Robertson,
              et al. London: William Collins Sons & Co.
BETZ, Hans Dieter
    1979   *Galatians* (Hermeniea Commentaries). Philadelphia: Fortress
              Press.
BLANKE, Fritz
    1961   *Brothers in Christ.* Trans. from German. Scottdale, Pa.: Herald
              Press.
BOETTNER, Loraine
    1942   *The Christian Attitude Toward War.* Grand Rapids: Wm. B.
              Eerdmans Publishing Co.
BONHOEFFER, Dietrich
    1930/1962 *The Communion of Saints.* Trans. from German. London: William
              Collins Sons & Co.
    1931/1962 *Act and Being.* Trans. from German. London: William Collins
              Sons & Co.
    1937/1963 *The Cost of Discipleship.* Trans. R. H. Fuller, with I. Booth. New
              York: Macmillan Publishing Co.
    1949/1965 *Ethics.* Trans. Neville H. Smith from the 6th German edition and
              ed. E. Bethge. New York: MacMillan Publishing Co.

1970   *No Rusty Swords*. Trans. from the collected works by E. H. Robertson, et al. London: William Collins Sons & Co.
1972a   *Letters and Papers from Prison*, enlarged ed. Trans. R. Fuller, et al., and ed. E. Bethge. New York: Macmillan Publishing Co.
1972b   *The Way to Freedom*. Trans. from the collected works by E. H. Robertson, et al. London: Collins and World.
1978   *Christ the Center*. Trans. E. H. Robertson. New York: Harper & Row, Publishers.

BRAITHWAITE, R. B.
1955   *An Empiricist's View of the Nature of Religious Belief*. Cambridge: Cambridge University Press.

BRANDON, S. G. F.
1967   *Jesus and the Zealots*. Manchester: Manchester University Press.
1968   *The Trial of Jesus of Nazareth*. London: B. T. Batsford Ltd.

BROWN, Peter
1969   *Augustine of Hippo*. Berkeley: University of California Press.
1983   "Augustine and Sexuality," *Protocol of the Forty-Sixth Colloquy*. Ed. Mary Ann Donovan. Berkeley: Center for Hermeneutical Studies, Graduate Theological Union.

BROWN, Robert McAfee
1961   *The Spirit of Protestantism*. New York: Oxford University Press.

BUBER, Martin
1944/1946   *Moses*. Trans. from German. Oxford: East and West Library.

BUNYAN, John
1666/1969   *Grace Abounding to the Chief of Sinners*, in *The Pilgrim's Progress and Grace Abounding*. Ed. James Thorpe. Boston: Houghton Mifflin Co.
1684/1969   *The Pilgrim's Progress* in Bunyan, 1666/1969.

BUSHNELL, Horace
1864   *Work and Play*. New York: Charles Scribner.
1874/1965   *Forgiveness and Law*, in *Horace Bushnell*. Ed. H. Shelton Smith. New York: Oxford University Press.

BUTLER, Joseph
1729/1970   *Butler's Fifteen Sermons Preached at Rolls Chapel and A Dissertation of the Nature of Virtue*. Trans. T. A. Roberts. London: SPCK.

CAIRD, George
1956   *Principalities and Powers, a Study in Pauline Theology*. Oxford: Clarendon Press.

CALVIN, John
1559/1960   *Institutes of the Christian Religion*. Trans. Ford Lewis Battles. (Library of Christian Classics, vols. 20 and 21). Philadelphia: Westminster Press.

CAMPBELL, Jeff H.
1980-81   "After Christianity, What? John Updike's Critique of Contemporary American Culture," in *Faculty Papers of Midwestern State University*, Wichita Falls, Tex. Ed. James R. King. Series 2, vol. 6.

CAMPBELL, Will D.
1979   *Brother to a Dragonfly*. New York: Seabury Press.
1982   *The Glad River*. New York: Holt, Rinehart, & Winston.

CARNEY, Frederick
1978   "Theological Ethics," *Encyclopedia of Bioethics*. Ed. W. T. Reich. Vol. 1. New York: Free Press.

CARSE, James
1967   *Jonathan Edwards and the Visibility of God*. New York: Scribner's.

CHERNUS, Ira
   1984   "War as Myth: 'The Show Must Go On,' " War and Peace
           Studies Consultation, American Academy of Religion, Paper no.
           1 (mimeographed).
CHILDS, Brevard S.
   1974   *The Book of Exodus: A Critical, Theological Commentary.* Philadel-
           phia: Westminster Press.
   1979   *Introduction to the Old Testament as Scripture.* Philadelphia:
           Fortress Press.
CLARKE, William Newton
   1894   *Outline of Christian Theology.* Cambridge: Wilson. Many subse-
           quent editions.
COBB, John B., Jr.
   1967   *The Structure of Christian Existence.* London: Lutterworth Press.
   1973   *Liberal Christianity at the Crossroads.* Philadelphia: Westminster
           Press.
   1975a   *Christ in a Pluralistic Age.* Philadelphia: Westminster Press.
   1975b   "Strengthening the Spirit," *Union Seminary Quarterly Review* 30
           (Winter-Summer), pp. 130-39.
   1976   "Spiritual Discernment in Whiteheadian Perspective," in
           Bernard Lee and Harry J. Cargas, eds., *Religious Experience and
           Process Theology.* Paramus, N. J.: Paulist/Newman.
   1977   "The Identity of Christian Spirituality and Global Conscious-
           ness," unpublished typescript.
   1982   *Beyond Dialogue.* Philadelphia: Fortress Press.
COBB, John B., Jr., and David Ray GRIFFIN
   1976   *Process Theology: an Introductory Exposition.* Philadelphia: West-
           minster Press.
CONE, Cecil W.
   1975   *The Identity Crisis in Black Theology.* Nashville: AMEC.
CONE, James H.
   1969   *Black Theology and Black Power.* New York: Seabury Press.
   1972   *The Spirituals and the Blues: An Interpretation.* New York: Seabury
           Press.
CONNER, Walter Thomas
   1936   *Revelation and God.* Nashville: Broadman Press.
   1945   *The Gospel of Redemption.* Nashville: Broadman Press.
CROSSAN, John Dominic
   1975   *The Dark Interval: Towards a Theology of Story.* Niles, Ill.: *Argus
           Communications.*
CULLMANN, Oscar
   1962   *Christ and Time.* Trans. Floyd V. Filson from the 3rd German ed.
           London: SCM Press.

DAGG, J. L.
  1858/1859 *Manual of Theology: A Treatise on Christian Doctrine and A Treatise on
           Church Order.* Charleston, S.C. Reprint. New York: Arno, 1980.
DAVIES, W. D.
   1962   "Conscience," in *Interpreter's Dictionary of the Bible.* Ed. G. A.
           Buttrick. 4 vols. New York: Abingdon Press.
DAWIDOWICZ, Lucy S.
   1975   *The War Against the Jews 1933-45.* New York: Holt, Rinehart, &
           Winston.
DAY, Dorothy
   1924   *The Eleventh Virgin.* New York: Albert and Charles Boni.

| 1938 | *From Union Square to Rome.* Silver Spring, Md.: Preservation of the Faith. |

1938   *From Union Square to Rome.* Silver Spring, Md.: Preservation of the Faith.

1948   *On Pilgrimage.* New York: Catholic Worker Books.

1952   *The Long Loneliness.* New York: Harper & Row, Publishers.

1960   *Therese.* Springfield, Ill.: Templegate.

1963   *Loaves and Fishes: the Story of the Catholic Worker Movement.* New York: Harper & Row, Publishers.

1983   *By Little and By Little.* Ed. Robert Ellsberg. New York: Alfred A. Knopf.

DELATTRE, Roland Andre

1968   *Beauty and Sensibility in the Thought of Jonathan Edwards.* New Haven: Yale University Press.

DILLARD, Annie

1974   *Pilgrim at Tinker Creek.* Boston: Harper's Magazine.

DIX, Gregory

1946   *The Theology of Confirmation in Relation to Baptism.* Westminster: Dacre.

DODDS, Elisabeth D.

1971   *Marriage to a Difficult Man: The "Uncommon Union" of Jonathan and Sarah Edwards.* Philadelphia: Westminster Press.

DuBOIS, W. E. B.

1902/1965   *The Souls of Black Folk.* Reprinted in *Three Negro Classics.* New York: Avon Books.

DURNBAUGH, Donald F.

1968   *The Believers' Church.* New York: Macmillan Publishing Co.

EDWARDS, Jonathan

1737   *A Faithful Narrative of the Surprizing Work of God,* in Edwards, 1972.

1741   *The Distinguishing Marks of a Work of the Spirit of God,* in Edwards, 1972.

1743   *Some Thoughts Concerning the Present Revival of Religion in New-England,* in Edwards, 1972.

1746/1959   *A Treatise Concerning Religious Affections.* Ed. John E. Smith. New Haven: Yale University Press.

1754/1957   *Freedom of the Will.* Ed. Paul Ramsey. New Haven: Yale University Press.

1755   (approx. date) "The Nature of True Virtue" and "The End for Which God Created the World," (first published 1765) in Edwards, 1830, and in Edwards, 1765/1960.

1758/1970   *The Great Christian Doctrine of Original Sin.* Ed. Clyde A. Holbrook. New Haven: Yale University Press.

1765/1960   *The Nature of True Virtue.* Ed. William K. Frankena. Ann Arbor: University of Michigan Press.

1830   *The Works of President Edwards.* Ed. Sereno Edwards Dwight. 10 vols. New York: Carvill. (Vol. 1 contains Dwight's biography of Edwards.)

1852   *Charity and Its Fruits.* Ed. Tryon Edwards. New York: Carter.

1962   *Jonathan Edwards Representative Selections.* Ed. Clarence H. Faust and Thomas H. Johnson. Rev. ed., New York: Hill & Wang.

1972   *The Great Awakening.* Ed. C. C. Goen. New Haven: Yale University Press.

1980   *Scientific and Philosophical Writings.* Ed. Wallace E. Anderson, New Haven: Yale University Press.

ELLIS, Marc H.

1978   *A Year at the Catholic Worker.* New York: Paulist.

1981   *Peter Maurin: Prophet in the Twentieth Century*. New York: Paulist.
ELLUL, Jacques
  1964   *The Technological Society*. Trans. J. Wilkinson. New York: Alfred
            A. Knopf.
  1969   *Violence: Reflections from a Christian Perspective*. Trans. C. G.
            Kings. New York: Seabury Press.
ESTEP, William R., Jr.
  1975   *The Anabaptist Story*. Rev. ed., Grand Rapids: Wm. B. Eerdmans
            Publishing Co.
  1976   *Anabaptist Beginnings* (1523–1533): *A Source Book*. Nieuwkopp: B.
            DeGraaf.

FIERING, Norman
  1981   *Jonathan Edwards's Moral Thought and Its British Context*. Chapel
            Hill: University of North Carolina Press.
FINGARETTE, Herbert
  1963   *The Self in Transformation*. New York: Harper & Row, Publishers.
FIORENZA, Elizabeth Schussler
  1976   "Eschatology of the NT," *Interpreter's Dictionary of the Bible*. Ed.
            G. A. Buttrick. Supplementary Vol. Nashville: Abingdon Press.
FLOYD, Wayne
  1984   "Christ, Concreteness, and Creation in the Early Bonhoeffer,"
            Union Seminary Quarterly Review, 39/1 and 2.
FOUCAULT, Michel
  1980   *The History of Sexuality*, Vol. 1. Trans. Robert Hurley. New York:
            Random House.
FRANKENA, William
  1963   *Ethics*. Englewood Cliffs, N. J.: Prentice-Hall.
  1967   "Value and Valuation," *The Encyclopedia of Philosophy*. Ed. Paul
            Edwards. 8 Vols. New York: Macmillan and Free Press.
FREI, Hans
  1974   *The Eclipse of Biblical Narrative*. New Haven: Yale University
            Press.
  1975   *The Identity of Jesus Christ*. Philadelphia: Fortress Press.
FREUD, Anna
  1966   *The Ego and the Mechanisms of Defense*. New York: International
            Universities Press.
FREUD, Sigmund
  1895/1954 "Project for a Scientific Psychology," in *The Origins of
            Psycho-Analysis*. Ed. Marie Bonaparte, et al., and trans. E.
            Mosbacher and James Strachey. New York: Basic Books.
  1905a   "Fragment of an Analysis of a Case of Hysteria" (the Dora case),
            in *The Standard Edition* (1953–74). Vol. 7.
  1905b   *Three Essays on the Theory of Sexuality*, in *The Standard Edition*
            (1953–74). Vol. 7.
  1917/1973 *Introductory Lectures on Psychoanalysis*. Trans. James Strachey.
            London: Penguin.
  1920   *Beyond the Pleasure Principle*, in *The Standard Edition* (1953–74).
            Vol. 18.
  1927/1964 *The Future of an Illusion*. Trans. W. D. Robson-Scott, and ed. James
            Strachey. Garden City, N.Y.: Doubleday & Co.
  1930/1962 *Civilization and Its Discontents*. Trans. James Strachey. New York:
            W. W. Norton & Co.
  1933   *Why War?* in *The Standard Edition* (1953–74). Vol. 22.
  1933/1965 *New Introductory Lectures on Psychoanalysis*. Trans. James Stra-
            chey. New York: W. W. Norton & Co.

1953-74   *The Standard Edition of the Complete Psychological Works of Sigmund Freud*. Trans. James Strachey, et al. 24 vols. London: Hogarth and the Institute of Psycho-Analysis.

FRIEDMANN, Robert
1959   "Restitution," in *Mennonite Encyclopedia*. Ed. Harold S. Bender, et al. 4 vols. Scottdale, Pa.: Herald Press.

FRONDIZI, Risieri
1963   *What Is Value?* Trans. Solomon Lipp. Lasalle, Ill.: Open Court.

FURNISH, Victor Paul
1968   *Theology and Ethics in Paul*. New York: Abingdon Press.

GANDHI, Mohandas K.
1951   *Non-Violent Resistance*. New York: Schocken Books.

GARRETT, James Leo, Jr.
1969   *The Concept of the Believers' Church*. Scottdale, Pa.: Herald Press.

GAUSTAD, Edwin S., ed.
1980   *Baptists, the Bible, Church Order, and the Churches: Essays from Foundations*. New York: Arno.

GENOVESE, Eugene D.
1974   *Roll, Jordan, Roll*. New York: Pantheon Books.

GEORGI, Dieter
1976   "Corinthians, First Letter to the," *Interpreter's Dictionary of the Bible*. Ed. G. A. Buttrick. Supplementary Vol. Nashville: Abingdon Press.

GILL, David
1984   *The Word of God in the Ethics of Jacques Ellul*. ATLA Monograph Series, no. 20. Metuchen, N. J.: ATLA and the Scarecrow Press.

GILL, John
1767-70   . . . *Complete Body of Practical and Doctrinal Divinity*. Ed. W. Staughton. Abridged ed. Philadelphia: Delaplaine & Hellings, 1810.

GILL, Theodore
1971   *Memo for a Movie: A Short Life of Dietrich Bonhoeffer*. New York: Macmillan Publishing Co.

GILLIGAN, Carol
1982   *In a Different Voice*. Cambridge, Mass.: Harvard University Press.
1984   "The Conquistadore and the Dark Continent: Reflections on the Psychology of Love," in *Daedalus* (Summer).

GOEN, C. C.
1962   *Revivalism and Separatism in New England 1740-1800*. New Haven: Yale University Press.

GOLDBERG, Michael
1982   *Theology and Narrative: A Critical Introduction*. Nashville: Abingdon Press.
1985   *Jews and Christians: Getting Our Stories Straight*. Nashville: Abingdon Press.

GOTTWALD, Norman
1976   "War, Holy," in *Interpreter's Dictionary of the Bible*. Ed. Keith Crim. Supplementary vol. Nashville: Abingdon Press.

GREAVES, Richard L.
1969   *John Bunyan*. Appleford, Abingdon, Berkshire: The Sutton Courtenay Press.

GREEN, Clifford J.
1972   *The Sociality of Christ and Humanity: Dietrich Bonhoeffer's Early Theology, 1927-1933*. Missoula, Mont.: Scholars Press.

1981   "Two Bonhoeffers on Psychoanalysis" in Klassen (1981).
1986   "The Text of Bonhoeffer's *Ethics*," in William J. Peck, ed., *Studies in Bonhoeffer's Ethics*. New York: The Edwin Mellen Press (forthcoming).

GREGORY THAUMATURGUS
          The Oration and Panegyric Addressed to Origen, in *The Ante-Nicene Fathers*. Ed A. Roberts and J. Donaldson, rev. A. C. Coxe. Vol. 6. Reprint. Grand Rapids: Wm. B. Eerdmans Publishing Co., 1978.

GUSTAFSON, James
1975   *Can Ethics Be Christian?* Chicago: University of Chicago Press.
1981-84   *Ethics From a Theocentric Perspective*. Vol. 1 *Theology and Ethics*. Vol. 2 *Ethics and Theology*. Chicago: University of Chicago Press.

HACKING, Ian
1982   "Language, Truth, and Reason," *Rationality and Relativism*. Ed. Martin Hollis and Steven Lukes. Cambridge, Mass.: MIT Press.

HAMERTON-KELLY, Robert
1976   "Matthew, Gospel of," in *Interpreter's Dictionary of the Bible*. Supplementary vol. Nashville: Abingdon Press.

HARE, Richard
1952   *The Language of Morals*. Oxford: Clarendon Press.
1963   *Freedom and Reason*. Oxford: Clarendon Press.

HARNED, David B.
1979   *Images for Self-Recognition. The Christian as Player, Sufferer, and Vandal*. New York: Seabury Press.

HARRELSON, Walter J.
1962   "Ten Commandments," *Interpreter's Dictionary of the Bible*. Ed. George A. Buttrick, et al. 4 vols. New York: Abingdon Press.

HARRISON, Paul M.
1959   *Authority and Power in the Free Church Tradition*. Princeton: Princeton University Press.

HARVEY, Van Austin
1967   *The Historian and the Believer*. New York: Macmillan Publishing Co.

HAUERWAS, Stanley
1974   *Vision and Virtue*. Notre Dame, Ind.: Fides.
1975   *Character and the Christian Life*. San Antonio: Trinity University Press.
1977   *Truthfulness and Tragedy* (with Richard Bondi and David B. Burrell). Notre Dame: University of Notre Dame Press.
1981   *A Community of Character*. Notre Dame: University of Notre Dame Press.
1983   *The Peaceable Kingdom: A Primer in Christian Ethics*. Notre Dame: University of Notre Dame Press.

HAUGHTON, Rosemary
1980   *The Transformation of Man*. Springfield, Ill.: Templegate.

HELLER, Joseph
1964   *Catch-22, a Novel*. New York: Dell Publishing Co.

HELM, Paul, ed.
1981   *Divine Commands and Morality*. Oxford: Oxford University Press.

HENGEL, Martin
1973/1977 *Christ and Power*. Trans. Everett R. Kalin. Philadelphia: Fortress Press.

HENRY, Carl F.
1976-83   *God, Revelation, and Authority*. 6 vols. Waco, Tex.: Word.

HERSHBERGER, Guy F.
1953   *War, Peace, and Nonresistance*. Rev. ed. Scottdale, Pa.: Herald Press.

HOPKINS, Samuel
  1765   *The Life and Character of the Late Reverend Mr. Jonathan Edwards*, in Levin (1969).
HUDSON, Winthrop S.
  1953   "Baptists Were Not Anabaptists," *Chronicle* 16:171-78.
HUGO, John J.
  1944   *Applied Christianity*. New York: Privately printed.
  n.d.   *A Sign of Contradiction*. 2 vols. No place of publication shown: Typed and duplicated by the author.
  1984   *Your Ways Are Not My Ways: The Radical Christianity of the Gospel*. Pittsburgh, Pa.: Mt. Nazareth Center, Encounter with Silence.

JAMES, Henry
  1884/1984 "The Art of Fiction," in *Henry James: Literary Criticism, Essays on Literature, American Writers, English Writers*. No place of publication listed: The Library of America (Viking).
JAMES, William
  1902/1958 *The Varieties of Religious Experience*. New York: The New American Library.
  1910/1971 *The Moral Equivalent of War and Other Essays*. Ed. John K. Roth. New York: Harper & Row, Publishers.

KAUFMAN, Gordon D.
  1968   *Systematic Theology: A Historicist Perspective*. New York: Scribner's.
KELLEY, Patrick
  1984   in Bonhoeffer Society *Newsletter*, 28:3.
KELSEY, David H.
  1975   *The Uses of Scripture in Recent Theology*. Philadelphia: Fortress Press.
KENNEDY, R. Scott
  1984   "The Golani Druze: A Case of Non-Violent Resistance" in *Journal of Palestine Studies* 13:2 (Winter), pp. 48-64. Reprinted in Mubarak E. Awad and R. Scott Kennedy, *Nonviolent Struggle in the Middle East*. Philadelphia: New Society Publishers, 1984.
KESEY, Ken
  1962   *One Flew Over the Cuckoo's Nest*. New York: The New American Library.
KIERKEGAARD, Søren
  1843/1944 *Either/Or*. Vol. 1 trans. David F. Swenson and Lillian M. Swenson. Vol. 2 trans. Walter Lowrie. Princeton: Princeton University Press.
  1843/1952 *Fear and Trembling, A Dialectical Lyric*. Trans. Walter Lowrie. Princeton: Princeton University Press.
  1845/1940 *Stages on Life's Way*. Trans. Walter Lowrie. Princeton: Princeton University Press.
KINGSBURY, Jack Dean
  1977   *Matthew*, Proclamation Commentaries. Philadelphia: Fortress Press.
KITTEL, Gerhard, ed.
  1964   *Theological Dictionary of the New Testament*. Trans. G. W. Bromiley. 10 vols. Grand Rapids: Wm. B. Eerdmans Publishing Co.
KLASSEN, A. J., ed.
  1981   *A Bonhoeffer Legacy*. Grand Rapids: Wm. B. Eerdmans Publishing Co.

KLASSEN, William
    1968   *Covenant and Community: The Life and Writings of Pilgram Marpeck.*
               Grand Rapids: Wm. B. Eerdmans Publishing Co.
    1984   *Love of Enemies: The Way to Peace.* Philadelphia: Fortress Press.

LASSERRE, Jean
    1962   *War and the Gospel.* Trans. Oliver Coburn. Scottdale, Pa.: Herald
               Press.
LEHMANN, Paul
    1963   *Ethics in a Christian Context.* New York: Harper & Row,
               Publishers.
    1975   *The Transfiguration of Politics.* New York: Harper & Row,
               Publishers.
LESSING, Gotthold E.
    1957   *Lessing's Theological Works.* Stanford: Stanford University Press.
LEVIN, David, ed.
    1969   *Jonathan Edwards: A Profile.* New York: Hill & Wang.
LIND, Millard
    1980   *Yahweh is a Warrior.* Scottdale, Pa.: Herald Press.
LINDSELL, Harold
    1976   *The Battle for the Bible.* Grand Rapids: The Zondervan Corp.
LINENTHAL, Edward T.
    1980   "From Hero to Anti-Hero: The Transformation of the Warrior in
               Modern America." *Soundings* (Spring).
LITTELL, Franklin Hamlin
    1952   *The Anabaptist View of the Church.* 2nd ed., Boston: Starr King.
    1957   *The Free Church.* Boston: Starr King.
LOEWEN, Howard John
    1985   *One Lord, One Church, One Hope, and One God.* Elkhart, Ind.:
               Institute of Mennonite Studies.
LOHFINK, Gerhard
    1984   *Jesus and Community.* Trans. John P. Galvin. Philadelphia:
               Fortress Press.
LOHSE, Eduard
    1971   *Colossians and Philemon.* Trans. William R. Poehlmann and
               Robert J. Karris, and ed. Helmut Koester (Hermeneia Commen-
               taries). Philadelphia: Fortress Press.
LONERGAN, Bernard J. F.
    1972   *Method in Theology.* New York: Herder & Herder.
LOVELL, John, Jr.
    1972   *Black Song: The Forge and the Flame.* New York: Macmillan
               Publishing Co.
LUMPKIN, William L.
    1959   *Baptist Confessions of Faith.* Philadelphia: Judson Press.

McCABE, Herbert
    1969   *What Is Ethics All About?* Washington: Corpus.
McCLENDON, James Wm., Jr.
    1966   "Baptism as a Performative Sign," *Theology Today,* 23/3 (October)
               pp. 403-16.
    1967   "Why Baptists Do Not Baptize Infants," *Concilium* 24 *(The
               Sacraments: An Ecumenical Dilemma).* New York: Paulist.
    1971   "Biography as Theology," *Cross Currents* (Fall).
    1974   *Biography as Theology: How Life Stories Can Remake Today's
               Theology.* Nashville: Abingdon Press.
    1978   "Three Strands of Christian Ethics," in *Journal of Religious Ethics,*
               6/1 (Spring), pp. 54-80.

1981   "The God of the Theologians and the God of Jesus Christ" in
            Axel Steuer and James Wm. McClendon, Jr., eds., *Is God GOD?*
            Nashville: Abingdon Press.
McCLENDON, James Wm., Jr., and James M. SMITH
1975   *Understanding Religious Convictions.* Notre Dame: University of
            Notre Dame Press.
McENTYRE, John E.
1981   *The Increasing Significance of Symbolic Resistance in Selected
            Fiction . . .* Ph.D. Dissertation, Graduate Theological Union,
            Berkeley, California.
MacGREGOR, G. H. C.
1954   *The New Testament Basis of Pacifism,* rev. ed., and *The Relevance of
            an Impossible Ideal: An Answer to the Views of Reinhold Niebuhr.*
            Nyack, N.Y.: Fellowship.
MacINTOSH, Douglas Clyde
1919   *Theology as an Empirical Science.* New York: Macmillan Publishing
            Co.
MacINTYRE, Alasdair
1984   *After Virtue.* 2nd ed., Notre Dame: University of Notre Dame
            Press.
MacKINNON, Alastair
1970   *Falsification and Belief.* The Hague: Mouton.
MANSPEAKER, Nancy
1981   *Jonathan Edwards: Bibliographical Synopses.* New York: The Edwin
            Mellen Press.
MARPECK, Pilgram
1544/1978   *Preface to the "Explanation of the Testaments"* in *The Writings of
            Pilgram Marpeck.* Trans. and ed. William Klassen and Walter
            Klaassen. Scottdale, Pa.: Herald Press.
MASTON, Thomas B.
1967   *Biblical Ethics, A Survey.* Cleveland: World.
MATHEWS, Donald G.
1977   *Religion in the Old South.* Chicago: University of Chicago Press.
MAURIN, Peter
1961   *Easy Essays.* Fresno, Cal.: Academy Guild.
MBITI, John S.
1969   *African Religions and Philosophy.* London: Heinemann.
MEEKS, Wayne
1983   *The First Urban Christians.* New Haven: Yale University Press.
MEILAENDER, Gilbert C.
1981   *Friendship: A Study in Theological Ethics.* Notre Dame: University
            of Notre Dame Press.
1984   *The Theory and Practice of Virtue.* Notre Dame: University of Notre
            Dame Press.
MENNO SIMONS
1539/1956   *Foundation of Christian Doctrine* in *The Complete Writings of Menno
            Simons.* Ed. J. C. Wenger. Scottdale, Pa.: Herald Press.
1552/1956   *Confessions of the Distressed Christians* in *The Complete Writings of
            Menno Simons.* Trans. Leonard Verduin, and ed. J. C. Wenger.
            Scottdale, Pa.: Herald Press.
METZ, Johann B.
1980   *Faith in History and Society.* Trans. David Smith. New York:
            Seabury Press.
MIDGLEY, Mary
1978   *Beast and Man: The Roots of Human Nature.* Ithaca: Cornell
            University Press.

MILES, Margaret
  1979   *Augustine on the Body.* Missoula, Mont.: Scholars.
  1981   *Fullness of Life: Historical Foundations for a New Asceticism.*
             Philadelphia: Westminster Press.
MILLER, Perry
  1949   *Jonathan Edwards.* (no place of publication listed): William Sloane
             Associates.
  1953   *Roger Williams: His Contribution to the American Tradition.* New
             York: Atheneum Publishers.
  1956   *Errand into the Wilderness.* Cambridge, Mass.: The Belknap Press
             of Harvard University.
MILLER, William D.
  1973   *A Harsh and Dreadful Love: Dorothy Day and the Catholic Worker
             Movement.* New York: Liveright.
  1982   *Dorothy Day: A Biography.* San Francisco: Harper & Row,
             Publishers.
MITCHELL, Henry H.
  1975   *Black Belief: Folk Beliefs of Blacks in America and West Africa.* New
             York: Harper & Row, Publishers.
MONTAGU, Ashley
  1976   *The Nature of Human Aggression.* New York: Oxford University
             Press.
MOODY, Dale
  1981   *The Word of Truth.* Grand Rapids: Wm. B. Eerdmans Publishing
             Co.
MORRIS, Herbert
  1976   *On Guilt and Innocence: Essays in Legal Philosophy and Moral
             Psychology.* Berkeley: University of California Press.
MOYD, Olin P.
  1979   *Redemption in Black Theology.* Valley Forge, Pa.: Judson Press.
MULLINS, Edgar Young
  1908   *The Axioms of Religion.* Philadelphia: American Baptist Publica-
             tion Society.
  1920   *The Christian Religion in Its Doctrinal Expression.* Philadelphia:
             Judson Press. Often reprinted.
MURDOCH, Iris
  1966   "Vision and Choice in Morality," in Ian T. Ramsey, ed., *Christian
             Ethics and Contemporary Philosophy.* New York: Macmillan
             Publishing Co.
  1970   *The Sovereignty of Good.* London: Routledge & Kegan Paul.

NAPIER, B. Davie
  1962   "Prophet, Prophetism," in *Interpreter's Dictionary of the Bible.* Ed.
             George A. Buttrick. 4 vols. New York: Abingdon Press.
NIEBUHR, H. Richard
  1941   *The Meaning of Revelation.* New York: Scribner's.
  1951   *Christ and Culture.* New York: Harper & Row, Publishers.
  1963   *The Responsible Self.* Ed. with intro. by James Gustafson. New
             York: Harper & Row, Publishers.
NIEBUHR, Reinhold
  1932   *Moral Man and Immoral Society.* New York: Scribner's.
  1934   *An Interpretation of Christian Ethics.* New York: Harper &
             Brothers. (Reprint. New York: Meridian, 1956.)
  1939   "Why the Christian Church Is Not Pacifist." Pamphlet.
             Reprinted in Niebuhr, 1940.
  1940   *Christianity and Power Politics.* New York: Scribner's.

1941-43   *The Nature and Destiny of Man.* Vol. 1 *Human Nature.* Vol. 2 *Human Destiny.* New York: Scribner's.
1957   *Love and Justice: Selections from the Shorter Writings.* Ed. D. B. Robertson. Reprint. Cleveland: World, 1967.
NIEBUHR, Richard R.
1957   *Resurrection and Historical Reason.* New York: Scribner's.
NYGREN, Anders
1932/1969 *Agape and Eros.* Trans. Philip Watson. New York: Harper & Row, Publishers.

O'CONNELL, Timothy E.
1978   *Principles for a Catholic Morality.* New York: Seabury Press.
ORIGEN
           De Principiis, in *The Ante-Nicene Fathers.* Ed. A. Roberts and J. Donaldson, rev. A. C. Coxe. Vol. 4. Reprint. Grand Rapids: Wm. B. Eerdmans Publishing Co., 1979.
OTTO, Rudolf
1923   *The Idea of the Holy.* (German, 1917) Trans. John W. Harvey. London: Oxford University Press.
OUTKA, Gene
1972   *Agape: An Ethical Analysis.* New Haven: Yale University Press.

PARKER, G. Keith
1982   *Baptists in Europe: History and Confessions of Faith.* Nashville: Broadman Press.
PHILLIPS, Dewi Z., and H. O. MOUNCE
1970   *Moral Practices.* London: Routledge & Kegan Paul.
PIEHL, Mel
1982   *Breaking Bread: The Catholic Worker and the Origin of Catholic Radicalism in America.* Philadelphia: Temple University Press.
PIEPKORN, Arthur
1977-79   *Profiles in Belief: The Religious Bodies of the United States and Canada.* 4 vols. in 3. New York: Harper & Row, Publishers.
PINCOFFS, Edmund
1971   "Quandary Ethics," *Mind* (October), pp. 552-71.
PIXLEY, George
1983   "God's Kingdom in First-Century Palestine: The Strategy of Jesus," in *The Bible and Liberation,* ed. Norman K. Gottwald. Maryknoll, New York: Orbis Books.

RABOTEAU, Albert J.
1978   *Slave Religion.* New York: Oxford University Press.
RAHNER, Karl
1965   *Theological Dictionary* (with H. Vorgrimler). Ed. C. Ernst, and trans. R. Strachan. New York: Herder & Herder.
1970   "Theology," in *Sacramentum Mundi, an Encyclopedia of Theology.* Ed. Karl Rahner. Vol. 6. New York: Herder & Herder.
RAMM, Bernard
1957   *The Pattern of Authority.* Grand Rapids: Wm. B. Eerdmans Publishing Co.
RAMSEY, Paul
1961   *War and the Christian Conscience: How Shall Modern War Be Conducted?* Durham, N.C.: Duke University Press.
RASMUSSEN, Larry
1972   *Dietrich Bonhoeffer: Reality and Resistance.* Nashville: Abingdon Press.

RAUSCHENBUSCH, Walter
  1917   *A Theology for the Social Gospel.* New York: Scribner's.
  1968   *The Righteousness of the Kingdom.* Ed. and intro. by Max L.
            Stackhouse. Nashville: Abingdon Press.
RAWICK, George P.
  1972   *The American Slave: A Composite Autobiography.* (19 vols.) Vol. 19,
            God Struck Me Dead. Westport, Conn.: Greenwood Press.
RIDEMAN, Peter
  1545/1970 *Confessions of Faith.* Trans. from German. Rifton, N.Y.: Plough.
ROBERTS, Nancy L.
  1984   *Dorothy Day and the Catholic Worker Movement.* Albany, N.Y.:
            State University of New York Press.
ROBINSON, James M.
  1981   "From Easter to Valentinus: Christian Beginnings in Relation to
            Gnosticism." Mimeographed paper, presented to the Pacific
            Coast Theological Society, Berkeley, Cal., Fall, 1981.
ROBINSON, John A. T.
  1962   "Resurrection in NT," *Interpreter's Dictionary of the Bible.* Ed.
            G. A. Buttrick. 4 vols. New York: Abingdon Press.
RORTY, Richard
  1979   *Philosophy and the Mirror of Nature.* Princeton: Princeton
            University Press.
ROUGEMONT, Denis de
  1939/1983 *Love in the Western World.* Trans. Montgomery Belgion. Rev. ed.
            Princeton: Princeton University Press.

SARTRE, Jean-Paul
  1943/1957 *Being and Nothingness.* Trans. Hazel E. Barnes. London: Methuen.
SCHELL, Jonathan
  1982   *The Fate of the Earth.* New York: Alfred A. Knopf.
SCHLEIERMACHER, Friedrich
  1830/1966 *Brief Outline of the Study of Theology.* Trans. T. N. Tice. Richmond,
            Va.: John Knox Press.
  1835/1928 *The Christian Faith.* H. R. MacKintosh and J. S. Stewart.
            Edinburgh: T. & T. Clark.
SCHWEITZER, Albert
  1906/1968 *The Quest of the Historical Jesus.* Trans. W. Montgomery. New
            York: Macmillan Publishing Co.
SCOFIELD, Cyrus Ingerson, ed.
  1917   *The Scofield Reference Bible: The Holy Bible, Containing the Old and
            New Testaments, Authorized Version.* New York: Oxford Univer-
            sity Press.
SCRIVEN, Charles
  1985   *Christ and Culture After H. Richard Niebuhr.* Doctoral Dissertation,
            Graduate Theological Union, Berkeley, Cal.
SCROGGS, Robin
  1972   "Paul and the Eschatological Woman," *Journal of the American
            Academy of Religion,* 40/3 (September) 282-303.
SEARLE, John R.
  1967   "Proper Names and Descriptions," *Encyclopedia of Philosophy.*
            Ed. Paul Edwards. 8 vols. New York: Macmillan and Free Press.
  1979   *Expression and Meaning: Studies in the Theory of Speech Acts.*
            Cambridge: Cambridge University Press.
SEGAL, Erich
  1970   *Love Story.* New York: Harper & Row, Publishers.

SHARP, Gene
 1973   *The Politics of Nonviolent Action.* Ed. Marina Finkelstein. Boston:
          Parter Sargent.
SHEA, Daniel B., Jr.
 1968   *Spiritual Autobiography in Early America.* Princeton: Princeton
          University Press.
SHIRER, William L.
 1960   *The Rise and Fall of the Third Reich.* New York: Simon & Schuster.
SLATER, Peter
 1978   "The Kerygma and the Cuckoo's Nest," *Scottish Journal of
          Theology,* 31:4 (August) 301-18.
SLOAN, Douglas
 1979   "Teaching Ethics to American Undergraduates, 1876–1976" in
          Hastings Center Report, 9:6 (December).
SLOSSON, Edwin E.
 1920   "Jonathan Edwards as a Freudian." *Science* (n.s.), 52:609.
SMITH, Archie
 1982   *The Relational Self.* Nashville: Abingdon Press.
SMITH, Ronald Gregor, ed.
 1967   *World Come of Age.* Philadelphia: Fortress Press.
SMUCKER, Donovan
 1945   "The Theological Triumph of the Early Anabaptist-Mennon-
          ites," *Mennonite Quarterly Review,* 19:1 (October).
SNYDER, C. Arnold
 1984   *The Life and Thought of Michael Sattler.* Scottdale, Pa.: Herald
          Press.
SPIEGEL, Shallom
 1967   *The Last Trial.* New York: Pantheon Books.
STASSEN, Glen
 1962   "Anabaptist Influences in the Origin of the Particular Baptists,"
          Mennonite Quarterly Review (October).
STATNICK, Roger A.
 1983   *Dorothy Day's Religious Conversion: A Study in Biographical
          Theology.* Dissertation, University of Notre Dame, Ind.
STENDAHL, Krister
 1968   *The School of St. Matthew* (new ed.). Philadelphia: Fortress Press.
 1976   "The Apostle Paul and the Introspective Conscience of the
          West," in *Paul Among Jews and Gentiles and Other Essays.*
          Philadelphia: Westminster Press.
STEVENSON, Charles L.
 1944   *Ethics and Language.* New Haven: Yale University Press.
STEVENSON, Robert Louis
 1893/1952 *Catriona,* in *Kidnapped and Catriona.* London: William Collins Sons
          & Co.
STRONG, Augustus Hopkins
 1886   *Systematic Theology.* Philadelphia: Judson Press. Many subse-
          quent eds.
SUGGS, M. Jack
 1970   *Wisdom, Christology, and Law in Matthew's Gospel.* Cambridge,
          Mass.: Harvard University Press.
SUITS, Bernard
 1978   *The Grasshopper: Games, Life, and Utopia.* Toronto: University of
          Toronto Press.
SWARTLEY, Willard
 1983   *Slavery, Sabbath, War, and Women.* Scottdale, Pa.: Herald Press.

1984   ed., *Explorations of Systematic Theology from Mennonite Perspectives* (Occasional papers no. 7). Elkhart, Ind.: Institute of Mennonite Studies.

SWINBURNE, Algernon Charles
1904   *The Poems, Vol. 4. Tristram of Lyonesse* . . . New York: Harper & Brothers.

TAYLOR, John V.
1963   *The Primal Vision.* Philadelphia: Fortress Press.
TEMPLE, William
1934   *Nature, Man and God.* Oxford: Clarendon Press.
TERTULLIAN
      On Baptism, in *The Ante-Nicene Fathers,* III. Reprint. Grand Rapids: Wm. B. Eerdmans Publishing Co., 1978.
THIEMANN, Ronald F.
1985   *Revelation and Theology.* Notre Dame: University of Notre Dame Press.
TILLEY, Terrence W.
1978   *Talking of God: An Introduction to Philosophical Analysis of Religious Language.* New York: Paulist Press.
1985   *Story Theology.* Wilmington, Delaware: Michael Glazier.
TILLICH, Paul
1952   *The Courage to Be.* New Haven: Yale University Press.
TOLSTOY, Leo
1864/1869 *War and Peace.* Trans. from Russian. London: J. M. Dent.
TRACY, David
1975   *Blessed Rage for Order.* New York: Seabury Press.
1981   *The Analogical Imagination.* New York: Crossroad.
TROELTSCH, Ernst
1912a   *The Social Teaching of the Christian Churches.* Trans. Olive Wyon. New York: Harper & Row, Publishers.
1912b   *Protestantism and Progress.* Trans. W. Montgomery. Boston: Beacon Press.

UPDIKE, John
1966   "More Love in the Western World," *Assorted Prose.* Greenwich, Conn.: Fawcett.
1968   *Couples.* New York: Alfred A. Knopf.
1976   *Marry Me: A Romance.* New York: Alfred A. Knopf.

WAINWRIGHT, Geoffrey
1980   *Doxology.* New York: Oxford University Press.
WAYLAND, Francis
1865   *The Elements of Moral Science.* (Rev. and impr. ed.). New York: Sheldon.
WEIL, Simone
1952   *The Need for Roots.* Trans. Arthur Wills. New York: Harper & Row, Publishers.
WENGER, J. C.
1954   *Introduction to Theology.* Scottdale, Pa.: Herald Press.
WESTIN, Gunnar
1954   *The Free Church Through the Ages.* Trans. Virgil Olson. Nashville: Broadman Press.
WICKER, Brian
1975   *The Story Shaped World: Fiction and Metaphysics.* Notre Dame: University of Notre Dame Press.

WILKEN, Robert
1984 "Alexandria: A School of Training in Virtue," in *Schools of Thought in the Christian Tradition* (Pelikan Festschrift). Ed. Patrick Henry. Philadelphia: Fortress Press.

WILLIAMS, Bernard
1972 *Morality: An Introduction to Ethics.* New York: Harper & Row, Publishers.

WILLIAMS, George H.
1962 *The Radical Reformation.* Philadelphia: Westminster Press.

WILLIAMS, George H., and Angel MERGAL
1957 *Spiritual and Anabaptist Writers* (Library of Christian Classics, vol. 25). Philadelphia: Westminster Press.

WILLIAMS, Roger
1644 *The Bloody Tenent, or Persecution, for Cause of Conscience,* in *Complete Writings.* Vol. 4 (1963).
1652a *The Bloody Tenent Yet More Bloody,* in *Complete Writings.* Vol. 4 (1963).
1652b *The Hireling Ministry None of Christ's,* in *Complete Writings.* Vol. 7 (1963).
1963 *The Complete Writings of Roger Williams,* 7 vols. New York: Russell and Russell (a reprint of the Narragansett ed., with a seventh vol. added).

WILMORE, Gayraud, and James H. CONE, eds.
1979 *Black Theology: A Documentary History, 1966–1979.* Maryknoll, N.Y.: Orbis Books.

WILSON, Peter J.
1980 *Man the Promising Primate.* New Haven: Yale University Press.

WINK, Walter
1984 *The Powers: Volume 1: Naming the Powers.* Philadelphia: Fortress Press.

WINSLOW, Ola E.
1940 *Jonathan Edwards, 1703-1758: A Biography.* New York: Macmillan Publishing Co.

WITTGENSTEIN, Ludwig
1953 *Philosophical Investigations.* Trans. G. E. M. Anscombe. New York: Macmillan Publishing Co.

WOGAMAN, J. Philip
1976 *A Christian Method of Moral Judgment.* Philadelphia: Westminster Press.

WOOD, Thomas
1952 *English Casuistical Divinity During the Seventeenth Century.* London: SPCK.
1967 "Caroline Moral Theology," in *Dictionary of Christian Ethics.* Ed. John Macquarrie. Philadelphia: Fortress Press.

YODER, John Howard
1954 "Peace Without Eschatology." Pamphlet. Scottdale, Pa.: Concern. Reprinted in Yoder, 1971a.
1955 *Reinhold Niebuhr and Christian Pacifism.* Pamphlet, reprinted. Scottdale, Pa.: Concern.
1964 " 'Christ and Culture': A Critique of H. Richard Niebuhr." Mimeographed paper available at library, Associated Mennonite Biblical Seminaries, Elkhart, Ind.
1971a *The Original Revolution.* Scottdale, Pa.: Herald Press.
1971b *Nevertheless.* Scottdale, Pa.: Herald Press.

1972   *The Politics of Jesus*. Grand Rapids: Wm. B. Eerdmans Publishing Co.

1973   Trans. and ed., *The Legacy of Michael Sattler*. Scottdale, Pa.: Herald Press.

1979   The Stone Lectures at Princeton Theological Seminary (unpublished typescript).

1984   *The Priestly Kingdom: Social Ethics as Gospel*. Notre Dame: University of Notre Dame Press.

ZIMMERMAN, Wolf-Dieter, and Ronald Gregor SMITH
1973   *I Knew Dietrich Bonhoeffer*. Trans. Käthe Gregor Smith. London: William Collins Sons & Co.

ZUURDEEG, Willem F.
1958   *An Analytical Philosophy of Religion*. Nashville: Abingdon Press.

Index of Names and Subjects

abortion, 97, 204, 287f
Achtemeier, Elizabeth, 248
act, action, 70 (*see also* speech-acts)
Adam, Karl, 27
Adams, Richard, 70, 172
Adams, Robert, 332
adultery, 53, 182f
African influences, 37, 80f
aggression, 91, 95
Ahlstrom, Sydney, 44, 111, 129, 305
Aho, J., 313, 317
Alley, Robert S., 25
Alston, William P., 57
Alter, Robert, 330
Anabaptists, 19f, 25, 28, 30, 198, 210, 299 (*see also* Radical Reformation; baptists)
animal. *See* beast
anastatic, (*see also* strands, moral: s. three) Part III
Ardrey, Robert, 92f
Aristotle, 48, 69f, 173, 341f, 348
Arminianism, 44, 129
art, 41, 182, 231
Auden, W. H., 90
Augustine of Hippo, 58, 129, 143-46, 160

Bainton, Roland H., 301
baptism, 106, 213, 218, 233, 253f, 255-59, 291, 306; believer's, 28, 248f, 271, 277; infant, 113f, 258

baptist(s), ch. 1 pass., 51, 60, 80, 105, 159, 211, 231, 254, 270, 277, 299
baptist vision, the, 19, 26, 37, 44, 70, 75, 155, 159, 179, 198, 212, 235, 257f, 332; defined, 27-35
Barth, Karl, 41, 63, 93, 191f, 230-32
Barth, Markus, 73, 249, 252
Beasley-Murray, G. R., 245
beasts, beastly, 91f
beauty, 124f, 348
Believers' Church, 19, 28, 34f
Bender, Harold S., 29-31, 35
Bentham, Jeremy, 57, 348
Berger, Peter, 313, 317
Berkhof, Hendrik, 174-76
Bethge, E., 188f, 192, 200
Betz, Hans-Dieter, 73, 257
Bible, 25, 31f, 37, 43, 52, 63, 192, 198, 206, 278, 286, 329, 349
biblicism, 28f, 32f
biography as theology, 110f
black(s), 34, 39, 79-84, 106f, 238f
blame, 98-104, 273
Blanke, Fritz, 269
body, 90-103, 331
Boettner, Loraine, 315
Bonhoeffer, Dietrich, 16f, 30, 59, 84-86, 100, 186, ch. 7, 209, 332; early years, 187-91; family of, 189f, 200f, 206f; visits America, 191, 193f; "becomes Christian," 193, 206; in

Bonhoeffer cont.
London, 192, 200; India plans of, 192; Finkenwalde period, 195-200, 206; as conspirator, 199-208; tragedy of, 205-8.
Braithwaite, R. B., 344
Brandon, S. G. F., 73, 303-6
Brown, Peter, 144f
Brown, Robert McAfee, 27
Buber, Martin, 179
Bultmann, Rudolf, 73, 339
Bunyan, John, 59-62, 161
Burrell, David, 334
Bushnell, Horace, 168, 225-27
Butler, Joseph, 68, 225

Caird, George, 174f
Calvin, J., 25, 36f, 44
Calvinism, 25, 36f, 44
Campbell, Alexander, 108; and Thomas, 36
Campbell, Jeff H., 137f
Campbell, Will D., 157, 237-39
Carney, Frederick, 44
Carse, James, 128
casuistry, 71
Catholic and Protestant (vs. baptist), 18f, 27, 35f, 38, 48, 62, 176, 178, 231, 269, 313 (*see also* Constantinian)
Catholic Worker, The, 276, 291-93, 295f
Celsus, 301, 321
character, 70, 331f, 354f
Chernus, Ira, 314, 317
Childs, Brevard S., 177, 311
Christology, 42, 188, 191, 267
church(es), 37, 71, 74, 198, 204, ch. 8 pass., 270, 289, 330, 349, 356; fall of the, 30f; gathered, ch. 8; New Testament, 34; social structures of, ch. 6 pass.; and state, 28-30; true, 18, 30, 128; and world, 17f, 212, 214, 230-32
Clarke, William Newton, 37
Cobb, John B., Jr., 88, 266-69, 273, 345
Coleridge, S. T., 168
Commandments, Ten, 160, 177-84, 222, 311, 315
commissioning, 214, 259
communion, 116, 128, 215-18 (*see also* Lord's supper, eucharist)
community, 28, 30-34, 70, 105, 188, 206, 211; civil, 232; intentional, 28, 34; of Matthew, ch. 8 pass.; Messianic, 74; Pauline, ch. 8 pass.; of Ten Commandments, 177-84
concupiscentia carnis, 144f
Cone, Cecil W., 82

Cone, James H., 81, 265
Confessing Church, 192, 194, 199
Conner, Walter Thomas, 37
conscience, 68f, 98-103, 210; liberty of, 29-34
conscientious objection, 203, 274
consent to being, 55, 128-31
Constantine, Emp., 301, 310
Constantinian(ism), 31, 73f, 176, 192, 208, 258f, 264, 274, 301, 318
conversation or dialogue, 222-24, 270-72
conversion, 43, 53, 82, 113, 192, 206, 213, 254; ethics of, 131
convictions, 22f, 34, 62, 70, 332, 355f
courage, 170
covenant, 66; meal, 214-18
coveting, 182
cross, way of, 73, 186, 274f, 325
Crossan, John Dominic, 306
Cullmann, Oscar, 249
culture, 93-95, 133, 231; and Christ, 230-32
Cyprian of Carthage, 157

Dagg, J. L., 37
David and Bathsheba, 95f, 330
Davies, W. D., 102
Dawidowicz, Lucy S., 205
Day, Dorothy, 127, ch. 10, 299; childhood, 278-80; in Chicago, 280-88; U. of Illinois, 282f; in New York, 283-88; in New Orleans, 288f; conversion, 288-95; birth of Tamar, 290; and Catholic Worker Movement, 276f, 291-93, 295-98; in WW II, 297f
decision(s) (ism), decide, 47, 52, 55, 56-59, 62, 70, 75, 171, 182, 203f, 263, 266-69, 332; etymology of, 58; proper use of, 223f
Delattre, Roland Andre, 129
delight (and horror), 86, 98-105, 273f
descriptions, def., 337f, 341f
despair, 86f
development (of doctrine), 32
Dillard, Annie, 91
discipleship, disciples, 28-30, 34, 106, 194-97, 211-14, 323, 338f (*see also Nachfolge Christi*)
discipline, 214, 323
divorce, 221, 275, 288-90
Dix, Gregory, 258
doctrine, 41, 44
Dodds, Elisabeth D., 112, 121

drives, needs, and capacities, 91-103, 133, 242
DuBois, W. E. B., 83
Durnbaugh, Donald F., 19, 27
Dwight, Sereno E., 112

ecology, ch. 3 pass., 322
Edwards, Jonathan, 55, 69, 77; youth, 111-13; pastor, 13-17; conversion autobiography, 126f; life w. Sarah, ch. 4, 149; ethical theory, 124-26, 131, 148-50, 152
Edwards, Sarah Pierpont, ch. 4, 149; collapse and conversion, 116, 118-20; autobiography, 118-20, 126f
Ellis, Marc H., 292, 298
Ellsberg, Daniel, 308
Ellsberg, Robert, 276
Ellul, Jacques, 161, 251f, 265
Enlightened, Enlightenment, 25, 36f, 79, 108, 129, 142, 263, 336, 342
eros, ch. 5 pass.
eschatology, 74, 185f, 217, ch. 9 pass., 306f; and peace, 318-21, 325f
Estep, William R., Jr., 269f
ethics, ch. 2; aesthetic, 131; body, chs. 3–5; Christian, 63; consequentialist, 50, 54f, 57; contextualist, 70, 259-63; definition of, 47; deontological, 57, 333; ecological, 88; emotivist, 333, 344; medical, 72; narrative, 55, ch. 12; qualified, 71; resurrection, chs. 9–11; situationist, 70, 200, 259f; social, 42, 44, 71, chs. 6–8; theological, 25, 40-45, 329
eucharist, 32, 106, 196, 214-19 (see also Lord's supper, communion)
euthanasia, 97, 204
evangelism, 28, 169, 188, 274
evil, 51, 75, 92, 198, 245f
Exodus, the, 177f, 316f

fall (into sin), fallenness, 89f, 160f
fallibility, principle of, 45
family, 93f
Faulkner, William, 107, 314
feminism (ists), 142, 175, 322
Fiering, Norman, 125
Fingarette, Herbert, 101
Fiorenza, Elizabeth S., 249
flesh, 78
Floyd, Wayne, 200
forgiveness, 102, 152, 212, 214, 273, 299; as act and attitude, 224-29; and law, 219-24; as norm of commu-

nity, 224; not forgetting, 225f; politics of, 219-29
Foucault, Michel, 146
Fox, George, 108
Frankena, William, 347f
free, freedom, 29-34, 40, 257, 348 (see also liberty)
Free Church, 19
Frei, Hans, 39-41, 243, 330, 336f, 353
Freud, Anna, 101
Freud, Sigmund, 139-43, 146, 152, 313
Friedmann, Robert, 30
friend (ship), 43, 46, 140, 172f, 348; erotic, 111
Frondizi, Risieri, 347
Fundamentalism, 25, 37, 44, 321
fundamental option, stance, 53, 55, 293
Furnish, Victor Paul, 102

game(s), 149, 162-67; Suits' def. of, 163; cooperative, 166
Gandhi, M. K., 192, 206, 308, 324
Garrett, J. Leo, 19
Gaustad, Edwin S., 25
genocide, 128
Genovese, Eugene D., 81
Georgi, Dieter, 251
GeschichtBuch (Hutterian Chronicle), 39
Gill, David, 252
Gill, John, 36f
Gill, Theodore, 195, 198, 200
Gilligan, Carol, 142f
God, 66, 90f, 125, 129f, 147, 174f, 180, 183, 186f, 356
gods, 161, 174, 182
Goen, C. C., 25
Goldberg, Michael, 37, 222, 313, 330
Golden Rule, 222
good, the, 95, 347
goods, 105, 169, 223f
gospel, 85, 178, 335-46
Gottwald, Norman, 316
gratitude, awed, 218
Greaves, Richard L., 60
Green, C. J., 193, 200, 206
Gregory Thaumaturgus, 42-44
Griffin, David Ray, 88
guilt, 89, 98-104, 273, 287f
Gustafson, James M., 63, 70, 73, 129, 247

Hacking, Ian, 350
Hamerton-Kelly, Robert, 212

Hammarskjøld, Dag, 158
Hare, Richard, 344
Harnack, Adolf von, 191, 302
Harned, David B., 93
Harrelson, Walter, 178
Harrison, Paul M., 40
Harvey, Van Austin, 353
Hauerwas, Stanley, 48, 69-72, 89, 105, 172f, 230-32, 306, 313, 320-34 pass., 353
Haughton, Rosemary, 150f
Hawthorne, Nathanael, 107
hedonism, 57, 67
Heller, Joseph, 314
Helm, Paul, 180f
Hengel, Martin, 174f
Henry, Carl F., 37
hermeneutics, 29, 31 (see also reading strategy)
Hershberger, Guy, 317
Hiroshima and Nagasaki—1945, 87
history, 24, 29f, 52, 300f, 340-42; church, 74f
Hitler, Adolf, ch. 7 pass.; plot against, 193, 199-205
Hoekstra, Sytse, 37
Holbrook, Clyde, 130
Holy Spirit, 67, 82, 89, 103, 120, 175, 320
holy war, 316f
homosexuality and heterosexuality, 140
hope, 105, 182, 247, 346
Hopkins, G. M., 54, 77, 248
Hopkins, Samuel, 112f
Hubmaier, Balthasar, 40, 259
Hudson, Winthrop S., 20
Hugo, John L., 293
human qualities, 54, 171
Hume, David, 142, 347f

identity, identification, 212ff, 257, 332, 353, in Gospels, 336-40
ideology, 24, 166
incarnation, 145
individual(ism), 67f, 71
instincts, 91-95, 104
institutions, 173f
intention(s), 171, 344; God's, 172f, 231f
Iseult, 288. See Tristan and
Israel, 37, 177-84, 198, 211, 330, 349

James, Henry, 330f
James, William, 37, 56-59, 121, 322-25, 343

Jesus of Nazareth, Jesus Christ, 17, 37, 43, 45, 55, 70f, 89, 101f, 105, 173, 189, 204f, 212, 218, 223, 267-69, 300-308, 317, 330, 337f, 349; cross of, 161, 217; eschatological, 73; final coming, 175, 305; life of, 153, 220f, 256f; lordship, 28, 30, 34, 231f; mighty signs, 306; resurrected, 66f, 150, 161, 186, 191, 243-59, 272, 326; work of, 187, 325
Jews, Jewish, 58, 139, 200; and Gentiles, 40, 214, 223, 257; and Holocaust, 205
JHWH, 99, 178-84, 218, 249
Jordan, Clarence, 107, 306
Joshua, 316f
joy, 345f
Judaism, 246
judgment(s), moral, 49-51, 91, 98-104
justice, 319, 348; vindication of, 248f
just war theory, 295, 319-21

Kant, Immanuel, 37, 56f, 62
Kantian, 333; post-K., 102
Kaufman, Gordon D., 37
Kelley, Patrick, 193
Kelsey, David H., 37
Kennedy, R. Scott, 308
Kermode, Frank, 330
Kesey, Ken, 351-53
Kierkegaard, S., 63, 65, 86f
King, M. L., Jr., 107, 265, 324
kingdom of God, 71, 256, 274, 300, 318-27, 330, 339
Kingsbury, J. D., ch. 8 pass.
kinship, 242
Kittel, Gerhard, 256
Klassen, A. J., 200
Klassen, William, 303, 308, 315
koinonia, 260, 269-72

Lassere, Jean, 193, 311
law, 49, 55, 66, 175-84, 187, 211-14, 219-21, 233, 260; canon, 301
Lehmann, Paul, 259-66
Lessing, Gotthold E., 342
liberal, liberalism, 32, 37, 166, 172, 246
liberty, 28-35, 46, 81; religious, 36, 236 (see also free, freedom)
Lind, Millard C., 316f
Lindsell, Harold, 25
Linenthal, Edward T., 314
Littell, F. H., 19, 30f
Loewen, Howard J., 29
Lohfink, Gerhard, 302
Lohse, Eduard, 257

Lonergan, Bernard J. F., 39
Lord's supper, 28, 214-19, 239, 306
  (*see also* eucharist, communion)
love, 107, 124f, 130f, ch. 5, 168, 299,
  333, 343, 348; of enemies, 221, 297,
  308; suffering, 319f
Lovell, John, Jr., 81
lower nature, 90 (*see also* flesh)
Lumpkin, William L., 38, 270
lusory attitude, 163-66
Luther, Martin, 58, 146, 192, 259f

McCabe, Herbert, 99
McClendon, James Wm., Jr., 37, 63,
  66, 70, 81, 108, 111, 186, 256, 266,
  306, 337; and J. M. Smith, 23, 35,
  44f, 170, 218, 249, 329, 350, 354
McEntyre, John, 314
MacGregor, G. H. C., 301-3, 320
MacIntosh, Douglas C., 37, 44
MacIntyre, Alasdair, 104f, 160, 162,
  169-74, 181, 218f, 328
MacKinnon, Alastair, 32
man, 93, 267 (*see also* human quali-
  ties)
mandates, divine, 177
Manichae(ism), 134, 149f, 162
Manspeaker, Nancy, 112
Marpeck, Pilgram, 159, 315
marriage, 146, 154, 166-68, 175, 183,
  242, 288-91
Marx, Karl, 189, 265
Marxian, 24, 166, 244f, 263, 280, 285,
  304
Maston, Thomas B., 63
Mathews, Donald G., 79f, 83
Maurin, Peter, 292, 296
Mbiti, John S., 82
Meeks, Wayne, ch. 8 pass.
Meilaender, Gilbert, 104, 146
Menno Simons, 36, 44, 159
Metz, Johann B., 354
Midgley, Mary, 91f
Miles, Margaret, 79, 146
Miller, Perry, 116, 315
Miller, Wm. D., 127, 277, 281, 292
mission(s), 25, 28f, 34, 275
Mitchell, Henry, 82
Modernism, 25, 37, 44
Montagu, Ashley, 92f
Moody, Dale, 37
morals, morality, 133, 266; begin-
  nings of, 210; Christian, 132; de-
  fined, 47; m. theology, 41
Morris, Herbert, 102, 223f
Moses, 33, 66, 98, 178, 316f; new, 66

Moyd, Olin P., 82
Mullins, E. Y., 27, 29, 31f, 37
murder, 53, 182
Murdoch, Iris, 70, 153f
myth(s), 133-41, 330; of war, 308-18

Nachfolge Christi, 29, 194-98, 206
Napier, B. Davie, 33
narrative, 24ff, 37·39, 47, 70f, 105,
  118-20, 142, 170-73, 182, 257, ch. 12
  (*see also* story)
natural, the, 84f, 204, 291
natural law, 54, 89, 235
nature (or Nature), 54, 79, 94, 112,
  322f
needs, 78, 95-98, 104; of the soul, 97,
  210; of society, 210
New Testament, 51, 69, 174, 198, 281,
  296, 300-308
new that comes in Christ, 45, 54, 185
Niebuhr, H. R., 38, 63, 70, 89, 230-32,
  323, 331
Niebuhr, Reinhold, 69f, 86f, 146,
  160f, 177, 194, 313, 319-21, 323f
Niebuhr, Richard R., 247
Niemoeller, Martin, 192
nonresistance, 221, 274f
nonviolence, 163, 198, 206, 324f (*see
  also* violence)
nuclear weapons, 322, 325
Nygren, Anders, 148

oath(s), 181, 203
obedience, 65, 177, 180f, 195f, 214;
  ethics of, 180f
O'Connell, T. E., 48, 52-55
Old Testament, 243, 248; and war,
  315-18
Origen, 42-44, 301
Otto, Rudolf, 98f
Outka, Gene, 148

pacifism, pacifist, 194, 199, 233,
  295-98, 301, 318f, 321-24; arguments against, 308-18
Paley, William, 68
Parker, G. Keith, 38
patriarchy, 175
Paul, Apostle, 40, 58, 175, 185f, 218f,
  248, 257f, 267; ethics of, 102, 228
peace (making), 188, 231, 274-77,
  295-98, ch. 11 pass.
perfect(ionist), 51, 222, 234
Perry, Rufus Lewis, 37
Peter, Simon, 33, 99, 212

Phillips, Dewi Z., 183
philosophy, 39; moral, 36, 44, 68, 329
Piehl, Mel, 298
Piepkorn, Arthur, 19
Pincoffs, Edmund, 49
Pixley, George, 303-8
Platonism, 70
pluralist(ism), 24, 36f
politics, 131, 174
possession, spiritual, 82f
powers, principalities and, 159-62, 184, 187, 218f, 233f, 245f, 274f; conquest of, 174-76, 275; fallen, 185f; religions as, 175f
practice(s), 66, 105, 159, 162-70, 332; of community formation, 182, 216, 218f,229; of marriage, 154, 221; of peace, 321-24; powerful, 173-77, 180, 187f, 274; of sacrifice, 65
praxis, 24, 166
prayer, 112, 167
presence, 82f, 100, 106-8, 121, 224, 267f
pride, 185f, 319
promise, 94
prophets, prophecy, 33, 56
propositions, moral, 52, 65, 332-46, 353
psychoanalysis, 26, 100-102, 121f, 139-43, 146
punishment, 223f, 237f, 312
Puritan(ism), 25, 36, 58, 111, 159, 210, 343

Raboteau, Albert J., 80
Radical Reformation, 25-30, 35, 147, 159, 198
Rahner, Karl, 21
Ramm, Bernard, 40
Ramsey, Paul, 130, 312
Rasmussen, Larry, 194
rational(ity), 39f, 333f
Rauschenbusch, Walter, 21, 37, 63, 244-47
Rawick, George P., 82
reading strategy, 34, 315-17, 330ff
Reformers, Protestant, 25, 198, 245
relativism, 8, 89, 231, 349f
religion, natural and revealed, 69, 178; mystical, 148
resentment and reproach, 102, 225-27
responsibility, 52, 74, 102, 231, 268
restitution, restoration, 28, 30f, 34
resurrection (believers'), 145
revival(ism), 25, 58, 114-16

revolution, 25, 285
rights, 81, 95, 347 (see also needs)
Ritschl, Albrecht, 246, 347
Roberts, Nancy L., 276
Robinson, James M., 253
Robinson, John A. T., 246
roles, social, 66, 268f, 355
Rorty, Richard, 42
Rougemont, Denis de, 132-39, 149
rules, 216, 260, 289; of games, 163-66; constitutive, 163

sabbath, 182
salvation, 53, 104, 151, 185f, 224, 356
Sartre, Jean-Paul, 57
Sattler, Michael, 269-73, 301
Schell, Jonathan, 325
Schleiermacher, Friedrich, 18f, 23, 37-39, 41, 129, 188
Schleitheim Confession, 269-72
Schweitzer, Albert, 246, 306
science(s), 24, 39, 52, 112
Scofield, C. I., 304-6, 318-21
Scripture. See Bible
Scriven, Charles, 63
Scroggs, Robin, 257f
Searle, John, 342
sectarian(ism), 71, 214
Segal, Erich, 135-38
self, selves, embodied, 88, 218, 273, 331
Sermon on the Mount, 194f, 211, 281, 291, 296, 308, 312
sex, ch. 5 pass., 262f, 280, 284, 286
sexes, relation of, 26, 94
Shakespeare, William, 56, 141, 309, 323, 327
shame, 88, 98-102, 287f
Sharp, Gene, 324
Shea, Daniel B., Jr., 118
Shirer, William L., 202
Sider, Ron, 42
signs, 249, 306
sin, 53, 62, 146, 185f, 223, 256, 294, 319f; confession of, 196; mortal, 53; original, 53, 130, 160-62, 320; social paradigm of, 145
skills, 104, 205f
Slater, Peter, 351
slavery, 25, 204, 257, 274
Sloan, Douglas, 44
Slosson, Edwin E., 123
Smith, Archie, Jr., 210
Smith, James M. See McClendon
Smith, Ronald Gregor, 200

Smucker, Donovan, 28, 31-34
Snyder, C. Arnold, 270
sociality, 188, 190
society, ch. 6 pass., 171-74; structures of, 242, 250
soul competency, 28f, 31f
speech-acts, 335-46
Spiegel, Shallom, 65
spirituality, 71, 323
spirituals, black, 80-88, 106
stability, integrity, liberty, plurality, 235-37
Stackhouse, Max, 245
Stassen, Glen, 20, 176f
Statnick, Roger A., 277
Stendahl, K., 58, 175, 211
Stevenson, Charles L., 98, 344
Stevenson, Robert Louis, 151-53
Stoddard, Solomon, 113f, 128
Stoics, 54, 69
story, stories, 47, 56-59, 62, 138, 141, 144, 147, 171-73, 222, 225-27, 256f, 330-32, 356; women's, 142 (see also narrative)
strands, moral: s. one Part I, 69, 209f, 218, 224-26, 322-24; s. two Part II, 101f, 153, 324f; s. three Part III, 160, 206, 218, 234, 324f; three strands, 48, 62-67, 75, 109, 131, 154f, 158, 184-87, 305f, 322; correlated w. narrative, 331f
Strong, A. H., 37, 41
suffering, 83f; redemptive, 151f
Suggs, M. Jack, ch. 8 pass.
suicide, 288
Suits, Bernard, 162-66, 355
Swartley, Willard, 315
Swinburne, Algernon, 281, 287
Swiss, Brethren, 36, 270, 343

Taylor, John V., 82
Teilhard de Chardin, P., 87
Temple, William, 99
temptation, 227
Tertullian, 256
theologies, baptist, ch. 1; black, 81f; Liberation, 98, 159, 166, 234, 244f, 259, 263-66, 306; Neo-orthodox, 85-89; polytheistic and atheistic, 21f; Process, 85-89
theology, ch. 1; definition of, 21-24; organizing principle of, 33, 128f
Thiemann, Ronald F., 339
Thomas Aquinas, 69f, 312, 329
Tillich, Paul, 86f
Tocqueville, Alexis de, 68

Tolstoy, Leo, 314
Torah, 183, 211, 222
torture, 204
Tracy, David, 23f
tradition, 29, 52, 74f
tragic, tragedy, 72, 205-8
Trinity, divine, 63
Tristan (Tristram) and Iseult (Isolde), 132-39, 149, 281-87
Troeltsch, E., 29-31, 191, 272
truth(fulness), 18, 40, 262, 340, 348-55
typology, 73, 230-32

Updike, John, 136-38
Utilitarianism, 50, 55, 57, 62, 68, 333

value(s), 168, 333
vice(s), 104, 258
violence, 29, 105, 252, 265f (see also nonviolence)
virtue(s), 43, 70, 89, 124, 154f, 258, 332, 348; embodied, 103-9, 169-73; related to practices, 169f; secondary and true, 124-26; as strand-encompassing, 108
vision, 70, 90, 153; moral, 89 (see also baptist vision)
voluntarism, 29, 59

Wainwright, Geoffrey, 256
war, 25, 128, 231, ch. 11 pass.
Wayland, F., 48, 67-69, 178
Weil, Simone, 97, 104
Weiss, Johannes, 246, 306
Wenger, J. C., 37
Westin, Gunnar, 19
White, T. H., 314
Whitefield, George, 115, 121
Whitehead, A. N., 87
white(s), 79f, 101, 238f
Wicker, Brian, 183
Wilken, Robert, 43
will, human, 47, 56, 130; of God, 222
Williams, Bernard, 99, 355
Williams, George H., 19
Williams, R., 36, 40, 45, 315
Wilmore, Gayraud, 82
Wilson, Peter J., 93f
Wink, Walter, 176
Winslow, Ola E., 112
wisdom, 52, 103, 253; Jesus as, 221
withdrawal, 197, 231, 273, 319
witness, 28, 169, 204, 274; false, 182
Wittgenstein, Ludwig, 64, 162
Wogaman, J. P., 48-52, 55, 74, 231

woman, women, 39, 45, 257, 269, 286
(*see also* Sarah Edwards, Dorothy
Day)
Wood, Thomas, 210
worship, 182, 188, 274, 323f (*see also*
baptism, Lord's supper)

Yoder, John Howard, 48, 51, 63,
72-75, 89, 161, 176f, 263, 270-72,
296, 301, 306, 312, 318, 320f, 328

Zimmermann, Wolf-Dieter, 198
Zuurdeeg, Willem F., 22
Zwingli, Ulrich, 36, 269f

Index of
Scripture References

Genesis, 1–3 *p189*; 1–11 *p183*; 26–31 *pp91-94*; 2:2f *p179*; 2:9 *p81*; 2:15 *p88*; 2:16f *p93*; 3 *pp93, 161*; 3:5 *p59*; 3:7b *p 100*; 4:10 *p99*; 22 *p64*; 22:1-15 *pp64-66*; 22:11 *p248*; 26 *p91*; 45:8 *p31*

Exodus, 2 *p178*; 3:1-5 *p99*; 3:14 *p183*; 13:14 *p316*; 19 *p178*; 193f *p249*; 19:4 *p178*; 20:1-17 *pp177-84*; 20:13 *p311*; 21:23-25 *p221*

Leviticus, 19:18 *p221*; 20:2-5 *p65*

Deuteronomy, 5:6-21 *pp177-84*; 6:1-8 *p180*; 24:1-4 *p221*; 32:35 *p127*

Joshua, *p317*; 2–6 *p317*

Judges, *p317*; 5 *p317*

1 Samuel, 15:22 *p65*; 8f *p316*; 18:1 *p42*

2 Samuel, 11 *p95*; 11:1 *p95*; 11:8 *p96*; 11:11 *p96*

Nehemiah, 8:1 *p183*

Psalms, *pp84, 281*; 24:1 *p197*; 32:3 *p102*; 39:1 *p174*; 39:7 *p38*; 82 *p174*; 89:6f *p174*; 8:10 *p174*; 104:4 *p174*; 127:1f *p250*; 139 *p90*; 146:3 *p250*

Ecclesiastes, (pass.) *p250*; 3:2 *p97*; 4:12 *p16*

Isaiah, 9:6 *p317*; 40–66 *p317*; 43:25f *p225*

Daniel, *p245*

Joel, *p33*

Amos, 3:3 *p159*

Matthew, *pp211f, 222, 222-34*; 2 *p326*; 3:1ff *p302*; 3:2 *p305*; 4:1-11 *p67*; 5–7 *pp211, 281, 308*; 5:1-20 *p214*; 5:2 *p305*; 5:9 *p321*; 5:14 *p197*; 5:18 *p220*; 5:20 *p214*; 5:21ff *p221*; 5:21-26 *p312*; 5:31f *p220*; 5:33-42 *p233*; 5:38-42 *pp198, 221*; 5:38-48 *p312*; 5:30 *p302*; 5:44 *p221*; 6:8 *p96*; 6:12 *pp157, 227, 234*; 7:12 *p222*; 9:9 *p228*; 10:34 *pp301, 305*; 10:34-39 *p214*; 11:20 *p305*; 12:30 *p213*; 12:46-50 *p214*; 13:1 *p305*; 13:22 *p234*; 13:51 *p220*; 13:52 *p214*; 15:1-20 *p220*; 15:19 *p234*; 16:17-19 *p214*; 16:18 *p219*; 17:28 *p90*; 18 *pp102, 105, 196, 211, 227, 234f*; 18:10 *p234*; 18:15 *pp223, 227*; 18:15-20 *pp214, 227f*; 18:17 *p223*; 18:21f *pp223, 228*; 18:21-35 *p234*; 19:8 *p221*; 19:21 *p213*; 19:25f *p239*; 20:25-28 *p214*; 22:36-40 *p222*; 23 *p101*; 23:8-12 *pp214, 234*;

Matthew cont.

23:23 *p220;* 24:3 *pp305, 318;* 24:6 *p318;* 24:35f *p95;* 25 *p59;* 25:26-29 *p214;* 25:35f *p97;* 25:37 *p59;* 25:45 *p234;* 26 *pp215f;* 26:26-30 *p215;* 26:29 *p217;* 27:51 *p233;* 28:18-20 *pp212-14, 233, 255-57, 326*

Mark, *p337;* 1:1 *p336;* 1:1-8 *p255;* 1:5 *p255;* 1:11 *p150;* 1:15 *p306;* 4:35-41 *p307;* 6:2 *p306;* 6:5 *p306;* 6:32-44 *p307;* 7:1-23 *p101;* 827 *p338;* 9:1 *p250;* 9:2-8 *p264;* 9:50 *p324;* 10:19 *p177;* 10:24 *p338;* 10:32 *p338;* 10:35ff *p338;* 10:42-45 *p274;* 12:38 *p101;* 13:27 *p307;* 13:30 *p250;* 13:35 *p307;* 13:50 *p307;* 14:50 *p338;* 16:7 *p338*

Luke, 1:1-4 *p340;* 2:14 *p318;* 5:8 *p99;* 6:20-49 *p308;* 9:31 *p264;* 9:58 *p323;* 10:18 *p175;* 13:34f *p307;* 15:22 *p248;* 19:42 *p324;* 19:45 *p304;* 23:24 *p234*

John, *p248;* 1:13 *p90;* 11:25 *p253;* 18:11 *p301;* 15:15 *p173;* 21:25 *p147*

Acts, 1:5ff *p256;* 1:11 *p305;* 2 *p33;* 2:16 *p33;* 2:22-24 *p331;* 2:28 *p33;* 2:36 *p340;* 2:42 *p272;* 5:31 *p248;* 8:36 *p259;* 10 *p213;* 10:40-42 *p248;* 13:33 *p248;* 15 *p235;* 16 *p213;* 17:28 *p189;* 17:31 *p248;* 19:5 *pp255f;* 22:16 *p256*

Romans, *p248;* 1:4 *p248;* 1:16 *p101;* 4:25 *p248;* 4:25-5:2 *p273;* 5 *p161;* 6:1 *p185;* 6:1f *p50;* 6:4f *p253;* 6:4f *p253;* 6:4-11 *p256;* 7 *p58;* 7:12 *p185;* 7:23 *p45;* 7:24f *p186;* 8:24f *p105;* 12:20f *p310;* 12:21f *p309;* 13 *pp311f;* 13:1-4 *pp174f;* 13:1-7 *pp309f;* 13:8 *p310;* 13:8-10 *p310;* 13:13f *p144*

1 Corinthians, 1:2 *p219;* 1:9 *p271;* 1:12f *p235;* 1:12-15 *p256;* 1:16 *p213;* 2:13 *p90;* 3:1-9 *p235;* 4:4 *p102;* 4:8-13 *p253;* 5:3f *p106;* 6:9-20 *p253;* 6:19 *p219;* 7:17 *p253;* 7:29-31 *p250;* 9:19-23 *p176;* 10 *p217;* 10–11 *p254;* 10–12 *pp215-17;* 10:14-22 *p215;* 10:16 *pp215, 271;* 10:18 *p271;* 11 *p216;* 11:2-16 *p257;* 11:20f *p217;* 11:24 *p216;* 11:26 *pp216f;* 12 *p217;* 12–14 *p254;* 12:12f *pp90, 219, 257;* 13 *p125;* 13:5 *p125;* 14:33b-36 *p257;* 15:8 *p254;* 15:12 *p253;* 15:12-58 *p254;* 16:15f *p213*

2 Corinthians, 5:16f *p186;* 5:17 *pp54, 249, 248, 320;* 5:18 *p241;* 8:4 *p271;* 8:23 *p271;* 9:13 *p271;* 10:10 *p106;* 13:14 *p271*

Galatians, 3:27 *p256;* 3:27f *p257;* 4:1-11 *p174;* 6:15 *p54;* 6:16 *p249*

Ephesians, 1:10 *p176;* 2:1-10 *p89;* 2:1ff *p174;* 2:9 *p185;* 2:15 *p176;* 3:9f *p176;* 3:10 *p176;* 4:5 *pp18, 256;* 4:13 *p45;* 4:17-24 *p176;* 4:32 *p229;* 5:25ff *p130;* 5:27 *p219;* 6:10-20 *p314*

Philippians, 2:9-11 *p248;* 3:9 *p185;* 3:10 *p186*

Colossians, 1:15-17 *p174;* 1:18 *p249;* 1:20 *p325;* 1:24-25a *p83;* 2:12 *p256;* 2:14 *p174;* 3:1–4:6 *p258;* 3:9-11 *p257*

1 Thessalonians, *p230;* 5:21 *p46*

2 Timothy, 1:10 *p253;* 1:12 *p101*

Philemon, *p213;* 15–17 *p257*

James, 1:8 *p59;* 2:1 *p248;* 5:8 *p248*

Hebrews, 13:20 *p326;* 13:20f *p326*

1 Peter, *p248;* 2 *p309;* 3:21 *p256*

1 John, 1:3, 7 *p271;* 3:16 *p155*

Revelation, *p245;* 3:16 *p219;* 6:9-11 *p250;* 13 *p175*